P9-BYV-351

Trieste

AST

Venice

**Emilia-Romagna**
Pages 258–273

**Trentino-Alto
Adige**
Pages 170–179

**The Veneto and
Friuli**
Pages 142–169

**Venice**
Pages 88–141

Ancona

Pescara
L'Aquila

ROME
D LAZIO

**Umbria**
Pages 352-367

**Le Marche**
Pages 368–377

**Abruzzo, Molise
and Puglia**
Pages 504–517

Foggia

Bari

SOUTHERN ITALY

Napoli
Salerno
Potenza

Taranto

**Basilicata and
Calabria**
Pages 518–525

Catanzaro

Palermo
Messina
Reggio di
Calabria

SICILY

Catania
Agrigento

**Sicily**
Pages 526–547

# DK EYEWITNESS TRAVEL

# Italy

DK EYEWITNESS TRAVEL

# Italy

Penguin
Random
House

**Project Editor** Fiona Wild

**Art Editors** Vanessa Courtier, Annette Jacobs

**Editors** Francesca Machiavelli, Sophie Martin, Helen Townsend, Nicky Tyrrell

**Designers** Jo Doran, Anthea Forlee, Paul Jackson, Marisa Renzullo

**Main Contributors**

Ros Belford, Susie Boulton, Christopher Catling, Sam Cole, Paul Duncan, Olivia Ercoli, Andrew Gumbel, Tim Jepson, Ferdie McDonald, Jane Shaw

**Maps**

Lovell Johns Ltd., Dorling Kindersley Cartography

**Photographer**

John Heseltine

**Illustrators**

Stephen Conlin, Donati Giudici Associati srl, Stephen Gyapay, Roger Hutchins, Maltings Partnership, Simon Roulstone, Paul Weston, John Woodcock

Printed and bound in China

First American edition 1996

17 18 19 20 10 9 8 7 6 5 4 3 2 1

Published in the United States
by DK Publishing,
345 Hudson Street, New York, NY 10014

Reprinted with revisions 1997, 1999, 2000, 2001, 2002, 2003, 2004, 2005, 2006, 2007, 2008, 2009, 2010, 2011, 2012, 2013, 2014, 2015, 2016, 2017

Copyright 1996, 2017
© Dorling Kindersley Limited, London
A Penguin Random House Company

A catalog record for this book is available from the Library of Congress.

ISSN 1542-1554

ISBN 978-1-46546-043-1

Floors are referred to throughout in accordance with American usage; ie the "first floor" is at ground level.

MIX
Paper from
responsible sources
FSC
www.fsc.org   FSC™ C018179

# Introducing Italy

# Northwest Italy

The Colosseum, Rome

# Northeast Italy

# Central Italy

◄ **Title page** Farmhouse and Cypress Trees, Pienza, Tuscany   **Front cover image** Venetian gondola moored to the Molo, San Marco
**Back cover image** Panoramic view of historic Assisi in the sunrise

# Contents

A gondola navigating the canals in Venice

Basilica of San Francesco in Assisi

# HOW TO USE THIS GUIDE

This guide helps you get the most from your visit to Italy, providing expert recommendations as well as detailed practical information. *Introducing Italy* maps the whole country and sets it in its historical and cultural context. The 15 regional chapters, plus *Rome, Florence* and *Venice,* describe important sights with the help of maps and images. Each section is introduced with features on regional architecture and food specialties. *Travelers' Needs* gives details of hotels and restaurants and the *Survival Guide* contains practical information on everything from transportation to personal safety.

## Rome

The centre of Rome has been divided into five sightseeing areas. Each area has its own chapter, which opens with a list of the sights described. All the sights are numbered and plotted on an area map. Each sight is presented in numerical order within the chapter, making it easy to locate.

**Sights at a Glance** lists the chapter's sights by category: Churches, Museums and Galleries, Historic Buildings, Streets and Piazzas.

**All pages** relating to Rome have the same colored thumb tabs.

**1 Area Map** For easy reference, the sights are numbered and located on a map. The sights are also shown on the *Street Finder* on pages 451–61.

**A locator map** shows where you are in relation to other areas of the city center.

**2 Street by Street Map** This gives a bird's-eye view of the heart of each sightseeing area.

**Stars** indicate the sights that no visitor should miss.

**A suggested route** for a walk is shown in red.

**3 Detailed Information** All the sights in Rome are described individually. Addresses and practical information are provided. The key to the symbols used in the information block is shown on the back flap.

## 1 Introduction

The landscape, history and character of each region is described here, showing how the area has developed over the centuries and what it offers to the visitor today.

## Italy Area by Area

Aside from Rome, Florence and Venice, Italy has been divided into 15 areas, each of which has a separate chapter. The most interesting towns and places to visit have been numbered on the section's *Regional Map*.

**Each area** of Italy can be identified quickly by its color coding, shown on the inside front cover.

## 2 Regional Map

This shows the main road network and gives an overview of the whole region. All entries are numbered and there are also useful tips on getting around the region by car and train.

## 3 Detailed Information

All the important towns and other places to visit are described individually. They are listed in order, following the numbering given on the *Regional Map*. Within each entry, information is given on the most important sights. The name of the provincial capital is given for smaller towns at the top of each entry.

**Story boxes** explore specific subjects further.

**For all the top sights,** a Visitors' Checklist provides the practical information you need to plan your visit.

## 4 Italy's Top Sights

These are given two or more full pages. Historic buildings are dissected to reveal their interiors; museums and galleries have color-coded floorplans to help you locate the most interesting exhibits.

# INTRODUCING ITALY

# DISCOVERING ITALY

The following tours have been designed to take in as many of the country's highlights as possible, while keeping long-distance travel to a minimum. First come three two-day tours of Italy's most glamorous cities: Rome, Florence, and Venice. These itineraries can be followed individually or combined to form a week-long tour. Additional suggestions are provided for those who want to extend their stay to ten days. Next come two seven-day tours, covering the north and the south of Italy. These can be combined to make a superb two-week tour of the whole country. Finally, two themed itineraries have been designed for anyone wanting to tailor their trip according to a specific interest. Pick, combine, and follow your favorite tours, or simply dip in and out and seek inspiration.

**Golden Fields of Tuscany**
The Tuscan countryside, with its rolling hills and pencil-thin cypress trees, is a dream for artists and visitors alike.

## A Week in Northern Italy

- See the artwork of the Pinoteca di Brera and shop in fashionable **Milan**.
- Take a relaxing cruise on **Lake Como** and walk in the surrounding countryside.
- Look up at Juliet's balcony in **Verona** and marvel at the architecture of **Vicenza**.
- Admire world-famous frescoes in **Padua**.
- Enjoy a *vaporetto* ride along **Venice's** magnificent waterway, the Grand Canal.
- Take in stunning views of **Florence** from the Duomo.
- Walk the dizzying pathways and hillsides of the **Cinque Terre** coastline.
- Explore the three enchanting Tuscan towns of **Lucca**, **Pisa**, and **Siena**.

## A Week in Southern Italy

- See treasures of the classical world in **Rome's** museums and people-watch from the Spanish Steps.
- Marvel at sculptures and mosaics in Museo Archeologico in **Naples**, and sample fantastic pizza in the city of its origin.
- Visit the evocative ruins of **Pompeii** and take a ferry to the island of **Capri**.
- Admire the beautiful views from the towns along the **Amalfi Coast** and enjoy the sea air at **Ravello**.
- Take a night ferry to Palermo in **Sicily** and visit the glittering Palazzo dei Normanni.
- Discover the Valley of the Temples near **Agrigento**.
- Explore the magnificent Baroque town of **Noto**.

**Key**

— A Week in Northern Italy

— A Week in Southern Italy

◀ *A Court Scene*, from Mantegna's 15th-century fresco in the Camera degli Sposi, Palazzo Ducale, Mantua

## A Gourmet Tour of Central Italy

- Try fine cheeses and ham in the delightful town of **Parma**.
- Sample vintage balsamic vinegar in **Modena**.
- Dine in style in **Bologna** and soak up the atmosphere in the city's *enoteche* (wine bars).
- Taste the Tuscan specialty *Bistecca Fiorentina* in **Pisa** and enjoy *panforte* in **Siena**.
- Visit **Perugia** and stock up on the town's famous Baci chocolates.
- Travel to **Norcia** to feast on truffles and pork from the region's black pigs.
- Spend a day in **Orvieto**, seeking out pecorino cheese, delicious salami, and Orvieto Classico wine.

## A Tour of Etruscan Italy

- Explore fabulous museums dedicated to the Etruscan civilization in **Rome**.
- Visit the vast "city of the dead" at **Cerveteri** and marvel at the frescoed tombs in **Tarquinia**.
- See remnants of Etruscan life at the Necropoli Etrusca in **Orvieto** and spend an afternoon in the hill-town of **Todi**.
- Travel to **Chiusi** for the fine Museo Nazionale Etrusco and visit medieval **Gubbio** to see the Eugubine Tablets.
- Spend a day in **Volterra** to view the remarkable collection of Etruscan funerary urns at the Museo Guarnacci.

**Key**

— A Gourmet Tour of Italy

— A Tour of Etruscan Italy

**Colosseum, Rome**
Once the site of deadly gladiatorial combat, the Colosseum is the highlight of a trip to Rome. Tickets include access to the Forum and Palatine Museum.

Beautiful spiral staircase leading down from the Vatican Museums, Rome

## 2 days in Florence

*Florence is the ultimate city for art lovers, with a wealth of breathtaking museums and galleries.*

- **Arriving** Florence is served by two airports – Amerigo Vespucci airport, 2 miles (4 km) from the center, and Pisa airport. From Amerigo Vespucci, buses run to Florence's Santa Maria Novella train station; from Pisa, catch a direct train to Santa Maria Novella.

- **Moving on** The journey from Florence to Venice is just 2 hours by fast train.

The dome of Florence's Duomo, designed by Brunelleschi and completed in 1436

## 2 days in Rome

*The nation's capital has an overwhelming array of memorable sights, including the wonderful Vatican Museums and the Colosseum.*

- **Arriving** Fiumicino (Leonardo da Vinci) is Rome's main airport, located about 18 miles (30 km) southwest of the city. The "Leonardo Express" train runs nonstop to Termini station, the city's main train station.

- **Moving on** The journey from Rome to Florence takes 1 hour 37 minutes by Eurostar.

### Day 1

**Morning** A couple of days in Rome *(pp380–463)* will only scrape its surface, but do devote one day to the Vatican and St. Peter's. The fast route through the **Vatican Museums** *(pp424–31)* takes in the **Sistine Chapel** *(pp428–30)*. Don't miss Michelangelo's *Creation of Adam* on the ceiling and his dynamic fresco *The Last Judgment*. The four **Raphael Rooms** *(p431)* show another Renaissance master at the peak of his artistic powers.
**Afternoon** Inside the awe-inspiring **St. Peter's** *(pp422–3)*, be sure to see Michelangelo's moving *Pietà*. Climb the dome for views, then descend to the grottoes for the papal tombs. Afterward, cross the Tiber to the centro storico. Look in at the **Pantheon** *(p408)*, the only ancient Roman temple to survive intact, then spend the

evening among the exuberant Baroque fountains and cafés of **Piazza Navona** *(pp402–3)*.

### Day 2

**Morning** Wander through the evocative ruins of the **Roman Forum** *(pp394–6)*, and on to the monumental **Colosseum** *(p397)*. Nearby, the church of **San Clemente** *(p439)* reveals its layers of history from pagan temple to 15th-century church.
**Afternoon** For great city views, head up to the **Capitoline Museums** *(pp390–91)*. The Palazzo Nuovo has a fine selection of Greek and Roman statues. For some respite, visit the pretty 17th-century pleasure gardens of **Villa Borghese** *(pp442–3)*. Visit **Piazza di Spagna** and the **Spanish Steps** *(p413)* and cast a coin in the Baroque **Trevi Fountain** *(pp414–15)*.

> ### To extend your trip…
> Take a day trip to the lovely hill-town of **Tivoli** and visit **Hadrian's Villa** *(p472)*, about 3 miles (5 km) west of Tivoli.

### Day 1

**Morning** Much more compact than Rome, **Florence** *(pp274–317)* is the embodiment of the Renaissance. Feel the pull of Brunelleschi's immense orange-tiled dome, which crowns the **Duomo** *(pp284–6)*. Climb the dome for stunning views, then admire Ghiberti's

The Vatican, with St. Peter's Basilica and Sant'Angelo bridge, Rome

Looking south from the upper terrace of the Boboli Gardens, Florence

famous bronze doors on the **Baptistery** *(pp284–6)*. A few streets away, the **Bargello** *(p287)* holds a fantastic collection of Renaissance sculpture.

**Afternoon** Take a stroll around **Piazza della Signoria** *(pp294–5)*, dominated by its towering city hall, the Palazzo Vecchio, and a copy of Michelangelo's *David*. Stop off at the famous Bar Vivoli Gelateria for an ice cream before tackling the **Uffizi** *(pp290–93)*. Caravaggio, Titian, Raphael – works by all the major artists of the Renaissance and beyond are on display here.

**Day 2**
**Morning** See the real statue of *David* by Michelangelo in the **Galleria dell' Accademia** *(p279)*, then visit the church of **Santa Maria Novella** *(pp300–301)* for Masaccio's *Trinity*, with its novel use of perspective.

**Afternoon** Visit the Gothic church of **Santa Croce** *(pp288–9)*, the final resting place of Michelangelo, Galileo, and Machiavelli. Next, cross **Ponte Vecchio** *(p289)* for the **Cappella Brancacci** *(pp302–3)*, to see more frescoes by Masaccio. The fountains, grottoes, and woods of the **Boboli Gardens** *(p307)* are perfect for a picnic, and there is plenty more art in the **Palazzo Pitti** *(pp306–7)*.

> **To extend your trip…**
> Spend a day in the **Cinque Terre** *(p245)* and another exploring **Pisa** *(pp328–30)* and **Lucca** *(pp324–7)*.

## 2 days in Venice

*This unique city on the water has romantic gondolas, magnificent churches, and wonderful art.*

- **Arriving** Marco Polo airport is located at Tessera, 5 miles (8 km) north of the city. Alilaguna ferries, which stop at various points in the city, can be picked up a short walk from the airport. The travel time is around 1 hour. Water taxis are also available, but they are very expensive. Venice's main train station is Venezia Santa Lucia station.

**Day 1**
**Morning** Merely getting lost in Venice *(pp88–141)* will exceed expectations, as will the reality of the familiar images. To make the most of a visit to this watery city, travel by *vaporetto* or gondola along the **Grand Canal** *(pp92–5)* to **Piazza San Marco** *(pp112–13)* and the **Basilica di San Marco** *(pp114–17)*. The mosaics inside and out are stunning, but so too are the Pala d'Oro (golden altarpiece), the jewels of the Treasury, and the four Horses of St. Mark on the balcony. Take the elevator to the top of the adjacent Campanile to be rewarded with a view stretching all the way to the Alps.

**Afternoon** Join a prebooked Secret Itineraries tour to get the most out of the **Palazzo Ducale** *(pp118–20)*, where the vast Sala del Maggior Consiglio, with its magnificent Tintoretto, is the highlight. Have coffee at Caffè Florian or Grancaffè Quadri on **Piazza San Marco** *(pp112–13)*, then cross the Grand Canal to the **Accademia** *(pp110–11)* for the best of the Venetian painters. If you prefer modern art, visit the **Peggy Guggenheim Collection** *(pp108–9)*, housed in the 18th-century Palazzo Venier dei Leoni.

**Day 2**
**Morning** Make for the **Rialto** *(p101)* to watch boats go by from the bridge, and stock up at the city's busiest market. Nearby is the church of **Santa Maria Gloriosa dei Frari** *(pp102–3)* with its exquisite altarpiece, a *Madonna and Child* by Bellini.

**Afternoon** Tour the islands of **Torcello** *(pp126–7)* for 12th- and 13th-century mosaics, **Murano** *(p125)* for the glass museum, and colorful **Burano** *(p125)* for lace. Be sure to sample some local snacks and drink an *aperitivo* in one of the many enticing bars back in Venice.

> **To extend your trip…**
> Take a day trip to **Verona** *(pp146–51)*, which has a fine Roman arena.

Stylish waiters serve drinks in refined Caffè Florian, Venice

## A Week in Northern Italy

- **Airports** Arrive at Milano Malpensa airport and depart from Pisa Galileo Galilei.

- **Transportation** Trains connect the cities in 2 hours or less. Use the bus to reach Siena from Florence, and rent a car for the Cinque Terre, leaving it at La Spezia for the local train. It is easy to make day trips to Lake Como from Milan, the Veneto from Venice, and the Cinque Terre from Florence.

- **Reservations** Milan: viewing of *Last Supper*; Venice: Basilica di San Marco; Florence: Accademia, Uffizi; Pisa: ascent of the Leaning Tower.

### Day 1: Milan

If you're looking for Italian style, high fashion, art, and architecture, **Milan** *(pp196–205)*, the largest city of the north, has it all. Heading up the list of sights is Leonardo da Vinci's world-famous *Last Supper* *(p204)*. Visit the enormous Gothic Duomo *(p197)*, which invites a climb to its roof for the best city view. For glorious paintings from the Renaissance to the present day, don't miss the Pinacoteca di Brera *(pp202–203)*, and for those who enjoy shopping, Galleria Vittorio Emanuele II *(p198)*, with its magnificent glass dome and floor mosaics, is a must.

### Day 2: Lake Como

**Lake Como** *(pp194–5)*, its long arms nestling between steep hillsides, is a prime example of Italy's exquisite landscapes. Cruise the lake or take short ferry hops across the water, admiring the resplendent villas along the way. Explore Bellagio, or take a funicular up into the hills.

### Day 3: Venice

*Pick a day from the city itinerary on p13.*

### Day 4: The Veneto – Verona, Vicenza, and Padua

Pick from a trio of towns, all within striking distance of Venice. Lively **Verona** *(pp146–151)* conjures up Shakespeare's *Romeo and Juliet*, and crowds still flock to see Juliet's balcony. Famous for concerts is the well-preserved Roman Arena *(p147)*, while the Romanesque church of San Zeno Maggiore *(pp150–51)* has a lovely cloister. Admirers of Palladio will appreciate **Vicenza** *(pp154–7)*, where his elegant Classical buildings surround the Piazza dei Signori. **Padua** *(pp158–63)* is known for its Cappella dei Scrovegni *(pp160–61)*, containing some wonderful frescoes by Giotto.

### Day 5: Florence

*Pick a day from the city itinerary on p12.*

### Day 6 : Cinque Terre

The five tiny villages of the **Cinque Terre** *(p245)* – Monterosso, Vernazza, Corniglia,

Rolling fields in Tuscany

Manarola, and Riomaggiore – are the jewels of Italy's northwest coast. Colorful houses cling to the rocky cliffs, making a hike along the connecting path a delight to the eye. You can do the whole trail (north to south is less steep) in 5 or 6 hours.

### Day 7: Tuscany – Lucca, Pisa, and Siena

These three Tuscan towns are less busy than Florence, yet they offer a cultural feast with the bonus of an enchanting landscape. If time is tight, visit two. In **Lucca** *(pp324–7)*, promenade the encircling 17th-century grassy ramparts and visit the church of San Michele in Foro, its exquisite Pisan-Romanesque facade bursting with decoration. **Pisa** *(pp328–30)* is the home of the iconic 13th-century Leaning Tower, which, together with the Duomo and Baptistery, forms the Campo dei Miracoli. **Siena** *(pp342–7)* is one of Italy's most appealing medieval towns and home to the twice-yearly Palio *(p345)*, when Piazza del Campo comes alive with spirited bareback horse racing. Within striking distance of the piazza are the Gothic Palazzo Pubblico, which contains a treasure trove of frescoes from the Middle Ages, and the magnificent Duomo *(pp346–7)*. En route from Pisa to Siena, try to catch a glimpse of the 13 medieval towers that pierce the skyline in **San Gimignano** *(pp348–9)*. The view is magical in the evening.

Pretty Bellagio, which sits on a peninsula at the top of Lake Como's two "arms"

## A Week in Southern Italy

- **Airports** Arrive at Rome Fiumicino and depart from Catania airport, Sicily.

- **Transportation** Train travel from Rome to Naples is fast and easy (1 hour and 10 minutes is the fastest). Take the ferry for Capri and Sicily, the bus for the coastal towns of Sorrento, Positano, Amalfi, and Ravenna, and for Agrigento from Palermo (2 hours). You will need a car to see inland Sicily: Piazza Armerina and Noto. Pompeii and Capri are easy to visit as day trips from Naples.

- **Reservations** Rome: Vatican Museums, Colosseum, Forum, and Palatine; Naples: Museo Archeologico Nazionale, Secret Cabinet Tour.

The evocative ancient temple ruins at Selinunte, Sicily

## Days 1 and 2: Rome
*See the city itinerary on p12.*

## Day 3: Naples
**Naples** *(pp490–97)* is chaotic, but the rewards of visiting are manifold. The main attraction is the world-renowned Museo Archeologico Nazionale *(pp494–5)* and its vast collection of Roman and Pompeiian treasures; allow at least half a day here. Reserve ahead for the Secret Cabinet tour to view the erotic works from Pompeii. Tiny Cappella Sansevero *(p491)* holds intriguing works from the 18th century, notably the virtuoso alabaster and marble *Veiled Christ* by Sammartino. Santa Chiara *(p493)* is worth seeing for its charming majolica-tiled cloisters. Don't leave without eating pizza in the city of its invention.

## Day 4: Pompeii and Capri
The Circumvesuviana train skirts the base of Vesuvius from Naples to Pompeii and on to Sorrento. **Pompeii** *(pp498–9)* gives you an insight into a Roman town as it was before it was destroyed in AD 79.

The body casts of the people who perished here are perhaps the most poignant. Arrange a trip up the infamous volcano, or take a ferry from Naples or Sorrento to the idyllic island of **Capri** *(pp502–503)*, best enjoyed in the quiet of evening. Blue Grotto sea cave and Villa Jovis of Emperor Tiberius are secondary attractions to the captivating vistas you will find here.

Marina Grande on the pretty island of Capri

## Day 5: Amalfi Coast
Take the hair-raising bus ride along the coast for views of a lifetime and stop off at your leisure at some of Italy's most beautiful towns. **Sorrento** *(p501)* is the most lively and popular, while chic **Positano** *(p501)* favors the jet set and comes with a good beach.

**Amalfi** *(p501)* has a stunning 9th-century cathedral, while **Ravello** *(p501)*, set high above terraces of lemon groves, has the best of the views. Lose yourself among the bougainvillea in the lush gardens of the Villa Cimbrone or Villa Rufolo.

## Days 6 and 7: Sicily
Sicily is a melting pot of Norman, Byzantine, Greek, and Arab influences and deserves at least 2 days' exploration. Taking the night ferry from Naples to Palermo, the island's largest town, will save you time. **Palermo** *(pp530–33)* exemplifies all these influences, notably in the Palazzo dei Normanni, whose Cappella Palatina is a glittering mix of mosaics, marble, and gold. The most famous Norman mosaics, however, are outside Palermo, at the highly ornamented Duomo of Monreale *(pp534–5)*. Seek out the intricate Norman cloisters here. To the south you can discover the ancient Greek legacy in the Valley of the Temples *(p540)*, near Agrigento, or at Selinunte *(p538)*, which has the benefit of a long and sandy beach. In the interior, the Villa Romana del Casale at **Piazza Armerina** *(p541)* sports some of Italy's liveliest mosaics, and beautiful **Noto** *(p547)*, aglow with golden stone, is a unique Baroque town rebuilt after the earthquake of 1693.

## A Gourmet Tour of Central Italy

- **Duration** 7 days – but extends to a 10-day tour with the extra suggestions.

- **Airports** Arrive at Milan Linate airport and depart from Rome Fiumicino airport. From Milan, travel by train or car to Parma for the first stop on the tour.

- **Transportation** This tour can be made using Italy's railroad network, but renting a car allows more flexibility.

This itinerary takes you to Italy's central regions – Emilia-Romagna, Tuscany, and Umbria – focusing on the regional food specialties along the way. If you are traveling in summer or fall, look for the copious food festivals held across the region.

### Day 1: Parma
Affluent **Parma** (p263) is synonymous with cheese and ham – *Parmigiano Reggiano* (Parmesan) and *prosciutto crudo* (Parma ham). The delicatessens here are a feast for the eyes, as are the city's main sights, which include a fascinating 12th-century baptistery and paintings by Correggio in the exquisite Duomo.

### Day 2: Modena
The handsome city of **Modena** (p264) has two main claims to

fame: it is the producer of fast cars (Ferrari and Maserati) and balsamic vinegar – try the city's market for the best vintage variety. In between sampling some of the region's other specialties, such as mortadella, spicy sausage, and pig's feet, be sure to visit the very fine Romanesque Duomo and the Este collection of paintings in the Palazzo dei Musei.

### Day: 3 Bologna
Dress up for dinner here – **Bologna** (pp266–9) has some of the country's finest restaurants and atmospheric *enoteche* (wine bars). Homemade pasta comes with the famous Bolognese (*ragù*) or cream sauce, or stuffed with ricotta, pork, or pumpkin. During the day, check out the medieval skyscrapers of the Due Torri and the Gothic church of San Petronio.

> **To extend your trip…**
> Cycle around the lagoons of the **Po Delta** (pp270–71), 60 miles (97 km) from Bologna.

### Day 4: Pisa
Spend a day in **Pisa** (pp328–30). The city's main draw is the Campo dei Miracoli, which contains the Duomo, Baptistery, and Leaning Tower. Pisa's culinary attractions include fish dishes, such as *cacciucco*, a hearty fish soup, and *baccalá alla Pisana*, salt cod with tomato sauce. Meat-eaters will love *bistecca alla fiorentina* (thick charcoal-grilled steak).

The iconic Leaning Tower of Pisa

### Day 5: Siena
Life in **Siena** (pp342–7) centers on the beautiful fan-shaped piazza of Il Campo, around which *pasticcerie* sell the city's famous *panforte* cake and *ricciarelli* (almond cookies). Admire the frescoes in the medieval Palazzo Pubblico and the treasures of the spectacular Duomo and its Museo.

> **To extend your trip…**
> Head for the coast at **Maremma Park** (pp350–51), 50 miles (81 km) from Siena.

### Day 6: Perugia and Norcia
Stop at **Perugia** (pp356–7) to stock up on Baci chocolate and see the frescoes in the Palazzo dei Priori, before traveling to the gastronomic hot spot of **Norcia** (pp366–7), where black truffles, salami, and pork from the local black pigs are the specialties.

> **To extend your trip…**
> Explore the mountains of the **Valnerina** (p367), 30 miles (48 km) from Norcia.

### Day 7: Orvieto
Pretty **Orvieto** (pp362–3) is headquarters of the Città Slow movement, which promotes locally sourced produce and traditional food. Look for pecorino cheese and salami, and, of course, Orvieto Classico wine. Take time to visit the Romanesque-Gothic Duomo and the 16th-century Pozzo di San Patrizio.

Atmospheric outdoor dining in Piazza della Mercanzia, Bologna

For practical information on traveling around Italy, see pp628–35

## A Tour of Etruscan Italy

- **Duration** 7 days – but extends to a 10-day tour with the extra suggestions.
- **Airports** Arrive at Rome Fiumicino airport and depart from Pisa Galileo Galilei (trains from Florence to Pisa take 1 hour).
- **Transportation** This tour is most easily done by car, though Cerveteri is accessible by bus from Rome and Tarquinia and Orvieto by train.

This tour focuses on the ancient Etruscan sights and museums of Lazio, Umbria, and Tuscany, as well as other interesting sights along the way. For more on Italy's first major civilization, see pp48–9.

### Day 1: Rome
Be inspired by the world's best collections of Etruscan treasures in the **Etruscan Museum of the Vatican** (p424) and the **Museo Nazionale Etrusco** in the **Villa Giulia** (p444). The tender portrayals of people on the sarcophagi, the delicate and intricate gold jewelry, and the lifelike bronze sculptures display amazing craftsmanship. Leave time for the lovely gardens of the **Villa Borghese** (pp442–3).

### Day 2: Cerveteri
Feel the mystery of the vast necropolis at **Cerveteri** (p470) as you stroll its silent streets. Here, see the tombs that were built as replicas of homes, decorated with frescoes and filled with domestic furnishings. Fifty thousand Etruscans were entombed here from the 7th to the 1st century BC in what was one of the most powerful of the 12 Etruscan cities. Visit the Museo Nazionale Cerite to see displays of objects that were buried with the bodies.

> **To extend your trip...**
> Head 40 miles (64 km) from Rome to the Etruscan amphitheater at **Sutri** (p470).

Well-preserved "street" of Etruscan tombs, Cerveteri

### Day 3: Tarquinia
Spend some time in **Tarquinia** (p470). The medieval center here was the capital of Etruria 2,500 years ago. Head uphill to the necropolis, a warren of tombs that hold lively and colorful frescoes depicting the lives of their inhabitants. For more revelations of everyday life and artistry, head for the Museo Archeologico, where, alongside the famous terra-cotta winged horses, are fine displays of jewelry, bronzes, and ceramics.

> **To extend your trip...**
> Visit the Renaissance gardens of Villa Lante at **Viterbo** (pp468–9), 40 miles (64 km) from Tarquinia.

### Day 4: Orvieto and Todi
You can see more Etruscan remains in **Orvieto** (pp362–3), at the Museo Archeologico Faina and Museo Civico, at the Necropoli Etrusca, and even during a tour of Orvieto Underground (www.orvieto underground.it). The fine, beautiful Duomo and the 16th-century Pozzo di San Patrizio add to the attractions. From here, travel to nearby **Todi** (p363). This dramatic hilltop town is home to the Museo Etrusco-Romano.

### Day 5: Chiusi and Gubbio
Make your way northward to **Chiusi** (p336) and the Museo Nazionale Etrusco for its fine display of urns and vases taken from the surrounding tombs.

Then head toward the forest-clad Apennines for charming **Gubbio** (p356), where the Palazzo dei Consoli houses the famous seven bronze Eugubine Tablets inscribed with Etruscan letters, and where the strange Porte della Morte, walled-up doors, were once supposedly used to transport coffins.

Volterra, once an important Etruscan city

### Day 6: Volterra
The city of **Volterra** (p338) is home to the excellent Museo Guarnacci and beautiful Etruscan funerary urns, made out of alabaster, for which the region is famous. For more alabaster, visit the Pinacoteca e Museo Civico and browse the craft shops.

> **To extend your trip...**
> A 20-mile (32-km) drive from Volterra takes you to **San Gimignano** (pp348–9) and its 13th-century towers.

### Day 7: Florence
Finish your tour in Florence and visit the Medici Etruscan collection in the **Museo Archeologico** (p281), which includes two outstanding sculptures – the Chimera and the Arringatore (Orator) bronze.

# Putting Italy on the Map

Italy sits at the heart of the Mediterranean, shielded from the rest of Europe by the vast sweep of the Alps. The Po, its longest river, arcs across the industrial north, while the Apennine mountains split the boot-shaped peninsula down its length. With a population of 58 million, governed from Rome, Italy covers 116,320 sq miles (301,268 sq km) and includes Sicily and Sardinia.

SWITZERLAND

Lago Maggiore
Lago di Como
Lecco
S38
Trento
S42
Aosta
Arona
Bergamo
Lago di Garda
S22
Ivrea
A5
Milan
Brescia
A4
Verona
Turin
A4
Po
A7
A1
Mantova
A21
Po
Tanaro
A26
A45
Parma
Modena
Cuneo
A6
Genoa
A15
A10
La Spezia
A12
Lucca
A11
Avignon
FRANCE
Nice
San Remo
Pisa
A7
Monaco
Ligurian
Livorno
A51
A8
Sea
S1
Marseille
Piombino
Bastia
Elba
Orbetell
Corsica
Tyrrhenian
Sea
Ajaccio
Olbia
Porto Torres
Alghero
Sardinia
Arbatax
Cagliari

**Key**

━━━ Freeway

─── Major highway

- - - Ferry service

━━━ International boundary

**Europe**

NORWAY
North Sea
SWEDEN
ESTONIA
LATVIA
DENMARK
LITHUANIA
REP. OF IRELAND
UNITED KINGDOM
NETH.
GERMANY
POLAND
BELARUS
BELGIUM
CZECH REPUBLIC
UKRAINE
SLOVAKIA
FRANCE
AUSTRIA
HUNGARY
Atlantic Ocean
CROATIA
ROMANIA
ITALY
SERBIA
MONTEN.
KOS.
BULGARIA
MAC.
SPAIN
ALBANIA
PORTUGAL
GREECE
MOROCCO
ALGERIA
TUNISIA

Mediterranean Sea

Bizerte
Annaba
Tunis
TUNISIA

# Northern Italy

Airline connections link Milan, Turin, Bologna, Pisa, Florence, Verona, and Venice with the rest of Europe. Major highways and railroads also provide excellent links to cities all over Europe. Transportation services are very efficient, with freeways and railroads along both coasts, and across the area's main east-to-west axis at the foot of the Alps. Milan, Verona, and Bologna are the key transportation hubs, while Florence provides the main link to the south.

**Florence by Road**
Good fast roads link Florence to Pisa to the west, Rome and Siena to the south, and Bologna to the north.

**Florence and Environs**

### Key

-‑‑ International boundary

-‑- Regional boundary

▦ Freeway

▬ Major highway

— Railroad line

**For additional map symbols** *see back flap*

**Venice by Road**
Venice is joined to the mainland by a causeway. This provides easy access to freeway links with Verona and Padua.

**Venice**

Mestre

Marco Polo

S14b

S14

Canale Osellino

FS

Veneta

S11

Laguna

FS Santa Lucia

San Marco

0 kilometres 4
0 miles 2

AUSTRIA

ortina d'Ampezzo

Tolmezzo

552

A23

Cividale del Friuli

SLOVENIA

Belluno

Udine

S13

A4

Gorizia

Pordenone

S13

A27

A28

Treviso

Aquileia

Trieste

VENICE
see inset above

Po Delta

Greece, Turkey, Egypt

Ravenna

Rimini

Pèsaro

SAN MARINO

Fano

Urbino

Ancona

S71

Conero Peninsula

Greece, Turkey, Cyprus

Sansepolcro

Jesi

Sibillini

S3B

Grotte di Frasassi

Loreto

ortona

Gubbio

S76

Perugia

S77

A14

Lago Trasimeno hiusi

Assisi

Spello

Ascoli Piceno

S3

Montefalco

S3B

Norcia

Todi

Spoleto

rvieto

Pescara

Viterbo

S2

L'Aquila

A24

A25

A1

Lanciano

A25

Sulmona

Isole Tremiti

ROME

S17

Scanno

San Severo

A14

A12

A1

S214

S17

S647

S89

**Key to Color Coding**

**Northeast Italy**

- Venice
- The Veneto and Friuli
- Trentino-Alto Adige

**Northwest Italy**

- Lombardy
- Valle d'Aosta and Piedmont
- Liguria

**Central Italy**

- Emilia-Romagna
- Florence
- Tuscany
- Umbria
- Le Marche

0 kilometres 100
0 miles 50

# Southern Italy

International airline services operate to
Rome, Naples, and Palermo in southern
Italy. Transportation links within the
region are generally slower than in the
north, particularly inland and on the
islands of Sicily and Sardinia, where buses
are often a faster option than trains.
Mainland coastal highway and railroad
links are good, however, especially
those linking Rome and Naples, the
region's main transportation hubs,
which are connected by a high-speed
train service. Two trans-Apennine
highways offer the quickest cross-
country routes.

## Sicily and Sardinia

Ferries operate to Sicily
from Naples, Villa San
Giovanni, and Reggio
di Calabria. Onward
connections include
boats to Malta and
Tunisia. Ferries run to
Sardinia from several
mainland ports, notably
Civitavecchia, Genoa,
and Livorno.

## Key

--- International boundary

-- Regional boundary

═══ Freeway

▭▭▭ Main highway

— Railroad

**Rome by Road**
Highway links approach Rome from Naples, Pescara, and Florence. All feed into the city's ring road, the Grande Raccordo Anulare.

## Rome and Environs

0 kilometers 10
0 miles 5

VATICAN CITY

FS

GRANDE RACCORDO ANULARE (GRA)

VIA CASSIA

VIA NOMENTANA

VIA TIBURTINA

A24

VIA CASILINA

VIA AURELIA

S1

VIA APPIA NUOVA

A12

Leonardo da Vinci di Fiumicino

A91

Tevere (Tiber)

VIA CRISTOFORO COLOMBO

S7

Ciampino

A1

S2

S3

A1

S5

Vasto

Isole Tremiti

Termoli

Rodi Garganico

Vieste

A14

Gargano Peninsula

Manfredonia

S647

San Severo

Lucera

S17

Troia

Foggia

S89

Trani

A16

Bari

A14

S98

Croatia, Greece, Egypt

Benevento

S582

Castel del Monte

Ruvo di Puglia

Caserta

Melfi

Matera

S16

Alberobello

Brindisi

Greece

Pompei

A3

Potenza

S407

Taranto

S7

Lecce

Salerno

Amalfi

Paestum

Sala Consilina

Metaponto

Galatina

Otranto

Cilento

S18

Policoro

S106

Greece

S275

Maratea

Castrovillari

S18

Rossano

S106

Cosenza

S107

Crotone

S280

Catanzaro

Lamezia

A3

Tropea

Vibo Valentia

Stilo

Isole Eolie

↑ Naples

Gerace

S106

Milazzo

Messina

Tindari

Reggio di Calabria

A20

A18

Taormina

↑ Naples

Enna

A19

Catania

Piazza Armerina

S417

Pantalica

Siracusa

↓ Malta

Gela

S115

Noto

Modica

0 kilometers 100
0 miles 50

## Key to Color Coding

**Rome and Lazio**

Rome

Lazio

**Southern Italy**

Naples and Campania

Abruzzo, Molise, and Puglia

Basilicata and Calabria

Sicily

Sardinia

# A PORTRAIT OF ITALY

Italy has drawn people in search of culture and romance for many centuries. Few countries can compete with its Classical origins, its art, architecture, musical and literary traditions, its scenery, or food and wine. The ambiguity of its modern image is also fascinating: since World War II Italy has climbed into the top ten world economies, yet at its heart it retains many of the customs, traditions, and regional allegiances of its agricultural heritage.

Italy has no single cultural identity. From the northern snowcapped peaks of the Alps to the rugged southern shores of Sicily lies a plethora of distinctive regions and peoples. Politically, Italy is a young country: it did not exist as a unified nation state until 1870, and its 20 regions have maintained their cultural individuality. Visitors to Italy are often pleasantly surprised by the diversity of its dialects, cuisines, and architecture. There is also a larger regional division. People speak of two distinct Italies: the rich industrial north and the poorer, agricultural south,

known as *Il Mezzogiorno* or Land of the Midday Sun. The frontier separating the two is indeterminate, lying somewhere between Rome and Naples.

The north is directly responsible for Italy's place among the world's top industrial nations. It has been the powerhouse behind the Italian economic miracle, its success achieved by internationally renowned names such as FIAT, Prada, Ferragamo, Pirelli, Olivetti, Zanussi, Alessi, and Armani. In contrast, the south, once a cradle of high culture and civilization, has been dogged by

The rooftops of Montalcino, viewed from the town's fortress

◀ Cobblestone lane in the coastal fishing town of Cefalù, Sicily unemployment and organized crime. Some of its areas rank among the most depressed in Europe, although many southern towns did benefit from an injection of Millennium funds.

The historic divide between north and south is a powerful factor in contemporary politics. The federalist party, the Northern League, owes its popularity to this split. Those in favor of separation complain that the south is a drain on resources: Milan is seen as efficient and rich, while Naples is viewed as chaotic, dirty, and corrupt.

History and geography have both contributed to the division. The north is closer in both location and spirit to Germany and France, while the south has suffered a succession of invasions from foreign powers: Carthaginians and Greeks in ancient times, Saracens and Normans in the Middle Ages, and, until the middle of the 19th century, the Bourbons from Spain held sway.

## Tradition

Distinctive variations in Italy's regions have much to do with the mountainous landscape and inaccessible valleys. Tuscan and Ligurian hill-towns, for instance, have quite different silhouettes, and the farmhouses in Puglia, the famous *trulli*, are unlike those found in the landscape of Emilia-Romagna.

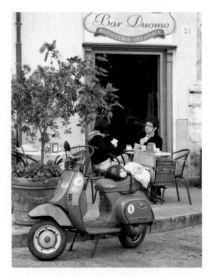

A scooter parked in front of The Bar Duomo, Piazza Duomo in Cefalù

In southern Italy the landscape, architecture, dialects, food, and even the appearance of the people have closer affinities with the Eastern Mediterranean and North Africa than with Europe. In the far south, study of the local dialects has revealed traces of ancient Greek and old Albanian, preserved in tightly knit communities isolated by the rugged geography. Christianity and pagan ritual are closely linked; sometimes the Virgin is portrayed as a thinly disguised Demeter, the Earth goddess.

Café-goers relaxing in Marina di Pisa, Tuscany

Medieval skyscrapers emerging from the Tuscan landscape of San Gimignano

Throughout Italy, ancient techniques of husbandry endure, and many livelihoods are closely connected to the land and the seasons. Main crops include sugar beet, corn, wheat, olives, and grapes; colorful Easter celebrations *(see p70)* pay tribute to the bounty of the soil. Although some of the north's postwar economic prosperity can be attributed to industry (especially car production in and around Turin), much of it has grown from the expansion of family-owned artisan businesses and the export of handmade goods abroad. This is recognized as a distinct sector of the economy. The internationally successful retail clothes chain Prada is a good example. The "Made in Italy" label, found on goods such as clothes, shoes, and leather bags, guarantees a high standard.

## Culture and Arts

The arts in Italy have had a long and glorious history and Italians are very proud of this. Given the fact that Italy has more than 100,000 monuments (archeological sites, cathedrals, churches, houses, and statues), all of which have major historical significance, it is not surprising that there is a shortage of funds to keep

them in good repair. Many museums in Italy, particularly those in the south, are closed, or partially closed. You may find churches in Venice hidden behind permanent scaffolding, or those in Abruzzo shut due to earthquake damage. However, with tourism accounting for around 12 percent of Italy's gross domestic product,

Bernini's 17th-century Fontana del Tritone, Rome

Roadside stall near Positano, Campania

reserve *ciao* (hello or good-bye) for friends your age or younger, and greet older people with *piacere* (pleased to meet you), *buon giorno* (good day), or *buona sera* (good evening); on parting, say *arrivederci* (good-bye). Strangers are met with a hand-shake, but family and friends receive a kiss.

Italian chic decrees that the clothes you wear should give the impression of wealth. Italians are conformists in fashion as in other aspects of daily life.

Italian politics, in contrast, are not so well regulated. Governments in the postwar era were characterized by short-lived coalitions, dominated by the Christian Democrats. In 1993 Italy experienced a political crisis when an organized network of corruption was exposed, disgracing a huge number of politicians and businessmen. The investigations may have failed to eradicate corruption, but they led to the formation of two large coalitions, center-left and center-right. Silvio Berlusconi, leader of Forza Italia, became prime minister in 1994 but lasted only a short while, as he, too, was accused of corruption. In 1998 Massimo D'Alema became Italy's first left-wing prime minister. For more than a decade, Italy saw an alternation between the two coalitions, with Berlusconi

efforts are being made to put as many buildings and collections on show as possible. The Jubilee 2000 helped matters by allocating large amounts of money for the restoration of buildings and sites belonging to the Catholic Church.

The performing arts are also underfunded, yet there are some spectacular cultural festivals. Almost every town of any size has its own opera house, and La Scala opera house in Milan stages world-class productions.

Film is another flourishing art form in Italy and has been so since its invention. The sound stages at Cinecittà, on the outskirts of Rome, have been used by many famous directors, including Fellini, Pasolini, de Sica, Visconti, and many others. Italian movies such as *La Vita è Bella* and *The Son's Room* have found critical acclaim and box-office success both in Italy and abroad. In Italy the arts belong to everyone: opera is attended by people from all backgrounds, regardless of social status, as are movie theaters and galleries.

## Social Customs and Politics

Italian society is still highly traditional, and Italians can be very formal. Between the generations degrees of familiarity exist:

Diners relaxing at a restaurant in Orta San Giulio, Piedmont

The solution to heavy traffic in Rome: motorbikes and scooters

dominating. In August 2013, Berlusconi was barred from holding any public office for seven years for tax fraud. In 2014, leftist Democrat Matteo Renzi became Italy's youngest prime minister. In December 2016, Renzi resigned after his plans for reform were defeated in a referendum.

## Modern Life

Food and soccer are the great constants; Italians live for both. Much time is spent on preparing food and eating. The Italian diet, particularly in the south, is among the healthiest in the world. Soccer is a national passion and inspires massive public interest and media attention, not least as a way of expressing regional loyalties.

As far as religion is concerned, the number of practicing Catholics has been in decline for some years. Although Rome lies at the center of world Catholicism, today many Italians are uninterested in religion, but still attend Mass in number on saints' days or feast days. As a result of immigration, other religions are now on the increase.

The emphasis on conformity and a commitment to the institution of the family remain key factors in Italian society despite the country's low birth rate. Grandparents, children, and grandchildren often still live in family units, although this is becoming less common. Women's Liberation fought a powerful campaign in the 1970s and did much to change attitudes to women in the workplace, particularly in metropolitan areas. However, the idea that men should help with housework and the care of the children is still a fairly foreign notion among the older generation.

With the miracle of its postwar economic recovery, where industry and technology were united with design, Italy became a success story. Although the economy was dented by the worldwide recessions of recent years, the exposure of corruption in many walks of public life, and political upheaval, Italy appears unchanged to foreign visitors. Its ability to keep its regional identities and traditional values seems to allow it to ride out any changes relatively unscathed.

# Medieval and Early Renaissance Art

The story of early Italian art, from the 13th century until the late 15th century, illuminates one of the richest periods in European art history. For the first time since Classical antiquity, painters and sculptors created a convincing pictorial space in which figures, modeled "in the round," were given life. Ethereal buildings were replaced by those firmly rooted in the real world, reproducing what artists actually saw. This revolution in art included the reintroduction of the fresco technique, giving artists huge surfaces for telling pictorial stories.

**c. 1305 Giotto di Bondone**, *The Meeting at the Golden Gate* (Cappella degli Scrovegni, Padua). Giotto broke away from the ornate Byzantine style to visualize naturalness and human emotions. His way of working would later be dubbed the Florentine style.

**1235 Bonaventura Berlinghieri**, *St. Francis Altarpiece* (San Francesco, Pescia)

**1285 Duccio di Buoninsegna**, *Rucellai Madonna*, panel (Uffizi, Florence). Duccio dominated the Sienese painting style, which combined bold linear movements with a new human intimacy.

**1339 Ambrogio Lorenzetti**, *Good Government Enthroned* (Sala dei Nove, Palazzo Pubblico, Siena)

| 1220 | 1240 | 1260 | 1280 | 1300 | 1320 | 1340 |
|------|------|------|------|------|------|------|
| **Middle Ages** | | | | **Forerunners to Renaissance** | | |
| 1220 | 1240 | 1260 | 1280 | 1300 | 1320 | 1340 |

**c. 1259 Nicola Pisano**, Pulpit (Baptistery, Pisa cathedral)

**c. 1316–18 Simone Martini**, *Vision of St. Martin* (Lower Church of San Francesco, Assisi)

**c. 1265 Coppo di Marcovaldo**, *Madonna and Child* (Santa Monica dei Servi, Orvieto)

**c. 1297 Giovanni Pisano**, Pulpit (Sant'Andrea, Pistoia)

**c. 1280 Cimabue**, *Madonna Enthroned with Angels and Prophets*, also known as *Santa Trinità Madonna* (Uffizi, Florence)

**c. 1336 Andrea Pisano**, *Baptism of St. John the Baptist*, panel on the South Doors (Baptistery, Florence cathedral)

**c. 1291 Pietro Cavallini**, *The Last Judgment*, detail (Santa Cecilia, Trastevere, Rome)

*c.* **1425–52 Lorenzo Ghiberti**, *Solomon and the Queen of Sheba*, panel on the East Doors (Baptistery, Florence cathedral). These elaborate doors mark a transition from the Gothic style to the Early Renaissance style, in Florence.

**1357 Andrea Orcagna**, *Enthroned Christ with Madonna and Saints* (Strozzi Altarpiece, Santa Maria Novella, Florence)

*c.* **1435 Donatello**, *David* (Museo del Bargello, Florence)

*c.* **1452–65 Piero della Francesca**, detail of *The Dream of Constantine* (San Francesco, Arezzo)

*c.* **1456 Paolo Uccello**, *Battle of San Romano* (Uffizi, Florence)

*c.* **1410 Nanni di Banco**, *Four Crowned Martyrs* (Orsanmichele, Florence)

| 1360 | 1380 | 1400 | 1420 | 1440 | 1460 |
|---|---|---|---|---|---|

**Early Renaissance**

| 1360 | 1380 | 1400 | 1420 | 1440 | 1460 |
|---|---|---|---|---|---|

**1423 Gentile da Fabriano**, *Adoration of the Magi* (Uffizi, Florence)

*c.* **1440 Fra Angelico**, *Annunciation* (San Marco, Florence)

*c.* **1350 Francesco Traini**, *Triumph of Death* (Campo Santo, Pisa)

*c.* **1463 Piero della Francesca**, *Resurrection* (Pinacoteca, Sansepolcro)

*c.* **1465 Fra Filippo Lippi**, *Madonna with Child and Angels* (Uffizi, Florence)

*c.* **1425–8 Masaccio**, *The Tribute Money* (Cappella Brancacci, Florence)

*c.* **1465–74 Andrea Mantegna**, *Arrival of Cardinal Francesco Gonzaga* (Palazzo Ducale, Mantova)

*c.* **1470 Andrea del Verrocchio**, *David* (Bargello, Florence)

## Fresco Technique

Fresco, meaning "fresh," refers to the technique of painting onto a thin layer of damp, freshly laid plaster. Pigments are drawn into the plaster by surface tension, and the color becomes fixed as the plaster dries. The pigments react with the lime in the plaster to produce strong, rich colors, such as those in Masaccio's *The Tribute Money*.

*The Tribute Money* by Masaccio (Cappella Brancacci, Florence)

# High Renaissance Art

The High Renaissance in the late 15th century was marked by an increasing sense of realism in many religious works and by the technical mastery of such renowned artists as Michelangelo, Leonardo da Vinci, and Raphael. The different schools of Renaissance painting, while drawing on Classical models, produced varying styles: Florentine painting was noted for its cool clarity, while sensuous color and warm light characterized many Venetian works. By the mid-16th century, however, these styles shifted to the fanciful, contorted imagery of Mannerism.

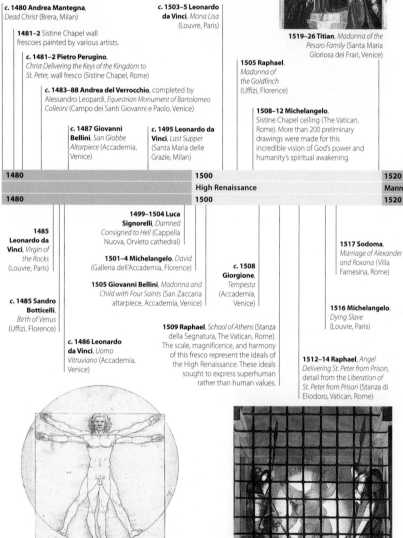

**c. 1480 Andrea Mantegna,** *Dead Christ* (Brera, Milan)

**1481–2** Sistine Chapel wall frescoes painted by various artists.

**c. 1481–2 Pietro Perugino,** *Christ Delivering the Keys of the Kingdom to St. Peter,* wall fresco (Sistine Chapel, Rome)

**c. 1483–88 Andrea del Verrocchio,** completed by Alessandro Leopardi, *Equestrian Monument of Bartolomeo Colleoni* (Campo dei Santi Giovanni e Paolo, Venice)

**c. 1487 Giovanni Bellini,** *San Giobbe Altarpiece* (Accademia, Venice)

**c. 1495 Leonardo da Vinci,** *Last Supper* (Santa Maria delle Grazie, Milan)

**c. 1503–5 Leonardo da Vinci,** *Mona Lisa* (Louvre, Paris)

**1505 Raphael,** *Madonna of the Goldfinch* (Uffizi, Florence)

**1519–26 Titian,** *Madonna of the Pesaro Family* (Santa Maria Gloriosa dei Frari, Venice)

**1508–12 Michelangelo,** Sistine Chapel ceiling (The Vatican, Rome). More than 200 preliminary drawings were made for this incredible vision of God's power and humanity's spiritual awakening.

| 1480 | 1500 | 1520 |
|---|---|---|
| | High Renaissance | Mannerism |
| 1480 | 1500 | 1520 |

**1485 Leonardo da Vinci,** *Virgin of the Rocks* (Louvre, Paris)

**c. 1485 Sandro Botticelli,** *Birth of Venus* (Uffizi, Florence)

**c. 1486 Leonardo da Vinci,** *Uomo Vitruviano* (Accademia, Venice)

**1499–1504 Luca Signorelli,** *Damned Consigned to Hell* (Cappella Nuova, Orvieto cathedral)

**1501–4 Michelangelo,** *David* (Galleria dell'Accademia, Florence)

**1505 Giovanni Bellini,** *Madonna and Child with Four Saints* (San Zaccaria altarpiece, Accademia, Venice)

**c. 1508 Giorgione,** *Tempesta* (Accademia, Venice)

**1509 Raphael,** *School of Athens* (Stanza della Segnatura, The Vatican, Rome). The scale, magnificence, and harmony of this fresco represent the ideals of the High Renaissance. These ideals sought to express superhuman rather than human values.

**1517 Sodoma,** *Marriage of Alexander and Roxana* (Villa Farnesina, Rome)

**1516 Michelangelo,** *Dying Slave* (Louvre, Paris)

**1512–14 Raphael,** *Angel Delivering St. Peter from Prison,* detail from the *Liberation of St. Peter from Prison* (Stanza di Eliodoro, Vatican, Rome)

**1523 Rosso Fiorentino**,
*Moses Defends the
Daughters of Jethro*
(Uffizi, Florence)

**1530–32 Giulio Romano**,
Ceiling and wall frescoes (Sala dei
Giganti, Palazzo del Tè, Mantova)

**c. 1532 Michelangelo**,
*"Blockhead" Captive*
(Galleria dell' Accademia,
Florence)

**1534–5 Paris
Bordone**, *Fisherman
Delivering the Ring*
(Accademia, Venice)

**1534–41
Michelangelo**, *The Last
Judgment*, wall fresco
(Sistine Chapel, Rome)

**c. 1540–42 Titian**, *David
and Goliath* (Santa Maria
della Salute, Venice)

**c. 1562–6 Jacopo Tintoretto**,
*Finding of the Body of St. Mark*
(Brera, Milan)

**c. 1550 Moretto**, *Ecce Homo
with Angel* (Pinacoteca Tosio
Martinengo, Brescia)

| 1540 | 1560 |
|---|---|

| 1540 | 1560 |
|---|---|

**1538 Titian**,
*Venus of Urbino*
(Uffizi, Florence)

**c. 1546 Titian**,
*Portrait of Pope Paul III
Farnese with his
Nephews* (Museo di
Capodimonte, Naples)

**c. 1534–40
Parmigianino**,
*Madonna and Angels or
Madonna with the Long
Neck* (Uffizi, Florence).
Attenuated
proportions and
contrasting colors
make this a fine
example of the
Mannerist style.

**c. 1540 Agnolo Bronzino**,
*Portrait of Lucrezia Panciatichi*
(Uffizi, Florence). Elongated
features, such as Lucrezia's
fingers, are typical of
the exaggerated
Mannerist style.

**1556 Veronese**,
*Triumph of Mordecai*
(San Sebastiano, Venice)

**c. 1526–30 Correggio**, *Assumption of the
Virgin* (Dome of Parma cathedral). Neither a
Mannerist nor a High Renaissance painter,
Correggio was a master of illusion, skilled at
making ascending figures float convincingly,
as seen in the fresco on the left.

# Italian Architecture

The buildings of Italy span almost 3,000 years, drawing influences from a wide variety of sources. Etruscan and Roman buildings borrowed heavily from ancient Greece, while in later centuries Norman, Arabic, and Byzantine styles colored Italy's Romanesque and Gothic architecture. Classical ideals infused the country's Renaissance buildings, later giving way to the inspired innovations of the Baroque period.

**Orvieto's Duomo** displays the ornate and intricate decoration, notably sculpture, common to many Gothic cathedrals. Building stretched from the 13th to the early 17th centuries.

The Basilica di San Marco

**The Basilica di San Marco** (AD 832–1094) in Venice combines Classical, Romanesque, and Gothic architecture, but its key inspiration was Byzantine *(see pp114–15).*

| 200 | 400 | 600 | 800 | 1000 |
|---|---|---|---|---|
| Classical | | Byzantine | | Romanesque |
| 200 | 400 | 600 | 800 | 1000 |

**Triumphal arches** such as Rome's Arch of Constantine (AD 315) were a uniquely Roman invention. Built to celebrate military victories, they were adorned with reliefs depicting episodes from successful campaigns *(see p384).*

**The round-arched** Romanesque style emerged from the Dark Ages in structures such as the Duomo in Modena. The churches usually had simple interiors that derived from Roman basilicas.

**The building of domes** over square or rectangular spaces was a major development of the Byzantine era.

## Etruscan Architecture

Virtually the only architectural memorials to the Etruscans are their necropolises (c.6th century BC), found primarily in Tuscany, Lazio, and Umbria. Little else survives, probably because most day-to-day buildings were made from wood. The Etruscans' close cultural and trading ties with Greece, however, suggest their architecture would have borrowed heavily from Greek models. Rome, in turn, looked to Etruscan architecture for inspiration, and most early Roman public buildings were probably Etruscan in style.

Model of Etruscan temple with Classical Greek portico

**The cathedral of Monreale** in Sicily, built in the 12th century, contains Norman elements blended with exotic Arabic and Byzantine decoration *(see pp534–5).*

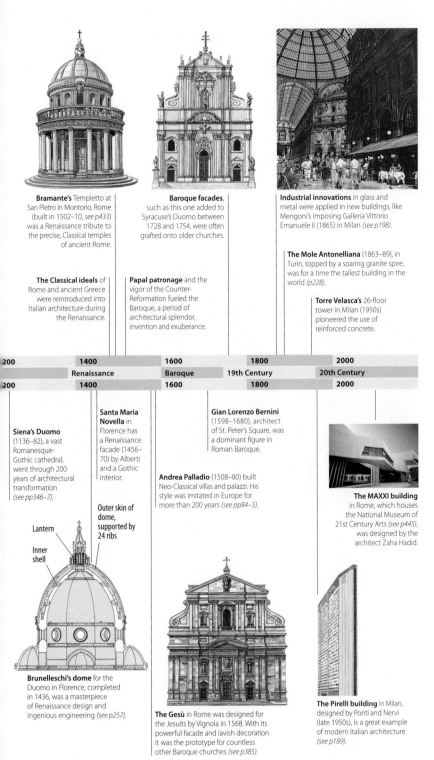

**Bramante's** Tempietto at San Pietro in Montorio, Rome (built in 1502–10, *see p433*) was a Renaissance tribute to the precise, Classical temples of ancient Rome.

**Baroque facades**, such as this one added to Syracuse's Duomo between 1728 and 1754, were often grafted onto older churches.

**Industrial innovations** in glass and metal were applied in new buildings, like Mengoni's imposing Galleria Vittorio Emanuele II (1865) in Milan *(see p198)*.

**The Mole Antonelliana** (1863–89), in Turin, topped by a soaring granite spire, was for a time the tallest building in the world *(p228)*.

**The Classical ideals** of Rome and ancient Greece were reintroduced into Italian architecture during the Renaissance.

**Papal patronage** and the vigor of the Counter-Reformation fueled the Baroque, a period of architectural splendor, invention and exuberance.

**Torre Velasca's** 26-floor tower in Milan (1950s) pioneered the use of reinforced concrete.

| 200 | 1400 | 1600 | 1800 | 2000 |
| --- | --- | --- | --- | --- |
| | Renaissance | Baroque | 19th Century | 20th Century |
| 200 | 1400 | 1600 | 1800 | 2000 |

**Santa Maria Novella** in Florence has a Renaissance facade (1456–70) by Alberti and a Gothic interior.

**Gian Lorenzo Bernini** (1598–1680), architect of St. Peter's Square, was a dominant figure in Roman Baroque.

**Siena's Duomo** (1136–82), a vast Romanesque-Gothic cathedral, went through 200 years of architectural transformation *(see pp346–7)*.

**Andrea Palladio** (1508–80) built Neo-Classical villas and palazzi. His style was imitated in Europe for more than 200 years *(see pp84–5)*.

**The MAXXI building** in Rome, which houses the National Museum of 21st Century Arts *(see p445)*, was designed by the architect Zaha Hadid.

Outer skin of dome, supported by 24 ribs

Lantern

Inner shell

**Brunelleschi's dome** for the Duomo in Florence, completed in 1436, was a masterpiece of Renaissance design and ingenious engineering *(see p257)*.

**The Gesù** in Rome was designed for the Jesuits by Vignola in 1568. With its powerful facade and lavish decoration it was the prototype for countless other Baroque churches *(see p385)*.

**The Pirelli building** in Milan, designed by Ponti and Nervi (late 1950s), is a great example of modern Italian architecture *(see p189)*.

# Saints and Symbols in Italian Art

Saints and symbols are especially important in Italian art. They form part of an established visual language used by artists to narrate stories of the Bible and the Catholic Church to churchgoers. Paintings of the saints were the focus for prayer and each offered assistance in a particular aspect of daily life. Patron saints protected specific cities or trades, and individuals who bore their name. Saints' days and religious festivals still play an important part in Italian life.

### The Evangelists

The four evangelists, Matthew, Mark, Luke, and John, are each represented by a winged creature, standing for a divine mission.

Eagle (St. John)

**St. John** carries a book of the Gospel bearing his name.

**St. Thomas Aquinas** is usually shown with a star, barely visible in this painting, on his Dominican habit.

**St. Dominic** is usually portrayed wearing the habit of his order. The lily is another of his attributes.

**St. Cosmas and St. Damian** are always shown together, dressed in physicians' clothing.

**St. Mark the Evangelist** often holds his book of the Gospels.

**St. Lawrence** carries a palm leaf as well as the gridiron on which he was roasted.

**Virgin Enthroned with the Child and Saints** (c.1450) was painted on dry plaster by the Dominican friar Fra Angelico. It is on display at the Museo di San Marco, Florence (see p280).

**The Virgin**, usually shown in blue robes, is depicted as Mater Amabilis – the "Mother Worthy of Love."

**St. Peter Martyr**, here with a palm leaf, is sometimes depicted with a head wound, carrying a sword.

## Symbols

In order to identify different saints or martyrs, they were given "attributes" or symbols – particular objects to carry, or clothing to wear. These were items that played a particular role in their life story. Martyrs were known by their instruments of torture or death. Symbolism also appears in the sky, animals, flowers, colors, and numbers.

**The lamb** symbolizes Christ, the Lamb of God, or, in early Christian art, the sinner.

**The skull** is a memento mori to remind us of death and impermanence.

Winged man
(St. Matthew)

Winged lion
(St. Mark)

Winged ox
(St. Luke)

Giovanni Bellini's painting *Madonna and Child with Four Saints (see p123)*

**St. Peter the Apostle**, the "rock" on which the Christian church was founded, carries the keys to Heaven.

**The Madonna**, with the Christ Child, is an emblem of perfect motherly love.

**St. Catherine of Alexandria** is shown here with a piece of the wheel on which she was martyred.

**St. Jerome** is always portrayed as an old man, often a hermit, whose life was devoted to scholarship.

**Detail from Madonna and Child with Four Saints**, by Giovanni Bellini. The painting was produced in 1505 for an altarpiece at San Zaccaria, Venice, where it is still on display.

**The angel**, a messenger of God to man, is portrayed in this scene as a musician of Heaven.

**St. Lucy** is depicted here holding her own eyes in a dish. She became the patron saint of the blind and symbolizes light.

**The lily**, flower of the Virgin, is the symbol of purity, resurrection, peace, and chastity.

**The cockle shell** most often represents pilgrimage. It is a particular attribute of St. Roch.

**The palm** represents, in Christian art, a martyr's triumph over death.

# Writers, Poets, and Dramatists

Italy has produced many writers (in Latin and Italian) who have won worldwide acclaim. Each of them provides an illuminating insight into the country's turbulent past: the Classical poets Virgil, Horace, and Ovid give vivid accounts of the concerns and values of ancient Rome; medieval Florence and Tuscany are brought to life in the poetry of Dante and Petrarch and the salacious tales of Boccaccio. These three great writers, in less than a century, created a new literary language to rank with any in Europe. Italy's modern literature still commands international attention – Umberto Eco has to his credit one of the most widely read books of the 20th century.

**Primo Levi** (1919–87) gave an astonishing account of his survival of the Jewish Holocaust and World War II's aftermath in *The Truce* and *If This Is a Man*.

Trentino Alto Adige

Lombardy

Valle d'Aosta and Piedmont

Emilia-Romagna

Liguria

**Dario Fo** (born 1926) won the Nobel Prize for Literature in 1997.

Tuscany

**Umberto Eco** (born 1932), a professor at the University of Bologna, wrote the novel *The Name of the Rose*, which explored his passion for the Middle Ages. The book was made into a movie (above) in 1986.

**Giovanni Boccaccio** (1313–75) is notable for providing a fascinating social record of his era. *The Decameron*, his captivating collection of 100 short stories, is set in the plague-stricken Florence of 1348.

**Pinocchio**, written by Carlo Collodi (1826–90) in 1883, is one of the world's best-known children's stories. "Collodi" was Carlo Lorenzini's pseudonym, taken after his mother's birthplace in Tuscany.

**Dante's** (1265–1321) *Divine Comedy* (c.1308–21) is a journey through Hell, Purgatory, and Paradise. It includes horrific accounts of the torments suffered by the damned.

The Veneto
and Friuli

**Venetian author**
Carlo Goldoni (1707–93)
reacted against the satirical
tradition of *commèdia
dell'arte*, preferring to write
more forgiving plays on
contemporary Venice society.

## Classical Roman Writers

Texts in Latin by Classical Roman philosophers, poets,
dramatists, and politicians are part of the bedrock of
Western culture. Today the names Virgil *(The Aeneid)*, Ovid
*(Metamorphoses)*, and Pliny *(Historia Naturalis)* are literary
legends. Fascinating histories such as Livy's *Early History of
Rome*, Caesar's Gallic Wars, Tacitus's *Annals*, and Suetonius's
*The Twelve Caesars* give us an invaluable window on
the distant Roman past, as do
the caustic *Satires* of Juvenal.
Many Latin works owe their
survival to the teams of medieval
monks who diligently copied
and illustrated them. In the
Renaissance the stories of Ovid's
*Metamorphoses* were plundered
by many writers and the works
of Cicero had a profound
influence on prose style; Seneca
was seen as a master of tragedy
and Plautus's *Pot of Gold* served
as a model for comedies.

Detail from medieval copy of
Pliny's *Historia Naturalis*

Le Marche

**Petrarch** (1304–74), one
of the earliest and greatest
lyric poets, produced works
that showed the first
indications of Humanism.

Umbria

Lazio

**St. Francis of Assisi** (1182–
1226) was the first author to
write in Italian instead of
formal Latin. As well as
letters and sermons, he
wrote poems and songs,
including the popular
*Canticle of the Sun*.

**Abruzzo, Molise,
and Puglia**

Campania

Basilicata
and
Calabria

**Roman writer** Alberto Moravia
(1907–90) is usually labeled a
"Neo-Realist." His novels and short
stories focus on the corrupt values
of contemporary society. Among
his best-known works are
*Gli Indifferenti* and *Agostino*.

Sicily

**The Sicilian** Nobel Prize winner
Luigi Pirandello (1867–1936)
was preoccupied with
themes of illusion and reality.
*Six Characters in Search of an
Author* is his most famous work.

0 kilometers 200
0 miles 100

# Music and Opera in Italy

Before Italy's unification, particularly during the 17th and 18th centuries, each major city had its own traditions of music-making. Rome, as the papal city, had musical traditions less hedonistic than elsewhere, and avoided opera. Florence had its day at the turn of the 16th century, with its celebrated *camerata* (groups set on reviving the traditions of ancient Greek spectacle). Venice fostered church music on a grand scale, and Naples, during the 18th century, was renowned for comic opera. In the 19th century, Milan became the undisputed heart of Italian opera, centered on La Scala.

## The Baroque Era

Claudio Monteverdi's music straddled the transition from the Renaissance period to 17th-century Baroque. The word *baroque* means "highly ornamented, even bizarre," and embellishment was rife. Monteverdi's madrigals began as standard pieces for four voices but ended up as mini-operas. This was due to the popularity of an individual instrumental style and the development of the *basso continuo* (a supporting organ, harpsichord or lute that unleashed the possibility for solos and duets). At this point, the beginnings of the string orchestra were in place.

A new fashion for declamation meant that various emotional states were being represented with sighs and sobs rather than just description. Monteverdi's *Vespers* followed others in exploiting the stereophonic possibilities of San Marco in Venice by contrasting different

## The Medieval and Renaissance Periods

Through Boccaccio *(see p38)*, among others, it is known that singing, dancing, and poetry often went hand in hand in medieval and Renaissance Italy. Italy concentrated on music as part of a spectacle rather than as a pure art form.

Important contributors to the music of these periods include Guido d'Arezzo (c.995–1050), a monk who perfected musical notation, and Francesco Landini (1325–97), one of the first known composers whose songs displayed a distinct concern for lyricism. The next 150 years were to be characterized by the *Ars Perfecta* style, culminating with composer Giovanni Pierluigi da Palestrina (1525–94). His vocal style subjected dissonance to strict control, and it was employed for most church music during his lifetime. Madrigals (vocal settings of poems by Petrarch and other poets) were also popular.

La Pietà, Venice, where Vivaldi performed

The early 17th century saw Italian composers such as Carlo Gesualdo da Venosa (c.1561–1613) and Claudio Monteverdi challenge these traditions by introducing more declamation and more of the unexpected.

## Major Italian Composers through the Ages

**Claudio Monteverdi** (1567–1643) was best known for his *Vespers* of 1610. His madrigals and operas are both considered major landmarks in the development of music.

**Antonio Vivaldi** (1678–1741) wrote over 600 concertos, many of which are for the violin. *The Four Seasons,* a set of concertos, is among the best-selling classical music of all time.

**Gioacchino Rossini** (1792–1868) was most famous for his comic operas, like *The Barber of Seville* and *La Cenerentola*. The romantic, expressive side of his more serious works, such as *Otello*, was often overlooked.

Luciano Pavarotti brought opera to a wider international audience

forces in different parts of the building. In the 1680s, Arcangelo Corelli (1653–1713) turned to classicism. Corelli was famous for the *concerto grosso,* a style that contrasted the solo string group with the full ensemble. He was followed by Antonio Vivaldi (1678–1741), who concentrated his efforts on developing the solo form of the *concerto grosso.* He used wind and plucked instruments as well as violins.

## The Emergence of Opera

Opera first emerged during the wedding celebrations of Italy's wealthy 16th-century families. Monteverdi was the first composer to establish his work

**Giuseppe Verdi** (1813–1901), whose first works were for the opera house La Scala *(see p197),* was the most important opera composer of the 19th century. His most celebrated works include *Rigoletto* and *Aida.*

firmly in the opera repertoire. During the 17th century, Alessandro Scarlatti (1660–1725) formulated a model which consisted of an orchestral overture followed by a sequence of narrative, set as *recitative,* and interrupted by *da capo* (three-part) arias. Themes for the weightier *opera seria* were largely drawn from mythology, while the lighter *opera buffa* had stock scenes that sometimes owed a large debt to the traditions of *commèdia dell'arte.* Famous for his comic operas, such as *The Barber of Seville,* was the composer Gioacchino Rossini. Among other contributors, Vincenzo Bellini (1801–35) and Gaetano Donizetti (1797–1848) developed *bel canto* singing, a style stressing fine tone and ornamentation.

The two most prominent opera composers of the latter half of the 19th century were Giuseppe Verdi and Giacomo Puccini (1858–1924). Verdi often turned to the works of Shakespeare as well as to contemporary subjects in order to form a basis for his work, while many composers, like Puccini, turned to the new trend of *verismo* (slices of realism) – *La Bohème* is one of the most refined examples of this style.

Puccini's *Tosca,* first staged in 1900

## The 20th Century

In the early 20th century, Puccini's *La Fanciulla del West* (The Girl of the West) brought cowboys into opera, *Turandot* looked toward the Orient and *Tosca* brought torture and murder. Some composers have attempted to emulate French and German music, and only a few Italian pieces, such as those by Ottorino Respighi (1879–1936), have been regularly performed. The most important name in post-war Italian music was Luciano Berio (1925–2003), who developed Music Theater, an art form lying somewhere between drama and opera. In later years, however, Berio continued the tradition of Grand Opera with his elaborate production of *Un Re in Ascolto.* But it is Luciano Pavarotti (1935–2007) who must be credited with renewing an international interest in opera. In the 1990s, his televised performances with "Three Tenors" co-stars José Carreras and Placido Domingo secured a massive world audience for opera. Another star of opera and classical music is internationally renowned conductor Riccardo Muti, former director of La Scala and now the director of Rome's Teatro dell'Opera.

The illuminated interior of Rome's Teatro dell'Opera

# Italian Design

Italy has had phenomenal success evolving stylish, desirable forms for everyday objects. Its 20th-century achievements can be credited to a handful of forward-thinking industrial giants, such as Olivetti, willing to entrust important product decisions to a group of inspired designers, like Ettore Sottsass. The design genius was to rethink the function of consumer objects, apply new technology, and then make the result look seductive.

**The streamlined** aesthetic of Italian design extends even to pasta; this Marille version was created by car designer Giorgio Giugiaro for Voiello in 1983.

**Sleek, sculptural Alessi cutlery** (1988), designed by Ettore Sottsass, combines maximum utility with elegance and aesthetic integrity.

**The Alessi kettle** (1985), designed by Michael Graves, achieved such popularity in its first year of production that more than 100,000 were sold.

**One of the best-known** coffeemakers is Bialetti's Moka Express. Although designed in 1930, it is still enormously popular today.

**Christophe Pilet's** chair, designed for Giulio Cappellini's collection of contemporary furniture, is a wonderful example of the 1990s aesthetic, and is still available for purchase.

**The folding Cumano** table, designed by Achille Castiglione for Zanotta in 1979, is still revered as a "designer object."

**The Patty Difusa** chair, with unusual wooden arms that curve into legs, was designed by William Sawaya for Sawaya & Moroni in Milan.

**Pininfarina's streamlined** form for the Ferrari Testarossa (1986) pushes car design almost into the realms of sculpture.

**Light in weight**, and compact in shape, Olivetti's Valentine typewriter revolutionized the role of the desk typewriter. Designed by Ettore Sottsass in 1969, its portability allowed the user to work anywhere.

**Italian printer** Giambattista Bodoni (1740–1813) designed the sophisticated typeface that bears his name and is still popular 200 years after its creation.

**Milan's Giorgio Armani** is best known for creating a flattering, smart, and comfortable look. He often relies on muted colors, such as beige, black, or gray.

**Prada, the Milan-based** fashion house headed by Miuccia Prada, features minimalist, cutting-edge designs and the use of innovative fabrics.

**Florence** has a long reputation as a producer of high-quality crafts, particularly fashion accessories such as purses, shoes, belts, jewelry, and briefcases.

**Gucci's** classic items, including purses and loafers, are a revered totem for the fashion-conscious.

**The Artemide** company is renowned for combining metal and glass in many of their designs, especially lamps and lighting fixtures.

**Piaggio's innovative** Vespa scooter (1946), by Corradino d'Ascanio, provided cheap, fast, and reliable transportation at a time when few could afford a car. Hugely successful, the Vespa is still a common sight on Italy's streets.

**The FIAT 500** (1957), like the Vespa, became a symbol of mobility and democratization, an expression of Italy's rapid postwar recovery.

# Scientists, Inventors, and Explorers

Italy has fostered a long tradition of important scientific thought and discovery, fueled in the Renaissance by such men as Galileo, who searched for a new understanding of the universe. Meanwhile, explorers such as Columbus had set off to find new worlds, a move heralded in the 13th century by Marco Polo. The spirit of scientific inquiry continued up to the 20th century, with the invention of radio and pioneering work in the field of nuclear physics.

Trentino Alto Adi

Lombardy

Valle d'Aosta and Piedmont

Liguria

Emilia-Romagna

Tuscany

**Genoese-born** Christopher Columbus sailed west from Spain in 1492. He reached the Indies in three months, navigating with such aids as an astrolabe.

**The explorer** Amerigo Vespucci established that the New World was a separate land mass. A pamphlet wrongly described him as its discoverer, and so, in 1507, America acquired its name.

**Guglielmo Marconi** invented the first practical system for sending radio signals. In 1901, he succeeded in picking up a signal that had been sent to England from Newfoundland.

**Leonardo da Vinci** was the ultimate Renaissance man, accomplished in both arts and sciences. He conceived his first design for a flying machine in c.1488, more than 400 years before the first airplane took off. This model is based on one of his technical drawings.

| 0 kilometers | 200 |
|---|---|
| 0 miles | 100 |

**The telescope** enabled astronomers to produce accurate lunar maps. Domenico Cassini, astronomy professor at Bologna University, refined the instrument. In 1665 he traced the meridian line in the church of San Petronio.

**Padua University**, founded in 1222, was a center of scientific learning in the Renaissance. Galileo, inventor of the telescope, taught physics here, and the lectern he used is still on view.

The Veneto and Friuli

**The Venetian Marco Polo** set off for the East as a youth in 1271. He stayed at the court of the Mongol emperor Kublai Khan for nearly two decades before returning home. He is seen here arriving at Hormuz in the Persian Gulf from India.

**Galileo Galilei** proved that the earth revolved around the sun, over-turning Church doctrine. He was convicted of heresy in 1633. Here he shows the rings of Saturn to Venetian senators.

Le Marche

Umbria

**Winner of** the Nobel Prize for Physics in 1938, Enrico Fermi directed the first controlled nuclear chain reaction. He built the world's first nuclear reactor for producing power at the University of Chicago.

Rome and Lazio

Abruzzo, Molise, and Puglia

Naples and Campania

**Pliny the Elder** wrote his catalog of human knowledge, *Natural History*, in AD 77. He died when Vesuvius erupted two years later, but his book retained its authority for 1,500 years.

Basilicata and Calabria

**Eyeglasses were invented** in Italy in the 13th century. They are first recorded in Venice, still an important center for glasswork today.

Sicily

**The mathematician Archimedes** was born in *c.*287 BC in Syracuse, Sicily, then a Greek colony. Legend has it that he discovered the principle of specific gravity while in the bath.

# THE HISTORY OF ITALY

The concept of Italy as a geographic entity goes back to the time of the Etruscans, but Italy's history is one of discord and division. Prior to the 19th century, the only time the peninsula was united was under the Romans, who by the 2nd century BC had subdued the other Italian tribes. Rome became the capital of a huge empire, introducing its language, laws, and calendar to most of Europe before succumbing to Germanic invaders in the 5th century AD. Another important legacy of the Roman Empire was Christianity and the position of the pope as head of the Catholic Church. The medieval papacy summoned the Franks to drive out the Lombards and, in AD 800, crowned the Frankish king Charlemagne Holy Roman Emperor. Unfortunately, what seemed to be the dawn of a new age turned out to be anything but. For five centuries, popes and emperors fought to decide which of them should be in charge of their nebulous empire.

Meanwhile, a succession of foreign invaders – Normans, Angevins, and Aragonese – took advantage of the situation to conquer Sicily and the south. The north, in contrast, saw a growth of independent city-states, the most powerful being Venice, fabulously wealthy through trade with the East. Other cities, such as Genoa, Florence, Milan, Pisa, and Siena, also had their days of glory. Northern Italy became the most prosperous and cultured region in western Europe, and it was the artists and scholars of 15th-century Florence who inspired the Renaissance. Small, fragmented states, however, could not compete with great powers. In the 16th century Italy's petty kingdoms fell prey to a foreign invader, this time Spain, and the north subsequently came under the control of Austria.

One small kingdom that remained independent was Piedmont, but during a war between Austria and France it fell to Napoleon in 1796. In the 19th century, however, it was Piedmont that became the focus for a movement toward a united Italy, a goal that was achieved in 1861, thanks largely to the heroic military exploits of Garibaldi. In the 1920s, the Fascists seized power and, in 1946, the monarchy was abandoned for today's republic.

16th-century map of Italy, of the kind used by Venetian and Genoese sailors

◄ *Fall of the Rebel Angels*, fresco by Giacinto Brandi on the ceiling of Sant'Ambrogio e Carlo al Corso, Rome

# The Age of the Etruscans

The Etruscans were Italy's first major civilization. The frescoes, jewelry and pottery found in their tombs are evidence of a highly artistic, cultured people. Their origin is a mystery, as is their language, but from the 9th century BC they spread through central Italy, their chief rivals being the Greeks in the south. Etruria was never a unified state, just a loose confederation of cities. In the 6th century Etruscan kings ruled Rome, the city that would ultimately eclipse them.

**Italy in 650 BC**

Etruscan kingdoms

Greek colonies

**Terracotta Winged Horses**
This beautiful relief of yoked horses (4th century BC) decorated the facade of the Ara della Regina temple at Tarquinia.

**The double flute** was a specialty of the Etruscans. The instrument was played at festivals and funerals alike.

**Bronze Sheep's Liver**
The inscriptions served as a guide for telling the future from animals' entrails.

**Terracotta Cremation Urn**
The lid of the urn shows the deceased holding a writing tablet. The Etruscans introduced the alphabet to Italy.

**Tomb of the Leopards**
*Feasts and revelry are common themes in the frescoes that decorate Etruscan tombs. These musicians are from a tomb fresco (c.500 BC) at Tarquinia (see p470).*

---

| | | |
|---|---|---|
| **9th century BC** Pre-urban communities established along river valleys in Etruria | | **c.700 BC** Growth of cities in Etruria; earliest Etruscan inscriptions |
| | **753 BC** Legendary date of foundation of Rome by Romulus | **616 BC** Etruscans become rulers of Rome under Tarquino the Older |

| **900 BC** | **800 BC** | **700 BC** |
|---|---|---|

**c.900 BC** First traces of Iron Age in Italy; Villanovan period

**c.800 BC** Greeks settle in Sicily and south of Italy

**715–673 BC** Reign of the wise Numa Pompilius, second king of Rome

*Etruscan gold earrings*

**A Boxing Contest**
Athletic competitions were held at funerals. This vase, which dates from about 500 BC, was made in Etruria, but imitates the Greek black-figure style of pottery.

**The musicians** and the dancer in the tomb painting are painted with a realism that indicates the influence of Greek art.

**The lyre** was made from a tortoiseshell and played with a plectrum.

**Apollo of Veii**
This magnificent statue of Apollo (c.500 BC) shows the stylized facial features characteristic of Etruscan art.

**Bronze Mirror**
Wealthy Etruscans lived in great luxury. The women used polished bronze mirrors with engraved backs. This one shows Helen of Troy and the goddess Aphrodite.

## Where to See Etruscan Italy

**Rock tombs** like these at Sovana (p350) are common in the volcanic tufa of central Italy.

Tuscany, Lazio, and Umbria are rich in Etruscan remains, especially tombs. There are huge necropolises in Lazio at Cerveteri and Tarquinia (p470). The latter also has an important museum. Other museums with major collections of Etruscan art and artifacts include Villa Giulia (p444) and the Vatican's Museo Gregoriano Profano (p426) in Rome, the Museo Archeologico in Florence (p281), the Museo Nazionale in Chiusi (p336), and the Museo Guarnacci in Volterra (pp338–9).

**Temple of Neptune**
This fine temple at Paestum (5th century BC) is a legacy of Greek colonization of the south.

**509 BC** Last Etruscan king, Tarquinius Superbus, expelled from Rome; establishment of Roman Republic

*Mixing bowl, imported from Greece*

**450 BC** Roman law codified in the Twelve Tables

**390 BC** Gauls sack Rome; Capitol saved thanks to alarm sounded by cackling geese

**600 BC**

**500 BC**

**400 BC**

**499 BC** Battle of Lake Regillus; Romans defeat alliance of Latins and Etruscans

**474 BC** Etruscan fleet defeated by Greeks off Cumae; blow to Etruscan naval power

**c.400 BC** Gauls start to settle along valley of the Po

**396 BC** Veii, a major Etruscan city in present-day Lazio, falls to Rome

*Relief of Capitoline geese, found in the Roman Forum*

# From Republic to Empire

From the scores of tribes inhabiting ancient Italy, one group of people, the Romans, emerged to conquer the peninsula and impose their language, customs, and laws on the rest. Rome's success was due to superb skill in military and civil organization. The State was a republic ruled by two consuls, elected each year, but as the extent of Rome's conquests grew, power passed to generals such as Julius Caesar. The Republic became unworkable and Caesar's heirs became the first Roman emperors.

**Cisalpine Gaul** was annexed in 202–191 BC.

**Etruria** was in Roman hands by 265 BC.

**Julius Caesar**
The great general, conqueror of Gaul, returned to Italy in 49 BC to defeat Pompey. His rise to absolute power marked the end of the Republic.

**Oscan Inscription**
The languages of the peoples conquered by Rome lived on for centuries before being replaced by Latin. The Oscans lived in what is now Campania.

**War Elephant**
In 218 BC the great Carthaginian general Hannibal brought 37 elephants across the Alps – to spread alarm in the Roman ranks.

**Roman Aqueduct**
The Romans' talent for engineering found its most spectacular expression in huge aqueducts. These could be up to 50 miles (80 km) long, though for most of that distance the water ran underground.

High ground

Cleaning vent

Reservoir

Underground water channel

Arches carrying water across low ground

**312 BC** Building of Via Appia and Aqua Appia aqueduct

**308 BC** Etruscan city of Tarquinii falls to Rome

**275 BC** Greek King Pyrrhus defeated by Romans at Beneventum

**264–241 BC** First Punic War (between Rome and Carthage)

**218 BC** Second Punic War; Hannibal crosses the Alps

**216 BC** Roman defeat at Battle of Cannae

**300 BC**

**250 BC**

**200 BC**

*Via Appia*

**287–212 BC** Life of Archimedes, the great Greek mathematician of Syracuse

**265 BC** Romans capture last Etruscan city

**237 BC** Romans occupy Corsica and Sardinia

*Hannibal, Carthaginian leader in the Second Punic War*

**191 BC** Gaulish territory south of the Alps falls to Rome

### Cicero Addresses the Senate
State business was debated in the Senate. The great orator Cicero (106–43 BC) argued for the Republic and against tyranny.

### Roman Legionary
This bronze shows a legionary in standard kit of helmet, breastplate, leather kilt with iron plates, greaves on his shins, and sandals.

**The Via Appia** was extended from Capua to Brindisi in 190 BC.

**INIUM**

*aleria*

**APUA**

*Via Appia*

**BRUNDISIUM**
**Brindisi**

**TARENTUM**
**Taranto**

**Sicily** became the first Roman province in 241 BC.

**RHEGIUM**
**Reggio di Calabria**

### Where to See Republican Era Italy

Republican structures are very rare, most having been rebuilt under the Empire. In Rome itself, two notable exceptions are the 2nd-century BC Temples of the Forum Boarium *(p437)*. However, the legacy of the age to modern Italy is not hard to appreciate. Countless roads, such as the Via Appia Antica *(p445)*, and towns were planned originally by Roman engineers. Two striking examples of towns with original Roman street plans are Lucca *(pp324–5)* and Como *(pp194–5)*.

These huge basalt blocks at Tharros in Sardinia *(p554)* were part of a Roman road.

### Roman Roads

*After conquering other tribes, the Romans imposed their authority by building roads along which legions could march rapidly to deal with any trouble. They also built towns. Many, such as Ariminum (Rimini), were "colonies", settlements for Roman citizens – often veteran legionaries.*

### Aerial View of Bologna
Roman street plans are still visible in city centers today. The route of the old Via Aemilia cuts straight through the center of Bologna.

---

**104 BC** Slave revolt in Sicily

**146 BC** End of Third Punic War; Carthage destroyed

**89 BC** Social War: Rome's Italian allies granted citizenship

**80 BC** Building starts on the first Roman amphitheater, at Pompeii

**31 BC** Octavian defeats Mark Antony at Battle of Actium

**30 BC** Suicide of Mark Antony and Cleopatra in Egypt

**150 BC**

**100 BC**

**50 BC**

**168 BC** End of Third Macedonian War; Romans now masters of Greece

*Milestone from the Via Aemilia*

**73–71 BC** Slave revolt led by Spartacus

**49 BC** Caesar crosses the Rubicon and drives Pompey from Rome

**44 BC** Murder of Julius Caesar; end of Roman Republic

**45 BC** Introduction of 12-month Julian calendar

# The Golden Age of Rome

From the age of Augustus to the reign of Trajan, Rome's power grew until her Empire stretched from Britain to the Red Sea. Despite the extravagance of emperors such as Nero, taxes and booty from military campaigns continually refilled the Imperial coffers. Under the wiser rule of Trajan, Hadrian, and Marcus Aurelius in the 2nd century AD, Roman citizens enjoyed wealth and comfort, with most of the work performed by slaves. Entertainment included visits to the baths, the theater, and the games. The town of Pompeii, buried when Vesuvius erupted in AD 79, preserves many fascinating details of everyday life.

**Roman Empire in AD 117**

▦ Maximum extent of the empire

**Mosaic of Gladiators**
Bloodthirsty gladiatorial combats were very popular. The gladiators were mostly slaves captured in war.

Frescoes of festoons and medallions

**Trajan's Column**
The carvings record Trajan's successful campaigns in Dacia (present-day Romania) in the first decade of the 2nd century AD.

**The triclinium**
(main dining room) had a beautiful frieze of cupids.

**House of the Vettii**
*This reconstruction shows one of Pompeii's finest houses (see pp498–9). The Vettii were not aristocrats, but freedmen, former slaves, who had made a fortune through trade. The rooms were richly decorated with frescoes and sculptures.*

**Roman Stores**
Buildings in towns were lined with small stores open to the street, like this pharmacy. The front was closed with wooden panels and locked at night.

**9 BC** Dedication of Ara Pacis *(see p414)* in Rome to celebrate peace after wars in Gaul and Spain

**AD 17** Tiberius fixes boundary of Empire along the Rhine and Danube

*Bronze cooking pots from kitchen at Pompeii*

**AD 79** Eruption of Vesuvius destroys Pompeii and Herculaneum

**50 BC**

**AD 1**

**AD 50**

**27 BC** Augustus takes title Princeps, in effect becoming the first Roman emperor

**AD 37–41** Reign of Caligula

**AD 43** Roman conquest of Britain in reign of Claudius

**AD 67** Traditional date for martyrdom of St. Peter and St. Paul in Rome

**AD 68** Deposition and suicide of Nero

**AD 80** Inaugural games in Colosseum

**Augustus**
The adopted son of Julius Caesar became the first emperor, reducing the Roman Senate to impotence and ruling by decree.

**The atrium** had a skylight in the roof with a pool that collected rainwater below.

Front entrance

## Where to See Imperial Rome

The best places to discover how people lived are Pompeii (pp498–9) and Herculaneum. Artifacts and works of art from these sites are held at the Museo Archeologico in Naples (pp494–5), while local museums all over Italy contain statues and other remains. Famous sights in Rome include the Pantheon (p408) and the Colosseum (p397). Hadrian's Villa, at Tivoli (p472), and Ostia (p471) are also fascinating to visit, but the whole country preserves traces of Rome's glory – from the Arch of Augustus in Aosta (p219) to Villa Romana del Casale (p541) in Sicily.

**The Forum** (pp394–5), with its temples and law courts, was the center of daily life in ancient Rome.

Reception room

**Mosaic of a Banquet**
The Romans ate reclining on low couches. A popular accompaniment for many dishes was *garum*, a salty sauce made of dried fish.

Peristyle or colonnade

**Household Shrine**
Religious rites were practiced both in public and in private. This shrine from the House of the Vettii was dedicated to the *lares*, the household gods.

**The internal garden** was a feature borrowed by the Romans from the Greeks.

**AD 97** Roman Empire reaches largest extent in reign of Trajan

**AD 161–180** Reign of Marcus Aurelius

**AD 193–211** Reign of Septimius Severus

**AD 212** Roman citizenship extended to include people from all parts of the empire

**AD 100**

**AD 150**

**AD 200**

Late 1st century AD Amphitheater of Verona built

**AD 134** Hadrian's Villa at Tivoli completed

*Emperor Septimius Severus*

**AD 125** Pantheon rebuilt by Hadrian

**AD 216** Baths of Caracalla completed in Rome

# The Splitting of the Empire

A decisive turning point in the history of the Roman Empire came with Emperor Constantine's conversion to Christianity in AD 312 and his decision to build a new capital at Constantinople (Byzantium). By the 5th century, the Empire was split in two. Rome and the Western Empire could not stem the tide of Germanic invaders migrating southward, and Italy fell first to the Goths and later to the Lombards. The Eastern Empire retained nominal control over parts of Italy from its stronghold at Ravenna, which became the richest, most powerful city of the age, while the great palaces and arenas of Rome were reduced to ruins.

**Italy in AD 600**

▨ Byzantine territories

☐ Lombard territories

**The Donation of Constantine**
A medieval legend, encouraged by the papacy, tells how Constantine granted Pope Sylvester temporal power over Rome.

**Belisarius**
(500–565) was a general who won much of Italy back from the Goths.

**Theodolinda of the Lombards**
The 6th-century queen converted her people to orthodox Catholicism. Here, gold is melted for the church she built at Monza *(see p205)*.

**Justinian** reigned from 527 to 565. He was a great lawgiver and one of the most powerful Byzantine emperors.

| | | | | |
|---|---|---|---|---|
| **303–5** Persecution of Christians throughout the Empire in the reign of Diocletian | **404** Ravenna becomes seat of the Western Empire | | *Gold coin of Theodoric* | **547** Church of San Vitale in Ravenna |
| | **312** Constantine defeats rival Maxentius at Battle of the Milvian Bridge | | **488** Italy invaded by the Theodoric the Ostrogoth | |

| 200 | 300 | 400 | 500 |
|---|---|---|---|

| | | | | |
|---|---|---|---|---|
| **270** Aurelian Wall built to protect Rome from Germanic invaders | **313** Edict of Milan grants freedom of worship to Christians | **324** Christianity becomes state religion | **476** End of the Western Empire | **535** Belisarius lands in Sicily; reconquest of most of Italy by Byzantine Empire |
| | | *c.* **320** Building of first St. Peter's in Rome | **410** Sack of Rome by Alaric the Visigoth | **564** Lombard invade Italy establishing their capita at Pavi |

### Charlemagne
The King of the Franks was invited by the pope to crush the Lombards. In return, he was crowned Holy Roman Emperor in AD 800.

**Saracens Besieging Messina**
In the 9th century, Sicily was conquered by Muslims from Africa. Saracen raiders even reached Rome, where Pope Leo IV built a new wall to defend the Vatican.

**The emperor** holds a large gold paten, the dish in which the bread is placed for Mass.

Maximian, Archbishop of Ravenna

## Where to See Early Christian and Byzantine Italy

Though the fall of the Roman Empire led to war, famine, and depopulation, the continuity of the Christian religion has preserved many monuments of the late Empire and Byzantine period. Rome has the catacombs (p446) and great basilicas, such as Santa Maria Maggiore (p417). In Ravenna, the administrative capital of the Byzantine Empire, are the churches of San Vitale and Sant' Apollinare (pp272–3) with their magnificent mosaics. Sicily and the south also preserve many Byzantine churches, while the finest example of late Byzantine architecture is San Marco in Venice (pp114–15).

**Stilo** in Calabria has a beautiful Byzantine church, the Cattolica (p524), dating from the 10th century.

### The Court of Justinian
*Byzantine churches were decorated with glorious mosaics of colored glass and gold leaf. This one, from the apse of the church of San Vitale in Ravenna (see p272), completed in 547, depicts members of the Imperial court.*

Priests

**Santa Costanza** in Rome (p445) was built in the 4th century as the mausoleum of Constantine's daughter. Late Roman mosaics decorate the vaults.

| | | | |
|---|---|---|---|
| **595** Lombards control two-thirds of Italy | **752** Lombard King Aistulf takes Byzantine stronghold of Ravenna | **774** Charlemagne conquers Italy and takes Lombard crown | **878** Saracens capture city of Syracuse from Byzantine Empire and gain control of Sicily |
| | | **800** Charlemagne crowned Holy Roman Emperor in St. Peter's | |
| **600** | **700** | **800** | **900** |
| *Gregory the Great (reigned 590–604)* | **754** Pope appeals to Franks for help; King Pepin invades Italy and defeats Lombards | | |
| **599** Pope Gregory negotiates peace between the Lombards and the Byzantine Empire | | | *6th-century Lombard gold helmet in the Bargello museum, Florence (see p287)* |

# The Rise of Venice

Medieval Italy saw waves of foreign invaders joining in the struggle for power between popes and emperors. In the confusion, many northern cities asserted their independence from feudal overlords. The most powerful was Venice, governed by its doge and Great Council, which grew rich through trade with the East and by shipping Crusaders to fight the Saracens in the Holy Land. Its maritime rivals on the west coast were Genoa and Pisa.

**The Mediterranean (1250)**
— Genoese trade routes
— Venetian trade routes

**Matilda of Tuscany**
Matilda, Countess of Tuscany (1046–1115), supported the radical Pope Gregory VII against the Emperor Henry IV. When she died, she left her lands to the Church.

Basilica San Marco

Doge's Palace

**Sails** – for added speed

**Canopy over the half-deck**

**The oars**, pulled by slaves, were the principal means of propulsion.

**Venetian Galley**
The galleys used by Venice, both as warships and for carrying cargo, were similar to ancient Greek vessels.

**The columns** of San Marco and San Teodoro had been erected in the 12th century.

## Marco Polo's Departure for China

*Venice traded in Chinese silks and spices imported via the Middle East, but no Venetian had been to China before Marco Polo's father Niccolò. Marco Polo set off with his father in 1271, returning 25 years later with fantastic tales of his time at the court of Kublai Khan.*

**1000** Doge of Venice, Pietro Orseolo II, defeats Dalmatian pirates in Adriatic

**11th century** School of Law at Bologna develops into Europe's first university

*Medieval students*

**1139** Naples incorporated into Kingdom of Sicily

**1000**

**1050**

**1100**

**1030** Norman knight Rainulf granted county of Aversa by Duke of Naples

**1061** Normans Robert Guiscard and Roger de Hauteville capture Messina from the Arabs

**1063** San Marco in Venice rebuilt

**1084** Normans sack Rome

**1076** Salerno, last Lombard city, falls to Normans

**1073–85** Pope Gregory VII reforms Church and papacy

**1130** Roger II crowned king of Sicily

**1115** Death of Countess Matilda

**St. Francis of Assisi**
(1181–1226)
In *The Dream of Pope Innocent III* by Giotto, painted around 1290–95, St. Francis holds up the tottering edifice of the Roman church. The Franciscans' rule of poverty brought about a religious revival in reaction to the wealth of the church.

Monastery of Sant'Apollonia

Today's Riva degli Schiavoni

**Where to See Early Medieval Italy**

Of the many churches built in this period, especially fine examples are Venice's San Marco *(p114)*, Sant'Antonio *(p162)* in Padua, and the Duomo in Pisa *(p328)*.

**Castello dell' Imperatore**, Prato, was built around 1240.

The Leaning Tower *(p330)* also dates back to the 12th century. Medieval castles include Frederick II's Castel del Monte in Puglia *(p513)* and Castello dell'Imperatore in Prato.

**Niccolò Polo**, his brother Maffeo, and son Marco prepare to embark. They sailed first to Acre in the Levant.

**Fourth Crusade**
Discord between the leaders of the crusade and Pope Innocent III culminated in the sacking of Constantinople in 1204.

**Frederick II**
(1194–1250) The emperor kept a court of poets and scholars in Sicily. He won Jerusalem from the Arabs by diplomacy, but was constantly at war with the pope and the cities of Lombardy.

---

**1155** Frederick Barbarossa crowned Holy Roman Emperor

**1198** Frederick II becomes king of Sicily

**1204** Sacking of Constantinople

**1209** Franciscan Order founded

**1216** Dominican Order founded

**1250** Death of Frederick II

**1260** Urban IV invites Charles of Anjou to rule Naples and Sicily

**1265** Birth of Dante

**1150**

**1200**

**1250**

*Frederick Barbarossa dressed as a Crusader*

**1220** Frederick II crowned Holy Roman Emperor

**1237** Lombard League defeats Frederick at Battle of Cortenuova

**1228** Gregory IX excommunicates Frederick II; struggle between Guelphs (the papal party) and Ghibellines (supporters of the emperor)

**1271** Marco Polo sets off on journey to China

# The Late Middle Ages

Old feuds between pope and emperor thrived throughout the 14th century, kept alive by two warring factions – the Guelphs, who backed the papacy, and the Ghibellines, who favored Imperial power. The cities of Lombardy and Tuscany used the political confusion to grow in strength. It was against this turbulent backdrop that a great new age in painting was inspired by artists such as Duccio and Giotto. Also at this time the Florentine poets Dante and Petrarch laid the foundations of Italian literature.

**Italy in 1350**

Papal States

Holy Roman Empire

Angevin Kingdom of Naples

The campanile or bell tower

A griffin, symbol of Perugia

## Medieval Town Square

*Throughout central Italy, the town square was an expression of civic pride and independence. Towns, such as Perugia (see pp356–7), tried to overshadow their rivals in the splendor of their town halls. The center of Perugia has changed little since the 14th century, when the town's main rival was Siena.*

### Condottieri

Cities paid *condottieri*, leaders of bands of mercenaries, to fight their wars. Siena hired Guidoriccio da Fogliano, seen here in a fresco by Simone Martini (1330).

**The main chamber** of the town hall, the Sala dei Notari, is decorated with the coats of arms of Perugia's mayors.

**The Fontana Maggiore** was begun in 1275 and includes panels by Nicola Pisano. Prominently placed, it is an emblem of the town's wealth.

### Dante's Inferno

One of the harshest punishments in Dante's vision of hell is reserved for corrupt popes, such as Boniface VIII (reigned 1294–1303), who are placed upside down in fiery pits.

**1282** Sicilian Vespers; uprising against French rule in Palermo; 2,000 French soldiers killed

**1296** Work begins on the Duomo in Florence

**1298** Marco Polo returns from China to Venice

**1309–43** Reign of Robert the Wise of Naples

**1310** Work begins on Palazzo Ducale in Venice

**1313** Birth of Boccaccio

**1339** Simon Boccanegra becomes first doge of Genoa; Giovanna I Queen of Naples

**1275**

**1300**

**1325**

**1282** Peter of Aragon lands at Trapani, conquers Sicily, and is crowned king in Palermo

**1304** Birth of Petrarch

**1309** Clement V moves papacy to Avignon

**1321** Dante completes *La Divina Commedia* and dies the same year

**1337** Death of Giotto

*The poet and scholar Petrarch*

**The Black Death**
Bubonic plague reached Italy in 1347, carried on Genoese ships from the Black Sea. It killed over one third of the population, reducing the remainder to a state of superstitious terror.

## Where to See Late Medieval Italy

Many central Italian cities and towns have public buildings from the 13th and 14th centuries; among the most impressive are Palazzo Vecchio (p295) in Florence and Siena's Palazzo Pubblico (p344). Smaller towns that preserve much of their medieval character include Volterra (p338) and the walled Monteriggioni (p338) in Tuscany, Gubbio (p356) and Todi (p363) in Umbria, and Viterbo (pp468–9) in Lazio. The Duomo in Orvieto (pp362–3) is a fine example of a late 13th-century Gothic cathedral.

**Piazza dei Priori** in Volterra (p338) is one of the most beautiful medieval squares in Italy.

**The cathedral** was started in 1350 and used to include an outside pulpit on the square.

**Construction of Alessandria**
Almost all towns were ringed with strong walls. This fresco (1407) by Spinello Aretino is a valuable record of medieval building techniques.

**Return of Pope Gregory XI to Rome** (1378)
For 70 years the popes had lived in Avignon, protected by the French kings, while nobles and republicans fought for control of Rome.

*Medieval doctor*

**1347–9** The Black Death

**1378–1415** Period of Schism, with rival popes and antipopes in Rome and Avignon

**1380** Genoese fleet surrenders to Venetians at Chioggia

| 1350 | 1375 | 1400 |
| --- | --- | --- |

**1354** Cola di Rienzo killed in Rome

**1385** Gian Galeazzo Visconti becomes ruler of Milan

**1406** Pisa annexed by Florence

**1347** Cola di Rienzo tries to re-establish Roman Republic

**1378** Gregory XI returns from Avignon to Rome

# The Renaissance

Fifteenth-century Italy saw a flowering of the arts and scholarship unmatched in Europe since the days of Greece and Rome. Architects turned from the Gothic to Classical models for inspiration, while painting, with its new understanding of perspective and anatomy, produced a generation of artists that included such giants as Leonardo da Vinci, Raphael, and Michelangelo. The patronage for this cultural "rebirth" came from the wealthy families that ruled the city-states of the north, led by the Medici of Florence. In spite of intense rivalry, they oversaw a period of uneasy stability out of which the Renaissance grew.

**Italy in 1492**
- Republic of Florence
- Papal States
- Aragonese possessions

**Christ Handing the Keys to St. Peter**
Perugino's fresco in the Sistine Chapel *(see p430)* links the authority of the pope to the New Testament and, through the Classical buildings in the background, to ancient Rome.

Self-portrait of the artist

**Execution of Savonarola** (1498)
Having assumed the leadership of Florence in 1494, the fanatical monk was hanged, then burned for heresy in Piazza della Signoria.

**Galeazzo Maria Sforza** was the son of Milan's ruler.

**Piero de' Medici**, Lorenzo's father, was given the nickname "the Gouty."

**1420** Martin V re-establishes papacy in Rome

**1435** Publication of *On Painting* by Alberti, which contains the first system for the use of linear perspective

**1436** Brunelleschi completes dome of Florence cathedral

**1458–64** War between Houses of Aragon and Anjou over Kingdom of Naples

**1469** Lorenzo the Magnificent becomes ruler of Florence

**1400**

**1425**

**1450**

**1434** Cosimo de' Medici comes to power in Florence

**1442** Naples captured by Alfonso of Aragon

**1452** Birth of Leonardo da Vinci

**1444** Federico da Montefeltro becomes Duke of Urbino

**1453** Fall of Constantinople

*Cosimo de' Medici*

*Filippo Brunelleschi*

**The Battle of Pavia** (1525)
The French King Francis I was captured at this battle against the army of the Habsburg Emperor Charles V, who won control of Italy.

## The Procession of the Magi

*Benozzo Gozzoli's fresco (1459) in the Palazzo Medici-Riccardi, Florence, depicts members of the Medici family and other contemporary notables. It contains many references to a great church council held in Florence in 1439.*

### Where to See Renaissance Italy

Many cities were flourishing centers of the arts in the 15th century. None can rival Florence (pp274–317) with its great palazzi and the Uffizi gallery (pp290–93), but Venice (pp88–141), Urbino (pp374–5), and Mantua (p211) all preserve great treasures. In Rome, do not miss the Vatican's Sistine Chapel and Raphael Rooms (pp428–31).

**The Spedale degli Innocenti** by Brunelleschi in Florence (p281) shows the Classical symmetry and restraint of Renaissance architecture.

**Humanism**
Carpaccio's painting of St. Augustine is thought to show Cardinal Bessarion (c. 1395–1472), one of the scholars who revived interest in Classical philosophy, especially Plato.

**Lorenzo de' Medici** (the Magnificent) was depicted as one of the three kings traveling to Bethlehem.

**Pope Julius II**
During his reign (1503–13), the worldly Julius made the papacy a major power in European politics. Raphael's portrait shows him as a shrewd old statesman.

**1487** Birth of Titian

**1483** Sixtus IV consecrates Sistine Chapel

**1494** Italy invaded by Charles VIII of France

**1503** Giuliano della Rovere elected Pope Julius II; he proves the most powerful of the Renaissance popes

**1527** Rome sacked by Imperial troops

*Niccolò Machiavelli*

**1475**

**1500**

**1525**

**1475** Birth of Michelangelo

*Raphael*

**1483** Birth of Raphael

**1498** Savonarola executed; Machiavelli secretary to ruling Council in Florence

**1512** Michelangelo completes Sistine Chapel ceiling

**1513** Giovanni de' Medici crowned Pope Leo X

**1525** Francis I of France captured at Battle of Pavia

**1532** Machiavelli's book *The Prince* is published, five years after his death

# The Counter-Reformation

After the Sack of Rome in 1527, Italy was at the mercy of Charles V, Holy Roman Emperor and King of Spain. Pope Clement VII, who had opposed Charles, crowned him emperor in Bologna. In response to the growing threat from Protestantism, a series of reforms, known as the Counter-Reformation and backed by the Inquisition, imposed rigid orthodoxy. New religious orders, such as the Jesuits, were set up to take the battle for men's souls far overseas. The missionary spirit of the age inspired the dramatic forms of the Baroque.

**Italy in 1550**

▨ Spanish possessions

▨ States allied with Spain

**Emperor Charles V and Pope Clement VII**
The two former enemies settled their differences and the future destiny of Italy in the Treaty of Barcelona (1529).

**The Virgin Mary** intervenes on the side of the Christians.

## Baroque Stucco Decoration

*This stucco relief by Giacomo Serpotta (c.1690) in the Oratory of Santa Zita in Palermo is a magnificent example of late Baroque exuberance. The subject is a favorite of the period, the Battle of Lepanto, a great naval triumph for the combined forces of Christendom against the Turks (1571).*

**The center** of the ingenious creation is, in effect, a framed painting in perspective.

**Baroque Architecture**
Guarino Guarini's decoration of the dome of the Chapel of the Holy Shroud in Turin *(see p225)* was completed in 1694.

**The young boy** rests his hand on a helmet, symbol of the victorious Christians.

**1530–37** Alessandro de' Medici ruler of Florence

**1542** Inquisition established in Rome

**1545–63** Council of Trent sets out agenda of Counter-Reformation

*Andrea Palladio*

**1580** Death of architect Palladio

**1589** Palestrina publishes setting of the Latin Hymnal

**1600** Philosopher Giordano Bruno burned for heresy in Rome

| 1525 | 1550 | 1575 | 160 |

**1540** Founding of Jesuit Order

**1541** Michelangelo completes *Last Judgment* in Sistine Chapel

**1529** Charles V crowned Holy Roman Emperor in San Petronio, Bologna

**1564** Birth of Galileo

**1560** San Carlo Borromeo appointed Bishop of Milan

**1571** Victory over Turkish fleet at Battle of Lepanto

*Giovanni Pierluigi da Palestrina*

## Trial of Galileo

The great astronomer was often in trouble with the Inquisition. He was summoned to Rome in 1633 and forced to deny that the Earth and planets moved round the sun.

**Lepanto** was the last major sea battle in which Venetian galleys played an important role.

**St. Ignatius Loyola** The Spanish saint was the founder of the Jesuits – sanctioned by the pope in Rome in 1540.

Cherubs, a favorite motif in Baroque decoration

The turban, symbol of the defeated Turks

## Where to See Baroque Italy

**The Ecstasy of St. Teresa** by Bernini *(p416)* has the dynamic theatricality characteristic of the best Baroque sculpture.

The Baroque is strongly associated with Rome and in particular with its great public spaces such as Piazza Navona *(pp402–3)* and the many churches by Borromini and Bernini. Other cities and towns with striking Baroque architecture include Lecce *(pp516–17)* in Puglia, Palermo *(pp530–33)*, Noto *(p547)*, and Siracusa *(pp546–7)* in Sicily, and Turin *(pp224–7)*.

**Revolt of Masaniello** (1647) High taxes made Spanish rule in Naples unpopular. A proposed tax on fruit sparked off this failed revolt.

| | | |
|---|---|---|
| **1626** New St. Peter's consecrated in Rome | **1669** Venice loses island of Crete to the Turks | **1694** Andrea Pozzo completes ceiling fresco for the church of Sant'Ignazio in Rome |
| **1631** Duchy of Urbino absorbed by Papal States | | **1678** Birth of Vivaldi |
| **1625** | **1650** | **1675** |
| **1633** Galileo condemned by papal authorities | **1642** *L'Incoronazione di Poppea* by Monteverdi | **1647** Revolt in Naples in response to tax on fruit | **1674** Revolt against Spanish rule in Messina | **1693** Eastern Sicily ruined by earthquake that kills 5 percent of the island's population |
| | | **1669** Major eruption of Mount Etna | | |

# The Grand Tour

The treaty of Aix-la-Chapelle in 1748 marked the start of 50 years of peace. It was around this time that Italy, with its great art treasures and Classical ruins, including the newly excavated Pompeii, became Europe's first great tourist destination. Young English "milords" visited Rome, Florence, and Venice as part of a new type of pilgrimage, the Grand Tour, while artists and poets sought inspiration in Rome's glorious past. In 1800, Napoleon, who conquered and briefly united Italy, threatened to destroy the old order, but in 1815 the status quo was restored.

**Charles III's Fleet at Naples** (1753)
Ruler of Naples from 1734 to 1759, when he became king of Spain, Charles attempted genuine political reforms.

**Goethe in the Roman Campagna**
Goethe toured Italy in the 1780s. Great poets who followed his example included the Romantics Keats, Shelley, and Byron.

Farnese Hercules
*(see p495)*

The Dying Galatian
*(see p390)*

**Venetian Carnival**
The colorful folklore of Carnival attracted many tourists, but Venice's days of greatness were over. In 1797, the proud maritime republic was ceded to Austria by Napoleon.

### Gallery of Views of Ancient Rome by Pannini

*Giovanni Pannini (1691–1765) painted views of Roman ruins for foreigners. This painting is a* capriccio, *an imaginary scene incorporating many well-known views and Classical statues.*

**1713** Treaty of Utrecht gives Naples and Sardinia to Austria and Sicily to Piedmont

*Medici coat of arms*

**1725** *The Four Seasons* by Vivaldi

**1735** Peace of Vienna confirms Charles III as King of the Two Sicilies (Naples and Sicily)

**1748** First excavations at Pompeii

**1700**

**1720**

**1740**

**1707** Birth of playwright Carlo Goldoni

**1737** End of Medici dynasty in Florence; Grand Duchy of Tuscany passes to Austrian House of Lorraine

*Antonio Vivaldi, great Venetian composer*

**1718** Piedmont and Sardinia united under House of Savoy; Sicily passes to Austria

**View of the Roman Forum by Piranesi**
The popular series of etchings *Vedute di Roma* (Views of Rome) by Giovanni Battista Piranesi (1720–78) inspired a new interest in excavating the ruins of ancient Rome.

## Where to See 18th-century Italy

The 18th century produced two of Rome's best-loved tourist attractions: the Spanish Steps (*p413*) and the Trevi Fountain (*pp414–15*). It was also the age of the first specially built museums, including the Vatican's Museo Pio-Clementine (*p425*). The Neo-Classical sculpture of Antonio Canova (1757–1822) was immensely popular during this period. His tomb is in Santa Maria Gloriosa dei Frari in Venice (*pp102–3*). Of Neo-Classical buildings, the most imposing is a vast monument to enlightened despotism: the Palazzo Reale at Caserta (*p500*).

**Pauline Borghese**, Napoleon's sister, was the model for Antonio Canova's *Venus (1805)*, in the Villa Borghese collection in Rome (*p443*).

**The Colosseum** was as popular a subject in the 18th century as it is on today's picture postcards.

The Laocoön
*(see p421)*

View of the Pantheon
*(see p408)*

**Napoleon**
When Napoleon conquered Italy in 1800, he was seen by many as a liberator. The enchantment wore off as he took priceless works of art back to Paris.

**Congress of Vienna** (1815)
The conference decided that Austria should keep Lombardy and Venice, thereby sowing the seeds of the Italian unification movement.

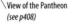

*La Scala Opera House, Milan (see p197)*

**1778** La Scala opened in Milan

**1797** Venice given to Austria by Treaty of Campo Formio; France controls rest of northern Italy

**1800–1801** Napoleon conquers Italy

**1808** Murat becomes King of Naples

**1809** Pope Pius VII exiled from Rome

| 1760 | 1780 | 1800 |

**1773** Pope dissolves Jesuit Order

**1780** Joseph II succeeds to Austrian throne; minor reforms in Lombardy

**1806** Joseph Bonaparte becomes King of Naples

**1768** Corsica sold by Genoa to France

**1765–90** Reign of Leopold, Grand Duke of Tuscany, who introduces enlightened reforms

**1796–7** Napoleon's first campaign in northern Italy

**1815** Congress of Vienna restores status quo in Italy, though Austria keeps Venice

# The Risorgimento

The word "Risorgimento" (resurgence) describes the five decades of struggle for liberation from foreign rule, culminating in the unification of Italy in 1870. In 1848, patriots rose up against the Austrians in Milan and Venice, the Bourbons in Sicily, and the pope in Rome, where a republic was declared. Garibaldi valiantly defended the republic, but all the uprisings were too localized. By 1859, the movement was better organized, with Vittorio Emanuele II at its head. Two years saw the conquest of all but Venice and Rome, both of which fell within a decade.

**Italy in 1861**
Kingdom of Italy

**Giuseppe Mazzini**
(1805–72)
An exile for much of his life, Mazzini fought alongside Garibaldi to unite Italy as a republic, rather than a kingdom.

**The guns** were rusty, old converted flintlocks.

**The red shirt** was the badge of the Garibaldini.

**Italian Railroads**
The short railroad line from Naples to Portici was opened in 1839. Politically fragmented, Italy was slow to create an effective rail network.

**Revolt of Messina**
When, in 1848, Messina revolted, Ferdinand II subjected the town to a savage bombardment, earning himself the nickname King Bomba.

**1831** Insurrection in Romagna and Le Marche against papal rule

**1840** First three major railroad lines established

**1849** Accession of Vittorio Emanuele II as ruler of Piedmont

**1852** Cavour becomes prime minister of Piedmont

**1820**

**1830**

**1840**

**1850**

**1820s** Carbonari secret society active in Papal States

**1847** Economic crisis

**1831** Mazzini founds *Giovine Italia* (Young Italy) movement

*Daniele Manin, hero of the Venetian uprising of 1848*

**1848** Revolutions throughout Italy

**1849** Republic of Rome crushed by French troops

**Battle of Solferino** (1859)
With the help of a French army led by
Napoleon III, the Piedmontese won Milan
and Lombardy from the Austrians.

## Where to See Risorgimento Italy

Almost every town in Italy honors the heroes of
the Risorgimento with a Via Garibaldi, a Via Cavour, a
Piazza Vittorio, a Via Mazzini, and a Via XX Settembre
(the date of the fall of Rome in 1870). Many cities
also have Risorgimento museums. One of the best
is in Turin (p227).

**The Victor Emmanuel Monument** (p388) is a
prominent, but largely unloved, Roman landmark.

**Two old paddle steamers**
brought the Thousand from
Quarto near Genoa.

**Count Camillo di
Cavour** (1810–61)
Cavour's diplomacy
as prime minister of
Piedmont ensured that
the House of Savoy
became rulers of the
new Italy. He also
coined the word
"Risorgimento."

**The skiffs** were lent
by other ships moored
in Marsala harbor.

## Garibaldi and the Thousand

*Giuseppe Garibaldi (1807–82) was a leader
of courage and genius. In 1860, he landed at
Marsala with 1,000 volunteers. The garrison
at Palermo surrendered, Sicily fell, and he
went on to conquer Naples, thus presenting
Vittorio Emanuele with half a kingdom.*

**Giuseppe Verdi**
(1813–1901)
Composers such as
Verdi, Donizetti, and
Rossini made the 19th
century the great era of
Italian opera. Verdi's
early operas inspired
the Risorgimento.

**1859** Battles of Magenta and Solferino;
Piedmont acquires Lombardy from Austria
and duchies of Parma, Modena, and Tuscany

**1861** Kingdom of Italy
proclaimed with capital at Turin

*Pope Pius IX, who remained a virtual
prisoner in the Vatican when Rome
became capital of Italy*

**1882** Deaths of Garibaldi
and Pope Pius IX

**1893** Troops
sent to suppress
insurrection
in Sicily

**1860**

**1866** Italy wins
Venice from Austria

**1860** Garibaldi and the Thousand
capture Kingdom of the Two Sicilies

**1870**

**1870** Rome falls to royalist
troops and is made capital
of new kingdom; Vatican
announces doctrine of
papal infallibility

**1878** Death of Vittorio Emanuele;
accession of King Umberto I

**1880**

**1890**

**1890** Italian colony
of Eritrea established
by royal decree

# Modern Italy

Fascism under Mussolini (1922–43) promised the Italians greatness, but delivered only humiliation. In spite of this, Italy has become one of Europe's leading economies, with a standard of living that could not have been imagined at the turn of the 20th century. This has been achieved in the face of great obstacles. Since 1946, the Republic has passed through many crises: a series of unstable coalitions, the terrorist outrages in the 1970s and, in the 1990s, corruption scandals involving numerous government ministers and officials.

**1936** FIAT produces first "Topolino" car

**1960** *La Dolce Vita*, Federico Fellini's movie satire on Rome's decadent café society, is released

**1922** Fascists march on Rome; Mussolini invited to form government

**1940** Italy enters World War II

**1918** Austrian advance halted at the river Piave, just north of Venice

**1900** Assassination of King Umberto I

**1911–12** Italy conquers Libya

**1943** Allies land in Sicily; Italy signs armistice and new Badoglio government declares war on Germany

| 1900 | 1910 | 1920 | 1930 | 1940 | 1950 | 196 |
|---|---|---|---|---|---|---|

| 1900 | 1910 | 1920 | 1930 | 1940 | 1950 | 196 |
|---|---|---|---|---|---|---|

**1908** Earthquake destroys many towns and villages in Calabria and eastern Sicily; Messina almost completely razed to the ground; over 150,000 die

**1915** Italy enters World War I

**1936** Italy conquers Abyssinia; pact with Germany, forming anti-Communist "Axis"

**1943** Mussolini imprisoned, then freed by Germans

**1946** Referendum in which Italy votes to become a republic; Christian Democrat party forms first of a long series of coalition governments

**1920s** Postwar years see continued emigration to the United States. Here, emigrants cheer as they reach New York aboard the *Giulio Cesare*

**1957** Treaty of Rome; Italy one of the six founder members of the European Economic Community

**1960** Olympic Games and first official Paralympic Games held in Rome

**1917** Defeat at Caporetto on Italy's northeastern border; Italian troops, such as these Alpini, retreat to defensive positions

**1909** In his *Futurist Manifesto*, Filippo Marinetti condemns all traditional art as too static. His idea of a new dynamic art is expressed in works such as Umberto Boccioni's bronze *Unique Forms of Continuity in Space*

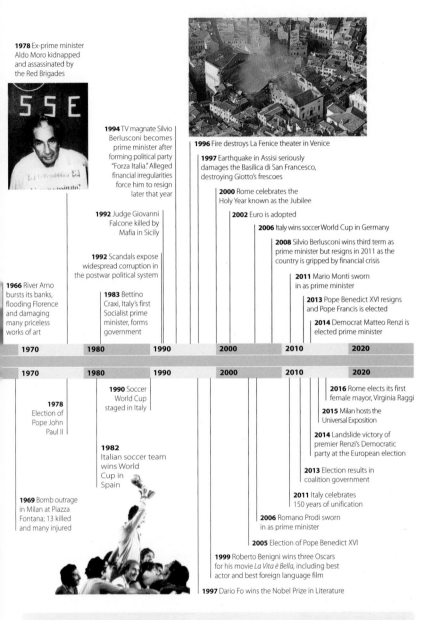

**1978** Ex-prime minister Aldo Moro kidnapped and assassinated by the Red Brigades

**1994** TV magnate Silvio Berlusconi becomes prime minister after forming political party "Forza Italia." Alleged financial irregularities force him to resign later that year

**1996** Fire destroys La Fenice theater in Venice

**1997** Earthquake in Assisi seriously damages the Basilica di San Francesco, destroying Giotto's frescoes

**2000** Rome celebrates the Holy Year known as the Jubilee

**2002** Euro is adopted

**1992** Judge Giovanni Falcone killed by Mafia in Sicily

**2006** Italy wins soccer World Cup in Germany

**2008** Silvio Berlusconi wins third term as prime minister but resigns in 2011 as the country is gripped by financial crisis

**1992** Scandals expose widespread corruption in the postwar political system

**2011** Mario Monti sworn in as prime minister

**1966** River Arno bursts its banks, flooding Florence and damaging many priceless works of art

**1983** Bettino Craxi, Italy's first Socialist prime minister, forms government

**2013** Pope Benedict XVI resigns and Pope Francis is elected

**2014** Democrat Matteo Renzi is elected prime minister

| 1970 | 1980 | 1990 | 2000 | 2010 | 2020 |
|------|------|------|------|------|------|
| 1970 | 1980 | 1990 | 2000 | 2010 | 2020 |

**1990** Soccer World Cup staged in Italy

**2016** Rome elects its first female mayor, Virginia Raggi

**2015** Milan hosts the Universal Exposition

**1978** Election of Pope John Paul II

**2014** Landslide victory of premier Renzi's Democratic party at the European election

**1982** Italian soccer team wins World Cup in Spain

**2013** Election results in coalition government

**2011** Italy celebrates 150 years of unification

**1969** Bomb outrage in Milan at Piazza Fontana; 13 killed and many injured

**2006** Romano Prodi sworn in as prime minister

**2005** Election of Pope Benedict XVI

**1999** Roberto Benigni wins three Oscars for his movie *La Vita è Bella*, including best actor and best foreign language film

**1997** Dario Fo wins the Nobel Prize in Literature

## Italian Cinema Since World War II

The social problems of late 1940s Italy inspired a wave of cinema known as Neo-Realism. Leading exponents included Roberto Rossellini, who made *Roma Città Aperta* (1945), Vittorio de Sica, the director of *Bicycle Thieves* (1948), Pier Paolo Pasolini, and Luchino Visconti. Since that time, the major Italian directors have cultivated their own personal styles. Visconti's later films,

**Vittorio de Sica**
**(1901–74)**

such as *Death in Venice* (1971), show formal beauty and decadence, while Federico Fellini's *La Dolce Vita* (1960) and *Roma* (1972) depict life as a grotesque carnival. Italy has also produced some commercially successful movies, such as Sergio Leone's late 1960s westerns and the Oscar-winning *Cinema Paradiso* and *La Vita è Bella*.

# ITALY THROUGH THE YEAR

Throughout Italy, the variety of local character and color is astonishing. This is mainly due to the survival of regionalism, particularly in the southern parts of the country. Old traditions, customs, and lifestyles are still greatly respected and there is a deep attachment to the land, which is reflected in a healthy interest in food and produce, as well as a perseverance of seasonal religious and secular events. Annual festivals, whether in rural or urban areas, range from wine-tasting and gastronomic celebrations to elaborate commemorations of every patron saint imaginable.

## Spring

The Italian spring begins early, particularly in the south. City streets and main sights are rarely overcrowded (except at Easter in Rome). The weather, however, can be unpredictable and wet in the central and northern parts of the country. Spring specialties, such as asparagus, spinach, and rocket, begin to feature on restaurant menus. This is a season of great celebration; festivals and fairs abound, especially in Sicily, and the Easter papal address always draws massive crowds to St. Peter's.

### March

**Dolomiti Ski Jazz Festival**, *(mid-Mar)*, Val di Fiemme, Trentino-Alto Adige. Live jazz on the ski slopes.

**Sa Sartiglia**, Oristano, Sardinia. Three-day carnival ending on Shrove Tuesday.

**Su e zo per i ponti** *(Sun, varies)*, Venice. A lively race through the city's streets, up and down the bridges.

*Tuscan asparagus*

### April

**Procession of the Grieving Madonna** (Good Friday), Procida, Campania. A colorful religious procession throughout the island.

**Holy Week** *(Easter Week)*. Numerous Easter celebrations from Palm Sunday to Easter Sunday, throughout the country.

**Papal Address** *(Easter Sunday)*, Rome. The pope makes his Easter address from the Vatican.

**Dance of the Devils** *(Easter Sunday)*, Prizzi, Sicily. Dance recital symbolizing the attempts of evil to vanquish the forces of good.

**Scoppio del Carro** *(Easter Sunday)*, Florence. Firework display is lit by a mechanical dove in front of the Duomo.

**Festa della Madonna che Scappa in Piazza** *(Easter Sunday)*, Sulmona, Abruzzo. Re-enactment of a meeting between the Virgin and the Risen Christ.

**Festa degli Aquiloni** *(first Sun after Easter)*, San Miniato, Tuscany. Kite lovers perform aerial acrobatics at this festival.

*Spring strawberries*

**Festa di San Marco** *(Apr 25)*, Venice. A gondola race across St. Mark's Basin commemorates the patron saint of Venice, St. Mark.

**Mostra Mercato Internazionale dell'Artigianato** *(last week)*, Florence. An important European exhibition of arts and crafts.

Scoppio del Carro (Explosion of the Carriage) festival in Florence

**Sagra Musicale Lucchese** *(dates vary)*, Lucca, Tuscany. Festival of sacred music held in Romanesque churches.

### May

**Festa di Sant'Efisio** *(May 1)*, Cagliari, Sardinia. Paraders in traditional Sardinian costume.

**Festa di San Nicola** *(May 7–9)*, Bari, Puglia. A statue of St. Nicholas is taken to the sea.

**Festa dei Ceri** *(May 15)*, Gubbio, Umbria. Festival, including a race with four teams carrying large candles.

**Festa di San Domenico Abate** *(first Thu)*, Cocullo, Abruzzo. Includes a procession with a statue of St. Dominic covered with live snakes.

**Festa dello Speck** *(late May)*, Bolzano, Trentino-Alto Adige. A celebration of the famed ham.

**Greek Drama in Theater** *(May–Jun)*, Syracuse, Sicily. Festival of Greek drama.

**Maggio Musicale** *(May–Jun)*, Florence. This is the city's biggest arts festival, including music, drama, and dance.

Procession of the Grieving Madonna on the isle of Procida

Street carpeted with flowers for the Infiorata in Genzano

## Summer

Summer brings the crowds to Italy, particularly the cities. Italians, however, flee and head for the coast, usually in August. The lines for tourist attractions can be long and hotels are often full. Festivals vary; religious events are interspersed with those of the arts and local folklore.

### June
**Festa della Fragola**
*(Jun 1)*, Borgo San Martino, Piedmont. Musical and folkloric performances in celebration of the strawberry.
**Biennale** *(Jun–Sep)*, Venice. The world's biggest exhibition of contemporary art takes place during odd-numbered years only.
**Infiorata** *(Corpus Christi day)*, Genzano, Lazio. A procession through streets carpeted with flowers.
**International Film Festival** *(mid-Jun)*, Taormina, Sicily.
**Festa di San Giovanni** *(mid-Jun–mid-Jul)*, Turin, Piedmont. Festival in honor of the city's patron saint, John.
**Calcio Storico** *(Jun 24 and two other days in Jun)*, Florence. Soccer in 16th-century costumes; fireworks.

**Festa di Sant'Andrea** *(Jun 27)*, Amalfi, Campania. Fireworks and processions.
**Festival dei Due Mondi** *(late Jun–early Jul)*, Spoleto, Umbria. International festival of drama, music, and dance.
**Gioco del Ponte** *(last Sun)*, Pisa. "The Bridge Parade" of marchers in antique armor.
**Estate Romana** *(late Jun–mid-Sep)*, Rome. Open-air movies, performances, ballet, and concerts.

### July
**Corsa del Palio** *(Jul 2)*, Siena. Tuscany's most famous event *(see p345)* presents a medieval flag-waving exhibition and horse race.
**Festa della Madonna della Bruna** *(first Sun)*, Matera, Basilicata. A lively procession of clergymen and knights in costume.
**Festa de' Noantri** *(last two weeks Jul)*, Rome. A colorful festival in Trastevere.
**Festa della Santa Maria del Carmine** *(Jul 16)*, Naples. Featuring the illumination of the city's bell tower.

Musician from Florence's Calcio

**Umbria Jazz** *(Jul)*, Perugia. World-famous jazz artists perform in various settings.

A crowded beach near Livorno, Tuscany, during the summer vacation

**Opera Festival** *(Jul & Aug)*, Verona, Veneto. Renowned opera festival overlapping with the **Shakespeare Festival**, providing music, drama, opera, and dance.

### August
**Medieval Palio** *(first weekend Aug)* Feltre, Veneto. Parades and archery competitions, medieval-style.
**Festa del Mare** *(Aug 15)*, Diano Marina, Liguria. This "Festival of the Sea" boasts a spectacular fireworks display.
**Festa dei Candelieri** *(Aug 14)*, Sassari, Sardinia. "Festival of the Candle", dating from the 16th century.
**Corsa del Palio** *(Aug 16)*, Siena, Tuscany. See July entry.
**Rossini Festival** *(mid-Aug)*, Pesaro, Le Marche. A celebration of the composer's work, in his birthplace.
**Venice Film Festival** *(late Aug–early Sep)*. International festival on the Lido.
**Settimane Musicali di Stresa** *(late Aug–end Sep)*, Stresa, Lombardy. Four weeks of concerts and recitals.

Flag-throwers in Piazza del Campo, Siena, just before the Corsa del Palio

## Fall

Fall is a slow, gentle season in Italy, but that doesn't mean there are fewer festivals and fairs. In addition to the various religious events at this time of year, gastronomic festivals are especially popular, commemorating such delectables as chestnuts, local cheeses, sausages, and mushrooms. Fall is the season of the *vendemmia*, the grape harvest, which is often used as an excuse for village festivities at which the latest local wines flow freely.

The climate *(see pp76–7)* in late fall is often cold and wet in the north. The south, however, can be quite warm right through October.

Advertisement for the September Palio in Asti, Piedmont

### September

**Festa di Santa Lucia** *(first Sun)*, Lodè, Sardinia. Includes a contest in which competitors improvise short poems.
**Procession of the Macchina di Santa Rosa** *(Sep 3)*, Viterbo, Lazio. Commemoration of the saint's body being transported to the Church of Santa Rosa in 1258.
**Giostra del Saracino** *(first Sun)*, Arezzo, Umbria. Joust of the Saracen and knights, dating from the 13th century.
**Regata Storica** *(first Sun)*, Venice. A procession of historic boats plus a colorful gondola race.
**Human chess game** *(second week)*, Marostica, near Vicenza. A popular costumed game held in the main square every even-numbered year.

The widely cultivated olive tree

**Rassegna del Chianti Classico** *(second week)*, Chianti, Tuscany. Celebration of the local wines.
**Auditorium Parco della Musica Season** *(Sep–Jul)*, Rome. The broad program includes classical, jazz, and rock music, as well as a circus and a popular modern dance festival.
**The Miracle of San Gennaro** (Sep 19), Naples. Reenactment of the liquefaction of the saint's blood, in a lively Mass at the Duomo.
**Palio** *(third Sun)*, Asti, Piedmont. Includes a costumed medieval procession and bareback horse racing.

### October

**Amici della Musica** *(Oct–Apr)*, Florence, Tuscany. The popular "Friends of Music" concert season begins.
**Fiera del Tartufo** *(Oct–Nov)*, Alba, Piedmont. A variety of events centered around the locally grown white truffle.
**Festa di San Francesco** *(Oct 4)*, Assisi, Umbria. Feast in honor of one of Italy's patron saints.

**Wine festivals** *(first week)*, Castelli Romani, Lazio.
**Sagra del Tordo** *(last Sun)* Montalcino, Tuscany. Celebration of the thrush; costumed archery contests.
**Festa dell'Uva** *(dates vary)*, Bolzano, Trentino-Alto Adige. Grape festival with live music and a costumed procession featuring allegoric carts.
**International Festival of Cinema** *(dates vary)*, Rome. A week of screenings, high-profile events, and celebrity spotting in the capital.

A roasted chestnut stand in autumn

### November

**Festa dei Popoli** *(Nov)*, Florence, Tuscany. Film festival showing documentary films in their original languages with Italian subtitles.
**Festa della Salute** *(Nov 21)*, Venice. Cherished by Venetian locals, this feast gives thanks to the Virgin Mary in memory of a 1630 plague.

The human chess game in the town square of Marostica

## Winter

There are fairs, markets, and religious events up and down the country at this time of year. Neapolitan Christmas cribs are famous and nearly every church has one. The Christmas holiday itself is low-key; more is made of other religious events such as the liquefaction of San Gennaro's blood in Naples and the Carnevale in Venice.

### December
**Festa di Sant'Ambrogio** *(early Dec)*, Milan. The official opening of La Scala Opera season *(see p197)*.
**Festa della Madonnadi Loreto** *(Dec 10)*, Loreto, Le Marche. Celebration of the Virgin's Holy House.
**Mercato della Befana** (mid-Dec–Jan 6), Rome. Well-known Christmas fair held in Piazza Navona.
**The Miracle of San Gennaro** *(Dec 16)*, Naples. See September. **Christmas fair** *(mid-Dec)*, Naples. Fair selling crib figures and decorations.
**Fiaccole di Natale** *(Christmas Eve)*, Abbadia di San Salvatore, Tuscany. Features carols and processions in memory of the first shepherds.
**Midnight Mass** *(Dec 24)*, at churches all over the country.
**Christmas Day** *(Dec 25)*, St. Peter's Square, Rome. Public blessing by the pope.

Rome during one of its rare snowfalls

Carnevale, Viareggio

La Befana at Piazza Navona, Rome

### January
**Capodanno** *(Jan 1)*, all over the country. New Year's Day is celebrated with fireworks and volleys from hunters firing into the air to scare off ghosts and spirits of the old year and to welcome in the new.
**La Befana** *(Jan 6)*, throughout Italy. Children's holiday with presents and candies.
**Pitti Immagine Uomo, Pitti Immagine Donna, Pitti Immagine Bimbo**, Fortezza da Basso, Florence. Month of international fashion shows for women, men, and children.
**Festa di San Sebastiano** *(Sun nearest Jan 20)*, Dolceacqua, Liguria. A laurel tree covered with colorful communion hosts is carried through town.
**Festa d'o'Cippo di Sant'Antonio** *(Jan 17)*, Naples. A procession for St. Anthony, protector of animals.
**Carnevale** *(a month-long event finishing Shrove Tue)*, Viareggio, Tuscany. A carnival famous for its lively, topically themed floats.
**Fair of St. Orsa** *(Jan 30 & 31)*, Aosta, Valle d'Aosta. Exhibition of traditional arts and crafts.

### February
**Carnevale** *(last 10 days before Lent, finishing Shrove Tuesday)*, Venice. Pre-Lent festival meaning "farewell to meat." Events are organized, but anyone can buy a mask and watch the array of gorgeous costumes on display.

Carnevale revelers in Venice

### Public Holidays

**New Year's Day** (Jan 1)
**Epiphany** (Jan 6)
**Easter Sunday & Monday**
**Liberation Day** (Apr 25)
**Labor Day** (May 1)
**Republic Day** (Jun 2)
**Ferragosto** (Aug 15)
**All Saints' Day** (Nov 1)
**Immaculate Conception** (Dec 8)
**Christmas Day** (Dec 25)
**Santo Stefano** (Dec 26)

**Sagra delle Mandorle in Fiore** *(first or second week)*, Agrigento, Sicily. Annual almond blossom celebration.
**Bacanal del Gnoco** *(dates vary)*, Verona. Traditional masked procession with both international and local allegorical floats. Masked balls are held in the town's squares.
**Carnevale** *(dates vary)*, Mamoiada, Sardinia. Processions include *mamuthones* wearing sinister black masks.

# The Sporting Year

Soccer is by far the most important sport in Italy, uniting the country when the national team *(Azzurri)* plays. A range of other sporting events, including bicycling, skiing, and tennis, also take place throughout the year, so fans are never at a loss for something to watch. For most big games or tournaments, tickets can be obtained for cash at club outlets such as the venue itself. Agencies provide hard-to-get tickets at often higher prices. Beware of the inevitable scalpers at popular events, as their expensive tickets may not be valid.

**Calcio Fiorentino,** one of Italy's few indigenous sports, is said to be the medieval precursor of modern soccer.

| Coppa Italia soccer final |

| Memorial d'Aloia rowing competition, held in Umbria |

**The professional water polo** season takes place from March through July. The Canottieri Napoli team play consistently well through the championship.

**The Giro d'Italia** bicycle race takes place over many stages. The Italian Vincenzo Nibali *(left)* won the race in 2013.

| January | February | March | April | May | June |
|---|---|---|---|---|---|

| Indoor Athletics Championships |

| Rome Marathon |

| International Showjumping, Rome |

**Rugby** is becoming increasingly popular. Italy takes part in the Six Nations Championship in February and March, along with England, Scotland, Wales, Ireland, and France.

**The Rome Masters,** previously known as the Italian Open, takes place in Rome during May. The event is one of the most prestigious clay court tennis competitions in the world.

**The Italian leg o**f the Circuito Mondiale in Mugello. Valentino Rossi has dominated the MotoGP World Championship for over a decade.

**The Italian Outdoor European Swimming Championships** are held every year in July. The Olympic gold medal winner Massimiliano Rosolino is pictured here celebrating a victory.

**Italy has some of the best** ski resorts in Europe, and in 2006 Turin hosted the Winter Olympics. Above is Alberto Tomba, once a champion of the slopes.

**The Italian Grand Prix**, held annually at Monza, is Italy's round of the international Formula One World Championship. Giancarlo Fisichella has been one of Italy's most successful drivers.

Trofeo dei Templi rowing competition, Sicily

**The Sanremo Car Rally**, held each year in October, was made famous by driver Miki Biasion and the Lancia Delta Integrale.

| August | September | October | November | December |
| --- | --- | --- | --- | --- |

Siena Palio (see p345), held on 2 July and 16 August

Italy won the soccer World Cup in 2006

**The Italian soccer** season runs from September through May. It culminates with the Coppa Italia final, which is equivalent to a superbowl. Italy's soccer obsession, however, reaches fever pitch when the World Cup takes place every four years.

**The Outdoor Athletics Championship** has become very popular. One of Italy's foremost athletes is race walker Alex Schwazer, winner of an Olympic gold medal in 2008.

**Key to Sporting Seasons**

Soccer
Water polo
Rugby
Basketball
Volleyball
Skiing

# The Climate of Italy

The Italian peninsula has a varied climate falling into three distinct geographical regions. Cold Alpine winters and warm, wet summers characterize the northern regions. In the extensive Po Valley, arid summers contrast with freezing, damp winters. The rest of Italy has a pleasant climate, with long, hot summers and mild winters. Cooler weather along the backbone of the Apennines can bring snow during the winter months.

**TRENTINO-ALTO ADIGE**

| °F | | | |
|---|---|---|---|
| 61 | 83 | | |
| 39 | 63 | 63 | |
| | 41 | 41 | |
| | | | 23 |
| 6 hrs | 8 hrs | 4 hrs | 2 hrs |
| 2.6 in | 3.9 in | 3.3 in | 0.8 in |
| month | Apr | Jul | Oct | Jan |

Average monthly maximum temperature

Average monthly minimum temperature

Average daily hours of sunshine

Average monthly rainfall

**LOMBARDY**

| °F | | | |
|---|---|---|---|
| 64 | 82 | 63 | |
| 46 | 64 | 50 | 43 |
| | | | 30 |
| 5 hrs | 9 hrs | 5 hrs | 3 hrs |
| 2.9 in | 3.1 in | 3.5 in | 2.5 in |
| month | Apr | Jul | Oct | Jan |

**VALLE D'AOSTA AND PIEDMONT**

| °F | | | |
|---|---|---|---|
| 83 | 79 | 63 | |
| 43 | 59 | 45 | 45 |
| | | | 28 |
| 5 hrs | 9 hrs | 4 hrs | 3 hrs |
| 3.7 in | 3.4 in | 3.3 in | 1.3 in |
| month | Apr | Jul | Oct | Jan |

**LIGURIA**

| °F | | | |
|---|---|---|---|
| 64 | 82 | 70 | |
| 53 | 68 | 57 | 54 |
| | | | 44 |
| 7 hrs | 9 hrs | 8 hrs | 4 hrs |
| 2.6 in | 1.2 in | 2.9 in | 2.7 in |
| month | Apr | Jul | Oct | Jan |

**SARDINIA**

| °F | | | |
|---|---|---|---|
| 66 | 84 | 72 | |
| 50 | 68 | 57 | 57 |
| | | | 45 |
| 8 hrs | 11 hrs | 6 hrs | 4 hrs |
| 31 mm | 7 mm | 48 mm | 50 mm |
| month | Apr | Jul | Oct | Jan |

**TUSCANY**

| °F | | | |
|---|---|---|---|
| 63 | 84 | 68 | |
| 46 | 61 | 59 | 50 |
| | | | 36 |
| 8 hrs | 11 hrs | 6 hrs | 5 hrs |
| 72 mm | 30 mm | 90 mm | 65 mm |
| month | Apr | Jul | Oct | Jan |

**EMILIA-ROMAGNA**

| °F | | | |
|---|---|---|---|
| 63 | 86 | 61 | |
| 47 | 66 | 50 | 39 |
| | | | 30 |
| 6 hrs | 11 hrs | 5 hrs | 3 hrs |
| 2.3 in | 1.5 in | 3.2 in | 1.8 in |
| month | Apr | Jul | Oct | Jan |

Trent

Aosta

Milan

Verona

Turin

Parma

Genoa

Bologna

Florence

Livorno

Olbia

Cagliari

## THE VENETO AND FRIULI

| °F | | | |
|---|---|---|---|
| | | 82 | |
| 63 | 64 | 64 | |
| 45 | | 48 | 45 |
| | | | 32 |
| 7 hrs | 9 hrs | 4 hrs | 2 hrs |
| 4.4 in | 4.3 in | 5.3 in | 3.5 in |
| month **Apr** | **Jul** | **Oct** | **Jan** |

## LE MARCHE

| °F | | | |
|---|---|---|---|
| | | 81 | |
| 61 | 68 | 66 | |
| 48 | | 55 | 47 |
| | | | 37 |
| 6 hrs | 10 hrs | 5 hrs | 3 hrs |
| 2.2 in | 2.2 in | 3 in | 2.6 in |
| month **Apr** | **Jul** | **Oct** | **Jan** |

## UMBRIA

| °F | | | |
|---|---|---|---|
| | | 84 | |
| 66 | 61 | 66 | |
| 43 | | 48 | 46 |
| | | | 34 |
| 5 hrs | 10 hrs | 6 hrs | 3 hrs |
| 3.1 in | 1.7 in | 3.6 in | 3 in |
| month **Apr** | **Jul** | **Oct** | **Jan** |

## ABRUZZO, MOLISE, AND PUGLIA

| °F | | | |
|---|---|---|---|
| | | 82 | |
| 64 | 68 | 70 | |
| 50 | | 57 | 55 |
| | | | 43 |
| 6 hrs | 10 hrs | 6 hrs | 4 hrs |
| 1.9 in | 1.1 in | 2.7 in | 2.4 in |
| month **Apr** | **Jul** | **Oct** | **Jan** |

## ROME AND LAZIO

| °F | | | |
|---|---|---|---|
| | | 84 | |
| 64 | 66 | 72 | |
| 48 | | 55 | 54 |
| | | | 40 |
| 6 hrs | 10 hrs | 7 hrs | 5 hrs |
| 2 in | 0.8 in | 3.7 in | 3.4 in |
| month **Apr** | **Jul** | **Oct** | **Jan** |

## NAPLES AND CAMPANIA

| °F | | | |
|---|---|---|---|
| | | 86 | |
| 66 | 70 | 72 | |
| 54 | | 64 | 55 |
| | | | 45 |
| 7 hrs | 11 hrs | 6 hrs | 4 hrs |
| 2.3 in | 0.5 in | 2.7 in | 3.3 in |
| month **Apr** | **Jul** | **Oct** | **Jan** |

## SICILY

| °F | | | |
|---|---|---|---|
| | | 84 | |
| 66 | 68 | 75 | |
| 54 | | 61 | 59 |
| | | | 48 |
| 8 hrs | 11 hrs | 7 hrs | 4 hrs |
| 1.1 in | 0.3 in | 2.3 in | 2.3 in |
| month **Apr** | **Jul** | **Oct** | **Jan** |

## BASILICATA AND CALABRIA

| °F | | | |
|---|---|---|---|
| | | 85 | |
| 64 | 65 | 71 | |
| 49 | | 57 | 55 |
| | | | 44 |
| 6 hrs | 10 hrs | 5 hrs | 4 hrs |
| 2.8 in | 0.5 in | 3.4 in | 3.5 in |
| month **Apr** | **Jul** | **Oct** | **Jan** |

Trieste
Venice
Padova
Ferrara
Ravenna
Ancona
Perugia
Pescara
L'Aquila
Foggia
Bari
Naples
Salerno
Potenza
Taranto
Catanzaro
Reggio di Calabria
Messina
Catania
Agrigento

# NORTHEAST ITALY

# Introducing Northeast Italy

The sheer variety to be found in northeast Italy makes it a fascinating area to explore. The majestic Dolomites dominate the north, straddling Trentino-Alto Adige and the Veneto, and are dotted with medieval castles and modern ski resorts. On the plain, the cities of Verona, Vicenza, and Padua are all noted for outstanding architecture and museums, while the rural hinterland boasts beautiful villas. The incomparable and spectacular city of Venice, with its magnificent monuments, rises from the lagoon. Farther east, in Friuli, there are important Roman remains. This map pinpoints some of the highlights.

Malles
Venosta

Merano
(Meran)

Bressanone

Bolzano
(Bozen)

TRENTINO-ALTO-ADIGE
*(See pp170–79)*

Trento

Riva del
Gardo

Rovereto

Bassano
del Grappo

THE VENETO AND FRIUL
*(See pp142–69)*

Lake
Garda

Vicenza

Villafranca
di Verona

Verona

Padua

Montagnana

Monse

*Adige*

Rovigo

**Alto Adige** is a dramatic region of snow-covered mountain valleys scattered with forbidding castles and onion-domed churches in the Tyrolean style *(see pp174–7)*.

**The Dolomites** *(see pp86–7)* form the spectacular back-drop to many towns in northeast Italy, among them Trento, the region's capital *(see pp178–9)*.

**Verona** is one of the loveliest cities in the Veneto, boasting the Castelvecchio and a Roman arena now used for performances of opera *(see pp146–51)*.

**Vicenza**, a model Renaissance city, is domi-nated by the buildings of Palladio, such as the Palazzo della Ragione and La Rotonda *(see pp154–7)*.

◄ Santa Maddalena with the Dolomites in the background

**Udine** in Friuli is an interesting city that centers on the elegant Piazza della Libertà. The piazza contains a number of imposing statues, including a colossal figure of Hercules, and the Porticato di San Giovanni *(see pp166–7)*.

**Locator Map**

0 kilometres    40
0 miles    20

nico

Cortina d'Ampezzo

Tarvisio

Tolmezzo

FRIULI-VENEZIA GIULIA

uno

Vittorio Veneto

Pordenone

Udine

Gorizia

Piave

Oderzo

Monfalcone

Treviso

ENETO

Caorle

Trieste

Mestre

**Padua** boasts several major sights, among them the Basilica di Sant'Antonio and the Cappella degli Scrovegni with its frescoes by Giotto *(see pp158–63)*.

Venice *(see inset below)*

Chioggia

**Aquileia**, once a splendid Roman city, is filled with ancient remains, such as this Mausoleum. Its Basilica houses early Christian mosaics *(see p168)*.

**Basilica di San Marco** in Venice is one of Europe's finest Byzantine buildings, with a magnificent gilded interior *(see pp114–17)*.

**VENICE** *(See pp88–141)*

**The Palazzo Ducale** is a masterpiece of Venetian Gothic architecture *(see pp118–20)*.

CANNAREGIO

Canal Grande

SANTA CROCE

SAN POLO

CASTELLO

SAN MARCO

DORSODURO

LA GIUDECCA

0 kilometres    1
0 miles    0.5

# The Flavors of Northeast Italy

This diverse region is the least Italian area of Italy. Bordering on Balkan and Austro-Hungarian territory, its food reflects its rich culture and landscape. Venice's traditional trading links have given a Middle Eastern flavor to some dishes, such as sweet and sour *saor* sauce, and spices like nutmeg, saffron, and cinnamon feature widely. While pasta is eaten, many dishes are accompanied by the more typical polenta, made from yellow corn flour, and risotto is also a favorite. Butter is sometimes used instead of olive oil. From hearty, rib-sticking fare to the most delicate and sophisticated of dishes, this is a region full of gastronomic surprises.

Saffron

Delicate, sweet fried pastries in a Trieste bakery

## The Veneto & Venice

The Veneto is one of Italy's main rice-growing regions. Rice was introduced from Spain by the Arabs and is a staple ingredient for many local dishes. Creamy risottos come in many guises, including *di mare* (with seafood), in which cuttlefish ink creates a dramatic, dark appearance. The Veneto's favorite pasta is *bigoli*, a thick spaghetti.

Vegetables are plentiful, including zucchini, asparagus, bitter red radicchio (endive) from Treviso, and variegated radicchio from Castelfranco.

Venetian specialties include *cichetti* and *antipasti* – snacks and appetizers such as marinated sardines, fried artichokes (*articiochi* in the Venetian dialect), and seafood in bite-size portions, especially mussels (*peoci*). Venetian crab (*granceola*) is highly prized, and the local fish soup (*sopa de pesce*) is deliciously hearty.

Finely sliced raw beef (*carpaccio*) had its origins here; it was created by Giuseppe Cipriani at Venice's Harry's Bar.

Delicious, traditional *tiramisù* is also said to originate from Venice, and sorbets are common too. It was the Venetians who introduced cane sugar to Europe and their sweet tooth is still evident in the rich candied fruit, sultana raisins, and pine nuts acquired from the Turks and Byzantines.

Caper berries    Marinated white anchovies    Olives wrapped in anchovies    Seafood cocktail

Selection of Venetian *antipasti*, the perfect appetizer

## Regional Dishes and Specialties

*Antipasto di frutti di mare* (a mixed seafood appetizer) is a special favorite in Venice, where the ingredients come fresh from the Adriatic. From lovely Lake Garda, *anguilla del pescatore* (stewed eel), *lavarelli al vino bianco* (lake fish in white wine), and *carpione* (a type of lake trout) are all fishy delights. Another fish specialty of the region is *baccalà alla veneziana*, made with dried salt cod. Pork and salamis feature throughout the area, but in Friuli goose is often used as an alternative to pork, with succulent cured meat offerings such as *salame d'oca* (goose salami). Game is also found on the menu, together with sauerkraut and filling goulash, while desserts often have an Austrian flavor too, such as *Apfelstrudel*. But the region is also proud of claiming as its own the decadent classic Italian dessert *tiramisù*.

Asparagus

**Sarde in saor** Venetian specialty of fried sardines in a sweet and sour onion marinade, with pine nuts.

Delivering fresh vegetables on the waterways of Venice

## Friuli-Venezia Giulia

A culinary crossroads, this region marks the meeting point of Slavic, Germanic, and Latin traditions and was once the poorest of the northern Italian regions. Varieties of Hungarian goulash and Austrian strudels often appear

Fresh radicchio and bell peppers piled high in a Treviso market

on local menus. The area produces fine sweet ham and prosciutto (including the fabled, succulent San Daniele). Goose is a staple dish, as is Istrian lamb, grazed in the open air on local herbs and grasses that impart a delicious flavor.

Trieste is famous for its Viennese pastries and sweet *gnocchi*, prune dumplings sprinkled with sugar and cinnamon. Friuli's dairy specialty is Montasio, a hard cheese made from cow's milk.

## Trentino & Alto Adige

Strong Austrian influences from the Alto Adige combine with hearty fare from the mountainous region of Trentino, as well as more southern Italian flavors. Staple dishes include cured meats such as *speck*

(smoked ham) and salamis, as well as warming soups including the classic minestrone. Bread dumplings – *canederli* in Italian but *knödel* in Alto Adige – feature more than pasta. Trentino risottos include sweet and savory variations. Especially good are those made with *finferli* mushrooms, highly prized and similar to Tuscan *porcini* in flavor and quality. Alpine trout is flavorsome, and game dishes, especially venison and rabbit, are popular in season, often served with polenta. The Trentino apple is crisp and delicious.

### ON THE MENU

**Carpaccio** *(Venice & the Veneto)* Wafer-thin slices of raw beef in extra virgin olive oil with arugula and slivers of Parmesan cheese.

**Fegato alla Veneziana** Calf's liver served on a bed of onions.

**Jota** *(Friuli–Venezia Giulia)* A soup of barley and sauerkraut. This cheap and filling dish is often mixed with *brovada* – turnips that have been steeped in a wooden cask of grape pressings.

**Strangolapreti** *(Trentino–Alto Adige)* Dumplings *(gnocchi)* made with bread, spinach, or potatoes, coated with butter and cheese. Literally means "priest stranglers."

**Risi e bisi** Soft and moist risotto mixing rice with fresh peas, sometimes with ham and Parmesan cheese.

**Polenta** Cornmeal porridge served plain as a side dish, often with rabbit, or *con baccalà* (with salt cod).

**Tiramisù** A rich dessert of mascarpone, sponge cake, coffee, and Marsala. The name means "pick me up."

# Understanding Architecture in Venice and the Veneto

Trade contact with the East led medieval Venice to develop its own exotic style – known as Venetian Gothic – blending Byzantine domes and Islamic minarets with European Gothic pointed arches and quatrefoils. In the 16th century, Palladio introduced his interpretations of Classical architecture through a series of churches, public buildings, and rural villas in Venice and the Veneto. The 17th century brought the Baroque style, though its exuberance was tempered by Palladio-influenced restraint.

Andrea Palladio (1508–80)

## The Architecture of Venice: Byzantine to Baroque

Upper loggia with copies of the Four Horses of St. Mark

Byzantine-style facade mosaics

Onion-shaped cupolas capping the main domes

Statues added in the 15th century

Central portal modeled on the Roman triumphal arch

**The Basilica di San Marco**, western Europe's finest Byzantine church (completed 11th century), was given lavish treatment to make it a dazzling shrine for the relics of St. Mark, the Evangelist, and a fitting symbol of Venetian aspirations *(see pp114–17)*.

## The Genius of Palladio

Doric columns supporting the second floor, Ionic above

Shaded loggias for escaping the heat

**Palazzo Chiericati** is a huge mansion of 1550, its simple style borrowed from the ancient Romans. It was once surrounded by water to reflect the statues of Classical deities along its roof *(see p156)*.

**Villa Barbaro at Maser** was one of the villas designed by Palladio from the 1550s, when it became fashionable for rich Venetians to acquire rural estates. This villa is typical, combining a working farm, housed in the side wings, with the elegant buildings of a country house *(see p153)*.

Symmetrical facade

Arcades linking the wings to the central block

## Where to See the Architecture

A *vaporetto* trip along the Grand Canal in Venice *(see pp92–5)* is a splendid way of getting an over-view of Venetian architecture. Ca' d'Oro, Ca' Rezzonico, and Ca' Pesaro may also be visited, for the museums they contain, and a visit

Typical Venetian Gothic window

to the Basilica di San Marco and the Palazzo Ducale is a must. There are numerous examples of Palladio's architecture in the Veneto, but the star is the Villa Barbaro *(see p153)*. Several of his villas line the Brenta Canal *(see p164)*, and the town of Vicenza *(see pp154–7)* is full of his buildings, including La Rotonda, his famous villa.

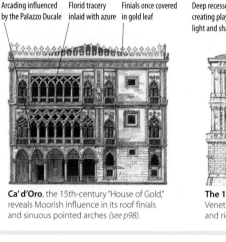

Arcading influenced by the Palazzo Ducale

Florid tracery inlaid with azure

Finials once covered in gold leaf

**Ca' d'Oro**, the 15th-century "House of Gold," reveals Moorish influence in its roof finials and sinuous pointed arches *(see p98)*.

Deep recesses creating play of light and shade

Keystones carved as helmeted heads

Festoons of fruit, ribbons, and flowers

**The 17th-century Ca' Pesaro** typifies the Venetian Baroque style – Classical columns and rich, but subtle, ornamentation *(see p93)*.

Giant composite columns

Istrian marble, chosen to catch the changing light of the lagoon

Statues and memorials to patrons of the church

**San Giorgio Maggiore**, built 1566–1610, is marvelously sited at the entrance to the Venetian inner harbor. It broke from the prevailing Gothic style, introducing the clean simplicity and harmonious proportions of Classical architecture to Venice, and more resembles an ancient Roman temple than a Christian church *(see pp124–5)*.

Pediment with coat of arms

Sundials at each end

# The Dolomites

The Dolomites are the most distinctive and beautiful mountains in Italy. They were formed of mineralized coral which was laid down beneath the sea during the Triassic era, and uplifted when the European and African continental plates dramatically collided 60 million years ago. Unlike the glacier-eroded saddles and ridges of the main body of the Alps, the pale rocks here have been carved by the corrosive effects of ice, sun, and rain, sculpting the cliffs, spires, and "organ pipes" that we see today. The eastern and western ranges of the Dolomites have slightly different characteristics; the eastern section is the more awe-inspiring, especially the Catinaccio (or Rosengarten) range, which is particularly beautiful, turning rose pink at sunset.

Onion dome, a common local feature

## Strada delle Dolomiti

One of the most spectacular routes through the Dolomites links Bolzano (*see p176*) with Cortina d'Ampezzo (*see p165*). It follows the lie of the land, passing some of the greatest peaks, and the most majestic landscape.

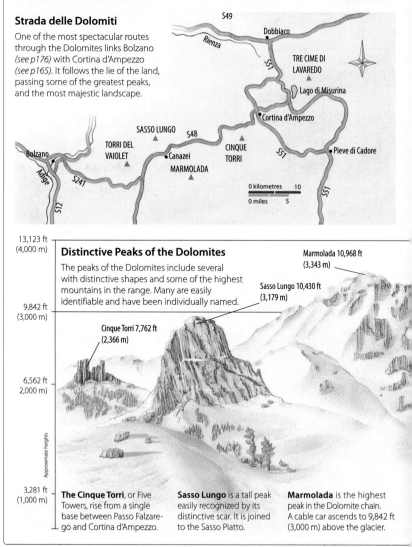

### Distinctive Peaks of the Dolomites

The peaks of the Dolomites include several with distinctive shapes and some of the highest mountains in the range. Many are easily identifiable and have been individually named.

Marmolada 10,968 ft (3,343 m)

Sasso Lungo 10,430 ft (3,179 m)

Cinque Torri 7,762 ft (2,366 m)

13,123 ft (4,000 m)

9,842 ft (3,000 m)

6,562 ft (2,000 m)

3,281 ft (1,000 m)

Approximate heights

**The Cinque Torri**, or Five Towers, rise from a single base between Passo Falzarego and Cortina d'Ampezzo.

**Sasso Lungo** is a tall peak easily recognized by its distinctive scar. It is joined to the Sasso Piatto.

**Marmolada** is the highest peak in the Dolomite chain. A cable car ascends to 9,842 ft (3,000 m) above the glacier.

**Lago di Misurina** is a large and beautiful lake lying beside the resort of Misurina. The crystal-clear waters reflect the surrounding mountains, mirroring various peaks such as the distinctive and dramatic Sorapiss, in shimmering colors.

**Outdoor activities** in this area of dramatic landscapes include skiing in winter, and walking and hiking along the footpaths, and to picnic sites, in summer. Chairlifts from the main resorts provide easy access up into the mountains themselves, transporting you into some breathtaking scenery.

Torri del Vaiolet
7,375 ft m (2,243)

Tre Cime di Lavaredo
9,839 ft (2,999 m)

**The Torri del Vaiolet** is part of the beautiful Catinaccio range, known for its color.

**Tre Cime di Lavaredo**, or Drei Zinnen, dominate the valleys north of the Lago di Misurina.

## Nature in the Dolomites

Forests and meadows support a breathtaking richness of wildlife in the region. Alpine plants, which flower between June and September, have evolved their miniature form to survive the harsh winds.

### The Flora

**Gentian roots** are used to make a bitter local liqueur.

**The orange mountain lily** thrives on sun-baked slopes.

**The pretty burser's saxifrage** grows in clusters on rocks.

**Devil's claw** has distinctive pink flower heads.

### The Fauna

**The ptarmigan** changes its plumage from mottled brown in summer to snow white in winter for effective camouflage. It feeds on mountain berries and young plant shoots.

**The chamois**, a shy mountain antelope prized for its soft skin, is protected in the national parks, where hunting is forbidden.

**Roe deer** are very common, as their natural predators – wolves and lynx – are decreasing in number. An appetite for tree saplings causes problems for foresters.

# VENICE

Lying in the extreme northeast of Italy, Venice, gateway to the Orient, became an independent Byzantine province in the 10th century. Exclusive trading links with the East and victory in the Crusade of 1204 brought wealth and power, which were only gradually eroded by European and Turkish rivals. Today, Venice's ties are with the local Veneto region, which stretches from the flat river plains to the Dolomites.

Venice is one of the few cities in the world that can be truly described as unique. It survives against all the odds, built on a series of low mudbanks amid the tidal waters of the Adriatic, and regularly subject to floods. During the Middle Ages, under the leadership of successive doges, Venice expanded its power and influence throughout the Mediterranean to Constantinople (modern Istanbul). The immense wealth of the city was celebrated in art and architecture throughout the town.

The riches of St. Mark's alone bear witness to Venice's position as a world power from the 12th to 14th centuries. After slowly losing ground to the new states of Europe, however, it fell to Napoleon in 1797. Finally, Venice joined the Kingdom of Italy in 1866, so bringing unity to the country for the first time in its history. Today, Venice has found a new role. Her palazzi have become museums, stores, hotels, and apartments, and her convents have been turned into centers for art restoration. Yet little of the essential fabric of Venice has altered in 200 years. The city's sounds are still those of footsteps and the cries of boatmen. The only engines are those of barges delivering supplies or waterbuses ferrying passengers between stops. The same well-worn streets are still trodden. More than 20 million visitors a year succumb to the magic of this improbable place whose "streets are full of water" and where the glories of the past are evident at every turn.

Tourists relax at cafés along a canal in Burano, Venice

◀ Dusk settles over St. Mark's Basin, Venice

# Exploring Venice

Venice is divided into six ancient administrative districts or *sestieri*: Cannaregio, Castello, San Marco, Dorsoduro, San Polo, and Santa Croce. You can walk to most places in Venice itself, and take a ride on a waterbus to any of the islands. The Venezia Unica Card *(see p634)* covers all transportation as well as admission to most museums, such as Ca' Rezzonico, the Palazzo Ducale, and Museo Correr.

## Sights at a Glance

### Churches

**①** Madonna dell'Orto
**③** San Giovanni Grisostomo
**④** Santa Maria dei Miracoli
**⑥** San Giacomo dell'Orio
**⑦** San Polo
**⑧** *Santa Maria Gloriosa dei Frari pp102–3*
**⑩** San Rocco
**⑪** San Pantalon
**⑬** San Nicolò dei Mendicoli
**⑭** San Sebastiano
**⑰** Santa Maria della Salute
**⑲** *Basilica di San Marco pp114–17*
**㉔** Santo Stefano
**㉕** Santi Giovanni e Paolo
**㉗** Santa Maria Formosa
**㉘** San Zaccaria
**㉚** San Giovanni in Bragora
**㉜** San Giorgio Maggiore

### Buildings and Monuments

**⑤** Rialto
**⑳** *Palazzo Ducale pp118–20*
**㉑** Torre dell'Orologio

**㉒** Campanile
**㉖** Statue of Colleoni
**㉙** Scuola di San Giorgio degli Schiavoni
**㉛** Arsenale

### Museums and Galleries

**②** Ca' d'Oro
**⑨** *Scuola Grande di San Rocco pp104–5*
**⑫** Ca' Rezzonico
**⑮** *Accademia pp110–11*
**⑯** Peggy Guggenheim Collection
**⑱** Punta della Dogana
**㉓** Museo Correr

### Lagoon

**㉝** Murano
**㉞** Burano
**㉟** *Torcello pp126–7*

0 meters    500
0 yards      500

Santa Maria della Salute, at the mouth of the Grand Canal

**For keys to symbols** *see back flap*

A gondola ride along the Grand Canal

**The Lagoon**

Marco Polo

Mestre

Canale Osellino

Mestre

Veneta

Laguna

VENICE

## Getting Around

The only road into Venice is the S11 from Mestre, which carries you over the causeway to the Tronchetto and Piazzale Roma, where there are parking lots and bus stops. Train travelers arrive at Santa Lucia station on the Grand Canal. In the city, public transportation is by *vaporetto*, or waterbus – the No.1 is best for sightseeing, as it travels the length of the Grand Canal *(see pp140–41)*.

# The Grand Canal: Santa Lucia to the Rialto

The best way to view the Grand Canal as it winds through the heart of the city is from a *vaporetto*, or waterbus. Two lines travel the length of the canal *(see p635)*. The palaces lining the waterway were built over a span of five centuries and present a panoramic survey of the city's history, almost all bearing the name of some once-great Venetian family.

**San Marcuola**
The church was rebuilt in the 18th century, but the planned new facade overlooking the canal was never completed.

**San Geremia** houses the relics of St Lucy, once kept in the church of Santa Lucia where the train station now stands.

**Palazzo Labia**
Between 1745 and 1750, Giambattista Tiepolo decorated the ballroom with scenes from the life of Cleopatra.

Canale di Cannaregio

**Palazzo Corner-Contarini**

San Marcuola

Riva di Biasio

Ferrovia

FS

**Ponte degli Scalzi**

**Fondaco dei Turchi**
A warehouse for Turkish traders in the 17th–19th centuries, this is now the Natural History Museum.

**San Simeone Piccolo**
This 18th-century domed church is based on the Pantheon in Rome.

## The Gondolas of Venice

The gondola has been a part of Venice since the 11th century. With its slim hull and flat underside, the craft is perfectly adapted to negotiating narrow, shallow canals. There is a slight leftward curve to the prow, which counteracts the force of the oar, preventing the gondola from going round in circles.

In 1562 it was decreed that all gondolas should be black, to stop people making an ostentatious show of their wealth. For special occasions they are decorated with flowers. Today, gondola rides are expensive and usually taken by tourists *(see p635)*. However, *traghetti* (gondola ferries) are a cheap, convenient way of crossing the Grand Canal.

Gondolas tied up by steps

### Ca' d'Oro
The delicate Gothic tracery of the facade makes this a striking landmark. Its art collection *(see p98)* includes Bernini's model for a fountain (c.1648).

**Locator Map**

*See Venice Street Finder maps 1, 2, 3*

### Palazzo Vendramin Calergi
This is one of the finest early Renaissance palaces in Venice. The German composer Richard Wagner *(left)* died here in 1883.

**The Pescheria** has been the site of a busy fish market for six centuries.

**Palazzo Sagredo**
Graceful Veneto-Byzantine and Gothic arches are both featured on the waterfront facade.

**Palazzo Michiel dalle Colonne** takes its name from its distinctive colonnade.

**The Rialto Bridge** *(see p101)* spans the canal in the commercial heart of the city.

San Stae

### San Stae
The facade of this Baroque church is richly adorned with statues. It regularly hosts exhibitions.

Ca' d'Oro

Rialto Mercato

### Ca' Pesaro
The huge, stately Baroque palace today houses a gallery of modern art and the Oriental Museum.

Rialto

# The Grand Canal: the Rialto to San Marco

After passing the Rialto, the canal doubles back on itself along a stretch known as La Volta (the bend). It then widens out and the views become more spectacular approaching San Marco. Facades may have faded and foundations battered with the tides, yet the canal remains, in the words of the French ambassador in 1495, "the most beautiful street in the world."

**Palazzo Mocenigo**
Lord Byron stayed in this huge 18th-century palace in 1818.

Sant' Angelo

**Palazzo Garzoni**
is a renovated Gothic palace.

San Tomà

**Ca' Rezzonico**
Now a museum of 18th-century Venice (see p107), the palace was the last home of the English poet Robert Browning, seen here with his son Pen.

San Samuele

Ca' Rezzonico

**Palazzo Grassi**
This elegant palazzo dates from the 1730s. Bought by French tycoon François-Henri Pinault in 2005, it is now used for art exhibitions.

Ponte dell'Accademia

**Palazzo Capello Malipiero**
The palace was rebuilt in 1622. Beside it stands the 12th-century campanile of San Samuele.

Accademia

**Accademia**
The world's greatest collection of Venetian paintings is housed here in the former Scuola della Carità (see pp110–11), which has a Baroque facade by Giorgio Massari.

**Palazzo Barbaro**
Novelist Henry James wrote The Aspern Papers here in 1888.

Rialto

 San Silvestro

**The Riva del Vin** is the quay where wine *(vin)* used to be unloaded. It is one of the few spots where you can sit and relax on the banks of the Grand Canal.

**Locator Map**
*See Venice Street Finder maps 6, 7*

**Palazzo Barzizza**, rebuilt in the 17th century, preserves its early 13th-century facade.

**Peggy Guggenheim Collection**
A one-story palazzo houses Guggenheim's great modern art collection *(see pp108–9).*

**Santa Maria della Salute**
The vast weight of this Baroque church is supported by over one million lumber piles *(see p109).*

**Palazzo Gritti-Pisani**
The former home of the Gritti family is now the luxury Gritti Palace hotel *(see p563).*

Santa Maria del Giglio

Salute

San Marco Vallaresso

**Harry's Bar**, founded in 1931 by Giuseppe Cipriani, is famous for its cocktails.

**Palazzo Dario**
Beautiful colored marbles give the 1487 palace a highly individual facade. According to legend, the building is cursed.

**The Punta della Dogana** customs house, built in the 17th century, now contains the François Pinault Foundation of contemporary art. It is crowned by a golden globe and a weather vane *(see p109).*

Gondolas moored along the Grand Canal at sunrise ▶

Madonna dell'Orto, with 15th-century facade statues of St. Christopher and the Apostles

# ❶ Madonna dell'Orto

Campo Madonna dell'Orto. **Map** 2 F2.
**Tel** 041 719933. 🚤 Madonna
dell'Orto. **Open** 10am–5pm Mon–Sat,
noon–5pm Sun & public hols.
**Closed** Jan 1, Dec 25. 🅿 🚳
**w** madonnadellorto.org

This lovely Gothic church,
founded in the mid-14th
century, was dedicated to
St. Christopher, patron saint of
travelers, to protect the boatmen
who ferried passengers to the
islands in the northern lagoon.
A 15th-century statue of the
saint, restored by the Venice in
Peril fund, stands above the
main portal. The dedication
was changed and the church
reconstructed in the early 15th
century, after the discovery, in a
nearby vegetable garden (orto),
of a statue of the Virgin Mary
said to have miraculous powers.

The interior, faced almost
entirely in brick, is large and
uncluttered. On the right is
a magnificent painting by
Cima da Conegliano, St. John
the Baptist and Other Saints
(c.1493). The vacant space in the
chapel opposite belongs
to Giovanni Bellini's Madonna
with Child (c.1478), stolen in
1993 for the third time.

The church's greatest
remaining treasures are the
works of art by Tintoretto, who
was a parishioner of the church.
His tomb lies with that of his
children, in the chapel to the
right of the chancel. The most

dramatic of his works are the
towering masterpieces that
decorate the chancel (1562–4).
On the right wall is The Last
Judgment, whose
turbulent content
caused John Ruskin's
wife, Effie, to flee the
church in horror. In The
Adoration of the Golden
Calf on the left wall,
the figure carrying the
calf, fourth from the
left, is believed to be a
portrait of the artist.
Inside the chapel of
San Mauro, off the
end of the right nave,
stands a statue of the
Madonna by Giovanni
de' Santi. Restored by the Venice
in Peril fund, it inspired the
rededication of the church.

# ❷ Ca' d'Oro

Calle Ca' d'Oro. **Map** 3 A4. **Tel** 041 520
03 45. 🚤 Ca' d'Oro. **Open** 8:15am–
2pm Mon, 8:15am– 7:15pm Tue–Sun
(last adm: 6:45pm). **Closed** Jan 1,
May 1, Dec 25. 🅿 🏛 🎧 🛗 partial.
🚳 **w** cadoro.org

In 1420 Marino
Contarini, a
wealthy patrician,
commissioned the
building of what
he hoped would be
the city's most mag-
nificent palace (see
p85). The building's
intricate carving was
entrusted to a team
of Venetian and Lombard
craftsmen, while the facade was
adorned with the most elaborate
and expensive decorative finishes,
including gold leaf, vermilion,

Tullio Lombardo's
Double Portrait

and ultramarine. Over the years
the palace was extensively
remodeled, and by the 18th
century was in a state of semi-
dereliction. In 1846 it was
bought by the Russian Prince
Troubetzkoy for the famous
ballerina Marie Taglioni. Under
her direction the palace
suffered barbaric restoration,
losing, among other things,
its staircase and much of its
original stonework. It was
finally rescued by Baron Giorgio
Franchetti, a wealthy patron of
the arts, who bequeathed both
the building and his private art
collection to the state in 1915.

Pride of place on the first of
the gallery's two floors goes to
Andrea Mantegna's St. Sebastian
(1506), the artist's last work,
which occupies a special alcove
of its own. Elsewhere, the floor's
main exhibits are ranged around
the portego (gallery). This is
largely dominated by the vivid
15th-century Double Portrait
(c.1493) by the sculptor Tullio
Lombardo; Sansovino's lunette
of the Madonna and Child
(c.1530); and several bronze
reliefs by the Paduan Andrea
Briosco, "Il Riccio"
(1470–1532). Rooms
leading off the
portego to the right
contain numerous
bronzes and
medallions, with
some examples by
Pisanello and
Gentile Bellini.

Paintings here also
include the famous Madonna of
the Beautiful Eyes, attributed to
Giovanni Bellini, a Madonna and
Child, attributed to Alvise Vivarini
(both late 15th century),
and Carpaccio's
Annunciation and
Death of the Virgin
(both c.1504). A room
to the left of the
portego contains non-
Venetian paintings,
notably a Flagellation
by Luca Signorelli
(c.1480). A lovely
staircase leads to the
second floor, which
opens with a room
hung with tapestries.
It has bronzes by

The magnificent Gothic facade of the Ca' d'Oro, or
House of Gold

*For hotels and restaurants in this region see pp562–5 and pp580–84*

Alessandro Vittoria and paintings by Titian and Van Dyck. The *portego* displays frescoes (*c.*1532) by Pordenone from the cloister of Santo Stefano, while an anteroom contains damaged frescoes by Titian taken from the Fondaco dei Tedeschi.

Giovanni Bellini's 1513 altarpiece in San Giovanni Grisostomo

## ❸ San Giovanni Grisostomo

Campo San Giovanni Grisostomo. **Map** 3 B5. 🚤 Rialto. **Open** 8:15am–12:15pm, 3–7pm daily. **Closed** during Mass. ♿

This terra-cotta-colored church is located near the Rialto. Built between 1479 and 1504, it is a lovely Renaissance design, the last work of Mauro Coducci.

The interior is built on a Greek-cross plan. The light meter illuminates Giovanni Bellini's painting, *St. Jerome with Saints Christopher and Augustine* (1513), above the first altar on the right. This was most probably Bellini's last painting, executed when the artist was in his eighties.

Over the high altar hangs Sebastiano del Piombo's *St. John Chrysostom and Six Saints* (1509–11).

## ❹ Santa Maria dei Miracoli

Campo dei Miracoli. **Map** 3 B5. **Tel** 041 275 04 62. 🚤 Rialto, Fondamenta Nuove. **Open** 10:30am–4pm Mon, 10:30am–4:30pm Tue–Sat. **Closed** Jan 1, Dec 25. 📷 ♿ 🌐 chorusvenezia.org

An exquisite masterpiece of early Renaissance architecture, the Miracoli is the church where many Venetians like to get married. Tucked away in a maze of alleys and waterways in eastern Cannaregio, it is small and somewhat elusive.

Santa Maria dei Miracoli is decorated in various shades of marble, with some fine bas-reliefs and sculpture. It was built in 1481–9 by architect Pietro Lombardo and his sons to enshrine *The Virgin and Child* (1408), a painting believed to have miraculous powers. The picture, by Niccolò di Pietro, can still be seen above the altar.

The interior of the church is embellished with pink, white, and gray marble. It is crowned by a barrel-vaulted ceiling (1528), which has 50 portraits of saints

Decorative column from inside Santa Maria dei Miracoli

and prophets. The balustrade, between the nave and the chancel, is decorated by Tullio Lombardo's carved figures of St. Francis, Archangel Gabriel, the Virgin, and St. Clare.

The screen around the high altar and the medallions of the Evangelists in the cupola spandrels are also Lombardo's work. Above the main door, the choir gallery was used by the nuns from the neighboring convent, who entered the church through an overhead gallery. Santa Maria dei Miracoli has undergone a major restoration program, which was funded by the American Save Venice organization.

### Santa Maria dei Miracoli

*This beautifully proportioned facade is composed of decorated panels and multicolored polished marble.*

Carving of saint

**The semicircular** crowning lunette emphasizes the church's jewel-box appearance.

**A false loggia** is formed of Ionic arches, inset with windows. The marble used was reportedly left over from the building of San Marco.

*Virgin and Child by Giorgio Lascaris*

**The marble panels** are fixed to the bricks by metal hooks. This method prevents the buildup of damp and saltwater behind the panels, and dates from the Renaissance.

# Street by Street: San Polo

The Rialto bridge and markets make this area a magnet for visitors. Traditionally the city's commercial quarter, it was here that bankers, brokers, and merchants conducted their affairs. Streets are no longer lined with stands selling spices and fine fabrics, but the food markets and pasta stores are unmissable. Away from the bridge, streets quickly become less crowded, leading to tiny squares and quiet churches.

**The Rialto Markets** have existed for centuries and are renowned for their produce. The Pescheria sells fresh seafood.

**The 17th-century** church of San Cassiano houses a carved altar (1696) and a *Crucifixion* by Tintoretto (1568).

**Key**

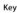 Suggested route

0 meters    75
0 yards     75

The Frari

**Sant'Aponal** has a facade decorated with worn Gothic reliefs. The church was founded in the 11th century, but is now deconsecrated.

**For keys to map symbols** *see back flap*

San Silvestro

**San Giovanni Elemosinario** is an inconspicuous church that was rebuilt in the early 16th century, although its campanile dates from the end of the 14th century. Inside are interesting frescoes by Pordenone

**Locator Map**
*See Venice Street Finder
maps 2, 3, 6, 7*

The lively Erberia, selling fresh fruit and vegetables

**San Giacomo di Rialto's**
clock face (1410), which
has sadly been a poor
timekeeper over the
years, adorns one
of Venice's oldest
churches.

DEGLI OREFICI

Market
entrance

**❺ ★ Rialto**
One of Venice's most famous
sights, the bridge offers fine
views of the Grand Canal, and
marks the heart of the city.

## ❺ Rialto

Ponte di Rialto. **Map** 7 A1. 🚤 Rialto.

The Rialto takes its name from
*rivo alto* (high bank) and was
one of the first areas of Venice
to be inhabited. A banking and
then market district, it remains
one of the city's busiest and
most bustling areas. Locals and
visitors alike jostle among the
colorful stands of the Erberia
(fruit and vegetable market)
and Pescheria (fish market).

Stone bridges were built
in Venice as early as the
12th century, but it was not
until 1588, after the collapse,
decay, or sabotage of earlier
wooden structures, that a solid
stone bridge was designed for
the Rialto. Completed in 1591,
the new bridge remained the
only means of crossing the
Grand Canal until 1854, when
the Accademia bridge was built.

Few visitors leave Venice
without crossing the famous
bridge. It is a wonderful place
to watch and photograph the
constant activity of boats on
the Grand Canal below.

## ❻ San Giacomo dell'Orio

Campo San Giacomo dell'Orio. **Map** 2
E5. **Tel** 041 275 04 62. 🚤 Riva di Biasio
or San Stae. **Open** 10:30am–
4pm Mon, 10:30am–4:30 Tue–Sat.
**Closed** Jan 1, Dec 25. 🖼 📷
🌐 **chorusvenezia.org**

This church is a focal point of
a quiet quarter of Santa Croce.
The name "dell'Orio" may derive
from a laurel tree *(alloro)* that
once stood near the church.
San Giacomo was founded
in the 9th century, rebuilt

in 1225, and thereafter
repeatedly modified, resulting
in a mixture of styles. The
campanile and basilica ground
plan date from the 13th century.
The ship's keel roof and the
columns are Gothic, and the
apses are Renaissance.

The sacristy has a beautiful
ceiling by Veronese and some
interesting altar paintings.

## ❼ San Polo

Campo San Polo. **Map** 6 F1.
**Tel** 041 275 04 62. 🚤 San Silvestro.
**Open** 10:30am–4pm Mon, 10:30am–
4:30pm Tue–Sat. **Closed** Jan 1, Dec 25.
🖼 🏠 📷 🌐 **chorusvenezia.org**

Founded in the 9th century,
rebuilt in the 15th century, and
revamped in Neo-Classical
style in the early 19th century,
this church is worth visiting
for the lovely Gothic portal and
the Romanesque lions at the
foot of the 14th-century
campanile – one holds a
serpent between its paws,
the other a human head.

Inside, follow the signs for the
*Via Crucis del Tiepolo* – 14 pictures
of the Stations of the Cross (1749)
by the painter Giandomenico
Tiepolo; many of these works
include vivid portraits of
18th-century Venetian life. The
church also has paintings by
Veronese and Palma il Giovane
(the Younger), and a dramatic
*Last Supper* by Tintoretto.

A Romanesque lion at the base of San Polo's
14th-century campanile

*For hotels and restaurants in this region see pp562–5 and pp580–84*

# ❽ Santa Maria Gloriosa dei Frari

More commonly known as the Frari (a corruption of *frati*, meaning "brothers"), this vast Gothic church dwarfs the eastern area of San Polo. The first church on the site was built by Franciscan friars in 1250–1338, but was replaced by a larger building completed in the mid-15th century. The airy interior is striking for its sheer size and for the quality of its works of art, including masterpieces by Titian and Giovanni Bellini, a statue by Donatello, and several grandiose tombs.

**★ Monks' Choir**
This consists of three-tiered stalls (1468), carved with bas-reliefs of saints and Venetian city scenes.

**★ Assumption of the Virgin**
Titian's glowing and spectacular work (1518) draws the eye through the monk's choir, to the altar, and heavenward.

**Rood Screen** (1475)
Pietro Lombardo and Bartolomeo Bon carved the rood screen and its decorative marble figures.

## KEY

① **The campanile** is 262 ft (83 m) high, the tallest in the city after that of San Marco.

② **The former monastery**, which houses the State Archives, has two cloisters: one in the style of Sansovino, another designed by Palladio.

③ *The Madonna di Ca' Pesaro* (1526) shows Titian's mastery of light and color.

## Floorplan

*The Frari's imposing cruciform interior, which is 295 ft (90 m) long, holds 12 sights that should not be missed.*

### Key to Floorplan

1 Tomb of Canova
2 Monument to Titian
3 Madonna di Ca' Pesaro by Titian
4 Choir stalls
5 Corner Chapel

6 Tomb of Monteverdi
7 Tomb of Doge Nicolò Tron
8 High altar with *Assumption of the Virgin* (1518) by Titian
9 Tomb of Doge Francesco Foscari

10 John the Baptist (c.1450) by Donatello
11 Bartolomeo Vivarini's altar painting (1474), Bernardo Chapel
12 Madonna and Child with Saints (1488) by Bellini

### VISITORS' CHECKLIST

**Practical Information**
Campo dei Frari. **Map** 6 D1–E1.
Tel 041 275 04 62. **Open** 9am–6pm Mon–Sat, 1–6pm Sun & religious hols. **Closed** Jan 1, Dec 25. 🚫 unless attending Mass. 🕋 frequent. 📷
🌐 **chorusvenezia.org**

**Transportation**
🚤 San Tomà.

★ **Madonna and Child**
The sacristy's altarpiece (1488) by Bellini, with its sublime use of color, is one of Venice's most beautiful Renaissance paintings.

Entrance

**Tomb of Canova**
Canova designed, but never constructed, a Neo-Classical marble pyramid like this as a monument for Titian. After Canova's death in 1822, the sculptor's pupils used a similar design for their master's tomb.

# ❾ Scuola Grande di San Rocco

Restored main entrance to the Scuola di San Rocco

Founded in honor of San Rocco (St. Roch), a saint who dedicated his life to helping the sick, the Scuola started out as a charitable confraternity. Construction began in 1515 under Bartolomeo Bon and was continued by Scarpagnino until his death in 1549. The work was financed by donations from Venetians keen to invoke San Rocco's protection and the Scuola quickly became one of the wealthiest in Venice. In 1564 its members decided to commission Tintoretto to decorate its walls and ceilings. His earliest paintings, the first of over 50 works he eventually left in the Scuola, fill the small Sala dell'Albergo off the Upper Hall. His later paintings occupy the Ground Floor Hall, immediately within the entrance.

Tintoretto's magnificent *Crucifixion*, painted in 1565 for the Sala dell'Albergo in the Scuola di San Rocco

## Ground Floor Hall

The ground floor cycle was executed in 1582–7, when Tintoretto was in his sixties, and consists of eight large paintings illustrating, among others, the life of Mary. The series starts with an *Annunciation* and ends with an *Assumption*.

The calm and tranquil scenes of *The Flight into Egypt*, *St. Mary Magdalene*, and *St. Mary of Egypt* are remarkable for their serenity. This is portrayed most lucidly by the repentant

Detail from *The Flight into Egypt* (1582–7) by Tintoretto

hermit's isolated spiritual contemplation in *St. Mary of Egypt*. In all three paintings, it is noticeable that the landscapes are rendered with rapid strokes, and are an important part of the final composition.

## Upper Hall and Sala dell'Albergo

Scarpagnino's great staircase (1544–6), its upper flight decorated with two vast paintings commemorating the plague of 1630, leads to the Upper Hall. Here, biblical subjects decorate the ceiling and walls, painted by Tintoretto from 1575 to 1581.

The ceiling paintings portray scenes from the Old Testament. The three large and dynamic square paintings in the center show episodes from the Book of Exodus: *Moses Strikes Water from the Rock*, *The Miracle of the Bronze Serpent*, and *The Fall of Manna in the Desert*. These all allude to the charitable aims of the Scuola

in alleviating thirst, sickness, and hunger, respectively. All three paintings are crowded compositions displaying much violent movement.

The vast wall paintings in the hall feature episodes from the New Testament, linking with the ceiling paintings. Two of the most striking paintings are *The Temptation of Christ*, which shows a handsome young Satan offering Christ two loaves of bread, and *The Adoration of the Shepherds*. Like *The Temptation of Christ*, *The Adoration* is composed of two halves, with a female figure, shepherds, and an ox below, and the Holy Family and onlookers above.

The breathtakingly beautiful carvings below the paintings were added in the 17th century by sculptor Francesco Pianta. The figures are allegorical and include (near the altar) a caricature of Tintoretto with his palette and brushes, representing Painting.

*For hotels and restaurants in this region see pp562–5 and pp580–84*

Detail from *The Temptation of Christ* (1578–81) by Tintoretto

The easel painting *Christ Carrying the Cross* was once attributed to Giorgione, though many believe it to be by Titian.

Near the entrance to the Sala dell'Albergo is the *Annunciation* by Titian. The Sala dell'Albergo itself holds the most breath-taking of Tintoretto's works – the *Crucifixion* (1565). Henry James

remarked of this painting: "No single picture contains more of human life; there is everything in it, including the most exquisite beauty." Tintoretto began the cycle of paintings in this room in 1564, when he won the commission with the ceiling painting *San Rocco in Glory*. On the wall opposite the *Crucifixion* are paintings of episodes from the Passion: *Christ before Pilate*, *The Crowning with Thorns*, and *The Ascent to Calvary*.

## ⑩ San Rocco

Campo San Rocco. **Map** 6 D1. **Tel** 041 523 48 64. 🚌 San Tomà. **Open** 9:30am–5:30pm daily (to 12:30pm Jan 1, Easter Sun, & Dec 25). ✉

On the same square as the celebrated Scuola Grande di San Rocco is the church of the same name. Designed by the sculptor and architect Bartolomeo Bon in 1489 and largely rebuilt in 1725, the exterior suffers from a mixture of styles. The facade was added in 1765–71. Inside, the chancel is decorated with a series of paintings by Tintoretto depicting scenes from the life of San Rocco.

## ⑪ San Pantalon

Campo San Pantalon. **Map** 6 D2. **Tel** 041 523 58 93. 🚌 San Tomà, Piazzale Roma. **Open** 10am–noon, 1–3pm Mon–Sat. ✉ 🌐 **sanpantalon.it**

Fumiani's epic ceiling painting (1680–1740) in San Pantalon

The overwhelming feature of this late 17th-century church is its vast painted ceiling, dark, awe-inspiring, and remarkable for its illusionistic effect of height. The ceiling comprises a total of 40 scenes, and admirers claim that this is the world's largest work of art on canvas.

The scenes show the martyrdom and apotheosis of the physician St. Pantalon. The artist, Gian Antonio Fumiani, took 24 years (1680–1704) to achieve the masterpiece, before allegedly falling to his death from the scaffolding.

## Key to Paintings

🔲 Ground Floor Hall **1** The Annunciation; **2** The Adoration of the Three Kings; **3** The Flight into Egypt; **4** The Massacre of the Innocents; **5** St. Mary Magdalene; **6** St. Mary of Egypt; **7** The Presentation in the Temple; **8** The Assumption.

🔲 Upper Hall Walls **9** San Rocco; **10** St. Sebastian; **11** The Adoration of the Shepherds; **12** The Baptism of Christ; **13** The Resurrection; **14** The Agony in the Garden; **15** The Last Supper; **16** The Vision of San Rocco; **17** The Miracle of the Loaves and Fishes; **18** The Resurrection of Lazarus; **19** The Ascension; **20** Christ Heals the Paralytic; **21** The Temptation of Christ.

🔲 Upper Hall Ceiling **22** Moses Saved from the Waters; **23** The Pillar of Fire; **24** Samuel and Saul; **25** Jacob's Ladder; **26** Elijah on a Chariot of Fire; **27** Elijah Fed by the Angels; **28** Daniel Saved by the Angels; **29** The Passover; **30** The Fall of Manna; **31** The Sacrifice of Isaac; **32** The Miracle of the Bronze Serpent; **33** Jonah Emerges from the Whale; **34** Moses Strikes Water from the Rock; **35** Adam and Eve; **36** Three Children in the Furnace; **37** God Appears to Moses; **38** Samson Brings out Water from the Jawbone of an Ass; **39** The Vision of the Prophet Ezekiel; **40** The Vision of Jeremiah; **41** Elisha Distributes Bread; **42** Abraham and Melchizedek.

Ground Floor Hall

Upper Hall

# Street by Street: Dorsoduro

Built on a stratum of solid subsoil is the *sestiere* of Dorsoduro – the name means "hard backbone." It has as its focal point the lively Campo Santa Margherita, the largest open space in this part of Venice. The square bustles with activity, particularly in the morning, when the market stands are open, and in the evening, when it is the haunt of students from nearby Ca' Foscari, now part of the University of Venice. The surrounding streets contain some architectural stunners, notably Ca' Rezzonico and the Scuola Grande dei Carmini, which has decorations by Tiepolo. Of the area's waterways, the delightful Rio San Barnaba is best appreciated from the Ponte dei Pugni, near the barge selling fruit and vegetables – itself a time-honored Venetian sight. Alongside the Rio Terà Canal there are some lively cafés and a fascinating store selling masks for Carnevale.

**Campo Santa Margherita** is an ideal place for relaxing in a café.

**Palazzo Zenobio**, built at the end of the 17th century, is now a guesthouse. With permission, visitors can see the fine 18th-century ballroom.

**Scuola Grande dei Carmini** contains nine ceiling panels (1739–44) in the hall on the upper floor, painted by Tiepolo for the Carmelite confraternity.

**Santa Maria dei Carmini** has a Gothic side porch carved with Byzantine reliefs.

**Fondamenta Gherardini** runs beside the Rio San Barnaba, one of the prettiest canals in the sestiere.

**Key**

— Suggested route

| | |
|---|---|
| 0 meters | 50 |
| 0 yards | 50 |

*For hotels and restaurants in this region see pp562–5 and pp580–84*

**Locator Map**
*See Venice Street Finder maps 5, 6*

Tiepolo's *New World* fresco, part of a series in Ca' Rezzonico

**⑫ ★ Ca' Rezzonico**
The ballroom covers the width of the palazzo once owned by Browning.

**Palazzo Giustinian** was home to Wagner in 1858.

**Ca' Foscari** was completed in 1437 for Doge Francesco Foscari.

RIO DI CA FOSCARI

C D ASEO

C SAONERI

ZEN

C FOSCARI

C DELLA VIDA

C D BOTTEGHE

CALLE BERNARDO

CANAL GRANDE

CAMPO SAN BARNABA

CALLE DEL TRAGHETTO

**Ponte dei Pugni** was a traditional scene of fistfights between rival factions. They were finally banned in 1705 for being too violent.

**San Barnaba** is a thriving community, with its own floating market barge crammed with fresh fruit and vegetables. It is a focal point for tourists and locals alike.

## ⑫ Ca' Rezzonico

Fondamenta Rezzonico 3136.
**Map** 6 E3. **Tel** 041 241 01 00. Ca' Rezzonico. **Open** 10am–6pm Wed–Mon (Nov–Mar: to 5pm, last adm: 1 hr before closing). **Closed** Jan 1, Dec 25.
**W** visitmuve.it

This palazzo houses the museum of 18th-century Venice, its rooms furnished with frescoes, paintings, and period pieces taken from other palaces or museums. Building began with Longhena (architect of La Salute, *see p109*) in 1667, but the funds of the Bon family, who commissioned it, ran dry before the second floor was started. In 1712 the unfinished palace was bought by the Rezzonico family of Genoa, who spent a large portion of their fortune on its completion.

The Rezzonico family sold it on, in 1888, to the famous poet Robert Browning and his son, Pen. The outstanding attraction in the palace today is Giorgio Massari's ballroom, which occupies the entire breadth of the building. It is adorned with gilded chandeliers, carved furniture by Andrea Brustolon, and a ceiling with *trompe l'oeil* frescoes. Other rooms have frescoes by Giambattista Tiepolo, including his lively *Nuptial Allegory* (1758), and one by his son, Giandomenico, originally in his villa at Zianigo. There are paintings by Longhi, Guardi, and – rare in Venice – Canaletto. On the top floor is a reconstructed 18th-century apothecary's shop and the Pinacoteca Martini.

Nave of San Nicolò dei Mendicoli, one of the oldest churches in Venice

### ⓭ San Nicolò dei Mendicoli

Campo San Nicolò. **Map** 5 A3. **Tel** 041 275 03 82. San Basilio. **Open** 10am–noon, 3–5:30pm Mon–Sat, 9am–noon Sun & public hols.

Contrasting with the remote and run-down area that surrounds it, this church still remains one of the most charming in Venice. Founded in the 7th century, it has been rebuilt extensively over the years. The little porch on the north flank is 15th century and once sheltered the beggars, or *mendicanti*, who gave the church its name.

Thanks to the Venice in Peril fund, in the 1970s the church underwent one of the most comprehensive restoration programs since the floods of 1966. Flooding had become such a problem that the priest often ferried himself around the church in a small wicker boat. The floor, which was 1 ft (30 cm) below the level of the canals, was rebuilt and raised slightly to prevent further flood damage. The roofs and lower walls were reconstructed, and paintings and statues restored.

The interior is delightfully embellished, particularly the nave with its 16th-century gilded wooden statues. These include the figure of San Nicolò himself. On the upper walls is a series of paintings of the life of Christ (*c.*1553) by Alvise dal Friso and other pupils of Veronese.

Outside, a small column supports a stone lion, in a humbler echo of the Column of San Marco in the Piazzetta.

### ⓮ San Sebastiano

Campo San Sebastiano. **Map** 5 C3. **Tel** 041 275 04 62. San Basilio. **Open** 10:30am–4pm Mon, 10:30am–4:30pm Tue–Sat. **Closed** Jan 1, Aug 15, Dec 25. **chorusvenezia.org**

This church has one of the most homogeneous interiors in Venice, created by Veronese. From 1555 to 1560 and again in the 1570s, he was commissioned to decorate the sacristy ceiling, the nave ceiling, the frieze, the east end of the choir, the high altar, the doors of the organ panels, and the chancel.

The paintings feature radiant colors and rich costumes. Those on the sacristy ceiling depict the *Coronation of the Virgin* and the *Four Evangelists*.

Of the other paintings, the finest are the three that tell the story of Esther, Queen of Xerxes I of Persia, famous for securing the deliverance of the Jewish people.

Veronese is buried here. His tomb is in front of the paved chapel to the left of the chancel.

### ⓯ Accademia

*See pp110–11.*

### ⓰ Peggy Guggenheim Collection

Palazzo Venier dei Leoni. **Map** 6 F4. **Tel** 041 240 54 11. Accademia. **Open** 10am–6pm Wed–Mon. **Closed** Dec 25. **guggenheim-venice.it**

Intended as a four-story palace, the 18th-century Palazzo Venier dei Leoni in fact never rose beyond the first floor. In 1949 the building was bought as a home by the American

The truncated palazzo housing the Peggy Guggenheim Collection

millionaire Peggy Guggenheim (1898–1979), a collector, dealer, and patron of the arts who befriended, and then furthered the careers of, many innovative abstract and Surrealist artists. One was Max Ernst, who became her second husband. The collection consists of 200 fine paintings and sculptures, each representing the 20th century's most influential modern art movements. The dining room has notable Cubist works of art, including *The Poet* by Pablo Picasso, and an entire room is devoted to Jackson Pollock, who was "discovered" by Guggenheim.

Other artists represented are Braque, Chagall, de Chirico, Dalí, Duchamp, Léger, Kandinsky, Klee, Mondrian, Miró, Malevich, Rothko, Bacon, and Magritte, whose Surreal *Empire of Light* (1953–4) shows a night scene of a darkened house in a wooded setting with a bright day sky above. The sculpture collection, which includes Constantin Brancusi's elegant *Maiastra* (1912), is laid out in the house and garden.

The large Baroque church of Santa Maria della Salute

*Maiastra* by Constantin Brancusi

Perhaps the most provocative piece is Marino Marini's *Angelo della Città* (Angel of the Citadel, 1948), located on the terrace overlooking the Grand Canal. This shows a prominently displayed man sitting on a horse, erect in all respects.

The Guggenheim is the best place in the city to see 20th-century art. Light-filled rooms and the large modern canvases provide a striking contrast to the Renaissance paintings in most Venetian churches and museums.

The garden has been paved and features an array of sculptures. Peggy Guggenheim's ashes are also preserved here. A shop and restaurant are located on the grounds. Check the website for information on temporary exhibits.

## ⓱ Santa Maria della Salute

Campo della Salute. **Map** 7 A4. **Tel** 041 241 10 18. Salute. **Open** Jun–Mar: 9am–noon, 3–5:30pm daily; sacristy: **Open** 10am–noon & 3–5:30pm; Apr & May: 10am–5pm Mon–Sat. May be closed mornings of religious holidays. to sacristy.

This great Baroque church standing at the entrance of the Grand Canal is one of the most imposing architectural landmarks of Venice. Henry James likened it to "some great lady on the threshold of her salon."

Santa Maria della Salute was built in thanksgiving for the city's deliverance from the plague epidemic of 1630; hence the name *Salute*, meaning "health and salvation." Each November, in celebration, worshippers light candles and approach the church across a bridge of boats spanning the mouth of the Grand Canal for the occasion.

Baldassare Longhena started the church in 1630 at the age of 32, and worked on it for the rest

of his life. It was completed in 1687, five years after his death.

The interior consists of a large octagonal space below the cupola and six chapels radiating from the ambulatory. The large domed chancel and grandiose high altar dominate the view from the main door.

The altar's sculptural group by Giusto Le Corte represents the Virgin and Child giving protection to Venice from the plague. The best of the paintings are in the sacristy to the left of the altar: Titian's early altarpiece of *St. Mark Enthroned with Saints Cosmas, Damian, Roch, and Sebastian* (1511–12) and his dramatic ceiling paintings of *Cain and Abel, The Sacrifice of Abraham and Isaac,* and *David and Goliath* (1540–9). *The Wedding at Cana* (1551) on the wall opposite the entrance is by Jacopo Tintoretto.

## ⓲ Punta della Dogana

Campo della Salute. **Map** 7 A4–B4. **Tel** 199 139 139; 041 271 90 39 from outside Italy. Salute. **Open** 10am–7pm Wed–Mon (ticket counter closes at 6pm). **Closed** Jan 1, Dec 25. **w** palazzograssi.it

The magnificent 17th-century Punta della Dogana (formerly a customs house) was restored by Japanese architect Tadao Ando and opened in 2009 as a contemporary art gallery. Together with the Palazzo Grassi, it houses the French billionaire François Pinault's large collection of contemporary art. Many well-known artists are represented here, including Jeff Koons and Takeshi Murakami.

Punta della Dogana, a contemporary art museum

# ⓯ Accademia

The art collection in the Accademia offers a complete spectrum of the Venetian School, from the Byzantine era through the Renaissance to the Baroque and later. The basis of the collection was the Accademia di Belle Arti founded in 1750 by the painter Giovanni Battista Piazzetta. In 1807 Napoleon moved the collection to these premises, enriching it with artworks removed from churches and monasteries. The Accademia is currently undergoing extensive restoration, which may result in changes to the floorplan.

**The Tempest** (c.1507)
In this enigmatic landscape, Giorgione was probably creating a fantasy rather than portraying any specific subject.

The former church of Santa Maria della Carità

*Feast in the House of Levi* (1573) by Paolo Veronese

The courtyard (1561) designed by Palladio

First floor

Second floor

**Key to Floorplan**

- 1300–1450
- 1300–1450 and 1450–1600
- 1450–1600
- 1600–1700
- 1600–1700 and 1450–1600
- 1700–1800
- 1600–1700 and 1700–1800
- Future access areas
- Temporary exhibitions

**Madonna and Child between St. John the Baptist and a Saint** (c.1504)
In this beautiful painting, Giovanni Bellini places the figures in a spacious landscape, so marking a new phase in his development.

Entrance

**Coronation of the Virgin** (1325)
Paolo Veneziano's polyptych has a central image of the Virgin surrounded by a panoply of religious scenes. This detail shows episodes from the Life of St. Francis.

*Healing of the Madman* (c.1496) by Vittore Carpaccio

## Byzantine and International Gothic

Room 1 shows the influence of Byzantine art on the early Venetian painters. In Paolo Veneziano's glowing *Coronation of the Virgin* (1325), the linear rhythms are unmistakably Gothic, but the gold background and central panel are distinctly Byzantine.

## Renaissance

The Renaissance came late to Venice, but by the second quarter of the 15th century it had transformed the city into a thriving art center rivaling Florence and Rome. Central to Venetian art in the 15th century was the *Sacra Conversazione*, in which the Madonna is portrayed with various saints in a harmonious composition. Giovanni Bellini's altarpiece for San Giobbe (c.1487) in room 2 is one of the finest examples of this subject.

In contrast, the High Renaissance exuberance of Paolo Veronese is exemplified in the monumental *Feast in the House of Levi* (1573). The painting occupies a whole wall in room 10. Tintoretto's huge masterpiece *The Miracle*

of *St. Mark Freeing a Slave* (1548) is also on display here. The Sala dell'Albergo (room 24) contains Titian's magnificent *Presentation of the Virgin* (1534–38), which was painted specifically for this space.

## Baroque, Genre, and Landscape

Venice lacked native Baroque painters, but a few non-Venetians kept the Venetian school alive in the 17th century. The most notable was the Genoese Bernardo Strozzi (1581–1644). The artist was a great admirer of the work of Veronese, as can be seen in his *Feast at the House of Simon* (1629) in room 11. Giambattista Tiepolo, the greatest Venetian painter of the 18th century, is represented in room 2 on the first floor.

Room 8 and the rooms that lead from it are largely devoted to light-hearted landscape and genre paintings from the 18th century. Among them are pastoral scenes by Francesco Zuccarelli, works by Marco Ricci, scenes of Venetian society by Pietro Longhi and a view of Venice by Canaletto (1763). This is a fine example of his sense of perspective.

## Ceremonial Painting

Rooms 20 and 21 return to the Renaissance, featuring two great cycles of paintings from the late 16th century. The detail in these large-scale anecdotal canvases provides a fascinating glimpse of the life, customs, and appearance of Venice at the time.

Room 20 houses *The Stories of the Cross* by Venice's leading artists. In room 21, minutely detailed *Scenes from the Legend of St. Ursula* (1490s) by Carpaccio mix reality and imagination by linking episodes from the life of the saint to the settings and costumes of 15th-century Venice.

*Feast in the House of Levi* (1573) by Paolo Veronese

# Street by Street: Piazza San Marco

Throughout its long history, Piazza San Marco has witnessed pageants, processions, political activities, and countless Carnival festivities. Visitors flock here in their thousands for two of the city's most important historic sights – the Basilica and the Palazzo Ducale. These magnificent buildings complement lesser sights, such as the Campanile, Museo Correr, and Torre dell' Orologio, not to mention the gardens of the Giardinetti Reali, outdoor orchestra concerts, elegant cafés – notably Quadri and Florian's – and numerous stylish shops.

**㉑ Torre dell'Orologio**
The clock tower, with hidden clockwork figures, dates from the Renaissance.

**Traditionally, gondolas** have moored in the Bacino Orseolo, which is named after Doge Orseolo.

**The Piazza** was described by Napoleon as the "most elegant drawing room in Europe."

**㉓ Museo Correr**
Giovanni Bellini's *Pietà* (1455–60) is one of many masterpieces hanging in the galleries of the Correr.

**Harry's Bar** has attracted American visitors since Giuseppe Cipriani and his friend Harry set it up in 1931. Shown here is Ernest Hemingway, one of the bar's many famous patrons.

San Marco Vallaresso

MERCE

PROCURATIE VECCH

PIAZZA SAN MARCO

PROCURATIE NUOV

**⑲ ★ Basilica di San Marco**
This 13th-century facade mosaic shows the body of St. Mark being carried into the basilica.

**Locator Map**
*See Venice Street Finder map 7*

**The Bridge of Sighs**
(1600) was built as a passageway between the Palazzo Ducale and the prison. It reputedly took its name from the sighs of prisoners being led to trial.

E LARGA SAN MARCO

RIO DEL PALAZZO

Ponte della Paglia

PIAZZETTA

**⑳ ★ Palazzo Ducale**
Once home to Venice's rulers, and to the offices of state, the Doges' Palace is a triumph of Gothic architecture.

**㉒ The Campanile**
The present Campanile replaced one that collapsed in 1902.

MOLO SAN MARCO

San Marco Giardinetti

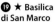

| 0 meters | 75 |
| 0 yards | 75 |

**The vaulting** of the stairway in the magnificent Libreria Sansoviniana (1588) is decorated with frescoes and gilded stucco. The national library of St. Mark is housed here.

**The Zecca**, designed by Sansovino and started in 1537, was the city mint until 1870, and gave its name to the *zecchino* or Venetian ducat.

*For hotels and restaurants in this region see pp562–5 and pp580–84*

# ⑲ Basilica di San Marco

Venice's famous Basilica blends the architectural and decorative styles of East and West to create one of the greatest buildings in Europe. The exterior owes its almost Oriental splendor to countless treasures from the Republic's overseas empire. Among these are copies of the famous bronze horses brought from Constantinople in 1204, and a wealth of columns, bas-reliefs, and colored marbles studded across the main facade. Mosaics from different epochs adorn the five doorways, while the main portal is framed by some of Italy's loveliest Romanesque carving (1240–65).

**St. Mark and Angels**
The statues crowning the central arch are additions from the early 15th century.

★ **Horses of St. Mark**
The four horses are replicas of the gilded bronze originals, now protected inside the Basilica's museum.

## KEY

① **The elegant arches** echo those of the lower floor, forming a repeat pattern.

② **The Pentecost Dome**, showing the Descent of the Holy Ghost as a dove, was probably the first dome to be decorated with mosaics.

③ **The Ascension Dome** features a magnificent 13th-century mosaic of Christ surrounded by angels, the 12 Apostles and the Virgin Mary.

④ **St. Mark's body**, believed lost in the fire of AD 976, supposedly reappeared when the new church was consecrated in 1094. The remains are housed in the altar.

⑤ **The Mosaic pavement** shows beautiful pictures of birds and beasts, some of which are allegorical.

⑥ **St. Mark's Treasury**

⑦ **Romanesque carvings** adorn the arches of the main portal.

Entrance

★ **Facade Mosaics**
A 17th-century mosaic shows the body of St. Mark being taken from Alexandria, reputedly smuggled past Muslim guards under slices of pork.

**Ciborium**
The fine alabaster columns of
the altar canopy, or baldacchino,
are adorned with scenes from
the New Testament.

## VISITORS' CHECKLIST

**Practical Information**
Piazza San Marco. **Map** 7 B2–C2.
**Tel** 041 270 83 11. Basilica. Pala
d'Oro, Loggia dei Cavalli, &
Treasury: **Open** Easter–Oct:
9:45am–5pm Mon–Sat, 2–5pm
Sun; Nov–Easter: 9:30am–5pm
Mon–Sat, 2–4pm Sun). Museum:
**Open** 9:45am–4:45pm daily. 🚻
no sightseeing during services. 🚫
except Sun (Basilica). 📷 📱 ♿
🏠 ✉ 🆆 **basilicasanmarco.it**

**Transportation**
🚤 San Marco.

## The Building of St. Mark's

Built on a Greek cross plan and
crowned with five huge domes,
this is the third church to stand
on the site. The first, which
enshrined the body of St. Mark
in the 9th century, was destroyed
by fire. The second was pulled
down in favor of a church that
reflected Venice's growing power.
The present design was inspired
by the Church of the Apostles
in Constantinople and was
completed and decorated over
the centuries. From 1075, all ships
returning from abroad had, by law,
to bring back a precious gift to
adorn "the House of St. Mark." The
mosaics inside are mostly 12th to
13th century and cover 45,622 sq ft
(4,240 sq m). Some were later
replaced by such artists as Titian
and Tintoretto. Until 1807 St. Mark's
was the doge's private chapel,
used for ceremonies of state, after
which it succeeded San Pietro di
Castello as the cathedral of Venice.

13th-century carving of a grape
harvester on the main portal

**The Tetrarchs**
This charming sculptured group
in porphyry (4th-century Egyptian)
is thought to represent Diocletian,
Maximian, Valerian, and Constantine.
Collectively they were the Tetrarchs,
appointed by Diocletian to help rule
the Roman Empire.

# Exploring the Basilica

St. Mark's magnificent interior is clad with dazzling mosaics, which begin in the narthex, or atrium, of the Basilica, and culminate in the glittering panels of the Pentecost and Ascension domes. The Genesis Cupola in the atrium has a stunning Creation of the World described in concentric circles. The *pavimento*, or floor, is also patterned with mosaics in marble and glass. Steps from the atrium lead to the Museo Marciano, home to the Basilica's famous horses. Other treasures include the jewel-encrusted Pala d'Oro, behind the high altar; the Nicopeia icon; and the precious hoards of silver, gold, and glassware in the Treasury.

**Madonna di Nicopeia**
This Byzantine icon, looted in 1204, is one of Venice's most revered images.

★ **Pentecost Dome**
Showing the Apostles touched by tongues of flame, the Pentecost Dome was lavishly decorated in the 12th century.

★ **Ascension Dome**
A mosaic of Christ in Glory decorates the enormous central dome. This masterpiece was created by 13th-century Venetian craftsmen, who were strongly influenced by the art and architecture of Byzantium.

★ **Treasury**
A repository for precious artifacts from both Italy and Constantinople, the treasury houses objects such as this 11th-century silver-gilt coffer.

**★ Pala d'Oro**
The altarpiece, created in the 10th century by medieval goldsmiths, is made up of 250 panels like this one.

## Mosaics

Clothing the domes, walls, and floor of the Basilica are over 43,000 sq ft (4,000 sq m) of gleaming golden mosaics. The earliest, dating from the 12th century, were the work of mosaicists from the East. Their delicate techniques were adopted by Venetian craftsmen, who gradually took over the Basilica's decoration, combining Byzantine inspiration with Western influences. During the 16th century, many sketches by Tintoretto, Titian, Veronese, and other leading artists were reproduced in mosaic.

Among the most dazzling mosaics – many of which have been heavily restored – are those in the 13th-century central Ascension Dome and the 12th-century Pentecost Dome over the nave.

## Pala d'Oro

Beyond the Cappella di San Clemente lies the entrance to the most valuable treasure of San Marco: the Pala d'Oro. This jewel-spangled altarpiece, located behind the high altar, consists of 250 enamel paintings on gold foil, enclosed within a gilded silver Gothic frame. Originally commissioned in Byzantium in AD 976, the altarpiece was further embellished over the centuries.

Napoleon stole some of the precious stones in 1797, but the screen still gleams with pearls, rubies, sapphires, and amethysts.

## Museo Marciano

From the atrium, steps signposted "Loggia dei Cavalli," take you up to the church museum, where the gallery offers a splendid view into the Basilica. The gilded bronze horses, housed in a room at the far end of the museum, were stolen from the top of the Hippodrome (ancient race track) in Constantinople (modern Istanbul) in 1204, but their origin, either Roman or Hellenistic, remains a mystery. Also on display are mosaics, medieval manuscripts, and antique tapestries.

## Baptistery and Chapels

The baptistery (closed to the public) was added by Doge Andrea Dandolo (1343–54), who is buried here, with Sansovino, who designed the font. The adjoining Cappella Zen (also closed to the public) became a funeral chapel for Cardinal Zen in 1504 in return for a bequest to the state. The left transept of the Cappella dei Mascoli is decorated with scenes from the life of Mary, while the third chapel in the same transept houses the icon of the Madonna of Nicopeia. Looted in 1204, it was once carried into battle at the head of the Byzantine army.

### KEY

① **The columns** of the inner facade are thought to be fragments of the first Basilica.

② **South side aisle**

③ **Baptistery**

④ **Cappella Zen**

⑤ **Steps to Museo Marciano**

⑥ **Atrium**

⑦ **North side aisle**

⑧ **The Porta dei Fiori**, or Gate of Flowers, is decorated with 13th-century reliefs.

⑨ **Cappella dei Mascoli**

⑩ **The sacristy door** has fine bronze panels by Sansovino that include portraits of himself with Titian and Aretino.

⑪ **The Altar of the Sacrament** is decorated with mosaics of the parables and miracles of Christ dating from the late 12th or early 13th century.

*Noah and the Flood*, atrium mosaic from the 13th century

# ⑳ Palazzo Ducale

The Palazzo Ducale (Doge's Palace), the official residence of Venice's rulers, was founded in the 9th century. The present palace owes its external appearance to the building work of the 14th and early 15th centuries. To create their airy Gothic masterpiece, the Venetians broke with tradition by perching the bulk of the palace (built in pink Veronese marble) on top of an apparent fretwork of loggias and arcades (built from white Istrian stone).

**★ Giants' Staircase**
This 15th-century staircase is crowned by Sansovino's statues of Mars and Neptune, symbols of Venice's power.

**★ Porta della Carta**
This 15th-century Gothic gate was once the main entrance to the palace. From it, a vaulted passageway leads to the Arco Foscari and the internal courtyard.

**★ Sala del Maggior Consiglio**
This vast hall was used as a meeting place for members of Venice's Great Council. Tintoretto's huge *Paradise* (1590) fills the end wall.

### Sala dello Scudo
The walls of this room, once part of the doge's private apartments, are covered with maps of the world. In the center of the room are two giant 18th-century globes.

## VISITORS' CHECKLIST

**Practical Information**
Piazzetta. **Map** 7 C2. **Tel** 041 271 59 11. **Open** Apr–Oct 8:30am–7pm daily; Nov–Mar 8:30am–5:30pm (last adm: 1 hr before closing. **Closed** Jan 1, Dec 25. 🕯 🔔 & partial. 📷 Secret tours (in English: 9:55am, 10:45am & 11:35am daily). Reserve in advance at the Palace or by phone. 🏠 💻 📧 🌐 **visitmuve.it**

**Transportation**
🚤 San Marco.

### Torture Chamber
Interrogations took place in the Torture Chamber. Suspects were hung by their wrists from a cord in the center of the room.

### Drunkenness of Noah
This early 15th-century sculpture, symbolic of the frailty of man, is set on the corner of the palace.

**Entrance**

### The Loggia
Each arch of the ground-level portico supports two arches of the loggia, which commands fine views of the lagoon.

## KEY

① **Exit**

② **The Arco Foscari** has copies of Antonio Rizzo's 15th-century Adam and Eve.

③ **Courtyard**

④ **Sala del Collegio**

⑤ **Sala del Senato**

⑥ **Anticollegio**

⑦ **Sala delle Quattro Porte**

⑧ **The Bridge of Sighs**

⑨ **Sala della Bussola**

⑩ **Sala del Consiglio dei Dieci**

⑪ **The Ponte della Paglia**, built of Istrian stone, has a pretty balustrade of columns and sculpted pine cones.

# Exploring the Palazzo Ducale

A tour of the Palazzo Ducale takes visitors through a succession of richly decorated chambers and halls, arranged over three floors, culminating with the Bridge of Sighs, which links the palace to the prisons. Casanova was once imprisoned here and made a daring escape from the Palazzo through a hole in the roof.

Jacopo and Domenico Tintoretto's *Paradise*, one of the world's largest paintings, in the Sala del Maggior Consiglio

### Scala d'Oro and Courtyard

A passage from the Porta del Frumento opens onto the palace courtyard. The ticket office and palace entrance are to the left. At the top of Antonio Rizzo's 15th-century Giants' Staircase, the new doge would be crowned with the *zogia* or dogal cap. The Scala d'Oro (golden staircase), designed by Jacopo Sansovino, leads to the palace's upper floors. It takes its name, however, from the elaborate gilt stucco vault created by Alessandro Vittoria (1554–8).

### Sala delle Quattro Porte to the Sala del Senato

The second flight of the Scala d'Oro leads to the Sala delle Quattro Porte, with a ceiling designed by Palladio and frescoed by Tintoretto. The end walls of the next room, the Anticollegio, are decorated with mythological scenes by Tintoretto, while Veronese's masterly *Rape of Europa* (1580), opposite the window, is one of the palace's most dramatic works. The adjoining Sala del Collegio was where the doge and his counselors met to receive ambassadors and discuss matters of state. Embellishing the magnificent ceiling are 11 paintings by Veronese. In the next room, the Sala del Senato, the doge and some 200 senators discussed foreign affairs. The paintings are by Tintoretto and pupils.

### Sala del Consiglio dei Dieci to the Armeria

The Sala del Consiglio dei Dieci was the meeting room of the powerful Council of Ten, founded in 1310 to protect state security. Two fine works by Veronese adorn the ceiling: *Age and Youth* and *Juno Offering the Ducal Crown to*

*Dialectic* (c.1577) by Veronese in the Palazzo Ducale's Sala del Collegio

*Venice* (both 1553–4). In the Sala della Bussola, offenders awaited their fate in front of the Council of Ten. The room's *bocca di leone* (lion's mouth) was used to post secret denunciations and was just one of several in the palace. The wooden door here leads to the State Inquisitors' Room and onward to the torture chamber and prisons. The Armory – one of the finest such collections anywhere in Europe – occupies the following rooms.

### Sala del Maggior Consiglio

The Scala dei Censori leads to the second floor and past the Sala del Guariento and Antonio Rizzo's statues of Adam and Eve (1480s) to the magnificent Sala del Maggior Consiglio. A vast chamber, it was used as a meeting place for the Great Council and for grand state banquets. By the mid-16th century the Great Council had around 2,000 members. Any Venetian of high birth over 25 was entitled to a seat unless he married a commoner. Tintoretto's huge *Paradise* (1587–90) occupies the eastern wall. Measuring 25 by 81 ft (7.45 by 24.65 m), it is one of the largest paintings in the world. The itinerary then continues in a more somber vein, crossing the Bridge of Sighs to enter the dank world of the prisons.

A *bocca di leone* for denunciations

## ㉑ Torre dell'Orologio

Piazza San Marco. **Map** 7 B2. **Tel** 848 082 000 (booking). 🚊 San Marco. 🚶 10 & 11am Mon–Wed, 2 & 3pm Thu–Sun (by reservation); meet at Correr Museum ticket office 5 mins before tour time. **Closed** Jan 1, Dec 25. 🌐 visitmuve.it

This richly decorated clock tower on the piazza's north side was built in the late 15th century. Mauro Coducci is thought to have worked on the design. With its phases of the moon and zodiac signs, the clock face was designed with sea-farers in mind. According to legend, once the clock was completed, the two inventors had their eyes gouged so they could never create a replica.

The clock face of the Torre dell'Orologio

On the upper level, the winged lion of St. Mark stands against a star-spangled blue backdrop. At the very top the two huge bronze figures, known as the *Mori*, or Moors, strike the bell on the hour.

## ㉒ Campanile

Piazza San Marco. **Map** 7 B2. **Tel** 041 270 83 11. 🚊 San Marco. **Open** Nov–Easter: 9:30am–3:45pm daily; Easter–Jun & Oct: 9am–7pm daily; Jul–Sep: 8:30am–9:30pm daily. 🌐 basilicasanmarco.it

From the top of St. Mark's campanile, high above the piazza, visitors can enjoy views of the city, the lagoon and, visibility permitting, the peaks of the Alps. It was from here that Galileo demonstrated his telescope to Doge Leonardo Donà in 1609. To do so he would have climbed the internal ramp. Access today is via an elevator.

The first tower, completed in 1173, was built as a lighthouse to assist navigators in the lagoon. It took on a less benevolent role in the Middle Ages, when offenders were imprisoned – and in some cases left to die – in a cage hung near its summit.

With the exception of 16th-century renovations, the tower survived until July 1902, when, with little warning, it collapsed. The only casualties were the Loggetta at the foot of the tower and the custodian's cat. Donations flooded in, and in 1903 the foundation stone was laid for a new campanile *"dov'era e com'era"* ("where it was and as it was"). The new tower opened on April 25 (the Feast of St. Mark), 1912. Due to small structural shifts, the foundations have been reinforced.

## ㉓ Museo Correr

Procuratie Nuove. Entrance in Ala Napoleonica. **Map** 7 B2. **Tel** 041 240 52 11. 🚊 San Marco. **Open** Apr–Oct: 10am–7pm; Nov–Mar: 10am–5pm (last adm: 1hr before closing). **Closed** Jan 1, Dec 25. 🚶 (includes adm to Libreria Sansoviniana and Museo Archeologico). 📷 📱 ✉ 🌐 visitmuve.it

Teodoro Correr bequeathed his extensive collection of works of art to Venice in 1830, thus forming the core of the city's fine civic museum.

Its first rooms form a suitably Neo-Classical backdrop for early statues by Antonio Canova (1757–1822). The rest of the floor covers the history of the Venetian Republic, with maps,

*Young Man in a Red Hat (c.1490)* by Carpaccio in the Museo Correr

coins, armor, and a host of doge-related exhibits. The second floor contains a picture collection second only to that of the Accademia.

The paintings, hung chrono-logically, trace the evolution of Venetian painting, and show the influence of Ferrarese, Paduan, and Flemish artists.

The gallery's most famous works are by Carpaccio: *Portrait of a Young Man in a Red Hat* (c.1490) and *Two Venetian Ladies* (c.1507). The latter is traditionally, but probably incorrectly, known as *The Courtesans* because of the ladies' low-cut dresses. The Museo del Risorgimento on the same floor looks at the history of Venice until unification with Italy in 1866.

The ceiling of Santo Stefano, built in the form of a ship's keel

## ㉔ Santo Stefano

Campo Santo Stefano. **Map** 6 F2. **Tel** 041 275 04 62. 🚊 Accademia or Sant'Angelo. **Open** 10:30am–4pm Mon, 10:30am–4:30pm Tue–Sat. **Closed** Jan 1, Easter Sun, Aug 15, Dec 25. 📷 🏛 ✉ 🌐 chorusvenezia.org

Deconsecrated six times on account of the blood spilled within its walls, Santo Stefano – one of Venice's most beautiful churches – is now remarkably serene. Built in the 14th century, and altered in the 15th, it has a carved portal by Bartolomeo Bon, and a campanile with a typical Venetian tilt. The splendid ship's keel ceiling with carved tie-beams, and the sacristy is full of valuable paintings.

# ㉕ Santi Giovanni e Paolo

Known more colloquially as San
Zanipolo, Santi Giovanni e Paolo
vies with the Frari *(see pp102–3)* as
the city's greatest Gothic church.
Built by the Dominicans in the
14th century, it is striking for its vast
scale and architectural austerity.
Known as the Pantheon of Venice,
it houses monuments to no fewer
than 25 doges. Among these are
several fine works of art, executed
by the Lombardi family and other
leading sculptors.

**The Nave**
The cross-vaulted interior
is tied by wooden beams
and supported by stone
columns.

**★ Tomb of Nicolò Marcello**
This magnificent Renaissance
monument to Doge Nicolò
Marcello (died 1474)
was sculpted by
Pietro Lombardo.

Entrance

**★ Tomb of Pietro Mocenigo**
Pietro Lombardo's superb tomb
(1481) commemorates the doge's
military pursuits when he was Grand
Captain of the Venetian forces.

**★ Polyptych by Bellini**
This painting (*c.*1465) shows
St. Vincent Ferrer, a Spanish cleric, flanked
by St. Sebastian and St. Christopher.

## KEY

① **The doorway**, which is decorated
with Byzantine reliefs and carvings
by Bartolomeo Bon, is one of Venice's
earliest Renaissance architectural
works.

② **The bronze statue** is a
monument to Doge Sebastiano
Venier, who was Commander of
the Fleet at Lepanto.

③ **Tomb of Andrea Vendramin**,
Lombardo's masterpiece (1476–8),
takes the form of a Roman
triumphal arch.

④ **The Baroque high altar**, begun
in 1619, is attributed to Baldassare
Longhena.

⑤ **16th-century altar statues
by Vittoria**

⑥ **16th-century frescoes attributed
to Palma il Giovane**

## 🄬 Statue of Colleoni

Campo Santi Giovanni e Paolo.
**Map** 3 C5. 🚤 Ospedale Civile.

Bartolomeo Colleoni, the
famous commander of
mercenaries, left his fortune to
the Republic on condition that
his statue was placed in front of
San Marco. A prominent statue
in the piazza would have broken
with precedent, so the Senate
cunningly had Colleoni
raised before the Scuola di San
Marco instead of the basilica.
A touchstone of early Renaissance
sculpture, the equestrian statue
of the proud warrior (1481–8)
is by the Florentine Andrea
Verrocchio, but was cast in
bronze after his death by
Alessandro Leopardi. The statue
has a strong sense of power
and movement, which arguably
ranks it alongside the works of
Donatello.

## 🄬 Santa Maria Formosa

Campo Santa Maria Formosa.
**Map** 7 C1. **Tel** 041 275 04 62.
🚤 Rialto. **Open** 10:30am–4pm Mon,
10:30–4:30pm Tue–Sat. **Closed** Jan 1,
Easter Sun, Aug 15, Dec 25. 🖼 ✉
🖥 chorusvenezia.org

Designed by Mauro Coducci
in 1492, this church is most
unusual in having two main
facades – one overlooks the
*campo*, the other the canal.
The bell tower, or campanile,
added in 1688, is noted for the
grotesque face at its base.

Two paintings stand out in
the interior: a triptych (1473) by
Bartolomeo Vivarini, and Palma
il Vecchio's *St. Barbara* (c.1510).

## 🄬 San Zaccaria

Campo San Zaccaria. **Map** 8 D2.
**Tel** 041 522 12 57. 🚤 San Zaccaria.
**Open** 10am–noon, 4–6pm Mon–Sat,
4–6pm Sun & public hols. 🏛 chapels
and crypt. ✉

Set on a quiet square just a
stone's throw from the Riva
degli Schiavoni, the church
of San Zaccaria is a successful
blend of Flamboyant Gothic
and Classical Renaissance styles.

Palma il Vecchio's *St. Barbara* (c.1510) in
Santa Maria Formosa

Founded in the 9th century,
its facade was later rebuilt by
Antonio Gambello in Gothic
style. When Gambello died in
1481, Mauro Coducci completed
the upper section, adding many
of its Renaissance panels.

The interior's artistic highlight
is Giovanni Bellini's serene and
sumptuously colored *Madonna
and Child with Four Saints* (1505)
in the north aisle. A door off the
right nave leads to the Chapel
of St. Athanasius, which in turn
leads to the Chapel of San
Tarasio. The chapel contains
vault frescoes (1442) by Andrea
del Castagno, and polyptychs
(1443–4) by Antonio Vivarini
and Giovanni d'Alemagna.

A Renaissance panel by Coducci on the
facade of San Zaccaria

## ㉙ Scuola di San Giorgio degli Schiavoni

Calle Furlani, Castello 3959a. **Map** 8 D1. **Tel** 041 522 88 28. 🚤 San Zaccaria. **Open** 1:30–4:30pm Mon; 9:15am–1pm, 1:30–4:30pm Tue–Sun. **Closed** Jan 1, May 1, Dec 25 and other religious hols. 🖼 🖼

This small gem houses some of Vittore Carpaccio's finest paintings, commissioned by the Schiavoni, or Dalmatian Slav community in Venice.

The Scuola was established in 1451 and rebuilt in 1551. It has changed very little since. The exquisite frieze, executed between 1502 and 1508, shows scenes from the lives of patron saints: St. George, St. Tryphone, and St. Jerome. Each episode of the narrative cycle is remarkable for its vivid coloring, minute detail, and historic record of Venetian life. Outstanding among them are *St. George Slaying the Dragon* and *St. Jerome Leading the Tamed Lion to the Monastery*.

## ㉚ San Giovanni in Bragora

Campo Bandiera e Moro. **Map** 8 E2. **Tel** 041 520 59 06. 🚤 Arsenale. **Open** 9–11am, 3:30–5pm Mon–Sat, 9:30am–noon Sun. 🖼

The existing church (1475–9) is essentially Gothic, and the interior contains major works of art that demonstrate the transition from Gothic to Early Renaissance. Bartolomeo Vivarini's altarpiece *Madonna and Child with Saints* (1478) is unmistakably Gothic.

Lagoon entrance
Arsenale Novissimo, 15th–16th century
Old sail factory
Arsenale Vecchio, 12th–13th century
Corderia
Arsenale Novo, 14th century

18th-century engraving of the Arsenale

Contrasting with this is Cima da Conegliano's *Baptism of Christ* (1492–5), on the main altar.

## ㉛ Arsenale

**Map** 8 F1–F2. 🚤 Arsenale. Museo Storico Navale: Campo San Biagio. **Map** 8 F3. **Tel** 041 244 13 62; 041 24 24 to reserve. **Open** June–Oct: 8:45am–1:30pm Mon–Fri, 8:45am–1pm Sat.; Nov–May 8:45am–1pm Mon–Thu, 8:45am–5pm Fri, 10am–5pm Sat & Sun. **Closed** public hols. 🖼 🌐 visitmuve.it

The Arsenale was founded in the 12th century. By the 16th century it had become the greatest naval shipyard in the world, capable of constructing a whole galley in 24 hours, using an assembly-line system. Surrounded by crenelated walls, it was like a city within a city. Now used by the Biennale for exhibitions, its impressive 15th-century gateway, twin towers and guardian lions can be viewed from the

*campo* or bridge. The gateway was built by Antonio Gambello and is often cited as Venice's first Renaissance construction.

Around the corner, on Campo San Biagio, the **Museo Storico Navale** charts Venetian naval history back to the heyday of the Arsenale. Exhibits include friezes from famous galleys and a replica of the *Bucintoro*, the doge's ceremonial barge.

## ㉜ San Giorgio Maggiore

**Map** 8 D4. **Tel** 041 522 78 27. 🚤 San Giorgio. **Open** 9:30am–12:30pm, 2:30–5:30pm daily (4:30pm in winter). 🖼 (Campanile). 🖼 Fondazione Cini: **Tel** 041 220 12 15. **Open** 10am–4pm Sat & Sun (to 5pm Apr–Sep). 🖼 in English: 11am, 1pm, & 3pm (also 5pm in summer). 🖼 🌐 cini.it

Appearing like a stage set across the water from the Piazzetta is the little island of San Giorgio Maggiore. The

*St. George Slaying the Dragon* (1502–8) by Carpaccio, in the Scuola di San Giorgio degli Schiavoni

church and monastery, built between 1566 and 1610, are among architect Andrea Palladio's greatest achievements. The church's temple front and the spacious interior, with its perfect proportions, are typically Palladian (see pp84–5). These qualities are echoed by the church of Il Redentore on the nearby island of Giudecca, built by Palladio in 1577–92.

On the chancel walls of San Giorgio Maggiore are two fine paintings by Tintoretto: *The Last Supper* and *Gathering of the Manna* (both 1594). In the Chapel of the Dead is his last work, *The Deposition* (1592–4), finished by his son Domenico.

The top of the campanile affords superb views of the city and lagoon. You can see the monastery cloisters below, now part of the **Fondazione Cini**, a cultural center that is used to host international exhibitions.

The colonnaded exterior of Murano's Basilica dei Santi Maria e Donato

### 🏛 Museo del Vetro
Palazzo Giustinian, Fondamenta Giustinian. **Tel** 041 73 95 86. **Open** Apr–Oct: 10am–6pm daily; Nov–Mar: 10am–5pm daily (last adm: 1 hr before closing). **Closed** Jan 1, Dec 25. 🖼 📷 ⓦ visitmuve.it

In the 15th and 16th centuries Murano was the principal glass-producing center in Europe, and most tourists visit for glass alone. In the Palazzo Giustinian, this museum houses antique pieces, most notably the dark blue Barovier wedding cup (1470–80), with enamel work by Angelo Barovier.

### ⛪ Basilica dei Santi Maria e Donato
Fondamenta Giustinian. **Tel** 041 73 90 56. **Open** Apr–Oct: 9am–noon & 3:30–7pm Mon–Sat, 3:30–7pm Sun; Nov–Mar: 9am–noon & 3:30–6pm Mon–Sat, 3:30-6pm Sun). 🚫

With its lovely colonnaded apse, this basilica is the architectural highlight of the island. Despite major restoration, this 12th-century church still retains much of its original beauty. Note the Gothic ship's keel roof, the mosaic Madonna in the apse, and the mosaic floor dating from 1140.

Palladio's San Giorgio Maggiore

### ㉝ Murano
🚤 4.1 and 4.2 from Fondamente Nuove; 3 from Ferrovia and Piazzale Roma.

Much like Venice, Murano comprises a cluster of small islands, connected by bridges. It has been the center of the glassmaking industry since 1291, when the furnaces were moved here from the city because of the risk of fire and the disagreeable effects of smoke. Some of the houses on the water date from this period.

Venetian glass goblet

### ㉞ Burano
🚤 12 from Fondamenta Nuove; 14 from San Zaccaria via Lido and Punta Sabbioni.

Burano is the most colorful of the lagoon islands and can be distinguished from a distance by the tilting tower of its church. In contrast with the haunting Torcello, the island is densely populated, its waterways fringed with brightly painted houses.

The main thoroughfare is Via Baldassare Galuppi, named after the Burano-born composer. It features traditional lace and linen stands and open-air trattorias serving fresh fish.

### 🏛 Museo del Merletto
Piazza Baldassare Galuppi 187. **Tel** 041 73 00 34. **Open** Apr–Oct: 10am–6pm Tue–Sun; Nov–Mar: 10am–5pm Tue–Sun (last adm: 30 min before closing). **Closed** Jan 1, Dec 25. 🖼 ⓦ visitmuve.it

The people of Burano are fishermen and lacemakers by tradition. You can still see fishermen scraping their boats or mending nets, but today lacemakers are rare.

In the 16th century the local lace was the most sought after in Europe – it was so delicate it became known as *punto in aria* ("point in the air"). After a slump in the 18th century, the industry revived and a lacemaking school was set up here in 1872. Authentic Burano lace is hard to find, but you can watch it being made at the school, now a museum, which displays fine examples of antique lace.

Brightly painted street in Burano

# ㉟ Torcello

Established between the 5th and 6th centuries, the island of Torcello boasts the oldest building in the lagoon – the cathedral of Santa Maria Assunta. Founded in AD 639, it contains some splendid ancient mosaics. The adjoining church of Santa Fosca, of pure Byzantine design, is another mark of Torcello's former glory. Before being eclipsed by Venice, the island had a population of 20,000.

**★ Doomsday Mosaics**
The highly decorative 12th-century mosaic of the Last Judgment covers the west wall.

**Pulpit**
The present basilica dates from 1008, but includes earlier features. The pulpit contains 7th-century fragments.

## KEY

① **The exquisite Byzantine marble panels** of the iconostasis, or rood screen, are carved with peacocks, lions, and flowers.

② **The Roman sarcophagus**, below the altar, is said to contain the relics of St. Heliodorus.

③ **The 13th-century apse mosaic** of the Madonna against a gold background, is one of the most beautiful in Venice.

④ **The central dome** and cross sections are supported by columns of Greek marble with Corinthian capitals.

⑤ **The portico** of Santa Fosca, with its elegant stilted arches, is built on three sides of the church, and probably dates from the 12th century.

⑥ **The altar** was rebuilt in 1939 and stands below a 15th-century wood relief of *Santa Fosca Sleeping*.

**Nave Columns**
Two rows of slender marble columns, 18 in all, separate the three naves. Their finely carved capitals date from the 11th century.

**Torcello's Last Canals**
Silted canals and malaria hastened Torcello's decline. One of the remaining waterways runs from the *vaporetto* stop to the basilica.

**Santa Fosca**
Built in the 11th and 12th centuries on a Greek-cross plan, the church has a serene Byzantine interior with a central pentagonal apse.

**Vaporetto boarding point** →

**The Museo dell'Estuario** houses many old church treasures.

**Attila's Throne**
It was said that the 5th-century king of the Huns used this marble seat as his throne.

# Shopping in Venice

The attractive storefronts that line the narrow streets of Venice are an irresistible attraction for any visitor. Myriad fashion brands are available in gleaming, ultramodern stores, but the city also has a strong artisan tradition. Expert craftspeople in tiny workshops open to the public create delightful and highly original objects in glass, wood, leather, and papier-mâché. Skilled hands transform colored glass rods into miniature animals and flowers, while plaster molds turn out shapes destined to become ornate masks. Interior-design establishments also abound, and sleek kitchenware and fabrics make unusual purchases. Beautiful boutiques offering antique furniture and accessories are concentrated in the city center.

## Where to Shop

The glittering Mercerie, which runs from Piazza San Marco to the Rialto, has been Venice's main shopping street since the Middle Ages and, along with the fashion avenue Calle Larga XXII Marzo, is still a draw for the crowds. The zigzagging Frezzeria is full of unusual shops, while across the Grand Canal the narrow streets from the Rialto southwest toward Campo San Polo are lined with a variety of less expensive stores. The bustling Lista di Spagna, near the station, and the Strada Nova, toward the Rialto, cater to the everyday needs of the locals.

The islands of Murano and Burano are the places to buy traditional glass and lace.

## Food and Markets

One of the delights of Venice is exploring the city's food markets and shops. Fruit and vegetable stands sprawl to the west of the Rialto Bridge and along the Grand Canal. The Pescheria, or fish market, occupies the farthest section. The neighboring streets are full of gourmet food stores. Wine, olive oil, vinegar, and grappa in decorative bottles, as well as dried pasta in many shapes, colors, and flavors, are all good purchases. **Aliani**'s cheese store offers a mouthwatering selection of picnic fare, while **Drogheria Mascari** has a fine range of dried fruit, coffee, and alcohol. **Rizzo**, on the other side of the bridge, is a master pasta-maker.

## Glass

The island of Murano is a good place to watch expert glass-blowing. However, for contemporary glass creations head back to Venice, around San Marco – try **Venini**'s showroom for stunning platters and huge vases, and **L'Isola** for Carlo Moretti's tumblers in rich colors.

The art of bead-making is flourishing thanks to sisters **Marina e Susanna Sent**'s simple, irresistible necklaces. At **Perle e Dintorni**, customers can sort through an astonishing range of beautiful glass beads and create their own costume jewelry.

## Clothing and Accessories

Mango, near the train station, has reasonably priced fun gear for the young set. Nearby is **Benetton**'s megastore, with its trademark bright clothes, while, opposite, **Max Mara** has superlative womenswear. Other leading names in fashion – **Armani**, **Roberto Cavalli**, **Missoni**, and **Gucci** – also have stylish stores around Piazza San Marco.

Just off San Lio, **Giovanna Zanella** can be found at her cobbler's bench crafting zany shoes and sandals. Her amazing range even includes eye-catching gondola decorations.

## Masks and Costumes

Mass-produced Carnival masks can be found all over the city, but a genuine one makes for a wonderful souvenir. With its striking designs, **Papier Mâché** has revived traditional mask-making. Near Campo San Polo, **Tragicomica** sells masks and costumes, as well as *commèdia dell'arte* figures. You will also find these at **Leon d'Oro**, where they make string puppets too. **Ca' Macana** has a great collection of eye-catching masks. You can even participate in a mask-making workshop. Down a winding street in Cannaregio, the husband-and-wife team at **Il Pirata** make papier-mâché masks in their store. Courses are available in the decoration and history of Venetian masks.

## Jewelry

**Nardi**, located in the arcades of Piazza San Marco, crafts an exquisite brooch with a Moor's head, among other things. A short distance away are the sparkling premises of **Bulgari**, while **Cartier**, with its beautiful collection of watches, can be found along the nearby Mercerie. Stores on the Rialto Bridge sell cheaper designs; this is a good place to find bracelets and chains, the prices of which are determined by the weight of the gold. Over the bridge, under the arcades of the ancient goldsmiths' district, is **Attombri** – two brothers who design unusual jewelry from antique Murano glass beads.

## Fabric and Interior Design

Venice is famed for fine silks and velvets and sumptuous brocades, many of which are still sold at **Trois**, close to the Gritti Palace hotel. On the Grand Canal, at Sant'Angelo, **Rubelli** is fabric heaven, with a wide range of designs and rich upholstery. More down-to-earth but good-quality household linen and brilliantly colored bath accessories are sold at **TSL**, which has several stores around town.

For original kitchen items, the choice at **Domus** is hard to beat; or head to **Il Canape**, on Calle San Pantalon, for fabulous fabrics and interior design pieces.

## Books and Gifts

**Cafoscarina 2**, the University of Venice's tiny bookstore, is close to Ca' Foscari. The store has an assortment of literature in English, including a good selection of books on the history of Venice. The **Libreria Marco Polo** bookstore offers a decent English-language section, while **Mare di Carta** sells a range of nautical books and magazines.

**Alberto Valese-Ebru** uses a distinctive marbling technique on fabric as well as paper. On the opposite side of the Grand Canal, at San Tomà, **Daniela Porto** has lovely old printed maps and frames, perfect as gifts, and **Signor Blum** on Campo San Barnaba has charming hand-made carved and painted wooden objects and toys. Nearby, **Paolo Olbi** has a wide range of papers and art books for sale.

# DIRECTORY

## Food and Markets

**Aliani (Casa del Parmigiano)**
Erberia Rialto, San Polo 214–8.
**Map** 3 A5.
**Tel** 041 520 65 25.

**Drogheria Mascari**
Calle dei Spezieri, San Polo 381.
**Map** 3 A5.
**Tel** 041 522 97 62.

**Rizzo**
Salizzada S. Giovanni Grisostomo, Cannaregio 5778.
**Map** 3 B5.
**Tel** 041 522 28 24.

## Glass

**L'Isola – Carlo Moretti**
Calle delle Botteghe, San Marco 2970.
**Map** 6 F2.
**Tel** 041 523 19 73.

**Marina e Susanna Sent**
Campo S. Vio, Dorsoduro 669.
**Map** 6 F4.
**Tel** 041 520 81 36.

**Perle e Dintorni**
Calle della Mandola, San Marco 3740.
**Map** 7 A2.
**Tel** 041 520 50 68.

**Venini**
Piazzetta dei Leoncini, San Marco 314.
**Map** 7 B2.
**Tel** 041 522 40 45.

## Clothing and Accessories

**Armani**
Calle Goldoni, San Marco 4412.
**Map** 7 A2.
**Tel** 041 523 47 58.

**Benetton**
Marzaria (Merceria) Due Aprile, San Marco 5051.
**Map** 7 B2.
**Tel** 041 296 04 93.

**Giovanna Zanella**
Calle Carminati, Castello 5641. **Map** 7 B1.
**Tel** 041 523 55 00.

**Gucci**
Calle Larga XXII Marzo, San Marco 2102.
**Map** 7 A3.
**Tel** 041 241 39 68.

**Mango**
Fondamente Santa Lucia, Cannaregio 23.
**Map** 1 C5.
**Tel** 06 477 868 67.

**Max Mara**
Campo San Salvador, San Marco 5033.
**Map** 7 A1.
**Tel** 041 522 66 88.

**Missoni**
Calle Vallaresso, San Marco 1312. **Map** 7 B3.
**Tel** 041 520 57 33.

**Roberto Cavalli**
Calle Vallaresso, San Marco 1314.
**Map** 7 B3.
**Tel** 041 520 57 33.

## Masks and Costumes

**Ca' Macana**
Calle delle Botteghe, Dorsoduro 3172.
**Map** 6 D3.
**Tel** 041 520 32 29.

**Leon d'Oro**
Calle Frezzeria, San Marco 1770. **Map** 7 A2.
**Tel** 041 520 33 75.

**Papier Mâché**
Calle Lunga Santa Maria Formosa, Castello 5175.
**Tel** 041 522 99 95.

**Il Pirata**
Salizzada San Canciano, Cannaregio 5559.
**Map** 3 B5.
**Tel** 041 520 65 29.

**Tragicomica**
Calle dei Nomboli, San Polo 2800. **Map** 6 F1.
**Tel** 041 721 102.

## Jewelry

**Attombri**
Sottoportego degli Orefici, San Polo 65.
**Map** 3 A5.
**Tel** 041 521 25 24.

**Bulgari**
Calle Larga XXII Marzo, San Marco 2282.
**Map** 7 A3.
**Tel** 041 241 05 53.

**Cartier**
Mercerie San Zulian, San Marco 606.
**Map** 7 B2.
**Tel** 041 522 20 71.

**Nardi**
Procuratie Nuove, Piazza San Marco, San Marco 69/71.
**Map** 7 B2.
**Tel** 041 522 57 33.

## Fabric and Interior Design

**Il Canape**
Calle San Pantalon, Dorsoduro 3736.
**Map** 6 D2.
**Tel** 041 528 75 81.

**Domus**
Campo Manin, San Marco 4296. **Map** 7 A2.
**Tel** 041 522 58 27.

**Rubelli**
Campiello del Teatro, San Marco 3877.
**Map** 6 F2.
**Tel** 041 523 61 10.

**Trois**
Campo San Maurizio, San Marco 2666.
**Map** 6 F3.
**Tel** 041 522 29 05.

**TSL Tessile San Leonardo**
Rio Terrà San Leonardo, Cannaregio 1318.
**Map** 2 D3.
**Tel** 041 718 524.

## Books and Gifts

**Alberto Valese-Ebru**
Campiello Santo Stefano, San Marco 3471.
**Map** 6 F3.
**Tel** 041 523 88 30.

**Cafoscarina 2**
Calle Giustinian, Dorsoduro 3259.
**Map** 6 D2.
**Tel** 041 240 48 02.

**Daniela Porto**
Rio Terrà dei Nomboli, San Polo 2753.
**Map** 6 E1.
**Tel** 041 523 13 68.

**Libreria Marco Polo**
Campo Santa Margherita, Dorsoduro 2899.
**Map** 5 C2.
**Tel** 041 822 48 43.

**Mare di Carta**
Fondamenta dei Tolentini, Santa Croce 222.
**Map** 5 C1.
**Tel** 041 716 304.

**Paolo Olbi**
Calle Foscari, Dorsoduro 3253.
**Map** 6 D2.
**Tel** 041 523 76 55.

**Signor Blum**
Campo San Barnaba, Dorsoduro 2840.
**Map** 6 D3.
**Tel** 041 522 63 67.

# VENICE STREET FINDER

All the map references given for sights, hotels, and restaurants in Venice refer to this section of the book. The key map below shows which areas of the city are covered by the Street Finder. The first figure of the map reference indicates which map to turn to, and the letter and number that follow are for the grid reference. Standard Italian spelling has been used on all the maps in this book, but when exploring Venice you will find that the names on many street signs are written in Venetian dialect. Mostly this means only a slight variation in spelling (as in the word *Sottoportico/Sotoportego* below), but some names look totally different. For example, the church of Santi Giovanni e Páolo *(see map 3)*, is frequently signposted as "San Zanipolo." A further map showing the *vaporetto* routes follows the street maps.

## Recognizing Street Names

The signs for street *(calle)*, canal *(rio)*, and square *(campo)* will soon become familiar, but the Venetians have a colorful vocabulary for the maze of alleys that makes up the city. When exploring, the following may help.

### FONDAMENTA S.SEVERO

**Fondamenta** is a street that runs alongside a canal, often named after the canal it follows.

### RIO TERRA GESUATI

**Rio Terrà** is a filled-in canal. Similar to a *rio terrà* is a *piscina*, which often forms a square.

### SOTOPORTEGO E PONTE S.CRISTOFORO

**Sottoportico** or **Sotoportego** means a covered passageway.

### SALIZADA PIO X

**Salizzada** is a main street (formerly a paved street).

### RIVA DEI PARTIGIANI

**Riva** is a wide *fondamenta*, often facing the lagoon.

### RUGAGIUFFA

**Ruga** is a street lined with stores.

### CORTE DEI DO POZZI

**Corte** means a courtyard.

### RIO MENUO O DE LA VERONA

**Many streets and canals** in Venice have more than one name: *o* means "or."

| 0 meters | 500 |
| 0 yards | 500 |

**MURANO**
*(Inset on maps 3 & 4)*

**Scale of Murano inset**

| 0 meters | 300 |
| 0 yards | 300 |

**Key to Street Finder**

- Major sight
- Place of interest
- FS Train station
- Vaporetto boarding point
- Traghetto crossing
- Gondola mooring
- Bus terminal
- *i* Tourist information
- Hospital with emergency room
- Police station
- Church
- Synagogue
- Train line

*Murano*

*Castello*

*San Marco*

*rande*

*Giudecca*

**Scale of map pages**

| 0 meters | 150 |
| 0 yards | 150 |

# Venice Vaporetto Routes

The ACTV network runs regular services around the city and out to most of the islands. Some services are circular; others extend their routes during the high season. There are also additional lines during the summer months. More details of the different types of *vaporetti* and how to use them are given on pages 634–5.

**Key**

🛪 Airport

**FS** Train station

🛳 Car ferry

**P** Parking

🚌 Main bus terminal

○ Waterbus stop

— City center route 1

═ City center route 2 (part seasonal)

— City center route 3

— City center route 4.1 (counterclockwise)

— City center route 4.2 (clockwise)

— City center route 5.1 (counterclockwise)

— City center route 5.2 (clockwise)

— City center route 6

═ City center route 7 (seasonal)

═ City center route 8 (seasonal)

--- City center route 10 (part seasonal)

--- Night service N

# THE VENETO AND FRIULI

The Veneto is a region of tremendous contrasts, encompassing the breathtaking natural beauty of the Dolomites, Lake Garda (Italy's largest lake) and the rolling Euganean Hills, and the man-made delights of magnificent ancient cities such as Verona, Vicenza, and Padua. Neighboring Friuli-Venezia Giulia lines the border with Slovenia to the east, taking in the Carnic Hills in the north, the Roman town of Aquileia, and the bustling Adriatic port of Trieste.

The Romans built frontier posts on this fertile land of silt deposits, and these survive today as the cities of Vicenza, Padua, Verona, and Treviso. Strategically placed at the hub of the empire's road network, the cities prospered under Roman rule, but suffered in the wave of Germanic invasions of the 5th century AD.

The region's fortunes revived under the benign rule of the Venetian Empire. The medieval cities of the Veneto lay on important trade routes such as the Serenissima, the road connecting the flourishing port cities of Venice and Genoa, and the Brenner Pass, used by commercial travelers crossing the Alps from northern Europe. Wealth from agriculture, commerce, and the spoils of war paid for the beautification of these cities through the building of Renaissance palaces and public buildings, many designed by the Veneto's great architect, Andrea Palladio. His palazzi and villas are telling symbols of the leisured existence once enjoyed by the area's aristocrats.

Today the Veneto is a thriving wine exporter, textile producer and agricultural center, and Friuli is a focus for new technology, while remaining largely agricultural. Both regions are popular tourist destinations, despite lying a little in the shadow of Venice, and boast an abundant and enchanting variety of attractions.

People strolling around Piazza Bra in Verona, with the Roman arena on the right

◀ The Renaissance Alpini Bridge by Palladio at Bassano del Grappa in the Veneto

# Exploring the Veneto and Friuli

The flat landscape of the Veneto plain is dramatically offset by the spectacular Dolomite mountains that form the northwestern border to the Veneto. Friuli, Italy's most northeasterly region, lies tucked up against Austria to the north and Slovenia to the east. Both the Veneto and Friuli are bordered to the south by the Adriatic, with its beaches and ports, which provide a contrast with the area's gently rolling countryside, the vast stretch of Lake Garda, and the many attractive resorts and ancient towns.

The stunning Teatro Romano in Verona

## Key

━━━ Freeway

━━━ Major highway

━━━ Secondary road

┄┄┄ Minor road

━━━ Scenic route

━•━ Main railroad

── Minor railroad

━━━ International border

━━━ Regional border

△ Summit

0 kilometres    25

0 miles    20

**For additional map symbols** *see back flap*

## Getting Around

An extensive railroad network and good bus services make this region easy to explore by public transportation, though only buses operate around Lake Garda. Freeways and highways provide good links between the main cities. The Venice Simplon-Orient-Express train, which operates from London to Venice, offers a novel approach to the area.

The bridge at Cividale del Friuli

A mountain chalet in Cortina d'Ampezzo

## Sights at a Glance

# ❶ Verona

Verona is a vibrant trading center, the largest city in the Veneto region (followed by Venice), and one of the most prosperous in northern Italy. Its ancient center boasts many magnificent Roman ruins, second only to those of Rome itself, and fine palazzi built of *rosso di Verona*, the local pink-tinged limestone, by the city's medieval rulers. Verona has two main focal points: the massive 1st-century-AD Arena, which is still the setting for major events including a large opera festival, and Piazza Erbe, with its colorful market. One of the main attractions, however, is the church of San Zeno Maggiore *(see pp150–51)*, which boasts unusual medieval bronze door panels: they are carved with extraordinary scenes, some biblical, others on the life of San Zeno.

Verona viewed from the Museo Archeologico

## Verona's Rulers

In 1263 the Scaligeri began their 124-year rule of Verona. They used ruthless tactics in their rise to power, but once established, brought peace to the city. They proved to be relatively just and cultured rulers – Dante was welcomed to their court in 1301, and he dedicated the final part of his epic *Divine Comedy* to the ruling Cangrande I. Today their legacy remains in their ornate tombs and in Castelvecchio.

In 1387 Verona fell to the Visconti of Milan, and a succession of outsiders – Venice, France, Austria – ruled the city until the Veneto was united with Italy in 1866.

## 🏛 Castelvecchio

Corso Castelvecchio 2. **Tel** 045 80 62 611. **Open** Dec–Oct: 1:30–7:30pm Mon, 8:30am–7:30pm Tue–Sun, (last adm: 45 mins before closing). **Closed** Jan 1, Dec 25 & 26. 🎨 📷 ♿
**W** museodicastelvecchio.comune. verona.it

This impressive castle, built by Cangrande II between 1355 and 1375, houses one of the finest art galleries in the Veneto outside Venice.

The first section contains late Roman and early Christian items, while medieval and early Renaissance art illustrates the influence of northern art on local painters: with emphasis on brutal realism as opposed to

Verona's enormous Roman Arena seen from Piazza Brà

Ponte Scaligero, part of the old defense system of Castelvecchio

serene idealism. Works of the late Renaissance include several 15th-century Madonnas, and jewelry, arms, armor, and Veronese's *Deposition* (1565) are also on display.

A walkway offers views of the River Adige, the Ponte Scaligero, and the 14th-century statue of Cangrande I from his tomb *(see p148)*.

## Sights at a Glance

**For keys to symbols** *see back flap*

### 🏛 Ponte Scaligero
This medieval bridge was built by Cangrande II between 1354 and 1376. Such is the Veronese affection for the bridge that it was rebuilt after the retreating Germans blew it up in 1945, which involved dredging the river for the masonry. The bridge leads from Castelvecchio to the Arsenal on the north bank, fronted by public gardens.

### 🏛 San Lorenzo
Corso Cavour. **Tel** 045 805 00 00.
**Open** daily. **Closed** during Mass. 🎫
San Lorenzo is one of Verona's lesser-known churches, but is one of the city's most beautiful. Built in 1117 on the remains of a Paleo-Christian basilica, the Romanesque exterior, with alternate strips of stone and bricks, is typical of Veronese churches. The bell tower dates to the 15th century, and inside there are some 13th-century frescoes. The church features two unusual cylindrical towers.

### 🏛 Arena
Piazza Brà. **Tel** 045 800 32 04.
**Open** 1:30–7:30pm Mon, 8:30am–7:30pm Tue–Sun, (last adm: 1 hr before closing). **Closed** Jan 1, Dec 25; Jun–Aug: from mid-afternoon on performance days. 🎫 🚹 partial.
🌐 **arena.it**

Completed in AD 30, this is the world's third-largest Roman amphitheater, after Rome's

Colosseum and the amphitheater at Santa Maria Capua Vetere, near Naples. It could hold almost the entire population of Roman Verona, and visitors came from across the Veneto to watch gladiatorial combats. Since then, the arena has seen executions, fairs, bullfights, and opera productions.

### 🏛 San Fermo Maggiore
Stradone San Fermo. **Tel** 045 59 28 13.
**Open** daily (pm only Sun). 🎫 🎫
San Fermo Maggiore is not one but two churches: this is most clearly seen from the outside, where the apse has pointed Gothic elements rising above a sturdy Romanesque base. The lower church, begun in 1065 by Benedictine monks on the site of an earlier sanctuary, has frescoes on the simple arcades.

The more impressive upper church dates from 1313 and is covered with a splendid ship's keel roof. The interior also boasts much medieval fresco work, including a 14th-century section by Stefano da Zevio. Nearby is the Brenzoni mausoleum (c.1440) by Giovanni di Bartolo, and above it a 1426 fresco of the Annunciation by Pisanello (1377–1455).

The 11th-century apse of the lower church of San Fermo Maggiore

# Exploring Verona

Since the days of the Roman Empire, Piazza Erbe – built on the site of the ancient Roman forum – has been the center of Verona. Many of the city's fine palazzi, churches, and monuments are nearly as ancient, several dating from the medieval period.

The fountain, erected in the 14th century at the center of Piazza Erbe

## 🏛 Piazza Erbe

Piazza Erbe is named after the city's old herb market. Today's stands, shaded by umbrellas, sell everything from herb-flavored roast suckling pig in bread rolls to succulent fresh-picked fruit and delicious wild mushrooms.

At the northern end of the square is the Baroque **Palazzo Maffei** (1668), surmounted by statues. In front of it rises a column supporting the **Venetian lion** marking Verona's absorption into the Venetian Empire (1405). On the west side is the **Casa dei Mercanti**, a largely 17th-century building that dates originally from 1301. Opposite, wall frescoes are still visible above the cafés.

The **fountain** in the middle of the piazza is often overshadowed by the market stands, though the statue at its center dates from Roman times. It serves as a reminder that this piazza has been used as a marketplace for 2,000 years.

## 🏛 Piazza dei Signori

Torre dei Lamberti. **Tel** 045 927 30 27. **Open** 10am–7pm daily. 📷
In the center of the square is a 19th-century **statue of Dante**, whose gaze seems fixed on the forbidding **Palazzo del Capitano**, once the home of Verona's

military commanders. Beside it is the equally intimidating **Palazzo della Ragione**, the palace of Reason, or law court; both were built in the 14th century. The courtyard has a handsome external stone staircase, added in 1446–50. Stunning views of the Alps can be enjoyed from atop the 275-ft (84-m) **Torre dei Lamberti**, which rises from the western side of the courtyard.

Behind the statue of Dante is the **Loggia del Consiglio** (1493), the council chamber. The building is topped by statues of Roman worthies born in Verona: they include Pliny the Elder, the natural historian, and Vitruvius, the architectural theorist.

The square is linked to Piazza Erbe by the Arco della Costa, or the Arch of the Rib, named after the whale rib said to have hung here for the past 1,000 years.

The frescoed Renaissance facade of the Loggia del Consiglio on Piazza dei Signori

## 🏛 Tombs of the Scaligeri

Via Arche Scaligeri.
Beside the entrance to the tiny Romanesque church of **Santa Maria Antica**, once the parish church of the powerful Scaligeri family, lie a profusion of bizarre tombs of the one-time rulers of Verona.

Over the entrance to the church is the impressive tomb of Cangrande I (died 1329), surmounted by an equestrian statue of the ruler, a copy of the original which is now in Castelvecchio *(see pp146–7)*.

The other Scaligeri tombs are next to the church, behind a wrought-iron fence that incorporates the ladder emblem of the family's original name *(della Scala*, meaning "of the steps"). Towering above the fence are the tombs of Mastino II (died 1351) and Cansignorio (died 1375), splendidly decorated with a profusion of tiny Gothic spires. Other members of the Scaligeri family lie within a series of plainer tombs that stand closer to the church wall.

14th-centu Scaligeri tor

## 🏛 Sant'Anastasia

Piazza Sant'Anastasia. **Tel** 045 59 28 13. **Open** daily (pm only Sun). 📷 🔊 📧
🌐 chieseverona.it
The huge and lofty church of Sant'Anastasia was begun in 1290. Faded 15th-century frescoes and carved scenes from the life of St. Peter Martyr adorn its Gothic portal.

Inside, there are two holy-water stoups, supported on figures of beggars, known as *i gobbi* (the hunchbacks). They were carved a century apart: the earlier one (on the left) dates from 1495.

The sacristy contains a fine (but damaged) fresco by Pisanello: *St. George and the Princess* (1433–8).

## Romeo and Juliet

The tragic story of Romeo and Juliet, two young lovers from rival families, was written by Luigi da Porto of Vicenza in the 1520s and has inspired countless dramas, movies, and ballets.

At the **Casa di Giulietta** (Juliet's house), No. 23 Via Cappello, Romeo is said to have climbed to Juliet's balcony; in reality this is a restored 13th-century inn. Crowds throng to see the simple facade and stand on the small marble balcony. The run-down **Casa di Romeo** is a few streets away, in Via Arche Scaligeri.

The so-called **Tomba di Giulietta** is displayed in a crypt below the cloister of San Francesco al Corso on Via del Pontiere. The stone sarcophagus lies in an extremely atmospheric setting.

Both the Casa and the Tomba di Giulietta are open daily (in the afternoon only on Mondays). There is an admission charge.

The so-called Casa di Giulietta

### ⬆ Duomo

Piazza Duomo. **Tel** 045 59 28 13. **Open** daily (pm only Sun). 🚫 ♿ ✉
🌐 **chieseverona.it**

Verona's cathedral was begun in 1139 and is fronted by a magnificent Romanesque portal carved by Nicolò, one of the two master masons responsible for the facade of San Zeno *(see pp150–51)*. Here he sculpted the figures of Oliver and Roland, two of Charlemagne's knights, whose exploits were much celebrated in medieval poetry. Alongside them stand evangelists and saints. To the south there is a second Romanesque portal carved with Jonah and the Whale and with comically grotesque caryatids.

The highlight of the interior is Titian's lovely *Assumption* (1535–40). Outside is a Romanesque cloister in which the excavated ruins of earlier churches are visible. The 8th-century baptistery, or San Giovanni in Fonte (St. John of the Spring), was built from Roman masonry; the marble font was carved in 1200.

### ⬆ Teatro Romano
### 🏛 Museo Archeologico

Regaste Redentore 2. **Tel** 045 800 03 60. **Open** 1:30–7:30pm Mon (all day if public hol); 8:30am–7:30pm Tue–Sun. The theater closes early on performance days. **Closed** Jan 1, Dec 25 & 26. 🚫 ♿

This Roman theater was built in the 1st century BC, and although little survives of the stage area, the semicircular seating area is largely intact. It offers great views over Verona: in the foreground is the only one of three Roman bridges to have survived, though it was rebuilt after World War II.

There is an elevator from the Teatro Romano to the monastery above, which now houses an archaeological museum. The exhibits around the tiny cloister and in the old monks' cells include mosaics, pottery, glass, and a fine bronze bust of the first Roman emperor, Augustus (63 BC–AD 14), who in 31 BC overcame his opponents to become the sole ruler of the Roman world.

Statuary and formal hedges in the Renaissance Giardino Giusti

### ♣ Giardino Giusti

Via Giardino Giusti 2. **Tel** 045 803 40 29. **Open** 9am–8pm daily (Oct–Mar: to 7pm). **Closed** Dec 25. 🚫 ♿

This fine Renaissance garden was laid out in 1580. As with other gardens of the period, there is a deliberate juxtaposition of nature and artifice: the formal lower garden of clipped box-wood hedges, gravel walks, and potted plants contrasts with wilder, natural woods above.

John Evelyn, the English author and diarist who visited Verona in 1661, thought this the finest garden in Europe.

### ⬆ San Giorgio in Braida

Lungadige San Giorgio. **Tel** 045 834 02 32. **Open** daily. **Closed** during Mass.

This lovely domed Renaissance church was begun in about 1530 by Michele Sanmicheli. The altar includes the famous *Martyrdom of St. George* (1566) by Veronese, and above the west door is the *Baptism of Christ*, usually attributed to Tintoretto (1518–94).

The imposing facade of Verona's Duomo, Santa Maria Matricolare

# Verona: San Zeno Maggiore

San Zeno, built in 1120–38 to house the shrine of Verona's patron saint, is the most ornate Romanesque church in northern Italy. The facade is adorned with an impressive rose window, marble reliefs, and a graceful porch canopy. The highlight, however, is the fascinating 11th- and 12th-century bronze door panels. A squat tower just north of San Zeno is said to cover the tomb of King Pepin of Italy (777–810).

**Nave Ceiling**
The nave has a magnificent example of a ship's keel ceiling, so called because it resembles the inside of an upturned boat. This ceiling was constructed in 1386 when the apse was rebuilt.

**Altarpiece by Mantegna**
The Madonna's halo in Andrea Mantegna's altarpiece of the Virgin and Child with saints (1457–9) echoes the shape of the church's rose window.

**VISITORS' CHECKLIST**

**Practical Information**
P. San Zeno. **Tel** 045 59 28 13.
**Open** Mar–Oct: 8:30am–6pm Mon–Sat, 12:30–6pm Sun, Nov–Feb: 10am–1pm & 1:30–5pm Mon–Sat, 12:30–5pm Sun.
**Closed** for Mass. & 5 times vary.
📧 🌐 chieseverona.it

★ **Cloister (1293–1313)**
The arches are rounded Romanesque on one side, pointed Gothic on another.

## Bronze Door Panels

The 48 bronze panels of the west doors are primitive but force-ful in their depiction of biblical stories and scenes from the life of San Zeno. Those on the left date from 1030 and survive from an earlier church on the site; those on the right were made after the earthquake in 1137. The panels are the work of three separate craftsmen and are linked with masks. Huge staring eyes and Ottoman-style hats, armor, and architecture feature prominently. Among the scenes, some of which are unclear, are Adam and Eve, Salome dancing for the head of John the Baptist, and a startling Descent into Limbo.

Descent into Limbo    Christ in Glory    Human head

**Nave and Main Altar**
The plan of the church is modeled on an ancient Roman basilica, the Hall of Justice. The main altar is located in the raised sanctuary where the judge's throne would have stood.

### KEY

① **Former washroom**

② **The bell tower**, started in 1045, reached its present height of 236 ft (72 m) in 1173.

③ **The rose window**, dating from the early 12th century, symbolizes the Wheel of Fortune: figures on the rim show the rise and fall of human luck.

④ **The Romanesque porch** is one of the finest examples of the style in northern Italy. Since 1138 it has shielded biblical bas-reliefs, above the west doors, from the elements.

⑤ **Marble side panels**, which were carved in 1140, depict events from the Life of Christ (to the left of the doors) and scenes from the Book of Genesis (to the right).

⑥ **Striped brickwork** is typical of Romanesque buildings in Verona. Courses of local pink brick are alternated with ivory-colored tufa.

⑦ **The vaulted crypt** contains the tomb of San Zeno, appointed eighth bishop of Verona in AD 362, who died in AD 380.

**★ West Doors**
Each of the wooden doors has 24 bronze plates nailed on to make the doors look like solid metal. A multicolored bas-relief above them depicts San Zeno, flanked by the people of Verona, vanquishing the devil.

# ❷ Lago di Garda

Garda, the largest and easternmost of the Italian lakes, borders three regions: Trentino to the north, Lombardy to the west and south, and the Veneto to the south and east. The low-lying countryside around the southern stretches becomes increasingly dramatic farther north, until impressive rocky cliffs, sometimes swathed in pines, hug the shoreline of the northern tip. The numerous sports amenities, many sights, and splendid scenery of snowcapped mountains help make the lake a favorite summer playground.

## VISITORS' CHECKLIST

**Practical Information**
Brescia, Verona & Trento. 🅸 Viale Marconi 8, Sirmione (030 91 61 14). open Easter–Oct. Il Vittoriale: Gardone. **Tel** 036 529 65 11. **Open** daily. & Rocca Scaligera: Sirmione. **Tel** 030 91 64 68. **Open** Tue–Sun. 🎫 🅿
Ⓦ sirmionebs.it

**Transportation**
Ⓕⓢ Peschiera del Garda, Desenzano del Garda. 🚌 🚢 to all towns.

**Eastern tip of Sirmione Peninsula**
Beyond the town is a path that follows the rim of the peninsula, passing boiling sulphur springs.

**Riva's waterfront** is dominated by a 12th-century fortress. Windsurfers favor this resort because of the consistent offshore winds.

**Gardone** is noted for its exotically planted park and for Il Vittoriale, the Art-Deco villa of the poet Gabriele d'Annunzio, which is filled with curiosities.

**The Republic of Salò** was established here by Mussolini in 1943. The cathedral in this elegant town of pastel-painted houses contains a 14th-century altarpiece by Veneziano.

**The hydrofoils**, catamarans, and steamers that ply the lake offer glimpses of villas and gardens, not visible from the lakeshore road.

**The streets** of Malcesine cluster below an imposing medieval castle. A cable car climbs to the summit of Monte Baldo (5,725 ft/ 1,745 m), offering far-reaching views.

**The lake** is named after this long-established town.

**Bardolino** gave its name to the well-known red wine.

**Peschiera's** attractive enclosed harbor and fortress were built by the Austrians in the 1860s, during the Italian Wars of Independence.

Riva del Garda
Torbole
Limone sul Garda
Tremosine
Malcesine
Campione del Garda
Assenza
Tignale
Brenzone
Gargnano
Castelletto
Bogliaco
Toscolano Maderno
Gardone Riviera
Salò
Torri del Benaco
Portese
San Felice del Bonaco
Garda
Manerba
Bardolino
Moniga
Lazise
Padenghe sul Garda
Sirmione
Desenzano
Peschiera del Garda

S45b
S249
S11
S572

0 kilometres 5
0 miles 5

**Sirmione**
A fascinating medieval castle, the Rocca Scaligera dominates the town of Sirmione. At the tip of the peninsula lie Roman ruins.

## Key

••• Steamer route
••• Car ferry

The 16th-century wooden bridge by Palladio at Bassano del Grappa

### ❸ Bassano del Grappa

Vicenza. 🗺 39,000. FS 🚌 ℹ Largo Corona d'Italia 35 (0424 52 43 51).
🚉 Thu & Sat am.
w **bassanodelgrappa.com**

In this peaceful town at the foot of Monte Grappa, the River Brenta is straddled by the graceful Ponte degli Alpini, designed in 1569 by Palladio. It is built of lumber so it will flex when hit by the spring meltwaters. Bassano is well-known for its majolica (decorated and glazed earthenware), some of which is on display in the **Palazzo Sturm**. The town is also synonymous with the clear spirit known as *grappa*. It is produced from the lees *(graspa)* left over from wine production; information about the process is given in the **Museo degli Alpini**.

🏛 **Palazzo Sturm**
Via Schiavonetti. **Tel** 0424 52 49 33.
**Open** Tue–Sun. 🚫
w **museibassano.it**

🏛 **Museo degli Alpini**
Via Angarano 2. **Tel** 0424 50 36 50.
**Open** Tue–Sun. 🚫 ♿ 🛒 📷
w **museibassano.it**

### ❹ Asolo

Treviso. 🗺 2,000. 🚌 ℹ Piazza Garibaldi 73 (0423 52 90 46) **Open**
Tue–Sun. 🚉 Sat. w **asolo.it**

Asolo is beautifully sited among the cypress-clad foothills of the Dolomites. This tiny walled town was once ruled by Queen Caterina Cornaro (1454–1510), the Venetian wife of the King of Cyprus, who poisoned her husband so that Venice would gain Cyprus. Cardinal Pietro Bembo, a poet, coined the verb *asolare* to describe the bittersweet life of enforced idleness she endured in exile here. Among others who fell in love with the narrow streets and grand houses was poet Robert Browning, who named a volume of poems *Asolanda* (1889) after it.

**Environs**
At Maser, 6 miles (10 km) east of the town, stands the magnificent **Villa Barbaro** *(see pp84–5)*. It was designed by Palladio in about 1555, in conjunction with the artist Veronese, and perfectly blends symmetry and light, airy rooms with sumptuous *trompe l'oeil* frescoes.

🏠 **Villa Barbaro**
Masèr. **Tel** 0423 92 30 04. **Open** 10:30am–6pm Tue–Sat, 11am–6pm Sun & public hols. **Closed** Jan 1, Easter Sun, Dec 25. 🚫 w **villadimaser.it**

### ❺ Castelfranco Veneto

Treviso. 🗺 30,000. FS 🚌 ℹ Via Riccati 14 (0423 49 50 00). **Open** Tue–Sat am. 🚉 Tue am & Fri am.

Fortified in 1199 by the rulers of Treviso as a defense against the neighboring Paduans, the historic core of this town lies within well-preserved walls. The **Casa di Giorgione** is said to be the birthplace of the painter Giorgione (1478–1511). It now houses a museum devoted to his life. Giorgione innovatively used landscape to create mood, adding figures to intensify the atmosphere – for instance, in his most famous work, the broodingly mysterious but evocative *The Tempest (see p110)*. Another of his few directly attributable works hangs here in the **Duomo**: the *Madonna and Child with Saints Liberal and Francis* (1504).

**Environs**
About 5 miles (8 km) northeast of the town, at Fanzolo, lies the **Villa Emo** (c.1555). Designed by Palladio, it is a typical example of his work: a cube flanked by two symmetrical wings. Inside there are lavish frescoes by Zelotti.

🏠 **Casa di Giorgione**
Piazza San Liberale. **Tel** 0423 73 56 26.
**Open** Tue–Sun (am only Tue–Thu).
**Closed** public hols. 🚫
w **museocasagiorgione.it**

🏠 **Villa Emo**
Via Stazione 5, Fanzolo. **Tel** 0423 47 63 34. **Open** May–Oct: daily (pm only Mon–Sat); Nov–Apr: daily. **Closed** Jan 1, Dec 25, 26 & 31. 🚫 📷 w **villaemo.org**

Fresco by Paolo Veronese adorning a ceiling in Villa Barbaro, near Asolo

# ❻ Street by Street: Vicenza

Vicenza is known as the adoptive city of
Andrea Palladio (1508–80), who started
out as a stonemason and became the most
influential architect of his time. The evolution
of his distinctive style is visible all around the
city. In the center is the monumental Basilica
he adapted to serve as the town hall, nearby
is the Teatro Olimpico, and all around are the
palaces he built for Vicenza's wealthy citizens.

**Contrà Porti** is
bordered by some
of the most elegant
palazzi in Vicenza.

**Loggia del Capitaniato**
This covered arcade
was designed by
Palladio in 1571.

**Palazzo Valmarana Braga**
Palladio's impressive building of 1566 is
decorated with giant pilasters and sculpted
scenes. It was not completed until 1680,
100 years after the architect's death.

**Duomo**
Vicenza's cathedral
was rebuilt after bomb
damage during World
War II left only the facade
and choir entirely intact.

San Lorenzo

Piazza Stazione

CORSO ANDREA PALLADIO

CONTRA CAVOUR

PIAZ

PISIC

PALL

VIA BATTISTI

CONTRA
GARIBALDI

C MUSCHERIA

CONTRA
PESCHERIA
VECCI

CONTRA P LAMPERTICO

PIAZZA DEL
DUOMO

CONTRA SAN
ANTONIO

CONT

**Andrea Palladio**
This memorial to
Vicenza's most
famous citizen is
usually surrounded
by market stands.

| 0 kilometers | | 2 |
| 0 miles | | 1 |

**Key**

— Suggested route

**A large hall** is all that remains of the 15th-century Palazzo della Ragione.

**Torre di Piazza**, built in the 12th century, is an impressive 269 ft (82 m) high.

Santa Corona

Teatro Olimpico Museo Civico

**★ Piazza dei Signori**
Palladio's elegant buildings flank the Piazza dei Signori, including the majestic two-tier colonnades of the 16th-century "Basilica," built around the old Palazzo della Ragione.

**The Quartiere delle Barche** contains numerous attractive palaces built in the 14th-century Venetian Gothic style.

CONTRÀ S BARBARA
PIAZZA DELLE BIADE
CONTRÀ CATENA
C GAZZOLE
CONTRÀ SAN PAOLO
CONTRÀ PIANCOLI
CONTRÀ PONTE SAN MICHELE
ERBE
CONTRÀ PESCARIA
RETRONE

**Ponte San Michele**
This elegant stone bridge, built in 1620, provides lovely views of the surrounding town.

La Rotonda
Monte Berico
Villa Valmarana ai Nani

**Piazza delle Erbe**, the city's market square, is overlooked by a 13th-century prison tower.

**Casa Pigafetta**
This striking 15th-century house was the birthplace of Antonio Pigafetta, who in 1519 set sail around the world with Magellan.

The lion of St. Mark gazing down on Piazza dei Signori

### 🏛 Piazza dei Signori
Basilica: **Tel** 0444 32 36 81. **Open** for exhibitions, concerts, and guided tours only, when it is possible to visit the loggia (call tourist office for schedule). 📷

This square at the heart of Vicenza is dominated by the Palazzo della Ragione, often referred to as the **Basilica**. Its green, copper-clad roof is shaped like an upturned boat with a balustrade bristling with the statues of Greek and Roman gods. The colonnades were designed by Palladio in 1549 as a facing to support the city's 15th-century town hall, which had begun to subside. The Basilica is now used as an exhibition space. Beside it stands the 12th-century Torre di Piazza.

The **Loggia del Capitaniato**, to the northwest, was built by Palladio in 1571: the Loggia's upper rooms contain the city's council chamber.

### 🏛 Contrà Porti
*Contrà* (an abbreviation of *contrada*, or district) is the Vicenza dialect word for street. On one side of the Contrà is a series of pretty Gothic buildings with painted windows and ornate balconies, reminiscent of Venice and a reminder that Vicenza was once part of the Venetian Empire.

Several elegant Palladian palazzi stand on this street. Palazzo Porto Barbarano (No. 11), Palazzo Thiene (No. 12), and Palazzo Iseppo da Porto (No. 21) illustrate the variety of Palladio's style – all share Classical elements, but each is unique. An intriguing detail is that Palazzo Thiene appears to be of stone, but it is in fact built of cheap brick, rendered to look like masonry.

# Exploring Vicenza

Vicenza, the great Palladian city and one of the wealthiest cities in the Veneto, is celebrated the world over for its splendid and varied architecture. It also offers the visitor a dazzling array of elegant stores and cafés to visit.

Brusazorzi's ceiling fresco in the large entrance hall of the Museo Civico

### 🏛 Museo Civico
Piazza Matteotti 37–39. **Tel** 0444 22 28 11. **Open** 9am–5pm Tue–Sun.
🅿 ♿ 🌐 museicivicivicenza.it

This museum is housed in **Palazzo Chiericati** *(see p84), built* by Palladio. Inside is a fresco by Domenico Brusazorzi of a naked charioteer, representing the Sun, who seems to fly over the entrance hall. Among the Gothic altarpieces from churches in Vicenza is Hans Memling's *Crucifixion* (1468–70), the central panel from a triptych whose side panels are now in New York.

Other rooms contain works by the local artist Bartolomeo Montagna (c.1450–1523).

### 🏛 Santa Corona
Contrà Santa Corona.
Tel 0444 22 28 11. **Open** Tue–Sun.

This Gothic church was built in 1261 to house a thorn donated by Louis IX of France and said to be from Christ's Crown of Thorns. The Cappella Porto houses the tomb of Luigi da Porto, author of *Giulietta e Romeo*, on which Shakespeare based his famous play. Notable paintings include Giovanni Bellini's *Baptism of Christ* (c.1500) and the *Adoration of the Magi* (1573) by Paolo Veronese.

### 🎭 Teatro Olimpico
Piazza Matteotti 11. **Tel** 0444 22 28 00.
**Open** 9am–5pm Tue–Sun (last adm: 4:30pm).
**Closed** during performances, Jan 1, Dec 25. 🅿
♿ 📷 🌐 olimpicovicenza.it

Europe's oldest surviving indoor theater is a remarkable structure, largely made of wood and plaster, and painted to look like marble. Palladio began work on the design in 1579, but he died the year after. His pupil Vincenzo Scamozzi took over the project, completing the theater in time for its opening performance of Sophocles' tragic drama *Oedipus Rex* on March 3, 1585.

**Odeon Frescoes**
The gods of Mount Olympus, after which the theater is named, decorate the Odeon, a room used for music recitals.

**The Anteodeon** contains frescoes depicting the theater's opening performance and oil lamps from the original stage set.

**Main ticket office**

**Stage Set**
Scamozzi's scenery represents the Greek city of Thebes. The streets are cleverly painted in perspective and rise at a steep angle to give the illusion of great length.

**The Auditorium** was designed by Palladio to resemble outdoor theaters of ancient Greece and Rome, such as the Arena at Verona *(see p147)*, with a semicircle of stone benches and a painted ceiling depicting the sky.

### 🏛 San Lorenzo

Piazza San Lorenzo. **Open** daily (pm only on public hols).

The portal of this church is a magnificent example of Gothic stone carving, richly decorated with the figures of the Virgin and Child, and St. Francis and St. Clare. Inside there are fine tombs and damaged frescoes. The lovely cloister, north of the church, is an attractive, flower-filled haven of calm.

### 🏛 Monte Berico

Basilica di Monte Berico. **Tel** 0444 55 94 11. **Open** daily (Sun pm only).

Monte Berico is the cypress-clad hill to the south of Vicenza to which wealthy residents once escaped, in the heat of summer, to enjoy the cooler air and pastoral charms of their country estates. Today, shady *portici*, or colonnades, adorned with shrines, line the wide avenue

**The facade statues** of stately toga-clad figures are portraits of sponsors who paid for the theater's construction.

**The courtyard** giving access to the Teatro is decorated with ancient sculptures. These were donated by members of the Olympic Academy, the learned body that built the theater.

Main entrance

La Rotonda (1550–52), most famous of all Palladio's works

linking central Vicenza to the basilica on top of the hill. The domed basilica itself, built in the 15th century and enlarged in the 18th, is dedicated to the Virgin, who appeared during the 1426–8 plague to announce that Vicenza would be spared.

The ornate interior contains a moving *Pietà* fresco (1500) by Bartolomeo Montagna, a fossil collection in the cloister, and Veronese's fine painting *The Supper of St. Gregory the Great* (1572) in the refectory.

The Baroque hilltop church, the Basilica di Monte Berico

### 🏛 Villa Valmarana ai Nani

Via dei Nani 8. **Tel** 0444 32 18 03. **Open** early Mar–early Nov: 10am–12:30pm & 3–6pm Tue–Sun; early Nov–early Mar: 10am–noon & 2–4pm Sat & Sun. 🅿 🌐 **villavalmarana.com**

The wall alongside the Villa Valmarana, built in 1688 by Antonio Muttoni, is topped by figures of dwarfs (*nani*) which give the building its name.

Inside, the walls are covered with frescoes by Tiepolo, in which the gods of Mount Olympus float

about on clouds watching scenes from the epics of Homer and Virgil. In the separate Foresteria (guesthouse), the 18th-century frescoes depicting peasant life and the seasons, painted by Tiepolo's son Giandomenico, are imbued with an earthy realism.

The villa can be reached by a 10-minute walk from the basilica on Monte Berico. Head downhill along Via Massimo d'Azeglio to the high-walled convent on the right where the road ends, then take Via San Bastiano.

### 🏛 La Rotonda

Via Rotonda 45. **Tel** 0444 32 17 93. Villa: **Open** Mar 13–Nov 4: Wed & Sat. 🅿 Garden: **Open** Tue–Sun. 🅿 🌐 **villalarotonda.it**

With its perfectly regular, symmetrical forms, this villa, also known as the Villa Capra Valmarana, is the epitome of Palladio's architecture *(see pp84–5)*. The design, consisting of a dome rising above a cube, received immediate acclaim for the way it blends perfectly with its surroundings. A pleasant contrast exists between the terra-cotta roof tiles, the white walls, and the green lawns.

The villa, built in 1550–52, has inspired many copies in cities as far away as London, St. Petersburg, and Delhi. Fans of *Don Giovanni* will enjoy spotting locations used in Joseph Losey's 1979 film.

La Rotonda can be reached by bus from town, or on foot, following the path alongside the Villa Valmarana ai Nani.

# ❼ Street by Street: Padua

Padua (Padova) is an old university town with an illustrious academic history. Rich in art and architecture, it has two particularly outstanding sights. The magnificent Cappella degli Scrovegni *(see pp160–61)*, north of the city center, is famous for Giotto's lyrical frescoes. Close to the train station, it forms part of the complex incorporating the Eremitani church and museums. The Basilica di Sant'Antonio, which forms the focal point in the southern part of the city, is one of the most popular pilgrimage destinations in Italy.

**Palazzo del Capitanio**
Built between 1599 and 1605 for the head of the city militia, the tower incorporate an astronomical clock made in 1344.

**Corte Capitaniato**, a 14th-century arts faculty (open for concerts), contains frescoes that include a rare portrait of the poet Petrarch.

Ufficio di Turismo ↑

PIAZZA CAPITANIATO

VIA SAN CLEMENTE

PIAZZA DEI SIGNORI

VIA MONTE DI PIETÀ

VIA MANIN

**Loggia della Gran Guardia**
This fine Renaissance building dating from 1523 once housed the Council of Nobles. It is now used as a conference center.

PIAZZA DEL DUOMO

V GRITT

VIA SONCIN

VIA VANDELLI

**★ Duomo and Baptistery**
The 12th-century baptistery of the Duomo contains one of the most complete medieval fresco cycles to survive in Italy, painted by Giusto de' Menabuoi in 1378.

**Key**

— Suggested route

```
0 meters        75
0 yards         75
```

**Piazza dei Signori** is bordered by attractive arcades that house small specialty store, cafés, and old-fashioned wine bars.

**The Palazzo del Monte di Pietà** has 16th-century arcades and statues enclosing a medieval building.

**Caffè Pedrocchi**
Built like a Classical temple, the Caffè Pedrocchi has been a famous meeting place for students and intellectuals since it opened in 1831.

**A bronze statue** of a woman (1973) by Emilio Greco stands at the center of this largely traffic-free square.

Stazione Chiesa Degli Eremitiani Cappella Degli Scrovegni Museo Civico

PIAZZA CAVOUR

VIA GORIZIA

PIAZZA DELLE FRUTTA

VIA OBERDAN

VIA VIII FEBBRAIO

PITTA GARZERIA

PIAZZA DELLE ERBE

V SAN CANZIANO

Basilica di Sant'Antonio
Orto Botanico
↓

**Padua University**
Founded in 1222, this is Italy's second-oldest university. Elena Piscopia was the first woman graduate, in 1678.

alazzo della Ragione, e medieval court of justice, ontains magnificent frescoes.

**Piazza delle Erbe**
There are some excellent views over the marketplace from the 15th-century loggia that runs alongside the 13th-century Palazzo della Ragione.

## VISITORS' CHECKLIST

### Practical Information
🏛 220,000. 🚌 Mon–Sat, Piazza delle Erbe. 🎭 Jun–Sep: Cultural Festival. 🌐 turismopadova.it

### Transportation
🚆 ℹ Piazzale della Stazione 13a (049 201 00 80). 🚌 Piazza Boschetti.

### 🏛 Duomo and Baptistery
Piazza Duomo. Baptistery: **Tel** 049 65 69 14. **Open** 10am–6pm daily. **Closed** Jan 1, Easter, Dec 25. 📷 📹
The Duomo was built in 1552 to plans partly by Michelangelo, on the site of an earlier 14th-century cathedral. Beside it stands a domed baptistery (c.1200). The interior is entirely decorated with vibrant frescoes painted by Giusto de' Menabuoi, dating from around 1378. The frescoes depict episodes from the Bible, including scenes of the Creation, the Miracles, the Passion, the Crucifixion, and the Resurrection of Christ.

### 🏛 Palazzo della Ragione
Piazza delle Erbe (entrance via the town hall). **Tel** 049 820 50 06. **Open** 9am–7pm Tue–Sun (Nov–Jan: to 6pm). **Closed** Jan 1, May 1, Dec 25 & 26. 📷 ♿ 🚻

The "Palace of Reason" was built in 1218 to serve as Padua's law court and council chamber. The vast main hall was originally decorated with frescoes by Giotto, but fire destroyed his work in 1420. The Salone is breathtaking in its sheer size. It is the largest undivided medieval hall in Europe, 260 ft (80 m) long, 90 ft (27 m) wide, and 90 ft (27 m) high. Frescoes painted in 1420–25 by Nicola Miretto cover its walls: the 333 panels depict the months of the year, with appropriate gods, signs of the zodiac, and seasonal activities. A 1466 copy of the huge Gattamelata statue *(see p162)* by Donatello stands at one end of the hall.

### 🏛 Caffè Pedrocchi
Via VIII Febbraio 15. **Tel** 049 878 12 31. **Open** daily (Jun–Oct: Tue–Sun). **Closed** Aug. Museum: **Open** Tue–Sun. 🌐 caffepedrocchi.it

Caffè Pedrocchi opened in 1831. Today people come as much to talk, play cards, or watch the world go by as to eat or drink. The upstairs rooms, decorated in Moorish, Egyptian, and other styles, house a museum documenting modern Italian history.

# Padua: Cappella degli Scrovegni

Enrico Scrovegni built this chapel in 1303, hoping thereby to spare his dead father, a usurer, from the eternal damnation in hell described by the poet Dante in his *Inferno*. The interior of the chapel is entirely covered with beautiful frescoes of scenes from the life of Christ, painted by Giotto between 1303 and 1305. As works of great narrative force, they exerted a powerful influence on the development of European art.

**The Nativity**
The naturalism of the Virgin's pose marks a departure from Byzantine stylization, as does the use of natural blue for the sky, in place of celestial gold.

**Expulsion of the Merchants**
Christ's physical rage, the cowering merchant and the child hiding his face show an animation that is characteristic of Giotto's style.

**The Coretti**
Giotto painted the two panels known as the Coretti as an exercise in perspective, creating the illusion of an arch with a room beyond.

View toward altar

West entrance — North side — Altar — South side — West entrance

## Gallery Guide

*Due to the Cappella degli Scrovegni's small size, the number of visitors allowed in at any one time is strictly limited. Prior to entering, visitors are required to spend 15 minutes in a decontamination chamber, where multimedia and multilingual information on the chapel is provided. The visit itself is also restricted to 15 minutes. Advance reservations are compulsory, by phone (049 201 00 20) or online (www.cappelladegliscrovegni.it), with a credit card payment.*

**Key**

- Episodes of Joachim and Anna
- Episodes from the Life of Mary
- Episodes from the Life and Death of Christ
- The Virtues and Vices
- The Last Judgment

**The Last Judgment**
This scene fills the entire west wall of the chapel. Its formal composition is closer to Byzantine tradition than some of the other frescoes, with parts probably painted by assistants. A model of the chapel is shown (center left, at the bottom) being offered to the Virgin by Scrovegni.

**Mary is Presented at the Temple**
Giotto sets many scenes against an architectural background, using the laws of perspective to give a sense of three dimensions.

**Injustice**
The Vices and Virtues are painted in monochrome. Here Injustice is symbolized by scenes of war, murder, and robbery.

View toward entrance

**Lament over the Dead Christ**
Giotto's figures express their grief in different ways: some huddle together, another gestures wildly.

## Giotto

The Florentine artist Giotto (1266–1337) is regarded as the father of the Renaissance, the great revival in the Classical traditions of Western art. His work, with its sense of pictorial space, naturalism, and narrative drama, marks a decisive break with the Byzantine tradition of the preceding 1,000 years. Although he was regarded in his lifetime as a great artist, few of the works attributed to him are fully documented. Some may have been painted by others, but his authorship of the frescoes in the Scrovegni Chapel need not be doubted.

# Exploring Padua

Padua is a city of many attractions, with a rich history: this is reflected in the major museum complex that occupies a group of 14th-century monastic buildings attached to the church of the Eremitani, a reclusive Augustinian order. Next door is the Cappella degli Scrovegni (see pp160–61). Padua is, in addition, the setting for one of Italy's most important churches – the splendid Basilica di Sant'Antonio – and for one of the earliest universities to be founded in Italy.

15th-century *Angels in Armor* by Guariento, Museo Civico Eremitani

### 🏛 Chiesa degli Eremitani and Museo Civico Eremitani

Piazza Eremitani 8. **Tel** 049 820 45 51. Chapel: **Open** daily. Museum: **Open** Tue–Sun. **Closed** Jan 1, May 1, Dec 25 & 26. 🅿️♿🚻📷
🆆 turismopadova.it

The Eremitani church, built from 1276 to 1306, contains magnificent roof and wall tombs. Among them is that of Marco Benavides (1489–1582), a professor of law at the city university, whose Renaissance tomb was the work of Florentine architect Ammannati (1511–92). Celebrated frescoes (1454–7) by Mantegna, portraying scenes from the lives of St. James and St. Christopher, were destroyed during a World War II bombing raid in 1944. Two scenes from this magnificent series survive in the Cappella Ovetari, to the south of the sanctuary: *The Martyrdom of St. James* and *The Martyrdom of St. Christopher*.

A 1st-century AD tomb in the archaeological collection

The Museo Civico Eremitani holds a coin collection featuring rare Roman medallions and an almost complete set of Venetian coinage, an archaeological section, and an art gallery.

The rich archaeological collection contains Roman tombs, fine mosaics, and statues. Renaissance bronzes include the comical *Drinking Satyr* by Il Riccio (1470–1532). The 14th-century crucifix from the Cappella degli Scrovegni is in the Quadreria Emo Capodilista, as well as works by Giotto and 15th- to 18th-century paintings from the Venetian and Flemish schools.

### 🏛 Basilica di Sant'Antonio

Piazza del Santo. **Tel** 049 822 56 52. **Open** 7am–7:30pm daily.

This exotic church, with its minaret-like spires and Byzantine domes, is also known as Il Santo. It was built from 1232 to house the remains of St. Anthony of Padua, a preacher who modeled himself on St. Francis of Assisi. Although he was a simple man who rejected worldly wealth, the citizens of Padua built a lavish church to serve as his shrine.

The influence of Byzantine architecture is clearly visible in the basilica's outline: a cone-shaped central dome rises above seven encircling domes; the facade combines Gothic and Romanesque elements.

Inside, the high altar features Donatello's magnificent reliefs (1444–5) on the miracles of St. Anthony, and his statues of the Crucifixion, the Virgin, and Paduan saints. The tomb of St. Anthony, hung with offerings, lies in the north transept; large marble reliefs depicting the saint's life, carved in 1505–77 by various artists, adorn the walls around it. A lively fresco scene of the Crucifixion by Altichiero da Zevio (1380s) adorns the south transept.

### 🏛 Statue of Gattamelata

Beside the entrance to the basilica stands one of the great works of the Renaissance: a statue of the mercenary soldier Gattamelata. This gritty portrait was created in 1443–52, in honor of a man who during his life did great service to the Venetian Republic. The artist Donatello won fame for the monument, the first equestrian statue made on such a large scale since Roman times.

The Basilica di Sant'Antonio, and Donatello's statue of Gattamelata

### ⊞ Scuola del Santo and Oratorio di San Giorgio

Piazza del Santo 11. **Tel** 049 822 56 52. **Open** daily. 🎦

Five excellent frescoes, including the earliest documented paintings by Titian, are to be found here. The Scuola del Santo contains two scenes from the life of St. Anthony, painted by Titian in 1511. The works in the San Giorgio oratory are by Altichiero da Zevio and Jacopo Avenzo, who painted them in 1378–84.

### ▣ Orto Botanico

Via Orto Botanico 15. **Tel** 049 827 39 39. **Open** Tue–Sun (Apr, May & Oct: daily). **Closed** Jan 1, Dec 25. 🎦 🔥 🔲 **ortobotanico.pd.it**

Padua's botanical garden, one of the oldest in Europe (1545), still retains much of its original appearance. The gardens and hothouses were used to grow the first lilac trees (1568), sunflowers (1568), and potatoes (1590) in Italy. The gardens also have a biodiversity section.

### ⊞ Palazzo del Bo

Via VIII Febbraio 2. **Tel** 049 827 51 11. **Open** for guided tours only. 🎦 Tue & Sat am; Mon, Wed, & Fri pm; Thu all day. Call for hours. 🎦 🔲 **unipd.it**

The historic main university building originally housed the medical faculty, renowned throughout Europe. Among its famous teachers and students was Gabriele Fallopio (1523–62), after whom the Fallopian tubes are named.

Guided tours include the pulpit Galileo used when he taught physics here from 1592 until 1610 and the wooden anatomy theater, built in 1594 and now the oldest surviving medical lecture theater in the world.

The 16th-century anatomy theater in the old medical faculty of the university's Palazzo del Bo, Padua

The Euganean Hills, formed by ancient volcanic activity

### ❽ Euganean Hills

🚉 🚌 to Terme Euganee, Montegrotto Terme. 🛈 Viale Stazione 60, Montegrotto Terme (049 892 83 11). 🔲 **turismopadova.it**

The conical Euganean Hills, remnants of extinct volcanoes, rise abruptly out of the plain. Hot-springs bubble up out of the ground at Abano Terme and Montegrotto Terme, where scores of establishments offer thermal treatments, ranging from mudbaths to immersion in the hot, sulfurated waters. Spa cures originated in Roman times; remains of the original baths and theater are still visible at Montegrotto Terme.

### ⌂ Abbazia di Praglia

Via Abbazia di Praglia 16, Bresseo di Teolo. **Tel** 049 999 93 00. **Open** Tue–Sun (pm only). **Closed** religious holidays. 🎦 Donations welcome. 🔲 **praglia.it**

The Benedictine monastery at Praglia, 4 miles (6 km) west of Abano Terme, is a peaceful haven in the hills where the monks grow herbs and restore manuscripts. They guide tours of parts of the abbey and the church (1490–1548), with its beautiful cloister, richly carved stalls in the choir and refectory, and paintings and frescoes by Zelotti, a 16th-century painter from Verona.

### ⊞ Casa di Petrarca

Via Valleselle 4, Arquà Petrarca. **Tel** 0429 802 06 56. **Open** Tue–Sun (also Mon if public hol). **Closed** public hols. 🎦 🎦

The picturesque town of Arquà Petrarca, on the southern edge of the Euganean Hills, is named after Francesco Petrarca (1304–74). This medieval poet, known in English as Petrarch, spent the final years of his life here, in a house frescoed with scenes from his lyrical poems, overlooking a landscape of olive groves and vineyards. He lies buried in a simple sarcophagus in front of the church.

The Casa di Petrarca (part 14th century) in Arquà Petrarca

### ⊞ Villa Barbarigo

Via Diana 2, Valsanzibio. **Tel** 049 931 065. **Open** Feb–Nov: daily. 🎦 🔥 🎦 🔲 **valsabzibiogiardino.it**

This 18th-century villa north of Arquà boasts one of the finest Baroque gardens in the Veneto, planned by Antonio Barbarigo in 1669. The gardens are a grandiose mix of statuary, fountains, a maze, formal parterres, lakes, and avenues of cypress trees.

The 16th-century Villa Foscari at Malcontenta, beside the Brenta Canal

## ❾ Brenta Canal

Padua and Venice. **FS** Venezia Mestre, Dolo, Mira. 🚌 to Mira, Dolo, and Strà. Canal trips on Il Burchiello: Venice. **Tel** 049 876 02 33. **Closed** Jan 25–Feb 7. 🚻
**w** ilburchiello.it

Over the centuries, in order to prevent the Venetian lagoon silting up, the rivers flowing into it were diverted. The River Brenta was canalized in two sections: the older branch, between Padua and Fusina (just west of Venice), dates back to the 1500s and flows for 22 miles (36 km). Its potential as a transportation route was quickly realized and fine villas were built along its length. Many of these elegant buildings can still be admired today – the S11highway runs alongside most of the canal's length – and several are open to the public.
The 18th-century **Villa Pisani** at Strà has an extravagant frescoed ceiling by Tiepolo. The **Barchessa Valmarana** at Mira (a pretty village) boasts 18th-century decorations. In the village of Malcontenta is **Villa Foscari**, or Villa Malcontenta, one of Palladio's loveliest villas *(see pp84–5)*. It was built in 1560 and the interior decorated with magnificent frescoes by Zelotti. These villas may also be visited as part of an indulgent

8.5 hour guided tour from Padua, traveling to Venice (or, on alternate days, from Venice to Padua) along the river in a leisurely fashion on board the *Burchiello* motor launch – the cost, however, is fairly prohibitive.

🏛 **Villa Pisani**
Via Pisani, Strà. **Tel** 049 50 20 74. **Open** Tue–Sun. **Closed** Jan 1, May 1, Dec 25. 🚻 🚻 🏠 Fri–Sun (in Italian). **w** villapisani.beniculturali.it

🏛 **Barchessa Valmarana**
Via Valmarana 11, Mira. **Tel** 041 426 63 87. **Open** Apr–Oct: 10am–6pm Tue–Sun. 🚻 🚻 ✉ **w** villavalmarana.net

🏛 **Villa Foscari**
Via dei Turisti 9, Malcontenta. **Tel** 041 547 00 12. **Open** Tue & Sat am. **Closed** Nov–Mar. 🚻
**w** lamalcontenta.com

## ❿ Treviso

🚹 81,700. 🚌 **FS** **ℹ** Via Fiumicelli 30, Piazza Borsa (0422 54 76 32). 🛒 Tue & Sat am.
**w** visittreviso.it

Despite comparisons with Venice, the fortified city of Treviso has its own distinctive character.
A good place to start a tour of the streets, some lined with attractive balconied houses, is **Calmaggiore**. The street links the Duomo with the Palazzo dei Trecento, the rebuilt 13th-century town hall. The **Duomo** was founded in the 1100s but rebuilt several times. Inside, Titian's *Annunciation* (1570) vies for attention with the striking *Adoration of the Magi* fresco (1520) by Titian's archrival, Il Pordenone. More paintings by Titian and other artists of the Renaissance may be seen in the **Museo Civico**.
The fish market, which dates from medieval times, is held on an island in the middle of Treviso's River Sile; this allows the remains of the day's trading to be flushed away.
The Dominican church of **San Nicolò**, nestling by the 16th-century city wall, contains interesting tombs and frescoes, including, on a wall of the chapterhouse, the first ever depiction of eyeglasses in art. A magnificent tomb (1500) by Antonio Rizzo is framed by a fresco of pageboys by Lorenzo Lotto.

🏛 **Museo Civico**
Chiesa di Santa Caterina, Piazzetta Mario Botter 1. **Tel** 0422 65 84 42. **Open** Tue–Sun. **Closed** public hols. 🚻 🚻
**w** museicivictreviso.it

The houses of the medieval town of Treviso overlooking ancient canals

The facade and entrance to the Renaissance Palazzo dei Rettori in Belluno

# ⓫ Conegliano

Treviso. 🚗 35,000. 🚉 🚌 *i* Via XX
Settembre 61 (0438 212 30). 🛒 Fri.

Conegliano lies among Prosecco-
producing vineyards, and
winemakers from all over Italy
learn their craft at Conegliano's
renowned wine school. Via XX
Settembre, the arcaded main
street, is lined with fine 15th- to
18th-century palazzi, many in the
Venetian Gothic style or decorated
with fading frescoes. The **Duomo**
contains the town's one great
work of art, an altarpiece
painted by local artist
Cima da Conegliano
(1460–1518) depicting
the *Virgin and Child*
*with Saints* (1493).

Reproductions
of Cima's most
famous works are on
show in the **Casa di
Cima**, the artist's birthplace. The
detailed landscapes in the
background of his paintings
were based on the hills around
the town; the same views can
still be seen from the gardens
surrounding the Castelvecchio
(old castle).

A mythical statue on
Conegliano's theatre

## ▦ Casa di Cima

Via Cima 24. **Tel** 0438 224 94.
**Open** Sat & Sun, pm only and during
temporary exhibitions. 🐾

# ⓬ Belluno

🚗 36,000. *i* Piazza Duomo 2. 🚉
🚌 🛒 Sat. 🖥 infodolomiti.it

Picturesque Belluno, capital of
Belluno province, serves as a
bridge between the two
different parts of the Veneto,
with the flat plains to the south
and the Dolomite peaks to the

north. Both are encapsulated
in the views to be seen from
the 12th-century **Porta Rugo**
at the southern end of Via
Mezzaterra, the main street of
the old town. More spectacular
still are the views from the bell
tower of the 16th-century
**Duomo** (subsequently rebuilt).
The nearby baptistery houses a
font cover with the figure of
John the Baptist carved by
Andrea Brustolon (1662–1732).
Brustolon's works also grace the
churches of San Pietro (on Via
San Pietro) and Santo Stefano
(Piazza Santo Stefano). North of
Piazza del Duomo stands the
elegant **Palazzo dei
Rettori** (1491) –
once home to the
town's Venetian
rulers – and the
12th-century **Torre
Civica**, all that now
survives of a medieval castle.

The **Museo Civico** contains
paintings by Bartolomeo
Montagna (1450–1523) and
Sebastiano Ricci (1659–1734),
and a notable archaeological
section. North of the museum
is Belluno's finest square, the
**Piazza del Mercato**, with its
arcaded Renaissance palaces
and its fountain of 1410.

South of the town are the ski
resorts of the Alpe del Nevegal;
in the summer a chair lift
operates from Faverghera up
the flank of the mountain to
a height of 5,250 ft (1,600 m),
offering extensive views.

## ▦ Museo Civico

Piazza Duomo 16. **Tel** 0437 94 48 36.
**Open** Tue–Sun. **Closed** Wed, Thu, Sat
& Sun pm. 🐾 🎫 📷 🖥 museo.
comune.belluno.it

# ⓭ Cortina
d'Ampezzo

Belluno. 🚗 6,800. 🚌 *i* Corso Italia
81 (0436 86 90 86). 🛒 Tue am & Fri
am. 🖥 infodolomiti.it

Italy's top ski resort, much
favored by the smart set from
Turin and Milan, is well supplied
with restaurants and bars. Cortina
is set amid the extremely
dramatic scenery of the Dolomites
*(see pp86–7)*, which explains
part of the resort's attraction: all
around, crags and spires thrust
their distinctive weather-beaten
shapes above the trees.

Cortina has better than average
sports amenities, thanks to hosting the 1956 Winter Olympics. In
addition to downhill and cross-
country skiing, there is also a
ski jump and a bobsled run for
those who favor something
more adventurous than usual, as
well as an Olympic ice stadium,
several swimming pools, tennis
courts, and horseback riding.

During the summer months,
Cortina becomes an excellent
base for walkers. Useful information on trails and guided walks
is available from the tourist office
or, during the summer, from the
Guides' office opposite.

Corso Italia in Cortina d'Ampezzo, Italy's most important ski resort

Traditional copper pans on display in the Museo delle Arti e Tradizioni in Tolmezzo

## ⓮ Tolmezzo

🏔 10,000. 🚌 ℹ️ Via della Vittoria 4 (0433 448 98). 🏛 Mon am.
🌐 turismofvg.it

Tolmezzo is the capital of the Carnia region, named after the Celtic tribe that inhabited the area around the 4th century BC. The town is surrounded by the high peaks of the Carnic Alps, including the pyramidal Monte Amariana (6,253 ft/1,906 m) to the east. The best place to begin a tour of the region is the **Museo delle Arti e Tradizioni**, which has displays of local costumes, crafts, textiles, and agriculture.

Southwest of the town, a scenic road climbs 9 miles (14 km) to the ski resort of **Sella Chianzutan**, a good base for walking in the summer. More resorts line the road, west of Tolmezzo, to **Ampezzo**, at which point a minor road heads north through the gorge of the River Lumiei. Following this road to the Ponte di Buso bridge and the **Lago di**

**Sauris** is an excellent introduction to the majestic Carnic Alps.

Above this point the road is often impassable in winter, but in summer there are flower-filled meadows all along the road up to Sella di Razzo, and then back along the **Pesarina Valley**, via Comeglians and Ravascletto. Returning south, **Zuglio** was once the Roman town of Forum Iulii Carnicum, guarding the road over the pass. Today it is worth a detour for the remains of its Roman basilica, baths, and forum.

🏛 **Museo delle Arti e Tradizioni**
Via della Vittoria 2. **Tel** 0433 432 33.
**Open** Tue–Sun (Aug: daily).
**Closed** Jan 1, Dec 25. 🎫 ♿ 📷

## ⓯ Pordenone

🏔 49,000. 🚊 🚌 ℹ️ Via Mazzini 2 (0434 52 03 81). 🏛 Sat am & Wed.
🌐 turismofvg.it

Old Pordenone consists of one long street, the **Corso Vittorio Emanuele**, lined with pretty arcaded houses of pink brick, some with the faded traces of decorative frescoes on their facades. The 13th-century **Palazzo Comunale** forms a striking conclusion to the street, with its eccentrically shaped roofline of curves and minaret-like side towers, and its 16th-century clock tower. Opposite is the **Museo d'Arte**,

housed in the 17th-century Palazzo Ricchieri, where works by the local artist Il Pordenone (1484–1539) are on display.

Around the corner stands the **Duomo**, which contains the lovely altar painting of the *Madonna della Misericordia* (1515) by Il Pordenone. The bell tower beside the Duomo is a fine example of Romanesque decorative brickwork.

🏛 **Museo d'Arte**
Corso Vittorio Emanuele II 51. **Tel** 0434 39 29 35. **Open** Tue–Sun (pm only Tue–Sat). 🎫 ♿ 📷

## ⓰ Udine

🏔 99,000. 🚊 🚌 ℹ️ Piazza I Maggio 7 (0432 29 59 72). 🏛 Sat. 🌐 turismofvg.it

Udine is a city of varied and surprising architecture. In the center lies **Piazza della Libertà**, where the Loggia del Lionello (1448–56), built of pink stone in Venetian Gothic style, stands beside the Art Deco Caffè Contarena. Opposite, the Renaissance symmetry of the **Porticato di San Giovanni** is interrupted by the Torre dell'Orologio (Clock Tower, 1527), crowned by two bronze Moors who strike the hours. Note also the fountain of 1542, the two 18th-century statues, and the column supporting the Lion of St. Mark.

Beyond the **Arco Bollani**, a gateway designed by Palladio in 1556, steps lead up to an 85-ft (26-m) hill with sweeping views over the city. On the hill is the 16th-century castle, now the **Musei Civici e Galleria di Storia e Arte Antica**, with fine art and archaeology collections.

Southeast of Piazza Matteotti, at the end of Via Savorgnana where a small market is held, stands the **Oratorio della Purità**, and the **Duomo** with its octagonal bell tower. Both contain important paintings and frescoes by Giambattista Tiepolo (1696–1770). More of Tiepolo's work can be seen in the **Museo Diocesano e Galleria Tiepolo**, formerly the Palazzo Arcivescovile, which the artist decorated with frescoes.

Lago di Sauris, an artificial lake lying in the Carnic Alps above Tolmezzo

The arcaded Porticato di San Giovanni on Piazza della Libertà, Udine

## Environs

Outside Codroipo, 15 miles (24 km) west, rises the imposing **Villa Manin**. A road passes through the villa's grounds, so it can be seen even when the house – once the retreat of Ludovico Manin, the last doge of Venice (1725–1802) – and its gardens are closed to the public.

### 🏛 Musei Civici e Galleria di Storia e Arte Antica
Castello di Udine. **Tel** 0432 27 15 91. **Open** Tue–Sun. **Closed** Jan 1, Easter, May 1, Dec 25. 🔊 ♿ ✉

### 🖼 Museo Diocesano e Galleria Tiepolo
Piazza Patriarcato 1. **Tel** 0432 29 80 56. **Open** Wed–Mon. **Closed** Jan 1, Easter, Dec 25. 🔊 ♿ 📷

### 🖼 Villa Manin
Piazza del Doge, Passariano. **Tel** 0432 82 12 10. **Open** Tue–Sun. **Closed** Jan 1, Dec 25. 🔊 for exhibitions only. ♿

## ⓱ Cividale del Friuli

🚗 11,000. 🚈 🚌 **i** Piazza Paolo Diacono 10 (0432 71 04 60). 🚆 Sat. 🌐 cividale.net

A gate in the medieval walls of Cividale leads down the main street and straight to the dramatic ravine of the River Natisone, which is spanned by the arch of the **Ponte del Diavolo** (Devil's Bridge).

Above the river's north bank stands the **Tempietto Longobardo** (Lombardic Chapel), a very rare example of an 8th-century church decorated with reliefs of saints, modeled in stucco. The town's history is traced in the excellent **Museo**

**Archeologico Nazionale**, which contains the excavated remains of buildings from a Roman town, and a collection of Lombardic items including jewelry, ivory, and weapons.

Next door is the **Duomo**, rebuilt in 1453 after a fire, with its beautiful silver altarpiece (13th century). The **Museo Cristiano**, off the south aisle, contains sculptures from the original church: of particular interest is the altar donated by Ratchis, the Lombardic Duke of Friuli and later King of Italy (737–44), which is finely carved with scenes from the Life of Christ. There is in addition the unusual baptismal font of Patriarch Callisto (737–56): this octagonal structure, with a roof supported by pillars, is decorated with symbols of the Evangelists.

### 🏛 Tempietto Longobardo
Via Monastero Maggiore 34. **Tel** 0432 70 08 67. **Open** daily. 🔊 ✉

Interior view of the Tempietto Longobardo in Cividale del Friuli

### 🏛 Museo Archeologico Nazionale
Palazzo dei Provveditori Veneti, Piazza del Duomo 13. **Tel** 0432 70 07 00. **Open** 9am–1:30pm Mon, 8:30am–7:30pm Tue–Sun. **Closed** Jan 1, May 1, Dec 25. 🔊 ♿

### 🏛 Museo Cristiano
Via Condotti 1. **Tel** 0432 73 04 03. **Open** Wed–Sun. **Closed** Jan 1, Dec 25. 🔊 ♿ 🌐 mucris.it

## ⓲ Gorizia

🚗 37,000. 🚈 🚌 **i** Corso Italia 9 (0481 53 57 64). 🚆 Thu, Fri. 🌐 turismofvg.it

Gorizia was at the center of fierce fighting during both world wars and was split in two by the 1947 Treaty of Paris, leaving part in Italy, part in Yugoslavia (now Slovenia).

The town's arcaded streets and pastel-painted houses have been carefully restored following substantial damage during World War II. The modern Museo Provinciale della Grande Guerra (Museum of the Great War), housed in the basement of the **Museo Provinciale di Storia e Arte**, provides a fascinating introduction to the realities of war. Videos, photographs, and life-size mock-ups of trenches, latrines, and gun emplacements are

The Lion of Venice above the entrance to Gorizia's castle

used to show the waste, squalor, and heroism of war.

The upper floor houses temporary exhibitions and items from the town's art collection.

On a mound nearby rises the castle, encircled by 16th-century fortifications. From here there are views over the town.

### Environs

Southwest of Gorizia, scenic country roads pass through the foothills of the **Carso**, a limestone plateau stretching down to Trieste. The plateau is dotted with fields enclosed by drystone walls and gouged with tunnels, caves, and underground rivers.

### 🏛 Museo Provinciale di Storia e Arte
Borgo Castello 13. **Tel** 0481 53 39 26. **Open** Tue–Sun. **Closed** Dec 25. 🔊 ✉

The attractive harborside at Grado, along the coast south of Aquileia

# ⑲ Aquileia

🏔 3,300. ⬜ 🛈 Via Julia Augusta (0431 91 94 91). 🏪 Tue.
🌐 turismofvg.it

Aquileia, now little more than a village but encircled by the ruins of palatial villas, baths, temples, and market buildings, provides a poignant reminder of the lost splendor of the Roman Empire.

It was here that Emperor Augustus received Herod the Great, King of Judea, in 10 BC, and it was here too, in AD 381, that the early Christian church held a major council attended by the learned saints Ambrose and Jerome to settle doctrinal issues. In the 5th century, however, the town was abandoned following several sackings. Fortunately, substantial parts of the early Christian **Basilica** have survived. These contain the town's particular treasure: ornate floor mosaics.

## 🏛 Basilica
Piazza Capitolo. **Tel** 0431 91 97 19. **Open** daily. **Closed** during Mass. Crypt 🐾 ♿

The Basilica was founded in about AD 313 and much of the original structure still survives, including the floor mosaics of the nave and **Cripta degli Scavi** below. The designs mix biblical stories, geometric patterns, and scenes from everyday life in ancient Aquileia. There is a lively portrayal of the tale of Jonah, who was swallowed by an extraordinary sea monster: the fishing boats are also surrounded by a rich array of creatures from the deep, including wide-eyed dolphins and squid.

## 🏛 Museo Archeologico Nazionale
Via Roma 1. **Tel** 0431 910 16.
**Open** 8:30am–7:30pm Tue–Sun. 🐾
♿ 🖂 🌐 museoarcheologico aquileia.beniculturali.it

The mosaics in the Basilica demonstrate a tradition of craftsmanship that flourished in the city from the 2nd century AD. Additional examples of mosaics and stone carvings from the 1st to 3rd centuries are on display in this museum, together with glass, amber, and a collection of flies, beautifully worked in gold, that formed the adornment of a Roman matron's veil.

## 🏛 Museo Paleocristiano
Località Monastero. **Tel** 0431 911 31.
**Open** 8:30am–1:45pm Thu. 🐾 ♿ 🖂
This museum, which stands not far from Aquileia's ancient harbor beside the once-navigable Natissa River, focuses on the development of art during the early Christian era.

## Environs
South of Udine, **Palmanova** is worth a visit for its remarkable octagonal layout and intact walls. The town was built in 1593 by the Venetians to commemorate the Battle of Lepanto.

**Grado** sits on a group of low islands in the middle of the Adriatic lagoon, attached to the mainland by a narrow causeway. The town grew into a port for Aquileia in the 2nd century and was used as a haven by Aquileia's citizens during the barbarian invasions. Today, Grado is a popular seaside resort. At the center of the old town is the **Duomo**, which contains 6th-century frescoes in the apse, similar to those on the vaults of San Marco in Venice (see pp114–17). Nearby, in the church of **Santa Maria delle Grazie**, there are more 6th-century mosaics.

---

## Symbolism in Early Christian Art

Christians were persecuted until their religion was granted official status by Constantine the Great in AD 313. Prior to this they had developed a language of secret symbols to express their beliefs, many of which can be seen in the mosaics and marble tomb chests of Aquileia. Many of these and other symbols later found their way into popular bestiaries and folk art.

Part of the 4th-century floor mosaic in the Basilica at Aquileia

**The winged figure of Victory** holding a laurel wreath was a Classical symbol of triumph and holiness. Later, it came to represent Christ's resurrection and, more generally, victory over death.

# ⑳ Trieste

🏠 218,000. ✈ FS 🚌 ℹ Via dell'Orologio 1 (040 347 83 12). 📅 Tue–Sat. 🌐 **turismofvg.it**

Trieste is an atmospheric city next to Slovenia, with a long, bustling harbor lined with handsome buildings and lapped by the waves of the Adriatic Sea.

## 🏛 Acquario Marino

Molo Pescheria 2, Riva Nazario Sauro 1. **Tel** 040 30 62 01. **Open** 9am–7pm Thu–Tue (Nov–Mar: to 1:30pm). 🌐 ♿

The aquarium, one of Trieste's most popular attractions, contains fascinating Adriatic marine life.

## 🏰 Castello di San Giusto

Piazza Cattedrale 3. **Tel** 040 30 93 62. **Open** Castle & museums: May–Sep: 10am–7pm Tue–Sun; Grounds 9am–7pm daily; Apr–Oct: 10am–5pm Tue–Sun. Grounds: 9am–5pm daily. 🌐

Above the harbor is a hilltop castle built by Trieste's Venetian governors from 1368. It is set on a terrace that offers sweeping views over the Gulf of Trieste

The Castello di Miramare on the bay of Trieste

and houses two museums with Roman mosaics, and a collection of weapons and armor.

## 🏰 Basilica Paleocristiana

Via Madonna del Mare 11. **Tel** 040 426 14 11. **Open** 10am–noon Wed; other times by appointment only.

Beside the castle lie the substantial ruins of the Roman Basilica or law court built around AD 100. Note the stone magistrates' bench and throne.

## 🏰 Duomo

Piazza Cattedrale 2. **Tel** 040 322 45 75. **Open** daily. ♿

In the church of **San Giusto**, the city's Duomo, a magistrates' bench and throne of the Roman Basilica were reinterpreted to become the seat of the bishop and clergy. Because the building was formed in the 14th century from two adjacent 5th-century churches, there are two thrones and benches here. The apses contain very fine 13th-century mosaics in the Venetian style.

## 🏛 Museo di Storia ed Arte ed Orto Lapidario

Piazza della Cattedrale 1. **Tel** 040 31 05 00. **Open** Apr–Oct: 10am–1pm & 4–7pm Tue–Sat; 10am–7pm Sun; Nov–Mar: 10am–5pm daily. **Closed** Jan 1, Dec 25. 🌐

The archaeological collection here documents Trieste's extensive trade links with the ancient Greek world.

13th-century mosaics in the apse of San Giusto, Trieste's Duomo

### Environs

From **Villa Opicina**, just north of Trieste, sweeping views may be had over the city, the bay, and south down the coast of Slovenia. A little beyond, at Borgo Grotta Gigante, lies the **Grotta del Gigante**, a huge cavern filled with stunning "organ pipe" formations and tall columns of stalagmites.

At Grignano, 5 miles (8 km) northwest of the city, stands the **Castello di Miramare**, a white castle set in lush green gardens beside the sparkling blue Adriatic. It was built by the Habsburg Archduke Maximilian in 1856–60 as his summer retreat, a few years before he was assassinated in Mexico. It is still furnished in contemporary style.

## 🌿 Grotta del Gigante

Borgo Grotta Gigante 42a. **Tel** 040 32 73 12. **Open** Tue–Sun (Jul & Aug: daily). 🌐 📷

## 🏰 Castello di Miramare

Viale Miramare, Grignano. **Tel** 040 22 41 43. **Open** daily. ♿ 🌐 (castle).

**The tortoise** hiding in his shell represented darkness and ignorance, while the cockerel, who crows at dawn, signified light and enlightenment.

**ICHTHUS, or fish**, was an acronym for Iesous CHristos THeou Uios Soter – Jesus Christ, Son of God, Savior, in ancient Greek.

**Colorful birds**, such as peacocks, symbolized immortality and the glorious transformation of the soul when it arrives in Heaven.

# TRENTINO-ALTO ADIGE

The Italian-speaking Trentino – named after Trento, the regional capital – and the German-speaking Alto Adige or Südtirol (South Tyrol, the region bordering the upper reaches of the River Adige) differ dramatically in culture. However, they do have one feature in common: the majestic Dolomites that form the backdrop to every town and village, covered in snow for three months of every year and carpeted with exquisite Alpine plants for another three.

The region's mountains have been cut by glaciers into a series of deep, broad valleys. Many of these face south, so it remains unusually warm and sunny, even in winter. Travelers have passed up and down these valleys for generations – as confirmed by the extraordinary discovery, of a 5,000-year-old man's body in 1991, found emerging from the surface of a melting glacier in Alto Adige. The frozen corpse wore leather boots, stuffed with hay for warmth, and was armed with a copper ice pick.

The paths that Neolithic man once trod became major road networks under the Romans, when many of the region's cities were founded. By the Middle Ages, Alto Adige had established its very own distinctive culture under the Counts of Tyrol, whose land (later appropriated by the Habsburgs) straddled both sides of today's Italy-Austria border. The Tyrolean nobility built the castles that still line the valleys and the mountain passes, in order to protect travelers from brigands.

Another ancient legacy is the tradition of hospitality to be found in the numerous guesthouses along the valleys. Many of these are built in the distinctive Tyrolean style, with beautiful wooden balconies for making the most of the winter sun, and overhanging roof eaves to keep snow at a distance. Cozy in winter, with log fires and warming food, and offering marvelous views, they make the ideal base for enjoying the region's mountain footpaths and ski slopes.

Skiers enjoying the slopes around Monte Spinale, near Madonna di Campiglio, in Trentino

◄ Hikers climbing the glowing peaks of the Rosengarten mountain range in the Dolomites, South Tyrol

# Exploring Trentino-Alto Adige

Trentino-Alto Adige is a region where unspoiled nature is complemented by a wealth of sports opportunities. The tributary valleys feeding into the Adige valley contain lakes, rivers, and streams, and also woodland, vineyards, and Alpine pasture full of butterflies, birds, and flowers. Southeast of the region rise the distinctive limestone peaks of the Dolomites, while farther north the area becomes more mountainous still, enclosed finally by the splendid heights of the Alps.

Via Ponte Aquila in Bressanone

## Sights at a Glance

1. Malles Venosta (Mals im Vinschgau)
2. Merano (Meran)
3. Vipiteno (Sterzing)
4. Brunico (Bruneck)
5. Bressanone (Brixen)
6. Bolzano (Bozen)
7. Ortisei (Sankt Ulrich)
8. Canazei
9. Cavalese
10. San Martino di Castrozza
11. Cembra
12. Madonna di Campiglio
13. Trento
14. Rovereto
15. Castello di Avio

## Key

═══ Freeway

═══ Major Highway

─── Secondary road

····· Minor road

─── Scenic route

══ Main railroad line

─── Minor railroad line

▬▬ International border

─── Regional border

△ Summit

0 kilometers    25

0 miles    10

**For additional map symbols** *see back flap*

Innsbruck

Brennero
Passo del Brennero
**A22**
Colle Isarco
**VIPITENO** ③
Mules
n Leonardo Passiria
bianco
a Cervina 084m
Pennes
Cima San Giacomo 2741m
Sarentino
Fortezza
Castello di Velturno
Chiusa
**S12**
**BOLZANO** ⑥
Siusi
San Giacomo
△ Passo di Croce Domini 3134m
△ Monte Gruppo 2809m
Rio di Pusteria
Abbazia di Novacella
Castello di Rodengo
Plancios
**S44**
Alpi Aurine
Lappago
Campo Tures
Anterselva
Rienza
Val Pusteria
**⑤ BRESSANONE**
Santa Maddalena
Pedraces
Selva di Val Gardena
Corvara
Vetta d'Italia 2912m
Monte Lovello 3378m
Casere
Cadipietra
Riva di Tures
**④ BRUNICO**
**S49**
Monguelfo
Dobbiaco
San Candido
Lienz
Sesto
Marebbe
Lago di Braies
Cima Dieci 3023m △
Cortina d'Ampezzo
Belluno
**S51**

Ponte Gardena
**ORTISEI** ⑦
Alpi di Siusi
Appiano
Laives
Caldaro
Ora
**CANAZEI** ⑧
Nova Levante
Vigo di Fassa
Moena
△ Marmolada 3343m
**S48**
Dolomitiche
Alpi
**D I G E**
Predazzo
Bellamonte
**S50**
San Lugano
**CAVALESE** ⑨
Tesero
Alpe Tognola 2163m
Catena dei Lagorai
**⑩ SAN MARTINO DI CASTROZZA**
Avisio
BRA
Piramidi di Segonzano
△ Monte Croce 2488m
aselga di Pinè
ergine alsugana
Val Sugana
Borgo Valsugana
**S47**
Levico Terme
Caldonazzo
Lavarone
Fiera di Primiero
Imer
**S50**
Castello Tesino
Grigno
Brenta
Padova Vincenza

The Val di Funes, South Tyrol

The snow-covered Dolomites viewed from Madonna di Campiglio

### Getting Around

The region's main artery is the Brenner Pass freeway: it runs from Austria in the north, following the River Adige from Bolzano to Trento, and southward on to Verona. Both the freeway and the highway beside it are among the busiest in Europe, and the valley roads can also be congested during the ski season. Winter driving can be hazardous, requiring winter tires and snow chains. An excellent train and bus network serves the whole area.

Abbazia di Monte Maria, founded in the 12th century, near Malles Venosta

# ❶ Malles Venosta

*Mals Im Vinschgau*

🚗 4,600. 🚆 🚌 ℹ️ Via San Benedetto 1 (0473 83 11 90). 🏪 Wed.
🌐 altavenosta-vacanze.it

Malles Venosta sits in high border country, close to Switzerland and Austria, and was a customs point during the Middle Ages. The town has several Gothic churches, whose spires and towers give an appealing skyline, mirroring the jagged peaks that rise all around. The oldest is the tiny church of **San Benedetto**, a 9th-century Carolingian building on Via San Benedetto, with frescoes of its patrons.

### Environs

The medieval **Castel Coira** (Churburg) rises at Sluderno (Schluderns), 2.5 miles (4 km) southeast of Malles. It contains an excellent collection of weapons and armor.

Clinging to the mountainside above the town of Burgusio (Burgeis), 3 miles (5 km) north of Malles, is the Benedictine **Abbazia di Monte Maria** (Marienberg), founded in the 12th century but enlarged in the 18th and 19th. The church's crypt shelters an outstanding series of 12th-century frescoes.

The glorious medieval town of **Glorenza** lies just 1 mile (2 km) south of Malles.

### 🏰 Castel Coira
Churburg, Sluderno. **Tel** 0473 61 51 13. **Open** Mar 20–Oct: Tue–Sun (& Mon if pub hol). 📷 compulsory. 🅿️

### 🏰 Abbazia di Monte Maria
**Tel** 0473 83 13 06 (abbey); 0473 84 39 80 (museum). **Open** mid-Mar–Oct: Mon–Sat; Nov–Apr: groups by appt only. **Closed** public hols. 🅿️ 📷

# ❷ Merano

*Meran*

🚗 35,000. 🚆 🚌 ℹ️ Corso della Libertà 45 (0473 27 20 00). 🏪 Tue, Fri.
🌐 meran.eu

Merano is an attractive spa town popular with Austrians, Germans, and Italians. On Corso Libertà, a street of chic stores and hotels, stands the **Kurhaus**, or Spa Hall, built in 1914, now a concert venue. Furnished in period style, the 15th-century **Castello Principesco** was home to the Habsburg Archduke Sigismund. Inviting gardens line the Passirio River, which winds

The Art Nouveau facade of the Kurhaus in Merano

its way through the town. The Passeggiata Lungo Passirio d'Inverno (Winter Walk) follows the north bank to the Roman bridge, Ponte Romano; the Passeggiata d'Estate (Summer Walk) on the south bank leads to the medieval Ponte Passirio.

### Environs

The romantic 12th-century **Castel Tirolo** lies 2.5 miles (4 km) to the north. It hosts a museum of Tyrolean history.

The grounds of **Castel Trauttmansdorff** house a fascinating botanical garden.

### 🏰 Castello Principesco
Via Galilei. **Tel** 3290 18 63 90. **Open** Tue–Sun & public hols. **Closed** Jan 7–Easter. 🅿️ 📷

### 🏰 Castel Tirolo
Via Castello 24, Tirolo. **Tel** 0473 22 02 21. **Open** mid Mar–Dec 10: Tue–Sun. **Closed** Dec–mid-Mar. 🅿️ ♿ 🏰 💻 🌐 schlosstirol.it

### 🏰 Castel Trauttmansdorff
Via S. Valentino 51a. **Tel** 0473 25 56 00. **Open** Apr 1–Nov 15: daily. 🅿️ 📷 📷 🌐 trauttmansdorff.it

# ❸ Vipiteno

*Sterzing*

🚗 5,600. 🚆 🚌 ℹ️ Piazza Città 3 (0472 76 53 25). 🏪 daily.

Surrounded by mineral-rich valleys, Vipiteno is very Tyrolean in feel. On Via Città Nuova, lined with fine mansions, rise the Gothic **Palazzo Comunale**, containing Renaissance sculpture and paintings, and the Torre dei Dodici, the symbol of the town. Wood carvings in the **Museo Multscher** are by Hans Multscher; the Bavarian sculptor came to Vipiteno in 1456–8 to carve the altar for the parish **church**, which lies just south of the town.

To the west, the charming **Val di Racines** includes waterfalls and a natural rock bridge.

### 🏛️ Palazzo Comunale
Via Città Nuova 21. **Tel** 0472 72 37 00. **Open** Mon–Fri. **Closed** Fri pm & public hols.

### 🏛️ Museo Multscher
Via della Commenda 11. **Tel** 0472 76 64 64. **Open** Apr–Oct: Tue–Sat. **Closed** public hols. 🅿️

The medieval castle dominating the town of Brunico

# ❹ Brunico

*Bruneck*

🗺 13,000. 🚇 🚌 ℹ Piazza Municipio 7 (0474 55 57 22). 🛒 Wed.
Ⓦ bruneck.com

This attractive town, overlooked by the imposing form of its medieval **castle**, retains 14th-century fortifications and narrow streets that can only be explored on foot. The church of **St. Ursula**, northwest of St. Ursula's Gate, holds a series of outstanding mid-15th-century altar reliefs of the Nativity. The **Museo Etnografico di Teodone** offers displays of traditional agricultural life and local costumes; this folklore museum also provides an ideal opportunity to visit a 16th-century farmhouse and barn.

St. Ursula's Gate sundial, Brunico

🏛 **Museo Etnografico di Teodone**
Via Duca Diet 24, Teodone.
**Tel** 0474 55 20 87. **Open** Easter–Oct: Tue–Sat, Sun and public hols pm (Aug: also Mon). 🅿 ♿
🅿 Ⓦ volkskundemuseum.it

# ❺ Bressanone

*Brixen*

🗺 18,000. 🚇 🚌 ℹ Viale Ratisbona 9 (0472 83 64 01). 🛒 Mon.
Ⓦ brixen.org

The narrow medieval alleys of Bressanone cluster around the cathedral and the palace of the prince-bishops who ruled the town for much of its history. The **Duomo**, on Piazza del Duomo, was rebuilt in the 18th century but retains its 12th-century cloister, decorated with superb 15th-century frescoes. The lavish interiors of Palazzo Vescovile, the bishops' Renaissance palace, house the **Museo Diocesano**. It contains precious items from the Middle Ages, as well as the **Museo dei Presepi**, with its collection of wooden crib figures that are carved locally.

## Environs

At Velturno (Feldthurns), 5 miles (8 km) southwest, stands the Renaissance **Castello di Velturno**, the summer retreat of the rulers of Bressanone, noted for its frescoed rooms. A little over 2 miles (3 km) north of Bressanone lies the **Abbazia di Novacella**, a picturesque group of fortified monastic buildings with outstanding cloister frescoes. Farther up the valley, at **Rio di Pusteria** (Mühlbach), are the remains of a 16th-century fortified barrier, to the east of the town. The barrier funneled ancient travelers through the customs post that divided Tyrol from the Görz district.

High above Rio di Pusteria, to the southeast, looms the huge outline of the **Castello di Rodengo** (Rodeneck), with wonderful 13th-century frescoes of battles, the Last Judgment, and courtly episodes from the *Iwein* romance by Hartmann von Aue, the medieval poet.

🏛 **Museo Diocesano & Museo dei Presepi**
Piazza Palazzo Vescovile 2.
**Tel** 0472 83 05 05. Museo Diocesano: **Open** 10am–5pm Tue–Sun. **Closed** Nov & Jan 8–mid-Mar. Museo dei Presepi: **Open** 10am–5pm Tue–Sun (Dec–Jan 6: open daily). **Closed** Dec 24 & 25.
🅿 Ⓦ hofburg.it

🏰 **Castello di Velturno**
Velturno. **Tel** 0472 85 55 25.
**Open** Mar–Nov: Tue–Sun. 📷 only.
🅿 Ⓦ castelvelturno.it

🏰 **Abbazia di Novacella**
Via Abbazia 1/2b, Varna. **Tel** 0472 83 61 89. **Open** Mon–Sat. **Closed** Mon (Jan–Mar) & public hols. 📷 only. 🅿

🏰 **Castello di Rodengo**
Rodengo. **Tel** 0472 45 40 56.
**Open** Jun–Oct: Sun–Fri. 📷 🅿

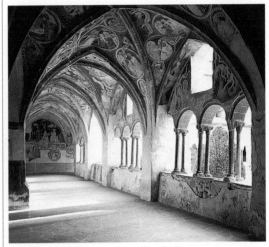

The cloisters of Bressanone Duomo with their 15th-century frescoes

The Baroque interior of the church of St. Ulrich in Ortisei

## ❻ Bolzano

*Bozen*

🗺 98,000. FS 🚍 ℹ️ Piazza Walther 8 (0471 30 70 00). 🚃 Mon–Sat.
W **bolzano-bozen.it**

Bolzano, the capital of the Alto Adige, is the gateway between the Italian-speaking Trentino region and the German-speaking Alto Adige, or Südtirol, and has a marked Tyrolean atmosphere. The old center, **Piazza Walther**, is dominated by the 15th-century Gothic **Duomo**, with its multicolored mosaic-patterned roof and elaborate spire. The "wine door" inside the Duomo is carved with figures at work among vines and reflects the importance of wine to the local economy. In the middle of Piazza Walther is a statue of Walther von der Vogelweide, the 13th-century troubadour – born, according to legend, in this area. North of the square, the streets are lined with houses adorned with intricate gables, balconies, and oriel windows. The outdoor market, starting at Piazza Grano, displays an inviting array of local produce that continues along the arcaded Via dei Portici. The modern **Museo Archeologico** houses impressive finds from the Stone Age, Bronze Age, Iron Age, Roman times, and the time of Charlemagne. A key exhibit is

The Duomo spire, Bolzano

Ötzi, the famous 5,000-year-old "Iceman." The **Chiesa dei Domenicani** (Dominican church), on Piazza Domenicani, has 14th-century *Triumph of Death* frescoes and a frescoed cloister.

### 🏛 Museo Archeologico
Via Museo 43. **Tel** 0471 32 01 00.
**Open** Tue–Sun (Jul, Aug, & Dec: daily).
**Closed** Jan 1, May 1, Dec 25. 🈳 🈯
🏠 W **iceman.it**

## ❼ Ortisei

*Sankt Ulrich*

🗺 4,500. 🚍 ℹ️ Via Rezia 1 (0471 77 76 00). 🚃 Fri. W **valgardena.it**

Ortisei is the prosperous main resort for the pretty Val Gardena and Alpe di Siusi region, and a major center for wood carving; examples of local craftsmanship may be seen in local stores, in the **Museo della Val Gardena** (which also focuses on local

archaeology), and in the church of **St. Ulrich**.

To the south is the **Alpe di Siusi** (Seiser Alm) region, noted for Alpine meadows, balconied farmsteads, and onion-domed churches. The best way to explore this beautiful area is by cableway from Ortisei: to the northeast a cable car runs to 8,260-ft- (2,518-m-) high Monte Seceda, and walks from here lead into the Odle Dolomites.

### 🏛 Museo della Val Gardena
Via Rezia 83. **Tel** 0471 79 75 54.
**Open** Jan 7–Mar: Tue–Fri; mid-May–Oct: Mon–Fri (Jul & Aug: Mon–Sat); Dec 26–Jan 6: daily. **Closed** Jan 1 & Dec 31. 🈳 W **museumgherdeina.it**

## ❾ Canazei

🗺 1,800. 🚍 ℹ️ Piazza Marconi 5 (0462 60 96 00). 🚃 Sat (Jul–Sep).
W **fassa.com**

Located at the base of some of the highest and most awe-inspiring groups of peaks, Canazei is a good base for exploring the Dolomites. In summer, chairlifts climb to viewpoints where the beauty of the encircling mountains can be appreciated to the fullest. The most popular viewpoints are Pecol and Col dei Rossi, reached by the Belvedere cableway from Via Pareda in Canazei: the cliffs of the Sella group are visible to the north, with Sasso Lungo to the west and Marmolada, the highest of the Dolomites at 10,965 ft (3,343 m), to the south.

Skiers enjoying views of the Dolomites above Canazei

## Environs

At **Vigo di Fassa**, 8 miles (13 km) southwest, the **Museo Ladino** focuses on the Ladin-speaking people of some of the valleys. Ladin – a Rhaeto-Romance language – is taught in local schools, and the traditions thrive.

### 🏛 Museo Ladino

Località San Giovanni, Vigo di Fassa. **Tel** 0462 76 01 82. **Open** Tue–Sat am & pm (Jun–mid-Sep: daily). **Closed** Jan 1, May 1, Jun 1–9, Nov & Dec 25. 🦽 🖼 🇼 istladin.net

The frescoed facade of the Palazzo della Magnifica Comunità, Cavalese

## ❾ Cavalese

🏔 3,600. 🚌 ℹ Via Fratelli Bronzetti 60 (0462 24 11 11). 🗓 last Tue of month (not Jul); smaller market Tue & Fri. 🇼 visitfiemme.it

Cavalese is the chief town in the Val di Fiemme, a pretty area of flower-filled aromatic pastures, delightful wooded valleys, and Tyrolean architecture. At the center of the town stands the **Palazzo della Magnifica Comunità**. Originally built in the 1200s, this was the seat of the medieval governing council that ruled the area as a semiautonomous region. Today the paneled interiors contain medieval paintings by local artists, and an archaeology collection. Most visitors come for the excellent summer and winter resort amenities, and to climb, by cable car, to the 7,311-ft (2,229-m) top of **Alpe Cermis**, the mountain that rises to the south of the town.

## Environs

The church in **Tesero**, the next village east, bears a 15th-century fresco by an unknown painter depicting Sabbath-breakers. The church, dating to 1450, has

Vines growing on the terraced slopes of the Cembra valley

Gothic vaulting, and a modern *Crucifixion*, painted against a background of the village.

At **Predazzo**, about 8 miles (13 km) east, the **Museo Geologico delle Dolomiti** explains the local geology.

### 🏛 Palazzo della Magnifica Comunità

Piazza Cesare Battisti 2. **Tel** 0462 34 03 65. **Open** Tue–Sun (mid-Sep–Nov & Jan–Jun by appt). 🗺 🖼 🦽 🇼 palazzomagnifica.eu

### 🏛 Museo Geologico delle Dolomiti

Piazza SS Filippo e Giacomo 1. **Tel** 0462 50 03 66. **Open** 10am–12:30pm & 4–7pm Tue–Sun (mid-Sep–Feb by appt). 🇼 muse.it

## ❿ San Martino di Castrozza

🏔 470. 🚌 ℹ Via Passo Rolle 165 (0439 76 88 67). 🗓 Tue (Jul & Aug). 🇼 sanmartino.com

The resort of San Martino occupies one of the most accessible and scenic valleys in the southern Dolomites, making it popular with walkers and skiers. Cable cars rise to the peak of **Alpe Tognola** (7,095 ft /2,163 m), southwest of the town, and up the **Cima della Rosetta** (8,557 ft/2,609 m) to the east. Both offer fabulous views of the Pale di San Martino, a stirring sight of massive rock peaks, split by glaciers, above a sea of green meadows and

woodland. San Martino is almost surrounded by forest, which once supplied the Venetian Republic with lumber for ships. The forest is now protected, and as a result it is possible to see Alpine flowers, mushrooms, birds, and other wildlife with relative ease.

## ⓫ Cembra

🏔 2,500. 🚌 ℹ Piazza San Rocco 10 (0461 68 31 10). 🗓 Wed am. 🇼 visitpinecembra.it

The wine-producing town of Cembra nestles on the terraced slopes of a scenic valley of flower-filled villages. Some 4 miles (6 km) east of Cembra stand the **Piramidi di Segonzano**, a rare series of erosion pillars, some over 100 ft (30 m) high, each topped by a rock. The footpath to the pillars is well signposted, with informative signboards along the way explaining the formation of the bizarre columns, which look like giant termite colonies.

Piramidi di Segonzano, near Cembra

Their setting amid bird-filled woodland makes the steep climb up to the site well worthwhile. A further reward is the fine view, from the top of the hill, along the Cembra valley and westward as far as the Brenta group of Dolomites.

### 🏛 Piramidi di Segonzano

Strada Statale 612 to Cavalese. **Open** daily.

The impressive falls of the Cascate di Nardis, Madonna di Campiglio

## ⓬ Madonna di Campiglio

🏔 1,300. 🚌 **ⓘ** Via Pradalago 4 (0465 44 75 01). 🗓 Jul & Aug: Tue & Thu. **🖥** campigliodolomiti.it

Madonna di Campiglio is the chief resort in the Val Meledrio. Nestling between the Brenta and Adamello groups of peaks, it makes the perfect base for walking or skiing amid the magnificent mountain terrain. Cableways radiate out from the town in every direction, giving easy access to the peaks.

**Environs**
The church at **Pinzolo**, 9 miles (14 km) south, has a well-preserved fresco depicting a Dance of Death (1539). The inevitable march of the figures, both rich and poor, is underlined by a text written in local dialect.

North of Pinzolo, the road west from Carisolo leads to the verdant and popular, yet unspoiled, **Val Genova**. About 2 miles (4 km) along the valley is the spectacular **Cascate di Nardis**, a waterfall that plunges down 300 ft (90 m). The two masses of rock at the bottom are said to be the forms of petrified demons.

## ⓭ Trento

🏔 105,000. 🚇 FS 🚌 **ⓘ** Piazza Duomo 24 (0461 21 60 00). 🗓 Thu am.

Trento, the capital of the region to which it gave its name, is also the most attractive town in Trentino. It has a fine Romanesque cathedral, a richly decorated castle, and streets lined with Renaissance mansions. Trento has a place in history as the venue for the **Council of Trent** (1545–63), set up by the Catholic Church to consider reforms that might encourage breakaway groups, in particular the German Protestants, to return to the fold. The reforms, which ushered in the period of the Counter-Reformation, were only partly successful.

The **Duomo**, site of some of the Council meetings, was begun in Romanesque style in the 1200s. It took three centuries to complete (in 1515), but the builders maintained its architectural harmony by ignoring the Gothic and Renaissance styles entirely. The result is a church of unusual integrity.

The Duomo stands on **Piazza Duomo**, the city's main square, which was first laid out by the Romans as their central marketplace or forum. Trento's Roman name, Tridentum, is commemorated in the figure of Neptune, who stands at the top of the fountain, which occupies the middle of the main square.

Inner courtyard of the Magno Palazzo

## 🏛 Museo Diocesano Tridentino

Piazza Duomo 18. **Tel** 0461 23 44 19. **Open** Wed–Mon. **Closed** Jan 1 & 6, Easter, June 26, Aug 15, Nov 1, Dec 25. 🅿 ♿ 🖥 museodiocesano tridentino.it

This museum is housed in the **Palazzo Pretorio**, an imposing medieval building that stands on the eastern side of Piazza Duomo. Its contents include early ivory reliquaries, Flemish tapestries, and paintings depicting the Council of Trent.

## 🏰 Castello del Buonconsiglio

Via Bernardo Clesio 5. **Tel** 0461 23 37 70. **Open** Tue–Sun (Jul & Aug: daily). **Closed** Jan 1, Dec 25. 🅿 🏛 🖥 buonconsiglio.it

This large castle, built in the 1200s and later enlarged with additional buildings, is part of the defenses of the town. Trento was an important frontier on the main road linking Italy to northern Europe, and thick walls still encircle the town.

The southern section of the castle consists of the magnificent **Magno Palazzo** (1530), built for the ruling prince-bishops of Trento, who were given extensive powers by the Holy Roman Emperor to foster loyalty and discourage defection to the pope. The lavish decoration (including frescoes of virile satyrs and nymphs by Gerolamo Romanino, 1531–2) speaks of huge wealth and a luxurious lifestyle. The palazzo houses the **Museo Provinciale**, with paintings, ceramics, 15th-century wood carvings, and prehistoric, Etruscan and Roman items.

Palazzo Pretorio and the Duomo in Trento's main square

The commanding form of the Ossario del Castel Dante in Rovereto

The **Torre dell' Aquila** (Eagle Tower) nearby contains frescoes painted around 1400 that depict the months of the year.

### Environs
To the west of Trento, a scenic round trip along a winding road leads up the north flank of **Monte Bondone** and back, via **Vezzano**, down the western slopes. The views are magnificent, particularly from Vaneze and Vason. East of Trento, Pergine marks the start of the **Val Sugana**, a broad valley with lakes. In the hills north of Lake Levico lies the spa town of **Levico Terme**, distinguished by elegant Neo-Classical buildings set amid beautifully wooded parkland.

## ⑭ Rovereto

🔼 33,000. 🚆 🚌 ℹ️ Corso Rosmini 6 (0464 43 03 63). 🚌 Tue.
🌐 **visitrovereto.it**

Rovereto was at the center of fierce fighting during World War I, after which the Venetian castle (built in 1416) that dominates the town was transformed into the **Museo Storico Italiano della Guerra**, a war museum. The displays include sections on wartime humor, propaganda, and spying. Near the museum entrance, stairs lead out onto the castle roof for a view of the imposing **Ossario del Castel Dante.**

Some distance away is the **Campana dei Caduti** (Bell of the Fallen), which was cast from melted-down cannons at the end of World War II and mounted in an imposing building above the town; it is rung daily at sunset.

Below the war museum is the Museo Civico, with collections of archaeology, art, natural history, and folklore. Another branch, on Corso Bettini, houses a collection of sculpture by Carlo Fait. The Mario Botta–designed **Museo di Arte Contemporanea di Trento e Rovereto (MART)** showcases 20th-century Italian art. A second site, in Via Portici, holds Italian Futurist art.

### Environs
A little over 5 miles (8 km) north of Rovereto is **Castel Beseno**, rising on a hill to the east. This enormous castle was built and rebuilt from the 12th century to the 18th to guard the junction of the three valleys.

Three miles (5 km) south of Rovereto, the main road passes through a valley littered with massive boulders created by landslides: these are known as Lavini di Marco or **Ruina Dantesca**, because they are mentioned in Dante's *Inferno* (XII, 4–9). Fossilized dinosaur footprints have been discovered there.

🏛️ **Museo Storico Italiano della Guerra**
Via Castelbarco 7. **Tel** 0464 43 81 00.
**Open** Tue–Sun. **Closed** public hols. 🎧
🌐 **museodellaguerra.it**

🏛️ **Museo Civico**
Borgo Santa Caterina 41.
**Tel** 0464 45 28 00; Palazzo Alberti, Corso Bettini 41. **Tel** 0464 45 28 00.
**Open** Tue–Sun. **Closed** Jan 1, Aug 5, Nov 1, Dec 25. 🎧 ♿
🌐 **fondazionemcr.it**

🏛️ **MART**
Corso Bettini 43. **Tel** 0464 43 88 87; Casa d'Arte Futurista Depero, Via Portici 38. Tel 0464 43 18 13.
**Open** Tue–Sun (Mon if public hol). 🎧
🔳 ♿ 🍴 📷 🛈 🌐 **mart.trento.it**

🏰 **Castel Beseno**
Besenello. **Tel** 0464 83 46 00.
**Open** Mar–Oct: Tue–Sun (& Mon if public hol); Nov–Feb: Sat & Sun. 🎧
🌐 **buonconsiglio.it**

## ⑮ Castello di Avio

Via Castello, Sabbionara d'Avio.
**Tel** 0464 68 44 53. 🚌 🚆 to Vo, then 2-mile (3-km) walk. **Open** Mar–Sep: 10am–6pm Wed–Sun (open Tue in Aug); Oct–Nov: 10am–5pm Wed–Sun; Mon and Tue if public hol. **Closed** 3rd week of Nov–Feb. 🎧 📷 🛈 🍴

Castles line the Adige valley to the Brenner Pass, but few are as accessible as the Castello di Avio. It was founded in the 11th century, extended in the 13th, and today offers far-reaching views. Among the many frescoes is a series in the Casa delle Guardie (Sentry House) depicting 13th-century battle scenes.

The extensive walls enclosing Castel Beseno above Rovereto

# NORTHWEST ITALY

# Introducing Northwest Italy

The northwest of Italy is made up of three very different geological characteristics: the jagged Alps, the flat plain, and the undulating shoreline of the Mediterranean. Within this varied landscape, some of it still wild and unspoiled, lie extremely rich and diverse vestiges of the area's substantial cultural heritage. The major sights, in the regions of Valle d'Aosta and Piedmont, Liguria and Lombardy, are shown on this map.

Aosta

VALLE D'AOSTA

Biella

Ivrea

Vercelli

Turin

Po

Moncalieri

Pinerolo

Asti

VALLE D'AOSTA
AND PIEDMONT
(See pp214–33)

Alessa

Alba

Cuneo

LIGU
(See pp2

Savona

Imperia

Sanremo

**The Parco Nazionale del Gran Paradiso** is a beautiful wilderness, and the habitat of rare Alpine fauna and flora *(see pp220–21).*

**The capital of Piedmont** is Turin, an elegant and bustling city of splendid Baroque architecture. Its skyline is dramatically dominated by the Mole Antonelliana *(see p228).*

**Sanremo** is a typical Riviera resort, with palm trees and a casino. The onion-domed outline of the Russian church adds an exotic flavor to the town *(see p238).*

**The Basilica di Sant'Andrea** in Vercelli is an important Romanesque building, one of the earliest to use Gothic elements *(see p232).*

◀ The picturesque Isola San Giulio in the center of Lake Orta, Valle d'Aosta

0 kilometers 50

0 miles 25

**Locator Map**

Sondrio

*Lake Como*

*re*

LOMBARDY
*(See pp190–213)*

Varese

Lecco

Como

Bergamo

Monza

Milan

Brescia

*Lake Garda*

Lodi

Pavia

Cremona

Po

*rtona*

*oa*

Portofino

La Spezia

**Isola Bella** is an enchanting island on romantic Lake Maggiore. Nearby lies beautiful Lake Como *(see pp194–5)*.

**Milan's Duomo**, with its distinctive bristling spires, is one of the many architectural gems in this stylish city *(see p197)*.

**Portofino** is one of Italy's most exclusive resorts. Nestling in a creek, its pretty pastel-colored houses surround a yacht-filled harbor *(see p244)*.

**The Certosa di Pavia**, a charming Carthusian monastery, includes a richly decorated Gothic church with a magnificent Renaissance facade, and a series of attractive cloisters *(see pp208–9)*.

# The Flavors of Northwest Italy

From Mediterranean Liguria to the Alps, the Lombardy plain, and Piedmont, this diverse area is characterized by its rich yet hearty cuisine. Along with the Veneto, Lombardy and Piedmont are Italy's main rice-growing areas and risotto features widely, especially delicious when made with local wild mushrooms. The white truffles of Alba are the "white gold" of Piedmont, while lush pastures produce some of the country's best meat and many of Italy's finest cheeses. The mild Ligurian climate favors olives and herbs – especially basil, used in pesto sauce – and fish teem in the sparkling Mediterranean.

Fresh basil

A precious haul of aromatic Piedmontese truffles

## Lombardy

This is the home of dishes prepared *alla Milanese*, rich in butter, *ossobuco* (shin of veal), vegetable soups, and boiled meats *(bollito misto)*. From veal to beef and from pork to poultry, Lombardy produces some of the country's finest meat, but it is also associated with *cucina povera* (cuisine of the poor), in which polenta (corn porridge) still features from its days as the staple diet of impoverished country folk. The other staple food, the short-grained rice that is used in risotto, grows abundantly in the area around Pavia. Lombardy is one of Italy's largest cheese-making regions, the most famous including Gorgonzola, Mascarpone, Bitto, and Grana Padano.

## Piedmont & Valle d'Aosta

The "Slow Food" movement was born in Piedmont in 1986. Its mission is "to defend biodiversity in our food supply, spread taste education, and connect producers of excellent food." The movement now has more than 100,000 members in more than 50 countries. Piedmontese flavors are robust,

Grana Padano · Gorgonzola · Fontina · Bitto · Mascarpone · Taleggio
Mouthwatering range of northwest Italy's finest cheeses

## Regional Dishes and Specialties

Veal is especially popular in Lombardy and Piedmont, and a great favorite with the Milanese is *ossobuco*. Another classic Piedmontese dish, *vitello tonnato*, is a surprisingly delicious blend of cold roast veal served with a sauce made with mayonnaise, tuna, gherkins, and capers. As well as pesto, a traditional dish from Genoa is *buridda alla Genovese* – a delicious fish soup or stew containing mussels, shrimps, octopus, squid, and clams. Shavings of truffle in dishes such as risotto and *fagiano tartufato* (pheasant stuffed with white truffle and pork fat) give a taste of sheer luxury, and fortunately, a little of this very expensive delicacy goes a long way. And, for those with a sweet tooth, *panettone* is a soft Christmas cake studded with dried and candied fruit, another Milanese specialty.

Gianduiotti

**Bagna Caôda** From Piedmont; a warm mix of olive oil, anchovies, and garlic into which raw vegetables are dipped.

Boxes of fresh fish are unloaded onto a Ligurian quayside

rich, and earthy, and laced with French flair, reflecting a history of French rule and influence.

The paddy fields of Vercelli are the rice capital of Europe, and truffle risotto, especially when flavored using the prized white variety from Alba, is truly memorable fare.

The mountains are famous for cow's-milk cheese, especially the semisoft Fontina from the Valle d'Aosta, cured meats, salamis, terrines, and game. Piedmont also produces Italy's greatest red wines, and the prized Barolo and Barbaresco often feature as a marinade in beef dishes.

The Turinese are passionate about chocolate, echoing Turin's tradition of chocolate-making originating in the 17th century. Most famous are the sublime ingot-shaped *gianduiotti*, filled with a rich chocolate-hazelnut cream. The

city is also the birthplace of *grissini*, crisp breadsticks that grace every restaurant table. The tradition of the *aperitivo* also originates in Turin. The spread that accompanies a glass of Prosecco or a cocktail in bars throughout the city between 6pm and 8pm is substantial.

Delicious focaccia bread made with Ligurian olive oil

## Liguria

The Mediterranean climate is perfect for growing herbs, fruits and vegetables, nuts, and olives. Ligurian olive oil is of the highest quality and is used in the preparation of many dishes. To accompany pasta, pesto is the signature sauce, made from basil, pine nuts, garlic, and olive oil, as well as a mix of pecorino and Parmesan. This use of aromatic herbs is typical of Ligurian cuisine in general.

Not surprisingly, seafood is as common as meat and dairy in this region, where the vast majority of people live on the coast.

### ON THE MENU

**Agnolotti** Piedmont pasta specialty – crescent-shaped ravioli stuffed with meat or vegetables. Served with *ragù* or a creamy sauce.

**Brasato al Barolo** Braised beef cooked gently with vegetables in Barolo wine.

**Lumache** Piedmontese snails, the best of which come from Cherasco, served either in garlic and butter or in a sauce of olive oil, tomatoes, and garlic.

**Oca alla Piemontese** Goose preserved in fat.

**Risotto alla Milanese** Rich, saffron-scented dish of rice with white wine, onion, and Parmesan cheese.

**Trenette con pesto** A Ligurian dish of flat noodles with a sauce of basil, garlic, pine nuts, and olive oil.

**Ossobuco** Milanese shin of veal, braised slowly in white wine. The bone marrow is considered a delicacy.

**Zabaione** A frothy dessert of egg yolks, sugar, and Marsala, *zabaione* is a specialty of the Piedmont region.

# The Wines of Northwest Italy

Grapes are grown throughout the northwest – from the cliffs of Liguria to the steep mountainsides of Valle d'Aosta. The best wines, however, come from Piedmont, in particular the Langhe hills southwest of Turin, source of two of Italy's finest reds: the rich, powerful, long-lived Barolo and Barbaresco. Both of these are now showing the benefits of modern techniques and a renewed interest in high-quality wine-making. Lighter, everyday red wines that go well with the local cuisine include Dolcetto and the popular Barbera. Another Piedmont specialty is sparkling *spumante*, Italians' instinctive choice whenever there is something around to celebrate.

Castiglione Falletto in the heart of Piedmont

**Barbera d'Alba** comes from the adaptable Barbera grape, which can grow on almost any slope. Its ubiquitous nature means that the wines it yields can be light and full of fruit, as well as dense, strong, and full-flavored. Good producers include Aldo Conterno, Voerzio, Pio Cesare, Altare, Gaja, Vaira, and Vietti.

**Dolcetto** is grown in seven different areas. Dolcetto d'Alba has a delicious perfume and deep purple color. Best drunk within one or two years, it ranges in flavor from fresh and fruity to the rich, concentrated plumminess of some of the top wines, such as those produced by Giuseppe Mascarello.

**Barolo**, prized the world over for its complex array of flavors and firm tannins, is made from the Nebbiolo grape and may take up to 20 years to mature. Vigna Colonnello is a top Barolo from Aldo Conterno, made only in the best years, like 2006, 2005, 2004, and 1993.

**The white truffle** of Alba is an autumn specialty from the Langhe hills. Highly prized for its earthy scent, it is excellent with Barolo.

**Key**

- Barolo
- Barbaresco
- Other vineyard areas

0 kilometers     25
0 miles     15

**Moscato d'Asti** is an excellent *aperitivo* or light dessert wine made from the aromatic, fruity Moscato grape. It is light in alcohol with a gently sweet finish and may have a slight sparkle. Ideal for refreshing the palate after a hearty Piedmontese meal, Araldica's versatile Moscato is delicious when served well chilled.

## Grapes of the Northwest

The Nebbiolo grape is used to produce two of Italy's finest red wines, Barolo and Barbaresco, as well as other regional wines in the Valtellina and north of Turin. It is a difficult grape to cultivate and requires a long growing season to soften its high acidity. However, the final results are worth it: in the Langhe region the Nebbiolo offers complex perfumes and a range of flavors, often encased within strong tannins. Easier to handle and lighter, the Dolcetto and Barbera both came from the Monferrato region originally. These reds yield lighter, fruitier wines but, when at their best, no less distinctive than those of the Nebbiolo. Of the white grapes, the Moscato is Piedmont's oldest known variety. Famous for the successful sparkling Asti Spumante, the best grapes are reserved for Moscato d'Asti.

Nebbiolo grapes

## How to Read the Label

**The name** of the wine is shown in the center of the label: *bricco* is local dialect for a good hilltop vineyard.

The producer's name

Producer's emblem

Year of production

ROCCHE DEI MANZONI®

BRICCO
MANZONI
1985

IMBOTTIGLIATO DA
PODERE ROCCHE DEI MANZONI
DI VALENTINO
MONFORTE D'ALBA (ITALIA)

VINO DA TAVOLA DELLE LANGHE

13,5% vol.                75cl ℮

Alcoholic strength

Size of bottle

**The official** category; in this case a table wine from the Langhe region.

The bottler's name and address

**Good Vintages**
Barolo and Barbaresco had good years in 2006, 2005, 2004, 2003, 2000, 1998, 1997.

**Barolo is aged** in wooden casks for at least two years before being put in bottles. This may be done in either the traditional, large *botte* or the smaller *barrique*, which imparts a strong oaky flavor to the wine.

Casale Monferrato

LOMBARDY

Voghera

Alessandria

Tortona

Nizza Monferrato

Novi Ligure

nelli

Acqui Terme

Ovada

Gavi

LIGURIA

Genoa

llo

Savona

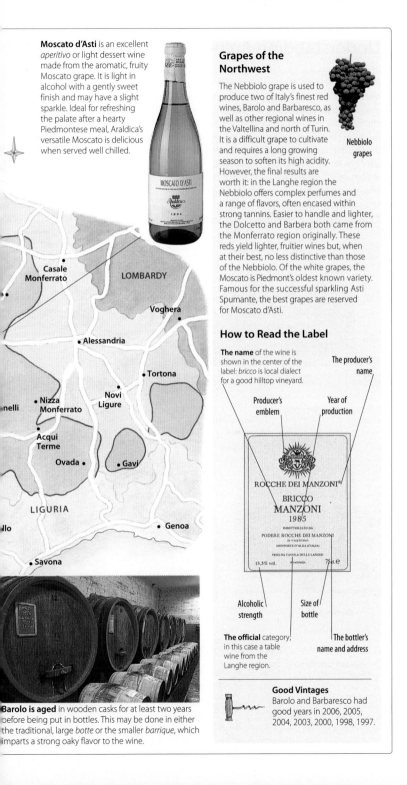

# Understanding Architecture in Northwest Italy

Although the buildings of the northwest tend to be solid and imposing – a result partly of the more severe climate – there is no distinctive architectural stamp as there is around Venice, Florence, or even Rome. Instead, a variety of buildings in different styles, many borrowed or reinterpreted from elsewhere, are dotted across the area: enchanting medieval castles, outstanding Romanesque and Gothic buildings, unusual Baroque structures. The northwest is also rich in modern architecture – in terms of both design and materials – influenced by the region's industrial developments and its strong flair for innovative design, which also often draws its inspiration from earlier architectural styles.

Castello Sforzesco, 1451–66 *(see p196)*

## Characteristics of Northwest Italian Architecture

Double row of defensive walls

Wooden balcony

Few windows

Massive square tower

Pointed turret

Battlements

**Castello di Fénis**, one of the finest castles in the Valle d'Aosta, is a 14th-century fortress with asymmetrical towers, turrets, and crenellated walls. Frescoes adorn the interior *(see p219)*.

Alternating bands of marble

Rose window

Lions support columns and porch above

Elaborate carving

Rose window

Octagonal drum influenced by the Duomo in Florence

Highly orn facade

**Cappella Colleoni**, Bergamo (1476), mixes rich, decorative elements in this early Renaissance masterpiece *(see p205)*.

Patterned marble design

**Monza's Duomo** (1390s) typifies the Lombard style of Romanesque architecture with its marble stripes and ornate carving *(see p205)*.

Massive scale

Ornate window surrounds

Rotunda

Balcony

Curved brickwork

**Palazzo Carignano** is perhaps the finest product of Turin's idiosyncratic Baroque school. Guarini's masterpiece (1679) boasts an extraordinary undulating brick facade and a fine rotunda *(see p227)*.

## Where to See the Architecture

The road to Aosta is flanked by numerous medieval castles (see p218), while inspirational Romanesque and Gothic churches are found in Lombardy – at Monza (p205), Pavia (p207), Milan (pp196–205), and Como (pp194–5). The 15th-century Certosa di Pavia (pp208–9) is a must, as well as the charming city of Mantua (p211). Turin (pp224–9) is famous for its unique Baroque school, and Bergamo for its exuberance. Architecture from the last two centuries is best represented in Milan and Turin, and in Genoa some exciting redevelopment projects are taking place.

Renzo Piano's mast structure (1992) in Genoa's redeveloped port and conference center

## 19th- and 20th-Century Architecture

Top reaches 550 ft (167 m)

Aluminum replaces original granite top

Square-sided dome

**Galleria Vittorio Emanuele II** in Milan, designed by Mengoni in 1865, was the first Italian building to use glass and iron structurally (see p198).

Central dome

Mosaics

Glass balcony

Overhanging upper stories

Struts support the top

**The Mole Antonelliana** (1863–97), designed by Antonelli, was the tallest building in the world when it was built (see p228).

**Torre Velasca, Milan**, is a 26-floor tower south of the Duomo. The design, from the 1950s, was influenced by medieval castles such as the Castello Sforzesco.

Elliptical shape

Taller windows

Tapering struts

Spiral ramps up to roof

Roof served as test track

Reinforced concrete

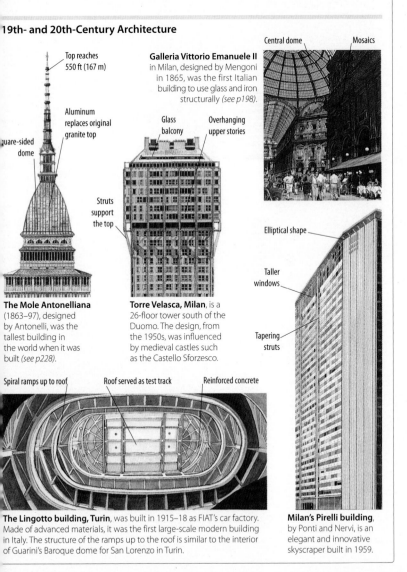

**The Lingotto building, Turin**, was built in 1915–18 as FIAT's car factory. Made of advanced materials, it was the first large-scale modern building in Italy. The structure of the ramps up to the roof is similar to the interior of Guarini's Baroque dome for San Lorenzo in Turin.

**Milan's Pirelli building**, by Ponti and Nervi, is an elegant and innovative skyscraper built in 1959.

# LOMBARDY

The region of Lombardy stretches from the Alps, on the border with Switzerland, down through the romantic lakes of Como and Maggiore to the broad, flat plain of the River Po. It is an area of lakeside villas with azalea-filled gardens, of wealthy towns with imposing palazzi and highly decorated churches, and of efficient, modern industry and large-scale agriculture, the financial heart of Italy. At its center stands Milan, the style-conscious capital of Lombardy.

The region was named after the Lombards or Longobards, a Germanic tribe that invaded Italy in the 6th century AD. During the Middle Ages, Lombardy was part of the Holy Roman Empire, but not always loyal to its German emperors. The Lombards, who had a talent for banking and commerce, resented any outside interference with their prosperity.

The 12th century saw the rise of the Lega Lombarda, or Lombard League, a band of forceful separatists founded to counter the brutal imperialism of Frederick Barbarossa (their most modern incarnation being the Lega Nord political party). Power was seized by the region's great families, most notably the Visconti and the Sforza of Milan, from the 14th to the early 16th century. These dynasties also became great patrons of the arts, commissioning exquisite palaces, churches, and artworks, many of which can still be seen. Bergamo, Mantua, and Cremona – not to mention Milan itself – contain a remarkably rich array of art treasures. Here are such pinnacles of European civilization as the charterhouse at Pavia, Leonardo da Vinci's *Last Supper*, and the magnificent paintings of the Pinacoteca di Brera in Milan.

Lombardy – famous as the birthplace of Virgil, Monteverdi, Stradivarius, and Donizetti – offers visitors the contrasting pleasures of lyrical lakeside landscapes (resorts on lakes Como and Maggiore have attracted poets, aristocrats, and gamblers for centuries) and beautiful, bustling cities.

Strolling through Milan's enormous Galleria Vittorio Emanuele II

◀ The village of Corenno Plinio on the peaceful eastern shores of the beautiful Lake Como

# Exploring Lombardy

The enormous plain of the River Po runs through much of Lombardy, providing a landscape that is flat and perfectly suited to the consequent expansion of industry in the region. This is, however, also a region of great contrasts. To the north, in a still unspoiled setting in the foothills of the mountains, lie the lakes Como and Maggiore, as well as the dramatic valleys and peaks of the Parco Nazionale dello Stelvio around Bormio, Sondrio, and Val Camonica. Farther south, busy industrialized areas give way to huge tracts of agriculture dotted with towns of great beauty such as Cremona, Mantua, and Pavia, which offer a splendid array of artistic treasures.

Isola Bella on Lake Maggiore

## Sights at a Glance

❶ Lago di Como
❷ Lago Maggiore
❸ *Milan (Milano) pp196–204*
❹ Monza
❺ Bergamo
❻ Parco Nazionale dello Stelvio
❼ Val Camonica
❽ Lago d'Iseo
❾ Brescia
❿ Lodi
⓫ Pavia
⓬ *Certosa di Pavia pp208–9*
⓭ Cremona
⓮ Sabbioneta
⓯ Mantua (Mantova)

The colorful facade of the Cappella Colleoni in Bergamo

**For additional map symbols** *see back flap*

Passo del Gavia in the Parco Nazionale dello Stelvio on the eastern fringes of Lombardy

### Key

=== Freeway
=== Major Highway
— Secondary road
···· Minor road
— Scenic route
⊷⊶ Main railroad line
---- Minor railroad line
▬▬ International border
▬▬ Regional border
△ Summit

## Getting Around

Milan has three international airports, which are obvious gateways into northern Italy, and the vast and flat Lombard plain has its advantages when it comes to transportation: highways and railroads criss-cross it and make trips between the larger towns very easy. The lakes, however, are better visited by car, as only two main towns are served by trains, though there are bus and boat services around the shores. The Parco Nazionale dello Stelvio and the mountains are more remote still, but offer good tourist amenities.

0 kilometers    25

0 miles    20

# ❶ Lago di Como

Set in an idyllic landscape of mountains and rugged hillsides, Lake Como has for centuries attracted visitors who come here to go boating, for walks in the hills, or for relaxation and inspiration. The northern stretches, in particular, are shrouded in an almost eerie calm. The long and narrow lake, shaped into a wishbone by glacial erosion, offers fine views up to the Alps and down to the towns of Como and Lecco.

**The northern** stretches are wilder and less populated than the southern part, offering visitors great tranquility.

The banks of the lake near Como

**Menaggio** is one of a string of popular resorts lining the west bank.

**Varenna**, a ferry port, is overlooked by a ruined 11th century castle. At Fiumelatte just south, there is a foaming stream, the "river of milk."

**Villa Carlotta** nestles among lush gardens with lovely views.

**Cernobbio** was a favorite resort of the exiled Queen Caroline of England in the early 19th century.

**The scenic route** just south of Bellagio climbs a hill to offer far-reaching lake views.

**Bellagio**
This delightful resort on the cusp of the lake's two arms has elegant lakeside promenades and cafés.

**The southeastern** arm of the lake is also called the Lago di Lecco.

**Lecco**, home to the 19th-century novelist Manzoni.

**Como**
The town, which gave its name to the lake, boasts a fine Duomo in mixed Gothic and Renaissance styles, with carvings on its facade.

Domaso • Gravedona • Còlico • S38 • Dèrvio • Bellano • Menaggio • Varenna • Fiumelatte • Griante • Tremezzo • Bellagio • Mezzegra • Argegno • Onno • Cernobbio • Como • Lecco

0 meters 10
0 miles 10

## Key

••• Car ferry route
••• Ferry route
━━ Freeway
━━ Major highway
┄┄ Minor road

For hotels and restaurants in this region see pp565–9 and pp584–90

## VISITORS' CHECKLIST

**Practical Information**
ℹ️ Piazza Cavour 17, Como (031 26 97 12); Piazza XX Settembre 23, Lecco (0341 29 57 20).
🌐 lakecomo.it

**Transportation**
FS Como, Lecco. 🚌 🚢 all towns.

Tadoline's copy (1834) of Canova's *Cupid and Psyche* in Villa Carlotta

### Exploring Lago di Como

In the heart of **Como** lies the elegant Piazza Cavour. Nearby rises the beautiful 14th-century **Duomo**, with its 15th- and 16th-century reliefs and paintings, and fine tombs. The 18th-century dome is by Turin's famous Baroque architect, Juvarra. Next to the Duomo stand the 13th-century Broletto (town hall), charmingly striped in white, pink, and gray, and the tall Torre del Comune. At Tremezzo, **Villa Carlotta** is an elegant 18th-century summer-house known for its gardens. In springtime, all sorts of flowers burst into color. The villa houses a collection of sculptures.

**Lecco**, a small industrial town to the south of the lake's eastern arm, was home to Alessandro Manzoni (1785–1873). The writer's childhood home, the **Villa Manzoni**, is devoted to memorabilia of his life and works. A monument in Piazza Manzoni depicts scenes from his most famous novel, *I Promessi Sposi (The Betrothed)* – set in 17th-century Lecco and Milan.

### 🏛 Villa Carlotta
Via Regina 2b, Tremezzo. **Tel** 0344 404 05. **Open** early Apr–mid-Oct: 9am–7:30pm daily; mid-Mar–early Apr & mid-Oct–Oct 31: 10am–6pm daily. 🅿️

### 🏛 Villa Manzoni
Via Guanella 1, Lecco. **Tel** 0341 48 12 47. **Open** 9.30am–6pm Tue–Fri; 10am–6pm Sat & Sun. **Closed** Jan 1, Easter, May 1, Aug 15, Dec 25. 🅿️

## ❷ Lago Maggiore

Verbania. FS 🚌 🚢 Stresa, Verbania, Baveno & the islands. ℹ️ Piazza Marconi 16, Stresa (0323 301 50).
🌐 distrettolaghi.it

Lake Maggiore, the second-largest Italian lake after Lake Garda, is a long expanse of water nestling right against the mountains and stretching into Alpine Switzerland; it is warmer in atmosphere and more romantic than Lake Como. The gently sloping shores are dotted with camellias, azaleas, and verbena – from which the ancient lake derived its Roman name, Verbanus.

A huge copper statue of Cardinal San Carlo Borromeo, the chief patron of the lake, stands in **Arona**, the town where he was born in 1538. It is possible to climb up and look out over the lake through his eyes and ears. Arona also boasts a ruined castle and a chapel, Santa Maria, dedicated to the Borromeo family.

Farther up the western coast of the lake is **Stresa**, the chief resort and main jumping-off point for visits to the islands; the town boasts many grand hotels, handsome villas, and pleasant gardens. Behind Stresa, a cable car ride away, rises Monte Mottarone, a snow-capped peak offering spectacular panoramic views of the surrounding mountains, including Monte Rosa.

The statue of Carlo Borromeo in Arona

The **Borromean islands**, at the center of the lake near Stresa, are small jewels of natural beauty augmented by artificial grottoes, architectural follies, and landscaped gardens. **Isola Bella** is home to the 17th-century **Palazzo Borromeo** and its splendid gardens, while Isola Madre is largely given over to a botanical garden. The only island inhabited year-round is Isola dei Pescatori, with a population of 50. The private Isola di San Giovanni is the smallest of the isles, with a villa that once belonged to the great conductor Arturo Toscanini (1867–1957).

The lake becomes quieter toward the Swiss border, but continues to be lined with attractive villas. The **Villa Taranto**, located on the outskirts of Verbania, houses a fine exotic botanical collection.

About 2 miles (3 km) west of **Cannobio**, a market town near Switzerland, is the dramatic gorge and tumbling waterfall of Orrido di Sant'Anna, accessible by boat.

### 🏛 Palazzo Borromeo
Isola Bella. 🚢 from Stresa. **Tel** 0323 305 56. **Open** early Mar–Oct: 9am–5:30pm daily. 🅿️
🌐 isoleborromee.it

### 🏛 Villa Taranto
Via Vittorio Veneto 111, Verbania, Pallanza. **Tel** 0323 40 45 55. **Open** mid-Mar–Oct: daily. 🅿️ ♿

Isola Bella's 17th-century Palazzo Borromeo and garden on Lago Maggiore

# ❸ Milan

Center of fashion, business, and finance, Milan has a bustling, businesslike feel about it. It is smart rather than attractive – a city of wealth as opposed to imagination and the heartland of the Italian economy. Its name is thought to come from a composite of the Latin words *medio* and *planum*, meaning "middle of the plain." It has long been an important trading center at the intersection of transalpine routes, and a prize for powerful dynasties. Today, it is the best place to see Italy at its most cosmopolitan and stylish.

*Portrait of a Young Woman* by Pollaiuolo, Museo Poldi-Pezzoli

### 🏰 Castello Sforzesco

Piazza Castello. **Tel** 02 88 46 37 03. Castello: **Open** daily. Musei del Castello: **Open** 9am–5:30pm Tue–Sun. **Closed** public hols. 🗝️ ♿
**w** milanocastello.it

The first castle on this site was built by the Visconti family, but demolished when their reign ended in the mid-15th century. Milan's new ruler, Francesco Sforza, built in its place this Renaissance palace. The castle is based on a series of courtyards, the most beautiful of which, the Cortile della Rocchetta, is a graceful arcaded square designed by Bramante and Filarete. The palace now contains, together with sections on Applied Arts, Archaeology, and Coins, the **Musei del Castello**. This fine collection of furniture, antiquities, and paintings includes Michelangelo's unfinished sculpture known as the *Rondanini Pietà*. The

canvases in the picture collection, dating from the Renaissance to the 18th century, are particularly impressive.

### 🏛️ Museo Poldi-Pezzoli

Via Alessandro Manzoni 12. **Tel** 02 79 48 89. **Open** 10am–6pm Wed–Mon. 📷 **w** museopoldipezzoli.it

Giacomo Poldi-Pezzoli was a wealthy nobleman who, on his death in 1879, bequeathed his magnificent art collection to the State. Its most famous painting is the 15th-century Renaissance *Portrait of a Young Woman* by Antonio Pollaiuolo, though there are also works by Piero della Francesca, Botticelli and Mantegna, among others. The applied arts section is richly endowed with fascinating items ranging from rugs and lace to glass, enamels and porcelain, as well as sculpture, jewelry and sundials.

### Sights at a Glance

① Castello Sforzesco
② *Pinacoteca di Brera pp202–203*
③ Museo Poldi-Pezzoli
④ Teatro alla Scala
⑤ Galleria Vittorio Emanuele II
⑥ Duomo
⑦ Palazzo Reale (Museo della Reggia)
⑧ San Satiro
⑨ Pinacoteca Ambrosiana
⑩ Sant'Ambrogio
⑪ San Lorenzo Maggiore
⑫ Civico Museo Archeologico
⑬ Parco Sempione

Michelangelo's *Rondanini Pietà* (c.1564) in the Castello Sforzesco

## 🎭 Teatro alla Scala

Piazza della Scala. Box office: **Tel** 02 72 00 37 44. 🎭 Museo Teatrale: Largo Ghiringhelli 1 (Piazza Scala). **Tel** 02 88 79 24 73. **Open** 9am–noon & 1:30–5pm daily. 🎫 🚻 📷

🌐 teatroallascala.org

This Neo-Classical theater opened in 1778 and is one of the world's most prestigious opera houses. It has one of the largest stages in Europe and hosts sumptuous productions. Two hours before each performance the box office

The façade of the world-famous Teatro alla Scala

opens to sell tickets at discount prices. The **Museo Teatrale** houses sets and costumes of past productions and theatrical items dating back to Roman times. There is also a good view of the auditorium, with its gilded box galleries, *trompe-l'oeil* effects and huge chandelier.

The Gothic Duomo, crowned with spires

## VISITORS' CHECKLIST

### Practical Information

🏛 1,325,000. 🛈 Galleria Vittorio Emanuele (02 88 45 55 55). 🛒 daily. 🎉 Dec 7: Sant'Ambrogio.
🌐 turismo.milano.it

### Transportation

✈ Malpensa 31 miles (50 km) NW; Linate 5 miles (8 km) E. 🚆 Stazione Centrale, Piazza Duca d'Aosta; Stazione Porta Garibaldi, Piazza Freud. 🚌 Lampugnano.

## 🏛 Duomo

Piazza del Duomo. **Tel** 02 72 02 26 56. **Open** 8am–7pm daily. Archaeological site: **Open** 8am–7pm daily. Museum: **Open** 10am–6pm Thu–Tue. Roof: **Open** 9am–7pm daily. 🎫 for roof. 🚻
🌐 duomomilano.it

Milan's cathedral is one of the largest Gothic churches in the world. It was begun in the 14th century under Prince Gian Galeazzo Visconti but not completed until more than 500 years later. The building's most startling feature is the extraordinary roof, with its 135 spires, innumerable statues, and gargoyles, and from which, on a clear day, there are views of the Alps. Below, the facade boasts an assortment of styles from Gothic through Renaissance and Neo-Classical. The bronze doors are faced with bas-reliefs recounting episodes from the life of the Virgin and of Sant'Ambrogio, and scenes retelling the history of Milan.

The aisles are divided by 52 giant pillars and well lit by stained-glass windows. Look out for the Visconti family symbol – a serpent swallowing a man – in the fine tracery of the apse windows. Among the many statues is a depiction of the flayed San Bartolomeo carrying his own skin.

The treasury, beneath the main altar, contains medieval gold and silverwork, and the remains of a 4th-century baptistery.

**For keys to map symbols** *see back flap*

# Exploring Milan

In addition to the great monuments in Milan, such as the cathedral and the castle, there is a host of varied and interesting museums, churches, and civic buildings, which provide an enthralling mix of old and new. This chic and busy metropolis offers plenty of opportunities for cultural activities, gastronomic adventures, designer-fashion shopping, or just strolling about, Milan-style.

The glass ceiling and dome covering the Galleria Vittorio Emanuele II

### 🎫 Galleria Vittorio Emanuele II

Main entrances on Piazza del Duomo and Piazza della Scala.

This ornate shopping arcade, known as *il Salotto di Milano* (Milan's drawing room), was designed by the architect Giuseppe Mengoni in 1865. The galleria had a tragic start, however, as Mengoni fell to his death from the scaffolding not long before its inauguration in 1877 (a year before the arcade was actually finished). Tourists are nevertheless attracted to its stylish stores and cafés, as well as Savini, one of Milan's historic restaurants.

The galleria itself has a floorplan in the shape of a Latin cross, with an octagonal center adorned with mosaics representing four continents (Europe, America, Africa, and Asia), together with others representing Art, Agriculture, Science, and Industry. Its finest feature is its metal and glass roof, crowned with a magnificent central dome. The roof was the first structure in Italy to use metal and glass in a structural way, rather than just decoratively. The floors are decorated with mosaics of the signs of the zodiac; tourists may be seen stepping on the genitals of Taurus the Bull, which is said to bring good luck.

### 🏛 Palazzo Reale

Piazza del Duomo. **Open** 2:30–7:30pm Mon, 9:30am–7:30pm Tue–Sun (Thu & Sat to 10:30pm). Museo della Reggia: 🔣 🖼 **w palazzorealemilano.it** Museo del Novecento: Via Marconi 1. **w museodelnovecento.org**

The former royal palace, for centuries home to the Visconti and other rulers of Milan, houses the **Museo della Reggia**. It displays the sumptuous interiors of the building and showcases the four historic phases of the palace, including the Neo-Classical era and the Restoration. Palazzo Reale is also a prestigious venue for temporary art exhibitions. The building abutting it to the west (the Arengario) now houses a modern art museum, the **Museo del Novecento**, and many Italian works from the 20th century are displayed here.

### 🏛 Villa Belgiojoso Bonaparte and Galleria d'Arte Moderna (GAM)

Via Palestro 16. **Tel** 02 88 44 59 47. **Open** 9am–7:30pm Tue–Sun. 🔣 🖼 **w gam-milano.com**

Milan's 19th-century and modern art collections are housed in a Neo-Classical villa built by Leopold Pollack in 1790 for Count Ludovico Barbiano di Belgiojoso. It was lived in by Napoleon in 1802 and later by Marshal Radetzky. The villa houses 19th-century Italian art, showing all the major art movements, as well as the Grassi and Vismara collections of 19th- and 20th-century Italian and foreign artists and the Marino Marini Museum. Of particular note are works by Giorgio Morandi (1890–1964) and Carlo Carrà (1881–1966), as well as by Modigliani (1884–1920) and De Chirico (1888–1978). Non-Italian artists include Van Gogh, Cézanne, Gauguin, Picasso, Matisse, Klee, Mondrian, and Kandinsky.

*Still Life* (1920) by Giorgio Morandi in the Galleria d'Arte Moderna

*Fruit Basket (c.1596) by Caravaggio in the Pinacoteca Ambrosiana*

### 🏛 Pinacoteca Ambrosiana

Piazza Pio XI 2. **Tel** 02 80 69 21.
**Open** 10am–6pm Tue–Sun. 🖼
**w** ambrosiana.eu

The Ambrosiana is home to Cardinal Federico Borromeo's magnificent library of 36,000 manuscripts. These include a 5th-century illustrated *Iliad*, early manuscripts of Dante's *Divine Comedy* (1353), and the *Atlantic Codex* (1478–1519) by Leonardo da Vinci. In order to exhibit as much of the *Atlantic Codex* as possible, the pages on display are changed every three months.

The building also houses an art gallery, bequeathed by Borromeo in 1618. The collection ranges from 14th-century pieces to works of the early 19th century. Among the canvases are *Portrait of a Musician* by Leonardo, the *Madonna of the Canopy* by Botticelli (15th century), a cartoon version of Raphael's Vatican fresco, *The School of Athens* (16th century), and Caravaggio's *Fruit Basket*. There is also a strong collection of Venetian art, with paintings by Giorgione, Titian, Bassano, and Tiepolo, and panel paintings by the late 15th-century Lombard painter Bergognone.

### 🏛 San Satiro

Via Speronari 3. **Tel** 02 87 46 83.
**Open** 9:30am–5:30pm Tue–Sat, 2–5:30pm Sun & public hols.

The church of Santa Maria presso San Satiro is one of the most beautiful Renaissance buildings in Milan. It was built on the site of a 9th-century sanctuary, little of which remains apart from the Cappella della Pietà, beside a bell tower dating back to the 11th century.

The interior seems to be in the shape of a Greek cross, but this is an illusion created by trompe-l'oeil effects, since space restrictions led Bramante to choose a T-shaped plan. Above the altar is a 13th-century fresco. An octagonal baptistery lies off the right aisle. The church's facade was finished in the 19th century.

### 🏛 Civico Museo Archeologico

Corso Magenta 15. **Tel** 02 88 44 52 08.
Ⓜ 1, 2 Cadorna. 🚎 16, 27. 🚌 50, 58, 94. **Open** 9am–5:30pm Tue–Sun. ♿ (phone ahead). 🖼 🏛 ✉

At the entrance to this museum is a model of Roman Milan, which illustrates urban planning and architecture in Milan from the 1st to the 4th century AD. The exhibition begins in a hall on the right, containing clay objects and Roman sculpture. At the end of this room is a huge fragment of a torso of Hercules and 3rd-century-AD floor mosaics. Also in this room are two of the most important works in the museum: the Parabiago Patera and the Diatreta Cup. The Patera is a gilded silver plate with a relief of the goddess Cybele (4th century AD). The Diatreta Cup, dating from the same period, is a single piece of colored glass, with finely wrought, intricate decoration.

### 🟦 Parco Sempione

Piazza Castello–Piazza Sempione.
Ⓜ 1 Cadorna, Cairoli, 2 Lanza, Cadorna. 🚉 Ferrovie Nord, Cadorna. 🚎 1, 2, 4, 12, 14, 27. 🚌 50, 57, 61, 94. **Open** May: 6:30am–10pm; Jun–Sep: 6:30am–11:30pm; Oct–Apr: 6:30am–9pm.

Although it covers an area of about 2 sq miles (5 sq km), this park occupies only a part of the old Visconti ducal garden, enlarged by the Sforza in the 15th century to make a 1 sq mile (3 sq km) hunting preserve. The present-day layout was designed by Emilio Alemagna between 1890 and 1893.

Among the trees are monuments to Napoleon III by Francesco Barzaghi, De Chirico's *Mysterious Baths*, the sulfur water fountain, and the Torre Branca, a tower of steel tubes made in 1932 to a design by Gio Ponti.

### 🏛 Gallerie d'Italia

Via Manzoni 10. **Tel** 800 16 76 19.
**Open** 9:30am–7:30pm Tue–Sun (to 10:30pm Thu). 🎫
**w** gallerieditalia.com

Housed in the Palazzo Anguissola Antona Traversi and Palazzo Brentani, Gallerie d'Italia has around 200 works of art from the 1800s. This collection offers a fascinating journey through one century of Italian art, with pieces by such artists as Antonio Canova, Angelo Inganni, and Umberto Boccioni.

The Parco Sempione with the Arco della Pace in the background

# Shopping in Milan

In Milan, one of the most affluent cities in Italy, shopping is synonymous with buying designer apparel. High-fashion flagship stores here are invariably smart and stylish, especially in the city center, and looking is almost as satisfying as making a purchase. However, Milan also has many independent boutiques with a range of styles to suit all tastes. If you are looking for gifts to take home, there are some excellent *pasticcerie* (pastry shops), where you can buy authentic delicacies and traditional local confectionery. Alternatively, a cutting-edge object of design will make for an impressive souvenir of your trip to the city.

## Where to Shop

All leading fashion designers have stores in the area between Via Montenapoleone, Via della Spiga, Via Manzoni, and Via Sant'Andrea, the so-called "fashion quadrilateral."

Those interested in interior design will enjoy Via Durini, while lovers of antiques should head to Brera or the Navigli, where antiques markets are held monthly.

If time is of the essence, call ahead to check on opening hours. In Milan generally, non-food stores may be closed on Monday mornings, while food stores might be closed on Monday afternoons. The largest stores tend to stay open through the day, but sometimes a lunch break is taken. Stores are closed on Sundays, except in the city center and for the run-up to Christmas and during the main fashion shows.

## Designer Fashion

Milan is renowned as a world capital of fashion, and most national and international designers have a flagship store here. In addition to all the designers you would expect to find in a fashion center, such as **Dolce & Gabbana**, **Giorgio Armani**, **Gucci**, **Prada**, **Versace**, and **Hugo Boss**, there are many smaller designer stores. For an overview of what's new, check out the multibrand boutiques such as **Banner**, which features a selection of the best from a wide array of names. For the latest on what the younger set is wearing, go to **Amedeo D** or to the Corso di Porta Ticinese area. Up-and-coming designers are gathering in the areas around Corso Garibaldi and Corso Como. As well as of-the-moment clothes and accessories, **10 Corso Como** offers a bookstore, a record store, an art gallery, a café, and a restaurant, and even a top-class B&B.

Most of the designers carry clothes for men as well as women's apparel. Specialized men's stores include **Pal Zileri**, **Ermenegildo Zegna**, and **Corneliani**.

## Regular Clothing

Designer outlets sell samples, seconds, and last season's goods at a discount. Among Milan's longest-established outlets are **Salvagente** and **DMagazine**. Many designers also have their own outlets: fans of Max Mara, for example, should head for **Diffusione Tessile**.

Milan's main department stores are **La Rinascente** and **Coin**. The former carries many leading-edge fashion designers, while the latter features smaller fashion labels, purses, costume jewelry, and home decor items. There is more to Milan than upscale, cutting-edge designer fashion, though. For good-value casualwear for the whole family, try **Oviesse**.

Many fashion shoppers also scour the stands at the Saturday market at Viale Papiniano, at the Piazza Sant'Agostino end, which starts at 8:30am and continues until 5pm. Corso Vercelli is also recommended.

## Accessories

Purses, shoes, hats, and jewelry are also worth seeking out. Chains such as **Furla** and **Coccinelle** offer a wide array of bags, while those looking for shoes can head to **René Caovilla** for stylish heels, or purchase comfortable shoes with a twist from **Tod's** and **Hogan**. **Garlando** carries a number of classic styles in a wide array of colors and sizes, while **Ghigodonna** has elegant shoes in larger sizes. **Borsalino** is synonymous with stylish hats.

Other jewelers include **Federico Buccellati**, and **Bulgari**, in the "fashion quadrilateral," and **Mereu** in the Brera area.

## Food and Wine

Gourmands will have a great time in Milan. **Peck** consists of three floors of the best that Italy can offer, in terms of both food and wine. **Eataly** also sells high-quality Italian products as well as housing eateries and arranging gastronomic events. **Giovanni Galli Marroni e Canditi** offers a different take on chocolate-coated delicacies.

For those who like a hands-on approach to their food, **High Tech** is a gold mine for kitchen tools, including all the top names such as Alessi, as well as plates and cutlery.

## Design, Books, and Gifts

Milan is the cradle of designer furniture. A stroll down Via Durini will reveal, among others, **Cassina** and **B&B**. For lighting, see **Flos** and **Artemide**. Those interested in 20th-century design could visit **Spazio 900**.

If an item of furniture is not an option, the next best thing might be a book on design or architecture. Visit the bookstore of the **Triennale** or that of the art-catalogue publisher **Skira** for the best on the market.

**Fabriano**, the company that developed the first paper mill in the 1200s, has a store selling handsome writing paper, envelopes, and gift items.

# DIRECTORY

## Designer Fashion

**10 Corso Como**
Corso Como 10.
**Tel** 02 2900 2674.
**Tel** 02 626 163 (B&B).
**Tel** 02 2901 3581
(bar & restaurant).
**Tel** 02 653 531 (gallery).
W 10corsocomo.com

**Amedeo D**
Galleria di Corso Vercelli
23. **Tel** 02 4800 4048.
W amedeod.it

**Banner**
Via Sant'Andrea 8.
**Tel** 02 7600 4609.
W bannerboutique.it

**Corneliani**
Via Montenapoleone 26.
**Tel** 02 7631 7955.
W corneliani.com

**Dolce & Gabbana**
Via della Spiga 26
(women).
**Tel** 02 7600 1155.
Corso Venezia 15 (men).
**Tel** 02 7602 8485.
Via della Spiga 2
(women's accessories).
**Tel** 02 795 747.
Corso Venezia 7 (D&G).
**Tel** 02 7600 4091.
W dolcegabbana.it

**Ermenegildo Zegna**
Via Montenapoleone 27.
**Tel** 02 7600 6437.
W zegna.com

**Giorgio Armani**
Via Montenapoleone 2
(boutique).
**Tel** 02 7600 3234.
Via Manzoni 31 (megastore).
**Tel** 02 7231 8600.
c/o La Riascente, Piazza
del Duomo (Collezioni).
Via Sant'Andrea 9 (Armani
Casa). **Tel** 02 7626 0230.
W armani.com

**Gucci**
Via Montenapoleone 5–7.
**Tel** 02 771 271.
Galleria Vittorio Emanuele II
11 (accessories).
**Tel** 02 859 7991.
W gucci.com

**Hugo Boss**
Corso Matteotti 11 (men
and women).
**Tel** 02 7639 4667.
W hugoboss.com

**Pal Zileri**
Via Manzoni 20.
**Tel** 02 7639 4680.
W palzileri.com

**Prada**
Galleria Vittorio Emanuele
63–65. **Tel** 02 876 979.
Galleria Vittorio Emanuele
62 (men). **Tel** 02 8721 145.
Via Montenapoleone 8
(women). **Tel** 02 777 1771.
Via Montenapoleone 6
(men). **Tel** 02 7602 0273.
Corso Venezia 3. **Tel** 02
7600 1426.
Via della Spiga 18
(accessories).
**Tel** 02 780 465.
W prada.com

**Versace**
Ottagono Galleria Vittorio
Emanuele II. **Tel** 02 8901
1479. W versace.com

## Regular Clothing

**Coin**
Piazza Cinque Giornate.
**Tel** 02 5519 2083.
Corso Vercelli 30.
**Tel** 02 4399 0001.
Piazza Cantore 12.
**Tel** 02 5810 4385.
W coin.it

**Diffusione Tessile**
Galleria San Carlo 6.
**Tel** 02 7600 0829.

**DMagazine**
Via Manzoni 44.
**Tel** 02 3651 4365.

**Oviesse**
Via Dante 11.
**Tel** 02 8909 5062.
Corso Garibaldi 72.
**Tel** 02 655 1649.
Corso Buenos Aires 35.
**Tel** 02 2952 1352.
W ovs.it

**La Rinascente**
Piazza del Duomo.
**Tel** 02 88 521.
W rinascente.it

**Salvagente**
Via Fratelli Bronzetti 16.
**Tel** 02 7611 0328.
W salvagentemilano.it

## Accessories

**Borsalino**
Galleria Vittorio Emanu-
ele II 92. **Tel** 02 8901 5436.
W borsalino.com

**Bulgari**
Via Montenapoleone 2.
**Tel** 02 777 001.
W bulgari.com

**Coccinelle**
Via Bigli 28 (cnr Manzoni).
**Tel** 02 7602 8161.
Corso Buenos Aires 42.
**Tel** 02 2940 7717.

**Federico
Buccellati**
Via Montenapoleone 23.
**Tel** 02 7600 2154.
W buccellati.com

**Furla**
Piazza Duomo 31.
**Tel** 02 8909 6794.
Corso Vercelli 11.
**Tel** 02 4801 4189.
Corso Buenos Aires
(corner Via Omboni)
**Tel** 02 2043 319
W furla.com

**Garlando**
Via Madonnina 1.
**Tel** 02 874 665.
W alfonsogarlando.it

**Ghigodonna**
Viale Tunisia 2.
**Tel** 02 2940 8414.
W ghigocalzature.com

**Hogan**
Via Montenapoleone 23.
**Tel** 02 7601 1174.
W hogan.com

**Mereu**
Via Solferino 22.
**Tel** 02 653 770.
W giolinaangelo.com

**René Caovilla**
Via Bagutta 28.
**Tel** 02 7631 9049.
W renecaovilla.com

**Tod's**
Via della Spiga 22.
**Tel** 02 7600 2423.
Galleria Vittorio
Emanuele II.
**Tel** 02 877 997.
W todsgroup.com

## Food and Wine

**Eataly**
Piazza XXV Aprile 10.
**Tel** 02 4949 7301.
W eataly.net

**Giovanni Galli
Marroni e Canditi**
Via Victor Hugo 2.
**Tel** 02 8646 4833.
Corso di Porta Romana 2.
**Tel** 02 8645 3112.
W giovannigalli.com

**High Tech**
Piazza XXV Aprile 12.
**Tel** 02 624 1101.
W cargomilano.it

**Peck**
Via Spadari 9.
**Tel** 02 802 3161.
W peck.it

## Design, Books, and Gifts

**Artemide**
Corso Monforte 19.
**Tel** 02 7600 6930.
Via Manzoni 12
(showroom).
**Tel** 02 778 712 201.
W artemide.com

**B&B**
Via Durini 14.
**Tel** 02 764 4411.
W bebitalia.com

**Cassina**
Via Durini 16.
**Tel** 02 7602 0745.
W cassina.it

**Fabriano**
Via Ponte Vetero 17.
**Tel** 02 7631 8754.
W fabriano.com

**Flos**
Corso Monforte 7.
**Tel** 02 3701 1080.
W flos.it

**Skira**
Via Torino 61.
**Tel** 02 724 441.
W skira.net

**Spazio 900**
Viale Campania 51.
**Tel** 02 7012 5737.
W spazio900.com

**Triennale**
Viale Alemagna 6.
**Tel** 02 724 341.
W triennale.it

# Milan: Pinacoteca di Brera

Milan's finest art collection is held in an imposing 17th-century building, the Palazzo di Brera. This is where, in the 18th century, the Accademia di Belle Arti was founded; the picture collection developed alongside the academy. Inside the Brera hang some of the finest examples of Italian Renaissance and Baroque painting, including works by Piero della Francesca, Mantegna, Canaletto, Bellini, Raphael, Tintoretto, Veronese, and Caravaggio. The collection also includes 20th-century works by some of Italy's most famous modern artists.

**★ Dead Christ by Mantegna**
The subtle lighting and dramatic perspective of this lamentation by Mantegna (1430–1506) make it one of his greatest masterpieces.

## Gallery Guide

*The collection is displayed in 38 rooms, and was first built up by paintings from churches, later from acquisitions. Not all of it is permanently on view – this is due to restoration work and research.*

**Twin staircases** lead up to the second-floor entrance of the Pinacoteca.

**The Kiss** (1859)
Francesco Hayez's painting is one of the most reproduced works of Italian 19th-century art. Patriotic and sentimental, it became a symbol of the optimism surrounding the unification of Italy.

**The bronze statue** (1809) by Canova depicts Napoleon as a demigod with Victory wings in his hand.

### Key to Floorplan

- 15th- to 16th-century Italian painting
- 16th- to 17th-century Dutch and Flemish painting
- 17th-century Italian painting
- 18th- to 19th-century Italian painting
- 20th-century Italian painting and sculpture and Jesi Collection
- Nonexhibition space

**Works by** Rubens and Van Dyck represent some of the non-Italian artists on show.

**Mother and Son**
(1917)
The metaphysical paintings of Carlo Carrà show a dream world full of strange and obscure symbols.

**Portrait of Moïse Kisling**
Modigliani's angular portrait of 1915 reflects his interest in African sculpture.

**Twinned columns** support the arcades in the courtyard.

**The stone facade** presents a regular and slightly austere appearance.

**Madonna della Candeletta** (*c.*1490)
This painting by Carlo Crivelli was the central part of a polyptych. It is richly detailed with much distinctive ornamentation.

Main entrance from Via Brera

12
13
15
20
21
22
23
24
27

**★ The Marriage of the Virgin by Raphael**
This graceful altarpiece was painted in 1504. The circular temple is signed with the artist's name.

# Milan: Southwest of the Center

Some of Milan's finest treasures are to be found in its religious buildings; the ancient monasteries and churches make up some very fine architectural ensembles in themselves, as well as incorporating important ruins and relics dating back to Roman times. It is also in Milan that one of the most famous images in the world is to be found: Leonardo's evocative masterpiece, *The Last Supper*.

San Lorenzo Maggiore viewed from the northeast

The entrance to Sant'Ambrogio, flanked by unequal bell towers

### 🔲 Sant'Ambrogio

Piazza Sant'Ambrogio 15. **Tel** 02 86 45 08 95. Basilica: **Open** 10am–noon, 2:30–6pm Mon–Sat, 3–5pm Sun. Museum: **Open** 10am–noon, 2:30–5:30pm Mon–Sat, 3–5pm Sun. 🔲
W **basilicasantambrogio.it**

Sant'Ambrogio, or St. Ambrose, Milan's patron saint and its bishop in the 4th century, was so eloquent that bees were said to fly into his mouth, attracted by his honey tongue. This is the basilica that he began in AD 379, though today most of it is 10th-century Romanesque. A gateway leads to the bronze doors of the entrance, flanked by two bell towers. Inside, note the fine rib vaulting and pulpit, and the 9th-century altar decorated with gold, silver, and

gems. In a chapel off the south aisle, fine mosaics line a stunning cupola. In the crypt lies the tomb of Sant'Ambrogio himself.

Above the portico, a small museum contains architectural fragments, tapestries, and paintings relating to the church.

### 🔲 San Lorenzo Maggiore

Corso di Porta Ticinese 39. **Tel** 02 89 40 41 29. **Open** 8am–6:30pm Mon–Sat, 9am–7pm Sun. Cappella Sant'Aquilino: **Open** 9am– 6:30pm daily.
🔲 for the Cappella.
W **sanlorenzomaggiore.com**

This church contains a vast collection of Roman and early Christian remains. The octagonal basilica was built in the 4th century, above what was probably a Roman amphi-theater, and rebuilt in the 12th and 16th centuries.

In front of the church stands a row of 16 Roman columns and a statue of Emperor Constantine. Fine 4th-century mosaics adorn the Cappella di Sant'Aquilino, a Romanesque chapel, with two early Christian sarcophagi. Other Roman architectural elements of this church are in a chamber below the chapel.

### 🔲 Santa Maria delle Grazie

Piazza Santa Maria delle Grazie 2. **Tel** 02 46 76 111 **Open** daily. Cenacolo: **Tel** 02 92 80 03 60 (reservations required – up to 60 days in advance). **Open** 8:15am– 6:45pm Tue–Sun. **Closed** public hols. 🔲 🔲
W **cenacolovinciano.org**

This beautiful 15th-century Renaissance convent, its lovely apse and calm small cloister designed by Bramante, contains one of the key images of Western civilization: the *Cenacolo (The Last Supper)* by Leonardo da Vinci. The image captures the moment at which Christ tells his disciples that one of them will betray him. The Christ figure is unfinished: Leonardo did not consider himself worthy enough to complete it.

The artist also spurned the standard fresco technique of painting on wet plaster, and applied tempera to the dry wall. It has deteriorated badly: paint is flaking off, and restoration has proved difficult. It is now pro-tected by a filtration system.

Leonardo da Vinci's *Last Supper* (1494–7) adorning the refectory wall of Santa Maria delle Grazie

# ❹ Monza

Monza. 🚉 120,000. 🚆 🚌 ℹ️ Piazza Carducci 2 (039 32 32 22). **Open** 9am–noon, 3–6pm daily. 🛍️ Thu & Sat.

Today Monza is mostly famous for its international Formula One **Autodromo**, which lies inside a vast park that also has an elegant Rococo hunting lodge, the Villa Reale, and a golf course. At one time, however, Monza was one of the most important towns in Lombardy. Theodolinda, the 6th-century Lombard queen, built its first cathedral and bequeathed her treasure to the town.

In the center is the **Duomo**, with its notable green and white 14th-century facade and beautiful 15th-century frescoes portraying Theodolinda's life. Behind the high altar is a small Iron Crown, believed to have belonged to Emperor Constantine: it is prized for the iron strip, said to have been a nail from the cross of Christ. More local treasures in the Duomo's **Museo e Tesoro del Duomo** include a silver hen standing over seven tiny chicks (which symbolize Lombardy and its seven provinces) and a relic said to be John the Baptist's tooth.

🏛️ **Autodromo**
Parco di Monza. **Tel** 039 248 21. **Open** daily. **Closed** public hols. 🎟️ ♿ 🌐 **monzanet.it**

🏛️ **Duomo**
Piazza Duomo. **Tel** 039 32 63 83 (museum). Museo e Tesoro del Duomo: **Open** 9am–6pm daily (from 3pm Mon). 🎟️ 🌐 **museoduomomonza.it**

Leonello d'Este (c.1440) by Pisanello in the Accademia Carrara, Bergamo

# ❺ Bergamo

🚉 120,000. 🚆 🚌 ℹ️ Via Gombito 13 (035 24 22 26). **Open** 9am–5:30pm daily. 🛍️ Mon. 🌐 **visitbergamo.net**

Bergamo owes much of its artistic inspiration and architectural splendor to the influence of Venice, which ruled it from the 15th to the late 18th century. The town is divided into two distinct parts: Bergamo Alta, crowning the hill with its cluster of attractive medieval and Renaissance buildings, and the more modern Bergamo Bassa below.

The jewel of the upper town is **Piazza Vecchia**, containing one of the most appealing architectural ensembles in the region. Its buildings include the 12th-century Torre del Comune with its fine clock and curfew bell that rings daily at 10pm, the late 16th-century Biblioteca Civica, and the attractive 12th-century Palazzo della Ragione, or law courts, adorned with a bas-relief of the Lion of Venice.

The arcades of the Palazzo della Ragione lead to Piazza del Duomo, the square of the Neo-Classical Duomo. The square is dominated by the **Cappella Colleoni** (see p188), a chapel built in 1476 to house the tomb of Bergamo's famous political leader, Bartolomeo Colleoni. It is flanked by two 14th-century buildings: an octagonal baptistery and the porch leading to the Romanesque basilica of Santa Maria Maggiore. The basilica's austere exterior contrasts with its Baroque interior, which contains the tomb of Bergamoborn composer Gaetano Donizetti (1797–1848).

The collection from the **Galleria dell' Accademia Carrara**, a major picture gallery with works by Venetian masters and local artists, as well as masterpieces from the rest of Italy, is housed temporarily in **Palazzo della Ragione** while the building is being restored. It includes 15th- and 16th-century works by Pisanello, Crivelli, Mantegna, Giovanni Bellini, Botticelli, Titian, Raphael, and Perugino, and 18th-century canvases by Tiepolo, Guardi, and Canaletto, as well as paintings by Holbein, Dürer, Bruegel, and Velázquez.

🏛️ **Palazzo della Ragione**
Città Alta. **Tel** 035 39 96 77. **Open** Jun–Sep: 10am–9pm Tue–Sun (to 11pm Sat); Oct–May: 9:30am–5:30pm Tue–Fri, 10am–6pm Sat & Sun. 🎟️ ♿

Emperor Constantine

## The Edict of Milan

Milan was colonized by the Romans in 222 BC and quickly grew to be an important city at the junction of various trading routes. As the Roman Empire grew and then split in two, the emperors began to neglect Rome for the better-placed Mediolanum (literally, "city in the middle of the plain"). It was here that Emperor Constantine declared his edict of AD 313, in which Christianity was recognized as one of the permitted religions of the Empire, ending centuries of persecution. The emperor is said to have converted following a vision, but by the 4th century adopting Christianity was also one way to unite the disparate Empire.

Detail from the Cappella Colleoni

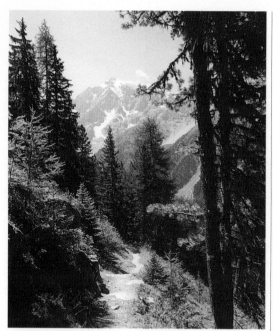

A leafy pathway through the Parco Nazionale dello Stelvio

## ❻ Parco Nazionale dello Stelvio

Trento, Bolzano, Sondrio, & Brescia. 🚌 from Bormio to Santa Caterina Valfurva & Madonna dei Monti. 🛈 Via de Simoni 42, Bormio (0342 90 08 11). 🖥 stelviopark.it

The Stelvio, Italy's largest national park, is the gateway from Lombardy to the glacier-strewn Dolomite mountains stretching into Trentino-Alto Adige. The glaciers are dotted with more than 50 lakes, and dominated by craggy peaks such as Gran Zebrù, Cevedale, and Ortles – the tallest mountain here is 12,811 ft (3,905 m).

For walkers, the area offers excellent hiking, and access to remote areas populated by ibexes, marmots, chamois, and eagles. The only real population center in the Lombardy part of the park is at **Bormio**, which boasts plenty of winter and summer sports amenities, and is a good base from which to explore the area. The town's **Giardino Botanico**, a 0.6 mile (1 km) walk from the center, displays some of the mountain plants found in the region.

### 🏵 Giardino Botanico Alpino Rezia
Via Sertorelli, Loc. Rovinaccia, Bormio. **Tel** 0342 92 73 70. **Open** Jun–Sep: daily. 🖼 🖥 ortobotanicoitalia.it

## ❼ Val Camonica

Brescia. 🚆 🚌 Capo di Ponte. 🛈 Via Briscioli 42, Capo di Ponte (0364 420 80). 🖥 proloco.capo-di-ponte.bs.it

This broad glacial valley contains an extraordinary series of prehistoric rock carvings that form an outdoor mural from the Lago d'Iseo to Capo di Ponte and beyond. The valley, a UNESCO cultural protection zone, has over 180,000 engravings from Neolithic to early Roman times; the best are in the **Parco Nazionale delle Incisioni Rupestri**. The Naquane rock is carved with nearly 1,000 figures from the Ice Age. The **Centro Camuno** focuses on the Roman settlement in the valley.

### 🏛 Parco Nazionale delle Incisioni Rupestri
Capo di Ponte. **Tel** 0364 421 40. **Open** mid-Oct–May: 8:30am–1:30pm Tue–Sun; Jun–mid-Oct 8:30am–6:30pm Tue–Sat, 8:30am–1:30pm Sun. **Closed** Jan 1, May 1, Dec 25. 🖥 parcoincisioni.capodiponte. beniculturali.it

### 🏛 Centro Camuno di Studi Preistorici
Via Marconi 7, Capo di Ponte. **Tel** 0364 420 91. **Closed** to tourists. ♿

## ❽ Lago d'Iseo

Bergamo & Brescia. 🚆 🚌 ⛴ Iseo. 🛈 Lungolago Marconi 2, Iseo (030 98 02 09). 🖥 lagodiseo.org

This glaciated lake is surrounded by tall mountains and waterfalls and boasts a mini-mountain of its own, in the form of the island of Monte Isola. Along the shores of the lake are a clutch of fishing villages such as Sale Marasino and Iseo itself. From Marone, on the east bank of the lake, a road leads to the village of **Cislano**, about 3 miles (5 km) away. Here, extraordinary spire-like rock formations rise from the ground, each spire topped by a boulder. These distinctive erosion pillars, one of the strangest natural wonders in Lombardy, are known as the "Fairies of the Forest."

Prehistoric engraving of a mounted hunter and stag in the Val Camonica

The partly Renaissance Ponte Coperto, straddling the River Ticino at Pavia

## ❾ Brescia

🏠 195,000. **FS** 🚌 **ℹ️** Via Musei 32 (030 374 96 16). 🚤 Sat.

Lombardy's second city after Milan boasts a rich artistic heritage, ranging from Roman temples to the triumphalist Mussolini-era architecture of Piazza Vittoriale. The major sights include the Roman ruins around Piazza del Foro, consisting of the **Tempio Capitolino** – a three-part temple incorporating the **Museo di Santa Giulia**, Brescia's main gallery – and a theater. The **Pinacoteca Civica Tosio Martinengo** has masterpieces by Raphael, Lorenzo Lotto, and Tintoretto; it is currently closed for restoration, but important paintings are on display at the Museo di Santa Giulia. The **Duomo** on Piazza Paolo VI, with its 11th-century core and 17th-century exterior, is another main attraction. One of the relics in the Duomo is the banner from the *Carroccio*, or sacred ox cart, which served as a symbol for the medieval Lega Lombarda. **Piazza della Loggia**, where the market is held, is named after the Renaissance loggia, built in Palladian style. The 18th-century church of San Nazaro e San Celso on Via Bronzoni contains an altarpiece by Titian.

🏛 **Tempio Capitolino**
Via Musei 57a. **Tel** 030 240 06 40. **Open** Tue–Sun. 🅿

🏛 **Museo di Santa Giulia**
Via Musei 81b.
**Tel** 030 297 78 34.
**Open** Tue–Sun. 🅿 ♿

🏛 **Pinacoteca Civica Tosio Martinengo**
Via Martinengo da Barcol.
**Tel** 030 377 49 99.
**Open** daily.

## ❿ Lodi

🏠 44,000. **FS** 🚌 **ℹ️** Piazza Broletto 4 (0371 40 92 38). 🚤 Tue, Thu, Sat, & Sun. **w** turismo.lodi.it

This is a charming medieval town of pastel-colored houses, pretty courtyards, and gardens. Just off Piazza della Vittoria, the arcaded square on which the 12th-century Duomo stands, is the fine Renaissance church of the **Incoronata**. The magnificent octagonal interior is entirely decorated with wall paintings and gilding, and crowned with a dome. One of the chapels has 15th-century works by Bergognone.

## ⓫ Pavia

🏠 71,000. **FS** 🚌 **ℹ️** Palazzo del Broletto, Piazza della Vittoria (0382 07 99 43). 🚤 Wed & Sat. **w** turismo.provincia.pv.it

During Pavia's golden age, the city was the Lombards' capital, and later witnessed coronations of Charlemagne and Frederick

The Roman Tempio Capitolino in Brescia

Barbarossa. Even after it lost its status to Milan in 1359, Pavia remained an important city, and great Romanesque churches, tall towers, and other monuments still reflect this.

As well as the Charterhouse (Certosa) *(see pp208–9)*, there is the sandstone **Basilica di San Michele** off Corso Garibaldi. The building was founded in the 7th century but largely rebuilt in the 12th. Its facade is decorated with symbols and friezes of fantastic animals, and inside there are intricate carvings on the columns; a chapel to the right of the main altar contains a 7th-century silver crucifix.

In the town center, around Piazza della Vittoria, are several ancient monuments, such as the medieval **Broletto** (town hall), with its 16th-century facade, and the **Duomo**, originally begun in 1488 and worked on in turn by Giovanni Antonio Amadeo, Leonardo, and Bramante. The dome was added in the 1880s. The 11th-century tower that stood next to it collapsed suddenly in 1989. Crossing the river is the **Ponte Coperto**, a Renaissance covered bridge with a consecrated chapel halfway along it. The bridge was rebuilt after World War II.

Pavia is also the site of one of Europe's oldest (1361) and most respected universities, now residing around a series of Neo-Classical courtyards off Strada Nuova. This road continues north to the 14th-century castle, now home to the **Museo Civico**.

Northwest of Piazza Castello is the 12th-century church **San Pietro in Ciel d'Oro**. The gilded ceiling after which it is named no longer exists, but it does still contain a magnificent shrine to St. Augustine, whose bones were allegedly brought to Pavia in the 8th century. The body of the philosopher Boëthius (*c.*480–524) is buried down in the crypt.

🏛 **Museo Civico**
Castello Visconteo, Viale XI Febbraio 35. **Tel** 0382 338 53. **Open** 10am–5:50pm Tue–Sun (Jan, Jul, Aug, & Dec: 9am–1:30pm). **Closed** public hols. 🅿 ♿ **w** museicivici.pavia.it

# ⑫ Certosa di Pavia

The Charterhouse 5 miles (8 km) north of Pavia is the pinnacle of Renaissance architecture in Lombardy, a gloriously decorated Carthusian monastery built over 200 years. Conceived as a monument to Gian Galeazzo Visconti, the Milanese ruler who founded the complex in 1396, this shrine was created by the great 15th-century craftsman Giovanni Antonio Amadeo, among others, who used innovative techniques of relief work and multicolored decoration. The Certosa is still home to Carthusian monks, who are under a strict vow of silence.

**Pietra Dura Altar**
Several of the 17th-century altars in the chapels have lavish designs worked in semiprecious stones (*pietra dura*).

## KEY

① **The side chapels** are richly decorated with marble, trompe l'oeil frescoes, and ornate altars and altarpieces.

② **The interior** of the church is largely Gothic.

③ **The grilles** date from c.1660.

④ **The choir stalls** (15th century) are deeply carved and inlaid with intricate marquetry.

⑤ **The tomb** of Gian Galeazzo Visconti (1351–1402) is in the south transept.

⑥ **The New Sacristy** is painted with colorful ceiling frescoes.

⑦ **Monk's cell**

⑧ **This delightful** arcaded Small Cloister, with fine terra-cotta ornamentation, contains a small garden, planted in formal designs.

⑨ **Main entrance** to the Certosa.

**Tomb of Ludovico il Moro and Beatrice d'Este**
This realistic marble portrait of Ludovico and his child bride was begun by Cristoforo Solari in 1497, some 11 years before Ludovico's death.

★ **Bergognone's Frescoes** (c.1488–93)
This striking portrait of Christ is one of several frescoes by Bergognone in the transept and chapels, together with an altar painting of Sant'Ambrogio.

**Great Cloister**
This huge cloister is reached through the Small Cloister. It is framed on three sides by the two-story monks' cells, each backed by a small garden. A hatch beside the door permits food to be delivered without any communication.

## VISITORS' CHECKLIST

**Practical Information**
Viale del Monumento 4, Pavia.
**Tel** 0382 92 56 13. 🚌 from Pavia & Milan. **Open** Oct–Mar: 9am–noon, 2:30–5pm Tue–Sun; Apr & Sep: 8:30am–noon, 2:30–6pm Tue–Sun (Apr: to 5:30pm). (Last adm: 30 mins before closing.) Donation to guide. 🅿 🕆 ♿ 📷

**Transportation**
🚆 Certosa. Followed by 0.5 mile (1 km) walk.

**★ Altarpiece by Perugino**
The six-panel altarpiece was painted in 1499, but now only one panel – that depicting God the Father – is original; it is flanked by two paintings by Bergognone.

**★ Renaissance Facade**
The 15th-century lower part of the facade is profusely decorated with statues and carvings of Roman emperors, saints (here St. Peter), apostles, and prophets. The upper part dates from 1500.

The Duomo on Piazza del Comune, Cremona

## ⓭ Cremona

🏛 72,000. 🚆 🚌 ℹ Piazza del Comune 5 (0372 40 63 91). 🛒 Wed & Sat. 🌐 turismo.comune.cremona.it

Cremona, a major agricultural market, is most famous for music, thanks to former inhabitants, such as the composer Claudio Monteverdi (1567–1643) and the violinmaker Stradivarius (1644–1737). The town itself is dominated by the beautiful Piazza del Comune.

The main attraction is the exuberant part-Romanesque **Duomo** and its bell tower – said to be the tallest medieval tower in Italy – known as the **Torrazzo**; the two are linked by a Renaissance loggia. The wonderful facade is dominated by the large 13th-century rose window and by a number of intricate touches, including a small portico with statues of the Virgin and saints. Inside, the Duomo is decorated with magnificent early 16th-century frescoes and Flemish tapestries, as well as paintings in the side chapels. The top of the Torrazzo offers sweeping views. Outside the Duomo, note the pulpit where itinerant preachers, including San Bernardino of Siena, spoke.

Next to the Duomo stands an octagonal 12th-century baptistery. On the other side of the piazza you can see the arcades of the late 13th-century

**Loggia dei Militi**, where the town's lords met. It is now a war memorial.

The Palazzo del Comune (town hall), rebuilt in the 1200s, is the square's other major building.

The **Museo Civico**, in a 16th-century palazzo, houses the Pinacoteca, containing paintings, wood carvings, the cathedral's treasure, and ceramics. The **Museo del Violino** has a large display of important historic instruments, including the Stradivari family collection of violins and masterpieces by Amati and Guarnieri. It also tells the history of the violin and the importance of Cremona in violin-making.

On the eastern outskirts of the town, on the road to Casalmaggiore, lies the Renaissance church of **San Sigismondo** (closed at lunchtime). It was here in a small chapel that Francesco Sforza married Bianca Visconti in 1441. The interior is decorated with 16th-century paintings, altarpieces, and frescoes by artists of the Cremona school (Campi family, Gatti, and Boccaccino).

🏛 **Torrazzo**
Piazza del Comune. **Tel** 0372 49 50 29. **Open** 10am–1pm, 2:30–6pm Tue–Sun. 🎫

🏛 **Palazzo del Comune**
Piazza del Comune. **Tel** 0372 40 72 91. **Open** 10am–5pm daily. **Closed** during meetings, public hols. ♿

🏛 **Museo Civico**
Via Ugolani Dati 4. **Tel** 0372 40 77 70. **Open** 10am–5pm Tue–Sun. **Closed** public hols. 🎫 ♿

🏛 **Museo del Violino**
Piazza Marconi 5. **Tel** 0372 80 18 01. **Open** 10am–6pm Tue–Sun. **Closed** public hols. 🎫 🌐 museodelviolino.org.

## ⓮ Sabbioneta

Mantua. 🏛 4,400. 🚌 from Mantua. ℹ Piazza d'Armi 1 (0375 520 39). 🛒 Wed am. 🎫 apply at tourist office. 🎫 🌐 iatsabbioneta.org

Sabbioneta is the result of a delightful experiment in the theory of Renaissance architecture. It was built by Vespasiano Gonzaga Colonna (1531–91) as an ideal city, and within its hexagonal walls is a perfect gridwork arrangement of streets and buildings designed on a human scale. The finest buildings include the splendid Teatro All'Antica designed by Scamozzi, the Palazzo Ducale, and the frescoed Palazzo del Giardino, which may be visited as part of a tour of the town.

### Antonio Stradivari and His Violins

The city of Cremona has been synonymous with violin-making since the 1530s, when Andrea Amati's instruments became sought after at the royal courts throughout Europe because of their superior tone to the medieval fiddle.

However, it was Antonio Stradivari, known as Stradivarius (1644–1737) – the pupil of Andrea Amati's grandson Niccolò – who raised the level of violin craftsmanship to genius. He went walking in the forests of the Dolomites in search of the perfect wood for his instruments. Stradivarius produced more than 1,100 violins in his workshop, of which more than 400 exist today. The main stopping-off points on a Stradivarius tour of Cremona are the Museo di Violino in the Museo Civico, the string collection in the Palazzo del Comune, and the great man's tombstone in the public gardens in Piazza Roma.

19th-century engraving of Antonio Stradivari

The ceiling of the Camera degli Sposi, by Mantegna, in the Palazzo Ducale

# ⑨ Mantua

🔺 49,000. **FS** 🚌 **ℹ** Piazza Andrea
Mantegna 6 (0376 43 24 32). 🏛 Thu.
**W** turismo.mantova.it

Mantua (Mantova in Italian) is
a striking place of fine squares
and aristocratic architecture,
bordered on three sides by lakes
formed by the River Mincio.
The climate can be humid as
a result, but the city makes up
for it with its cultural history: it
was the birthplace of the poet
Virgil and the playground of
the Gonzaga dukes for three
centuries. It was also the refuge
where Shakespeare sent Romeo
into exile from Verona, and the
setting for Verdi's opera *Rigoletto*.
These links are all celebrated in
street names, signposts, and
monuments around the town.
The theatrical connections are
enhanced by the 18th-century
**Teatro Accademico Bibiena**, on
Via Accademia, which Mozart's
father claimed was the finest
he had ever seen.

Mantua is focused on three
attractive main squares: Piazza
delle Erbe, Piazza Broletto,
named after the 13th-century
building adorned with a statue
of the poet Virgil, and the
cobblestone Piazza Sordello. On
one side of Piazza Sordello is the
**Duomo**, with an 18th-century
facade and fine interior stuccoes
by Giulio Romano (c.1492–1546);
on another side, the forbidding
facade of the Palazzo Bonacolsi,
with its tall prison tower. Piazza
delle Erbe is dominated by
the **Basilica di Sant'Andrea**

(15th century), designed largely
by Leon Battista Alberti, the
early Renaissance architect and
theorist, and now flanked by an
arcade of stores. The square is
also notable for the
appealing 11th-
century Rotonda
di San Lorenzo,
and the part-13th-
century Palazzo
della Ragione with
its 15th-century
clock tower.

Detail from the 15th-century clock
tower on Piazza delle Erbe

## 🏛 Palazzo
Ducale

Piazza Sordello 40. **Tel** 0376 22 48 32.
**Open** 8:15am–7:15pm (to 8:15pm Fri)
Tue–Sun. Last adm: 6pm. **Closed** Jan 1,
May 1, Dec 25. 🎫 🎫 Camera degli
Sposi: make advance reservations at
**Tel** 041 241 18 97 or
**W** ducalemantova.org

The vast, 500-room home of
the Gonzaga family covers
the northeastern corner of the
town and incorporates Castello
San Giorgio (a 14th-century
fortress), a basilica, and the
palace proper. The many works

of art include an unfinished
series of 15th-century frescoes
by Pisanello, retelling episodes
from the Arthurian legends;
a large portrait by Rubens (17th
century) of the ducal family in
the Salone degli Arcieri; and –
most absorbing of all – the
frescoes by Mantegna in the
**Camera degli Sposi** (1465–74).
These portray Lodovico
Gonzaga and members of his
family and court in all their
magnificence *(pp8–9)*. The
entire room is decorated with
images of people, animals, and
fantastic landscapes, and is
completed by a lighthearted
*trompe l'oeil* ceiling of figures,
*putti*, and a blue sky.

## 🏛 Palazzo Tè

Viale Tè. **Tel** 0376 32 32 66.
**Open** 1–6pm Mon, 9am–6pm
Tue–Sun. **Closed** Jan 1, May 1,
Dec 25. 🎫 🕿
**W** palazzote.it

At the other end
of town stands
the early 16th-
century Palazzo
Tè, built by Giulio
Romano for the
Gonzaga family
as a base from
which they could
go horseback riding. Here the
artworks conspire with the
architecture to produce striking
effects: in the **Sala dei Giganti**,
for instance, the frescoed Titans
seem to be tearing down the
very pillars of the room. Also
remarkable is the **Sala di Amore
e Psiche**, decorated with erotic
scenes from Apuleius' *Golden Ass*
and said to celebrate Federico II's
love for his mistress. Other
rooms are lavishly painted with
horses and signs of the zodiac.

The 13th-century facade of Palazzo Ducale overlooking Piazza Sordello

Late Renaissance fresco, by Romano, in the Duomo di Mantua, Mantua ▶

# VALLE D'AOSTA AND PIEDMONT

Piedmont and the neighboring Valle d'Aosta are – apart from Turin and its cultural splendors – essentially countryside. To the north lie the Alps, with ski resorts such as Courmayeur, and the wild stretches of the Parco Nazionale del Gran Paradiso. To the south lie the vineyard-clad hills around Barolo, and seemingly endless fields of grain and rice, used in the local dish, risotto.

The northwest is also rich in culture. From the 11th century to the 18th, both the verdant Valle d'Aosta and Piedmont were part of the French-speaking principality of Savoy and enjoyed the influences of both sides of the Alpine divide. Even today, French and dialectal variants are still spoken in the remote valleys of Piedmont and in much of the Valle d'Aosta. It was only under Duke Emanuele Filiberto in the 16th century that the region was brought definitively into the Italian sphere of influence, and later it was to play the key role in the Risorgimento *(see pp66–7)*, the ambitious movement that united Italy under a king from Piedmont. The vestiges of this history are to be found in the medieval castles of the Valle d'Aosta and the clusters of chapels known as *sacri monti* (sacred mountains) built into the foothills of the Alps. Piedmont also spawned a school of painting, which is in evidence in the small parish churches and excellent fine art collections in the region. The most impressive architecture in the northwest, however, is undoubtedly to be found in Turin, a much underrated and surprisingly elegant Baroque city that boasts, among other things, one of the best Egyptian museums in the world. Piedmont is also known for its industry – FIAT in Turin, Olivetti in Ivrea, Ferrero in Alba – but it has not forgotten its agricultural roots, and food and drink play an important role in the life of the region: the hills of southern Piedmont produce many of the great Italian red wines.

Traditional sidewalk café in the heart of Turin

◀ Banners hanging outside of the Gothic Duomo in Asti, Piedmont

# Exploring Valle d'Aosta and Piedmont

The vast flat plain of the Po, covered with the watery expanse of rice fields around Vercelli and Novara, eventually gives way, in the west, to the majestic heights of the Alps. Turin, the largest city in the area and the capital of Piedmont, stands at the edge of the plain, nestling almost in the shadow of the mountains. Farther northwest, attractive Alpine valleys headed by dramatic peaks provide the setting for the traditional villages, ancient towns, and castles around Aosta. The Parco Nazionale del Gran Paradiso is an unspoiled tract of breathtaking scenery.

Rice fields around Vercelli

## Sights at a Glance

1. Monte Bianco
2. Colle del Gran San Bernardo
3. Monte Cervino
4. Monte Rosa
5. Aosta
6. *Parco Nazionale del Gran Paradiso pp220–21*
7. *Ceresole Reale*
8. *Alta Val Susa*
9. *Susa*
10. *Sacra di San Michele*
11. *Avigliana*
12. *Pinerolo*
13. *Turin (Torino) pp224–9*
14. *Palazzina di Caccia Stupinigi*
15. *Basilica di Superga*
16. *Venaria Reale*
17. *Santuario d'Oropa*
18. *Domodossola*
19. *Varallo*
20. *Lago d'Orta*
21. *Novara*
22. *Vercelli*
23. *Asti*
24. *Cuneo*
25. *Bossea Caves*
26. *Garessio*

**For additional map symbols** *see back flap*

Corno Cieco
3374m
Riale
Formazza
Goglio
Baceno
Crodo
Pizzo la Scheggia
△ 2466m
Varzo
S33
Bellinzona
nanco
Craveggia
18 DOMODOSSOLA
S34
adossola
Cannobio
an Martino
naga
ella
Ornavasso
Lago di
Maggiore
nasco
Omegna
Stresa
Verbania
ALLO 19
20 LAGO D'ORTA
Scopello
Gozzano
Orta San Giulio
Arona
S299
orgosesia
Borgomanero
Varese
Valle Mosso
A26
S32
ella
S142
Gattinara
S229
Oleggio
Carpignano Sesia
Buronzo
Gallianta
A4
Milano
NOVARA 21
Trecate
Santhià
S11
Borgo
Vercelli
Vespolate
S11
no
22 VERCELLI
Desana
Stroppiana
Trino
A26
rescentino
Casale
Monferrato
nato
S31
Ottiglio
Occimiano
Po
Milano
Calliano
Vignale
Monferrato
Valenza
Montemagno
Sale
Piacenza
Pontecurone
23 ASTI
S10 Tanaro
Alessandria
Tortona
S456
Villalvernia
Agliano
S30
Nizza
Monferrato
Mombaruzzo
Novi
Ligure
San Sebastiano
Curone
a
Canelli
Cassine
A26
Bubbio
Acqui
Terme
Gavi
Arquata Scrivia
nilia
Molare
Ovada
Montaldo
di Cosola
S30
Voltaggio
Genova
vghe
Ponzone
Spigno Monferrato
zzano
0 kilometers          25
0 miles          20

vona
nasco

RESSIO

Turin, the capital of Piedmont, in the valley of the Po

## Getting Around

The Fréjus Pass and the Mont Blanc Tunnel link France with northwest Italy, while the tunnel under the Simplon or Sempione Pass provides a direct train route from Switzerland. From the rest of Italy there are excellent highway connections across the plain to Turin and up to Aosta. The region is well served with railroad links, and buses connect the main towns and outlying resorts. Getting around the mountains is more difficult, making the car the best method of transportation.

Castello di Fénis in the Valle d'Aosta

## Key

≡ Freeway
▬ Major highwaay
▬ Secondary road
⋯ Minor road
▬ Scenic route

— Main railroad line
— Minor railroad line
▬ International border
▬ Regional border
△ Summit

## ❶ Monte Bianco

Aosta. **FS** Pré-St-Didier. 🚌 Cour-mayeur. 🛈 Piazzale Monte Bianco 13, Courmayeur (0165 84 20 60).
**W** lovevda.it

Monte Bianco (Mont Blanc), the tallest mountain in the Alps at 15,780 ft (4,810 m), dominates the western Aosta valley and its attractive year-round resort, **Courmayeur**. A series of cable car rides from Entrèves, 3 miles (5 km) farther north, leads to Chamonix. Passing its highest point (12,606 ft, 3,842 m) at Aiguille du Midi, it offers a spectacular view. From Pré-St.-Didier, below Courmayeur, the **Little St. Bernard Pass**, with its small glaciers, forests, and ravines, can be explored.

## ❷ Colle del Gran San Bernardo

Aosta. **FS** 🚌 Aosta. 🛈 Strada Nazionale Gran San Bernardo 13, Etroubles (0165 785 59). **Open** daily.

The Great St. Bernard Pass is synonymous with the hardy mountain rescue dogs that have been trained locally by Catholic monks since the 11th century.

The **Monks' Hospice,** founded around 1050 by St. Bernard of Aosta, lies just over the Swiss border (bring your passport), on the shores of a lovely lake; the dogs are still being trained here. The pretty Great St. Bernard valley itself includes the town of Etroubles, set in a forest of conifers, the hamlet of St.-Oyen with its attractive parish church, and the resort of St.-Rhémy-en-Bosses.

A St. Bernard dog

🏛 **Monks' Hospice**
Colle San Bernardo, Switzerland.
**Tel** 00 41 277 87 12 36. **Open** daily.

## ❸ Monte Cervino

Aosta. **FS** 🚌 Breuil-Cervinia. 🛈 Via Circonvallazione 2, Breuil-Cervinia (0166 94 91 36).

The distinctive triangular peak of Monte Cervino (the Matterhorn) rises to 14,691 ft (4,478 m) and is easily recognizable. Below the mountain lies a scattering of attractive villages like Antey-St.-André, Valtournanche (which gave its name to the valley), and the resort of **Breuil-Cervinia**.

From Breuil a cable car rises to the Plateau Rosa (11,418 ft/3,480 m), offering dramatic views of the surrounding mountains. This entire area is a paradise for both skiers and walkers.

## ❹ Monte Rosa

Aosta. **FS** Verrès. 🚌 St.-Jacques. 🛈 Route Varasc, Champoluc/Ayas (0125 30 71 13).

Monte Rosa, Italy's second-highest mountain, overlooks the picturesque Ayas and Gressoney valleys. The rolling lower Ayas valley is dominated by the ruins of the 11th-century **Castello di Graines** and its Romanesque chapel, dedicated to St. Martin. Higher up, the resort of Champoluc has a cable car connection with the striking **Testa Grigia** (10,877 ft/3,315 m). The Gressoney valley is home to the Walser people, who speak a German dialect. At the bottom of the valley, north of Pont-St.-Martin, lies **Issime**: the 16th-century church here has a fresco of the Last Judgment on its facade.

🏠 **Castello di Graines**
Graines, Strada Statale 506.

## Medieval Castles and Forts in the Valle d'Aosta

The mountains alone provided insufficient protection to the fragmented fiefs that covered the Valle d'Aosta in the Middle Ages. The medieval lords, who ruled ruthlessly over their small domains, built castles to enforce their often fragile power. Of the many built, 70 castles survive in some form to this day. You will pass a number of them if you drive into Italy by the Mont Blanc tunnel; they stretch from Aosta to Pont-St.-Martin.

Originally, Aosta castles were designed to be defensive and threatening, such as the looming tower of **Montmayer**, perched high on a huge rock by the Valgrisenche valley. Nearby, the equally forbidding dark tower of **Ussel** throws a melancholy, brooding watchfulness over the valley.

**Fénis** and **Verrès** represent an important shift in the function of the feudal castle. Both Fénis, a splendid 14th-century showpiece (see p188), and Verrès were not just important military outposts but also examples of palatial opulence and good living. **Issogne**, too, furthered this luxurious trend with its elaborate frescoes, loggias, and fountains. Decoration

was also important to Vittorio Emanuele II, owner of **Sarre**, who turned the halls of his fortress into a plush hunting lodge. The owners of **Châtelard**, set in some of the highest vineyards in Europe, placed fine wine production alongside military aims.

The strategically sited 14th-century castle at Verrès

The 12th-century cloister, with 40 carved columns of darkened marble, in Sant'Orso

## ❺ Aosta

🗺 35,000. 🚉 🚌 ℹ️ Piazza Porta Pretoria 3 (0165 23 66 27). 🗓 Tue. 🌐 lovevda.it

Lying on a plain surrounded by dramatic mountains, the town of Aosta provides a remarkable mixture of ancient culture and spectacular scenery. The Romans captured it from the Salassian Gauls in 25 BC, and Aosta is still dotted with fine Roman architecture built in honor of Emperor Augustus – indeed the town was once called Augusta Praetoria, its name only evolving into Aosta over the centuries. The medieval town was later fortified by the Challant family and then by the Dukes of Aosta, who added towers to the old Roman walls.

Modern Aosta is a bustling intersection for local industries and tourists on their way to the mountains. The center, however, still consists of a delightful grid of large squares and surprising architectural treasures, which justify Aosta's nickname of "Rome of the Alps."

### 🏛 Roman Ruins

Roman Theater: Via Baillage. **Open** Apr–Sep: 9am–7pm daily; Mar: 9am–6pm; Oct: 9am–6:30pm; Nov–Feb: 9am–5pm. Roman Forum: Piazza Papa Giovanni XXIII. **Open** daily.

In Roman times, entry to Aosta was over the **bridge** to the east of the town (beyond the modern bridge) and through the **Arch of Augustus**. This triumphal arch is today marred by a roof added in the 18th century. Ahead stands the **Porta Pretoria**, its double row of stone arches flanked by a

medieval tower; the gateway originally stood about 8 ft (2.5 m) higher than at present. Also worth a look is the 65 ft- (20 m-) high facade of the **Roman Theater**. A little to the north is the elliptical amphitheater, although this is buried apart from three columns, which form part of the convent of San Giuseppe. In the old town, next to the cathedral, lies the **Roman Forum**, or marketplace, with its huge cryptoporticus: the function of this impressive underground gallery remains the subject of speculation.

Detail of a medieval mosaic on the floor of Aosta's Cattedrale

### 🏛 Cattedrale

Piazza Papa Giovanni XXIII. **Open** 6:30am–12:30pm & 2–7:30pm Mon–Fri, 7am–noon & 2–6pm Sat & Sun (early Sep–Easter: 6:30am–noon & 3–7pm). Museo del Tesoro: **Tel** 0165 404 13. **Open** 3–5:30pm Sat & Sun. **Closed** during religious services.

This relatively modest shrine to St. John the Baptist was first built in the 12th century, but has been altered many times since. The interior is Gothic, with finely carved 15th-century choir stalls and floor mosaics. Next door, the **Museo del Tesoro** contains a rich collection of statuettes and reliquaries, and a number of impressive medieval tombs.

### 🏛 Sant'Orso

Via Sant'Orso. **Open** daily. ♿

East of the town walls is the architectural highlight of Aosta: a medieval complex of church buildings. Sant'Orso itself has an unusual Gothic facade with a narrow, tall portal. The interior has 11th-century frescoes, a crypt holding the tomb of St. Orso, patron saint of Aosta, and a beautiful **cloister** with carved columns and capitals.

### Environs

The castle at **Fénis** (see p188), 8 miles (12 km) east, is one of the few castles in the Aosta valley with a well-preserved interior, including beautiful frescoes and wooden galleries. **Issogne**, 23 miles (38 km) south-east, is the setting for another highly decorated castle, remodeled around 1490. It has many frescoes and decorative motifs, including an octagonal fountain with a centerpiece in the shape of a pomegranate tree.

### 🏛 Castello di Fénis

Fénis. **Tel** 0165 76 42 63. **Open** daily. **Closed** Tue (Oct–Feb), Jan 1, Dec 25.

### 🏛 Castello di Issogne

Issogne. **Tel** 0125 92 93 73. **Open** daily. **Closed** Wed (Oct–Feb), Jan 1, Dec 25.

Some of the impressive ruins standing in the Roman Forum in Aosta

# ❻ Parco Nazionale del Gran Paradiso

A breathtaking wilderness of dramatic mountains and lush meadows, the Gran Paradiso is Italy's foremost national park, created in 1922 from part of a former royal hunting preserve of the House of Savoy. It is mainly a summer resort for walkers due to its unspoiled scenery, rare wildlife, and unusual Alpine flowers, though there is also cross-country skiing during the winter months. The king of the park is the ibex, a relative of the goat family all but extinct in the rest of Europe. The park is also prized by naturalists for its chamois, ptarmigan, golden eagles, rare butterflies, and marmots.

**Castello di Aymavilles**
The 18th-century core of this castle is framed by medieval corner towers.

**Val di Rhêmes-Notre-Dame**
This peaceful and broad valley offers magnificent scenery, with waterfalls and fast-flowing streams running from the glacier at its head.

## KEY

① **Goletta Waterfall** is an impressive cascade near the Lago di Goletta.

② **Cogne** is the main resort and a good base from which to explore the park. Maps of the park's routes and hiking trails are available here.

③ **Lillaz** is sedate and off the beaten track, while Valnontey and Cogne are two of the busiest resorts.

**★ Paradisia Alpine Garden**
The botanic garden contains a collection of Alpine plants, including the delicate "twinflower."

**Cascata di Lillaz**
This tall, dramatic waterfall, located a little to the east of the rustic village of Lillaz, is best observed after the spring snowmelt.

## VISITORS' CHECKLIST

**Practical Information**
Piemonte and Valle d'Aosta.
ℹ️ Segreteria Turistica, Cheriettes Aymavilles (0165 90 26 93); Centro Visitatori Parco Nazionale del Gran Paradiso, Ceresole Reale (0124 95 31 66). Paradisia Alpine Garden: Valnontey, Cogne. **Tel** 0165 753 01. **Open** mid-Jun–early Sep: 10am–5:30pm daily (Jul & Aug: to 6:30pm). 🅿️ ♿
W pngp.it W grand-paradis.it

**Transportation**
FS Aosta & Pont Canavese.
🚌 from Aosta or Pont Canavese to the different valleys.

**★ Valnontey**
This lovely valley, after which the resort is named, provides dramatic views of glaciers and easy access to various hiking trails.

**Male Ibex**
The ibex lives largely above the tree line. Groups are often seen around Col Lauson at dawn and dusk, and also around Pont in June.

**Key**

═ Main highway

0 kilometers      5
0 miles            5

The small resort of Ceresole Reale under winter snow

# ❼ Ceresole Reale

Turin. 🚌 to Ceresole Reale.
ℹ️ Palazzo Comunale, Ceresole Reale (0124 95 32 00).
🌐 **turismotorino.org**

On the southern, Piedmont side of the extensive Parco Nazionale del Gran Paradiso *(see pp220–21)* lies the small resort of Ceresole Reale. The route from Cuorgnè traverses rolling countryside and follows the S460 along a narrow gorge with a cascading stream. At **Noasca**, a spectacular waterfall may be seen high above the houses.

Ceresole Reale lies in a basin surrounded by meadows and forests of larch, and framed by mountains – the Gran Paradiso range to the north, Levanna to the southwest. The mountains are reflected in the clear waters of a spectacular artificial mountain lake, which is actually a dammed reservoir, providing energy to supply Turin with electricity. This nevertheless unspoiled corner of the country is an excellent base for walking, climbing, and hiking, and also offers amenities for skiing during the winter months.

# ❽ Alta Val Susa

Turin. 🚉 Oulx. 🚌 to Sauze d'Oulx.
ℹ️ Via Louset, Sestriere (0122 75 54 44). 🌐 **turismotorino.org**

The closest ring of mountain resorts to Turin, and as a consequence popular for weekend excursions, is also known colloquially as the Via Lattea or "Milky Way." Villages such as **Bardonecchia** and **Sauze d'Oulx** preserve traditional old stone and wood buildings that have been a feature of the region for centuries. The small church in Bardonecchia has, in addition, a fine 15th-century carved choir. In contrast, the supermodern complex at **Sestriere** was purpose-built to accommodate skiers in winter and hikers in summer.

From Bardonecchia, a chairlift operates some of the way up **Punta Colomion**, which rises immediately to the south of the resort. The summit, at 6,738 ft (2,054 m), offers fine views, and numerous hiking and walking possibilities.

# ❾ Susa

Turin. 👥 6,500. 🚉 🚌 ℹ️ Corso Inghilterra 39 (0122 62 24 47). 🛒 Tue.
🌐 **turismotorino.org**

This attractive mountain town flourished in Roman times: the **Arch of Augustus**, built in 8 BC, commemorates the alliance between the local Gaulish

The impressive part-Roman gateway, Porta Savoia, in Susa

chieftain and the Emperor Augustus. Other relics from the Roman period include two arches of an aqueduct, sections of an amphitheater, and traces of the old town walls. **Porta Savoia**, an imposing Roman gateway dating from the 4th century, was remodeled in the Middle Ages.

Most of the historic center of the town is medieval, including the castle of Countess Adelaide and the **Duomo**, both originally 11th century. The Duomo, much altered since then, houses a polyptych (c.1500) attributed to Bergognone, and a copy of a precious 14th-century Flemish triptych portraying the *Virgin and Saints*. South of the town lies the Gothic church of **San Francesco**, surrounded by an area of early medieval houses.

A street in the traditional village of Bardonecchia, in Alta Val Susa

Carved capitals on the Porta dello Zodiaco at the Sacra di San Michele

# ⑩ Sacra di San Michele

Strada Sacra San Michele. **Tel** 011 93 91 30. 🚌 May–Sep: Sun pm from Avigliana & Turin. **Open** 9:30am–noon & 2:30–6pm Tue–Sun (mid-Oct–mid-Mar: to 5pm). Call ahead to arrange group visits. 🚻 **w sacradisan michele.com**

This somewhat forbidding abbey complex is perched on a ridge halfway up Monte Pirchiriano, at 3,156 ft (962 m). Its monastic community was founded around the year 1000, possibly on the site of a previous sanctuary, though the exterior looks every bit as much a fortress as the spiritual refuge that it was for 600 years.

During its prime, the abbey attracted pilgrims on their way to Rome, and as a result it grew enormously wealthy and powerful, controlling over 100 other abbeys in Italy, France, and Spain. It was subsequently looted several times, despite being fortified, before falling into decline and eventually being suppressed in 1662.

The sanctuary is reached by climbing 154 steep steps hewn out of the rock, with wonderful views over the surrounding countryside and up to the Alps. At the very top of this stairway, known as the Scalone dei Morti (Stairway of the Dead), is the Romanesque **Porta dello Zodiaco**, a doorway carved with creatures and symbols relating to the signs of the zodiac. Beyond the doorway a few more steps lead into the church itself, which dates from the 12th–13th centuries and incorporates traces of an earlier building. The interior houses

15th- and 16th-century paintings and frescoes, and a 16th-century triptych by the Piedmontese artist Defendente Ferrari. The crypt holds tombs of the early dukes and princes of the House of Savoy-Carignano.

# ⑪ Avigliana

Turin. 🔼 12,000. 🚆 🚌 **i** Corso Laghi 389 (011 93 11 873). 🗓 Thu. **w turismoavigliana.it**

On a fine day, this small town perched beside two glacier-fed lakes and encircled by tall mountains looks breathtakingly beautiful. Avigliana is overlooked by a castle, first erected in the mid-10th century but now in ruins, which was once the home of the Counts of Savoy. Until the early 15th century the town was one of their favorite bases.

The medieval houses here are largely unspoiled, particularly in the two main piazzas, Santa Maria and Conte Rosso. Other buildings of note are the Casa della Porta Ferrata and the 15th-century Casa dei Savoia, both on Via XX Settembre. The church of San Giovanni

(13th–14th century) contains early 16th-century paintings by Defendente Ferrari.

# ⑫ Pinerolo

Turin. 🔼 36,000. 🚆 🚌 **i** Viale Giolitti 7/9 (0121 79 55 89). 🗓 Wed & Sat. **w turismotorino.org**

Pinerolo lies in an attractive setting beside hills at the confluence of the Lemina and Chisone valleys. The town was the capital of the Acaia family, a branch of the House of Savoy, and in the 14th and 15th centuries it was known for the cultural atmosphere that prevailed here under the family's patronage. However, the town enjoyed none of the stability of Turin: it was occupied by the French five times between the 15th and 18th centuries. During the 17th century the French demolished many of the town's ancient buildings in order to make Pinerolo a defensive stronghold; among the political prisoners allegedly held here was the notorious "Man in the Iron Mask." Today the town is a busy center of commerce.

A number of monumental buildings do remain, however. The **Duomo**, at the center of the town, was remodeled in Gothic style in the 15th–16th centuries and has a fine portal and an impressive bell tower. Via Principi d'Acaia climbs up to the 14th-century palace of the Princes of Acaia, and to the 15th-century church of **San Maurizio**, where the Acaia princes are buried; beside it rises a 14th-century bell tower.

The medieval arcades surrounding Piazza Conte Rosso in Avigliana

# ⑬ Turin

Mention Turin (Torino) and most people will think of industry and prosperity. It is certainly an economic powerhouse, but it is also a town of grace and charm, with superb Baroque architecture, elegant arcades of stores, and excellent museums set against the dramatic scenery of the foothills of the Alps. Turin is also, of course, home to the famous Turin Shroud, the FIAT car company, and the Juventus soccer team.

### Exploring Turin

Though settled by the Romans (**Porta Palatina** is an impressive 1st-century AD relic), and the seat of a university since the Middle Ages, Turin came into its own only after 1563, when Emanuele Filiberto of Savoy moved his capital here. Three centuries of prosperity ensued. Turin then became the base for Italy's unification movement and, from 1861 to 1865, the first capital of the newly united country. Subsequently its main power

The FIAT car factory logo

was economic. In 1899 the Agnelli family created the car company **FIAT** (Fabbrica Italiana Automobili Torino), which grew to be one of the biggest in Europe. After World War II, Turin attracted thousands of poor Italians from the south who came to work in its factories. Though there have been social conflicts and labor disputes as a result, managers and workers unite over soccer: the Juventus team is owned by the Agnelli family.

Statue of Emperor Augustus in front of the Roman Porta Palatina

### ⛪ Duomo

Via XX Settembre 87/Piazza San Giovanni. **Tel** 011 436 15 40. **Open** daily (closed 12:30–3pm). ♿

The cathedral, built in 1491–8 and dedicated to St. John the

## Turin Town Center

① Porta Palatina
② Duomo
③ San Lorenzo
④ Palazzo Reale
⑤ Armeria Reale
⑥ Palazzo Madama
⑦ Museo Egizio and Galleria Sabauda
⑧ Palazzo Carignano
⑨ Mole Antonelliana

0 meters          500

0 yards            500

**For keys to map symbols** *see back flap*

The 15th-century Duomo, with the Cappella della Sacra Sindone beyond

Baptist, is the only example of Renaissance architecture in Turin. The sober square bell tower, which pre-dates the rest of the church by 20 years, stands in refreshing contrast to Turin's sumptuous Baroque buildings; its top was designed by Filippo Juvarra in 1720. Inside, the Duomo is heavy with statuary and paintings. On the right side of the church is the **Cappella della Sacra Sindone** (Chapel of the Holy Shroud), which is incorporated into the Palazzo Reale *(see p228)*. The chapel is a remarkable feat, designed by Guarino Guarini (1624–83), with an extraordinary mesh-like cupola; the exterior view is equally eccentric.

### 🏛 Palazzo Madama
Piazza Castello 10. **Tel** 011 443 35 01.
**Open** 10am–6pm Wed–Mon ( to 7pm Sun) Last adm: 1 hour before closing.
🎟 free 1st Wed of month. 📷
🆆 palazzomadamatorino.it

Turin's main square once featured a medieval castle, which incorporated elements of the original Roman city walls. It was later enlarged and remodeled, and a new facade by Juvarra was added, requested by a royal widow, in the 18th century. The Palazzo Madama – as it was renamed – sits in the center of the square with a stately facade. The interior, with its grand staircase and second floor, both designed by Juvarra, houses the **Museo Civico d'Arte Antica**, with treasures from the Greco-Roman era to the 19th century. The display includes *Portrait of an Unknown Man* by Antonello da Messina (15th century) and reproductions of the Duc de Berry's *Book of Hours* from around 1420. Glass, jewelry, textiles, and furniture are also on display.

The facade of the Palazzo Madama, designed by Filippo Juvarra in 1718–21

Detail of the mysterious 12th-century Holy Shroud

### The Holy Shroud

The most famous – and most dubious – holy relic of them all is kept in Turin's Duomo. The Shroud, said to be the winding-sheet in which the body of Christ was wrapped after his crucifixion, owes its fame to the fact that the Shroud bears the imprint of a crucified man with a wound in his side, and bruises from what might have been a crown of thorns.

The Shroud is one of the most famous medieval relics. Its early history is unclear, but the House of Savoy was in possession of it around 1450, and had it displayed in Guarini's chapel from 1694. The "original" Shroud – which sits in a silver casket inside an iron box within a marble coffer – is not on display, though a replica is, together with a welter of scientific explanations as to the Shroud's possible origins. In 1988, however, the myth of the Shroud was exploded: a carbon-dating test showed that it dates back no farther than the 12th century. The Shroud nevertheless remains an object of religious veneration.

# Exploring Turin

Turin boasts numerous interesting museums, often housed in splendid palazzi and civic buildings. The center is fairly small, with broad, straight streets, many lined with historic cafés and stores. The Polo Reale, which includes the Palazzo Reale, Museo Archeologico, Galleria Sabauda, Biblioteca Reale, Armeria Reale, Royal Gardens, and Palazzo Chiablese, gives an insight into the importance of the House of Savoy.

Granite statue of Ramses II (13th century BC) in the Museo Egizio

### ▥ Museo Egizio
Via Accademia delle Scienze 6.
**Tel** 011 440 69 03. **Open** 9am–2pm Mon; 9am–6:30pm Tue–Sun. ▨ ⬥
W **museoegizio.it**

Turin owes its magnificent Egyptian Museum – one of the most important in the world – largely to the Piedmont-born Bernardo Drovetti, who was stationed in Egypt as French Consul General at the time of the Napoleonic Wars. It was the booty he brought back that formed the basis of this very fine collection of Egyptian artifacts.

The Egyptian Museum provides a modern, easy-to-navigate layout, virtual reconstructions, and video guides available in six languages explaining the important history of archaeological missions. The items on display are arranged in chronological order, from 4000 BC to AD 700.

The first floor hosts monumental statues in rooms decorated by the Oscar-winning set designer Dante Ferretti, plus the reconstruction of the 15th-century BC **Rock Temple of Ellesija**.

On the second floor is the Coffin Gallery, featuring fine coffins, such as the 14th-century-BC Tomb of Kha and Merit, complete with the food, tools, and ornaments buried with them for the afterlife. The Papyrus Room holds a collection of enormous interest to scholars: one document, the Royal Papyrus, lists all the pharaohs up to the 17th dynasty, with their dates. The museum holds three different versions of the *Book of the Dead*, including the oldest known copy. On the third floor are artifacts from the Old Kingdom to the New Kingdom.

Gaudenzio's *St. Peter and a Donor* (16th century), Galleria Sabauda

### ▥ Galleria Sabauda/ Polo Reale
Via XX Settembre 86. **Tel** 011 56 41 29 31. **Open** 9am–6:30pm Tue–Sun (last adm: 6pm). ▨ ⬥ W **galleria sabauda.beniculturali.it**

The collection of artworks that make up the Galleria Sabauda was started in the mid- to late 1400s, and it has been expanded over the centuries by the Savoy family. Carlo Alberto of Savoy opened it to the public and King Vittorio Emanuele II donated it to the nation.

The collection has moved a few times, arriving at the Manica Nuova of the Royal Palace in December 2014. The artworks are exhibited on four floors in chronological order, from medieval times to the 1700s, in large, bright rooms with self-explanatory paths and multimedia aids that enrich the visit.

Among works of particular interest from the Italian schools are Antonio and Piero Pollaiolo's

Detail from an 18th-dynasty papyrus *Book of the Dead*, Museo Egizio

*For hotels and restaurants in this region see pp565–9 and pp584–90*

spacious arcades on Turin's Via Roma

5th-century *Tobias and the Archangel Raphael*, the *Ritratto di Gentiluomo* by Bronzino, and a Madonna con Bambino by Beato Angelico. Bellini, Mantegna, and Veronese are among the other Italian artists represented in the Galleria. Dutch and the Flemish works include some important paintings by Jan Van Eyck, such as St. Francis (15th century), in addition to several portraits by Van Dyck.

The fourth floor is home to the Gualino Collection, which contains archaeological finds from the Roman era, Oriental works of art, and a *Venere* (Venus) by Botticelli.

### 🏛 Palazzo Carignano

Via Accademia delle Scienze 5.
Tel 011 562 11 47. **Open** 10am–6pm
Tue–Sun (last adm: 5pm). 🚫 ♿
W museorisorgimentotorino.it

This Baroque palazzo is not only Guarini's masterpiece; it is arguably the finest building in Turin, with its magnificent brick facade and ornate rotunda. It was built in 1679 for the Carignano family – an offshoot of the main House of Savoy and ancestors of the Italian kings – but came into its own in the 1800s. The first king of Italy, Vittorio Emanuele II, was born here in 1820. After Italy was unified in 1861 by a series of referenda, the former royal residence was used as the first national parliament building.

The palazzo is home to the Museo Nazionale del Risorgimento Italiano, which, through paintings and a collection of artifacts tells the story of unification. It introduces Mazzini, Cavour, and Garibaldi – key figures in the Risorgimento (*see pp66–7*).

### 🚇 Via Roma

Running through the historic center, Turin's main street Via Roma leads from Piazza Castello (north) through Piazza San Carlo to the distinctive arched facade of Stazione Porta Nuova (south). Via Roma is a magnificent concourse lined with stylish stores and shaded arcades, interrupted only by cobblestone squares. A grid pattern of side streets branches off either side of Via Roma, revealing additional shopping arcades.

### 🚇 Piazza San Carlo

The ensemble of Baroque architecture on this square, now a pedestrian-only area, has earned it the nickname "Turin's drawing room." At its southern end are the twin churches of Santa Cristina and San Carlo; both were built in the 1630s, though Santa Cristina has a Baroque facade, crowned with statues, which was designed by Juvarra in the early 18th century.

At the center of the square stands a 19th-century statue of Duke Emanuele Filiberto, by Carlo Marocchetti, which has become an emblem of the city.

At the corners of the square, frescoes depict the Holy Shroud. The Galleria San Federico, on the northwestern corner, is a stylish shopping arcade.

Piazza San Carlo is known for its society cafés. In one such establishment, in 1786, Antonio Benedetto Carpano invented vermouth, a drink that is still very popular all over Italy today.

### 🏛 Pinacoteca Giovanni e Marella Agnelli

Lingotto, Via Nizza 230/130. **Tel** 011
0062 713. **Open** 10am–7pm Tue–Sun
(last adm: 6:15pm). 🚫 🅿 ♿ 🔲 ∅
W pinacoteca-agnelli.it

Located on the roof of the former FIAT factory, redesigned by architect Renzo Piano, this museum displays art dating from the 18th to 20th centuries, including Manet, Picasso, Matisse, and Modigliani, as well as two statues by Canova.

### 🌳 Parco del Valentino

Corso Massimo d'Azeglio. **Open** daily.
Borgo Medioevale: Viale Virgilio 107.
**Tel** 011 443 17 01/02. **Open** Borgo:
9am–7pm daily (to 8pm Apr–Oct);
Castle: 10am–6pm Tue–Sun. Orto
Botanico: **Tel** 011 670 59 80 or 338 958
15 69. **Open** mid-Apr–mid-Oct: 9am–
noon Mon–Fri, 3–7pm Sat, 10am–1pm
& 3–7pm Sun. 🚫 ♿
W parcovalentino.it

This park contains the Borgo Medioevale, a complex of medieval-style buildings from the 1884 General Italian exhibition. They show traditional architecture of the region.

The Orto Botanico, beside the medieval complex, is an impressive botanical garden.

Looking south across the elegant Piazza San Carlo, "Turin's drawing room"

# Turin: Symbols of the City

Turin's architecture mirrors the city's transition from monarchic power to industrial power. Witness the ostentation of the Baroque apartments of the Savoy family in Palazzo Reale, and contrast them with the futuristic Mole Antonelliana, a tall structure that heralded the dawn of the modern industrial age. Much of Turin's history in the 20th century has been dominated by the automobile: FIAT is synonymous with Turin. For the curious, the city's extensive motor museum is worth a visit, since it maps out the history of Italian car design.

The 19th-century tower, Mole Antonelliana, dominating Turin

### 🎞 Mole Antonelliana/Museo del Cinema

Via Montebello 20. **Tel** 011 813 85 60/61. Panoramic elevator: **Open** 9am–8pm Wed–Mon (to 11pm Sat).
🎞 Museo del Cinema. **Open** 9am–8pm Wed–Mon (to 11pm Sat) (last adm: 1 hr before closing). 🅿 ♿
**W** museocinema.it

The Turin equivalent of the Eiffel Tower in Paris, this unmissably tall landmark is a signature for the city. It looks like a glorified lightning conductor: indeed in 1953 an electric storm struck down the top 155 ft (47 m), later replaced. The 550 ft (167 m) Mole, by Alessandro Antonelli (1798–1888), was meant to be a synagogue. Upon completion in 1889, it was left without a proper use for years. Eventually, it housed the Risorgimento museum. The Mole ("massive structure") – for a time Europe's tallest brick building – provides panoramic views and houses the National Cinema Museum.

*The interior of San Lorenzo's dome*

### 🏛 Palazzo Reale/Polo Reale

Piazzetta Reale. **Tel** 011 436 14 55.
**Open** 8:30am–7:30pm Tue–Sun (last adm: 6:20pm). ♿ (free 1st Sun of month) 🎫 🅿
**W** poloreale.beniculturali.it

This palace was the seat of the Savoy royal family from 1660 until the unification of Italy in 1861. Behind the austere facade, designed by Amedeo di Castellamonte, lie richly decorated state apartments with ceilings painted by Morello, Miel, and Seyter in the 17th century. Splendid furnishings, tapestries, and ornaments date from the 17th to the 19th centuries; they include the elaborate Chinese Cabinet, the Alcove Room, the lavishly decorated Throne Room, and the innovative Scala delle Forbici, or Scissor Stairs, created by Juvarra in 1720. Behind the palace are extensive gardens designed by André le Nôtre.

To the left of the main entrance **San Lorenzo** is a fine Baroque church, begun in 1634, by Guarino Guarini, its ornate interior boasting another of his extraordinary, geometric domes.

### ⚔ Armeria Reale/Polo Reale

Piazzetta Reale. **Tel** 011 436 14 55.
**Open** 9am–6:30pm Tue–Sun (last adm: 30 mins before closing).
**Closed** Jan 1, Dec 25. 🅿 ♿
**W** poloreale-beniculturali.it

One wing of the Palazzo Reale, on the northern side of the main square, provides the splendid setting for one of the most extensive and breathtaking collections of arms and armory in the world.

Opened to the public in 1832, the armory originally belonged to the House of Savoy. The fine rooms, such as the splendid Galleria Beaumont, designed by Juvarra in 1733, hold treasures ranging from Roman and Etruscan times to the 1800s. The collection has magnificent medieval and Renaissance items from some of the world's greatest armorers and gunsmiths, including a pistol that belonged to Emperor Charles V. One section is devoted largely to Oriental arms and armor.

The Royal Library contains a collection of drawings, including a self-portrait by Leonardo da Vinci on display during special exhibitions only.

### Environs

About 3 miles (5 km) out of the city center is the vast **MAUTO – Museo Nazionale dell'Automobile di Torino**.

A lavishly decorated gallery in the 17th-century Palazzo Reale, a royal residence until unification

*For hotels and restaurants in this region see pp565–9 and pp584–90*

Founded in 1932, and renovated in 2013 by architect Cino Zucchi, MAUTO is a pioneer in exhibiting cars. Its collection of 200 vehicles includes FIATs, Bugattis, Maseratis, Lancias, and some fine foreign cars. The first gas-driven car made in Italy (1896) is here, as are the first FIAT (1899) and the 1929 Isotta Fraschini *coupé de ville* used by Gloria Swanson in the movie *Sunset Boulevard*. Note that many of the sports cars from the 1950s are right-hand drive, in deference to great British brands such as Aston Martin.

Designs from 1949 for the Ferrari 166 MM

### 🏛 MAUTO – Museo Nazionale dell'Automobile di Torino

Corso Unità d'Italia 40. **Tel** 011 67 76 66. **Open** 10am–7pm daily (to 9pm Fri & Sat; am only Mon, pm only Tue). ♿ 🅆 museoauto.it

An interior view of the 18th-century Palazzina di Caccia di Stupinigi

### 🔟 Palazzina di Caccia di Stupinigi

Piazza Principe Amedeo 7, Stupinigi, about 8 miles (13 km) from city center. **Tel** 011 358 12 20. 🚌 4 from Porta Nuova train station to Piazza Caio Mario, then 41. **Open** Tue–Sun. ♿ 📷♿🅆 ordinemauriziano.it

In 1729–30 the architect Filippo Juvarra (1676–1736) designed a magnificent hunting lodge at Stupinigi, 5 miles (9 km) southwest of Turin. Known as the Palazzina di Caccia di

Stupinigi, the building was created for Duke Vittorio Amedeo II of Savoy and is one of the very finest hunting lodges, built on an impressive scale, reminiscent of the palace of Versailles in France.

The dynamic and complex plan incorporates semicircles and an octagon, with the main block consisting of a dome rising above a circular building from which wings jut out, not unlike the sails of a windmill.

The mass of the central section is lightened by balustrading topped with urns and figures, while the dome is crowned with an 18th-century bronze figure of a stag.

The huge interior includes rooms sumptuously decorated with *trompe l'oeil* paintings and frescoes on a hunting theme – the 18th-century *Triumph of Diana*, for instance, in the main *salone*. About 40 of those rooms house the interesting **Museo d'Arte e di Ammobiliamento**, specializing in 17th- and 18th-century furniture and furnishings. Many of the ornate items on display in these rooms were originally kept in other former royal residences.

Outside, extensive grounds feature spectacular broad avenues, parkland, and colorful formal parterres.

### 🔟 Basilica di Superga

Strada Basilica di Superga 73, about 6 miles (10 km) from city center. 🚌 15, 61, 68, or Sassi-Superga Rack Tramway from Piazzale Modena. **Open** daily. **Closed** Sep 8. Royal Tombs & Royal Apartment: **Tel** 011 899 74 56. **Open** Mar–Oct: Thu–Tue; Nov–Jan: Sat, Sun, & Dec 25–Jan 6; Feb: Sun & hols. **Closed** public hols. 🅆 basilicadisuperga.com

On a hill to the east of Turin stands the superb Baroque Basilica of Superga, built by Juvarra in 1717–31. The commission came from Duke Vittorio Amedeo II, in fulfillment of a vow made to the Virgin Mary in 1706 while the French were besieging the duke and his army in Turin.

The beautiful yellow and white facade is dominated by a large portico designed like a Classical temple, with a 213-ft- (65-m-) high dome immediately beyond. It is flanked by twin bell towers. The magnificently decorated interior contains fine paintings and carvings.

Beneath the Basilica lies the great mausoleum housing the tombs of the Savoy royal family from the 18th and 19th centuries. The victims of a 1949 aircrash here, including the Turin soccer team, are commemorated on a plaque behind the Basilica.

Another benefit of visiting the Basilica is seeing the views over Turin.

The imposing facade of the 18th-century Baroque Basilica di Superga designed by Filippo Juvarra

The 17th-century Basilica dell'Assunta dominating Sacro Monte, Varallo

## ❶ Venaria Reale

Piazza della Repubblica 4. **Tel** 011 499 23 33. **FS** **Open** palace: 9am–5pm Tue–Fri; 9am–7pm Sat & Sun; garden: 9am–dusk. **W** **lavenaria.it**

This grandiose complex dates from the mid-17th century, when Charles Emanuel II of Savoy decided to build a royal hunting lodge on the site of the existing town of Altessano Superiore. Venaria Reale incorporates the **Reggia di Diana**, a formal palace and garden built between 1660 and 1671, as well as **La Mandria**, the 12-sq-mile (30-sq-km) park surrounding it.

Venaria's historical center was designed by Amedeo di Castellamonte between 1667 and 1690; its focal point is the Piazza dell'Annunziata, with statues depicting the Angel Gabriel and the Virgin Mary.

## ❷ Santuario d'Oropa

Via Santuario d'Oropa 480, Comune di Biella. **Tel** 015 255 512 00. **FS** Biella. from Biella. **Basilica Antica: Open** 7:30am–7pm daily. Basilica Superiore: **Open** 8:30am–4:30pm (Jun–Sep: to 6:30pm) daily. **W** **santuariodioropa.it**

Perched above the wool town of Biella stands this tranquil church and hospice complex, a series of three squares surrounded by pale buildings with stone-shingled roofs, cut into the hillside. The sanctuary was founded in the 4th century by Sant'-Eusebio, Bishop of Vercelli. It was intended as a hospice for the poor, and to honor the "Black Madonna," which he had brought back from the Holy Land. The Madonna, said to be the work of St. Luke, is the object of some of the region's most important pilgrimages.

The statue of the Madonna is kept in the restored **Basilica Antica** (Old Church). Beyond it, at the top of the complex, is the imposing Neo-Classical **Basilica Superiore** (Upper Church), which was begun in 1885 but completed only in 1960.

## ❸ Domodossola

Verbania. 19,000. **FS** Stazione entrance, Piazza Matteotti 24 (0324 24 82 65). Sat. **W** **prodomodossola.it**

At the center of this pretty mountain town of Roman origin lies the **Piazza Mercato**, or market square, framed by attractive arcades and houses from the 15th and 16th centuries. The Ossola valley, where the town lies, sits in an Alpine landscape of pasture and forest sliced by rivers and streams. Pretty villages north of the town include **Crodo**, with its cold-water mineral spas, and **Baceno**, where the 14th- to 16th-century church contains fine frescoes and wood carvings.

## ❹ Varallo

Vercelli. 7,500. **FS** **i** Corso Roma 38 (0163 56 44 04). Tue. **W** **atlvalsesiavercelli.it**

The small town and tourist resort of Varallo lies halfway up the attractive Sesia valley, and boasts a remarkable church, **Santa Maria delle Grazie**. The late 15th-century church is notable for its beautiful frescoed wall depicting the Life of Christ and trompe l'oeil architectural elements; the paintings are the work of Gaudenzio Ferrari (1484–1546).

A long stairway behind the church (and also a cableway) climbs up to the extraordinary **Sacro Monte**, a religious community built at an altitude of about 2,000 ft (610 m). This "Sacred Mount" was founded as a sanctuary of the New Jerusalem in 1486 under the patronage of the Archbishop of Milan, San Carlo Borromeo.

The Basilica dell'Assunta, with a 19th-century facade, is set in a tranquil courtyard with palm trees and a fountain; the interior is a riot of ornate Baroque architecture. Dotted around it are over 40 chapels representing the sacred sites of Jerusalem, with statues and painted figures positioned in front of frescoed backdrops painted by Gaudenzio Ferrari, Tanzio da Varallo, and others.

*Christ Condemned* (16th century) in a chapel at Varallo's Sacro Monte

The interior of the church of San Giulio in the center of Lago d'Orta

## ⓴ Lago d'Orta

Novara. 🚈 🚌 ⛴ Orta. 🛈 Via Panoramica, Orta San Giulio (0322 90 51 63). 🌐 **distrettolaghi.it**

Lago d'Orta is one of Italy's least-visited lakes – unjustly, as it is delightfully set among the foothills of the Alps.

The lake's main resort is **Orta San Giulio**, a small town containing handsome palazzi, and houses decorated with wrought-iron balconies. In the lakeside **Piazza Principale** stands the Palazzo della Comunità, a frescoed building of 1582 resting on arcades. A cobblestone pathway leads up to the 15th-century church of **Santa Maria Assunta** (rebuilt in the 17th century), with a Romanesque doorway and an interior that is richly decorated with 17th-century frescoes and paintings.

Above Orta San Giulio is the sanctuary of **Sacro Monte**, a UNESCO World Heritage Site built from 1591 to 1770 and dedicated to St. Francis of Assisi. A winding path, offering lovely views of the lake, climbs to the church. The path is lined by 21 chapels, most of them Baroque, in which frescoes and life-size figure groups by various artists depict scenes from the life of St. Francis.

In the center of the lake rises the picturesque **Isola San Giulio**. The island was said to have been liberated from snakes and monsters by the 4th-century Christian preacher Julius, from whom the island's name derives. The basilica here is notable for its 12th-century black marble pulpit and for the 15th-century frescoes – including one attributed to Gaudenzio Ferrari, of the *Virgin and Child Enthroned*.

Fresco detail of a horseman (17th century) by Morazzone in San Gaudenzio, Novara

## ㉑ Novara

🏛 105,000. 🚈 🚌 🛈 Baluardo Quintino Sella 40 (0321 39 40 59). 🛒 Mon, Thu, & Sat. 🌐 **turismonovara.it**

Novara has distant origins as the Roman city of Nubliaria – meaning "surrounded in mist." Nowadays its delightful arcaded streets and squares, and historic buildings, exude a quiet affluence. Many of the most important buildings stand around Piazza della Repubblica. They include the beautiful Renaissance courtyard of the **Broletto** (town hall), with its graceful 15th-century red-brick arcades and covered stairway.

Across the piazza is the **Duomo**, rebuilt by the architect Alessandro Antonelli in around 1865 in Neo-Classical style, with a huge central doorway. The interior contains Renaissance paintings of the Vercelli school and Flemish tapestries, as well as the remains of an earlier sanctuary on this site: these include the frescoed 12th-century chapel of San Siro and the 15th-century cloisters. The octagonal **Baptistery** next door dates in part from the 5th century and is painted with medieval scenes of the Apocalypse. The **Museo della Canonica del Duomo** beside the Duomo has tombstones and inscriptions from the Roman and early Christian eras.

A few streets away stands the **Basilica di San Gaudenzio**. It is strikingly crowned by an elongated four-tiered dome and spire. Designed by Antonelli, it is reminiscent of his Mole Antonelliana in Turin *(see p228)*. Atop the spire, which is 400 ft (121 m) high, is a statue of San Gaudenzio. Inside, the late 16th-century church has a fine collection of Renaissance and Baroque paintings by artists from Piedmont. These include a notable 17th-century battle scene by Tanzio da Varallo, a 16th-century altarpiece by Gaudenzio Ferrari, and a fresco painting by Pier Francesco Morazzone (*c.*1572–1626).

🏠 **Baptistery**
Piazza della Repubblica. **Tel** 0321 66 16 35. **Open** 9:30am–noon & 3–5:30pm Sat & Sun.

🏛 **Museo della Canonica del Duomo**
Vicolo della Canonica 9. **Tel** 331 16 59 568. **Open** 3–6pm Sat & Sun.
🌐 **novarlae.it**

View across Lago d'Orta to the Isola San Giulio

## ㉒ Vercelli

🏙 47,000. 🚋 🚌 ℹ️ Viale Garibaldi 90 (0161 58 002). 🛒 Tue & Fri.
🌐 atlvalsesiavercelli.it

Vercelli is the rice capital of Europe, set in a vast plain of paddy fields that create the appearance of shimmering sheets of water stretching far into the distance. Vercelli also developed its own school of painting in the 16th century, and has one major architectural treasure, the 13th-century **Basilica di Sant'Andrea**.

The Basilica, standing just across from the train station, is famous as the first example of Italian architecture to be influenced by the Gothic style of northern France – note the beautiful vaulted nave and the flying buttresses, typical Gothic elements. Overall, however, the Basilica remains a stunning achievement in Romanesque architecture, built from 1219 to 1227 as part of an abbey for the papal legate Cardinal Guala Bicheri. The facade, curiously, changes color halfway up, the blue-gray of the lower part turning to red and white in the twin towers; these are linked by a double arcade. A carving attributed to Antelami (12th century) adorns the central lunette.

The three-aisled interior is gently illuminated through rose windows. The muted decoration is largely focused on the vaulting, which is supported by tall, slender shafts. Off the north side is the simple 13th-century cloister, beautifully framed by arcades rising from clustered columns.

Vercelli's other important historic buildings include the imposing 16th-century **Duomo**, the church of **San Cristoforo**, with frescoes and a fine Madonna degli Aranci (both c.1529) painted by Gaudenzio Ferrari, and the **Piazza Cavour** with its medieval arcades. The **Museo Borgogna** is the best place to admire the masterpieces of the Vercelli school. The main shopping street, Corso Libertà, has a handful of attractive 15th-century houses and courtyards.

🏛 **Museo Borgogna**
Via A. Borgogna 4/6. **Tel** 0161 25 27 76. **Open** Tue–Fri pm, Sat am (Mar–mid-May also pm), Sun am & pm. **Closed** Jan 1, Aug 15, Nov 1, Dec 25. 🎫 📷
🌐 museoborgogna.it

The 13th-century cloisters of the Basilica di Sant'Andrea in Vercelli

## ㉓ Asti

🏙 77,000. 🚋 🚌 ℹ️ Piazza Alfieri 34 (0141 53 03 57). 🛒 Wed & Sat.
🌐 astiturismo.it

Renowned for its *spumante* (sparkling) wine, Asti is at the center of Italy's most prestigious wine region *(see pp186–7)* and is

Detail of the carving on the 15th-century porch at the entrance to the Duomo in Asti

also a tranquil and noble city of medieval towers, elegant churches, and warm red roofs.

Just north of the main train station lies the Piazza del Campo del Palio, the largest square in Asti and formerly the site of its annual horse race, now in Piazza Alfieri. The race, held on the third Sunday of September to coincide with the local wine fair, rivals the Palio in Siena *(see p345)* for outrageous horsemanship and medieval pageantry.

Beyond this square lies the triangular-shaped **Piazza Alfieri**. A statue here commemorates the local poet and dramatist Vittorio Alfieri (1749–1803), in whose honor both this square and the main street were renamed.

Corso Alfieri runs the entire length of the old city center. At its eastern end stands the 15th-century church of **San Pietro in Consavia**, with its terra-cotta decoration, 17th-century frescoes, and attractive cloister. Beside it is the circular Romanesque **baptistery** which dates from the 10th–12th centuries; it was once the church of the Knights of the Order of St. John of Jerusalem, who had their headquarters here.

West of Piazza Alfieri is the **Collegiata di San Secondo** (13th–15th century), named after Asti's patron saint, which houses a Renaissance polyptych by Gandolfino d'Asti and 15th-century frescoes. The area around the western section of Corso Alfieri contains a few of the medieval towers for which the town was once famous; they include the Torre dei Comentini, the very elegant

The watery expanses of the rice fields around Vercelli

orre Troyana, and, at the far
nd, the Torre Ropa. This was
uilt on the ruins of a tower
 which San Secondo, a
oman soldier, was held.
he nearby 14th-century
othic **Duomo** has a 15th-
entury porch and, inside,
8th-century frescoes and
wo 12th- to 13th-century
arvings on the west corner
f the transept.

## Cuneo

55,000. FS 🚌 ℹ️ Via Amedeo II
a (0171 69 02 17). 🔺 Tue.
🌐 cuneoholiday.com

*uneo* in Italian means "wedge-
haped," and this perfectly
escribes the sliver of land
hat the town occupies at the
onfluence of two rivers, the
iesso and the Stura di
Demonte. In early November
he town hosts the regional
heese fair, with unusual local
heese varieties.

The town centers on a large
quare, **Piazza Galimberti**, with
ts old arcades, where the traders
ome to hawk their wares every
uesday. Much of the town was
ebuilt in the 18th and 19th
enturies, providing Cuneo with
vide, tree-lined boulevards,
hough the impressive viaduct
hat takes the railroad track into
own dates from the 1930s. The
leconsecrated 13th-century
hurch of **San Francesco** has
 fine 15th-century portal. The

Market day in the enormous Piazza Galimberti at the
center of Cuneo

18th-century church of **Santa
Croce** has a concave facade by
Francesco Gallo.

Cuneo is a good base for exploring the pretty local valleys,
such as the Valle Stura, where
rare flowers grow.

## Bossea Caves

Località Bossea, Comune Frabosa
Soprana. **Tel** 0174 34 92 40.
FS Mondovì. 🚌 from Mondovì.
**Open** daily for guided tours only. 📷
🌐 grottadibossea.com

Some 16 miles (25 km) south
of Mondovì, near the end of a
scenic route that follows the
valley of the Torrente Corsaglia
up into the Maritime Alps, are
the caves of Bossea, some of
the finest in Italy. The series of
caves contains remarkable
stalactite columns
and shapes that
have formed over
many hundreds of
thousands of years.
Guided tours lead
through different
chambers – some of
them surprisingly
vast – following the
underground rivers
and lakes. The
skeleton of a pre-
historic bear, *Ursus
spelaeus*, which was
discovered here, is
also on display.

Bring a sweater –
the temperature
rarely rises above
50°F (9°C).

The Castello di Casotto in the hills above the resort of Garessio

## Garessio

Cuneo. 🏔️ 3,400. FS 🚌 ℹ️ Corso
Statuto 1 (0174 80 31 45). 🔺 Fri.
🌐 garessio.net

One of the prettier resorts of the
Maritime Alps, Garessio is just a
sprinkling of houses spread out
over the hills, surrounded by
woods of chestnut trees. It is
also a popular spa.

According to legend, the
waters here have miraculous
powers: in about AD 980 an
octogenarian nobleman found
instant relief from his kidney
and circulatory problems by
drinking the mineral-rich water.
Since then, the waters have
been drunk for their remedial
properties – linked in particular
with the relief of diuretic and
digestive problems – and for
their refreshing taste.

### Environs

About 6 miles (10 km) west of
Garessio stands the **Castello di
Casotto**, the dramatically sited
summer palace used by the
House of Savoy. The royal family
used to come here to enjoy
the local mineral water, the
attractive scenery and the
exceptionally pure air of the hills.

The town of **Ormea**, 7 miles
(12 km) southwest, is interesting
for its ruined 11th-century
castle, its church with late
14th-century Gothic frescoes,
and its attractive houses.

🏰 **Castello di Casotto**
Garessio. **Tel** 0174 81 409. **Open** call
ahead for opening times. 📷

# LIGURIA

Liguria is a long, thin coastal strip nestling at the foot of pine-covered mountains. Here pastel-colored houses bask in the Mediterranean sun, while their gardens, flourishing in the mild climate, are a riot of colorful plants. In contrast with resorts like Portofino and even Sanremo, the bustling city of Genoa, for centuries a trading port of immense power, is the only major population center.

Genoa has a long history as a seafaring power, achieving greatness first as a trading post with ancient Greece and Phoenicia, and later as the capital of a small commercial empire that at one stage eclipsed even Venice. The great sea admiral Andrea Doria came from Genoa, as did the 15th-century explorer of the Americas, Christopher Columbus.

Genoa's rise began in the 12th century, when it succeeded in beating the Saracen pirates who plagued the Ligurian coast. Thereafter, the maritime republic prospered, profiting from the Crusades to set up trading posts in the Middle East and marshaling its naval might to humble its rivals. The golden age lasted from the 16th to the mid-17th century, and included the glorious reign of Andrea Doria, who enriched the city by financing the wars of Genoa's European allies through the offices of the city's bank. Factionalism among the ruling aristocracy, however, and foreign conquest, by the French in 1668 and the Austrians in 1734, led to the region's decline. It was only in the early 19th century, with unification fervor spreading thanks to native son Giuseppe Mazzini and the revolutionary Garibaldi, that Liguria ever recaptured a glimpse of its former prominence. Today, sheltered by the steep slopes that rise from the sea, faded, elegant mansions lie along the coast, particularly in Sanremo, where aristocrats came to spend the winter at the end of the 19th century.

Green shutters and rich ocher walls characterize the houses of Portofino

◀ The sunlit harbor of Riomaggiore, one of the Cinque Terre

# Exploring Liguria

Liguria divides neatly into two parts. The western coastline, known as the Riviera di Ponente, is a thin strip of coastal plain stretching across to the French border, while the eastern coastline, or Riviera di Levante, is more rugged and picturesque, descending directly into the sea. Between the two lengths of coast lies the region's capital and biggest port, Genoa (Genova). The faded elegance of the tranquil coastal villages contrasts with this cramped and busy port that snakes along the coast, hemmed in between the sea and the mountains rising steeply behind it.

Stag motif of the city of Cervo, above the cathedral doors

Genoese street market selling fruit and vegetables

### Sights at a Glance

1. Balzi Rossi
2. Villa Hanbury
3. Dolceacqua
4. Sanremo
5. Bussana Vecchia
6. Cervo
7. Albenga
8. Grotte di Toirano
9. *Genoa (Genova) pp240–43*
10. Camogli
11. Portofino Peninsula
12. Rapallo
13. Cinque Terre
14. Portovenere
15. Lerici

### Key

━━━ Freeway
━━━ Major highway
──── Secondary road
···· Minor road
──── Scenic route
━··━ Main railroad line
──── Minor railroad line
▦▦▦▦ International border
──── Regional border
△ Summit

**For additional map symbols** *see back flap*

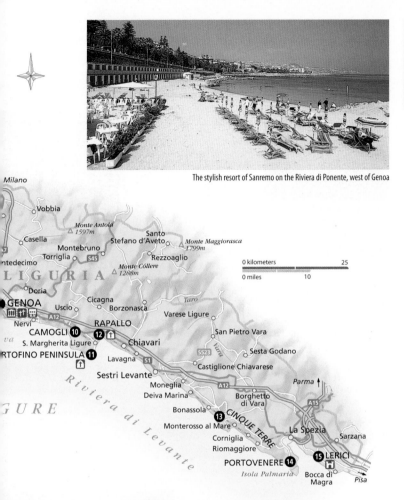

The stylish resort of Sanremo on the Riviera di Ponente, west of Genoa

*Milano*

Vobbia

Casella

Montebruno

Torriglia

*Monte Antola*
△ *1597m*

Santo
Stefano d'Aveto

*Monte Maggiorasca*
△ *1799m*

Rezzoaglio

ntedecimo

**L I G U R I A**

*Monte Còllere*
△ *1288m*

Doria

Cicagna

Uscio

Borzonasca

**GENOA**

Nervi

**A12**

**RAPALLO**

**CAMOGLI** 10

12

S. Margherita Ligure

Varese Ligure

San Pietro Vara

**RTOFINO PENINSULA** 11

Chiavari

*Taro*

Sesta Godano

**S523**

Lavagna

**S1**

Castiglione Chiavarese

**A12**

Sestri Levante

Moneglia

Deiva Marina

Borghetto
di Vara

*Parma* ↑

**A15**

*Riviera*

Bonassola

13

**CINQUE TERRE**

**G U R E**

Monterosso al Mare

*di*

Corniglia

Riomaggiore

La Spezia

Sarzana

**PORTOVENERE** 14

15 **LERICI**

*Isola Palmaria*

*Levante*

Bocca di
Magra

*Pisa* →

0 kilometers 25

0 miles 10

ouses wedged into the cliffs in Riomaggiore, Cinque Terre

## Getting Around

If you keep to the coast, transportation in Liguria is straightforward. Both the A10–E80 freeway (becoming the A12–E80 at Genoa) and a major railroad track hug the shore from the French border to Tuscany. The main stations along the route are at Ventimiglia, Sanremo, Imperia, Savona, Genoa, and La Spezia. There are good road and railroad links between Genoa and Milan and Turin. Access to inland Liguria is harder because of the mountains. Bus services link many of the coastal towns with the prettiest hill villages. You can explore some of the countryside by car by following the smaller routes, such as the S28 from Imperia toward Garessio in Piedmont, the S334 from Albisola, or the S456 from Voltri toward Milan.

The spectacular gardens of the Villa Hanbury near Ventimiglia

## ❶ Balzi Rossi

Imperia. 🚉 Ventimiglia & Menton. 🚌 from Ventimiglia to Ponte San Luigi, then a 10-minute walk. 🌐 **archeoliguria.beniculturali.it**

An unassuming promontory is the setting for some of the most important caves in northern Italy. Guided tours lead through the traces of the cave-dwelling civilization of pre-Iron Age Liguria. The caves contain excavated burial sites where the dead were adorned with seashells. The **Museo Nazionale dei Balzi Rossi** contains tools, weapons, and stone-etched female figures dating from 100,000 years ago. There is also a reproduction of an etching of a horse.

🏛 **Museo Nazionale dei Balzi Rossi**
Via Balzi Rossi 9. **Tel** 0184 381 13. **Open** 8:30am–7:30pm Tue–Sun. **Closed** Jan 1, May 1, Dec 25. 🌐

## ❷ Villa Hanbury

Corso Monte Carlo 43, Località La Mortola. **Tel** 0184 22 95 07.
🚉 Ventimiglia. 🚌 from Ventimiglia. **Open** 9:30am–5pm (Mar–mid-Jun & mid-Sep–mid-Oct: to 5pm; mid-Jun– mid-Sep: to 6pm; mid-Oct–Feb: to 4pm) daily. **Closed** Mon Nov–Feb. 🌐
🌐 **giardinihanbury.com**

In 1867, the English botanist Sir Thomas Hanbury and his brother bought this villa on the Mortola promontory. They took full advantage of the exceptionally mild Ligurian climate to establish a garden of exotic plants along the sloping pathways of the seaside villa.

The collection, gathered by Hanbury on trips to Africa and Asia, has grown to number more than 3,000 varieties of tropical flora, including rubber trees, palms, and wild cacti.

The garden is now run by the state and is one of the most impressive botanical gardens in Italy, even during the winter.

## ❸ Dolceacqua

Imperia. 🚹 2,000. 🚉 🚌 ℹ️ Via Barberis Colomba 3 (0184 20 66 66). 🛒 Thu. 🌐 **dolceacqua.it**

This pretty village, 5 miles (8 km) north of Ventimiglia, is built on either side of the churning Nervia River, its two halves joined by an arching 108-ft (33-m) medieval stone bridge. The highlight is the ruined 12th- to 15th-century **castle**, inhabited for a while in the 16th century by the powerful Doria family from Genoa. The two square towers at the

front dominate the village. The terraced vineyards in the surrounding hills produce grapes for general consumption, as well as for a robust red wine known as Rossese or vino di Dolceacqua.

The Casinò Municipale in Sanremo, completed in 1906

## ❹ Sanremo

Imperia. 🚹 57,000. 🚉 🚌 ℹ️ Corso degli Inglesi 14 (0184 58 05 00). 🛒 Tue & Sat am. 🌐 **turismoinliguria.**

Sanremo is a pleasant resort of faded elegance. The composer Tchaikovsky, Alfred Nobel (the father of modern explosives), and the nonsense poet Edward Lear all stayed in the stuccoed mansions of the palm-lined seafront avenue, the Corso Imperatrice. The focus of the town, then as now, is the Casinò. A little farther down the Corso stands the ornate Russian Orthodox church of San Borilic.

The old town, La Pigna ("fir cone"), is a huddle of narrow lanes with medieval houses and pastel-colored shutters. A bus service goes from Sanremo to San Romolo, a small village 2,579 ft (786 m) above sea level that offers beautiful views of the area.

A delightful flower market is held in Valle Armea (5–7am, Oct–Jun, by appt, 0184 517 11) while the Italian Song Festival takes place here in February.

## ❺ Bussana Vecchia

Imperia. Off Sanremo–Arma di Taggia road.

Bussana Vecchia is a marvelous atmospheric ghost town. In February 1887 an earthquake shook the village, reducing its Baroque church and surround-

The village of Dolceacqua with its medieval bridge and ruined castle ing houses to ruins. (One survivor, Giovanni Torre del Merlo, went on to invent the ice-cream cone.)

The town was rebuilt closer to the sea, and since then the original village has been taken over by artists, who have restored some interiors, providing a venue for summer concerts and exhibitions.

## ❻ Cervo

Imperia. 🗺 1,200. 🚋 🚌 🅸 Piazza Santa Caterina 2 (0183 40 81 97). 🚇 Thu. 🆆 **cervo.com**

Cervo is the prettiest of the many old seafront villages just east of Imperia, with a narrow complex of streets and houses rising dramatically up from the pebble beach. At the top of the village stands the concave Baroque facade of **San Giovanni Battista**. Charming chamber orchestra performances are held in front of the church in July and August. The church is also known as the *"dei corallini,"* after the coral fishing which once brought prosperity to the local people. Now Cervo is an unassuming but characteristic Ligurian vacation resort, with unspoiled hotels near the beach.

San Giovanni Battista at Cervo

Spectacular rock formations in the grottoes of Toirano

## ❼ Albenga

Savona. 🗺 24,000. 🚋 🚌 🅸 Piazza del Popolo 11 (0182 55 84 44). 🚇 Wed. 🆆 **turismoinliguria.it**

Until the Middle Ages, the Roman port of Albium Ingaunum played an important maritime role. The sea, however, gradually moved farther out, leaving the town, now called Albenga, stranded on the Centa River. Most striking now is its Romanesque brick architecture, in particular the three 13th-century towers clustered around the cathedral of **San Michele**. The cathedral's interior was restored to its medieval form in the late 1960s. To the south is an intriguing 5th-century **Baptistery** with a ten-sided exterior and octagonal interior. Inside, the original 5th-century blue-and-white mosaics of doves represent the 12 Apostles. To the north of the cathedral is the small Piazza dei Leoni, named after its three stone lions imported from Rome.

In a 14th-century palace on Piazza San Michele is the **Museo Navale Romano**, founded in 1950 following the salvage of a Roman ship that had sunk in the 1st century BC. The museum contains ancient amphorae as well as exhibits salvaged from more recent shipwrecks.

The 5th-century Baptistery at Albenga

### 🏠 Baptistery

Piazza San Michele. **Tel** 0182 502 88. **Open** 9:30am–12:30pm & 3:30–6:30pm (Oct–Apr: 3–6pm) Tue–Sat (Oct–Apr: 5pm Tue); 10am–12:30pm & 3:30–6pm Sun (Oct–Apr: groups only Sun). **Closed** Jan 1, Easter, Dec 25. 🖼

### 🏛 Museo Navale Romano

Piazza San Michele 12. **Tel** 0182 512 15. **Open** 9:30am–12:30pm & 3:30–7:30pm (Oct–Apr: from 10am, 2:30–6pm) Tue–Sun. **Closed** Jan 1, Easter, Dec 25. 🖼

## ❽ Grotte di Toirano

Via alle Grotte, Toirano. **Tel** 0182 980 62. 🚌 from Albenga to Borghetto Santo Spirito. 🚋 to Borghetto Santo Spirito or Loano. **Open** 9:30am–12:30pm, 2–5pm daily. **Closed** Dec 25–Jan 1. 🎟 reserve in advance. 🆆 **toiranogrotte.it**

Beneath the delightful medieval town of Toirano a series of caves contain relics of Paleolithic life dating from 100,000 years ago.

The **Grotta della Basura** (Witch's Cave) has remarkable prehistoric human and animal footprints, and ancient bear bones and teeth in the "bear cemetery."

The **Grotta di Santa Lucia** reveals the full beauty of the yellow and gray stalactites and stalagmites formed here over hundreds of thousands of years.

The **Museo Etnografico della Val Varatella**, housed in the 16th-century stables of the Palazzo del Marchese, has a collection of agricultural and domestic tools from the 17th to the early 20th century.

### 🏛 Museo Etnografico della Val Varatella

Via G Polla, Toirano. **Tel** 0182 98 99 68. **Open** 10am–1pm, 3–8pm daily. 🖼

# ❾ Street by Street: Genoa

There is something refreshingly rough-edged about Genoa (Genova in Italian), Italy's most important commercial port. In contrast to the genteel resorts along the neighboring coast, the narrow streets of the old town are the haunts of sailors and streetwalkers.

With its natural harbor and the mountains to protect it, Genoa rose to prominence as a sea-based power. During the 16th century, Andrea Doria cemented Genoa's importance, and also proved an astute patron of the arts.

**Piazza San Matteo**
The houses and church of San Matteo were built by the Doria family in 1278. Palazzo Quartara has a bas-relief of St. George above the doorway.

↖ Musei di
Strada Nuova

PIAZZA CAMPETTO

PIAZZA SAN MATTEO

SALITA SAN T

VIA DI SCURRERIA

VIA ARCHIVESCOVATO

← The port and Palazzo Reale

VIA SAN LORENZO

PIAZZA MATTEOTT

SALITA POLLAIUOLI

PIAZ ERBE

**San Lorenzo**
The black-and-white-striped Gothic facade of the Duomo dates from the early 12th century.

**Palazzo Ducale**
Once the seat of the doges of Genoa, this elegant building, with its two fine 16th-century courtyards and arcades, now contains a major arts and cultural center.

**San Donato** has a splendid 12th-century octagonal bell tower.

VICO DEI TRE RE MAGI

**Sant'Agostino**
The 13th-century church and convent were bombed during World War II, but the bell tower remains. The cloisters now house sculpture like this fragment from the tomb of Margaret of Brabant by Pisano (1312).

**Key**

— Suggested route

| 0 meters | | 100 |
| 0 yards | | 100 |

*For hotels and restaurants in this region see pp565–9 and pp584–90*

**Church of Gesù**
This Baroque church, built between 1589 and 1606, is also known as the church of Santi Ambrogio e Andrea.

**Piazza de Ferrari** is the site of the Neo-Classical Banco di Roma and the Accademia, as well as the restored Teatro Carlo Felice.

**The bronze fountain** in Piazza de Ferrari was constructed in 1936.

**Porta Soprana**
The eastern gateway to the city has curved outer walls and stands close to the site of Christopher Columbus's house.

**Sant'Andrea**
The 12th-century cloisters standing in a small garden are all that remain of the convent that once stood here.

### San Lorenzo (Duomo)
Piazza San Lorenzo. **Tel** 010 247 18 31. **Open** daily. Museo del Tesoro: **Tel** 010 254 12 50. **Open** 9am–noon & 3–6pm Mon–Sat.

The Duomo, with its black-and-white-striped exterior, blends many architectural styles, from the 12th-century Romanesque side portal of San Giovanni to the Baroque touches of some of its side chapels. The three portals at the west end are in French Gothic style.

The most sumptuous of the chapels is dedicated to St. John the Baptist, patron saint of the city; it includes a 13th-century sarcophagus that once held the venerated saint's relics.

Steps lead down from the sacristy to the **Museo del Tesoro di San Lorenzo**. It houses such treasures as the Roman green glass dish said to have been used at the Last Supper, and a blue chalcedony plate on which the head of John the Baptist was allegedly presented to Salome.

### The Port
Aquarium Ponte Spinola. **Tel** 010 234 56 78. **Open** 9:30am–7:30pm daily (to 8:30pm Sat, Sun & hols); Jul & Aug: 8:30am–10pm daily. Last adm: 90 mins before closing. **acquariodigenova.it**

The port is the heart of Genoa and the origin of its power as a seafaring city-state in the 11th and 12th centuries. A workaday place, it is ringed by busy roads and 1960s buildings.

Among the vestiges of its medieval glory is the **Lanterna** lighthouse (restored in 1543) near the Stazione Marittima. In the old days, fires would be lit at the top of the Lanterna to guide ships into port. Today, regeneration of the port is in part due to the Renzo Piano–designed conference center (see p189) and the **Aquarium**, one of the largest in Europe and an ideal place to discover the richness of marine life.

# Exploring Genoa

Visitors are well rewarded when they explore Genoa – a city proud of its history and legends. The palazzi of Via Balbi and Via Garibaldi, and the paintings and sculptures dotted around the city in churches and museums, are among the finest in northwestern Italy. The environs, too, provide scenic and relaxing locations for excursions along the coast or in the steep hills behind.

The courtyard of the University on Via Balbi

### ⬆ Sant'Agostino

Piazza Sarzano 35. **Tel** 010 251 12 63.
Museo di Architettura e Scultura Ligure:
**Tel** 010 251 12 63. **Open** 9am–7pm
Tue–Sat (to 6pm Tue), 9am–7:30pm
Sun (Nov–Mar: 8:30am–6pm Tue–Fri,
9:30am–6:30pm Sat & Sun).
**Closed** public hols. 🖼 ♿

This Gothic church was begun in 1260, but it was bombed to pieces in World War II. It is now deconsecrated and all that remains of the original building is the fine Gothic bell tower, decorated with colored tiles. The monastery, of which the church of Sant'Agostino was once a part, was also bombed.

What remained were two ruined cloisters – one of which forms the only triangular building in Genoa. The cloisters have been converted into the **Museo di Architettura e Scultura Ligure**. The museum contains the city's collection of architectural pieces, some dating back to the Roman era, along with fragments of sculpture and frescoes – all salvaged from Genoa's other destroyed churches. The finest piece is a magnificent fragment from the tomb of Margaret of Brabant, who died in 1311. She was the wife of Emperor Henry VII, who invaded Italy in 1310. Carved by Giovanni Pisano around 1313, the sculptures from her tomb were restored and repositioned in 1987. The figures, whose garments are arranged in simple folds, seem to be helping Margaret to lie down to rest.

### 🏛 Palazzo Reale

Via Balbi 10. **Tel** 010 271 02 36.
**Open** 9am–7pm Tue–Sat, 1:30–7pm
Sun (last adm: 30 mins before closing).
**Closed** Jan 1, May 1, Dec 25. 🖼 ♿
🌐 palazzorealegenova.
beniculturali.it

This austere-looking residence, used by the Kings of Savoy from the 17th century onward, has a highly ornate Rococo interior – notably its ballroom and its Hall of Mirrors. Among the paintings is a *Crucifixion* by Van Dyck. The garden, which slopes down toward the old port, includes an intriguing cobblestone mosaic around the central fountain, depicting houses and animals.

Opposite the palace is the old **University** (1634) designed by Bartolomeo Bianco, as was much of Via Balbi. The large building brilliantly overcomes Genoa's hilly topography, and is constructed on four levels.

### 🏛 Palazzo Bianco

Via Garibaldi 11. **Tel** 010 557 21 93.
**Open** 9am–7pm Tue–Sat (to 6pm Tue,
9pm Fri), 9:30am–7:30pm Sun (Nov–
Mar: 8:30am–6pm Tue–Fri,
9:30am–6:30pm Sat & Sun). 🖼
Palazzo Rosso: **Tel** 010 275 91 85.
**Open** as for Palazzo Bianco. 🖼
Palazzo Tursi: **Tel** 010 557 21 93. **Open**
as for Palazzo Bianco. 🖼 ♿

The Palazzo Bianco is on Genoa's most beautiful street, **Via Garibaldi**, where there are many 16th-century mansions and palazzi. It houses the city's prime collection of paintings, including works by many

## Christopher Columbus in Genoa

A portrait of Columbus,
Villa Doria at Pegli

The name of Cristoforo Colombo, or Christopher Columbus, as English speakers know him, is in evidence all over Genoa. A statue of the explorer of the New World greets you as soon as you emerge in Piazza Acquaverde from the Porta Principe train station; various public buildings bear his name; even the airport is named after him. In the 17th-century Palazzo Belimbau, built on top of the old city walls, is a series of frescoes by the local artist Tavarone celebrating the explorer's life, and you can see three of his letters in the Sala del Sindaco in Palazzo Tursi (the city hall) on Via Garibaldi. It is not certain whether Columbus (c.1451–1506) was born in Genoa, in Savona, 9 miles (15 km) to the west, or even outside Italy. However, city registers mention his father, a weaver, and various family homes within the city. The small ivy-clad house adjacent to Porta Soprana may have been Columbus's childhood home, where he first discovered his passion for the sea.

The house where Columbus
may have lived

The romantic gardens at Villa Durazzo-Pallavicini in Pegli

Genoese artists such as Luca Cambiaso, Bernardo Strozzi, and Domenico Piola. Better-known artists include Filippino Lippi, Van Dyck, Veronese, and Rubens. At No. 9 Via Garibaldi, **Palazzo Tursi** hosts the Lord Mayor's boardrooms and an extension of the Palazzo Bianco Gallery. Across the street in the **Palazzo Rosso** are paintings, including works by Dürer and Caravaggio, as well as ceramics and furniture.

Fine tomb architecture from the huge Staglieno Cemetery

### 🏛 Staglieno Cemetery

Piazzale Resasco, Staglieno. **Tel** 010 87 01 84. **Open** 7:30am–5pm daily. **Closed** public hols. 🔲

This grandiose cemetery, just over the hills northeast of Genoa along the Bisagno River, is so big (81.5 acres/33 ha) that it has its own internal bus system. Founded in 1844, its tombs and monuments make up an eerie city of miniature cathedrals, Egyptian temples, and Art Nouveau palaces. Its most famous resident is Giuseppe Mazzini, the Genoese revolutionary who died near Pisa in 1872.

### Environs

Until World War II, **Pegli**, 4 miles (6 km) west of the city center, was a popular weekend retreat for rich Genoese. Now it forms part of the city, but maintains an air of tranquility thanks to its parks and two villas, the 19th-century **Villa Durazzo-Pallavicini** and the 16th-century **Villa Doria, Museo Navale**. The latter is a naval history museum celebrating Genoa's glorious past: you can see compasses, astrolabes, globes, model ships, and a portrait of Columbus, ascribed to Ghirlandaio, probably dating from 1525. An archaeological museum in the Villa Durazzo-Pallavicini relates the pre-Roman history of the Ligurian coast. The villa's garden is landscaped with romantic grottoes, pavilions, and fountains.

**Nervi**, 5 miles (8 km) to the east of the city, is another former resort town, famous for its seafront promenade, the **Passeggiata Anita Garibaldi** (named after Garibaldi's wife). The walk follows a route that has been cut into the rock face, giving panoramic views of the coast. The lush **Parco Municipale** is another feature of Nervi. It once formed the grounds of two aristocratic villas – Villa Serra and Villa Gropallo. The former, on Via Capolungo, now houses the **Galleria**

d'Arte Moderna featuring modern Italian painting. The **Villa Luxoro** on Via Aurelia is notable for its collection of clocks, fabrics, furniture, and lace. The area is also famous as Garibaldi's departure point when he set off for Sicily with his *Mille* (the famous "Thousand" men) to help bring about the unification of Italy. A large monument at Quarto dei Mille, about 2 miles (3 km) back toward the city, marks the place where the volunteers met in May 1860 to follow the intrepid revolutionary (*see p66–7*). **Villa Grimaldi** houses the Frugone brothers art and sculpture collection of late 18th- and early 19th-century works by Fattori, Boldi, and Messina.

### 🏛 Villa Durazzo-Pallavicini

Via Pallavicini 11, Pegli. **Tel** 010 698 10 48. **Open** 9am–7pm Tue–Fri; 10am–7pm Sat & Sun. **Closed** public hols. 🔳 🔲

### 🏛 Villa Doria, Museo Navale

Piazza Bonavino 7, Pegli. **Tel** 010 696 98 85. **Open** 9am–1:30pm Tue–Sun (6pm Sat; 1pm Sun). **Closed** public hols. 🔳 🔲

### 🏛 Galleria d'Arte Moderna

Villa Serra, Via Capolungo 3, Nervi. **Tel** 010 372 60 25. **Open** Tue–Sun. 🔳

### 🏛 Villa Luxoro

Via Mafalda di Savoia 3, Nervi. **Tel** 010 32 26 73. **Open** Tue–Sat. **Closed** public hols. 🔳

### 🏛 Villa Grimaldi

Via Capolungo 9, Nervi. **Tel** 010 32 23 96. **Open** Tue–Sun.

*Pini (c.1920)* by Rubaldo Merello in the Galleria d'Arte Moderna at Nervi

Pastel-colored houses near the pebble beach at Camogli

## ⑩ Camogli

Genoa. 🏠 5,500. 🚉 🚌 ⛴ 🛈 Via
XX Settembre 33 (0185 77 10 66).
🍴 Wed. 🌐 camogliturismo.it

Built on a pine-wooded slope,
Camogli is a fishing village where
seashells adorn the pastel-
painted house walls, and the
smell of frying fish wafts out from
the small restaurants into the
streets. Near the pebble beach
and fishing port is the medieval
Castello della Dragonara.

Camogli celebrates its famous
festival of the Blessing of the
Fish on the second Sunday of
May, when sardines are fried
in a huge pan 13 ft (4 m) in
diameter. The fish is distributed
free to everyone.

## ⑪ Portofino Peninsula

Genoa. 🚌 ⛴ Portofino. 🛈 Via Roma
35 (0185 26 90 24).
🌐 parcoportofino.com

Portofino is the most exclusive
harbor and resort town in Italy,
crammed with the yachts of
the wealthy. You can reach
Portofino by road (although cars
are not allowed into the village),
or by boat, from the resort of
Santa Margherita Ligure. Above
the town are the church of **San
Giorgio**, containing relics said to
be those of the dragon-slayer,
and a castle.

On the other side of the
peninsula, which you have to
reach on foot (a 2-hour walk)
or by boat, is the **Abbazia di
San Fruttuoso**, named after
a 3rd-century
saint whose
followers were
shipwrecked
here and,
according
to legend,
protected by
three lions. The
white abbey
buildings, set
among pines
and olive trees,
date mostly

The 16th-century castle jutting
into Rapallo harbor

from the 11th century, although
the imposing Torre dei Doria
was added 500 years later. You
can take a boat to try to locate
the **Cristo degli Abissi**, a bronze
statue of Christ that sits on
the seabed near San Fruttuoso,
protecting sailors. Farther

west along the coast is Punta
Chiappa, a rocky promontory
famous for the changing colors
of the surrounding sea.

🏛 **Abbazia di San Fruttuoso**
San Fruttuoso. **Tel** 0185 77 27 03.
**Open** Mar–Oct: daily; Nov–Feb:
Tue–Sun. **Closed** Feb. 🔲

## ⑫ Rapallo

Genoa. 🏠 31,000. 🚉 🚌 ⛴ 🛈
Lungomare Vittorio Veneto 7 (0185 23
03 46). 🍴 Thu. Cable car: **Tel** 0185
523 41. 🌐 **turismoinliguria.it**

Historians know Rapallo as the
place where two post-World
War I treaties were signed,
while classic movie buffs might
recognize it from the 1954
movie *The Barefoot Contessa*,
which was shot here. Rapallo
was also a haven for writers
such as D. H. Lawrence and
Ezra Pound. Its villas still have
a patrician feel, as do the horseback riding
stables, golf
course, and
tennis courts.
The palm-lined
esplanade ends
in a small
16th-century
**castle**, where art
exhibitions are
occasionally
held. A cable car
from the center
of the town leads
to the 16th-century **Santuario di
Montallegro**, which houses a
Byzantine icon said to possess
miraculous powers.

🏛 **Santuario di Montallegro**
Montallegro. **Tel** 0185 23 90 00.
**Open** daily. **Closed** noon–2:30pm.

Large yachts moored in Portofino's famous harbor

The dramatic coastline near Corniglia in the Cinque Terre

## ⓭ Cinque Terre

La Spezia. 🚊 to all towns.
🚢 Monterosso, Vernazza.
ℹ️ Via Fegina 40, Monterosso
(0187 81 70 59) (summer only);
Piazza Rio Finale 26, Riomaggiore
(0187 92 06 33).
W **parconazionale5terre.it**

The Cinque Terre are five self-contained villages – Monterosso al Mare, Vernazza, Corniglia, Manarola, and Riomaggiore – located on the rocky coastline of the Riviera di Levante. Clinging dramatically to the steep cliffs, these villages are linked only by an ancient footpath known as the Sentiero Azzurro (Blue Path), which offers spectacular views of the rocky coastline and terraced vineyards that produce the local dry white Cinque Terre wines. The footpath also provides access to secluded beaches.

These days the five villages suffer from some depopulation. The largest, **Monterosso al Mare**, on the northwestern edge of the Cinque Terre, overlooks a wide bay with its own sandy beach. **Vernazza**, farther down the coast, has streets linked by steep steps or *arpaie*. **Corniglia**, perched at the pinnacle of rocky terraces, seems untouched by the passage of time, as does **Manarola**, which is linked by the famous Via dell'Amore, or Lovers' Lane, to **Riomaggiore**, a 15-minute walk away.

The best way to visit the villages is by boat (from La Spezia, Lerici, or Porto Venere) or by train (La Spezia–Genoa service).

## ⓮ Portovenere

La Spezia. 🔼 3,900. 🚌 🚢 ℹ️ Piazza Bastreri 7 (0187 79 06 91). 🚢 Mon.
W **prolocoportovenere.it**

Named after the goddess Venus, Portovenere is one of the most romantic villages on the Ligurian coast, with its cluster of narrow streets lined with pastel-colored houses. In the upper part of the village is the 12th-century church of **San Lorenzo**. A sculpture over the doorway here depicts the martyrdom of the saint who was roasted alive on a grill. On the stone promontory that curls out into the sea is the small,

Above the doorway of San Lorenzo in Portovenere

black-and-white, 13th-century church of **San Pietro**. From here, or from the 16th-century castle on the cliffs on the north-western side of the village, there are superb views of the Cinque Terre and the small island of Palmaria, about 435 yards (400 m) offshore.

## ⓯ Lerici

La Spezia. 🔼 10,500. 🚌 🚢 ℹ️ Via Biagini 6, Località Venere Azzurra (0187 96 73 46). 🚢 Sat am.
W **parconazionale5terre.it**

This stretch of coast, along the Gulf of La Spezia or Poets' Gulf, was once popular with such literati as Yeats and D. H. Lawrence. The village of San Terenzo, across the bay from Lerici, was where the poet Shelley spent the last four years of his life. It was from his home, the Casa Magni, that he set out in 1822 on a voyage to meet Leigh Hunt in Livorno. Tragically, he was shipwrecked near Viareggio and drowned.

The popular resort of Lerici sits on the edge of a beautiful bay overlooked by pastel-colored houses. The forbidding medieval **Castello di Lerici** (13th century), built by the Pisans and later passed to the Genoese, dominates the vacation villas below. Today it houses a museum of geo-paleontology and hosts art exhibitions and concerts.

🏰 **Castello di Lerici**
Piazza San Giorgio. **Tel** 0187 96 90 42.
**Open** Tue–Sun. **Closed** Dec 9–26.
W **castellodilerici.it**

The harbor of Vernazza in the Cinque Terre

Brightly painted buildings in Manarola, one of the villages that make up the Cinque Terre ▶

# CENTRAL ITALY

# Introducing Central Italy

The central regions of Italy offer a range of beautiful landscapes, towns rich in culture and history, and outstanding churches, towers, and palaces. Emilia-Romagna is home to the impressive Po Delta, which provides a haven for wildlife. Tuscany is dominated by Florence, one of Italy's most celebrated cities. Umbria and Le Marche offer gentle pastoral countryside and picturesque hill-towns. The major sights of this popular area are shown here.

**The Leaning Tower** of Pisa and the Duomo *(see pp328–30)*, splendid examples of 12th- and 13th-century architecture, are decorated with Arabic-inspired, complex geometric patterns.

**Florence**
*(See pp274–317)*

SAN LORENZO

S. MARIA NOVELLA

CENTRO STORICO

*Arno*

SANTA CROCE

OLTRARNO

*Giardino di Boboli*

**The Duomo** and the Baptistery, in the heart of Florence, dominate the city *(see pp284–6)*. The dome dwarfs many surrounding buildings.

**The Uffizi** contains a superb collection of Florentine art from Gothic to High Renaissance and beyond *(see pp290–93)*.

**The Palazzo Pitti,** begun in 1457 for the banker Luca Pitti, became the main residence of the Medici. It now houses their treasures *(see pp306–7)*.

0 kilometers  1
0 miles  0.5

Piacenza

*Po*

Fiorenzuola d'Arda

Parma

Reggio Em

*Parma*

Massa

Lucca

Pisa

Livorno

Volt

Campiglia Marittima

Piombino

0 kilometers  50
0 miles  25

◀ Sun setting over a tranquil vineyard in Tuscany

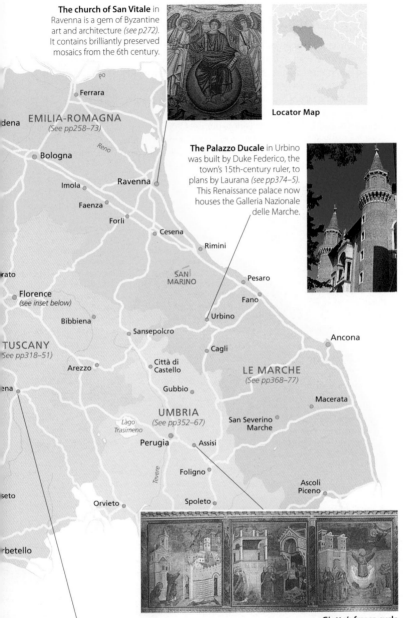

**The church of San Vitale** in Ravenna is a gem of Byzantine art and architecture *(see p272)*. It contains brilliantly preserved mosaics from the 6th century.

**Locator Map**

**The Palazzo Ducale** in Urbino was built by Duke Federico, the town's 15th-century ruler, to plans by Laurana *(see pp374–5)*. This Renaissance palace now houses the Galleria Nazionale delle Marche.

**Giotto's fresco cycle** from the Basilica of San Francesco in Assisi was executed in the 13th century *(see pp358–61)*. The church is visited by thousands of pilgrims each year.

**Siena**, a medieval town steeped in tradition, centers around the Campo, the large piazza shaped like a scallop shell *(see pp342–7)*. The lively horse race, the Corsa del Palio, is held here in July and August.

# The Flavors of Central Italy

Emilia-Romagna is Italy's gourmet capital, and home to Parmesan, Parma ham, and balsamic vinegar. Bologna has earned the epithet *La Grassa* ("The Fat") for rich dishes in which butter, cheese, and velvety sauces feature strongly. The lush lands and rolling hills of Tuscany, Umbria, and Le Marche tend to offer simpler flavors and more rustic, peasant cuisine. Top-quality pork from the Cinta Senese pig, beef from the Chianina cattle of Tuscany, fabulous *funghi* and Umbrian truffles, superb wild boar, and saffron-scented fish soups from the coast of Le Marche are all gastronomic delights of Central Italy.

Italian tomatoes

Tray of perfect, freshly made tortellini pasta

## Emilia-Romagna

Not only is this rich, fertile land the home of many of Italy's most classic ingredients, but it has also given the world *bolognese* sauce (*ragù*). The authentic sauce contains some 20 ingredients and is usually served with tagliatelle – never spaghetti. Pasta is an art form here. Legend has it that tagliatelle was invented in honor of Lucrezia Borgia's golden hair, while tortellini pasta is said to be modeled on the shape of Venus's navel.

The region's pork butchers are the most famous in Italy, making excellent sausages, *salumi*, and mortadella, and using every part of the animal including the feet, which are stuffed to form the local specialty *zamponi*. Emilia and coastal Romagna were once two provinces, and there is still a culinary distinction between them. While Emilia's gastronomy is liberally laced with butter, cheese, and mushrooms, Romagna's keynotes tend to be olive oil, garlic, and onions – and fish. The Adriatic in this region teems with life and is an especially good catching ground for turbot (*rombo*) – the "pheasant of the sea."

Nostrano    Milano    Finocchiona    Bococcini

Porchetta

Spianatta romana

Mortadella

Selection of the finest Italian salumi and other cold cuts

## Regional Dishes and Specialties

Tuscan olive oil is outstanding in quality. It has many uses and is an integral part of *crostini*, slices of toasted bread smeared with olive oil on which different toppings are spread, such as chicken livers in *crostini alla Toscana*. *Salumi* producers are a great feature of the region and *prosciutto di cinghiale* (wild boar ham) is a rich, gamey delicacy. As well as *tagliatelle al ragù* in Bologna, other very popular pastas include tortellini and tortelloni (the latter being larger than the former), often filled with cheese, butter, and herbs. *Panforte* is the Italian Christmas specialty – a delicious confection of fruits, nuts, honey, sugar, and spices originating in Siena. Try also *ricciarelli*, diamond-shaped almond biscuits, and *torta di riso* – a rich, golden cake made with rice.

Crostini alla Toscana

**Cacciucco** A fish and seafood soup from Livorno, flavored with herbs and tomatoes and ladled over garlicky toast.

Just part of a gigantic wheel of Parmigiano-Reggiano, or Parmesan

## Tuscany

Tuscany is the orchard and vegetable garden of Italy. It is also famous for red meat, especially from the prized Valdichiana cattle, from south of Arezzo. Pork is also excellent, and the Tuscan passion for hunting ensures that hare, pheasant, and wild boar, often served with local chestnuts, feature prominently on menus.

If there is one staple Tuscan ingredient it is fruity olive oil, liberally used in cooking and for seasoning everything from bread to salads, vegetables, stews, and soups.

Broths and soups are very popular, often made with beans, especially white cannellini beans. Not for nothing are Tuscans known as *toscani mangiafagioli* (Tuscan bean-eaters).

## Umbria and Le Marche

Umbria, "the green heart of Italy," is the only area outside Piedmont where truffles are found in such high concentration. Norcia is the capital of the black truffle, and stores everywhere

Tuscan market stand piled high with fresh, ripe vegetables

sell truffle paste and truffle oils. Norcia is also famous for its pigs, and a favorite dish is *porchetta* – whole roast suckling pig stuffed with herbs. Wild mushrooms are plentiful in season, in particular *porcini*. Game features too, usually in the form of pheasant, guinea fowl, or pigeon, with the odd songbird thrown in, although it is now illegal to catch wild songbirds. The rural interior of Le Marche also features *porchetta*; lamb and rabbit are popular, too. The long coastline yields a bounty of fish, often made into fish broths, and a specialty of Ancona, *zuppa di pesce*, fish soup with saffron.

### ON THE MENU

**Baci** From Perugia, these are chocolate-coated hazelnuts, their name literally meaning "kisses" in Italian.

**Bistecca Fiorentina** Steak, marinated in herbs, garlic, and finest extra virgin olive oil, rapidly grilled over wood coals. The meat for this has to be Chianina beef.

**Cinghiale in umido** Traditional Tuscan wild boar stew with red wine, tomatoes, garlic, and vegetables. Usually served with polenta.

**Vincisgrassi** A baked, layered dish from Le Marche of ham, pasta, and béchamel sauce, sprinkled with truffle shavings.

**Tagliatelle al ragù** Flat strips of pasta are tossed with the quintessential Italian meat sauce from Bologna.

**Arista alla Fiorentina** Pork loin is roasted in the oven with garlic and rosemary, a specialty of Florence.

**Zuccotto** A Tuscan specialty of light sponge cake filled with hazelnuts, almonds, chocolate, and cream.

# The Wines of Central Italy

Vineyards are seen everywhere in Central Italy, from the rolling cypress-fringed hills of Tuscany to the flatter, Lambrusco-producing plains of Emilia-Romagna. The finest red wines are made in the hills of southeastern Tuscany: Chianti Classico, Brunello di Montalcino, and Vino Nobile di Montepulciano. Today's innovative mix of modern and traditional techniques is steadily improving the quality of much of the region's wine.

**Chianti Classico** is the heart of the Chianti zone. Chianti may be light and fruity or dense and long-lived – price is the usual guide. Rocca delle Macie is very reasonably priced.

**Vernaccia di San Gimignano** is a Tuscan white wine with a long, distinguished history. Traditionally a golden, often oxidized wine, it is now also produced in a fresher style, for early drinking. Teruzzi & Puthod make consistently good Vernaccia.

**Vino Nobile di Montepulciano** is made from the same grapes as Chianti. It can be of superior quality, hence its claim to be a "noble wine." The vineyards are set around the delightful hilltop village of Montepulciano.

Parma

Modena

Bologna

EMILIA-ROMAGNA

Pistoia

Lucca

Florence

Pisa

Greve

San Gimignano

Siena

TUSCANY

Montep

Montalcino

**Brunello di Montalcino** is made from Sangiovese, Brunello being its local name. Its firm tannins may need up to 10 years to soften before the rich, spicy flavors are revealed. Rosso di Montalcino, on the other hand, can be enjoyed much younger.

## Super-Tuscans

During the 1970s, innovative wine-makers set out to create new, individual wines, even though under the existing rules they would be labeled as simple table wine. A trend that started with Antinori's Tignanello (a Sangiovese–Cabernet Sauvignon blend), this approach has reinvigorated Tuscan wine, to produce some exciting, if expensive, variations.

Sassicaia, a red wine made from the Cabernet Sauvignon grape

| 0 kilometers | 50 |
| 0 miles | 25 |

Chianti estate at Badia a Passignano in Tuscany

**Key**
- ☐ Chianti
- ☐ Chianti Classico
- ☐ Vernaccia di San Gimignano
- ☐ Brunello di Montalcino
- ☐ Vino Nobile di Montepulciano
- ☐ Orvieto Classico
- ☐ Orvieto
- ☐ Verdicchio dei Castelli di Jesi
- ☐ Lambrusco

Rimini
Marino
Pèsaro
Urbino · Ancona
LE MARCHE · Jesi
Gubbio
UMBRIA
Perugia · Assisi

**Verdicchio** is a dry white wine from Le Marche with a crisp, slightly salty taste. The single-vineyard Verdicchio, such as Umani Ronchi's Casal di Serra, is winning much acclaim.

**Orvieto Classico** is a popular Umbrian white wine. This fresh, dry *(Secco)* version from the Antinori estate is a good example of a modern-style Orvieto. The wine also comes in a sweeter form, known as *Abboccato*.

## Grapes of Central Italy

The versatile Sangiovese grape dominates wine-making in Central Italy. It is the main grape in Chianti, in Vino Nobile di Montepulciano, in Brunello di Montalcino, and in many of the Super-Tuscan wines. Of the established whites, Trebbiano and Malvasia head the list. Imported varieties such as Chardonnay and Cabernet Sauvignon play a role, often being used to complement and enhance native varieties, of which there has been a resurgence.

Sangiovese grapes

## How to Read the Label

**The DOCG name** guarantees the origin of the wine.
Producer's name
Year of production

**The bottler's** name and address are given, so the region of production is clear.
Alcoholic content

## Good Wine Producers

**Chianti**: Antinori, Badia a Coltibuono, Brolio, Castello di Ama, Castello di Rampolla, Fattoria Selvapiana, Felsina Berardenga, Il Palazzino, Isole e Olena, Monte Vertine, Riecine, Rocca delle Macie, Ruffino, Tenuta Fontodi.
**Brunello di Montalcino**: Argiano, Altesino, Caparzo, Castelgiocondo, Costanti, Il Poggione, Villa Banfi.
**Vino Nobile di Montepulciano**: Avignonesi, Le Casalte, Poliziano. In **Umbria**: Adanti, Lungarotti.

### Good Chianti Vintages

2008, 2007, 2004, 2003, 2001, 2000, 1999, 1997, 1995, 1993, 1990, 1988.

# Understanding Architecture in Central Italy

Central Italy has countless fine Renaissance buildings, many of them concentrated in and around Florence. Their clear lines, elegant simplicity, and harmonious proportions came out of a re-evaluation of the past. Turning their backs on the Gothic style, the architects of the Renaissance returned to Classical Rome for inspiration. Most of the large buildings had been started by the late 15th century, paid for by the Catholic Church or by powerful noble families, such as the Medici of Florence.

The Palazzo Ducale in Urbino (begun 1465)

## Religious Buildings

**Arched bays** trisect the facade.

Pope Pius II's coat of arms

One of 12 roundels by Luca della Robbia

Small circular windows

Square plan topped by small dome

Harmonious proportions

**Symmetrical floorplan** is based on a Greek cross.

**Pienza's Duomo** was built by Bernardo Rossellino in 1459 for Pope Pius II as part of his vision of the ideal Renaissance city *(see p337)*.

**The Pazzi Chapel** of Santa Croce in Florence (begun in 1441) is one of Brunelleschi's most famous works, decorated with terra-cotta roundels by Luca della Robbia *(see pp288–9)*.

**Santa Maria della Consolazione** in Todi, begun in 1508, owes much to the ideas of the architect Bramante *(see p363)*.

## Town and Country Houses

Wedge-shaped masonry

Strong horizontal line

**The cornice** was designed to cast a shadow over the face of the palace around midday.

**Square windows** are found only on the first floor.

**The Palazzo Strozzi** in Florence (1489–1536) is typical of many Tuscan city palaces *(see p332)*. The three stories are given equal importance, and the massive rusticated stonework conveys the impression of strength and power *(see p297)*.

## Where to See the Architecture

The simple canons of the Renaissance were interpreted differently away from the hotbed of artistic thought and cultural endeavor of Florence, which has the greatest number of churches and palaces. Alberti's Tempio Malatestiano at Rimini *(see p270)* evokes the sobriety of ancient Roman architecture yet

Vista in the Boboli Gardens, Florence

seeks to reinterpret it in his own unique fashion. Urbino's Palazzo Ducale *(pp374–5)* perfects the grace and polish of the era and is a truly noble period residence. On a smaller scale are the planned Renaissance centers of elegant towns such as Ferrara *(pp264–5)*, Pienza *(p337)*, and Urbania *(p373)*. All three centers are examples of enlightened patronage, and pay homage to the art of antiquity.

**The weight** of the lantern prevents the dome from springing apart.

**Wooden ribs** provide the main support.

Outer shell

Inner shell

**The Duomo in Florence** is crowned by the revolutionary dome (1436) by Brunelleschi, which had to be built without scaffolding due to its size. The wooden structure is covered by an inner and outer shell *(see pp284–5)*.

Classical triangular pediment

**The top edge** of the frieze divides the facade in two.

**Volute connects** the lower and upper parts.

**The facade of Santa Maria Novella** in Florence (1458–70) was designed by Leon Battista Alberti. He incorporated some of the existing Gothic features into an overall design typical of the Renaissance *(see pp300–301)*.

**The villa at Poggio a Caiano** (1480) was redesigned in the Renaissance by Giuliano da Sangallo *(see p332)*. The graceful, curved staircase was added around 1802.

Clock, a later addition

Classical frieze

Colonnade derived from a Classical temple

Classical portico

# EMILIA-ROMAGNA

Emilia-Romagna is the heartland of central Italy, a broad corridor through the hills and plains of the Po Valley that marks the watershed between the cold north of the Alps and the hot Mediterranean south. With its rich agricultural land, historic cities, and thriving industry, it is one of the most prosperous areas in Italy.

Most of the major towns in Emilia-Romagna lie near the Via Aemilia, a Roman road built in 187 BC, which linked Rimini on the Adriatic coast with the garrison town of Piacenza. Prior to the Romans, the Etruscans had ruled from their capital, Felsina, located on the site of present-day Bologna. After the fall of Rome, the region's focus moved to Ravenna, which became a principal part of the Byzantine Empire administered from Constantinople.

During the Middle Ages pilgrims heading for Rome continued to use the Via Aemilia. Political power, however, passed to influential noble families – the Malatesta in Rimini, the Bentivoglio in Bologna, the d'Este in Ferrara and Modena, and the Farnese in Parma and Piacenza. Great courts grew up around the families, attracting poets such as Dante and Ariosto, as well as painters, sculptors, and architects whose works still grace the medieval centers of these towns. Cobbled together from separate Papal States in 1860, modern Emilia-Romagna was given its present borders in 1947. Emilia, the western part of the region, is traditionally associated with a more northern outlook and a tendency toward the left in politics. Romagna, on the other hand, has witnessed an increase in the support for right-wing parties calling for political independence from Rome.

The entire region has a reputation as a great gastronomic center. Agriculture has long thrived on the Po's alluvial fringes, earning the Pianura Padana (Po Plain) epithets such as the "breadbasket" and "fruit bowl" of Italy. Pigs still outnumber humans in many areas, and some of the country's most famous staples – Parma ham and Parmesan cheese – originate here.

The Palazzo del Comune, or "il Gotico," in Piacenza

◄ The statue of Garibaldi that stands in front of the Palazzo del Governatore, Parma

# Exploring Emilia-Romagna

Emilia-Romagna is a checkerboard of fields and plains between the Po River to the north and the forest-covered Apennine mountain slopes to the south. The best place to begin a tour of the region is centrally located Bologna. Modena, its long-time rival, boasts one of the country's loveliest Romanesque cathedrals. Parma has a more provincial feel, and Ferrara, too, has an easygoing air. Castell'Arquato offers a taste of the smaller villages that dot the hills south of the Po.

Piazza Cavalli, Piacenza's central square

Reed-lined shores along the Po Delta

## Sights at a Glance

1. Piacenza
2. Castell'Arquato
3. Fidenza
4. Parma
5. Modena
6. Ferrara
7. *Bologna pp266–9*
8. Faenza
9. Rimini
10. Po Delta
11. *Ravenna pp271–3*

## Getting Around

Excellent roads and railroads, aided by mostly flat terrain, make this region quick and easy to get around. Bologna is connected by the A1–E35 to Florence and by the A13 to Ferrara and Venice. The busy A1–E35 links Bologna to Milan via Piacenza, Fidenza, and Parma. The A15–E31 connects Parma with La Spezia, and the A21–E70 joins Piacenza and Cremona. Fast, frequent train services run along almost parallel routes.

The beach at Cesenatico, north of Rimini on the Adriatic coast

### Key

━━ Freeway

━━ Major highway

━━ Secondary road

┄┄ Minor road

━━ Scenic route

━━ Main railroad line

── Minor railroad line

━━ International border

━━ Regional border

△ Summit

The 13th-century Palazzo Pretorio in Castell'Arquato

# ❶ Piacenza

🏛 105,000. **FS** 🚌 **ℹ** Piazza Cavalli 2 (0523 49 22 23). 🗓 Wed & Sat.

Piacenza traces its history back to Roman times. Located near the Po, it served as a fortified camp protecting the Emilian plain from invasion. The center is still based on the Roman plan.

Piacenza has a pleasantly understated old center full of fine medieval and Renaissance buildings. Pride of place goes to two bronze equestrian **statues** in the central Piazza Cavalli, the work of the 17th-century sculptor Francesco Mochi, a pupil of Giambologna. Lauded as master-pieces of Baroque sculpture, the statues represent Alessandro Farnese, a soldier of fortune, and his son, Ranuccio: both were rulers of 16th-century Piacenza.

Behind the statues is the red-brick **Palazzo del Comune**, also known as "Il Gotico," an evocatively battlemented Lombard-Gothic palace begun at the end of the 13th century. It is one of Italy's most beautiful medieval buildings. The **Duomo**, at the end of Via XX Settembre,

has a rather leaden Lombard-Romanesque exterior (begun in 1122) and a 14th-century campanile. The interior features Guercino's painted cupola and medieval frescoes. There are also frescoed saints near the main door, painted to resemble members of the congregation.

The **Museo Civico** offers an eclectic mixture of sculpture and paintings – the star among these is the *Madonna and Child with John the Baptist* by Botticelli (1444–1510). There is also an armory and archaeology section. The highlight here is the so-called *Fegato di Piacenza*, an Etruscan bronze representation of the sheep livers once used by priests for divination, inscribed with the names of deities.

🏛 **Museo Civico**
Palazzo Farnese, Piazza Cittadella. **Tel** 0523 49 26 61. **Open** Tue–Sun. **Closed** public hols. ♿

# ❷ Castell'Arquato

Piacenza. 🏛 4,500. 🚌 **ℹ** Piazza Municipio 1 (0523 80 32 15). 🗓 Mon.

Tucked into the folded hills between Fidenza and Piacenza, Castell'Arquato is one of the prettiest villages in the countryside south of the Po. Day visitors come on the weekends to escape Emilia's larger cities, thronging the restaurants and bars around the beautiful **Piazza Matteotti**. The best medieval building on the piazza is the 13th-century **Palazzo Pretorio**, a Romanesque basilica. The impressive **Rocca Viscontea** (14th century), a former fortress, is on Piazza del Municipio. The village's hilltop site offers good views, particularly over the verdant Arda Valley to the east.

# ❸ Fidenza

Parma. 🏛 25,000. **FS** 🚌 **ℹ** Piazza Duomo 16 (0524 833 77). 🗓 Wed & Sat.

Like many towns hugging the line of the Po, Fidenza owed its early prominence to the Via Aemilia (the old Roman road). The town assumed greater importance as a medieval way station for pilgrims en route to Rome. Today Fidenza is visited for its superb **Duomo** on Piazza Duomo (13th century), a composite piece of architecture that embraces Lombard, Gothic, and transitional Romanesque elements. The most immediately eye-catching feature is the opulent facade, most probably created by the craftsmen who worked with Benedetto Antelami on Parma's Duomo. Inside, the walls are dotted with fragments of medieval frescoes, while the crypt contains the relics of San Donnino, the Duomo's patron.

Detail from facade of Duomo in Fidenza

Interior of Parma Baptistery

## ❹ Parma

🔺 190,000. **FS** 🚌 *i* Piazza
Garibaldi 1 (0521 21 88 89).
🛒 Wed & Sat; Thu (flea market).
**w** turismo.comune.parma.it

Few Italian towns are as
prosperous as Parma, not only
a byword for fine food and
good living but also a treasure
trove of excellent paintings,
superlative sculpture, and fine
medieval buildings. It boasts
one of Italy's top opera houses
and a panoply of elegant
stores and first-rate bars
and restaurants.

The Lombard-Romanesque
**Duomo** on Piazza Duomo,
among the greatest in
northern Italy, is renowned for
the painting that fills its main
cupola, the *Assumption* (1526–
30) by Antonio da Correggio.
The nave is adorned with the
work of Correggio's pupils. The

south transept features a carved
frieze of *The Deposition* (1178)
by Benedetto Antelami, who
was also responsible for much
of the exquisite **Baptistery**
(1196) just south of the
cathedral. The reliefs inside and
outside the latter – particularly
those describing the months of
the year – are among the most
important of their age in Italy.

East of the Duomo is the
church of **San Giovanni
Evangelista** (rebuilt 1498–1510),
whose dome features a fresco
(c.1520) of the *Vision of St. John
at Patmos* by Correggio.
Frescoes by Parmigianino can
be seen here and in the 16th-
century church of **Madonna
della Steccata** on Via Dante.

### 🏛 Palazzo della Pilotta

Piazzale della Pilotta 15.
Galleria: **Tel** 0521 23 36
17. **Open** Tue–Sun am.
🚫 ♿ Museo: **Tel** 0521
23 37 18. **Open** Tue–Sat,
Sun am. 🚫 ♿

This vast palace was
built for the Farnese
family during the
1500s and rebuilt
after bomb damage
from World War II.
It comprises several
parts, including the
**Teatro Farnese**
(1628), a copy of
Palladio's ravishing
theater in Vicenza,
built entirely
of wood.

Both Correggio and Parmigianino
are represented in the palace's
**Galleria Nazionale**, which also
houses works by Fra Angelico,
El Greco, and Bronzino, and two
by Ludovico Carracci: the
*Apostles at the Sepulchre* and the
*Funeral of the Virgin* (late 1500s).

The **Museo Archeologico
Nazionale**, on the lower floor, has
exhibits from Velleia, an Etruscan
necropolis, and from prehistoric
sites in the hills around Parma.

### 🏛 Camera di Correggio

Via Melloni. **Tel** 0521 23 33 09.
**Open** Tue–Sun (am only; to 6pm Sat).
🚫 ♿
Originally the refectory of the
Benedictine convent of San
Paolo, this room was frescoed
by Correggio in 1518 with
mythological scenes.

Campanile and Baptistery in Parma

## The Making of Parmesan Cheese and Parma Ham

No cheese is as famous or
as vital to Italy's cuisine as
Parmesan *(Parmigiano)*. There
are two types: the superior
Parmigiano-Reggiano and
the lower-quality Grana.
The cheese is made using
techniques that have barely
altered in centuries. Partially
skimmed milk is added
to whey, to promote fermen-
tation, and rennet is used to
curdle the milk. The cheese
is then salted and shaped.
Parmesan is not only used in
cooking but is delicious eaten
on its own, or with pears –
an Italian specialty. Parma

Store selling Parmesan cheese
and Parma ham

ham owes its excellence to
techniques perfected over
many years and to the special
conditions in which it is cured.
It is made from pigs fattened
on whey left over from the
making of Parmesan cheese.
The meat has a character that
requires little more than salt
and pepper to produce the
famous *prosciutto crudo*. The
breezy hills of Langhirino,
south of Parma, are ideal for
curing the hams, which are
aged for up to 10 months.
Each ham is branded with the
five-pointed crown of the old
Duchy of Parma.

*Flora* by Carlo Cignani (1628–1719) in the Galleria Estense in Modena

## ❺ Modena

185,000. FS 🚍 ℹ Piazza Grande 14 (059 203 26 60). 🗓 Mon.
**w** turismo.comune.modena.it

To most Italians Modena means fast cars, for both Ferrari and Maserati have factories in its industrial outskirts, and opera, since this is the birthplace of Luciano Pavarotti. Monuments to an earlier age, however, make this one of Emilia's most enticing historic destinations. A thriving colony since Roman times, the city rose to medieval prominence on the back of its broad agricultural hinterland and the arrival in 1598 of the d'Este nobles from Ferrara. This family continued to rule the city until the 18th century.

### 🔼 Duomo

Corso Duomo. **Tel** 059 21 60 78. **Open** daily. Torre Ghirlandina: **Open** Tue–Sun & hols (closed at lunchtime Tue–Fri). 🅿

Modena's superlative **Duomo** rises alongside the old Roman Via Emilia. One of the region's greatest Romanesque buildings, it was founded by Countess Matilda of Tuscany, ruler of Modena in the 11th century. It was designed by Lanfranco and dedicated to San Geminiano, the city's patron saint, whose stone coffin lies under the choir. Its most noticeable feature is the **Torre Ghirlandina**, a perilously leaning tower begun at the same time as the Duomo and completed two centuries later. It once housed the *Secchia*, a wooden bucket whose 1325 theft from Bologna allegedly sparked a war between the two cities. It also inspired Tassoni's 17th-century mock epic poem *La Secchia Rapita* (The Stolen Bucket), and became the symbol of a rivalry between the cities.

The large reliefs on the Duomo's main (west) facade are the work of the 12th-century sculptor Wiligelmus. The highlight of the somewhat severe interior is a large carved *tribuna* (rood screen) decorated with 12th-century scenes from the Passion.

### 🏛 Palazzo dei Musei

Largo di Porta Sant'Agostino 337. Galleria Estense: **Tel** 059 203 31 00. **Open** daily. 🅿 ♿ Biblioteca Estense: **Tel** 059 22 22 48. **Open** Mon–Thu (Fri, & Sat am). **Closed** public hols. 📷

Northwest of the Duomo, and reached through an attractive warren of old streets, is the Palazzo dei Musei. Formerly an arsenal and workhouse, it is now home to the city's best museums and galleries. Its finest section is the **Galleria Estense**, given over to the d'Este private art collection, which was transferred here when the city of Ferrara, the family's former dominion, became part of the Papal States. Most of the paintings are by Emilian and Ferrarese artists (notably Reni and the Carracci), but there are also works by Velázquez, Tintoretto, Bernini, and Veronese.

Among the permanent displays in the **Biblioteca Estense**, the d'Este Library, are a 1481 edition of Dante's *Divine Comedy* and dozens of fascinating maps and diplomatic letters, many dating back centuries. A map dated 1501 was among the first to show the 1492 voyage made by Columbus to the New World. The jewel of the collection is the magnificent illuminated Borso d'Este Bible, with gloriously decorated pages containing more than 1,200 miniatures by 15th-century artists of the Ferrara school, most notably Taddeo Crivelli and Franco Russi.

### Environs

The **Ferrari** factory, 12 miles (20 km) to the south, was founded by Enzo Ferrari in 1945. The FIAT-owned manufacturer now produces around 2,500 automobiles annually. The **Galleria Ferrari** has an excellent exhibition featuring auto memorabilia, classic engines, and many vintage cars.

### 🏛 Museo Ferrari

Via Dino Ferrari 43, Maranello. **Tel** 0536 94 97 13. **Open** 9:30am–6pm daily (to 7pm summer). **Closed** Jan 1, Dec 25. 🅿 ♿

## ❻ Ferrara

135,000. FS 🚍 ℹ Castello Estense, Largo Castello (0532 20 93 70). 🗓 Mon & Fri.

The d'Este dynasty has left an indelible mark on Ferrara, one of the region's greatest walled towns. The noble family took control of the town under Nicolò II in the late 13th century, holding power until 1598, when the family was forced by the papacy to move to Modena.

Ferrari 250 SWB, produced between 1959 and 1962

### 🏰 Castello Estense

Largo Castello. **Tel** 0532 29 92 33.
**Open** Tue–Sun (Sep–Mar: daily).
**Closed** public hols. 🖼

With its towers and battlements, the Este family's dynastic seat (begun 1385) looms over the town center. Ferrante and Giulio d'Este were incarcerated in its dungeons for plotting to overthrow Alfonso I d'Este. Parisina d'Este, wife of Nicolò III, was executed here for having an affair with Ugo, her illegitimate stepson.

### 🏛 Palazzo del Comune

Piazza Municipale.
Bronze statues of Nicolò III and Borso d'Este, one of Nicolò's reputed 27 children, adorn this medieval palace (begun 1243). Both are copies of the 15th-century originals by Leon Battista Alberti.

The impressive medieval Castello Estense in Ferrara

Facade of the Duomo in Ferrara

### 🏛 Museo della Cattedrale

Via San Romano. **Tel** 0532 76 12 99.
**Open** Tue–Sun. **Closed** Jan 1 & 6, Easter, Dec 25 & 26. 🖼

Ferrara's 12th-century Duomo is a Romanesque-Gothic hybrid designed by Wiligelmus, who is widely regarded as the first great Italian sculptor. Fine reliefs on the facade depict scenes from the Last Judgment. The excellent **museum** (in a deconsecrated church opposite the cathedral) contains a fine set of marble reliefs of the *Labors of the Months* (late 1100s), two painted organ shutters (1469) of *St. George* and the *Annunciation* by Cosmè Tura, and the *Madonna of the Pomegranate* (1408) by Jacopo della Quercia.

### 🏛 Museo Schifanoia

Via Scandiana 23. **Tel** 0532 641 78.
**Open** Tue–Sun. **Closed** public hols. 🖼

Building work in the d'Este summer retreat began in 1385. The estate is famous for its Salone dei Mesi (Room of the Months), decorated with beautiful 15th-century murals by Tura and other Ferrarese painters with detailed scenes depicting months of the year.

### 🏛 Museo Archeologico Nazionale

Palazzo di Ludovico il Moro, Via XX Settembre 122. **Tel** 0532 662 99.
**Open** 9:30am–5pm Tue–Sun (last adm: 4:30pm). **Closed** May 1, Dec 25. 🖼 ♿

The most interesting exhibits in the Museo Archeologico Nazionale are artifacts that were excavated from Spina, a Greco-Etruscan trading post near Comacchio on the Po Delta.

### 🏛 Palazzo dei Diamanti

Corso Ercole d'Este 21.
**Tel** 0532 24 49 49. **Open** 9am–7pm daily. 🖼 🖼 📷

Named after the diamond motifs on its facade, the Palazzo dei Diamanti houses a modern art gallery, an interesting museum devoted to the Risorgimento, and the Pinacoteca Nazionale, which contains works from leading exponents of the local Renaissance school.

### The d'Este Family Dynasty

During their medieval heyday, the d'Este family presided over one of Europe's leading courts, combining the roles of blood-crazed despots with enlightened Renaissance patrons. Nicolò III, for example, had his wife and her lover brutally murdered. Alfonso I (1476–1534) married Lucrezia Borgia, descendant of one of Italy's most notorious families, while Ercole I (1471–1505) attempted to poison a nephew who tried to usurp him (and eventually had him executed). At the same time the d'Este court attracted writers like Petrarch, Tasso, and Ariosto, and painters such as Mantegna, Titian, and Bellini. Ercole I also rebuilt Ferrara, creating one of Europe's finest Renaissance cities.

*Portrait of Alfonso I d'Este (c.1523) by Titian*

# ❼ Street by Street: Bologna

The historic city center of Bologna is a
handsome ensemble of brick buildings and
charming porticoed streets. Medieval palaces
are clustered around the two central squares,
Piazza Maggiore and Piazza del Nettuno,
flanked to the south by the churches of San
Petronio and San Domenico. The university
of Bologna is the oldest in Europe and the
venerable Archiginnasio was its first official
building. Farther afield, the skyline is dominated
by the Asinelli and Garisenda towers, and by
the campanile of Santo Stefano.

**Fontana di Nettuno**
The famous Neptune Fountain (1566) was designed
by Tommaso Laureti and decorated with magnificent
bronze figures by Giambologna.

**The Palazzo
del Podestà**
(13th century) was
remodelled in 1484.

**★ San Petronio**
*The Martyrdom of St. Sebastian*
(15th century) in the Cappella
di San Sebastiano is by Lorenzo
Costa of the Ferrarese School.

Archiginnasio

**Piazza Cavour**
The flagstone medieval
streets and shady porticoed
buildings found in this
pleasant piazza are typical of
Bologna's elegant city center.

**Key**

— Suggested route

| 0 metres | 150 |
| 0 yards | 150 |

**San Domenico**
(1251) is dedicated to
St. Dominic, who is
buried here in a
magnificent tomb.

VIA UGO BASSI
Modena ←
Train station ↑
VIA RIZZO
VIA OREF
PIAZZA MAGGIORE
VIA IV NOVEMBRE
VIA DELL'ARCHIGINNASIO
VIA FARINI
PIAZZA CAVOUR
VIA GARIBALDI

**San Giacomo Maggiore**
The *Triumph of Death* fresco by Costa (1483–6) adorns the Cappella Bentivoglio.

↗
Pinacoteca Nazionale
Museo delle Cere
Anatomiche

VIA ZAMBONI

VIA SAN VITALE → Ravenna

STRADA MAGGIORE

ZZA DI
ORTA
EGNANA

VIA SANTO STEFANO

VIA CASTIGLIONE

Firenze ↙

**Torri degli Asinelli e Garisenda**
The colossal towers are two of the few remaining towers begun by Bologna's important families in the 12th century.

**Abbazia di Santo Stefano**
The Fontana di Pilato, or Pilate's Fountain, in the courtyard features a basin with Lombard inscriptions from the 8th century.

## VISITORS' CHECKLIST

**Practical Information**
380,000. Airport; Piazza Maggiore 1/e; Stazione Centrale (051 23 96 60). Fri & Sat. Mar–Jun: Bologna Music Festival.
**W** bolognawelcome.com

**Transportation**
Marconi 5 miles (9 km) NW.
Piazza Medaglia d'Oro.
Piazza XX Settembre.

### San Giacomo Maggiore
Piazza Rossini. **Open** daily.
This Romanesque-Gothic church, begun in 1267 but altered substantially since, is visited mainly for the Cappella Bentivoglio, a superb family chapel founded by Annibale Bentivoglio in 1445 and consecrated in 1486. Pride of place naturally goes to a portrait with subtle characterization of the patrons by Lorenzo Costa (1460–1535), who was also responsible for the frescoes of the *Apocalypse*, the *Madonna Enthroned* and the *Triumph of Death*. The chapel's altarpiece, depicting the *Virgin and Saints with Two Angel Musicians* (1488), is the work of Francesco Francia. The Bentivoglio family is further glorified in the tomb of Anton Galeazzo Bentivoglio (1435) opposite the chapel. It was among the last works of the noted Sienese sculptor Jacopo della Quercia. The Oratory of Santa Cecilia features frescoes on the lives of Santa Cecilia and San Valeriano by Costa and Francesco Francia (1504–6).

The Bentivoglio tomb (1435) by Jacopo della Quercia

# Exploring Bologna

Monuments to Bologna's rich cultural heritage are scattered across the city, from the leaning towers and the church of San Petronio in the old center to the Pinacoteca Nazionale in the university district.

### ▦ Torri degli Asinelli e Garisenda

Piazza di Porta Ravegnana. Torre degli Asinelli: **Open** daily. 🚻

The famous leaning towers – Torre degli Asinelli and Torre Garisenda – are among the few survivors of the original 200 that once formed the skyline of Bologna. Both were begun in the 12th century, though there were probably earlier towers on the site – Dante mentioned a pair of towers here in his *Inferno*. Torre Garisenda was shortened as a safety measure within only a few years of its construction,

and still leans some 10 ft (3 m) from the vertical. At 318 ft (97 m) tall, Torre degli Asinelli is the fourth-highest tower in Italy after those in Cremona, Siena, and Venice. Its 500-step ascent offers fine views over the city's rooftops to the hills beyond.

### 🏛 Abbazia di Santo Stefano

Via Santo Stefano 24. **Tel** 051 648 06 11. **Open** 8am–7pm daily.

Santo Stefano is a curious collection of four medieval churches (originally seven) jumbled together under one roof. The 11th-century church of the Crocifisso provides little more than a corridor to

Exterior of the Abbazia di Santo Stefano

### 🏛 San Petronio

Piazza Maggiore. **Tel** 051 23 14 15. **Open** daily. ♿

Dedicated to the city's 5th-century bishop, this church ranks among the greatest of Italy's brick-built medieval buildings. Founded in 1390, it was originally intended to be larger than St. Peter's in Rome, but its size was scaled down when the church authorities diverted funds to the nearby Palazzo Archiginnasio. The resulting financial shortfall left the church decidedly lopsided, with a row of columns on its eastern flank that were intended to support an additional internal aisle. The project's financial profligacy, nonetheless, was said to have been instrumental in turning Martin Luther against Catholicism.

**The altarpiece of** the *Martyrdom of St. Sebastian* is from the late Ferrarese School.

**The pink and white interior** adds to the overall light and airy effect.

**The canopied main portal** features beautiful biblical reliefs (1425–38) by Jacopo della Quercia.

**Gothic Interior**
The interior is airy, with graceful pillars supporting the roof. Twenty-two chapels, shielded by screens, open off the nave. In 1547 the Council of Trent was temporarily moved here due to the plague.

Entrance

Unfinished upper facade

**The meridian line** was traced in 1655 by the astronomer Gian Domenico Cassini. It is 219 ft (67 m) long.

**The stained-glass windows** (1464–6) in this chapel are by Jacob of Ulm.

polygonal San Sepolcro, the most appealing of the quartet. Also dating from the 11th century, its centerpiece is the tomb of St. Petronius, a marvelously overstated affair modeled on the Holy Sepulchre of Jerusalem. The courtyard contains the so-called Fontana di Pilato, an 8th-century basin.

The 5th-century Santi Vitale e Agricola is the oldest church in the city. It was rebuilt in the 8th and 11th centuries. Inside are the sarcophagi of saints Vitalis and Agricola, martyred in the 4th century. Santa Trinità features a small museum of minor paintings and religious artifacts, including wooden statues of the *Adoration of the Magi* painted by Simone dei Crocifissi (*c.*1370).

Bell tower

**Choir Stalls** The exquisite inlaid choir stalls of the Chapel of the Holy Sacrament were made by Raffaello da Brescia in 1521.

## 🏛 Pinacoteca Nazionale

Via delle Belle Arti 56. **Tel** 051 420 94 11. **Open** 9am–1:30pm Tue & Wed; 2–7pm Thu–Sun & Hols. **Closed** Jan 1, May 1, Aug 15, Dec 25. 🖼 ♿

Bologna's principal art gallery, and one of northern Italy's most important collections, stands on the edge of the university district, a bustling area of bars, bookstores, and cheap restaurants. The gallery is mainly devoted to work by Bolognese painters, notably Vitale da Bologna, Guido Reni, the Carracci family, and Guercino. Members of the Ferrarese School are also represented, in particular Francesco del Cossa and Ercole de' Roberti. The two highlights are Perugino's *Madonna in Glory* (*c.*1491) and Raphael's famous *Ecstasy of St. Cecilia*, painted around 1515, both artists having worked in Bologna.

*The Ecstasy of St. Cecilia* (c.1515) by Raphael in Bologna's Pinacoteca Nazionale

## 🏛 Museo delle Cere Anatomiche

Via Irnerio 48. **Tel** 051 209 15 33 or 051 209 15 56. **Open** 10am–1pm, 2–6pm Mon–Thu, 10am–1pm Fri. **Closed** Jan 1, Easter, May 1, Dec 25, public hols. 📷

The Museum of Anatomical Waxworks is one of the more memorable of Bologna's smaller museums, featuring occasionally gruesome visceral waxworks and numerous models of organs, limbs, and flayed bodies. Sculpted rather than made from casts, they have an artistic as well as scientific appeal. The models were used as medical teaching aids until the 19th century. Exhibits from the 18th century are in Palazzo Poggi, which also contains the Geografia e Nautica collection.

## 🏛 San Domenico

Piazza di San Domenico 13. **Tel** 051 640 04 11. **Open** daily. ♿

Bologna's San Domenico can lay claim to being the most important of Italy's many Dominican churches. Begun in 1221, after St. Dominic's death, it was built to house the body of the saint, who died here and lies buried in a tomb known as the Arca di San Domenico. A magnificent composite work, the tomb's statues were executed by Nicola Pisano; the reliefs of scenes from the *Life of St. Dominic* were the work of Nicola Pisano and his assistants; the canopy (1473) is attributed to Nicola di Bari; while the figures of the angels and saints Proculus and Petronius are early works by Michelangelo. The reliquary (1383) behind the sarcophagus contains St. Dominic's head.

Arca di San Domenico in the Basilica di San Domenico

Fresco of Malatesta and St. Sigismund (1451) by Piero della Francesca in the Tempio Malatestiano, Rimini

## ❽ Faenza

Ravenna. 🗺 54,000. 🚇 🚌
ℹ️ Voltone Molinella 2 (0546 252 31).
🛒 Tue, Thu & Sat.

Faenza is synonymous with the *faïence* ceramic-ware to which it gave its name. Renowned across Europe for over 500 years, the pottery, with its distinctive blue and ocher coloring, is still made in countless small factories around the town.

The highlight of Faenza is the **Museo Internazionale delle Ceramiche**, one of the largest ceramic collections in Italy. Its exhibits feature not only examples of local ware, but also pottery from other countries and other periods, including Roman ceramics and medieval majolica. There is also a section devoted to the modern ceramic art of Picasso, Matisse, and Chagall.

### 🏛 Museo Internazionale delle Ceramiche
Viale Baccarini 19. **Tel** 0546 69 73 11.
**Open** Apr–Oct: Tue–Sun; Nov–Mar: Tue–Sun (Tue–Thu am only). **Closed** Jan 1, May 1, Aug 15, Dec 25. 🚻 📷

## ❾ Rimini

🗺 140,000. 🚇 🚌 ℹ️ Piazzale Fellini 3 (0541 70 45 87). 🛒 Wed & Sat.
🌐 riminiturismo.it

Rimini was once a quaint seaside resort, whose charms were celebrated in the early movies of Federico Fellini (1920–93), the

director born and raised here. Today it is the largest beach resort in Europe. The seafront, which stretches unbroken for almost 9 miles (15 km), is lined with clubs, bars, and restaurants. The crowded beaches are clean and well groomed, though entrance fees are charged at private beaches.

The town's old quarter, by contrast, is pleasantly quiet. Its charming cobblestone streets gather around **Piazza Cavour**, dominated by the 14th-century **Palazzo del Podestà**. Rimini's finest building is the **Tempio Malatestiano**, built as a Franciscan church but converted in 1450 by Leon Battista Alberti, the great Florentine architect, into one of Italy's great Renaissance monuments. It was commissioned by Sigismondo Malatesta (1417–68), a descendant of Rimini's medieval rulers, and reputedly one of the most evil and debauched men of his

time. Ostensibly designed as a chapel, the Tempio became little more than a monument to Malatesta. Inside are sculptures by Agostino di Duccio and a fresco, by Piero della Francesca, of Malatesta kneeling before St. Sigismund (1451) .

The entwined initials of Malatesta and his fourth wife, Isotta degli Atti, are a recurring decorative motif, and there are reliefs depicting bacchanalian excess and oddities such as strangely posed elephants (a Malatesta family emblem). All this led Pope Pius II to condemn the building as "a temple of devil-worshippers," and to burn Malatesta's effigy for acts of "murder, violation, adultery, incest, sacrilege, and perjury."

### Environs
Farther along the coast, the resorts become relatively quieter. **Cesenatico**, 11 miles (18 km) north, has all the usual amenities, yet the beaches are less crowded.

### 🏛 Tempio Malatestiano
Via IV Novembre. **Tel** 0541 511 30.
**Open** 8:30am–12:30pm, 3:30–7pm Mon–Sat; 9am–12:30pm, 3:30–6:30pm Sun. 🚻

## ❿ Po Delta

Ferrara. 🚇 Ferrara Ostellata. 🚌 to Goro or Gorino. 🚢 from Porto Garibaldi, Goro & Gorino. ℹ️ Via Mazzini 4, Comacchio (0533 31 41 54). Parco Delta del Po: **Tel** 0533 31 40 03.
🌐 parcodeltapo.it

The Po is Italy's longest river. Its vast basin covers some 15 percent of the country and supports

Facade of the Renaissance Tempio Malatestiano in Rimini

*For hotels and restaurants in this region see pp569–73 and pp590–96*

around a third of the nation's population. Although ravaged in many places by industrial pollution, at its finest it offers beautifully subtle landscapes – rows of poplar trees across misty fields and vistas over the shifting sands of its vast delta, an estuary of marshes, dunes, and islands.

The immense **Parco Delta del Po** is a national park stretching for 234 sq miles (600 sq km), all the way to the Veneto. Wetland areas such as the **Valli di Comacchio** north of Ravenna have long been nature preserves, a winter home to thousands of breeding and migrating birds. Ornithologists gather here to see gulls, coots, bean geese, and black terns, and far rarer species such as the white egret, hen harrier, and pygmy cormorant. **Comacchio**, the nearest settlement, comprises 13 tiny islands connected by bridges. It is one of several fishing villages in the area, and its most famous catch is eels, often caught using methods, like water gates, that date back as far as Roman times.

Piazza del Popolo, Ravenna's central square

Other nature preserves include the **Bosco della Mesola**, a tract of ancient woodland planted by the Etruscans and cared for by generations of monks. You can either walk or bicycle through it, with excellent opportunities for seeing large herds of deer. For a good look at the entire region, follow the S309 – part of the old Via Romea pilgrimage trail to Rome – that runs north to south through 60 miles (100 km) of the park. A number of smaller lanes branch off into the wilderness. There are also boat trips to some of the delta's remote corners: key departure points include the villages of Ca'Tiepolo, Ca'Vernier, and Taglio di Po. Most areas also offer the possibility of renting bicycles. The 78 mile (125 km) ride along the right bank of the Po is very popular with bicyclists.

Hen harrier, found in the Po Delta

## ⓫ Ravenna

🏠 160,000. 🚆 🚌 🛈 Via Salara 8/12 (0544 357 55/354 04). 🗓 Wed & Sat; antiques on 3rd weekend of each month. 🌐 **turismo.ra.it**

Most people visit Ravenna for its superb mosaics from the Byzantine period *(see pp54–5)*, but the town itself is a surprisingly pleasant medley of old streets, fine stores, and peaceful piazzas. The **Museo Nazionale** has a wide range of icons, paintings, and archaeological displays. The best place to take a break from sightseeing is Piazza del Popolo, a lovely ensemble of medieval buildings.

**🏛 Museo Nazionale**
Via Fiandrini. **Tel** 0544 21 56 18.
**Open** Tue–Sun. **Closed** Jan 1, May 1, Dec 25. 🖼 🚻

The peaceful landscape along the banks of the river in the Po Delta

# A Tour of Ravenna

Ravenna rose to power in the 1st century BC under the Emperor Augustus, who built a port and naval base at nearby Classe, currently the site of a major excavation project. As Rome's power declined, Ravenna was made the capital of the Western Empire (AD 402), a role it retained during the Ostrogoth and Byzantine rule in the 5th and 6th centuries. Ravenna is renowned for its early Christian mosaics – the town had converted to Christianity in the 2nd century AD. The mosaics span the years of Roman and Byzantine rule, offering comparisons between Classically inspired designs and later Byzantine motifs.

**② The Good Shepherd**
This mosaic adorns the tiny Mausoleo di Galla Placidia. Begun in 430, this exquisite building probably never received the remains of Placidia, wife of a barbarian emperor.

**① San Vitale**
San Vitale's apse mosaics (526–547) show Christ, San Vitale (being handed a martyr's crown), two angels, and Bishop Ecclesius, who began the church (see pp54–5).

**③ Baptism of Jesus**
The 5th-century Battistero Neoniano (Neonian Baptistery) is named after the bishop who may have commissioned its decoration, including this beautiful mosaic. It was built near the remains of a Roman bathhouse and is Ravenna's oldest monument.

## ⑤ Battistero degli Ariani

The cupola of this late 5th-century baptistery has a mosaic showing the Apostles ringed around a centerpiece depicting the Baptism of Christ.

### VISITORS' CHECKLIST

**Practical Information**
San Vitale & Mausoleo di Galla Placidia: **Via Fiandrini. Tel** 0544 54 16 88. **Open** Apr–Sep: 9am–7pm daily; Nov–Feb: 9:30am–5pm; Mar & Oct: 9am–5:30pm (last adm: 15 mins before closing). **Closed** Jan 1, Dec 25. Battistero Neoniano: Via Battistero. **Tel** 0544 54 16 88. **Open & Closed** as above, except Nov–Feb: 10am–5pm. 🅿 🎫 Sant'Apollinare Nuovo: Via di Roma. **Tel** 0544 54 16 88. **Open & Closed** as above. 🎫 ♿ Tomba di Dante: Via Dante Alighieri. Tel 0544 21 56 76. **Open** Apr–Sep: 10am–8pm daily; Oct–Mar: 10am–4pm daily. **Closed** Jan 1, Dec 25. ♿ Battistero degli Ariani: Via degli Ariani. **Tel** 0544 54 37 11. **Open** 8:30am–7:30pm daily (winter to 4:30pm) (last adm: 15 mins before closing). **Closed** Jan 1, May 1. 7. A combined ticket is available. For reservations (mandatory for Mausoleo di Galla Placidia): **Tel** 800 303 999 or 0544 54 16 88. 🆆 **ravennamosaici.it**

*Map labels:*

VIA ROCCA AL FOSSI
GHISELLI
VIA UGO BASSI
VIA DI ROMA
VIA LUIGI RAVA
OLO COSTA
Basilica dello Spirito Santo
PIAZZA MAMELI
Stazione 130m (150 yards)
FS
⑤ Battistero degli Ariani
RMANDO DIAZ
VIA LUIGI CARLO FARINI
VIA G. CARDUCCI
VIA A. MARIANI
VIA DI ROMA
Museo Dantesco
VIA F. NEGRI
⑥ Sant'Apollinare Nuovo
Palazzo di Teodorico
Tomba di Dante
LARGO FIRENZE
an cesco
UACCIMANNI
RIMINI
VIGILIO PORTICINO
VIA ALBERONI

## ⑥ Sant'Apollinare Nuovo

This glorious 6th-century church, named after Ravenna's first bishop, is dominated by two rows of mosaics. Both show processions of martyrs and virgins bearing gifts for Christ and the Virgin.

## ④ Tomba di Dante

Dante's wanderings around Italy after his exile from Florence eventually brought him to Ravenna, where he died in 1321. A lamp in his sepulchre (1780) is fed by oil given by the city of Florence.

**Key**

— Suggested route

0 metres        200
0 yards        200

**For additional map symbols** *see back flap*

# FLORENCE

Florence is a vast and beautiful monument to the Renaissance, the artistic and cultural reawakening of the 15th century. Writers such as Dante, Petrarch, and Machiavelli contributed to its proud literary heritage, though it was the paintings and sculptures of artists such as Botticelli, Michelangelo, and Donatello that turned the city into one of the world's greatest artistic capitals.

While the Etruscans had long settled in the hills around Fiesole, Florence first sprang to life as a Roman colony in 59 BC. Captured by the Lombards in the 6th century, the city later emerged from the Dark Ages as an independent city-state. By the 13th century a burgeoning trade in wool and textiles, backed by a powerful banking sector, had turned the city into one of Italy's leading powers. Political control was wielded first by the guilds, and later by the Florentine Republic. In time, power passed to leading noble families, of which the most influential were the Medici, a hugely wealthy banking dynasty. Florence, and later Tuscany, remained under the family's almost unbroken sway for three centuries. During this time the city was at the cultural and intellectual heart of Europe, its cosmopolitan atmosphere and wealthy patrons providing the impetus for a period of unparalleled artistic growth. Artists, sculptors, and architects flocked to the city, filling its streets, churches, and palaces with some of the world's greatest Renaissance works. By 1737 the Medici had died out, leaving the city under Austrian (and briefly Napoleonic) control until Italian Unification in 1861. Between 1865 and 1871 Florence was the capital of the new Kingdom of Italy. The historic streets and artistic heritage were ravaged by the Arno floods of November 1966.

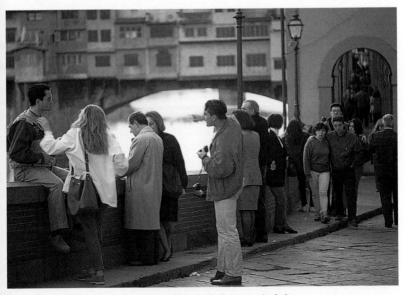

Florentines strolling in front of Ponte Vecchio (1345), the old bridge lined with stores spanning the Arno

◀ A replica of Michelangelo's *David* in Piazza della Signoria

# Exploring Florence

Historic Florence is a surprisingly compact area, and the majority of the sights described on the following pages can easily be reached on foot. Most visitors head for the Duomo, the city's geographical and historical focus, ideally placed to explore the Campanile, Baptistery, and Museo dell'Opera del Duomo. To the south is Piazza della Signoria, long the city's political heart, flanked by the Palazzo Vecchio, Florence's town hall, and the Uffizi, one of Italy's leading art galleries. To the east lies the church of Santa Croce, home to frescoes by Giotto and the tombs of some of Florence's greatest men. To the west stands Santa Maria Novella, the city's other great church, also adorned with fresco-filled chapels. Across the Ponte Vecchio and the Arno – the river that bisects the city – is the district of Oltrarno, dominated by Santo Spirito and the vast Pitti Palace, containing galleries with works by great Renaissance artists including Raphael and Titian.

### Getting Around

Florence has excellent bus service. One trolley line, with two more under construction, also operates in the city. The compact city center, a restricted traffic area, is best negotiated on foot.

### Key

▨ Major sight
▨ Place of interest
▨ Pedestrian-only street
— City walls

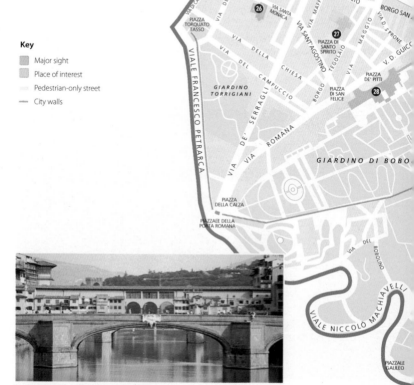

Ponte Vecchio with Ponte Santa Trinità in the foreground

**For additional map symbols** *see back flap*

## Sights at a Glance

### Churches

- ❷ Convento di San Marco
- ❸ Santissima Annunziata
- ❼ *Duomo and Baptistry pp284–6*
- ❽ *Orsanmichele*
- ❿ *Santa Croce*
- ⓲ San Lorenzo
- ⓳ *Cappelle Medicee*
- ㉑ *Santa Maria Novella*
- ㉕ Ognissanti
- ㉖ *Cappella Brancacci pp202–3*
- ㉗ Santo Spirito
- ㉙ Santa Felìcità
- ㉛ San Miniato al Monte

### Buildings, Monuments, and Squares

- ❺ Spedale degli Innocenti
- ⓬ Ponte Vecchio
- ⓮ Piazza della Signoria
- ⓯ Palazzo Vecchio
- ⓰ Palazzo Davanzati
- ⓱ Palazzo Strozzi
- ⓴ Mercato Centrale
- ㉒ Palazzo Antinori
- ㉓ Palazzo Rucellai
- ㉚ Piazzale Michelangelo

### Museums and Galleries

- ❶ Galleria dell'Accademia
- ❹ Museo Archeologico
- ❻ Museo dell'Opera del Duomo
- ❾ Bargello
- ⓫ Museo Galileo
- ⓭ *Uffizi pp290–93*
- ㉔ Museo Nazionale Alinari della Fotografia
- ㉘ *Palazzo Pitti pp306–7*

**Bell tower, Palazzo Vecchio**

| 0 meters | 500 |
|---|---|
| 0 yards | 500 |

# Street by Street: Around San Marco

The buildings in this part of Florence once stood on the fringes of the city, serving as stables and barracks. The Medici menagerie of lions, elephants, and giraffes was housed here. Today it is a student quarter and the streets are often busy with young people attending the university or the Accademia di Belle Arti, the world's oldest art school, founded in 1563.

**③ Santissima Annunziata**
This fine Renaissance church has an opulent Baroque interior.

**Palazzo Pandolfini** was designed by Raphael in 1516.

**② ★ Convento di San Marco**
*The Annunciation* (c.1445) is an example of Fra Angelico's exquisite fresco decoration.

**Sant'Apollonia** features a fresco of the *Cenacolo* (*Last Supper*) by Andrea del Castagno (1450).

VIA CAVOUR

VIA DELLA DOGANA

LA PIRA

VIA GIORGIO

VIA DEGLI ARAZZIERI

PIAZZA DI

SAN MARCO

VIA SAN GALLO

VIA CESARE BATISTI

VIA RICASOLI

PIAZZA DELLA
**④ SANTISSIMA
ANNUNZIATA**

**Luigi Cherubini** (1760–1842), the Florentine composer, trained at the Conservatorio.

**Giambologna's statue** of Duke Ferdinando I was cast by Tacca in 1608.

**① ★ Galleria dell'Accademia**
This detail is from a 14th-century altarpiece, the *Madonna and Saints*, by an unnamed master.

*For hotels and restaurants in this region see pp569–73 and pp590–96*

**Locator Map**
*See Florence Street Finder map 2*

0 meters 50
0 yards 50

**Key**

— Suggested route

**The Giardino dei Semplici** was opened in 1543.

**④ Museo Archeologico**
Many of the Etruscan objects in the museum were originally in the Medici collections.

**⑤ Spedale degli Innocenti**
Opened in 1444, the city orphanage by Brunelleschi was decorated with cameos by Andrea della Robbia.

Part of the 15th-century *Cassone Adimari* by Lo Scheggia in the Accademia

# ❶ Galleria dell'Accademia

Via Ricasoli 60. **Map** 2 D4.
**Tel** 055 238 86 12 (information).
**Open** 8:15am–6:50pm Tue–Sun (occasional extended hours in the summer). **Closed** public hols.
🅿 ♿ 🚻 ⬇ 🔲 **accademia.org**

The Academy of Fine Arts, founded in 1563, was the first school established in Europe specifically to teach the techniques of drawing, painting, and sculpture. The art collection displayed here was formed in 1784 to provide material for students to study and copy.

The most famous work is Michelangelo's *David* (1504), a colossal (17-ft-/ 5.2-m-) nude of the biblical hero who killed the giant Goliath. The sculpture was commissioned by the city for Piazza della Signoria, but it was moved to the Accademia for safe-keeping in 1873. One copy now stands in its original position (*see pp294–5*) and a second is on Piazzale Michelangelo. The *David* established Michelangelo, at the age of 29, as the foremost sculptor of his time.

Michelangelo's other master-pieces in the Accademia include the *Quattro Prigionieri* (Four Prisoners), sculpted between 1521 and 1523 and intended to adorn the tomb of Pope Julius II. The muscular figures struggling to free

Michelangelo's *David*

themselves from the stone are among the most dramatic of Michelangelo's works. The statues were presented to the Medici family in 1564 by the artist's nephew, Leonardo. They were then moved to the Grotta Grande in the Boboli Gardens, where casts of the originals can now be seen.

The Accademia also contains an important collection of paintings by 15th- and 16th-century Florentine artists, among them Filippino Lippi, Fra Bartolomeo, Bronzino, and Ridolfo del Ghirlandaio. The major works include the *Madonna del Mare* (Madonna of the Sea), attributed to Botticelli (1445–1510), and *Venus and Cupid* by Jacopo Pontormo (1494–1556), based on a preparatory drawing by Michelangelo. Also here is an elaborately painted wooden chest, the *Cassone Adimari* (1440–45) by Lo Scheggia, the step-brother of Masaccio. Originally part of a wealthy bride's trousseau, it is decorated with details of Florentine life, clothing and architecture. A scene of the bridal party appears on the chest in front of the Baptistery.

The Salone della Toscana (Tuscany Room) features modest paintings and sculptures by 19th-century members of the Accademia and plaster models by sculptor Lorenzo Bartolini.

The light and airy former library, designed by Michelozzo

## ❷ Convento di San Marco

Piazza di San Marco. **Map** 2 D4.
**Tel** 055 28 76 28 (information).
**Open** 7am–noon, 4–8pm. 🕏 Museo di San Marco: **Tel** 055 238 86 08 (reservations). **Open** 8:15am–1:50pm daily (to 4:50pm Sat & Sun). **Closed** Jan 1, May 1, Dec 25, 2nd & 4th Mon of month; 1st, 3rd, & 5th Sun of month. 🏛 ♿ 🚌

The Convent of San Marco was founded in the 13th century and enlarged in 1437, when Dominican monks from nearby Fiesole moved there at the invitation of Cosimo il Vecchio. He paid a considerable sum to have the convent rebuilt by his favorite architect, Michelozzo, whose simple cloisters and cells provide the setting for a remarkable series of devotional frescoes (c.1438–45) by Florentine painter and Dominican friar Fra Angelico. The convent and art collections form the **Museo di San Marco**.

Michelozzo's magnificent **Chiostro di Sant'Antonino** was named after the convent's first prior, Antonino Pierozzi (1389–1459), who later became the Archbishop of Florence. Most of the faded frescoes in this cloister describe scenes from the saint's life by Bernardino Poccetti. The panels in the corner are by Fra Angelico. A door in the right side of the cloister leads to the **Ospizio dei Pellegrini** (Pilgrims' Hospice). Today it houses the museum's freestanding paintings, including three famous

A detail from Fra Angelico's poignant *Lamentation over Christ* (c.1436–41)

masterpieces: Fra Angelico's *Deposition* (c.1432–4), an altar-piece painted for the church of Santa Trinità; the *Madonna dei Linaiuoli*, commissioned by the Linaiuoli (flaxworkers' guild) in 1433; and the moving *Lamentation over Christ* (c.1436–41), painted for Santa Maria della Croce al Tempio.

In the courtyard, right of the convent's former bell, is the vaulted **Sala Capitolare** (Chapterhouse), decorated with a noted but over-restored *Crucifixion and Saints* (1440) painted by Fra Angelico.

Covering one wall of the small **Refettorio** (refectory) is a fresco of the *Last Supper* (c.1480) by Domenico Ghirlandaio. Stairs from the courtyard lead to the second floor, where you suddenly see Fra Angelico's *Annunciation* (c.1440), thought by many to be among the city's most beautiful Renaissance paintings. Beyond, ranged around three sides of the cloister, are the **Dormitory Cells**. These 44 tiny monastic cells are frescoed with scenes from *The Life of Christ* by Fra Angelico and assistants (1439–45). The cells numbered 1 to 11 are generally attributed to Fra Angelico personally, as is the lovely fresco of the *Madonna and Saints* on the right of the corridor *(see p36)*.

Cells 12–14 were once occupied by Savonarola, the zealous Dominican monk who became Prior of San Marco in 1491. Among other deeds, Savonarola incited Florentines to rebel against the Medici and was responsible for the burning of many works of art. Denounced as a heretic, he was burned at the stake in 1498.

On the third corridor lies an airy colonnaded hall, formerly a public **library** designed by Michelozzo in 1441 for Cosimo il Vecchio. Beyond lie two cells (38 and 39) used by Cosimo when he went on retreat here. They are both larger than any of the neighboring rooms.

Fra Angelico's allegorical fresco, the *Mocking of Christ* (c.1442), showing Jesus blindfolded and being struck by a Roman guard

A large section on the third floor is dedicated to Greek vases, notably the famed François Vase, found in an Etruscan tomb near Chiusi.

*The Birth of the Virgin* (1514) by del Sarto in Santissima Annunziata

## ❸ Santissima Annunziata

Piazza della Santissima Annunziata. **Map** 2 E4. **Tel** 055 239 80 34. **Open** 7:30am–12:30pm, 4pm–6:30pm daily.

Founded by the Servite order in 1250, the church of the Holy Annunciation was later rebuilt by Michelozzo between 1444 and 1481. Its atrium contains frescoes by the Mannerist artists Rosso Fiorentino, Andrea del Sarto, and Jacopo Pontormo. Perhaps the finest of its panels are *The Journey of the Magi* (1511) and *The Birth of the Virgin* (1514) by del Sarto.

The heavily decorated, dark interior has a frescoed ceiling completed by Pietro Giambelli in 1669. Here is one of the city's most revered shrines, a painting of the Virgin Mary begun by a monk in 1252 but miraculously completed by an angel, according to devout Florentines. Newlywed couples traditionally visit the shrine (on the left as you enter the church) to present a bouquet of flowers to the Virgin and to pray for a long, fruitful, and fecund marriage.

A door from the north transept leads to the **Chiostrino dei Morti** (Cloister of the Dead), so called because it was originally used as a burial ground. Today it is best known for del Sarto's beautiful fresco *The Madonna del Sacco* (1525). The church is located on the northern flank of **Piazza della Santissima Annunziata**, one of the finest Renaissance squares in Florence. Designed by Brunelleschi, the delicate nine-bay arcade fronts the Spedale degli Innocenti to its right, while at the center of the square stands a bronze equestrian statue of Duke Ferdinando I. Started by Giambologna, it was finished in 1608 by his assistant Pietro Tacca (who designed the square's bronze fountains).

## ❹ Museo Archeologico

Via della Colonna 36. **Map** 2 E4. **Tel** 055 235 75. **Open** 8:30am–7pm Tue–Fri, 8:30am–2pm Sat–Mon. **Closed** Jan 1, May 1, Dec 25.

The Archaeological Museum in Florence is in a palazzo built by Giulio Parigi for the Princess Maria Maddalena de' Medici in 1620. It now exhibits an outstanding collection of Etruscan, Greek, Roman, and Egyptian artifacts.

The second floor contains a splendid series of Etruscan bronzes as well as the famous *Chimera* (4th century BC), a mythical lion with a goat's head imposed on its body and a serpent for a tail. Equally impressive is the 1st-century *Arringatore* bronze found near Lake Trasimeno in Umbria. It is inscribed with the name of Aulus Metellus.

Etruscan warrior, Museo Archeologico

## ❺ Spedale degli Innocenti

Piazza della Santissima Annunziata 12. **Map** 2 E4. **Tel** 055 203 71. **Open** Museum: 10am–7pm daily. **Closed** Jan 1, Easter, Dec 25.

Named after Herod's biblical Massacre of the Innocents, the "Hospital" opened in 1444 as Europe's first orphanage. Part of the building is still used for this purpose. Brunelleschi's arcaded loggia is decorated with glazed terra-cotta roundels, added by Andrea della Robbia around 1498, showing babies wrapped in swaddling bands. At the left end of the portico you can see the *rota*, a rotating stone cylinder on which anonymous mothers could place their unwanted children and ring the bell for them to be admitted.

Within the building lie two elegant cloisters: the **Chiostro degli Uomini** (Men's Cloister), built between 1422 and 1445 and decorated with *sgraffito* roosters and cherubs, and the smaller Women's Cloister (1438). The upstairs gallery contains a handful of fine works, including terra-cottas by della Robbia and pictures by Botticelli, Piero di Cosimo, and Domenico Ghirlandaio. There is a vast space for temporary exhibitions and a beautiful terrace, complete with a cafeteria.

Part of Brunelleschi's arcaded loggia, Spedale degli Innocenti

# Street by Street: Around the Duomo

While much of Florence was rebuilt during the Renaissance, the eastern part of the city retains a distinctly medieval feel. With its maze of tiny alleys, it is an area that would still be familiar to Dante (1265–1321), whose birthplace allegedly lay somewhere among these lanes. The poet would recognize the church of Santa Maria de' Cerchi, where he first glimpsed Beatrice, as well as the gaunt outlines of the Bargello. He would also be familiar with the Baptistery, one of the city's oldest buildings, though he would not know either the Campanile or the Duomo, whose foundations were laid in the poet's old age.

**❼ ★ Duomo and Baptistery**
The exteriors of the Duomo and Baptistery are richly decorated with marbles and reliefs, such as this detail from the Duomo's facade.

**Key**

— Suggested route

**The Loggia del Bigallo** (1358) is where abandoned children were once left. They were then sent to foster homes if they remained unclaimed.

```
0 meters            100
0 yards             100
```

**❽ Orsanmichele**
The church's niche carvings depict patron saints of trade guilds, such as this copy of Donatello's *St. George*.

**Via dei Calzaiuoli**, lined with stylish stores, is the city's liveliest street.

PIAZZA DI SAN GIOVANNI

PIAZZA DEL DUOMO

VIA DELL'OCHE

VIA D. STUDIO

VIA DE' MEDICI

VIA ROMA

VIA D. SPEZIALI

VIA DEI CALZAIUOLI

VIA DE' CERCHI

V.D. TAVOLINI

V.D. CIMATORI

V. DE'LAMBERTI

CALIMALA

VIA PORTA ROSSA

Piazza della Signoria

**6 Museo dell'Opera del Duomo**

Works from the Duomo, Campanile, and Baptistery are displayed in this museum.

**Pegna** sells a range of fine wines, oil, and honey.

**Locator Map**
See Florence Street Finder map 6

**Badia Fiorentina**, the abbey church founded in 978, is home to *The Virgin Appearing to St. Bernard* (1485) by Filippino Lippi.

**Casa di Dante**, a restored medieval house, is reputedly Dante's birthplace.

**9 ★ Bargello**
The city's old prison is home to a rich collection of applied arts and sculpture, including this figure of *Mercury* by Giambologna (1564).

Carving from Luca della Robbia's choir loft in the Museo dell'Opera

## 6 Museo dell'Opera del Duomo

Piazza del Duomo **Map** 2 D5 (6 E2). **Tel** 055 230 28 85. **Open** 9am–7pm daily (to 9pm Mon, Fri, & Sat). **Closed** 1st Tue of month. 🐾 ♿ 🌐 ilgrandemuseodelduomo.it

The Cathedral Works Museum has so far undergone extensive remodeling, and now a series of rooms is dedicated to the history of the Duomo. The main first-floor room holds statues from Arnolfo di Cambio's workshop that were once placed in the cathedral's niches. Nearby is Donatello's *St. John*. Another room contains 14th- and 15th-century religious paintings and reliquaries.

Michelangelo's *Pietà* has pride of place on the staircase. The hooded figure of Nicodemus is widely believed to be a self-portrait.

The first room on the upper floor contains two choir lofts, dating to the 1430s, by Luca della Robbia and Donatello. Carved in crisp white marble and decorated with colored glass and mosaic, both depict children playing musical instruments and dancing.

Other works by Donatello in this room are his statue of *La Maddalena* (1455) and several Old Testament figures.

The room to the left contains an exhibition of the tablets that used to decorate the bell tower. A lower level houses examples of the tools used by Brunelleschi's workmen and a copy of di Cambio's original cathedral facade.

# ❼ Duomo and Baptistery

Rising above the heart of the city, the richly decorated Duomo – Santa Maria del Fiore – and its orange-tiled dome have become Florence's most famous symbols. Typical of the Florentine determination to lead in all things, the cathedral is Europe's fourth-largest church, and to this day it still remains the city's tallest building. The Baptistery, with its celebrated bronze doors, may date back to the 4th century, making it one of Florence's oldest buildings. The Campanile, designed by Giotto in 1334, was completed in 1359, 22 years after his death.

**Campanile**
At 276 ft (85 m), the Campanile is 20 ft (6 m) shorter than the dome. It is clad in white, green, and pink Tuscan marble.

**★ Baptistery**
Colorful 13th-century mosaics illustrating the Last Judgment decorate the ceiling above the octagonal font, where many famous Florentines, including Dante, were baptized. The doors are by Andrea Pisano (south) and Lorenzo Ghiberti (north, east).

**Campanile Reliefs**
Copies of reliefs by Andrea Pisano on the Campanile's first story depict the Creation of Man, and the Arts and the Industries. The originals are kept in the Museo dell'Opera del Duomo *(see p283)*.

North Doors

Main entrance

East Doors
*(see p286)*

South Doors

## KEY

① **The Neo-Gothic marble facade** echoes the style of Giotto's Campanile, but was only added in 1871–87.

② **Gothic windows**

③ **The top of the dome** offers spectacular views over the city.

④ **The Last Judgment** frescoes (1572–4) by Vasari were completed by Zuccari.

⑤ **Bricks were set** between marble ribs in a self-supporting herringbone pattern – a technique

Brunelleschi copied from the Pantheon in Rome.

⑥ **The marble sanctuary** around the High Altar was created by Baccio Bandinelli in 1555.

★ **Dome by Brunelleschi**
Brunelleschi's dome, finished in 1463, was the largest of its time to be built without scaffolding. The outer shell is supported by a thicker inner shell that acts as a platform for it.

## VISITORS' CHECKLIST

**Practical Information**
Piazza del Duomo. **Map** 2 D5 (6 E2). **Tel** 055 230 28 85. Cathedral: **Open** 10am–5pm Mon–Fri (to 4:30pm Thu), 10am–4:45pm Sat, 1:30–4:45pm Sun. Crypt: **Open** 10am–5pm Mon–Fri (to 4:30pm Thu), 10am–4:45pm Sat. Baptistery: **Open** 8:15–10:15am & 11:15am–6:30pm Mon–Wed & Fri, 8:15am–6:30pm Thu & Sat, 8:15am–1:30pm Sun. Dome: **Open** 8:30am–6:20pm Mon–Fri, 8:30am–5pm Sat, 1–4pm Sun. Campanile: **Open** 8:15am–6:50pm daily. All buildings: **Closed** Jan 1, Easter, Aug 15, Sep 8, Dec 25.
**w** ilgrandemuseodelduomo.it

**Transportation**
1, 6, 14, 17, 23.

**Chapels at the East End**
The three apses, crowned by smaller copies of the dome, have five chapels each. The 15th-century stained glass is by Ghiberti.

Entrance leading to the dome

**...rble Pavement**
...e colorful, intricately inlaid pavement (16th ...tury) was designed in part by Baccio ...gnolo and Francesco da Sangallo.

**Dante Explaining the Divine Comedy** (1465)
This painting by Michelino shows the poet outside Florence against a backdrop of Purgatory, Hell, and Paradise.

# The East Doors of the Baptistery

Lorenzo Ghiberti's famous bronze Baptistery doors were commissioned in 1401 to mark the city's deliverance from the plague. Ghiberti was chosen to make them after a competition that involved seven leading artists, including Donatello, Jacopo della

Ghiberti's winning panel

Quercia, and Brunelleschi. The trial panels by Ghiberti and Brunelleschi are so different from Florentine Gothic art of the time – notably in the use of perspective and individuality of figures – that they are often regarded as the first works of the Renaissance.

### "Gate of Paradise"

Having spent 21 years working on the North Doors, Ghiberti was commissioned to make the East Doors (1424–52). Michelangelo enthusiastically dubbed them the "Gate of Paradise." The original ten relief panels showing scriptural subjects are now exhibited in the Museo dell'Opera del Duomo (see p283); those on the Baptistery are copies.

**Abraham and the Sacrifice of Isaac**
The jagged modeled rocks symbolizing Abraham's pain are carefully arranged to emphasize the sacrificial act.

**Joseph Sold into Slavery**
Ghiberti, a master of perspective, formed the architectural elements in shallower relief behind the figures to create the illusion of depth in the scene.

### Key to the East Doors

| | | | |
|---|---|---|---|
| 1 | 2 | 1 | Adam and Eve Are Expelled from Eden |
| | | 2 | Cain Murders His Brother, Abel |
| 3 | 4 | 3 | The Drunkenness of Noah and His Sacrifice |
| | | 4 | Abraham and the Sacrifice of Isaac |
| 5 | 6 | 5 | Esau and Jacob |
| | | 6 | Joseph Sold into Slavery |
| 7 | 8 | 7 | Moses Receives the Ten Commandments |
| | | 8 | The Fall of Jericho |
| 9 | 10 | 9 | The Battle with the Philistines |
| | | 10 | Solomon and the Queen of Sheba |

Detail of carvings by Donatello on the wall of Orsanmichele

## ❽ Orsanmichele

Via dell'Arte della Lana.
**Map** 3 C1 (6 D3). **Tel** 055 28 49 44.
**Open** 10am–5pm daily. **Closed** Jan 1, May 1, Mon in Aug, Dec 25.

Built in 1337 as a grain market, Orsanmichele was later converted into a church which took its name from *Orto di San Michele*, a monastic garden long since vanished. The arcades of the market became windows, which are today bricked in, but the original Gothic tracery can still be seen. The decoration was entrusted to Florence's major *Arti* (guilds). Over 60 years they commissioned sculptures of their patron saints to adorn the 14 exterior niches; however, today many of the figures are copies. Among the sculptors were Lorenzo Ghiberti, Donatello, and Verrocchio.

The beautifully tranquil interior contains an opulent 14th-century altar by Andrea Orcagna, a *Virgin and Child* by Bernardo Daddi (1348), and a statue of the *Madonna and Child with St. Anne* by Francesco da Sangallo (1522).

## ❾ Bargello

Via del Proconsolo 4. **Map** 4 D1 (6 E3).
**Tel** 055 238 86 06. 🚌 14, A. **Open** 8:15am–1:30pm daily (to 5pm mid-Jul–Sep. **Closed** 1st, 3rd & 5th Sun and 2nd & 4th Mon of each month; Jan 1, May 1, Dec 25. 🅿️ ♿ 🚫 ♿

Florence's second-ranking museum after the Uffizi, the Bargello contains a wonderful medley of applied arts and Italy's finest collection of Renaissance sculpture. Begun in 1255, the fortresslike building was initially the town hall (making it the oldest seat of government in the city), but it later became a prison and home to the chief of police (the *Bargello*). It also became known for its executions, which took place in the main courtyard until 1786, when the death sentence was abolished by Grand Duke Pietro Leopoldo. Following extensive renovation, the building opened as one of Italy's first national museums in 1865.

The key exhibits range over three floors, beginning with the Michelangelo Room, redesigned after extensive damage during the 1966 flood of the Arno. Three contrasting works by Michelangelo lie dotted around the room, the most famous a tipsy-looking *Bacchus* (1497), the sculptor's first large free-standing work. Close by is a powerful bust of *Brutus* (1539–40), the only known portrait bust by Michelangelo, and a delicate circular relief depicting the *Madonna and Child* (1503–5). Countless works by other sculptors occupy the same room. Among them is an exquisite *Mercury* (1564) by the Mannerist genius, Giambologna, as well as several virtuoso bronzes by the sculptor and goldsmith Benvenuto Cellini (1500–71).

Across the courtyard, full of fragments and the coats of arms of the Bargello's various incumbents, two more rooms contain exterior sculptures removed from sites around the city. The courtyard's external staircase leads to the first floor, which opens with a wonderfully

Brunelleschi's *Sacrifice of Isaac* (1402) in the Bargello

Donatello's *David (c.1430)* in the Bargello

eccentric bronze menagerie by Giambologna. To the right is the Salone del Consiglio Generale, a cavernous former courtroom that contains the cream of the museum's Early Renaissance sculpture. Foremost among its highlights is Donatello's heroic *St. George* (1416) – the epitome of "youth, courage, and valor of arms" in the words of Vasari. Commissioned by the Armorers' Guild, the statue was brought here from Orsanmichele in 1892. At the center of the room, in direct contrast, is Donatello's androgynous *David* (c.1430), famous as the first freestanding nude by a Western artist since antiquity. Among the room's more easily missed works, tucked away on the right wall, are two reliefs depicting *The Sacrifice of Isaac* (1402). Created by Brunelleschi and Lorenzo Ghiberti respectively, both were entries in the competition to design the Baptistery doors.

Beyond the Salone, the Bargello's emphasis shifts to the applied arts, with room after room devoted to rugs, ceramics, silverware, and a host of other beautiful *objets d'art*. The most celebrated of these rooms is the Salone del Camino on the second floor, which features the finest collection of small bronzes in Italy. Some are reproductions of antique models, others are small copies of Renaissance statues. Giambologna, Cellini, and Antonio del Pollaiuolo are represented here.

*Bacchus* (1497) by Michelangelo

# ⑩ Santa Croce

Work began around 1294 on the Gothic church of Santa Croce, which contains tombs and monuments of famous Florentines, such as Michelangelo, Galileo, and Machiavelli, as well as radiant early 14th-century frescoes by Giotto and his pupil Taddeo Gaddi. In the cloister alongside the church stands the Cappella de' Pazzi (Pazzi Chapel), a Renaissance masterpiece designed by Filippo Brunelleschi.

**★ Cappella de' Pazzi**
Brunelleschi's domed chapel with Classical proportions was begun in 1441. The roundels (c.1442–52) are by Luca della Robbia.

**Tomb of Leonardo Bruni** (1447)
Rossellino's effigy of this great humanist was unusual in its sensitive realism and lack of monumental pomp.

Ticket booth and entrance

**Cimabue's Crucifixion**
Badly damaged in the Florence flood of 1966, this 13th-century masterpiece is among the highlights of the collection, as is Taddeo Gaddi's magnificent *Last Supper* (c.1355–60).

## KEY

① **Refectory**

② *Tree of Life* **by Taddeo Gaddi**

③ **Vasari's Tomb of Michelangio** is decorated with figures representing sculpture and architecture.

④ **The Neo-Gothic facade** by Niccolò Matas was added in 1863.

⑤ **Tomb of Galileo**

⑥ **Tomb of Machiavelli**

⑦ *Annunciation* **by Donatello** (15th century)

⑧ **The Cappella Baroncelli**, frescoed by Taddeo Gaddi between 1332 and 1338, contains the first true night scene in Western art.

⑨ **Sacristy**

⑩ **The Neo-Gothic campanile** was added in 1842, after the original was destroyed in 1512 by lightning.

Exit

★ **Cappella Bardi Frescoes**
Giotto frescoed the Bardi
and Peruzzi chapels to the
right of the high altar between
1315 and 1330. This touching
scene from the left-hand
wall of the chapel shows
*The Death of St. Francis* (1317).

## ⓫ Museo Galileo

Piazza de' Giudici 1. **Map** 4 D1 (6 E4).
**Tel** 055 26 53 11. **Open** 9:30am–6pm
daily (to 1pm Tue). **Closed** Jan 1 & 6,
May 1, Easter, Jun 24, Aug 13, Nov 1
& 8, Dec 25 & 26. 📷 📷

This lively and superbly
presented museum devotes
two floors to various scientific
themes, illustrating each with
countless fine displays and a
panoply of old and beautifully
made scientific instruments.
It is also something of a shrine
to the Pisa-born scientist Galileo
Galilei (1564–1642), and
houses the only
surviving
instruments
he designed
and built,
including two
telescopes and
the objective
lens from the
telescope with
which he discovered
Jupiter's moons.
    A number of rooms
are devoted to astro-

**Astrolabe, Museo Galileo**

nomical, mathematical, and
navigational instruments, with
galleries concentrating on
Galileo, telescopes, and optical
games. The museum also
houses the scientific collections
of the two dynasties that once
ruled Florence: the Medici and
the House of Lorraine.
    Some of the best exhibits on
display are early maps, globes
and astrolabes, antique micro-
scopes, thermometers, and
barometers. There are also some
fine old clocks, mathematical
instruments, calculators, a horri-
fying collection of 19th-century
surgical instruments, and some

graphic anatomical models.
The museum has installed a
large bronze sundial outside
the entrance that can be used
to read the hour and the date.

## ⓬ Ponte Vecchio

**Map** 4 D1 (6 E4).

Ponte Vecchio, the oldest
surviving bridge in the city,
was built in 1345, the last in a
succession of bridges and fords
on the site that dated back to
Roman times. Designed by
Giotto's pupil Taddeo
Gaddi, it was originally
the domain of
blacksmiths,
butchers, and
tanners (who
used the river
for disposing
of waste). They
were reviled for
their noise and
stench and were
evicted in 1593 by
Duke Ferdinando I and
replaced by jewelers
and goldsmiths. The elevated
Corridoio Vasariano runs along
the eastern side of the bridge,
above the stores. Giorgio Vasari
designed the corridor in 1565
to allow the Medici family to
move about their residences
without having to mix with the
public. This was the city's only
bridge to escape destruction
during World War II and visitors
today come as much to admire
the views as to browse among
the antiques shops and specialty jewelry stores. A bust of the
famous goldsmith Benvenuto
Cellini stands in the middle of
the bridge.

**Ponte Vecchio viewed from the Ponte Santa Trinità**

# ⑬ Uffizi

The Uffizi, Italy's greatest art gallery, was built in 1560–80 to house offices *(uffici)* for Duke Cosimo I. The architect Vasari used iron as reinforcement, enabling his successor, Buontalenti, to create an almost continuous wall of glass on the upper story. This was used as a gallery for Francesco I to display the Medici art treasures. In the 19th century, the collection's ancient objects were moved to the archaeological museum and the sculpture to the Bargello, leaving a priceless collection of paintings. Continuing renovations may mean some room closures; check the website for details.

**Corridor ceilings** are frescoed in the "grotesque" style of the 1580s, inspired by Roman grottoes.

Second floor

Main Entrance

**The Loggia dei Lanzi terrace** merits a visit for its unusual views of the Piazza della Signoria *(see pp294–5).*

Bar

First floor

**Annunciation** (1333)
The Sienese painter Simone Martini was strongly influenced by French Gothic art, and this is one of his masterpieces.

**Bacchus** (*c.* 1589)
Caravaggio's early work depicting the god of wine can be found in the first-floor exhibition rooms.

**The Venus of Urbino** (1538)
Titian's sensuous nude, inspired by Giorgione's *Sleeping Venus*, may in fact be a portrait of a courtesan deemed sufficiently beautiful to represent a goddess.

## Gallery Guide

*The paintings are hung in a series of rooms to show the development of Florentine art from the Gothic to Renaissance and beyond. The earliest works are on the second floor – start here to explore the collection in a broadly chronological order. There are many well-known Early Renaissance paintings in rooms 7–18. Some familiar High Renaissance masterpieces are hung on the first floor, and masters from other European countries are in rooms 44–55.*

Main
staircase

**The Duke and Duchess of Urbino** (*c.*1465–70)
Piero della Francesca's portraits of Federico da
Montefeltro and his wife Battista Sforza were
painted after Battista died aged 26. Her portrait
was probably based on her death mask.

**The Tribune**,
decorated in red and
gold, contains the
works most valued
by the Medici.

Buontalenti
staircase

**Ognissanti
Madonna** (*c.*1310)
Giotto's grasp of
spatial depth and
substance in this
altarpiece was
a milestone in
the mastery of
perspective.

**The Birth of Venus** (*c.*1485)
Botticelli shows the goddess
of love flanked by Zephyrus,
god of the west wind, who
blows the risen Venus to
shore on a half-shell.
The myth may symbolize
the birth of beauty through
the divine fertilization
of matter.

Entrance to the Vasari Corridor

**The Holy Family** (1507)
Michelangelo's
painting, the first
to break with the
convention of
showing Christ on
the Virgin's lap,
inspired Mannerist
artists through
its expressive
handling of color
and posture.

Vasari's Classical
Arno facade

### Key to Floorplan

- East Corridor
- West Corridor
- Arno Corridor
- Gallery Rooms 1–45
- 17th- to 18th-century painting
  in Europe
- 17th-century painting in Italy
- 16th-century painting in Italy
- Sculpture gallery
- Temporary exhibitions
- Nonexhibition space

# Exploring the Uffizi

The Uffizi offers not only the chance to see the world's greatest collection of Italian Renaissance paintings, but also the opportunity to enjoy masterpieces from as far afield as Holland, Spain, and Germany. Accumulated over the centuries by the Medici, the collection was first housed in the Uffizi in 1581, and eventually bequeathed to the Florentine people by Anna Maria Ludovica, the last of the Medici.

*Madonna and Child with Angels* (1455–66) by Fra Filippo Lippi

## Gothic Art

Room 1 largely features paintings in the International Gothic style, a highly decorative style that represented the height of Gothic expression and a move away from the stilted conventions of Byzantium. The style is exemplified by Gentile da Fabriano's exquisite, glittering *Adoration of the Magi*, which was painted in 1423.

Rooms 2 to 6 of the gallery are devoted to Tuscan Gothic art from the 12th to the 14th century. Giotto (1266–1337) introduced a degree of naturalism that was new in Tuscan art. The angels and saints in his *Ognissanti Madonna* (1310), in room 2, express a range of emotions, from awe and reverence to puzzlement. This new feeling for depth and naturalistic detail is also shown by the carefully evoked three-dimensionality of the Virgin's throne. The temple in Lorenzetti's *Presentation in the Temple* (1342), in room 3, also shows a concern for three-dimensional depth quite at odds with the flatness of much Gothic art.

Giotto's naturalistic influence can also be seen among the paintings of room 4, which is devoted to the 14th-century Florentine School, an interesting counterpoint to the Sienese works of Duccio and his followers in room 3. Among the paintings here are works by Ambrogio and Pietro Lorenzetti, and Simone Martini's *Annunciation*.

## Early Renaissance

A new understanding of geometry and perspective during the 15th century increasingly allowed artists to explore the complexities of space and depth. None became more obsessed with these new compositional possibilities than Paolo Uccello (1397–1475), whose picture of *The Battle of San Romano* (1456) in room 7 is one of the gallery's most fevered creations.

Room 7 also contains two panels from 1460 by Piero della Francesca, another artist preoccupied with the art of perspective. The panels, which are among the earliest Renaissance portraits, depict the Duke and Duchess of Urbino on one side and representations of their virtues on the other.

While such works can seem coldly experimental, Fra Filippo Lippi's *Madonna and Child with Angels* (1455–66), in room 8, is a masterpiece of warmth and humanity. Like many Renaissance artists, Lippi uses a religious subject to

Sandro Botticelli's allegorical painting, *Primavera* (1480)

celebrate earthly delights such as landscape and feminine beauty. A similar approach is apparent in the works of Botticelli, whose famous paintings in rooms 10–14 are for many the highlight of the gallery. In *The Birth of Venus*, for example, Venus takes the place of the Virgin, expressing a fascination with Classical mythology common to many Renaissance artists. The same is true of the *Primavera* (1480), which breaks with Christian religious painting by illustrating a pagan rite of spring.

Detail from *The Annunciation* (1472–5) by Leonardo da Vinci

## High Renaissance and Mannerism

Room 15 features works attributed to the young Leonardo da Vinci, notably a sublime *Annunciation* (1472–5), which reveals hints of his still emerging style, and the *Adoration of the Magi* (1481), which remained unfinished when he left Florence for Milan to paint *The Last Supper* (1495–8).

Room 18, better known as the Tribune, was designed in 1584 by Buontalenti in order to accommodate the best-loved pieces of the Medici collection. Its most famous work is the so-called Medici Venus (1st century BC), a Roman copy of a Greek statue deemed to be the most erotic in the ancient world. The copy proved equally salacious and was removed from Rome's Villa Medici by Cosimo III to keep it from corrupting the city's art students.

Rooms 19 to 23 depart from the gallery's Florentine bias, demonstrating how rapidly Renaissance ideas and techniques spread beyond Tuscany. Painters from the German and Flemish schools are well represented, together with painters from Umbria like Perugino, but perhaps the most captivating works are the paintings by Venetian and northern Italian artists such as Mantegna, Carpaccio, Correggio, and Bellini.

Room 35, which returns to the Tuscan mainstream, is dominated by Michelangelo's *Holy Family*, or *Tondo Doni* (1456), notable for its vibrant colors and the Virgin's unusually twisted pose. The gallery's only work by Michelangelo, it was to prove immensely influential with the next generation of painters, especially Bronzino (1503–72), Pontormo (1494–1556), and Parmigianino (1503–40). The last of these was responsible for the *Madonna of the Long Neck* (c.1534) in room 29. With its contorted anatomy, unnatural colors, and strange composition, this painting is a masterpiece of the style that came to be called Mannerism. Earlier, but no less remarkable masterpieces in rooms 26 and 28 include Raphael's sublime *Madonna of the Goldfinch* (1506) and Titian's notorious *Venus of Urbino* (1538), censured by Mark Twain as the "foulest, the vilest, the obscenest picture the world possesses." Others hold it to be

*Madonna of the Goldfinch* (1506) by Raphael

*Madonna of the Long Neck* (c.1534) by Parmigianino

one of the most beautiful nudes ever painted. Other works of note include, in room 65, Agnolo Bronzino's portraits of Cosimo I and Eleonora di Toledo, both painted around 1545, and Pontormo's *Charity* (1530) and his portrait of Cosimo il Vecchio (1517) in room 61.

## European Art and Later Italian Paintings

The works in room 45 show how the naturalism pursued by Northern European masters, such as Dürer (1471–1528) and Cranach (1472–1553), had a profound influence on Renaissance painters such as Pietro Perugino (1446–1523) and Jacopo da Sallaio (1441–1523). A selection of works by Flemish painter Hans Memling (1430–94) is displayed in room 43, and later Flemish paintings, including those by Rubens (1577–1640) and Van Dyck (1599–1641), are in room 55. Dutch paintings of the 17th and 18th century, including a number of Rembrandt self-portraits, are in room 49.

Later Italian artists are represented in rooms 90 to 93. There are works by Caravaggio (1571–1610) and several of his followers, such as Dutch artist Gerard van Honthorst (1592–1656) and Artemisia Gentileschi (1593–1656), best known for her brutal masterpiece *Judith Slaying Holofernes* (1611–12).

# ⑭ Piazza della Signoria

Piazza della Signoria and Palazzo Vecchio have been at the heart of Florence's political and social life for centuries. The great bell once used to summon citizens to *parlamento* (public meetings) here, and the square has long been a popular promenade for both visitors and Florentines. The piazza's statues (some are copies) commemorate the city's major historical events, though its most famous episode is celebrated by a simple sidewalk plaque near the loggia: the execution of the fanatical religious leader Girolamo Savonarola.

**David**
This copy of the famous Michelangelo statue symbolizes triumph over tyranny. The original *(see p279)* stood in the piazza until 1873.

**Heraldic Frieze**
The crossed keys on this shield represent Medici papal rule.

## KEY

① **The Fontana di Nettuno**, created by Ammannati (1575), represents Roman sea god surrounded by water nymphs and commemorates Tuscan naval victories.

② **Sala dei Gigli**

③ **The Uffizi**

④ **The Loggia dei Lanzi**, designed by Orcagna (1382), is named after the Lancers, the bodyguards of Cosimo I who were billeted here.

⑤ **Roman statues**, possibly of emperors, line the Loggia.

⑥ **The Marzocco** is a copy of the heraldic lion of Florence, carved by Donatello in 1420. The original is in the Bargello *(see p287)*.

**Salone dei Cinquecento** (1495)
This vast chamber contains a statue of Victory by Michelangelo and frescoes by Vasari describing Florentine triumphs over Pisa and Siena.

★ **Palazzo Vecchio** (completed 1332)
This Republican frieze over the palace entrance is inscribed with the words "Christ is King," implying that no mortal ruler has absolute power.

★ **The Rape of the Sabine Women by Giambologna** (1583)
The writhing figures in Giambologna's famous statue were carved from a single block of flawed marble.

★ **Perseus by Cellini**
This bronze statue (1554) of Perseus beheading Medusa was intended to warn Cosimo I's enemies of their probable fate.

## ⓯ Palazzo Vecchio

Piazza della Signoria (entrance on via della Ninna). Map 4 D1 (6 E4). **Tel** 055 276 83 25. 🚌 A, B. **Open** Apr–Sep: 9am–11pm (to 2pm Thu); Oct–Mar: 9am–7pm (to 2pm Thu).
**Closed** Jan 1, Easter, May 1, Aug 15, Dec 25. 🎫 ♿ Secret Itineraries & Children's Museum tours (by reservation only). **Tel** 055 276 83 25.

The "Old Palace" still fulfills its original role as town hall. It was completed in 1322 when a huge bell, used to call citizens to meetings or warn of fire, flood, or enemy attack, was hauled to the top of the imposing bell tower. While retaining much of its medieval appearance, the interior was remodeled for Duke Cosimo I in 1540. The redecoration was undertaken by Vasari, who incorporated bombastic frescoes (1563–5) of Florentine achievements. Michelangelo's *Victory* statue (1525) graces the Salone dei Cinquecento, which also has a tiny study decorated by Florence's leading Mannerist painters in 1569–73. Other highlights include the Cappella di Eleonora, painted by Bronzino (1540–45); the loggia, with its views over the city; the Sala dei Gigli (Room of Lilies) with Donatello's *Judith and Holofernes* (c.1455); and frescoes of Roman heroes by Ghirlandaio (1485); as well as the excellent museum for children and the secret rooms and passageways.

A copy of Verrocchio's putto fountain in Vasari's courtyard

# Street by Street: Around Piazza della Repubblica

Underlying the street plan of modern Florence is the far older pattern of the ancient Roman city. Nowhere is this more evident than in the grid of narrow streets around Piazza della Repubblica, site of the old Roman forum. This pivotal square housed the city's main food market and the Jewish ghetto until the 1860s, when redevelopment tidied up the area and added the triumphal arch in today's café-filled square.

VIA DEL CAMPIDOGLIO

VIA DE BRUNELLESCHI

VIA DE PESCIONI

VIA DE VECCHETTI

PIAZZ

VIA DEGLI STROZZI

REPUB

VIA DE TORNABUONI

VIA DE SASSETTI

ANSELMI

PELLIC

PIAZZA DEGLI STROZZ

VIA DEGLI

VIA MONALDA

PIAZZA DE DAVANZATI

VIA PORTA ROSSA

VIA PARIONE

VIA DELLE TERME

PIAZZA DI S. TRINITA

V D FIORDALISO

O CORNINO

BORGO SS APOSTOLI

LUNGARNO DEGLI ACCIAIUOLI

**Santa Trìnita** has frescoes by Ghirlandaio on the Life of St. Francis (1486), depicting events that took place in this area. Here, a child is revived after falling from the Palazzo Spini-Ferroni.

Palazzo Spini-Ferroni

**Ponte Santa Trìnita** was built in wood in 1290 and then rebuilt by Ammannati in 1567 to celebrate the defeat of Siena.

**17 Palazzo Strozzi**
This monumental palazzo dominates the square.

**Santi Apostoli**
was reputedly founded by Charlemagne.

**16 Palazzo Davanzati**
Frescoes with exotic birds decorate the Sala dei Pappagalli, which was once the dining room of this 14th-century palazzo.

**Key**

— Suggested route

| 0 meters | 200 |
|---|---|
| 0 yards | 200 |

*For hotels and restaurants in this region see pp569–73 and pp590–96*

**Locator Map**
*See Florence Street Finder maps 5, 6*

**Piazza della Repubblica**, which dates from the 19th century, is lined by some of Florence's oldest and best-known cafés.

**Mercato Nuovo**, the "New Market" (1547), now deals mainly in souvenirs.

**Palazzo di Parte Guelfa** was the headquarters of the Guelphs, the dominant political party of medieval Florence.

Ponte Vecchio
*(see p289)*

Detail of a frieze illustrating a medieval romance in Palazzo Davanzati

## ⑯ Palazzo Davanzati

Via Porta Rossa 13. **Map** 3 C1 (5 C3). **Tel** 055 238 86 10. **Open** 8:15am–1:50pm daily. **Closed** 1st, 3rd, & 5th Mon and 2nd and 4th Sun of the month, Jan 1, May 1, Dec 25. 10am, 11am, noon (2nd floor only).

This wonderful museum, also known as the Museo dell'Antica Casa Fiorentina, uses original fittings and furniture to recreate a typical well-to-do 14th-century town house. Among the highlights are the Salone Madornale, where large gatherings would have been held, and the Sala dei Pappagalli (Parrots Room), with its frescoes and rich tapestries.

Pelting holes in the vaulted ceiling of the entrance courtyard were for dropping missiles on unwanted visitors. In one corner of the inner courtyard is a well and a pulley system to raise pails of water to each floor – a real luxury, since most medieval households had to fetch water from a public fountain.

## ⑰ Palazzo Strozzi

Piazza degli Strozzi. **Map** 3 C1 (5 C3). **Tel** 055 264 51 55. **Open** 10am–8pm daily (to 11pm Thu) for exhibitions. **w** palazzostrozzi.org

Sheer size accounts for the impact of the Palazzo Strozzi, and although it is only three stories high, each floor exceeds the height of a normal palazzo. It was commissioned by the wealthy banker Filippo Strozzi, who had 15 buildings demolished to make way for the palazzo. He hoped it would rival the Medici palaces elsewhere in the city. Strozzi died in 1491, just two years after the first stone was laid.

Work on the building continued until 1536, with three major architects contributing to its design – Giuliano da Sangallo, Benedetto da Maiano, and Simone del Pollaiuolo (also known as Cronaca). The exterior, built of huge rusticated masonry blocks, remains unspoiled. Look out for the original Renaissance torch-holders and lamps and the rings for tethering horses that still adorn the corners and facades. The palace is now primarily used as an exhibition venue, when visitors can also access "La Strozzina," a vaulted gallery space in the basement, where small temporary exhibitions are held.

Exterior of Palazzo Strozzi, with masonry block rustication

# ⑱ San Lorenzo

San Lorenzo was the parish church of the Medici family, and in 1419 Brunelleschi was commissioned to rebuild it in the Classical style of the Renaissance. Almost a century later, Michelangelo submitted some plans for the facade and began work on the Medici tombs in the Sagrestia Nuova (the Old Sacristy). He also designed a library, the Biblioteca Mediceo-Laurenziana, to house the family's collection of manuscripts. The lavish family mausoleum, the Cappella dei Principi, was started in 1604.

**Cappella dei Principi**
The Medici mausoleum, behind the high altar, was begun in 1604 by Matteo Nigetti, and forms part of the Cappelle Medicee.

**Biblioteca Staircase**
Michelangelo's Mannerist staircase, one of the artist's most innovative designs, was built by Ammannati in 1559.

## KEY

① **St. Joseph and Christ in the Workshop**, a striking work showing the young Christ with his father, is by Pietro Annigoni (1910–88), one of the few modern artists whose work is seen in Florence.

② **The cloister garden** is planted with boxwood hedges and pomegranate and orange trees.

③ **Michelangelo** designed the desks and ceiling of the Biblioteca, where exhibitions of Medici manuscripts are often held.

④ **The Old Sacristy** was designed by Brunelleschi and decorated by Donatello.

⑤ **The huge dome** by Buontalenti echoes that of the Duomo *(see pp284–6)*.

⑥ **Campanile**

⑦ **The Cappelle Medicee** complex comprises the Cappella dei Principi and its crypt, the New Sacristy *(see opposite)*.

⑧ **A simple stone** slab marks the unostentatious grave of Cosimo il Vecchio (1389–1464), founder of the Medici dynasty.

⑨ **Michelangelo** submitted several designs for the facade of San Lorenzo, but it remains unfinished.

The Martyrdom of St. Lawrence

Entrance to church

*The Tomb of the Duke of Nemours (1520–34)
by Michelangelo in the Cappelle Medicee's
New Sacristy*

tombs of six Medici Grand
Dukes. A corridor leads to
Michelangelo's **New Sacristy**,
designed as a counterpoint to
Brunelleschi's Old Sacristy in
San Lorenzo. Three groups
of statues, all carved by
Michelangelo between 1520
and 1534, stand around the
walls: that on the near left-hand
wall is *The Tomb of the Duke of
Urbino* (grandson of Lorenzo the
Magnificent). Opposite is *The
Tomb of the Duke of Nemours*
(Lorenzo's third son). Close to
the unfinished *Madonna and
Child* (1521) is the simple
tomb containing Lorenzo the
Magnificent and his murdered
brother, Giuliano (died 1478).

**Pulpits by Donatello**
The bronze pulpits in the
nave were Donatello's last
works. Completed by his
pupils in 1460, the reliefs
capture the flinching pain of
Christ's Passion and the glory
of the Resurrection.

## ⑲ Cappelle Medicee

Piazza di Madonna degli Aldobrandini.
**Map** 1 C5 (6 D1). **Tel** 055 238 86 02
(reservations). 🚌 many routes.
**Open** 8:15am–5pm daily (Nov & Dec:
8:15am–1:50pm daily). Last adm:
30 mins before closing. **Closed** 1st,
3rd, & 5th Mon of each month, 2nd &
4th Sun, Jan 1, May 1, Dec 25. 🚻 🔋

The Medici Chapels divide into
three distinct areas. Beyond the
entrance hall lies a low-vaulted
crypt, a suitably subdued space
for the brass-railed tombs of
many lesser members of the
Medici family. From here, steps
lead to the octagonal **Cappella
dei Principi** (Chapel of Princes),
a vast family mausoleum begun
by Cosimo I in 1604. The ceiling
is garishly frescoed and the
walls are smothered in huge
swaths of semiprecious *pietre
dure* (inlaid stone). Spaced
around the walls are the

## ⑳ Mercato Centrale

Piazza del Mercato Centrale. **Map** 1 C4
(5 C1). **Open** 7am–2pm Mon–Sat.

At the heart of the San Lorenzo
street market is the bustling
Mercato Centrale, Florence's
busiest food market. It is housed
in a vast two-story building of
cast iron and glass, built in
1874 by Giuseppe Mengoni.
The first-floor stands sell
meat, poultry, fish, hams, oils,
and cheeses. There are also
Tuscan takeout foods such as
*porchetta* (roast suckling pig),
*lampredotto* (pig's intestines),
and *trippa* (tripe). The second
floor houses a large bar/
restaurant, with seating. There
are food stands, a bank, a
bookstore, and a cooking school.
There is also a pizzeria and a
restaurant on the mezzanine.

**The Martyrdom of
St. Lawrence**
Bronzino's vast Mannerist
fresco of 1569 is a
bravura, choreographed
study of the human
form, rather than a
reverential response to
the agony of the saint.

Yellow zucchini flowers and other vegetables in the Mercato Centrale

# ㉑ Santa Maria Novella

The Church of Santa Maria Novella was built by the Dominicans between 1279 and 1357. The lower Romanesque part of its facade was incorporated into one based on Classical proportions by the pioneering Renaissance architect Leon Battista Alberti in 1456–70. The Gothic interior contains superb frescoes, including Masaccio's powerful *Trinity*. The famous Green Cloister, frescoed with perspective scenes by Paolo Uccello, and the dramatically decorated Spanish Chapel now form a museum.

**The Nave**
The piers of the nave are spaced closer together at the altar end. This trick of perspective creates the illusion of an exceptionally long church.

**Trinity by Masaccio**
This pioneering fresco (*c.*1428) is renowned as a masterpiece of perspective and portraiture. The kneeling figures flanking the arch are the painting's sponsors, judge Lorenzo Lenzi and his wife.

## KEY

① **Chiostro Verde** takes its name from the green base used in Uccello's frescoes, which were sadly damaged by the 1966 floods.

② **Cappellone degli Spagnuoli**, the chapel used by the Spanish courtiers of Eleonora of Toledo, has frescoes of salvation and damnation.

③ **Monastic buildings**

④ **The arcade arches** are emphasized by gray and white banding.

⑤ **The Strozzi Tomb** is by Benedetto da Maiano (1493).

⑥ **Cappella di Filippo Strozzi** features Filippino Lippi's frescoes of St. John raising Drusiana from the dead and St. Philip slaying a dragon.

Main door

Entrance to museum

Entrance (via courtyard)

**Cappella Strozzi**
The 14th-century frescoes by Nardo di Cione and his brother Andrea Orcagna were inspired by Dante's epic poem, *The Divine Comedy*.

Ghirlandaio's *Madonna della Misericordia* (1472) in Ognissanti

## ㉒ Palazzo Antinori

Piazza Antinori 3. **Map** 1 C5 (5 C2).
**Closed** to the public. Cantinetta
Antinori: **Tel** 055 29 22 34. **Open**
12:30–2:30pm & 7–10:30pm Mon–Fri.

Palazzo Antinori was built in
1461–6 and is one of the finest
small Renaissance palazzi in
Florence. It was acquired by
the Antinoris in 1506 and has
remained with the family ever
since. The dynasty produces a
range of wines, oils, and liqueurs
that can be sampled – along
with fine Tuscan dishes – in the
Cantinetta Antinori, the wine
bar off the main courtyard.

## ㉓ Palazzo Rucellai

Via della Vigna Nuova 16. **Map** 1 C5
(5 B3). **Closed** to the public.

Built in 1446–51, this is one of
the most ornate Renaissance
palaces in the city. It was
commissioned by Giovanni
Rucellai, whose enormous
wealth derived from the import
of a rare and costly red dye
made from lichen found
only on the Spanish island
of Majorca. The precious
dye was called *oricello*,
from which the name
Rucellai is derived.
Giovanni commissioned
several buildings from the
architect Leon Battista
Alberti, who designed this
palace as a virtual textbook
illustration of the major
Classical orders. The palazzo
used to house the Museo
Alinari, but the collection has
moved to Piazza Santa Maria
Novella and is being renovated.

## ㉔ Museo Nazionale Alinari della Fotografia

Piazza Santa Maria Novella 14ar.
**Map** 1 B5 (5 B2). **Tel** 055 21 63 10.
**Closed** for renovation. 🚻
🎫 📷 🆆 mnaf.it

The Alinari brothers began
taking pictures of Florence in
the 1840s. They supplied high-
quality postcards and prints
to visitors to Florence in the
19th century. The exhibits
offer a vivid insight into the
social history of Florence at
that time. The museum also
houses a collection of
cameras, documents, and
objects that illustrate the
history of photography.

## ㉕ Ognissanti

Borgo Ognissanti 42. **Map** 1 B5 (5 A2).
**Tel** 055 239 87 00. Church: **Open**
7am–12:30pm, 4–8pm daily.
♿ Ghirlandaio's *The Last Supper*:
**Open** 9am–noon Mon, Tue, & Sat.

Ognissanti, or All Saints, was the
parish church of the Vespucci,
one of whose members, the
15th-century navigator
Amerigo, gave his name to the
New World. The young Amerigo
is depicted in Ghirlandaio's
fresco of the *Madonna della
Misericordia* (1472) in the
second chapel on the right;
Ghirlandaio's *The Last Supper*
(1480) can be seen in the
convent next door.

In a chapel to the left of the
transept hangs the 14th-century,
16-ft- (5-m-) high Ognissanti
Crucifix by Giotto di Bondone.

**Cappella Tornabuoni**
Ghirlandaio's famous fresco cycle,
*The Life of John the Baptist* (1485),
peoples the biblical episodes
with Florentine aristocrats in
contemporary dress.

# ㉖ Cappella Brancacci

The Church of Santa Maria del Carmine is famous for the Brancacci Chapel, which contains frescoes on *The Life of St. Peter* commissioned by the Florentine merchant Felice Brancacci around 1424. Although the paintings were begun by Masolino in 1425, many of the scenes are by his pupil, Masaccio (who died before completing the cycle), and by Filippino Lippi, who finished the work in 1480. Masaccio's revolutionary use of perspective, his narrative drama, and the tragic realism of his figures placed him in the vanguard of Renaissance painting. Many great artists, including Michelangelo, later visited the chapel to study his pioneering work.

**St. Peter Healing the Sick**
Masaccio's realistic portrayal of cripples and beggars was revolutionary in his time.

## KEY

① **Masaccio's simple style** allows us to focus on the figures central to the frescoes without distracting detail.

② **The grouping** of stylized figures in Masaccio's frescoes reflects his interest in the sculpture of Donatello.

③ **In every scene**, St. Peter is distinguished from the crowds as the figure in the orange cloak.

④ **St. Peter** is depicted against a background of Florentine buildings.

⑤ **Masolino's Temptation of Adam and Eve** is gentle and decorous, in contrast with the emotional force of Masaccio's painting on the opposite wall.

**Expulsion of Adam and Eve**
Masaccio's ability to express emotion is well illustrated by his harrowing portrait of Adam and Eve being driven out of the Garden of Eden, their faces wracked by misery, shame, and the burden of self-knowledge.

**Key to the Frescoes: Artists and Subjects**

- [ ] Masolino
- [ ] Masaccio
- [ ] Lippi

| | | | | | |
|---|---|---|---|---|---|
| 1 | 2 | 3 | 7 | 8 | 9 |
| 4 | 5 | 6 | 10 | 11 | 12 |

**1** Expulsion of Adam and Eve
**2** The Tribute Money
**3** St. Peter Preaching
**4** St. Peter Visited by St. Paul
**5** Raising the Emperor's Son;
St. Peter Enthroned
**6** St. Peter Healing the Sick

**7** St. Peter Baptizing the Converts
**8** St. Peter Healing the Cripple;
Raising Tabitha
**9** Temptation of Adam and Eve
**10** St. Peter and St. John Giving Alms
**11** Crucifixion; Before the Proconsul
**12** The Release of St. Peter

**VISITORS' CHECKLIST**

**Practical Information**
Piazza del Carmine.
**Map** 3 A1 (5 A4).
**Tel** 055 276 82 24.
**Open** 10am–5pm Mon,
Wed–Sat; 1–5pm Sun.
**Closed** public hols.

**Transportation**
D.

**Woman in a Turban**
The freshness of Masaccio's original colors is seen in this rediscovered roundel, hidden behind the altar for 500 years.

**Two Figures**
Masolino's work tends to be more formal, less naturalistic, and less animated than that of Masaccio.

**Before the Proconsul**
Filippino Lippi was called in to complete the cycle of frescoes in 1480. He added this emotional scene showing the Proconsul sentencing St. Peter to death.

# Street by Street: Oltrarno

For the most part, the Oltrarno is a homey area of small houses, quiet squares and stores selling antiques, bric-a-brac and foodstuffs. The Via Maggio, a busy thoroughfare, breaks this pattern, but step into the side streets and you escape the bustle to discover a corner of old world Florence. The restaurants serve authentic, reasonably priced food, and the area is full of studios and workshops restoring antique furniture. Among the things to see are Santo Spirito and Palazzo Pitti, one of the city's largest palaces, whose medley of museums contains an art collection second only to that of the Uffizi.

**㉗ Santo Spirito**
Brunelleschi's simple church was completed after the architect's death.

Ponte Santa Trinità

**Cenacolo di Santo Spirito**, the old refectory of a monastery that once stood here, contains a dramatic fresco attributed to Orcagna (c.1360).

**★ Palazzo Guadagni**
(1500) was the first palace in the city to be built with a rooftop loggia, setting a trend among the aristocracy.

**★ Palazzo di Bianca Cappello**
(1579) is covered in ornate *sgraffito* work and was the home of the mistress of Grand Duke Francesco I.

**Traditional inlaid mosaics** can be purchased at this store, Pitti Mosaici.

PIAZZA DI S. FELICE

**The 16th-century fountain** and gargoyle in Piazza de' Frescobaldi were designed by Buontalenti, as was the facade (1593–4) of the nearby church of Santa Trinità.

**Locator Map**
*See Florence Street Finder maps 3, 5*

**Ponte Vecchio**
*(see p289)*

BORGO SAN JACOPO

V. DI RAMAGLIANTI

VIA DE' GUICCIARDINI

**Palazzo Guicciardini**
was the birthplace of historian Francesco Guicciardini.

**❷❽ ★ Palazzo Pitti**
Several museums are contained in this massive palazzo, including an outstanding collection of paintings. This painting of Palazzo Pitti is by Giusto Utens (1599).

**Key**

— Suggested route

0 metres        100
0 yards          100

# ❷❼ Santo Spirito

Piazza di Santo Spirito 30. **Map** 3 B2 (5 B4). 💬 D. **Tel** 055 21 00 30. **Open** 9:30am–12:30pm & 4–5:30pm Mon–Sat; 11:30am–12:30pm & 4–5:30pm Sun. **Closed** Wed.

The Augustinian foundation of this church dates from 1250. The present building, dominating the northern end of the pretty Piazza di Santo Spirito, was designed by the architect Brunelleschi in 1435, but not completed until the late 15th century. The unfinished, modest facade was added in the 18th century.

Inside, the harmony of the proportions has been some-what spoiled by the elaborate Baroque *baldacchino* and the High Altar, which was finished in 1607 by Giovanni Caccini. The church has 38 side altars, decorated with 15th- and 16th-century Renaissance paintings and sculpture, among them works by Cosimo Rosselli, Domenico Ghirlandaio and Filippino Lippi. The latter painted a magnificent *Madonna and Child* (1466) for the Nerli Chapel in the south transept.

In the north aisle, a door beneath the organ leads to a vestibule with an ornate coffered ceiling. It was designed by Simone del Pollaiuolo, more commonly known as Cronaca, in 1491. The sacristy adjoining the vestibule, in which 12 huge columns are crammed into a tiny space, was designed by Giuliano da Sangallo in 1489.

Interior of Santo Spirito with colonnaded aisle

# ㉘ Palazzo Pitti

The Palazzo Pitti was originally built for the banker Luca Pitti. The huge scale of the building, begun in 1457 and attributed to Brunelleschi, illustrated Pitti's determination to outrival the Medici family through its display of wealth and power. Ironically, the Medici later purchased the palazzo when building costs bankrupted Pitti's heirs. In 1550 it became the main residence of the Medici, and subsequently all the rulers of the city lived here. Today the richly decorated rooms exhibit countless treasures from the Medici collections.

*Judith* (1620–30) by Artemisia Gentileschi

*The Three Ages of Man* (c.1510), attributed to Giorgione

## Galleria Palatina

The Palatine Gallery, which forms the heart of the Pitti museum complex, contains countless masterpieces by artists such as Botticelli, Titian, Perugino, Andrea del Sarto, Tintoretto, Veronese, Giorgione, and Gentileschi. The works of art, accumulated by the Medici family and the house of Habsburg-Lorraine, are still hung much as the grand dukes wished, regardless of subject or chronology. The gallery consists of 11 main salons, the first 5 of which are painted with allegorical ceiling frescoes glorifying the Medici. Begun by Pietro da Cortona in 1641, they were completed in 1665 by his pupil Ciro Ferri. Room 1

(Sala di Venere) contains Antonio Canova's statue of the *Venus Italica* (1810), commissioned by Napoleon to replace the Venus de' Medici (which was to be taken to Paris). Room 2 (Sala di Apollo) features Titian's *Portrait of a Gentleman* (1540), perhaps the finest of several paintings by the artist in the gallery. Still finer pictures adorn rooms 4 and 5, including some by Perugino and Andrea del Sarto and a host of paintings by Raphael. The most beautiful of the last group are

Raphael's High Renaissance *Madonna della Seggiola* or "Madonna of the Chair" (c.1513–14) and the *Donna Velata* or "Veiled Woman" (c.1516), whose model was reputedly the artist's mistress. Other paintings in the remaining gallery rooms include Fra Filippo Lippi's lovely *Madonna and Child*, painted in the mid-15th century, and Caravaggio's *The Sleeping Cupid* (1608)

*Madonna della Seggiola* (c.1513–14) by Raphael

### Galleria Palatina

**The Museo degli Argenti**, or the Silverware Museum, also displays precious *objets d'art.*

The Boboli Gardens

Entrance to museums and galleries

**Brunelleschi** designed the palace facade, which was eventually extended to three times its original length.

**Appartamenti Reali**

**The Galleria d'Arte Moderna** is a 30-room gallery featuring paintings from the years 1784 to 1924.

*The Palmieri Rotonda* by Giovanni Fattori (1825–1908)

## Appartamenti Reali

The Royal Apartments on the first floor of the south wing of the Palazzo were built in the 17th century. They are decorated with frescoes by various Florentine artists, a series of portraits of the Medici by the Flemish painter Justus Sustermans, who worked at the court between 1619 and 1681, and a group of 18th-century Gobelins tapestries. In the late 18th and early 19th centuries, the apartments were revamped

The Throne Room of the Appartamenti Reali

Galleria del Costume

Piazza della Signoria depicted in precious stones

in Neo-Classical style by the Dukes of Lorraine when they succeeded the Medici dynasty as the rulers of Florence.

The apartments are lavishly appointed with ornate gold and white stuccoed ceilings and rich decoration, notably the walls of the Parrot Room, which are covered with an opulent crimson fabric detailed with a bird design. The Tapestry Rooms are hung with 17th- and 18th-century tapestries of French, Belgian, and Italian manufacture. The apartments reflect the tastes of three distinct historical periods.

## Other Collections

The Museo degli Argenti (Silverware Museum) is housed in rooms formerly used by the Medici as summer apartments. The family's lavish taste is reflected in the vast array of precious objects on display. These embrace beautiful examples of Roman glassware, ivory, carpets, crystal, amber, and fine works by Florentine and German goldsmiths. Pride of place goes to 16 *pietre dure* vases (decorated with hard or semiprecious inlaid stones), once owned by Lorenzo the Magnificent.

The Galleria del Costume, which opened in 1983, reflects the changing taste in the courtly fashion of the late 18th century up to the 1920s.

The highlights of the Galleria d'Arte Moderna (Modern Art Gallery) are the wonderful paintings of the *Macchiaioli* (spotmakers), who were a group of Tuscan artists with a style very similar to that of the French Impressionists.

A copy of Giambologna's *Oceanus Fountain* (1576)

## The Boboli Gardens

The Boboli Gardens, a lovely place to escape the rigors of sightseeing, were laid out for the Medici after they bought the Palazzo Pitti in 1549. An excellent example of stylized Renaissance gardening, they were opened to the public in 1766. The more formal parts of the garden, nearest the Palazzo, consist of box hedges clipped into symmetrical geometric patterns. These lead to wilder groves of ilex and cypress trees, planted to create a contrast between artifice and nature. Countless statues adorn the gardens, particularly along the Viottolone, an avenue of cypress trees planted in 1637. High above the gardens stands the Forte di Belvedere, designed by Buontalenti in 1590 for the Medici Grand Dukes.

The Virgin from *The Annunciation* (1525–8) by Pontormo

## ㉙ Santa Felìcita

Piazza di Santa Felicita. **Map** 3 C2 (5 C5). ⊞ D. **Tel** 055 21 30 18. **Open** 9:30am–noon & 3:30–5:30pm daily (only am Sun). ♿

There has been a church on this site since the 4th century. The present structure, begun in the 11th century, was remodeled in 1736–9 by Ferdinando Ruggieri, who retained Vasari's earlier porch (added in 1564) as well as many of the church's original Gothic features.

The Capponi family chapel to the right of the entrance contains two works by Jacopo da Pontormo: *The Deposition* and *The Annunciation* (1525–8). Their strange composition and remarkable coloring make them two of Mannerism's greatest masterpieces.

## ㉚ Piazzale Michelangelo

Piazzale Michelangelo. **Map** 4 E3. ⊞ 12, 13.

Of all the great Florentine viewpoints – such as the Duomo and Campanile – none offers such a magnificent panorama of the city as Piazzale Michelangelo. Laid out in the

1860s by Giuseppe Poggi, and dotted with copies of Michelangelo's statues, its balconies attract many visitors and the inevitable massed ranks of souvenir sellers. However, this square remains an evocative spot, especially when the sun sets over the Arno and distant Tuscan hills.

## ㉛ San Miniato al Monte

Via del Monte alle Croci. **Map** 4 E3. **Tel** 055 234 27 31. ⊞ 12, 13. **Open** 8am–1pm & 3:30–7pm daily. **Closed** public hols. ♿

San Miniato is one of the most beautiful Romanesque churches in Italy. Begun in 1018, it was built over the shrine of San Miniato (St. Minias), a rich Armenian merchant beheaded for his beliefs in the 3rd century. The facade, begun around 1090, has the geometric marble patterning typical of Pisan-Romanesque architecture. The statue on the gable shows an eagle carrying a bale of cloth, the symbol of the powerful Arte di Calimala (guild of wool importers), who financed the church in the Middle Ages. The 13th-century mosaic shows Christ, the Virgin, and St. Minias. The same

The facade of the church of San Miniato al Monte

protagonists appear in the apse mosaic inside the church, which sits above a crypt supported by columns salvaged from ancient Roman buildings. The floor of the nave is covered with seven mosaic panels of animals and signs of the zodiac. These mosaics date back to 1207.

Other highlights include Michelozzo's freestanding Cappella del Crocifisso (1448) and the Renaissance Cappella del Cardinale del Portogallo (1480) with terra-cotta roundels (1461) on the ceiling by Luca della Robbia. There is a fresco cycle of *Scenes from the Life of St. Benedict* by Spinello Aretino in the sacristy, which was completed in 1387.

Ponte Vecchio and the Arno from the heights of Piazzale Michelangelo

# Shopping in Florence

Few cities of comparable size can boast such a profusion and variety of high-quality stores as Florence. As you wander through its medieval streets, you will find all the big names in Italian fashion and jewelry alongside artisan workshops and family-run businesses. The city has translated its reputation as a center of artistic excellence into a wealth of antiques and fine-art shops. Tuscan tanneries are justifiably renowned, and there is nowhere better than Florence to buy shoes, purses, and other leather goods. Those searching for unusual gifts and souvenirs – from handmade stationery to delicious foodstuffs – will also be spoiled for choice.

## Where to Shop

The center of Florence is packed with all sorts of stores, from fashion designer flagships to secondhand bookstores. The tiny jewelry stores on the Ponte Vecchio sell both antique gems and high-quality new gold pieces. Antiques shops are mostly clustered around Via dei Fossi, Via dei Serragli, and Via Maggio. The best bargains can be found in the January and July sales.

## Clothing

Most leading Italian designer names – **Gucci**, **Armani**, **Versace**, and **Prada**, for example – can be found on Via de'Tornabuoni. Opposite Palazzo Strozzi is **Louis Vuitton**, with its collections of footwear, clothing, and luggage. **Dolce & Gabbana** is nearby, as is **Patrizia Pepe**, while **Valentino** is in Via dei Tosinghi. **La Perla**, specializing in sophisticated lingerie, is located in Via della Vigna Nuova, but more affordable lingerie styles can be found at **Intimissimi**.

Most department stores sell clothing. For mid-range fashion, try **Coin**. The more upscale **La Rinascente** has designer clothing, lingerie, and a great rooftop bar.

For discounts on designer fashion, visit **The Mall** or **Barberino Designer Outlet**, both about 30 minutes away from Florence.

There are fine silks and handwoven fabrics at **Casa dei Tessuti**.

## Shoes and Leather Goods

The main meccas for fans of designer Italian shoes are **Ferragamo**, **Gucci**, and **Prada**. For more classic styles, head to **Quercioli**, which stocks handmade leather footwear. The mid-priced range is well represented by **Peppe Peluso** and the chain store **Bata**.

The streets around Piazza di Santa Croce are filled with leather stores. Inside the cloisters of the church itself is the **Scuola del Cuoio**, where customers can watch the leather craftsmen at work.

Classic leather bags are sold at **Il Bisonte** and **Beltrami**; for more contemporary styles, head to **Coccinelle** and **Furla**.

Bound leather books, leather boxes, and leather-covered wooden desk objects are sold at **Scriptorium**.

## Jewelry

Florence has always been noted for its gold- and silversmiths. Visit **Torrini**, whose family has produced jewelry for six centuries, and **Pomellato's** stunning store for its chunky white gold rings with huge semi-precious gems. **Bulgari** is on the same street, and so is **Parenti**, which has unique antique jewels. Try **Aprosio & Co** for decorative jewelry made from precious metals and tiny glass stones.

## Art and Antiques

**Galleria Romanelli** has bronze statuary and works encrusted in semiprecious stones. The gallery also stocks marble sculptures and statues. Established in 1860, it is still run by the same family. For Art Nouveau and Art Deco, there is **Galleria Tornabuoni**, while **Ugo Poggi** has a selection of elegant porcelain. **Ugolini** and **Mosaico di Pitti** create tables and framed pictures using age-old technique of marble inlay.

## Books and Gifts

**Feltrinelli** and **Feltrinelli RED** (the latter also a restaurant) sell publications in several languages, while **Paperback Exchange** has a wide selection of new and secondhand books in English.

Typical Florentine crafts include bookbinding and handmade marbled paper, used to decorate a variety of objects. These are available at **Il Torchio** and **Il Papiro**.

For terra-cotta and ceramics, try **Sbigoli Terracotte**; for chandeliers and decorative glass objects, head to **La Bottega dei Cristalli**.

**Signum** sells postcards, posters, and prints, while **Mandragora** has a wide range of gifts based on famous artworks in the city.

## Food and Markets

Florence's main food market is the covered **Mercato Centrale** (*see p299*), but fruit and vegetable stands can also be found at the **Mercato di Sant'Ambrogio**. On Tuesday morning, there is a large market at the **Parco delle Cascine** with food, affordable clothing, and shoes.

**Pegna** is a mini-supermarket that sells fresh foods, as well as a range of gourmet items. The **Bottega dell'Olio** sells Tuscan extra-virgin olive oils, and **Grom** is famous for its artisan gelato.

**Dolceforte** sells chocolate souvenirs in the shape of the Duomo and the statue of *David*. Cookies and chocolates fill the front half of **Enoteca Alessi**, while at the back are fine wines, spirits, and liqueurs. At **Procacci,** stop for a glass of Italian wine while choosing between black or white truffles and other delicacies to eat or buy.

# DIRECTORY

## Clothing

**Armani**
Via de'Tornabuoni 48.
**Map** 1 C5 & 5 C2.
**Tel** 055 21 90 41.

**Barberino Designer Outlet**
A1 Firenze-Bologna, Exit Barberino di Mugello.
**Tel** 055 84 21 61.

**Casa dei Tessuti**
Via dei Pecori 20–24r.
**Map** 1 C5 & 6 D2.
**Tel** 055 21 59 61.

**Coin**
Via dei Calzaiuoli 56r.
**Map** 6 D3.
**Tel** 055 28 05 31.

**Dolce & Gabbana**
Via degli Strozzi 12–18r.
**Map** 1 C5 & 5 C3.
**Tel** 055 28 10 03.

**Gucci**
Via de'Tornabuoni 73r.
Map 1 C5 & 5 C2.
**Tel** 055 26 40 11.

**Intimissimi**
Via dei Calzaiuoli 99r.
**Map** 3 C1 & 6 D3.
**Tel** 055 21 21 47.

**Louis Vuitton**
Piazza degli Strozzi 1.
**Map** 1 C5 & 5 C3.
**Tel** 055 26 69 81.

**The Mall**
Via Europa 8,
Leccio Reggello.
**Tel** 055 865 77 75.

**Patrizia Pepe**
Via degli Strozzi 11/19r.
**Map** 3 C1 & 6 D2.
**Tel** 055 230 25 18.

**La Perla**
Via degli Strozzi 24r.
**Map** 1 C5 & 5 C3.
**Tel** 055 21 52 42.

**Prada**
Via de'Tornabuoni 67r.
**Map** 1 C5 & 5 C2.
**Tel** 055 26 74 71.

**La Rinascente**
Piazza della Repubblica 1.
**Map** 1 C5 & 6 D3.
**Tel** 055 21 91 13.

**Valentino**
Via de'Tornabuoni 23.
**Map** 1 C5 & 5 C2.
**Tel** 055 29 31 42.

**Versace**
Via de'Tornabuoni 13–15r.
**Map** 1 C5 & 5 C2.
**Tel** 055 28 26 38.

## Shoes and Leather Goods

**Bata**
Via dei Calzaiuoli 110r.
**Map** 3 C1 & 6 D2.
**Tel** 055 21 16 24.

**Beltrami**
Piazza dell'Olio 1r.
**Map** 1 C5 & 5 D2.
**Tel** 055 21 63 21.

**Il Bisonte**
Via di San Niccolò 24r.
**Map** 3 E2.
**Tel** 055 234 25 85.

**Coccinelle**
Via Calzaiuoli 28r. **Map** 3 C1 & 6 D4.
**Tel** 055 29 52 00.

**Ferragamo**
Via de'Tornabuoni 14r.
**Map** 1 C5 & 5 C2.
**Tel** 055 29 21 23.

**Furla**
Via de'Calzaiuoli 47r.
**Map** 3 C1 & 6 D3.
**Tel** 055 23.8 28 83.

**Peppe Peluso**
Via del Corso 5–6r.
**Map** 3 C1 & 6 D3.
**Tel** 055 26 82 83.

**Quercioli**
Via Calzaiuoli 18/20r.
**Map** 3 C1 & 6 D2.
**Tel** 055 21 39 41.

**Scriptorium**
Via dei Servi 5–7r.
**Map** 2 D5 & 6 E2.
Tel 055 21 18 04.

**Scuola del Cuoio**
Piazza di Santa Croce 16.
Map 3 C1 & 6 F4.
**Tel** 055 24 45 33.

## Jewelry

**Aprosio & Co**
Via del Moro 75/77r.
**Map** 1 B5 & 5 B2.
**Tel** 055 21 01 27.

**Bulgari**
Via de'Tornabuoni 61r.
Map 1 C5 & 5 C3.
**Tel** 055 239 67 86.

**Parenti**
Via de'Tornabuoni 93r.
Map 1 C5 & 5 C2.
**Tel** 055 21 44 38.

**Pomellato**
Via de'Tornabuoni 89–91r.
Map 1 C5 & 5 C2.
**Tel** 055 28 85 30.

**Torrini**
Piazza del Duomo 12r.
Map 2 D5 & 6 D2.
**Tel** 055 230 24 01.

## Art and Antiques

**Galleria Romanelli**
Borgo San Frediano 70.
**Map** 3 C1 & 5 C4.
**Tel** 055 239 60 47.

**Galleria Tornabuoni**
Borgo San Jacopo 53r.
Map 3 C1 & 5 C4.
**Tel** 055 28 47 20.

**Mosaico di Pitti**
Piazza de' Pitti 16–18r.
Map 3 B2 & 5 B5.
**Tel** 055 28 21 27.

**Ugo Poggi**
Via degli Strozzi 26r.
**Map** 1 C5 & 5 C3.
**Tel** 055 21 67 41.

**Ugolini**
Lungarno degli Acciaiuoli 66–70r.
**Map** 3 C1 & 5 C4.
**Tel** 055 28 49 69.

## Books and Gifts

**La Bottega dei Cristalli**
Via dei Benci 51r.
**Map** 3 C1 & 6 F4.
**Tel** 055 234 48 91.

**Feltrinelli**
Via dè Cerretani 30/32r.
**Map** 2 D4.
**Tel** 199 151 173.

**Feltrinelli RED**
Piazza della Repubblica 27r.
**Map** 1 C5 & 6 D3.
**Tel** 055 21 31 10.

**Mandragora**
Piazza del Duomo 50r.
**Map** 2 D5 & 6 D2.
**Tel** 055 29 25 59.

**Paperback Exchange**
Via dell'Oche 4r.
**Map** 2 D5 & 6 E2.
**Tel** 055 29 34 60.

**Il Papiro**
Piazza del Duomo 24r.
**Map** 2 D5 & 6 D2.
**Tel** 055 28 16 28.

**Sbigoli Terracotte**
Via Sant'Egidio 4r.
**Map** 6 F2.
**Tel** 055 247 97 13.

**Signum**
Borgo dei Greci 40r.
**Map** 3 C1 & 6 E4.
**Tel** 055 28 06 21.

**Il Torchio**
Via de' Bardi 17.
**Map** 3 C2 & 6 D5.
**Tel** 055 234 28 62.

## Food and Markets

**Enoteca Alessi**
Via dell'Oche 27r.
**Map** 3 C1 & 6 D2.
**Tel** 055 21 49 66.

**Bottega dell'Olio**
Piazza del Limbo 2r.
**Map** 3 C1 & 6 D4.
**Tel** 055 267 04 68.

**Dolceforte**
Via della Scala 21.
**Map** 1 C5 & 5 B2.
**Tel** 055 21 91 16.

**Grom**
Via del Campanile (on the corner of Via dell'Oche).
Map 2 D5 & 6 D2.
**Tel** 055 21 61 58.

**Mercato Centrale**
Via dell'Ariento 10–14.
**Map** 1 C4 & 5 C1.

**Mercato di Sant'Ambrogio**
Piazza Sant'Ambrogio.
**Map** 4 F1. **Open**
7am–2pm Mon–Sat.

**Parco delle Cascine**
Piazza Vittorio Veneto.
Open 8am–2pm Tue.

**Pegna**
Via dello Studio 26r.
**Map** 6 E2.
**Tel** 055 28 27 01.

**Procacci**
Via de'Tornabuoni 64r.
**Map** 1 C5 & 5 C2.
**Tel** 055 21 16 56.

# FLORENCE *STREET* FINDER

Map references given for sights in the Florence section refer to the maps on the following pages. Where two references are provided, the one in brackets relates to the large-scale maps, 5 and 6. References are also given for Florence hotels *(see pp562–77)* and restaurants *(see pp580–605)*, and for useful addresses in the *Travelers' Needs* and *Survival*

*Guide* sections at the back of the book. The map below shows the area of Florence covered by the *Street Finder*. The symbols used for sights and other features on the *Florence Street Finder* maps are listed below. Streets in Florence have double sets of numbers: red numbers are for businesses, and black or blue for domestic residences.

**Scale of Maps 1–4**

| 0 meters | 200 |
| 0 yards | 200 |

1:11,000

**Scale of Maps 5 & 6**

| 0 meters | 125 |
| 0 yards | 125 |

1:6,000

| 0 kilometers | 1 |
| 0 miles | 0.5 |

**Key to Street Finder**

- Major sight
- Place of interest
- **FS** Train station
- Bus station
- Streetcar stop

- **i** Tourist information
- Hospital with emergency room
- Police station
- Synagogue
- Church

- Railroad track
- City walls
- Pedestrian-only street

# TUSCANY

Renowned for its art, history, and evocative landscapes, Tuscany is thought to offer the quintessential Italian experience, and is understandably popular as a result. Hill-towns gaze across the countryside, many encircled by Etruscan walls and slender cypress trees. Handsome palaces testify to the region's wealth, while medieval town halls indicate a long-standing tradition of democracy and self-government.

In the countryside, among the vineyards and olive groves, there are hamlets and farmhouses, as well as fortified villas and castles – reminders of the violence and intercommunal strife that tore Tuscany apart during the Middle Ages. Several imposing castles and villas were built for the Medici family, the great patrons of the Renaissance who supported eminent scientists, such as Galileo.

Northern Tuscany, and the heavily populated plain between Florence and Lucca, is dominated by industry, with intensively cultivated land between the cities and the wild mountainous areas.

The area centered around Livorno and Pisa is now the region's economic hub. Pisa, at the height of its powers, dominated the western Mediterranean from the 11th to the 13th centuries.

Its navy opened up extensive trading routes with North Africa, and brought to Italy the benefits of Arabic scientific and artistic achievement. During the 16th century the Arno estuary began to silt up, ending Pisan power.

At the heart of central Tuscany lies Siena, which was involved in a long feud with Florence. Its finest hour came with its victory in the Battle of Montaperti in 1260, but it was devastated by the Black Death in the 14th century and finally suffered a crushing defeat by Florence in the siege of 1554–5.

Northeastern Tuscany, with its mountain peaks and woodland, provided refuge for hermits and saints, while the east was home to Piero della Francesca, the early Renaissance painter whose timeless and serene works are imbued with an almost spiritual perfection.

A view across treetops toward the medieval town of San Gimignano in central Tuscany

◄ The picturesque farmlands of Pienza in Tuscany

# Exploring Tuscany

Tuscan cities such as Florence (*see pp274–317*), Siena, and Pisa, together with smaller towns like Lucca, Cortona, and Arezzo, contain some of Italy's most famous artistic treasures. Medieval villages such as San Gimignano, with its famous towers, or Pienza, a tiny Renaissance jewel, sit at the heart of the glorious pastoral countryside for which the region is equally renowned. Elsewhere landscapes range from the spectacular mountains of the Alpi Apuane to the gentle hills of Chianti.

## Sights at a Glance

Cortona, a small town in eastern Tuscany

**For additional map symbols** *see back flap*

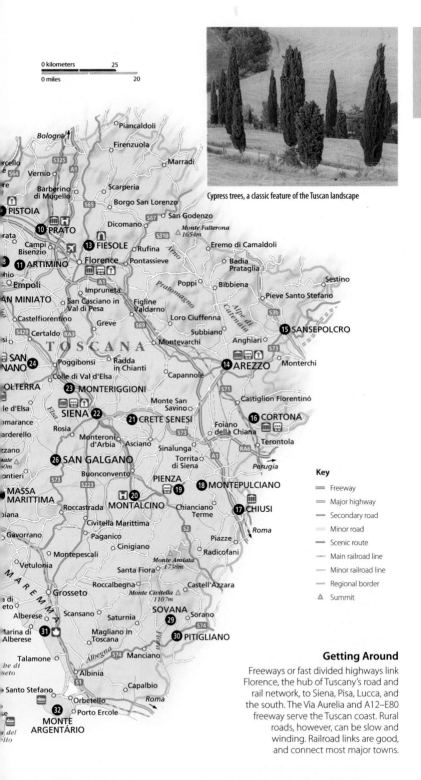

Cypress trees, a classic feature of the Tuscan landscape

0 kilometers 25
0 miles 20

Bologna

Piancaldoli
Firenzuola
Marradi

rcello
è
re

Vernio
Barberino
di Mugello
S325
A1
S64

Scarperia
Borgo San Lorenzo
S65
San Godenzo
S67

PISTOIA
rata
10 PRATO
Campi
Bisenzio
13 FIESOLE
Dicomano
S310
Monte Falterona
△ 1654m

Eremo di Camaldoli

9
11 ARTIMINO
Florence
Rufina
Pontassieve
Arno
Badia
Prataglia
Sestino

hio
Empoli
A1
Impruneta
Poppi
Bibbiena
Pieve Santo Stefano

AN MINIATO
San Casciano in
Val di Pesa
Figline
Valdarno
Pratomagno
Alpe di Catenaia
S3b

Castelfiorentino
Greve
S69
Loro Ciuffenna
Subbiano
Anghiari
15 SANSEPOLCRO
S73

si
Certaldo
S429
RA3
TOSCANA
Montevarchi
Monterchi

SAN
NANO 24
Poggibonsi
Radda
in Chianti
Capannole
14 AREZZO

Colle di Val d'Elsa
23 MONTERIGGIONI
S71
Castiglion Fiorentino

OLTERRA
le d'Elsa
Monte San
Savino
16 CORTONA

omarance
arderello
Rosia
SIENA 22
21 CRETE SENESI
Foiano
della Chiana
Terontola

ezzon
uate △
Om
ontieri
Monteroni
d'Arbia
Asciano
S73
Sinalunga
Torrita
di Siena
A1
RA6
Perugia

26 SAN GALGANO
Buonconvento
S223
PIENZA
18 MONTEPULCIANO

MASSA
MARITTIMA
20
19
17 CHIUSI

piana
Roccastrada
MONTALCINO
Chianciano
Terme

Gavorrano
Civitella Marittima
Paganico
S2
Roma

Vetulonia
Montepescali
Cinigiano
Piazze
Radicofani

Santa Fiora
Monte Amiata
△ 1738m

MAREMMA
a di
eto
Grosseto
Roccalbegna
Castell'Azzara

Monte Civitella △
1107m

Alberese
Scansano
Saturnia
SOVANA
29
Sorano
S74

larina di
Alberese
31
Magliano in
Toscana
S74
Manciano
30 PITIGLIANO

Talamone
be di
seto
Albinia
S1
Capalbio
Roma

Santo Stefano
Orbetello
Porto Ercole

se
32
MONTE
ARGENTÁRIO
s del
rito

## Key

— Freeway
— Major highway
— Secondary road
····· Minor road
— Scenic route
≈≈ Main railroad line
— Minor railroad line
— Regional border
△ Summit

## Getting Around

Freeways or fast divided highways link
Florence, the hub of Tuscany's road and
rail network, to Siena, Pisa, Lucca, and
the south. The Via Aurelia and A12–E80
freeway serve the Tuscan coast. Rural
roads, however, can be slow and
winding. Railroad links are good,
and connect most major towns.

# ❶ Carrara

Massa Carrara. 🏔 200,000. FS 🚌
*i* Lungomare Vespucci 24 (0585 24
00 63). 🏛 Mon.

Internationally renowned for its
marble quarries, Carrara's almost
flawless white stone has been
prized for centuries by famous
sculptors from Michelangelo to
Henry Moore (the stone for
Michelangelo's *David* came
from Carrara). The region's 300
or more quarries date back to
Roman times, making this one
of the oldest industrial sites in
continuous use in the world.
Many of the town's marble-
sawing mills and workshops
welcome visitors, offering them
the chance to see the ways in
which marble and quartz are
worked. These techniques –
along with marble artifacts old
and new – can be seen at the
**Museo Civico del Marmo**.

   Local marble is put to good
use in the town's **Duomo** in
Piazza del Duomo, particularly
in the fine Pisan-Romanesque
facade with its delicate rose
window. The cathedral square
also contains Michelangelo's
house, used by the sculptor

A quarry in the marble-bearing hills around Carrara

during his visits to select blocks
of marble. The town has some
lovely corners to explore, in
particular the elegant Piazza
Alberica. Most visitors head
for the stone quarries that are
open to the public at nearby
**Colonnata** and at **Fantiscritti**
(take one of the regular town
buses or follow the signs to the
"Cave di Marmo"). The latter
features a small museum with
displays of various marble
quarrying techniques.

🏛 **Museo Civico del Marmo**
Viale XX Settembre. **Tel** 0585 84 57 46.
**Open** Mon–Sat.

# ❷ Garfagnana

Lucca. FS 🚌 Castelnuovo di
Garfagnana. *i* Via Cavalieri di Vittorio
Veneto, Castelnuovo di Garfagnana
(0583 64 10 07).

A verdant, silent valley wedged
between the Orecchiella mountains and the Alpi Apuane, the
Garfagnana region can be
explored from **Seravezza**,
**Barga**, or **Castelnuovo di
Garfagnana**. While the town
of Barga makes the prettiest
base, thanks to its tawny stone
cathedral and charming streets,
Castelnuovo is more convenient
for drives and walks in the
surrounding mountains.
**San Pellegrino in Alpe** in the
Orecchiella has a fascinating
folklore museum, the **Museo
Etnografico**. It is easily seen in
conjunction with the **Orto
Botanico Pania di Corfino** at
the headquarters of the **Parco
dell'Orecchiella** at Pania di
Corfino, with its collection of
local Alpine trees.
   To the west is the Parco
Naturale delle Alpi Apuane,
an area where spectacular
jagged peaks and wooded
valleys are criss-crossed by
hiking trails and scenic
mountain roads.

🏛 **Museo Etnografico**
Via del Voltone 15, San Pellegrino in
Alpe. **Tel** 0583 64 90 72. **Open** Tue–
Sun (Jul–Aug: daily). 🔲

🌱 **Orto Botanico Pania di Corfino**
Parco dell'Orecchiella. **Tel** 0583 64 49
11. **Open** May–Sep: daily.

🌱 **Parco dell'Orecchiella**
Centro Visitatori, Orecchiella. **Tel** 0583
61 90 02. **Open** Jun–Sep: 9am–7pm
daily; Apr, May, & Oct: Sun only. ♿

The Parco Naturale delle Alpi Apuane on the edge of the Garfagnana

One of many seaside cafés lining the waterfront in the popular beach resort of Viareggio

## ❸ Bagni di Lucca

Lucca. 🅼 7,400. 🚍 *ℹ* Via E. Wipple c/o Chiesa Inglese (0583 80 57 45). 🛍 Sat.

All over Tuscany there are hot springs of volcanic origin, like Bagni di Lucca. The Romans first exploited the springs and built bath complexes where army veterans who settled in the area could relax. More spas came into prominence in the Middle Ages and the Renaissance, and they have continued to be recommended for relieving a variety of ailments, such as arthritis.

Tuscan spas really came into their own in the early 19th century, when Bagni di Lucca reached its heyday as one of Europe's most fashionable spas, frequented by emperors, kings, and aristocrats. Visitors came not only for thermal cures, but also for the **Casino** (1837), one of Europe's first licensed gambling houses. These days the town is rather sleepy, and its main sights are the 19th-century monuments, including the Neo-Gothic **English Church** (1839) on Via Crawford and the **Cimitero Anglicano** (Protestant Cemetery) on Via Letizia.

### Environs

Southeast of Bagni di Lucca lies another popular spa town, **Montecatini Terme**. Developed in the 18th century, this town is one of the most interesting, with a wide range of spa architecture, from Neo-Classical to Art Nouveau establishments.

## ❹ Viareggio

Lucca. 🅼 65,000. 🚊 🚍 *ℹ* Viale Carducci 10 (0584 96 22 33). 🛍 Thu.

Known for its carnival, held in January and early February, this is also the most popular of the resorts on the Versilia coast. Its famous "Liberty" (Art Nouveau) style of architecture can be seen in the grand hotels, villas, and cafés built in the 1920s after the resort's original boardwalk and wooden chalets went up in flames in 1917. The finest example of the architecture is the **Gran Caffè Margherita** at the end of Passeggiata Margherita, designed by the prolific father of Italian Art Nouveau, Galileo Chini.

## ❺ Torre del Lago Puccini

Lucca. 🅼 11,000. 🚊 🚍 *ℹ* Viale Kennedy 2 (0584 35 98 93). 🛍 Fri.

A glorious avenue of linden trees, the Via dei Tigli, connects Viareggio with Torre del Lago Puccini, once the home of the opera composer Giacomo Puccini (1858–1924). He and his wife are buried in their former home, now the **Museo Villa Puccini**, a small museum that features the piano on which the maestro composed many of his works. Equal prominence is given to the villa's original fixtures, including the gun room that housed Puccini's hunting rifle. **Lago Massaciuccoli**, a nature preserve for rare and migrant birds, provides a pretty backdrop for open-air performances of Puccini's works.

🏛 **Museo Villa Puccini**
Piazzale Belvedere Puccini 226.
**Tel** 0584 34 14 45. **Open** Mon pm–Sun. **Closed** Nov, Dec 25. ⚑ ♿

Near Puccini's lakeside home at Torre del Lago Puccini

# ❻ Street by Street: Lucca

Lucca's regular grid of streets still follows the pattern of the Roman colony founded in 180 BC. Great, solid ramparts, built in the 16th to 17th century, help to shut out traffic, making the city a pleasant place to explore on foot. San Michele in Foro – one of the town's many fine Pisan-Romanesque churches – stands on the site of the Roman forum *(foro)*, the city's main square laid out in ancient times. It is still Lucca's main square today.

**San Frediano**
**Palazzo Pfanner**

**In Via Fillungo,**
Lucca's main shopping street, several storefronts are decorated with Art Nouveau details.

**VIA BUIA**

**VIA S. LUCIA**

**PIAZZA SAN MICHELE**

**VIA FILLUNGO**

**Casa Natale di Puccini**
Giacomo Puccini (1858–1924), composer of hugely popular operas, including *La Bohème*, was born in this house.

**VIA VENETO**

**VIA BECCHERIA**

**VIA ROMA**

**VIA SANTE C**

**VIA CENAMI**

**Piazza Napoleone**
This sprawling square is named after Napoleon, whose sister, Elisa Baciocchi, ruled Lucca from 1805 to 1815.

**PIAZZA NAPOLEONE**

**VIA XX SETTEMBRE**

**VIA DEL BATTISTERO**

**PIAZZA DEL GIGLIO**

**Train station**

**VIA DEL DUOMO**

**PIAZZA ANTELMINELLI**

**PIAZZA SAN MARTINO**

**★ San Michele in Foro**
The extraordinary Pisan-Romanesque facade (11th to 14th century) has three tiers of twisted or carved columns, each one different from the rest.

**San Giovanni**

**The Museo dell'Opera del Duomo** features treasures removed from San Martino.

## Key

— Suggested route

| 0 meters | 300 |
|---|---|
| 0 yards | 300 |

## VISITORS' CHECKLIST

**Practical Information**

🗺 85,000. 🛈 Piazza Santa Maria 35 (0583 91 99 31). 🗓 3rd Sun of month (antiques), Wed, Sat. 🎭 Jul 12: Palio della Balestra; Jul: Lucca Summer Festival; Sep 13: Luminara di Santa Croce. 🌐 **luccaturismo.it**

**Transportation**

🚉 Piazza Ricasoli.
🚌 Piazzale Verdi.

Anfiteatro Romano and tourist information

Torre dei Guinigi

Villa Bottoni
Pinacoteca Nazionale

Giardino Botanico

**San Martino**

…ca's beautiful 11th-century …omo is one of the outstanding …mples of the exuberant Pisan-…nanesque style.

Apostles from the mosaic on the facade of San Frediano

### 🏛 San Frediano

Piazza San Frediano. **Open** daily.

San Frediano's striking facade features a colorful 13th-century mosaic, *The Ascension*, a fine prelude to the church's wonderfully atmospheric interior. Pride of place goes to a splendid Romanesque font on the right, its sides carved with scenes from the Life of Christ and the story of Moses. Note the scene of Moses and his followers (dressed as medieval knights) as they pass through the divided Red Sea. In the second chapel in the north aisle, Aspertini's frescoes (1508–9) tell the story of Lucca's precious relic, the Volto Santo – a carving said to date from the time of the Crucifixion. The fine altarpiece (1422) in the fourth chapel of San Frediano's north aisle is by Jacopo della Quercia.

### 🏛 San Michele in Foro

Piazza San Michele. **Open** daily.

Built on the site of the old Roman forum *(foro)*, San Michele's rich mixture of twisted marble columns and Cosmati work (inlaid marble) adorns one of the most exuberant Pisan-Romanesque facades in Tuscany. Built between the 11th and 14th centuries, its decoration is overwhelmingly pagan. Only the huge winged figure of St. Michael on the pediment marks this out as a church. The interior has little of interest except for the beautiful

painting of *Saints Helena, Jerome, Sebastian, and Roch* by Filippino Lippi (1457–1504).

### 🏠 Casa Natale di Puccini

Corte San Lorenzo 9. **Tel** 0583 58 40 28. **Open** May–Sep: 10am–7pm daily; Mar, Apr, & Oct: 10am–6pm Wed–Mon; Nov–Feb: 10am–1pm & 3–5pm Wed–Mon. **Closed** Dec 25. 🎟

The fine 15th-century house in which Giacomo Puccini (1858–1924) was born is now a shrine to the great opera composer. It contains portraits of Puccini, costume designs for his operas, and the piano he used to compose his last opera, *Turandot*.

### 🏠 Via Fillungo

Lucca's principal shopping street winds its way through the heart of the city toward the Anfiteatro Romano. Its northern end has several stores with Art Nouveau ironwork; halfway down lies the deconsecrated church of San Cristoforo, built in the 13th century, with a lovely interior.

One of the many bars and stores along Via Fillungo

# Exploring Lucca

Lucca's peaceful narrow lanes wind among the medieval buildings, opening suddenly to reveal churches, tiny piazzas, and many other reminders of the city's long history, including a Roman amphitheater.

Medieval buildings mark the outline of Lucca's old Roman amphitheater

### 🏛 Anfiteatro Romano
Piazza del Mercato.

Roman *Luca* was founded in 180 BC, and stones from the ancient Roman amphitheater have been ransacked over the centuries to build churches and palaces, leaving only a handful of original fragments studded into today's arena-shaped Piazza del Mercato. Slum housing clogged the piazza until 1830, when it was cleared on the orders of Marie Louise, the city's Bourbon ruler of that time. It was then that the amphitheater's original shape was revealed, a graphic and evocative reminder of Lucca's rich Roman heritage. Low archways at the piazza's cardinal points mark the gates through which beasts and gladiators would once have entered the arena.

### 🏛 Museo dell'Opera del Duomo
Piazza Antelminelli 5. **Tel** 0583 49 05 30. **Open** daily. **Closed** Jan 1, Easter (am), Dec 25. 🅿 ♿

The museum, housed in the former Archbishop's Palace (14th century), displays the treasures of the Duomo of San Martino. These include the 11th-century carved stone head of a king and a rare

### 🏛 San Martino
Piazza San Martino. **Tel** 0583 95 70 68. **Open** daily.
📷 for sacristy.

Lucca's cathedral was built after the campanile; hence the facade's cramped and asymmetric appearance. The main portals contain remarkable 13th-century carvings by Nicola Pisano and Guidetto da Como. The Tempietto inside houses a painting by Tintoretto and the Volto Santo, a revered 13th-century effigy once believed to have been carved at the time of the Crucifixion.

**Domed chapels encircling the apse**

**Romanesque blind arcades and carved capitals**

**Facade**
The cathedral facade is decorated with Romanesque sculptures and colonnading (1204).

**The campanile** was begun in 1060 as a defensive tower.

**Ghirlandaio's** painting of *The Madonna and Saints* (1449–94) is in the Sacristy.

**Tomb of Ilaria del Carretto**
This beautiful portrait in marble by Jacopo della Quercia (1405–6) is of the youthful bride of Paolo Guinigi.

**Matteo Civitali's marble Tempietto** (1184)

**Circular clerestory** windows, in the nave and above the aisle roof, illuminate the church's unusually tall nave.

**Nicola Pisano** (1200–78) carved the *Journey of the Magi* and *Deposition* on the left portal.

Baroque gods and goddesses in the garden of the Palazzo Pfanner

12th-century Limoges casket, possibly created for a relic of St. Thomas à Becket. The Croce dei Pisani, made by Vincenzo di Michele in 1411, is a sublime masterpiece of the goldsmith's art. It shows Christ on the Tree of Redemption, surrounded by angels, the Virgin, St. John, and the other Evangelists.

### 🏛 Palazzo Pfanner
Via degli Asili 33. **Tel** 0583 95 40 29.
**Open** Apr–Oct: 10am–6pm; Nov 1–15: 11am–4pm; rest of year: by appt.

This elegant, imposing house (1667) has a beautiful outside staircase. It also boasts one of Tuscany's most delightful formal gardens. Laid out in the 18th century, the garden's central avenue is lined with Baroque statues of the gods and goddesses of ancient Roman mythology. The garden can also be viewed while walking along the ramparts.

The house itself contains an interesting collection of furniture, antiques, and medical instruments.

### 🏛 Ramparts
One of the pleasures of visiting Lucca is strolling along the ramparts – the magnificent city walls, whose tree-lined promenade offers some entrancing views of the city. Work on the ramparts began

around 1500, when advances in military technology made the old medieval defenses ineffective. On their completion in 1645, the walls were some of the most advanced of their time. One of their most curious features was the open space that lay beyond them, and which survives to this day, cleared to prevent the enemy taking cover in trees and undergrowth. Ironically, the walls never actually had to be defended, and they were eventually converted into a public park in the early 19th century.

Part of the imposing 17th-century ramparts that encircle Lucca

### 🏛 Santa Maria Forisportam
Piazza di Santa Maria Forisportam.
**Open** daily.

This church was built at the end of the 12th century, beyond the Roman walls of Lucca. Its name, Forisportam, means "outside the gate." The unfinished marble facade, in Pisan-Romanesque style, has blind arcading. Above the central portal is a relief of the *Coronation of the Virgin* (17th century). The interior was redesigned in the early 16th century, resulting in the nave and transepts being raised. The fourth altar of the south aisle contains a painting of *St. Lucy*, and the north transept has an *Assumption*, both by Guercino (1591–1666).

### 🏛 Museo Nazionale di Villa Guinigi
Via della Quarquonia. **Tel** 0583 555 70.
**Open** 8:30am–7:30pm Tue–Sat.
**Closed** Jan 1, May 1, Dec 25.

This massive Renaissance villa was built in 1418 for Paolo Guinigi, leading light of the noble family who ruled Lucca in the early 15th century. A familiar landmark of the city is the battlemented tower, the Torre dei Guinigi, with oak trees growing at the top. It offers good views over the city and the Apuan Alps. The garden features traces of a Roman mosaic, together with a pride of Romanesque lions removed from the city's walls.

Romanesque lion in the Museo Nazionale Guinigi

Inside, the museum's first floor is devoted to sculptures and archaeological displays. The highlights are works by Matteo Civitali and Jacopo della Quercia and fine Romanesque reliefs removed from several of Lucca's churches. Most of the paintings in the gallery on the floor above are by minor local artists, with the exception of two by Fra Bartolomeo (c.1472–1517): *God the Father with Saints Catherine and Mary Magdalene* and the *Madonna della Misericordia*. The floor also has furnishings, church vestments, and choir stalls from Lucca's cathedral, inlaid with marquetry views of the city carved in 1529.

# ⑦ Pisa

For much of the Middle Ages, Pisa's powerful navy ensured its dominance of the western Mediterranean. Trading links with Spain and North Africa in the 12th century brought vast mercantile wealth and formed the basis of a cultural revolution that is still reflected in Pisa's splendid buildings – especially the Duomo, Baptistery, and Campanile (the eponymous leaning tower). Pisa's decline began in 1284, with its defeat by Genoa, and was hastened by the silting up of the harbor. The city fell to the Florentines in 1406, but suffered its worst crisis in 1944 when it fell victim to Allied bombing.

A detail from the Duomo pulpit

*Emperor Henry VII* (1315) by Tino da Camaino, and a mosaic of *Christ in Majesty* in the apse, completed by Cimabue in 1302.

The circular Baptistery was begun in 1152 along Roman-esque lines, and finished a century later (the delay caused by a shortage of money) in a more ornate Gothic style by Nicola and Giovanni Pisano. The former was responsible for the marble pulpit (1260) in the interior, carved with reliefs of the *Nativity*, the *Adoration of the Magi*, the *Presentation*, the *Crucifixion*, and *The Last Judgment*. The pillars that support the pulpit feature statues of the Virtues. The inlaid marble font (1246) is by Guido da Como.

### 🏛 Camposanto

Piazza dei Miracoli. **Tel** 050 83 50 11. **Open** daily. Closed Jan 1, Dec 25.

The Camposanto (cemetery) is the fourth element in the Campo dei Miracoli's lovely ensemble. Begun in 1278 by Giovanni di Simone, the vast marble arcades of this long building are said to enclose soil from the Holy Land. Bombs in World War II all but destroyed its once-famous frescoes, leaving only traces of *The Triumph of Death* (1360–80). Nearby is the Orto Botanico, one of Europe's oldest botanical gardens.

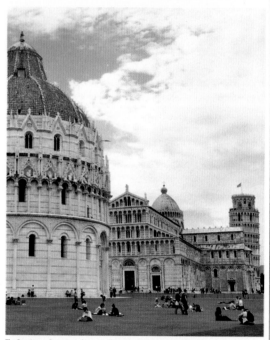

The Baptistery, Duomo, and Leaning Tower in Pisa's Campo dei Miracoli

### 🏛 Leaning Tower

See p330. **Tel** 050 83 50 11/12. **Open** daily. Mid-Jun–Aug: 8:30am–10pm; Sep–mid-Jun: times vary. ⏱ Visits last 30 mins. No children under 8. 🅿
🖥 opapisa.it (reservations).

### 🏛 Duomo and Baptistery

Piazza Duomo. **Tel** 050 83 50 11. **Open** daily (Duomo: pm only on Sun). 🖥 opapisa.it

Pisa's famous Leaning Tower is now the best-known building in the Campo dei Miracoli (Field of Miracles). Originally, however, it was intended as a campanile to complement the Duomo, which was begun by Buscheto in 1064.

Today the Duomo stands as one of the finest Pisan-Romanesque buildings in Tuscany, its wonderful four-tiered facade a medley of creamy colonnades and intricate blind arcades. Buscheto's tomb is in the left arch of the facade. Other important features of the exterior include the Portale di San Ranieri (leading to the south transept) and the bronze doors (1180), decorated with reliefs cast by Bonanno Pisano, the first architect of the Leaning Tower. Inside, the highlights are the carved pulpit (1302–11) by Giovanni Pisano, the *Tomb of*

A fresco from the *Triumph of Death* cycle in the Camposanto

Santa Maria della Spina alongside the River Arno in Pisa

## VISITORS' CHECKLIST

**Practical Information**

90,000. Piazza Duomo
(050 56 04 64); Piazza Vittorio
Emanuele 16 (050 422 91).
Wed & Sat. Jun 17: Regata di
San Ranieri; last Sun in Jun: Gioco
del Ponte. **pisaunicaterra.it**

**Transportation**

Galileo Galilei 3 miles (5 km) S.
Pisa Centrale, Piazza della
Stazione. Viale Gramsci.

## Museo dell'Opera del Duomo

Piazza del Duomo 6. **Tel** 050 83 10 11.
**Open** Apr–Sep: 8am–8pm daily; Oct–
Mar: 9am–6pm daily.

Housed in the cathedral's 13th-
century former Chapter House,
this museum displays exhibits
removed over the years from
the Duomo, Baptistery, and
Camposanto. Among the
highlights is an imposing
10th-century hippogriff
(half horse, half griffin).
Cast in bronze by
Moorish craftsmen,
this statue was looted
by Pisan adventurers
during the wars against
the Saracens. There are
also works by Nicola
and Giovanni Pisano,
notably Giovanni's ivory
*Virgin and Child* (1300), carved
for the Duomo's high altar. Other
exhibits include paintings,
Roman and Etruscan remains,
and ecclesiastical treasures.

**10th-century
bronze hippogriff**

## Museo Nazionale di San Matteo

Lungarno Mediceo, Piazza San Matteo 1.
**Tel** 050 54 18 65. **Open** 8:30am–7pm
Tue–Sun (Sun: am only).

This museum is located on the
banks of the Arno in San Matteo,
an elegantly fronted medieval
convent that in the 1800s also
served as a prison. Much of the
building has been closed for
years – several of the rooms
have no numbers and some of
the exhibits are poorly labeled.
Nevertheless, the museum
presents a unique opportunity to
examine the complete sweep of
Pisan and Florentine art from
the 12th to the 17th centuries.

The first rooms are devoted to
sculpture and early Tuscan
paintings. The best exhibits
include a 14th-century polyptych
by Francesco Traini of *Scenes
from the Life of St. Dominic*,
Simone Martini's fine polyptych
of *The Madonna and Saints*
(1321), and a 14th-century
statue of the *Madonna del
Latte*, attributed to
Andrea Pisano, another
member of Pisa's
talented school of
medieval sculptors.
The half-length statue,
in gilded marble,
shows Christ feeding
at his mother's breast.
In room 6 are some of
the highlights of the
museum, including
Masaccio's *St. Paul*
(1426), Gentile da Fabriano's
radiant 15th-century *Madonna
of Humility*, and Donatello's
reliquary bust of *San Rossore*
(1424–7). Additional rooms
contain paintings by Guido Reni,
Benozzo Gozzoli, and Rosso
Fiorentino, and an important
picture of *Christ* attributed to
Fra Angelico (*c.*1395–1455).

## Santa Maria della Spina

Lungarno Gambacorti. Tel 055 12 19
19. **Open** Tue–Sun.

The roofline of this tiny church,
located just beyond the Ponte
Solferino, bristles with spiky
Gothic pinnacles, spires, and
niches sheltering statues of saints
and apostles. The decoration
reflects the history of the church,
which was built between 1230
and 1323 to house a thorn
(*spina*) from Christ's Crown of
Thorns – the gift of a Pisan
merchant. The church was once
even closer to the Arno, but was
rebuilt on the present site in
1871 to protect it from flooding.

## Piazza dei Cavalieri

The huge building on the north
side of this square is the Palazzo
dei Cavalieri, home to one of
Italy's most prestigious
universities: the Scuola Normale
Superiore. Designed by Vasari in
1562, the building, which is
covered in black and white
*sgraffito* decoration (designs
scratched into wet plaster),
served as the headquarters of
the Cavalieri di Santo Stefano,
an order of knights created
by Cosimo I in 1561.

*The Madonna and Saints* (1321) by Simone Martini in the Museo Nazionale

# The Leaning Tower of Pisa

Begun in 1173 on sandy silt subsoil, the Leaning Tower (Torre Pendente) started to tilt even before the third story was finished in 1274. Despite the shallow foundations, construction continued, and the structure was completed in 1350. The tower's apparent flouting of the laws of gravity has attracted many visitors over the centuries, including the Pisan scientist Galileo, who climbed to the top to conduct his experiments on the velocity of falling objects. After several engineering interventions that decreased the lean by 14 inches (38 cm), the tower is once again safe and open to the public.

Galileo Galilei
(1564–1642)

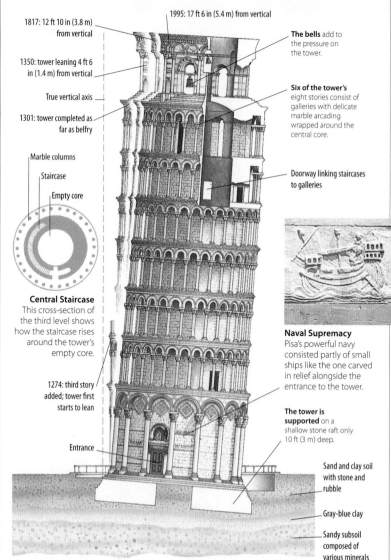

1995: 17 ft 6 in (5.4 m) from vertical

1817: 12 ft 10 in (3.8 m) from vertical

1350: tower leaning 4 ft 6 in (1.4 m) from vertical

True vertical axis

1301: tower completed as far as belfry

Marble columns

Staircase

Empty core

**Central Staircase**
This cross-section of the third level shows how the staircase rises around the tower's empty core.

1274: third story added; tower first starts to lean

Entrance

**The bells** add to the pressure on the tower.

**Six of the tower's** eight stories consist of galleries with delicate marble arcading wrapped around the central core.

**Doorway linking staircases** to galleries

**Naval Supremacy**
Pisa's powerful navy consisted partly of small ships like the one carved in relief alongside the entrance to the tower.

**The tower is supported** on a shallow stone raft only 10 ft (3 m) deep.

Sand and clay soil with stone and rubble

Gray-blue clay

Sandy subsoil composed of various minerals

# ❽ Vinci

Florence. 🚗 15,000. 🚉 ℹ️ Corso Gramsci 110 (0573 37 44 01). 🛒 Wed.

The birthplace of Leonardo da Vinci (1452–1519), this hilltop town celebrates the genius in the **Museo Leonardiano**, in the 13th-century castle. Among the displays are wooden models of Leonardo's machines and inventions; most are based on drawings from his notebooks, copies of which are shown alongside. These include a bicycle, his conception of a car, an armored tank, and even a machine gun.

## 🏛️ Museo Leonardiano

Castello dei Conti Guidi. **Tel** 0571 93 32 51. **Open** Mar–Oct: 9:30am–7pm daily; Nov–Feb: 9:30am–6pm daily. 📷

Model bicycle based on designs by Leonardo da Vinci, Museo Leonardiano

# ❾ Pistoia

🚗 93,000. 🚉 🚌 ℹ️ Palazzo dei Vescovi, Piazza del Duomo (0573 216 22). 🛒 Wed & Sat.

Pistoia's citizens were once known for violence and intrigue, a reputation grounded in the medieval disputes between the city's rival factions, the Bianchi and Neri (Whites and Blacks). Their favored weapon was a tiny, locally made dagger known as a *pistola*. Long a center of metalwork, everything from buses to mattress springs are now made here. In the center, several fine historic buildings are preserved.

## 🏛️ Duomo

Piazza del Duomo. **Open** daily.
Piazza del Duomo, Pistoia's main square, is dominated by the Duomo (San Zeno) and its bulky 12th-century campanile, originally built as a watchtower in the city walls. The interior of the Duomo is rich in funerary

Detail of frieze (1514–25) by Giovanni della Robbia, Ospedale del Ceppo

monuments. The finest of these, in the south aisle, is the tomb of Cino da Pistoia. He was a friend of Dante and fellow poet, and is depicted in a relief (1337) lecturing to a class of young boys.

Nearby is the chapel of St. James and its extraordinary silver altar decorated with more than 600 statues and reliefs. Although the earliest of these dates from 1287, the altar was not completed until 1456. One of the craftsmen involved was Brunelleschi, who began his career as a silversmith before turning to architecture. Also in the Piazza del Duomo is the octagonal Baptistery, completed in 1359.

## 🏛️ Ospedale del Ceppo

Piazza Giovanni XXIII.
This hospital and orphanage, founded in 1277, was named after the *ceppo* (hollowed-out tree trunk) that was used to collect donations for its work. The main facade features colored terra-cotta panels (1514–25) by Giovanni della Robbia illustrating the *Seven Works of Mercy*. The portico is by Michelozzo.

The Pisan-Romanesque facade of Pistoia's Duomo (San Zeno)

## 🏛️ Cappella del Tau

Corso Silvano Fedi 70. **Tel** 0573 322 04. **Open** 8:30am–1:30pm Mon–Sat.
The Cappella del Tau (1360) is so called because the monks who built it wore on their cloaks the letter T (*tau* in Greek), symbolizing a crutch and their work with the sick and disabled. Inside there are frescoes by Niccolò di Tommaso on *The Creation* and the *Life of St. Anthony Abbot* (1370). Two doors down, the **Palazzo Tau** has work by Marino Marini, Pistoia's best-known 20th-century artist.

*The Fall* (1372) by Niccolò di Tommaso in the Cappella del Tau

## 🏛️ San Giovanni Fuorcivitas

Via Cavour. **Open** daily.
Built in the 12th to 14th centuries, the striking church of San Giovanni Fuorcivitas (literally "St. John Outside the City") once stood beyond the city walls. Its north flank is clad in banded marble and there is a Romanesque relief of the Last Supper over the portal. Inside, the holy water stoup, carved in marble with figures of the Virtues, is by Giovanni Pisano (1245–1320). A masterly pulpit, carved in 1270 with scenes from the New Testament, is by Guglielmo da Pisa. Both are among the finest works of this period, when artists were reviving the art of carving.

# ⑩ Prato

🏛 190,000. 🚃 ℹ Piazza Buonamici 7 (0574 241 12). 🏛 Mon.

While textile factories gird its outskirts, the center of Prato retains several important churches and museums. The **Duomo** (begun 1211) is flanked by the Pulpit of the Holy Girdle (1434–8), designed by Donatello and Michelozzo, used once a year to display a girdle reputedly given to Thomas the Apostle before the Assumption of the Virgin. Inside the Duomo is *The Life of John the Baptist* (1452–66) by Fra Filippo Lippi, and a fresco cycle (1392–5) by Agnolo Gaddi.

Other sights include the **Museo di Palazzo Pretorio**; **Santa Maria delle Carceri**, a Renaissance church in Piazza delle Carceri; the **Castello dell' Imperatore**, a fortress built by Emperor Frederick II in 1237; the **Centro per l'Arte Contemporanea Pecci**; and the **Museo del Tessuto**, which traces the history of Prato's textile industry.

🏛 **Museo di Palazzo Pretorio**
Palazzo Pretorio, Piazza del Comune. **Tel** 0574 193 49 96. **Open** Wed–Mon.

🏛 **Castello dell'Imperatore**
Piazza delle Carceri. **Open** Wed–Mon.

🏛 **Centro per l'Arte Contemporanea Pecci**
Viale della Repubblica 277. **Tel** 0574 53 17. **Open** Wed–Mon. 🖼

🏛 **Museo del Tessuto**
Via Puccetti 3. **Tel** 0574 61 15 03. **Open** Tue–Sun. 🖼

*Madonna del Ceppo* by Fra Filippo Lippi in Prato's Museo Civico

Buontalenti's Villa di Artimino, or "Villa of a Hundred Chimneys"

# ⑪ Artimino

Prato. 🏛 400. 🚃

A small fortified hamlet, Artimino is remarkable for the unspoiled Romanesque church of **San Leonardo**. Outside the walls lies the **Villa di Artimino**, designed by Buontalenti in 1594 for Grand Duke Ferdinando I. Also known as the "Villa of a Hundred Chimneys," it used to house a collection of beautiful exhibits that are now in the **Museo Archeologico Comunale**.

**Environs**
Lovers of Pontormo's paintings should visit the church of **San Michele** in Carmignano, 3 miles (5 km) north of Artimino, because it contains *The Visitation* (1530). East of here lies the villa of **Poggio a Caiano**. Built in 1480 by Giuliano da Sangallo for Lorenzo de' Medici *(see p257)*, it was the first Italian villa in the Renaissance style.

🏛 **Villa di Artimino**
Viale Papa Giovanni 23. **Tel** 055 87 51 41. **Open** Sat & Sun by appt.

🏛 **Museo Archeologico Comunale di Artimino**
Piazza San Carlo 3. **Tel** 055 871 81 24. **Open** 9:30am–1:30pm Mon, Tue, Thu & Fri; 9:30am–1:30pm & 3–6pm Sat & Sun. **Closed** Wed. 🖼

🏛 **Poggio a Caiano**
Piazza Medici. **Tel** 055 87 70 12. **Open** daily. 🖼 ♿

# ⑫ San Miniato

Pisa. 🏛 3,900. 🚃 ℹ Piazza del Popolo (0571 427 45). 🏛 Tue.

This hilltop town manages to remain aloof from the vast industrial sprawl of the Arno valley. Its key building is the semiderelict Rocca (castle), built for Frederick II, German Holy Roman Emperor, in the 13th century. Close by stands the **Museo Diocesano**, which is home to a *Crucifixion* (*c.*1430) attributed to Filippo Lippi, a terra-cotta bust of Christ attributed to Verrocchio (1435–88), and the *Virgin of the Holy Girdle* by Andrea del Castagno (*c.*1417–57). Next door, the red-brick Romanesque facade of the **Duomo** dates from the 12th century. Its strange inset majolica plates, evidence of trade with Spain or North Africa, probably represent the North Star and the constellations of Ursa Major and Minor (all three were key points of reference for early navigators).

🏛 **Museo Diocesano**
Piazza Duomo. **Tel** 342 686 08 73. **Open** Apr–Sep: daily; Oct–Mar: Fri–Tue. 🖼

Facade of the Duomo in San Miniato

# ⑬ Fiesole

Florence. 🏛 15,000. 🚃 ℹ Via Portigiani 3 (055 596 13 23/296). 🏛 Sat.

Fiesole stands in rolling hilly countryside 5 miles (8 km) north of Florence. Idyllically located among olive groves, it is a popular retreat from the city thanks to its hilltop position, which brings cool breezes. Founded in the 7th century BC, the original Etruscan colony was a powerful force in central Italy,

The hills and rooftops of Fiesole viewed from Via di San Francesco

only surrendering its supremacy after the foundation of Florence (1st century BC).

The restored **Duomo** of San Romolo in Piazza Mino da Fiesole was begun in 1028. It has a massive bell tower and a bare Romanesque interior. Behind the Duomo, an archaeological area contains the remains of a 1st-century-BC **Roman theater**, traces of **Etruscan walls** from the 4th century BC, and the **Museo Civico Archeologico**, with a collection of bronzes, ceramics, and jewelry dating from the Bronze Age.

Via di San Francesco, a steep lane offering lovely views, leads to the Franciscan friary of **San Francesco** (14th century) and the interesting 9th-century church of **Sant'Alessandro**, with a Neo-Classical facade.

Via Vecchia Fiesolana leads to the hamlet of **San Domenico**, where the 15th-century church of the same name contains a painting of the *Madonna with Angels and Saints* (c.1430) by Fra Angelico and the Chapter House contains a fresco of *The Crucifixion* (c.1430), also by him. Close by, on the Via della Badia dei Roccettini, is the **Badia Fiesolana**, a pretty Romanesque church with a striped marble facade and interior of local gray sandstone, *pietra serena*.

🏛 **Museo Civico Archeologico**
Via Portigiani 1. **Tel** 055 596 12 93.
**Open** daily (Oct–Mar: Wed–Mon). 🏷

## ⑭ Arezzo

🔼 100,000. 🚊 ℹ Piazza della Repubblica 28 (0575 268 50). 🛍 Sat.

Arezzo is one of Tuscany's wealthiest cities, its prosperity based on a thriving jewelry industry. Although much of its medieval center was destroyed during World War II, resulting in extensive rebuilding and many medieval alleys being replaced by broad avenues, the city preserves some outstanding sights: foremost are Piero della Francesca's famous frescoes in the church of **San Francesco** *(see pp334–5)*. Close to the church on Corso Italia, the main street, stands the **Pieve di Santa Maria**, which boasts one of the most ornate Romanesque facades in the region. To its rear stretches the steeply sloping **Piazza Grande**, flanked by an arcade (1573) designed by Vasari, and by the **Palazzo della**

**Fraternità dei Laici** (1377–1552). The latter features a *Madonna* relief by Bernardo Rossellino. The huge **Duomo** to the north is best known for its 16th-century stained glass and a small fresco of *Mary Magdalene* by Piero della Francesca (1416–92). The **Museo Diocesano (Mudas)** features three wooden crucifixes, dating from the 12th and 13th centuries, a bas-relief of *The Annunciation* (1434) by Rossellino, and paintings by Vasari. More works by Vasari can be seen in the **Casa di Vasari**, a house built by the artist in 1540. Still more frescoes by him are displayed in the **Museo d'Arte Medioevale e Moderna**, a museum that is famed for its excellent collection of majolica pottery.

The **Fortezza Medicea**, a ruined Medici castle built by Antonio da Sangallo during the 16th century, has fine views.

🏛 **Museo Diocesano (Mudas)**
Piazzetta Dietro il Duomo 12.
**Tel** 0575 402 72 68. **Open** daily. 🏷

🏛 **Casa di Vasari**
Via XX Settembre 55. **Tel** 0575 40 90 40. **Open** Wed–Mon. 🏷

🏛 **Museo d'Arte Medioevale e Moderna**
Via di San Lorentino 8.
**Tel** 0575 40 90 50. **Open** Tue–Sun. 🏷

🏰 **Fortezza Medicea**
Parco il Prato. **Tel** 0575 37 76 78.
**Open** daily.

The monthly antiques market held in Arezzo's Piazza Grande

# Arezzo: San Francesco

The 13th-century Church of San Francesco houses one of Italy's greatest fresco cycles, the *Legend of the True Cross* (1452–66), Piero della Francesca's masterpiece. The scenes, on the walls of the choir, are now visible again after a long restoration. They describe the history of the Cross used to crucify Christ, from sprig to Tree of Knowledge to its use as a bridge during the reign of Solomon, and ultimately its discovery by Helena, mother of Constantine, the first Christian emperor.

**A Group of Onlookers**
These figures kneel in wonder while Heraclius returns the True Cross to Jerusalem.

**Excavation of the Cross**
The town, meant to be Jerusalem, gives a fair representation of 15th-century Arezzo.

## KEY

① **The prophets** appear to play no part in the narrative cycle; their presence may be for purely decorative reasons.

② **The Queen of Sheba** recognizes the wood of the Cross.

③ **The wood** of the Cross is buried in a pit.

④ **Judas reveals** where the Cross is hidden.

⑤ **The 13th-century Crucifix** forms the focal point of the fresco cycle. The figure at the foot of the Cross represents St. Francis, to whom the church is dedicated.

⑥ **The Cross** returns to Jerusalem.

⑦ **Constantine dreams** of the Cross on the eve of battle against rival emperor Maxentius.

⑧ **Constantine leads** his cavalry into battle.

⑨ **The Defeat of Chosroes** depicts the defeat of a Persian king who had stolen the Cross.

⑩ **The buildings** in the fresco reflect the newly fashionable styles of Renaissance architecture.

**Key to Frescoes**

1  The Death of Adam; a sprig from the Tree of Knowledge is planted over his grave.

2  The Queen of Sheba visits Solomon and foresees that a bridge made from the Tree will be used to crucify the greatest king in the world.

3  Solomon, assuming he is the greatest king in the world, orders the bridge to be buried.

4  The Annunciation: Christ's death is foreshadowed in the panel's cruciform structure.

**The Death of Adam**
Piero's vivid portrayal of Adam and Eve in old age shows an adept treatment of anatomy. He was one of the first Renaissance artists to paint nude figures.

**5** Constantine has a vision of the Cross and hears a voice saying "In this sign you shall conquer."

**6** Constantine defeats his rival Maxentius.

**7** The Levite Judas is tortured and reveals the location of the True Cross.

**8** Three crosses are dug up; Constantine's mother Helena recognizes the True Cross.

**9** The Persian king Chosroes is defeated after stealing the Cross.

**10** The True Cross is returned to Jerusalem.

**Solomon's Handshake**
The handshake between the Queen of Sheba and Solomon, King of Israel, portrays 15th-century hopes for a union between the Orthodox and Western churches.

Piero's *The Resurrection* (1463) in Sansepolcro

## ⑮ Sansepolcro

Arezzo. 🏠 16,000. 🚌 ℹ️ Via
Matteotti 8 (0575 74 05 36).
🗓 Tue, Sat.

Sansepolcro is the birthplace
of Piero della Francesca
(1410–92). The town's **Museo
Civico** contains two of his
masterpieces: *The Resurrection*
(1463) and the *Madonna della
Misericordia* (1462). It also has
a 15th-century *Crucifixion* by
Luca Signorelli. In the church of
**San Lorenzo** on Via Santa Croce
there is a *Deposition* in the
Mannerist style by Rosso
Fiorentino (1494–1541).

Another renowned painting
by Piero della Francesca, the
*Madonna del Parto* (1460),
can be seen at Via Reglia 1 in
Monterchi, 8 miles (13 km)
southwest of Sansepolcro.

🏛 **Museo Civico**
Via Aggiunti 65. **Tel** 0575 73 22 18.
**Open** daily. **Closed** public hols. 🅿️ 📷

## ⑯ Cortona

Arezzo. 🏠 23,000. 🚆 🚌 ℹ️ Piazza
Signorelli 9 (0575 63 72 23). 🗓 Sat.

Cortona was founded by the
Etruscans and aside from being
one of the oldest hill-towns in
Tuscany, it is also one of the
most scenic. A major power in
the Middle Ages, it was able to
hold its own against Siena and
Arezzo. Today it is a charming
maze of old streets and medieval
buildings, like the **Palazzo**
Comunale on
Piazza della
Repubblica.
The town's early
history is traced
in the **Museo
dell'Accademia
Etrusca**, which
contains Etruscan
artifacts and a
wide variety of
Egyptian and
Roman remains.
The small **Museo
Diocesano**
features several
fine paintings,
in particular a
*Crucifixion* by the
Renaissance artist
Pietro Lorenzetti, a *Deposition*
(1502) by Luca Signorelli,
and a sublime *Annunciation*
(c.1434) by Fra Angelico.
Signorelli, born in Cortona,
is buried in the church of
**San Francesco** (built in
1245), which contains an
*Annunciation* painted in
Baroque style by
Pietro da Cortona,
another native
artist. The
**Madonna del
Calcinaio** (1485),
a gem of Renais-
sance architecture,
is located on the
southern outskirts
of town.

The 13th-century Palazzo
Comunale in Cortona

🏛 **Museo dell'Accademia Etrusca**
Palazzo Casali, Piazza Signorelli 9.
**Tel** 0575 63 72 35. **Open** daily (except
Mon in winter). 📷

🏛 **Museo Diocesano**
Piazza del Duomo 1. **Tel** 0575 628 30.
**Open** daily (Tue–Sun in winter). 📷

## ⑰ Chiusi

Siena. 🏠 10,000. 🚆 🚌 ℹ️ Via
Porsenna 79 (0578 22 76 67). 🗓 Tue.

Chiusi is now a largely modern
town, but in the past it was one
of the most powerful cities in the
Etruscan league, reaching the
height of its influence in the 7th
and 6th centuries BC (*see p48–9*).
Numerous Etruscan tombs lie
dotted in the surrounding
countryside, the source of the
exhibits in the town's **Museo
Archeologico Nazionale**.
Founded in 1871, the museum
is packed with cremation urns,
vases decorated with black
figures and Bucchero ware,
burnished to resemble bronze.

The Romanesque **Duomo** in
Piazza del Duomo incorporates
recycled Roman pillars and
capitals. The wall decorations in
the nave, resembling frescoes,
were painted by Arturo
Viligiardi in 1887. There is a
Roman mosaic underneath the
high altar. Visits can be made
to several Etruscan
tombs under the
town from the
**Museo della
Cattedrale**, a
museum in the
cloister of the
Duomo that has
displays of Roman,
Lombardic and
medieval sculpture.

🏛 **Museo Archeologico Nazionale**
Via Porsenna 93. **Tel** 0578 201 77. **Open**
9am–8pm daily (last adm: 7:30pm; to
2pm Sun & public hols). 📷 📷

🏛 **Museo della Cattedrale**
P. del Duomo. **Tel** 0578 22 64 90. **Open**
daily (Jan–Mar: Tue, Thu, Sat, Sun). 📷

Etruscan frieze in the Museo Archeologico Nazionale in Chiusi

Pienza's Piazza Pio II, designed by Bernardo Rossellino (1459)

# ⑱ Montepulciano

Siena. ⚊ 14,000. ▦ **i** Piazza Don Minzoni 1 (0578 75 73 41). ⬢ Thu.
**w** prolocomontepulciano.it

This is one of Tuscany's highest hill-towns, its walls and fortifications offering broad views over Umbria and southern Tuscany, and the vineyards providing the Vino Nobile wine that has made its name famous. The streets are brimming with Renaissance palazzi. The main street, the Corso, climbs to the **Duomo** (1592–1630), the setting for one of the masterpieces of the Sienese School, the *Assumption* (1401) by Taddeo di Bartolo. The High Renaissance church, **Tempio di San Biagio** (1518–34), lies off the road to Pienza.

# ⑲ Pienza

Siena. ⚊ 2,300. ▦ **i** Piazza Dante Alighieri 18 (0578 74 83 59). ⬢ Fri.

Pienza is a delightful village whose intimate little center was almost completely redesigned in the 15th century by Pope Pius II. Born as Aeneas Sylvius Piccolomini in 1405, when the village was known as Corsignano, he became a leading Humanist scholar and philosopher. Elected pope in 1458, he decided to rebuild his birthplace, renaming it Pienza in his own honor. The Florentine architect and sculptor, Bernardo Rossellino, was commissioned to build a cathedral, papal palace, and

town hall (all completed in the three years from 1459 to 1462), but the grander scheme for a planned model Renaissance town was never realized. Some idea of what might have been, however, can still be gained from the **Palazzo Piccolomini**, the former papal palace, which continued to be inhabited by Pius's descendants until 1968. The rooms open to the public include Pius's bedroom and library, though the highlight of a visit is the superb panorama from the loggia and arcaded courtyard at the palace's rear.

Pleasant walks and more great views can be had from the village walls. The airy **Duomo** *(see p256)* next door contains six altarpieces of the *Madonna and Child*, each commissioned from the leading Sienese painters of the day. Rossellino was forced to build the Duomo on a cramped site with poor foundations, and cracks appeared in the building

before it was even completed. Today, the church's eastern end suffers from severe subsidence.

### 🏛 Palazzo Piccolomini
Piazza Pio II. **Tel** 0577 28 63 00.
**Open** 10am–6:30pm Tue–Sun (to 4:30pm mid-Oct–mid-Mar). **Closed** Jan–mid-Feb & mid-end Nov. ▨ ▮

# ⑳ Montalcino

Siena. ⚊ 5,100. ▦ **i** Costa del Municipio 1 (0577 84 93 31). ⬢ Fri.

Hilltop Montalcino sits at the heart of vineyards that produce Brunello, one of Italy's finest red wines. It can be sampled in the Enoteca (wine store) located in the 14th-century **Fortezza** with its impressive ramparts. The town's timeless streets are a pleasure to wander, and there are some buildings of interest. On the way from the fortress into town is the monastery of Sant' Agostino and its 14th-century church and, just beyond, the Palazzo Vescovile. On Piazza del Popolo the slim tower of the Palazzo Communale, constructed in the 13th and 14th centuries, stands tall above the town.

### 🏰 Fortezza
Piazzale della Fortezza. **Tel** 0577 84 92 11. ▨ for ramparts. Enoteca:
**Open** Apr–Oct: 9am–8pm daily;
Nov–Mar: 9am–6pm Tue–Sun.

The Tempio di San Biagio on the outskirts of Montepulciano

The landscape of the Crete Senesi

## ㉑ Crete Senesi

Asciano. FS 🚌 ℹ️ Via delle Fonti (0577 71 88 11).

To the south of Siena and central Tuscany is the area known as the Crete Senesi, which is characterized by round clay hillocks eroded by heavy rain over the centuries. Dubbed the "Tuscan desert," it is almost completely barren. Cypress and pine trees, planted to provide windbreaks along roads and around isolated farmhouses, are an important feature in this empty, primeval landscape. Shepherds tend flocks of sheep here; the milk is used to produce the strongly flavored pecorino cheese that is popular throughout Tuscany.

## ㉒ Siena

*See pp342–7.*

## ㉓ Monteriggioni

Siena. 🏛️ 99,000. 🚌 ℹ️ Piazza Roma (0577 30 48 34).
🌐 monteriggioniturismo.it

Monteriggioni is a gem of a medieval hilltop town. It was built in 1203 and 10 years later became a garrison town. It is completely encircled by high walls with 14 heavily fortified towers, built to guard the northern borders of Siena's territory against invasion by Florentine armies.

Dante used Monteriggioni as a simile for the deepest abyss at the heart of his *Inferno*, which compares the town's "ring-shaped citadel… crowned with

towers" with giants standing in a moat. The perfectly preserved walls are best viewed from the Colle di Val d'Elsa road. Within the walls, the sleepy town consists of a large piazza, a pretty Romanesque church (on the piazza), a few houses, a couple of craft shops, restaurants, and stores selling many of the locally produced Castello di Monteriggioni wines.

**Environs**
West of Monteriggioni by 2 miles (3 km) lies the former Cistercian Abbey of **Abbadia dell' Isola** (12th century). This Romanesque church was largely rebuilt in the 18th century, after the cupola fell apart. It contains frescoes by Taddeo di Bartolo and Vincenzo Tamagni.

## ㉔ San Gimignano

*See pp348–9.*

## ㉕ Volterra

Pisa. 🏛️ 13,000. 🚌 ℹ️ Piazza dei Priori 20 (0588 872 57). 🛒 Sat.
🌐 volterratur.it

Like many Etruscan cities, Volterra is located on a high plateau, offering fine views over the surrounding hills. In many places the ancient Etruscan

Detail from the pulpit in Volterra's Duomo

walls still survive. The **Museo Etrusco Guarnacci** contains one of the best collections of Etruscan artifacts in Italy. Of special interest is the group of over 600 cinerary urns, made from alabaster or terracotta, many of which were gathered from local tombs.

The **Palazzo dei Priori**, the medieval seat of government on Piazza dei Priori, is the oldest of its kind in Tuscany. It was begun in 1208 and there are 14th-century frescoes inside. The Pisan-Romanesque **Duomo**, located on Piazza San Giovanni, has a fine 13th-century pulpit with sculptured panels. Volterra's excellent art gallery and museum, the **Pinacoteca e Museo Civico**, features works by Florentine artists. *Christ in Majesty* (1492) by Ghirlandaio shows Christ hovering above an idealized Tuscan landscape. Luca Signorelli's *Virgin and Child with Saints* (1491) states his debt to Roman art through the reliefs on the base of the Virgin's throne. Painted in the same year, his *Annunciation* is a beautifully balanced composition. Another highlight is Rosso Fiorentino's Mannerist painting, *The Deposition* (1521).

The city is famous for its craftsmen who have been

The beautifully preserved walls of Monteriggioni in central Tuscany

The ruined abbey at San Galgano, surrounded by dense woodland

carving elaborate statues and objets d'art from locally mined alabaster for 2,500 years.

🏛 **Museo Etrusco Guarnacci**
Via Don Minzoni 15. **Tel** 0588 863 47.
**Open** daily. **Closed** Jan 1, Dec 25. 📷

🏛 **Pinacoteca e Museo Civico**
Via dei Sarti 1. **Tel** 0588 875 80.
**Open** daily. **Closed** Jan 1, Dec 25. 📷

## ㉖ San Galgano

Siena. 🚌 from Siena. Abbey & oratory:
**Open** daily. 🌐 www.comune.
chiusdino.siena.it

The remote Cistercian abbey at San Galgano lies in a superb setting. San Galgano (1148–81) was a brave but dissolute knight who turned to God, renouncing the material world. When he tried to break his sword against a rock as a symbol of his rejection of war, it was swallowed by the stone. This he interpreted as a sign of God's approval. He built a hut on a hill above the abbey (the site of today's beehive-shaped chapel at **Montesiepi**, built c.1185). Here he later died a hermit. Pope Urban III declared him a saint.

The abbey, begun in 1218, is Gothic in style, reflecting the French origins of the Cistercian monks who designed it. They avoided contact with the outside world and divided their lives between prayer and labor. Despite an emphasis on poverty, the monks became wealthy from the sale of wood, and by the

middle of the 14th century the abbey was corruptly administered and gradually fell into decline.

In the late 14th century, the English mercenary Sir John Hawkwood sacked the abbey, and by 1397 the abbot was its sole occupant. It was eventually dissolved in 1652.

St. Galgano's sword stands embedded in a stone just inside the door of the circular **oratory**. The 14th-century stone walls of the side chapel are covered with worn frescoes showing scenes from Galgano's life by Ambrogio Lorenzetti (1344).

## ㉗ Massa Marittima

Grosseto. 🗺 9,500. 🚌 ℹ Amatur, Via Todini 3–5 (0566 90 27 56). 🗓 Wed.

Set in the Colline Metallifere (metal-bearing hills) where lead, copper, and silver ores were mined as early as Etruscan times, Massa Marittima is far from being a grimy industrial town. Examples of Romanesque architecture survive from the time when the town became an independent republic (1225–1335). The Romanesque-Gothic **Duomo** in Piazza Garibaldi is dedicated to St. Cerbone,

a 6th-century saint whose story is sculpted in stone above the main portal. Inside the building, the *Maestà* is attributed to Duccio (c.1316).

The **Museo della Miniera** (Museum of Mining) is located partially inside a former mine shaft and has exhibits that explain mining techniques, tools, and minerals.

The **Museo Archeologico e Museo d'Arte Sacra** has material from Paleolithic to Roman times. Other attractions are the Fortezza Senese and the Torre della Candeliera.

🏛 **Museo della Miniera**
Via Corridoni. **Tel** 0566 90 22 89.
**Open** Tue–Sun. 📷 compulsory. 📷

🏛 **Museo Archeologico e Museo d'Arte Sacra**
Palazzo del Podestà, Piazza Garibaldi. **Tel** 0566 90 22 89.
**Open** Tue–Sun. 📷

The rooftops of Massa Marittima

Panoramic view of Siena, with the Duomo on the right ▶

# ㉒ Street by Street: Siena

Siena's principal sights cluster in the maze of narrow
streets and alleys around the fan-shaped Piazza del
Campo. One of Europe's greatest medieval squares, the
piazza sits at the heart of the city's 17 *contrade*, a series
of parishes whose ancient rivalries are still acted out in
the twice-yearly Palio *(see p345)*. Loyalty to the *contrada*
of one's birth is fierce, and as you wander the streets you
will see the parishes' animal symbols repeated on flags,
plaques, and carvings. Siena's hilly position also means
that city walks offer delightful hidden corners and
countless sudden views.

The Duomo dominating Siena's skyline

**Via della Galluzza** leads to
the house of St. Catherine.

**The Baptistery** has
fine frescoes and a
font with reliefs by
Donatello,
Jacopo della
Quercia, and
Ghiberti.

**★ Duomo**
Striped black-and-white
marble pillars, surmounted by
a carved frieze of the popes,
support the Duomo's vaulted
ceiling, painted blue with
gold stars to resemble
the night sky.

**Each tier** of the Duomo's bell
tower has one more window
than the floor below.

**Museo dell'Opera del Duomo**
Duccio's *Maestà*, one of the
greatest Sienese paintings, was
paraded around Siena's streets
on its completion in 1311, and
influenced the city's painters
for decades to come.

Bus station ↑

Train
station ↖

VIA D. GALLUZZA

PIAZZA INDIPENDENZA

VIA DI DIACCETO

VIA DI CITTÀ

VIA DI FONTEBRANDA

VIA FRANCIOSA

PIAZZA SAN
GIOVANNI

VIA DEI PELLEGRINI

VIA DEL FUSARI

VIC. D. CAMPANE

VIA DEL POGGIO

PIAZZA
DEL
DUOMO

VIA DI CITTÀ

VIA DEL CAPITANO

**Key**

— Suggested route

0 meters          300
0 yards            300

**Loggia della Mercanzia**
Built in 1417, the arcade is where Siena's medieval merchants and money dealers carried out their business.

**VISITORS' CHECKLIST**

**Practical Information**
60,000. Palazzo Squarcialupi, Piazza Duomo 1 (0577 28 05 51). Wed. Jul 2, Aug 16: Palio; Jul: Settimana Musicale Chigiana (classical music). **terresiena.it**

**Transportation**
Piazzale Rosselli.
Piazza S. Domenico.

**The Logge del Papa**, or Pope's Colonnade, was built in honor of Pius II in 1462.

Tourist information

**BANCHI DI SOTTO**
VIA DI PANTANETO
VIA RINALDINA
VIA DEL PORRIONE
VIA DI SALICOTTO
PIAZZA DEL MERCATO
VIA DUPRE

**Fonte Gaia**
These reliefs are 19th-century copies of originals by Jacopo della Quercia.

Drummer in Siena's Palio

**Piazza del Campo**
Italy's loveliest piazza occupies the site of the old Roman forum, and for much of Siena's early history was the city's principal marketplace. It began to assume its present shape in 1293, when the Council of Nine, Siena's ruling body at the time, began to acquire land with a view to creating a grand civic piazza. The red-brick paving was begun in 1327 and completed in 1349, its distinctive nine segments designed to reflect the authority of the Council of Nine and to symbolize the protective folds of the Madonna's cloak. The piazza has been the focus of city life ever since, a setting for executions, bullfights, and the twice-yearly drama of the Palio (see p345), a festival centered around a bareback horse race. Cafés, restaurants, and fine medieval palazzi now line the Campo's fringes, dominated by the **Palazzo Pubblico** (1297–1342) and **Torre del Mangia**, built in 1348 (see p344). This imposing ensemble tends to overshadow the little **Fonte Gaia** on the piazza's northern edge. The fountain is a 19th-century copy of an original carved by Jacopo della Quercia in 1409–19. Its reliefs depict the *Virtues*, *Adam and Eve*, and the *Madonna and Child* (the originals are on the rear loggia of the Palazzo Pubblico). The fountain's water is still supplied by a 500-year-old aqueduct.

**★ Palazzo Pubblico**
The graceful Gothic town hall was completed in 1342. At 330 ft (102 m), the bell tower, Torre del Mangia, is the second-highest medieval tower ever built in Italy.

The Piazza del Campo and Fonte Gaia from the Torre del Mangia

# Exploring Siena

Once a capital to rival Florence, Siena is Italy's prettiest medieval town, still endowed with the grandeur of the age in which it was at its peak (1260–1348). Begin an exploration of its historic center in Piazza del Campo and the surrounding maze of medieval alleys.

Lorenzetti's *Allegory of Good Government* (c.1338–40), Palazzo Pubblico

### 🏛 Palazzo Pubblico

Piazza del Campo 1. **Tel** 0577 29 22 32. Museo Civico & Torre del Mangia: **Open** Mid-Mar–end Oct: 10am–7pm daily; Nov–mid-Mar: 10am–6pm daily (tower: to 4pm); (last adm: 45 mins before closing). 🖼

Although it continues in its ancient role as Siena's town hall, the Palazzo Pubblico's medieval rooms, some decorated with paintings of the Sienese School, are open to the public. The **Museo Civico** is housed here. The main council chamber, or Sala del Mappamondo, is named after a map of the world painted by Ambrogio Lorenzetti in the early 14th century. One wall is covered by Simone Martini's fresco of the *Maestà* (1315), depicting the Virgin in Majesty as Queen of Heaven, attended by the Apostles, saints, and angels. Opposite is a fresco (attributed to Simone Martini, but possibly later) of the mercenary *Guidoriccio da Fogliano* (1330). The walls of the chapel are covered with frescoes of the *Life of the Virgin* (1407) by Taddeo di

Bartolo, and the choir stalls (1428) have wooden panels inlaid with biblical scenes. The Sala della Pace contains the famous *Allegory of Good and Bad Government* (c.1338–40), a pair of frescoes by Ambrogio Lorenzetti. They form one of the most important series of secular medieval paintings. In the *Good Government* fresco, civic life flourishes, while the *Bad Government*, headed by a demon, reveals garbage-strewn streets and ruins.

The Sala del Risorgimento is covered with late 19th-century frescoes illustrating the events leading up to the unification of Italy under King Vittorio Emanuele II.

In the palace courtyard is the entrance to the magnificent **Torre del Mangia**, the palace's huge bell tower. Rising 330 ft (102 m), it is a prominent feature of Siena's skyline. Built by the brothers Muccio and Francesco di Rinaldo

between 1338 and 1348, it was named after the first bell-ringer, whose idleness led to the nickname *Mangiaguadagni* (literally "eat the profits"). There are 505 steps to the wonderful views at the top.

### 🏛 Santuario e Casa di Santa Caterina

Costa di Sant'Antonio. **Tel** 0577 28 81 75. **Open** daily.

Siena's patron saint, Catherine Benincasa (1347–80), was the daughter of a tradesman. At the age of eight she devoted herself to God and had many visions, as well as later receiving the stigmata (wounds of Christ). Like her namesake, St. Catherine of Alexandria, she was believed to have been betrothed to the Christ child in a vision – a scene that inspired many artists. Her eloquence persuaded Pope Gregory XI to return the seat of the papacy to Rome in 1376, after 67 years of exile in Avignon. St. Catherine died in Rome and was canonized in 1461.

Today Catherine's house is surrounded by chapels and cloisters. Among them is the Church of the Crucifixion, which was built in 1623 in her orchard to house the late 12th-century Crucifixion in front of which she received the stigmata in 1375. The house is decorated with paintings of events from her life by artists including her contemporaries Francesco Vanni and Pietro Sorri.

Cloister of Santuario e Casa di Santa Caterina, birthplace of Siena's patron saint

## Palazzo Piccolomini

Piazza Pio II. **Tel** 0577 24 71 45.
**Open** 10am–6:30pm Tue–Sun (to
4:30pm Oct–Mar). **Closed** Jan 7–
Feb 14, Nov 16–30.

Siena's most imposing private
palazzo was built for the wealthy
Piccolomini family in the 1460s
by the Florentine architect and
sculptor Bernardo Rossellino. It
now contains the Sienese state
archives, account books, and
taxation documents dating back
to the 13th century. Some of the
leading artists of the day were
employed to paint the wooden
bindings used to enclose the
tax and account records. The
paintings, now on display in
the Sala di Congresso, often
show scenes of Siena itself or
episodes from the city's past.

Other records include a will
attributed to Boccaccio, and
the council's contract with
Jacopo della Quercia for the
Fonte Gaia *(see p343)*.

A detail from Martini's *Blessed Agostino Novello* (c.1330)

## Pinacoteca Nazionale

Via San Pietro 29. **Tel** 0577 28 61 43.
**Open** daily (Sun & Mon am only).
**Closed** Jan 1, May 1, Dec 25.

This fine gallery, which is housed
in the 14th-century Palazzo
Buonsignori, contains an unsur-
passed collection of paintings
by artists of the Sienese School.
Arranged in chronological order,
from the 13th century through
to the Mannerist period (1520–
1600), highlights include Duccio's
*Madonna dei Francescani* (1285)
and Simone Martini's masterpiece *The Blessed Agostino Novello
and Four of His Miracles* (c.1330).
Pietro Lorenzetti's *Two Views,* from
the 14th century, are early examples of landscape painting, and
Pietro da Domenico's *Adoration
of the Shepherds* (1510) shows

how the art of Siena remained
visibly influenced by its Byzantine
roots long after the naturalism
of the Renaissance had reached
across the rest of Europe.

The austere exterior of the church of San Domenico (begun 1226)

## San Domenico

Piazza San Domenico. **Open** daily.
The preserved head of the
city's patroness, St. Catherine of
Siena (1347–80), can be seen in
a gilded tabernacle on the altar
of a chapel dedicated to her
in the huge, barnlike Gothic
church of San Domenico
(begun 1226). The chapel
itself was built in 1460 for this
purpose and is dominated
by Sodoma's frescoes (1526),
to the right and left of the altar,
which show Catherine in
states of religious fervor and
her early life. The church has
the only portrait of St. Catherine
considered authentic, painted
by her friend Andrea Vanni. The
fresco by Vanni can be found in
the Chapel of the Vaults.

### The Palio of Siena

The Palio is Tuscany's most
celebrated festival, and it
occurs in the Campo
each year on July 2
and August 16 at 7pm.
This special event is
a bareback horse race
first recorded in 1283,
but it may have had
its origins in Roman
military training. The
jockeys represent 10 of
Siena's 17 *contrade* (districts);
the horses are chosen by the
drawing of lots and are blessed

A *contrada* symbol

at the local *contrada* churches.
Preceded by days of colorful
pageantry, costume
processions, and heavy
betting, the races
themselves last only
90 seconds each.
Thousands of spect-
ators crowd into the
piazza to watch the race,
and rivalry between
competitors is intense.
The winner is rewarded with a
silk *palio* (banner). Festivities for
the winners can last for weeks.

The Sienese displaying their flag-throwing skills before the Palio

# Siena: Duomo

Siena's Duomo (1136–1382), one of Italy's greatest cathedrals, is a spectacular mixture of sculpture, paintings, and Pisan-influenced Romanesque-Gothic architecture. Had 14th-century plans to create a new nave come to fruition, the building would have become the largest church in Christendom. In the end, the plan came to nothing, abandoned when the plague of 1348 virtually halved the city's population. Among the Duomo's treasures are sculptural masterpieces by Nicola Pisano, Donatello, and Michelangelo, a fine inlaid pavement, and a magnificent fresco cycle by Pinturicchio.

**Baptismal Font**
This Renaissance font by della Quercia, Ghiberti, and Donatello stands in the Baptistery.

**Pulpit Panels**
Carved in 1265–8 by Nicola Pisano, with help from Arnolfo di Cambio and his son Giovanni, the panels on the octagonal pulpit depict scenes from the *Life of Christ*.

## KEY

① **In the nave** black and white marble pillars support the vault.

② **The Campanile** was added in 1313.

③ **Archway** leading to the Baptistery.

④ **The Museo dell'Opera del Duomo** occupies the side aisle of the unfinished nave, which was roofed over to house the museum.

⑤ **The facade** gives an indication of the planned size of the nave.

⑥ **The unfinished nave**, if completed, would have measured 162 ft (50 m) in length and 97 ft (30 m) in breadth.

⑦ **The doors** were built in 1284–97, the rest of the facade a century later.

⑧ **The north aisle** contains sculptures by Michelangelo of saints Peter, Pius, Gregory, and Paul (1501–4).

⑨ **Chapel of St. John the Baptist**

Inlaid marble floor

**Piccolomini Library**
Pinturicchio's frescoes (1509) portray the life of the Piccolomini Pope, Pius II. Here he presides at the betrothal of Frederick III to Eleonora of Portugal.

**Inlaid Marble Floor**
*The Massacre of the Innocents* is one of a series of scenes in the inlaid marble floor. The marble is usually uncovered in September and October.

🏛 **Museo dell'Opera del Duomo**
Piazza del Duomo 8. **Tel** 0577 28 63 00. **Open** Mar–Oct:10:30am–7pm daily; Nov–Feb: 10:30–5:30pm. 🖼

Part of this museum is devoted to items from the Duomo, including a tondo of a *Madonna and Child*, probably by Donatello, and some badly eroded Gothic statues by Giovanni Pisano and Jacopo della Quercia. The highlight is Duccio's huge *Maestà* (1308–11), one of the Sienese School's finest works, with the Madonna and Child on one side, and scenes from the Life of Christ on the other. It was originally on the Duomo's high altar, where it replaced the striking *Madonna of the Large Eyes* (1220–30) by an anonymous Sienese painter, also in the museum.

Statues from the Duomo now on display in the Museo dell'Opera

🏰 **Fortezza Medicea**
Piazza Libertà 1. **Open** daily. Enoteca: **Tel** 0577 22 88 43. **Open** noon–1am Mon–Sat. 🖼

This huge red-brick fortress was built for Cosimo I by Baldassarre Lanci in 1560, following Siena's defeat by the Florentines in the 1554–5 war. After an 18-month siege, during which more than 8,000 Sienese died, the town's banking and wool industries were suppressed by the Florentine masters and all major building work ended.

The fortress now houses the Enoteca Italiana, offering visitors the chance both to taste and to buy quality wines from all over Italy. There is also a restaurant on the site.

Entrance to Duomo

**Facade Statues**
Many facade statues have been replaced by copies; the originals are in the Museo dell'Opera del Duomo.

# ⓔ Street by Street: San Gimignano

The 13 towers that dominate San Gimignano's skyline were built by noble families in the 12th and 13th centuries, when the town's position – on the main pilgrim route from northern Europe to Rome – brought it great prosperity. The plague of 1348, and the diversion of the pilgrim route, led to its decline as well as its preservation. Today only one of the towers, the Torre Grossa, is open. San Gimignano is rich in works of art as well as good stores and restaurants, although many close from November to March.

San Gimignano's famous skyline, almost unchanged since the Middle Ages

**The Museo Civico** provides access to the tallest of the town's 13 remaining towers.

**Collegiata**
This 11th-century church's interior is full of frescoes, including *The Creation* (1367) by Bartolo di Fredi.

**Palazzo del Popolo**
The council chamber of the town hall (1288–1323) features a large *Maestà* (1317) by Lippo Memmi.

**The Annunciation by Ghirlandaio**
This painting, completed in 1482, is located in a courtyard loggia alongside the Collegiata.

**Via San Giovanni** is lined with stores selling local goods.

Sant' Agostino

VIA SAN MATTEO
VIA CAPASSI
VIA DIACCETO
PIAZZA NOMI
PIAZZA DEL DUOMO
PIAZZA DELLA CISTERNA
VIA DELLA COSTERELLA
VIA DI QUERCECCHIO
VIA BERINANO
VIA SAN GIOVANNI

Bus station
Museo San Gimignano 1300

Among the Piazza del Duomo's
historic buildings is the Palazzo
Vecchio del Podestà (1239),
whose tower is probably
the town's oldest.

**Piazza della Cisterna**
This square
is named after
the well at
its center and is
the heart of
the old town.

### 🏛 Museo Civico

Palazzo del Popolo, Piazza del Duomo.
**Tel** 0577 28 63 00. Museum & tower:
**Open** Apr–Sep: 9:30am–6:30pm daily;
Oct–Mar: 11am–5pm daily.
**Closed** Dec 25. 🅿 🎫

Frescoes in the courtyard of
this museum feature the coats
of arms of city mayors, as well as
a 14th-century *Virgin and Child*
by Taddeo di Bartolo.

The first room is the Sala di
Dante, where an inscription
recalls a visit by the poet in
1300. The floor above has an
art collection, which includes
excellent works by Pinturicchio,
Bartolo di Fredi, Benozzo Gozzoli,
and Filippino Lippi. The famous
*Wedding Scene* frescoes by
Memmo di Filippucci (early 14th
century) show a couple sharing
a bath and going to bed –
an unusual record of life in
14th-century Tuscany.

### 🏛 Collegiata

Piazza del Duomo. **Open** daily.
This 12th-century Romanesque
church contains a feast of
frescoes. In the north
aisle the frescoes
comprise 26 episodes
from the Old
Testament (1367) by
Bartolo di Fredi.
The opposite wall
features scenes from
the *Life of Christ* (1333–
41) by Lippo Memmi,
while at the back of the church
there are scenes from the
Last Judgment painted by
Taddeo di Bartolo.

The ceiling of the Collegiata, painted
with gold stars

### 🏛 Sant'Agostino

Piazza Sant'Agostino. **Open** daily.
Consecrated in 1298, this
church has a simple facade,
contrasting markedly with the
heavily decorated Rococo
interior (c.1740) by Vanvitelli.
Above the main altar is the
*Coronation of the Virgin* by
Piero del Pollaiuolo, dated
1483. The choir is covered in
a cycle of frescoes of *The Life
of St. Augustine* (1465) painted
by the Florentine artist
Benozzo Gozzoli.

Bartolo di Fredi's *Christ*,
Sant'Agostino

### 🏛 Museo San Gimignano 1300

Via San Giovanni 50.
**Tel** 327 439 51 65. **Open**
10am–5pm daily (May–
Nov: to 6pm). 🅿 🅱

This museum houses
a reconstruction of
San Gimignano as
it was in the 13th and
14th centuries. The exhibits – all
entirely handmade – include 72
"tower houses," symbols of the
city's power in the Middle Ages.

Fresco from the early 14th-century *Wedding Scene* cycle by Memmo di Filippucci
in the Museo Civico

**Key**

— Suggested route

0 meters ——————— 250
0 yards ——————— 250

## ㉘ Elba

Livorno. 🗺 30,000. 🚢 Portoferraio.
🚌 ℹ Viale Elba 4 (0565 91 46 71).
🗓 Portoferraio: Fri.

Elba's most famous resident
was Napoleon, who spent nine
months here after the fall of
Paris in 1814. Today Italy's
third-largest island is mainly
populated by vacationers, who
come by ferry from Piombino,
6 miles (10 km) away on the
mainland. The main town is
Portoferraio, with an old port
and a modern seafront of hotels
and fish restaurants.

The landscape of the island is
varied. On the west coast, which
tends to be a little quieter, there
are sandy beaches suitable for
all water sports. The east coast,
centered on the town of Porto
Azzurro, the island's second
port, is more rugged, with high
cliffs and stony beaches. Inland,
olive groves and vineyards line
hillsides, and vegetation covers
the mountains. A good way to
see the interior is to take the road
from Marciana Marina to the old
medieval village of Marciana
Alta. Close by, a minor road leads
to a cable car that runs to Monte
Capanne (3,300 ft /1,018 m),
a magnificent viewpoint.

Marciana Marina on Elba

## ㉙ Sovana

Grosseto. 🗺 100. ℹ Piazza Busatti 8
(0564 61 40 74).

Sovana is one of southern
Tuscany's prettiest villages.
Its single little street ends in
Piazza del Pretorio, home to the
ancient church of Santa Maria,

The dramatic cliffs and caves of Pitigliano

which contains frescoes and
a 9th-century altar canopy.
A lane beyond leads through
olive groves to the Romanesque
Duomo, filled with reliefs and
carvings from an earlier church
on the site. Some fine Etruscan
tombs lie in the surrounding
countryside, many of them
clearly signed and easily visited
from the village.

## ㉛ Maremma

Grosseto. ℹ Piazza del Popolo 3,
Grosseto (0564 42 79 18). 🚌 to
entrances from Alberese. **Open** daily.
🎫 📷 Inner Park Areas: 🚌 from
Alberese to tour departure point. 📷
🌐 parco-maremma.it

The Etruscans, followed
by the Romans, were
the first to cultivate the
marshes and low hills
of the Maremma.
Following the collapse
of the Roman Empire,
however, the area fell prey
to flooding and malaria, twin
scourges that left it virtually
uninhabited until the 18th
century. The land has since
been reclaimed, the irrigation
canals unblocked, and
farming developed on the
fertile soil. The stunning Parco
Naturale della Maremma was
set up in 1975 to preserve the
area's native flora and fauna,
and to prevent development
on one of Italy's few pristine
stretches of coastline. Entrance
to much of the park is restricted
to access on foot or by a
park bus from Alberese.
Other more marginal areas,
however, such as the excellent
beach at Marina di Alberese
and the countryside around
Talamone in the south, are
easier to see.

## ㉚ Pitigliano

Grosseto. 🗺 4,400. 🚌 ℹ Piazza
Garibaldi 51 (0564 61 71 11). 🗓 Wed.

Pitigliano is spectacularly located
high above the cave-riddled cliffs
of the Lente valley. Its maze of
tiny medieval streets includes a
small Jewish ghetto, formed in
the 1600s by Jews fleeing from
persecution in the papal states.

The Ombrone estuary is a mixture of
pines, marsh, and dunes and is home
to birds such as the flamingo,
sea eagle, roller, and bee-eater.

### Key

— Roads
▦ Paths
▤ Canals and rivers
— Itineraries

0 kilometres  2
0 miles  1

offffofffofffff

The **Palazzo Orsini** has its water supply brought in by an impressive aqueduct, built in 1545. It houses the **Museo di Palazzo Orsini** with its exhibit of painted, engraved and sculptured works dating from the 14th century. Within the display are pieces by local artist Francesco Zuccarelli (1702–88). He also painted two of the altarpieces in the **Duomo** in Piazza San Gregorio. The **Museo Etrusco** contains finds from ancient local settlements.

**Ⅲ Museo di Palazzo Orsini**
Piazza della Fortezza Orsini 4. **Tel** 0564 61 60 74. **Open** 10am–1pm & 3–7pm Tue–Fri (to 5pm in winter).

**Ⅲ Museo Etrusco**
Piazza della Fortezza Orsini 59c. **Tel** 0564 61 40 67. **Open** 10am–5pm Thu–Mon (call for winter times).

## ㉜ Monte Argentario

Grosseto. 13,000. *i* Piazzale Sant'Andrea, Porto Santo Stefano (0564 81 42 08). Tue.

Monte Argentario was an island until the early 1700s, when the shallow waters separating it from the mainland began to silt up, creating two sandy spits of land, known as *tomboli,* which enclose the Orbetello lagoon. Today the lagoon hosts a beautiful nature preserve. **Orbetello** itself, a lively and relatively unspoiled little town, was linked to the island in 1842, when a dyke was constructed from the mainland. The harbor towns of **Porto Ercole** and **Porto Santo Stefano** are upscale resorts, busy with

Porto Ercole, Monte Argentario

visitors in summer. Interior highways – notably the Strada Panoramica – offer peaceful drives past rocky coves and bays.

**Spergolaia**

Entry tickets are sold at Alberese's park headquarters.

**Wild Boar**
The most impressive of the Maremma's many wild animals is the indigenous wild boar, a smaller creature than the Eastern European boar found elsewhere in Tuscany.

**Alberese**

San Rabano, a ruined Cistercian abbey (12th century), is close to the park's highest point.

**Pratini**

**Pine nuts** for cooking are still collected from the park's woodlands.

**Stazione di Alberese**

**Torre dell Uccellina**

re di elmarino

**The Uccellina Hills** are crowned by old Spanish watchtowers, pinewoods, and scented *macchia.*

**Torre di Collelungo**

**San Rabano**

**Birds of prey,** such as the hobby and peregrine, hunt in more remote parts of the park.

Unspoiled coastline

**Stazione di Talamone**

**Marked Footpaths**
Several gentle footpaths are marked around the park, but in practice you can wander almost at will among most of its dunes and pinewoods.

**This fishing village** is set against pretty countryside.

**For additional map symbols** *see back flap*

# UMBRIA

Long dismissed as Tuscany's "gentler sister," Umbria has finally emerged from the shadow of its more famous western neighbor. Forming an expanse of gentle pastoral countryside and high mountain wilderness, the picturesque region has been dubbed the "Green Heart of Italy." Umbria is also well known for the beauty and profusion of its medieval hill-towns.

The region was inhabited in the 8th century BC by the Umbrians, a peaceable farming tribe, and later colonized by the Etruscans and Romans. In the Middle Ages, the Lombards established a dukedom centered around Spoleto. By the 13th century much of the region was scattered with independent city-states, most of them eventually absorbed by the Papal States, where they remained until Italian unification in 1860.

Today the old towns are Umbria's chief glory. In Perugia, the region's capital, and the smaller centers of Gubbio, Montefalco, and Todi, there are numerous Romanesque churches, civic palaces, vivid fresco cycles, and endless medieval nooks and crannies. Spoleto, renowned for its summer arts festival, blends grandiose medieval monuments with Roman remains and some of

Italy's oldest churches. Assisi, the birthplace of St. Francis, contains the Basilica di San Francesco, frescoed in part by Giotto. At Orvieto, magnificently located on its volcanic crag, there are Etruscan remains and one of Italy's finest Romanesque-Gothic cathedrals.

Umbria's oak woods, ice-clear streams, and rich soils yield many delicacies. Chief among these are trout and truffles, olive oils to rival those of Tuscany, prized lentils from Castelluccio, cured meats from Norcia, and tangy mountain cheeses. A variety of well-regarded wines are produced from the vineyards of Torgiano and Montefalco.

Sadly, this beautiful area is also frequently hit by earthquakes (such as the devastating tremors of November 2016, for example), which cause considerable damage to its many artistic monuments.

store in Norcia selling a selection of Italy's finest hams, sausages, and salamis

◀ The Palazzo dei Consoli in Gubbio, as seen from the Palazzo Ducale's hanging gardens

# Exploring Umbria

Assisi and Spoleto, Umbria's loveliest towns, are the most convenient bases for exploring the region. Both these medieval gems are unmissable, as is the old center of Perugia, the region's capital, and the hill-towns of Orvieto, Gubbio, Spello, Montefalco, and Todi. Umbria's landscapes are just as compelling, from the eerie wastes of the Piano Grande and the mountain splendor of the Monti Sibillini National Park (best reached from Norcia) to the gentler countryside of the Valnerina and the beach-fringed shores of Lake Trasimeno.

### Sights at a Glance
1. Gubbio
2. *Assisi pp358–61*
3. Perugia
4. Lake Trasimeno
5. Orvieto
6. Todi
7. Spoleto
8. Montefalco
9. Spello
10. Monti Sibillini
11. Norcia
12. Valnerina

Olive harvest in the Umbrian countryside near Orvieto

### Getting Around

Excellent road, railroad, and bus links exist in the region. The A1 from Florence passes Orvieto, which is linked to Todi by the S448. The S75 connects Perugia, Assisi, and Spello, then the S3 continues to Trevi, Spoleto, and Terni. Rome–Florence trains serve Orvieto, and Rome–Ancona trains serve Spoleto, with branch lines connecting Perugia, Spello, and Assisi.

**For additional map symbols** *see back flap*

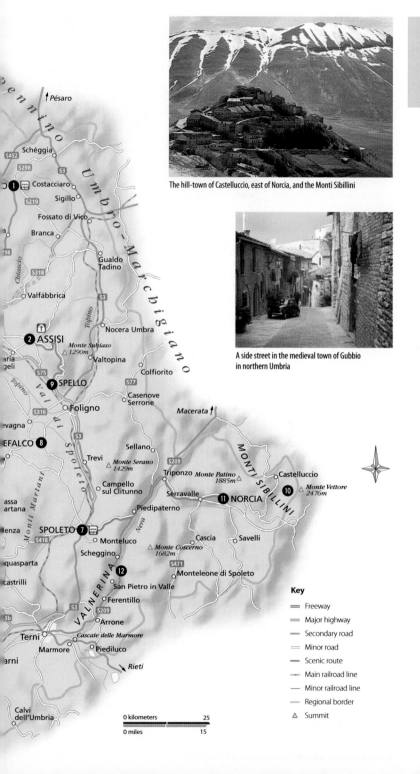

The hill-town of Castelluccio, east of Norcia, and the Monti Sibillini

A side street in the medieval town of Gubbio in northern Umbria

↑Pésaro

Schéggia

S452
S298
S3

① Costacciaro

Sigillo

S219

Fossato di Vico

Branca

S98

S318

Gualdo Tadino

Chiascio

Valfábbrica

S3

Topino

Nocera Umbra

② ASSISI

*Monte Subiaso*
△ *1290m*

Valtopina

aria
geli

S75

⑨ SPELLO

Colfiorito

Topino

Casenove
Serrone

○ Foligno

S316

Macerata ↑

evagna

EFALCO ⑧

S3

Sellano

Trevi

*Monte Serano*
△ *1429m*

S209

Campello
sul Clitunno

Triponzo *Monte Patino*
*1885m* △

Castelluccio

⑩

*Monte Vettore*
*2476m* △

assa
artana

Serravalle

Piedipaterno

⑪ NORCIA

Nera

SPOLETO ⑦

S418

Monteluco

Cascia

Savelli

lenza

Scheggino

*Monte Coscerno*
*1682m* △

quasparta

S471

castrilli

Monteleone di Spoleto

⑫

San Pietro in Valle

Ferentillo

S3

S209

3b

Arrone

Terni

*Cascate delle Marmore*

Marmore

Piediluco

arni

↘ *Rieti*

Calvi
dell'Umbria

### Key

━━ Freeway

━━ Major highway

━━ Secondary road

═══ Minor road

━━ Scenic route

╍╍ Main railroad line

── Minor railroad line

── Regional border

△ Summit

| 0 kilometers | 25 |
| 0 miles | 15 |

# ❶ Gubbio

Perugia. 🏛 33,000. 🚉 Fossato di Vico-Gubbio. 🚌 ℹ Via della Repubblica 15 (075 922 06 93). 🕒 Tue.

Gubbio vies with Assisi for the title of Umbria's most medieval town. The beauty of its twisting streets and terracotta-tiled houses is enhanced by the forest-swathed Apennines. Founded by the Umbrians in the 3rd century BC as Tota Ikuvina, it assumed greater prominence in the 1st century AD as a Roman colony (Eugubium). It emerged as an independent commune in the 11th century, having spread up the slopes of Monte Ingino. From 1387 to 1508 Gubbio was ruled from Urbino by the Dukes of Montefeltro.

The 13th-century **Duomo** is distinguished by a wagon-vaulted ceiling whose curved arches symbolize hands in prayer. Medieval Via dei Consoli leads to the 13th-century **Palazzo del Bargello** – a stone-faced building formerly the headquarters of the chief of police. Also here is the **Fontana dei Matti** (Fountain of the Mad), named after the tradition that anyone who walks around it three times will go insane.

Macabre legends surround the walled-up **Porte della Morte** (Doors of Death) that can be seen in Via dei Consoli and elsewhere in the town. Reputedly used for the passage of coffins from houses, the doors, once tainted, were sealed and never used again. Their purpose was probably defensive. In the lower town, the church of **San Francesco** (1259–82) is known for 17

Facade of the Palazzo dei Consoli in Gubbio

faded frescoes showing scenes from the *Life of the Virgin* (1408–13) by Ottaviano Nelli. Opposite is the **Tiratoio** (Weavers' Loggia). Wool was stretched out to dry in its shady arcade. West of here are the ruins of a 1st-century-AD Roman amphitheater.

### 🏛 Palazzo dei Consoli

Piazza Grande. **Tel** 075 927 42 98.
**Open** 10am–1pm & 3–6pm daily (Nov–Mar: 10am–1pm & 2:30–5:30pm).
**Closed** Jan 1, May 13–15, Dec 25. 🎟

Dominating the sky-line of Gubbio is this mighty civic palace, begun in 1332 by Gattapone. Its Salone dell'Arengo houses the Museo Civico, best known for the Eugubine Tablets (250–150 BC). Discovered in 1444, the seven bronze slabs are inscribed with Etruscan and Roman characters, probably a phonetic translation of prayers and rituals from the ancient Umbrian and Etruscan languages. Upstairs a small art gallery shows works by local painters.

One of the Eugubine Tablets in Gubbio

### 🏛 Palazzo Ducale

Via Federico da Montefeltro.
**Tel** 075 927 58 72. **Open** 8:30am–7:30pm Tue–Sun.
**Closed** Jan 1, Dec 25. 🎟 ♿

Attributed to Francesco di Giorgio Martini, this palace was built in 1470 for the Montefeltro as a copy of the family home in Urbino *(see pp374–5)*. It also has a pretty Renaissance courtyard.

The interior of Perugia's San Pietro, rebuilt in the 15th century

# ❷ Assisi

See pp358–9.

# ❸ Perugia

🏛 160,000. 🚉 🚌 Piazza Vittorio Veneto. ℹ Piazza Matteotti 18 (075 573 64 58). 🕒 Tue, Sat.
🌐 turismo.comune.perugia.it

Perugia's old center hinges around the traffic-free Corso Vannucci, named after the local painter Pietro Vannucci (Perugino). At its northern end is Piazza IV Novembre, dominated by the **Fontana Maggiore**, a 13th-century fountain by Nicola and Giovanni Pisano. To the rear rise the 15th-century **Duomo**, its entrance flanked by a statue of Pope Julius II (1555) and a pulpit built for Siena's San Bernardino (1425). Its Cappella del Santo Anello contains the Virgin's "wedding ring," a weighty piece of agate said to change color according to the character of the person wearing it. The third pillar in the south nave holds a Renaissance painting of the *Madonna delle Grazie* by Gian Nicola di Paolo. The figure is credited with miraculous powers and mothers bring newly baptized children to kneel before it. Buried in the transepts are Popes Urban IV and Martin IV.

Away from the Corso is the **Oratorio di San Bernardino** (1457–61) on Piazza San Francesco, with a colorful facade by Agostino di Duccio. Beyond the old city walls on Borgo XX Giugno stands **San Pietro**. Founded in the 10th century and rebuilt in 1463, the best feature of the fine interior is the wooden choir (1526).

Piazza Giordano Bruno is home to **San Domenico** (1305–1632), Umbria's largest church, which is known for the Gothic tomb of Benedict XI (c.1304) and decoration by Agostino di Duccio.

### 🏛 Museo Archeologico Nazionale dell'Umbria

San Domenico, Piazza Giordano Bruno 10. **Tel** 075 572 71 41. **Open** daily. **Closed** 1 Jan, 1 May, 25 Dec. 🈲 🚻

Housed in the cloisters of San Domenico, this museum exhibits prehistoric, Etruscan, and Roman artifacts.

### 🏛 Palazzo dei Priori

Corso Vannucci 19. **Tel** 075 573 64 58. **Open** daily (am only Sun). **Closed** Jan 1, May 1, Dec 25 & 1st Mon each month. 🚻 Collegio del Cambio: **Open** daily.

**Entrance of Palazzo dei Priori, Perugia**

The monumental walls and bristling crenellations of this palace mark it as Umbria's finest public building (*see pp58–9*). Among its fine rooms is the Sala dei Notari (c.1295), the former lawyers' hall, vividly frescoed with scenes from the Old Testament – the work of a follower of Pietro Cavallini. The doorway is guarded by a pair of large bronzes made in 1274: a Guelph lion and a griffin, the medieval emblem of

**Medieval street in Perugia**

Perugia. The Sala di Udienza del Collegio della Mercanzia, built around 1390, was formerly used by the Merchants' Guild. This room is late Gothic in style, with exquisite paneling and 15th-century inlaid wood.

Also in the palace is the **Collegio del Cambio**, Perugia's former money exchange, which was begun in 1452. This room was used by the Bankers' Guild. Its walls are covered with superlative frescoes (1498–1500) by Perugino, works devoted to Classical and religious scenes. A glum self-portrait scowls down from the center of the left wall, while the hand of Perugino's pupil Raphael may be evident in some panels on the right wall.

### 🏛 Galleria Nazionale dell'Umbria

Palazzo dei Priori, Corso Vannucci 19. **Tel** 075 58 66 84 10. **Open** Tue–Sun. **Closed** Jan 1, May 1, Dec 25. 🈲 🚻

Umbria's greatest collection of paintings is displayed here on the third floor of the palace. Most of the works are 13th- to 18th-century paintings by local artists, but the highlights are altarpieces by Piero della Francesca and Fra Angelico.

## ❹ Lake Trasimeno

Perugia. 🚉 🚌 Castiglione del Lago. 🛈 Piazza Mazzini 10, Castiglione del Lago (075 965 24 84). 🌐 umbriatourism.it

Edged with low hills, this is Italy's fourth-largest lake. Its miles of placid water and reed-lined shores have a tranquil, melancholy beauty.

Drainage of the lake began under the Romans, but today the lake is gently drying up of its own accord. The town of **Castiglione del Lago**, jutting out on a fortified promontory, has an easy-going atmosphere and small sandy beaches. The 16th-century **castle** is used for summer concerts. The church of **Santa Maria Maddalena**, begun in 1836, has a fine *Madonna and Child* (c.1500) by Eusebio di San Giorgio.

Like Castiglione, **Passignano sul Trasimeno** offers boat trips to **Isola Maggiore**. The island's charming village is known for lace-making.

### The Battle of Lake Trasimeno

In 217 BC the Romans suffered one of their worst ever military defeats on the shores of Lake Trasimeno. The Carthaginian general, Hannibal, lured the Romans (who were led by the consul Flaminius) into a masterful ambush close to present-day Ossaia (Place of Bones) and Sanguineto (Place of Blood). Some 16,000 legionaries perished, hacked down on the lake's marshy fringes. Hannibal, by contrast, lost only 1,500 men. Today you can explore the battlefield, which includes over 100 mass graves found near Tuoro sul Trasimeno.

**Portrait of General Hannibal**

**Colourful facade of Perugia's Oratorio di San Bernardino**

# Assisi: Basilica di San Francesco

The burial place of St. Francis, this basilica was begun in 1228, two years after the saint's death. Over the next century its Upper and Lower Churches were decorated by the foremost artists of their day, among them Cimabue, Simone Martini, Pietro Lorenzetti, and Giotto, whose frescoes on the *Life of St. Francis* are some of the most renowned in Italy. The Basilica, which dominates Assisi, is one of the great Christian shrines and receives vast numbers of pilgrims throughout the year.

**Lower Church**
Side chapels were created here in the 13th century to accommodate the growing number of pilgrims.

**St. Francis**
Cimabue's simple painting (*c.*1280) captures the humility of the revered saint, who stood for poverty, chastity, and obedience.

### KEY

① **The crypt** contains the tomb of St. Francis.

② **Steps to the Treasury**

③ **The choir** (1501) features a 13th-century stone papal throne.

④ **The campanile** was built in 1239.

⑤ **Faded paintings** by Roman artists line the walls above Giotto's *Life of St. Francis*.

⑥ **The facade** and its rose window are early examples of Italian Gothic.

**★ Frescoes by Lorenzetti**
The bold composition of Pietro Lorenzetti's fresco, entitled *The Deposition* (1323), is based around the truncated Cross, focusing attention on the twisted figure of Christ.

**Upper Church**
The soaring Gothic lines of the 13th-century Upper Church symbolized the heavenly glory of St. Francis. This style also influenced later Franciscan churches.

## VISITORS' CHECKLIST

**Practical Information**
Piazza San Francesco. **Tel** 075 81 90 01. **Open** 6am–6pm daily (Upper Church: from 8:30am). Longer hours Sun & summer.
🛈 ♿
W sanfrancescoassisi.org

**Transportation**
🚌 FS

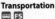

**Entrance to Upper Church**

**Entrance to Lower Church**

★ **Frescoes by Giotto**
*The Ecstasy of St. Francis* is one of 28 panels that make up Giotto's cycle on the *Life of St. Francis* (c.1290–95).

★ **Cappella di San Martino**
The frescoes in this chapel on the *Life of St. Martin* (1315) are by the Sienese painter Simone Martini. This panel shows the *Death of the Saint*. Martini was also responsible for the fine stained glass in the chapel.

## ❷ Assisi

Perugia. 🔼 25,000. FS 🚌 𝒊 Piazza del Comune 22 (075 813 86 80). 🚽 Sat. W umbriatourism.it

This beautiful medieval town, with its geranium-hung streets, lovely views, and fountain-splashed piazzas, is heir to the legacy of St. Francis (c.1181–1226), who is buried in the **Basilica di San Francesco**. The town suffered serious damage during the earthquake of September 1997, but restoration was relatively swift – completed in approximately two years. The tourist office can give information on which sights are open to visitors.

Piazza del Comune, Assisi's main square, is dominated by the columns of the **Tempio di Minerva**, a Roman temple-front from the Augustan age. The Palazzo Comunale, opposite, is home to the **Pinacoteca Comunale**, an art gallery with works by local medieval artists.

Down Corso Mazzini lies the **Basilica di Santa Chiara**, the burial place of St. Clare – Francis's companion and the founder of the Poor Clares (an order of nuns). One of its chapels contains the crucifix that is said to have bowed its head and ordered Francis to "Repair God's church." It came from **San Damiano**, a sublime church set amid olive groves south of the Porta Nuova.

The **Duomo (San Rufino)**, built during the 12th and 13th centuries, has a superb Romanesque facade. Inside is a small museum of paintings, and there are archaeological items in the crypt. From the Duomo, Via Maria delle Rose leads to the **Rocca Maggiore** (rebuilt in 1367), an evocative if much-restored castle.

Thirteenth-century **San Pietro**, on Piazza San Pietro, is a simple and carefully restored Romanesque church. The nearby **Oratorio dei Pellegrini**, a 15th-century pilgrims' hospice, contains well-preserved frescoes by Matteo da Gualdo.

Giotto's fresco, *St. Francis Appearing to the Friars at Arles* (c.1295), in the Basilica di San Francesco, Assisi ▶

## ❺ Orvieto

Terni. 🚇 22,000. 🚆 🚌 ℹ️ Piazza Duomo 24 (0763 34 17 72). 🛒 Thu & Sat. 🌐 orvietoonline.com

Perched on a 984 ft (300 m) plateau, Orvieto looks down over a vineyard-spotted plain. Visitors flood into the town to admire the **Duomo**, among the greatest of Italy's Romanesque-Gothic cathedrals.

The tiny 14th-century church of **San Lorenzo de'Arari** is at the end of Via Scalza. Its walls feature frescoes describing the martyrdom of St. Lawrence, who was grilled to death. The altar is made from an Etruscan sacrificial slab. Via Malabranca leads to **San Giovenale** at Orvieto's western tip, a church that is beautifully and almost completely covered in detailed frescoes from the 15th and 16th centuries. It offers broad views over the surrounding countryside. **Sant'Andrea**, in Piazza della Repubblica, is distinguished by a curious 12-sided campanile, part of the original 12th-century building.

### 🏛️ Museo dell'Opera del Duomo & Museo d'Arte Moderna "Emilio Greco"

Piazza Duomo. **Tel** 0763 34 35 92. **Open** Apr–Sep: 9:30am–7pm daily; Nov–Feb: 10am–1pm & 2–5pm Wed–Mon; Mar & Oct: 10am–5pm Wed–Mon. 🔲 🌐 opsm.it

The Museo dell'Opera del Duomo is an interesting little museum containing an eclectic collection of treasures given to the Duomo. Among the highlights are paintings by Lorenzo Maitani (died 1330) and sculptures by Andrea Pisano (c.1270–1348).

The "Emilio Greco" museum is devoted to the modern Sicilian sculptor Emilio Greco, who made the bronze doors (1964–70) of the Duomo in Orvieto.

The view into the Pozzo di San Patrizio in Orvieto

### 🏛️ Museo Archeologico Faina & Museo Civico

Piazza Duomo 29. **Tel** 0763 34 10 39. **Open** 8:30am–7:30pm daily. **Closed** Jan 1, May 1, Dec 25. 🔲 🔲 🔲

The first of these two museums has a well-known, low-key collection of Etruscan remains including a large number of Greek vases that were found in Etruscan tombs in the surrounding area. The Museo Civico contains ancient Greek artifacts and Etruscan copies of Greek works.

### 🏠 Duomo of Orvieto

Piazza Duomo. **Tel** 0763 34 11 67. **Open** daily. 🔲

Some 300 years in the building, Orvieto's Duomo (begun 1290), with its breathtaking facade, is one of Italy's greatest cathedrals. It was inspired by the Miracle of Bolsena in which real blood from a consecrated host supposedly fell on the altar cloth of a church in nearby Bolsena.

Carved choir stalls

**The exterior** is characterized by horizontal bands of white travertine and blue-gray basalt.

Cappella Nuova

14th-century rose window by Orcagna

Bronze doors by Emilio Greco (1964–70)

**The reliquary of the Corporal** contains the altar cloth from Bolsena.

**Cappella del Corporale**
This chapel contains Lippo Memmi's *Madonna dei Raccomandati* (1320). There are also frescoes (1357–64) by Ugolino di Prete Ilario of the *Miracle of Bolsena* and *Miracles of the Sacrament*.

### 🏛 **Pozzo di San Patrizio**

Viale San Gallo. **Tel** 0763 34 37 68.
**Open** daily. 🏛 allows entry at Museo
d'Arte Moderna.

This well was commissioned in
1527 by Pope Clement VII and
designed by the Florentine
architect Antonio da Sangallo to
provide the town with a water
supply in case of attack. Two
248-step staircases drop into its
dank interior, cleverly arranged
as a double helix (spiral) so as
not to intersect. The 203 ft (62 m)
shaft took ten years to complete.

### 🏛 **Necropoli Etrusca – Crocifisso del Tufo**

Strada Statale 71 to Orvieto Scalo, km
1,600. **Tel** 0763 34 36 11. **Open**
10am–7pm (Oct–Mar: to 5pm) daily.
**Closed** Jan 1, May 1, Dec 25. 🏛 🏛

This Etruscan necropolis from
the 6th century BC has burial
chambers built of blocks of tufa.
Etruscan letters, thought to be
the names of the deceased, are
inscribed on the tombs.

**Cappella Nuova**
Luca Signorelli's great fresco cycle
of the *Last Judgment* (1499–1504)
features prominently in this chapel.
Fra Angelico and Benozzo Gozzoli
worked here before Signorelli.

**The Facade**
There are detailed carvings
(c.1320–30) at the base of its four
main pilasters. By Lorenzo Maitani,
they depict scenes from the Old
and New Testaments, including
Hell and Damnation.

The beautiful hill-town of Todi in
southern Umbria

## ➏ **Todi**

Perugia. 🏛 17,000. 🚆 🚌 🛈 Piazza
Umberto I 6 (075 894 54 16). 🚌 Sat.

Looking down over the Tiber
valley from its hilltop eyrie, Todi
is one of the most strikingly
located of Umbria's famous
hill-towns. An ancient Etruscan
and then Roman, settlement,
it still preserves an uncorrupted
medieval air, with several tiny
churches, three austere
public palaces, and many
sleepy corners.

Most people are drawn here
by the **Piazza del Popolo**, the
main square, flanked by the
lovely plain-faced **Duomo**. Built
in the 13th century on the site
of a Roman temple to Apollo, it
has a dusky interior and one of
Umbria's finest choirs (1521–30).
Note Ferraù da Faenza's
huge painting (1596) on the
rear wall, a less than totally
successful copy of Michelangelo's
*The Last Judgment*, and the
altarpiece at the end of the
right aisle by Giannicola di
Paolo (a follower of Perugino).

Also flanking the piazza are
the **Palazzo dei Priori** (1293–
1337) and the linked **Palazzo
del Capitano** (1290) and
**Palazzo del Popolo**
(1213). In the Palazzo
del Capitano,
distinguished by
its redoubtable
medieval interior, lies
the **Museo Etrusco-
Romano**. The
museum contains a
collection of local
Etruscan and Roman
artifacts. There are

altarpieces and sacred objects
in the **Pinacoteca Comunale**,
also housed in the palace.

A few steps from the piazza
rises **San Fortunato** (1292–
1462), named after Todi's first
bishop, with a florid Gothic
doorway (1415–58). The high-
vaulted plan is based on
German Gothic "hall" churches
and the "barn" churches of
Tuscany, characterized by a low-
pitched vault, polygonal apse,
and naves and aisles of equal
height. The choir (1590) is
superb, but the church's most
famous work is *Madonna and
Child* (1432) by Masolino da
Panicale (fourth chapel on the
right). The crypt contains the
tomb of Jacopone da Todi
(c.1228–1306), a noted medieval
poet and mystic.

To the right of the church
are some shady gardens, from
which a path (past the tiny
castle) drops through the trees
to emerge in front of **Santa
Maria della Consolazione**
(1508–1607), near the N79.
One of central Italy's finest
Renaissance churches, and
based on a Greek cross, it may
have been built to a plan by
Bramante. The stark, chill
interior is overshadowed by
the harmonious exterior.

### 🏛 **Museo Etrusco-Romano and Pinacoteca Comunale**

Piazza del Popolo 29/30. **Tel** 075 894 41
48. **Open** 10am–1pm & 2:30–5pm
Tue–Sun. 🏛 🏛

Santa Maria della Consolazione in Todi

## ❼ Spoleto

Perugia. 🗺 38,000. 🚆 🚌 ℹ Piazza della Libertà 7 (0743 21 86 20 or 0743 21 86 21). 🛒 Fri. 🌐 conspoleto.com

Founded by the Umbrians, Spoleto was one of central Italy's most important Roman colonies, a prominence maintained by the Lombards, who in the 7th century made it the capital of one of their three Italian dukedoms. After a spell as an independent city-state, in 1354 Spoleto fell to the papacy.

Spoleto, within its wooded setting, is the loveliest of the Umbrian hill-towns. Its urbane atmosphere is enhanced by the Festival dei Due Mondi, one of Europe's leading arts festivals, held annually in June and July, and by its superb monuments.

The church of **San Pietro**, set on a hill overlooking Spoleto, was founded in 419 AD and built on an ancient necropolis. Its facade is covered in fascinating Romanesque relief sculptures, considered some of the finest examples in Umbria. From here, head north toward the town center on Viale Giacomo Matteotti and Via San Carlo.

At the southern end of Piazza del Mercato is the **Arco di Druso**, a 1st-century-AD Roman arch. It is flanked by the church of **Sant'Ansano**, whose crypt is covered in 6th-century frescoes. Via Aurelio Saffi, at the piazza's northern end, leads to Romanesque church **Sant'Eufemia**.

A short way beyond, the fan-shaped Piazza del Duomo opens out to reveal Spoleto's 12th-century **Duomo**, graced with an elegant Romanesque facade. Filling the apse of the Baroque interior is a great fresco cycle. The final work of Fra Lippo Lippi, 1467–9, it describes episodes from the *Life of the Virgin*. The Cappella Erioli is adorned with Pinturicchio's unfinished *Madonna and Child* (1497).

The best of the exceptional churches in the lower town is 4th-century **San Salvatore**, located in the main cemetery. Nearby stands **San Ponziano**,

Facade of San Pietro in Spoleto

fronted by a captivating three-tiered Romanesque facade typical of Umbria. It has a 10th-century crypt, decorated with Byzantine frescoes.

Romanesque **San Gregorio** in Piazza Garibaldi dates from 1069, but its facade and campanile incorporate fragments of Roman buildings. Inside is a raised presbytery and a lovely multi-columned crypt. Well-preserved patches of fresco dot the walls. Some 10,000 Christian martyrs are supposedly buried near the church. They were reputedly slaughtered in the town's Roman **amphitheater**, traces of which can be seen in the barracks on Via del Anfiteatro.

### 🌉 Ponte delle Torri

This magnificent 14th-century aqueduct, the "bridge of towers," is 262 ft (80 m) high. Designed by Gattapone (from Gubbio), it is the town's single most famous monument.

Ponte delle Torri, Spoleto

## Romanesque Churches in Umbria

Umbria's church-building tradition had its roots in ancient Roman basilicas and in the chapels built over the shrines of its many saints and martyrs. The region's Romanesque facades are usually divided into three tiers, often with three rose windows arranged above a trio of arched portals. The three doors usually correspond to the interior's nave and two aisles, which derive from the simple barnlike plan of Roman basilicas. Inside, the presbytery is often raised in order to allow for the building of a crypt, which usually contained the relics of a saint or martyr. Many of the churches took centuries to build, or were repeatedly modified over time, often acquiring elements of Gothic, Baroque, or Renaissance styles.

**San Lorenzo de'Arari** in Orvieto takes its name from an Etruscan altar *(arari)*. This 14th-century church has a very simple facade *(see p362)*.

12th-century campanile

Renaissance portico

**Spoleto's Duomo** (1198) has eight rose windows, a mosaic (1207), and a Renaissance portico (1491). The tower was built from old Roman ruins.

From the bridge, there are views of the bastions of the **Rocca Albornoz**, a huge papal fortress built in 1359–64, also by Gattapone. Across the bridge, a path leads to the Strada di Monteluco and the church of **San Pietro**, famous for the fascinating 12th-century carvings on its facade.

**Rocca Albornoz**
Piazza Campello 1. **Tel** 0743 22 49 52.
**Open** Tue–Sun. compulsory.

**Museo del Tessile e del Costume**
Via delle Terme. **Tel** 0743 459 40.
**Open** 3:30–7pm Sat & Sun.
**Closed** Jan 1, Dec 25.
Among the exhibits in this exquisite collection are sacred vestments complete with headgear, ties, and gold chains, and a series of 17th-century tapestries that once belonged to Queen Christina of Sweden.

## ❽ Montefalco

Perugia. 4,900. Mon.

Montefalco, whose name (Falcon's Mount) draws inspiration from its lofty position and sweeping views, is the best of the fascinating villages in the Vale of Spoleto. Criss-crossed by streets almost too narrow for cars, it takes less than 5 minutes to walk through the village. Yet you might happily spend a morning here, most of it in the polished **Museo Civico** housed

A panel from Gozzoli's fresco cycle (1452) in Montefalco's Museo Civico

in the former church of San Francesco. Its highlight is Benozzo Gozzoli's *Life of St. Francis* (1452), a radiant fresco cycle that borrows heavily from Giotto's cycle in Assisi (*see pp358–61*). Other painters represented here are Perugino, Tiberio d'Assisi, and Niccolò Alunno, all leading medieval Umbrian artists.

The simple Gothic church of **Sant'Agostino** (begun 1279) on Corso Mameli is dotted with frescoes from the 14th–16th centuries. The church also contains three mummies.

In the main square, local wines for sale include the rich red Sagrantino di Montefalco. Just outside the town walls, the church of **Sant'Illuminata** is covered with charming frescoes, the work of the local 16th-century artist

Francesco Melanzio. About 1 mile (2 km) beyond, the prettily located church of **San Fortunato** is decorated with frescoes by Gozzoli and Tiberio d'Assisi.

**Environs**
The village in the Vale of Spoleto with the most spectacular setting is **Trevi**. The churches of **San Martino** (16th century), on Passeggiata di San Martino, and **Madonna delle Lacrime** (1487–1522), south of Trevi on the road into the village, contain paintings by Perugino and Tiberio d'Assisi, among others.

**Museo Civico di San Francesco**
Via Ringhiera Umbra 9. **Tel** 0742 37 95 98. **Open** daily (Nov–Feb: Tue–Sun). **Closed** Jan 1, Dec 25.

**The Duomo** (1253) in Assisi is a fine example of the three-tiered facades found across central Italy (*see p359*). It has a pointed arch and a row of arcading.

11th-century campanile
Carved figures

**Todi's Duomo** was begun in the 12th century, but work on its windows and portals continued until the 17th century (*see p363*).

Rose window
Rounded portal

**San Michele** (*c.*1195), in Bevagna, has a beautiful portal that combines both Romanesque and old Roman fragments (*see p366*).

18th-century rose window

## ❾ Spello

Perugia. 🚗 8,000. 🚆 🚌 ℹ️ Piazza Matteotti 3 (0742 30 10 09). 🗓️ Wed.

Spello is one of the better-known villages in the Vale of Spoleto. It is renowned for a fresco cycle by Pinturicchio in the Cappella Baglioni of the church of **Santa Maria Maggiore** (12th–13th century) on Via Consolare. Executed around 1500, the frescoes depict scenes from the New Testament. Toward the center of the village is the Gothic church of **Sant'Andrea** (13th century) on Via Cavour. This road becomes Via Garibaldi, which leads to **San Lorenzo**, a Baroque gem of a church dating from the 12th century.

Spello also boasts Roman ruins from the age of Augustus: the **Porta Consolare** at the end of Via Consolare, and the twin-towered **Porta Venere** by Via Torri di Properzio.

The road to Assisi over **Monte Subasio** offers stunning views from the top of the mountain above Spello.

### Environs

The least-known village in the Vale of Spoleto is **Bevagna**. Like Spello, it sprang to life as a waystation on the Via Flaminia (the Roman road that ran through this part of Umbria). The medieval Piazza Silvestri is the setting for two Roman-esque churches.

The lofty peaks of the Monti Sibillini in eastern Umbria

**San Silvestro** (1195) is the more atmospheric of the pair, thanks to its shadowy interior and ancient crypt, but **San Michele** (late 12th century) has an elegant portal, famed for the little gargoyles on either side. Both churches are the work of Maestro Binello.

## ❿ Monti Sibillini

Macerata. 🚆 Spoleto. 🚌 Visso. ℹ️ Piazza del Forno 1, Visso (0737 97 27 11). 🌐 sibillini.net

The national park of the Monti Sibillini in eastern Umbria provides the region's wildest and most spectacular scenery. A range 25 miles (40 km) long, the mountains form part of the Apennines, a chain that runs the length of the Italian peninsula. **Monte Vettore** is the loftiest point, and the peninsula's third highest; it stands at 8,123 ft (2,476 m), a great whale-backed peak close to the cave of the mythical sybil that gave the region its name.

Good maps and trails make this a superb walking area, while drivers can follow hairpin roads to some of Italy's most magical landscapes. Chief of these is the **Piano Grande**, a huge upland plain surrounded by a vast amphitheater of mountains. Bare but for flocks of sheep and bedraggled haystacks, the plain blazes with wildflowers in spring and with lentils later in the year. The only habitation was **Castelluccio**, a beautiful, neglected mountain village that has sadly now been nearly destroyed by the 2016 November earthquake.

Storefront in Norcia displaying the town's varied meats

## ⓫ Norcia

Perugia. 🚗 4,700. 🚌 ℹ️ Piazza San Benedetto (0743 82 49 11). 🗓️ Thu.

The birthplace of St. Benedict, Norcia is a robust mountain town and an excellent base for exploring Valnerina and Monti Sibillini. One of Italy's culinary capitals, it is renowned for truffles and for some of Italy's best hams, sausages, and salamis. Indeed, the local word for a pork butcher's (*norcineria*) derives from the name of the town.

Norcia's main sights are in **Piazza San Benedetto**. On the eastern flank, the church of **San Benedetto** has a 14th-century portal adorned with statues of Benedict and his sister (Santa Scolastica). Legend claims that the church marks the site of Benedict's birth, and there are the remains of a 5th-century building in the crypt. However,

Pinturicchio's *Annunciation* (c.1500) in Spello's Santa Maria Maggiore

The 8th-century monastery of San Pietro in Valle, set in the beautiful Valnerina

the church was more likely to have been built over the site of an old Roman temple, since the forum of the Roman colony of Nursia once occupied this spot.

Left of the church stands the **Palazzo Comunale**, a monument to the town's period as a free commune during the 13th and 14th centuries. On the opposite side of the square rises the **Castellina** (1554), a blunt papal fortress designed by Vignola to help impose order on an unruly mountain district. The **Duomo** (1560), to the left of the Castellina, has been ravaged by earthquakes over the centuries. Indeed, Norcia has been the victim of successive earthquakes – the most recent being in November 2016, which led to the collapse of the church. Its complete reconstruction is

underway, but this is a long term project. **Sant'Agostino** on Via Anicia features a range of good 16th-century frescoes. A little way beyond, the **Oratorio di Sant'Agostinaccio** in Piazza Palatina contains a superb 17th-century ceiling. Via Umberto shelters the **Edicola** (1354), a strange tabernacle believed to have been carved for a Holy Week procession.

## ⑫ Valnerina

Perugia. 🚆 Spoleto, then bus. 🛈 Via G. da Chiavano 2, Cascia (0743 714 01).

The Valnerina (Valley of the River Nera) curves through a broad swathe of eastern Umbria, draining the mountains around Norcia and the Sibillini before

emptying into the Tiber. It is edged with craggy, tree-covered slopes and dotted with upland villages and fortified hamlets.

The high spot is **San Pietro in Valle**, an idyllically located monastery in the hills above the village of Colleponte. Founded in the 8th century, it is one of the few surviving memorials to the Lombards, whose central Italian duchy had its capital in Spoleto. The main body of the monastery church dates from this period, as does the high altar. The nave walls are covered in a wealth of 12th-century frescoes. Some of the best Romanesque carvings in Umbria can be found here.

More popular than the monastery are the **Cascate delle Marmore** near Terni, among Europe's highest waterfalls at 541 ft (165 m). Created by the Romans during drainage work, their waters are now diverted to produce hydroelectric power except for a few hours a day. You can view the falls from Marmore village or the S209.

🏠 **San Pietro in Valle**
Località Ferentillo, Terni. **Tel** 0744 78 01 29. **Open** daily (Sat & Sun in winter).

🌊 **Cascate delle Marmore**
4 miles (7 km) along S209 Valnerina, Terni. **Tel** 0744 629 82. **Open** daily.
🌐 marmorefalls.it

The remains of the church of San Benedetto in Norcia

# LE MARCHE

Tucked away in a remote corner between the Adriatic Sea and the Apennine mountains, Le Marche (the Marches) is an enchanting rural patchwork of old towns, hill country, and long, sandy beaches. In pre-Christian times the area was settled by the Piceni, a tribe eventually assimilated by the Romans.

In the 4th century BC, exiles from Magna Graecia colonized much of the region. The most notable town was Ancona, also the northernmost point of Greek influence on the Italian peninsula. During the early Middle Ages the region marked the edge of the Holy Roman Empire, giving rise to its present name (*march* meant "border area").

The region's historical peak was reached in the 15th century under Federico da Montefeltro, whose court at Urbino became one of Europe's leading cultural centers. Much of Urbino's former grandeur survives, particularly in Federico's magnificent Renaissance Palazzo Ducale, now home to a regional art collection. Ascoli Piceno is almost as enchanting as Urbino, its central Piazza del Popolo among the most evocative

old squares in Italy. Smaller towns like San Leo and Urbania and the republic of San Marino also boast fine medieval monuments.

Today, probably as many people come to Le Marche for its beaches and towns as for its hilly, unspoiled interior. Especially beautiful are the snowcapped peaks of the Monti Sibillini, located in magnificent walking and skiing country.

Regional cuisine encompasses the truffles and robust cheeses of the mountains, tender hams and salamis, *olive ascolane* (olives stuffed with meat and herbs), and *brodetto*, fish soup made in several versions up and down the coast. Dry, white Verdicchio is the best-known wine, although more unusual names, such as Bianchello del Metauro, are gaining in popularity.

A field of poppies and olive trees in the heart of Le Marche's countryside

◀ The Piazza del Popolo, built in travertine marble, in the town of Ascoli Piceno

# Exploring Le Marche

The medieval towns of Urbino and Ascoli Piceno are the highlights of the region, but the rolling hills of the interior contain an abundance of smaller towns and secluded villages. San Leo, with its dramatic fortress, is one of the best. Most of the countryside is a pretty mixture of woods and remote hills, rising in the west to the majestic Monti Sibillini. Ancona and the attractive town of Pèsaro are the pivotal points of the vast coastline.

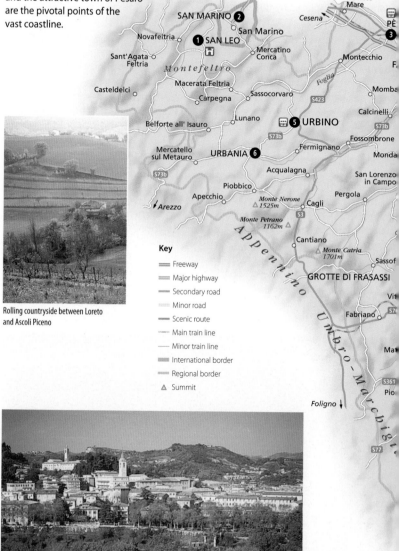

**Key**

═══ Freeway

─── Major highway

─── Secondary road

┄┄┄ Minor road

─── Scenic route

┈┈┈ Main train line

─── Minor train line

▬▬▬ International border

▬▬▬ Regional border

△ Summit

Rolling countryside between Loreto and Ascoli Piceno

Ascoli Piceno, one of the prettiest towns in Le Marche

**For additional map symbols** *see back flap*

## Sights at a Glance

1. San Leo
2. San Marino
3. Pèsaro
4. Fano
5. Urbino pp374–5
6. Urbania
7. Grotte di Frasassi
8. Jesi
9. Ancona
10. Conero Peninsula
11. Loreto
12. Ascoli Piceno

The rocky reef near Portonovo on the Conero Peninsula

### Getting Around

The A14–E55 provides easy access to the coastal resorts. Divided highway spurs from the A14–E55 lead to Jesi, Urbino, and Ascoli Piceno, but north–south roads in the interior can be slow. Bus services are generally good, but they can be infrequent in the interior. The train service along the coast is excellent, with a good service through the heart of the region, though it can be slow.

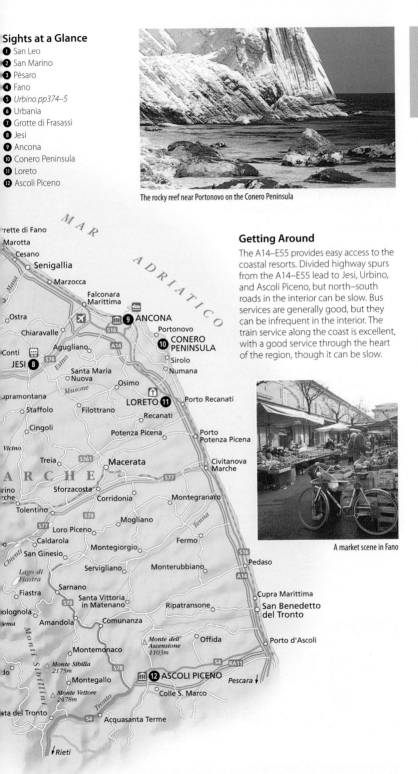

A market scene in Fano

The bell tower of the Duomo rising above the village of San Leo

# ❶ San Leo

Pèsaro. 🚗 3,000. 🅸 Piazza Dante Alighieri 14 (0541 92 69 67). 🚌 from Rimini, change at Villanova. 🆆 san-leo.it

Few castles are as impressive as the great **Fortress** that towers over the village of San Leo. Dante used this crag-top site as a model for the landscapes of *Purgatorio*, while Machiavelli considered the citadel to be the finest piece of military architecture in Italy. Its rocky ramparts once contained the Mons Feretrius, a Roman temple dedicated to Jupiter.

An earlier Roman fortress on the site became a papal prison in the 18th century. Its most famous inmate was the larger-than-life Conte di Cagliostro. A swindler, womanizer, necromancer, quack, and alchemist, Cagliostro was imprisoned for heresy in the 1790s. His cell was specially built so that its window faced the village's two churches. It is still visible, together with a small picture gallery, state rooms, and the majestic Renaissance ramparts, built by Francesco di Giorgio

Martini for the dukes of Monte-feltro in the 15th century.

The captivating village has a quaint cobblestone square with a superb 9th-century **Pieve** (parish church). Built partly with stone from the ruined Mons Feretrius, the church is on the site of a 6th-century chapel.

Just behind is the 12th-century **Duomo**, a fine Romanesque building with Corinthian capitals and Roman columns from the Mons Feretrius. The lid of St. Leo's sarcophagus is in the crypt. Ancient pagan carvings can be seen on the wall behind the altar.

## 🏠 Fortress

Via Leopardi. **Tel** 0541 91 63 06. **Open** daily. **Closed** lunch Oct–Mar. 🔲

# ❷ San Marino

🚗 26,000. 🚌 San Marino Città (from Rimini). 🅸 Contrada Omagnano (0549 88 29 14). 🆆 visitsanmarino.com

Europe's oldest republic, tiny San Marino was reputedly founded by St. Marinus, a 4th-century monk and stone-mason forced to flee the religious persecution of the Emperor Diocletian. With him was St. Leo, founder of the nearby town of San Leo. Located on the slopes of Monte Titano, the country has its own mint, stamps, soccer team – even its own 1,000-strong army. It is also famous for Formula One racing. There are no customs

Duty-free store in San Marino

formalities in this country, whose borders are just 7 miles (12 km) apart at the widest point. The capital, **San Marino**, is overrun with visitors and souvenir stands through the year. Garibaldi sought shelter here after fleeing Venice in 1849 and is honored by a monument in Piazza Garibaldi. The town of **Borgomaggiore** lies at the foot of Monte Titano, with a cable car to the capital above.

# ❸ Pèsaro

🚗 110,000. 🚆 🚌 🅸 Viale Trieste 164 (0721 693 41). 🔲 Tue & 1st Thu of month.

One of the Adriatic's larger seaside resorts, Pèsaro has managed to retain a stylish air. Behind the promenade and the wall of white stucco hotels is a lively, attractive medieval area.

The art gallery of the **Musei Civici** contains Giovanni Bellini's sumptuous polyptych, the *Coronation of the Virgin* (*c.*1470). The museum also features Renaissance ceramics.

The **Museo Archeologico Oliveriano** presents historical displays from Roman remains to Iron Age artifacts from the necropolis of nearby Novilara.

The best of the town's churches is **Sant'Agostino** on Corso XI Settembre, remarkable for its choir stalls, each a patchwork of inlaid landscapes and narrative scenes.

Pèsaro is also a point of musical pilgrimage because the composer Gioacchino Rossini was born here in 1792. His home, **Casa Rossini**, contains memorabilia, while his piano and some

Detail of the *Coronation of the Virgin* by Bellini (*c.*1470) in the Musei Civici

original manuscripts lie in the **Conservatorio Rossini**. His operas are performed in **Teatro Rossini** in Piazza Lazzarini during the annual August music festival.

🏛 **Musei Civici**
Piazza Mosca 29. **Tel** 0721 38 72 95. **Open** Tue–Sun. **Closed** Jan 1, Dec 25. 🖼

🏛 **Museo Archeologico Oliveriano**
Via Mazza 97. **Tel** 0721 333 44. **Open** Mon–Sat. ♿

🏠 **Casa Rossini**
Via Rossini 34. **Tel** 0721 38 73 57. **Open** Tue–Sun. 🖼

🏠 **Conservatorio Rossini**
Piazza Olivieri 5. **Tel** 0721 336 71. **Open** Mon–Fri, but call in advance to arrange. **Closed** public hols.

## ❹ Fano

Pèsaro. 🚍 65,000. 🚊 🚌 🚢 ℹ Via Cesare Battisti 10 (0721 80 35 34). 🛒 Wed & Sat.

Ancient Fano stands out from the string of beach resorts south of Pèsaro, thanks to its fine old center and historic monuments. Named after Fanum Fortunae, a pagan temple to the goddess Fortuna, it became the terminal of the Via Flaminia (an important consular road from Rome) and the largest Roman colony on the Adriatic coast. The **Arco d'Augusto** (AD 2), on Via Arco d'Augusto, is Fano's most significant ancient monument, having narrowly escaped destruction at the hands of Federico da Montefeltro in 1463. He destroyed its upper section while besieging the town as a papal *condottiere*.

The 16th-century **Fontana della Fortuna**, in Piazza XX Settembre, is dedicated to the goddess Fortuna. The imposing **Palazzo Malatesta**, which stands behind the fountain, was built around 1420 and enlarged in 1544 for Fano's rulers, the Rimini-based Malatesta family. Inside is the small **Museo Civico** and the **Pinacoteca Malatestiana**, with works by Guercino, Guido Reni, and the Venetian artist Michele Giambono.

🏛 **Museo Civico and Pinacoteca Malatestiana**
Piazza XX Settembre. **Tel** 0721 88 78 44. **Open** Tue–Sun. **Closed** Jan 1, Dec 25 & 26. 🖼

Entrance to the Palazzo Ducale in Urbania

## ❺ Urbino

*See pp374–5.*

## ❻ Urbania

Pèsaro. 🚍 7,200. 🚌 ℹ Corso Vittorio Emanuele 21 (0722 31 31 40). 🛒 Thu.

Urbania, with its elegant arcaded center, takes its name from Pope Urban VIII (1623–44), who entertained the notion of converting the old medieval village known as Castel Durante into a model Renaissance town.

Its chief attraction is a monument from an earlier age, the huge **Palazzo Ducale**, built by the dukes of Montefeltro as one of several residential alternatives to the Palazzo Ducale in nearby Urbino. It was begun in the 13th century, and then rebuilt in the 15th and 16th centuries. Beautifully located alongside the River Metauro, it houses a small art gallery, a modest museum, old maps and globes, and the remnants of Duke Federico's famous library.

🏛 **Palazzo Ducale**
Palazzo Ducale. **Tel** 0722 31 31 51. **Open** Tue–Sun. **Closed** public hols. 🖼

Fontana della Fortuna in Fano

# Urbino: Palazzo Ducale

Italy's most beautiful Renaissance palace was built for Duke Federico da Montefeltro, ruler of Urbino (1444–82). He was a soldier, but also a man of the arts, and his palace, with its library, paintings, and refined architecture, is a tribute to courtly life and to the artistic and intellectual ideals of the Renaissance. The Palazzo Ducale houses the Galleria Nazionale delle Marche.

★ **The Flagellation by Piero della Francesca**
Dramatic perspective creates an unsettling effect in this 15th-century painting of the scourging of Christ.

The palace rising above Urbino

## KEY

① **The library** was one of Europe's largest in its day.

② **The simple east side** of the palace was designed by Maso di Bartolomeo before 1460.

③ **Towers attributed to Laurana**

④ *The Ideal City*, attributed to Luciano Laurana, is a 15th-century painting of an imaginary Renaissance city. The piece is notable for its measured perspective and lack of people.

⑤ **Hanging garden**

⑥ **The rooms** in this wing are known as the Appartamento della Duchessa.

**Cortile d'Onore**
This early Renaissance courtyard was designed by the Dalmatian-born artist Luciano Laurana (1420–79).

★ **Studiolo**
The former study of Federico da
Montefeltro is decorated with
intarsia (inlaid wood), some of it
designed by Botticelli.

*Duke Federico
by Pedro
Berruguete*
The duke, shown
with his son in
this 15th-century
painting, was
always portrayed
in left profile
after an injury
to his face.

Main
entrance

⑤

⑥

★ **La Muta by Raphael**
*The Mute Woman* may be a
portrait of Maddalena Doni,
a Florentine noblewoman.

## ⑤ Urbino

Pèsaro. 16,000. *i* Piazza
Rinascimento (0722 26 13). Sat.
**W** turismo.pesarourbino.it

Amid a tangle of medieval and
Renaissance streets stands the
Neo-Classical **Duomo**, on Piazza
Federico, built in 1789. Of
interest is the painting of *The
Last Supper* by Federico Barocci
(*c*.1535–1612). The **Museo
Diocesano** contains ceramics,
glass, and religious artifacts.

Urbino's famous son, the
painter Raphael (1483–1520),
lived in the **Casa Natale di
Raffaello**. It has a highly
evocative interior, especially
the kitchen and courtyard.

In Via Barocci is the medieval
**Oratorio di San Giuseppe**,
known for its *presepio*
(Christmas crib), and the
14th-century **Oratorio di San
Giovanni Battista**, with its
15th-century frescoes of the
*Crucifixion* and the *Life of John
the Baptist* by Giacomo and
Lorenzo Salimbeni.

The 15th-century **Fortezza
dell'Albornoz**, on Viale Bruno
Buozzi, is the defensive focus of
Urbino's surviving 16th-century
walls and bastions.

**Museo Diocesano**
Piazza Pascoli 2. **Tel** 0722 48 18.
**Open** 9:30am–1pm, 2:30–6:30pm
Wed–Mon.

**Casa Natale di Raffaello**
Via di Raffaello 57. **Tel** 0722 32 01 05.
**Open** Mar–Oct: 9am–1pm & 3–7pm
Mon–Sat; 10am–1pm Sun & hols;
Nov–Feb: 9am–2pm Mon–Sat; 10am–
1pm Sun. **Closed** Jan 1, Dec 25.

A street scene in the medieval town
of Urbino

Fresh seafood and fishing boats in the harbor at Ancona

# ❼ Grotte di Frasassi

Ancona. **Tel** 0732 97 21 66. 🚆 Genga San Vittore Terme. **Open** daily. Guided tours only (70 mins). **Closed** Jan 1, Jan 10–30, Dec 4, Dec 25. 🚫 🅿️
🌐 **grotte-di-frasassi.it**

Some of Europe's largest publicly accessible caverns lie in the cave network gouged out by the River Sentino southwest of Jesi. Of the vast network of 11 miles (18 km), an area of about 3,281 ft (1,000 m) is open to the public. The colossal **Grotta del Vento** is large enough to contain Milan cathedral – its ceiling extends to a height of 787 ft (240 m). This cavern has been used for a range of experiments, from sensory deprivation to an exploration of the social consequences of leaving a group of people alone in its depths for long periods.

# ❽ Jesi

Ancona. 🚹 41,000. 🚆 🚌 ℹ️ Piazza della Repubblica 11 (0731 53 84 20). 🛒 Wed & Sat.

Perched on a long, rocky ridge, Jesi lies in the heart of the verdant hill country where Verdicchio is produced. A crisp, white wine, Verdicchio is bottled in unique containers – glass models of the terra-cotta amphorae once used to export the wine to ancient Greece. There are many vineyards in the surrounding countryside.

Housed in the town's 18th-century Palazzo Pianetti is the **Pinacoteca e Musei Civici**, which contains fine late-period paintings by Lorenzo Lotto. Almost as alluring as the gallery's paintings, however, is the great central salon – a riot of Rococo decoration that once formed the centerpiece of the Palazzo Pianetti. The nearby **Palazzo della Signoria** features an interesting collection of archae-ological finds, while beyond the old town's Renaissance walls stands the 14th-century church of **San Marco**, known for its collection of well-preserved Giottesque frescoes.

🏛️ **Pinacoteca e Musei Civici**
Via XV Settembre. **Tel** 0731 53 83 42.
**Open** Tue–Sun. 🚫

🏛️ **Palazzo della Signoria**
Piazza Colocci. **Tel** 0731 53 83 45.
**Open** Mon–Sat. **Closed** Mon am & Sat pm.

# ❾ Ancona

🚹 98,000. ✈️ 🚆 🚌 ⛴️ ℹ️ Via della Loggia 50 (071 35 89 91). 🛒 Tue & Fri.
🌐 **turismo.marche.it**

The capital of Le Marche and its largest port (with ferries to and from Greece and Croatia), Ancona dates back to at least the 5th century BC, when it was settled by Greek exiles from Siracusa. Its name derives from *ankon* (Greek for "elbow"), a reference to the rocky spur that juts into the sea to form the town's fine natural harbor.

Heavy bombing during World War II destroyed much of the medieval town. The 15th-century **Loggia dei Mercanti** (Merchants' Exchange) on Via della Loggia survives as a monument to the town's medieval heyday.

Just north of the loggia is the Romanesque church of **Santa Maria della Piazza**, with a lovely facade. The nearby **Pinacoteca Comunale F. Podesti e Galleria d'Arte Moderna** includes canvases by Titian and Lorenzo Lotto. In the **Museo Archeologico Nazionale delle Marche** there are displays of Greek, Gallic, and Roman art. The **Arco di Traiano**, by the harbor, was erected in AD 115 and is one of Italy's better preserved Roman arches.

An impressive cavern in the cave system of the Grotte di Frasassi

The beach at the village of Sirolo on the Conero Peninsula

🏛 **Pinacoteca Comunale F Podesti e Galleria d'Arte Moderna**
Via Pizzecolli 17. **Tel** 071 222 50 41.
**Open** Tue–Sat daily (Sun pm).
**Closed** public hols. 🔲 ♿

🏛 **Museo Archeologico Nazionale delle Marche**
Via Ferretti 1. **Tel** 071 20 26 02.
**Open** 8:30am–7pm Tue–Sun. **Closed** Jan 1, May 1, Aug 15, Dec 25. 🔲 ♿

# ⑩ Conero Peninsula

Ancona. 🚆 ⛴ Ancona. 🚌 from Ancona to Sirolo or Numana. ⓘ Via della Loggia 50, Ancona (071 35 89 91).
ⓦ **parcodelconero.eu**

The beautiful, cliff-edged Conero Peninsula is the only natural feature to disturb the almost unbroken line of beaches along the coast of Le Marche. Easily accessible from Ancona to the north, it is a semi-wild area known for its scenery, its wines (notably Rosso del Conero), and for a collection of coves, beaches, and little resorts.

The best of these resorts is **Portonovo**, above whose beach stands **Santa Maria di Portonovo**, a pretty 11th-century Romanesque church mentioned by Dante in Canto XXI of *Paradiso*. **Sirolo** and **Numana** are busier and more commercialized, but you can escape the crowds by hiking the flower-swathed slopes of Monte Conero, which stands at 1,877 ft (572 m), or by taking a boat trip to the smaller beaches beyond the resorts.

# ⑪ Loreto

Ancona. 🏘 11,000. 🚆 🚌 ⓘ Via Solari 3 (071 97 02 76). 🍴 Fri.

Legend has it that in 1294, the house of the Virgin Mary (**Santa Casa**) miraculously uprooted itself from the Holy Land and was brought by angels to a laurel grove *(loreto)* south of Ancona. Each year several million pilgrims visit the **Santa Casa** in Loreto and its **Basilica**. Begun in 1468, the latter was designed and built in part by Renaissance architects Bramante, Sansovino, and Giuliano da Sangallo. Its paintings include works by Luca Signorelli. The **Museo-Pinacoteca** has 16th-century paintings by Lorenzo Lotto.

Santa Casa in Loreto

🏰 **Basilica and Santa Casa**
Piazza Santuario. **Tel** 071 97 01 04.
**Open** daily. ♿

🏛 **Museo-Pinacoteca**
Palazzo Apostolico. **Tel** 071 974 71 98.
**Open** Apr–Oct: Tue–Sun; Nov–Mar: Fri–Sun. 🔲

# ⑫ Ascoli Piceno

🏘 54,000. 🚌 ⓘ Palazzo Comunale, Piazza Arringo (0736 25 30 45).
🍴 Wed & Sat.

This alluring town takes its name from the Piceni, a tribe eventually conquered by the Romans in 89 BC. The gridiron plan of Roman Asculum Picenum is visible in the streets today, but it is the town's medieval heritage that attracts most visitors.

The enchanting **Piazza del Popolo** is dominated by the 13th-century **Palazzo dei Capitani del Popolo**, whose facade was designed by Cola dell'Amatrice, and the church of **San Francesco**, a large and faintly austere Gothic ensemble built between 1262 and 1549.

Via del Trivio leads north to a medieval district overlooking the River Tronto. Along Via Cairoli lies the 13th-century church of **San Pietro Martire**. Opposite is the church of **Santi Vincenzo e Anastasio** (11th century), with an ancient crypt built over a spring said to cure leprosy.

Around Piazza dell'Arringo is the 12th-century **Duomo**, spoiled by a Baroque overlay. Its Cappella del Sacramento contains a polyptych by the 15th-century artist Carlo Crivelli. The **Pinacoteca Civica** has more works by Crivelli and by Guido Reni, Titian, and Alemanno. The **Museo Archeologico** contains Roman, Piceni, and Lombard artifacts.

🏛 **Pinacoteca Civica**
Palazzo Comunale, Piazza Arringo.
**Tel** 0736 29 82 13. **Open** Tue–Sun.
🔲 ♿

🏛 **Museo Archeologico**
Palazzo Panighi, Piazza Arringo.
**Tel** 0736 25 35 62. **Open** Tue–Sun.
**Closed** Jan 1, May 1, Dec 25. 🔲 ♿

The medieval town of Ascoli Piceno

# ROME AND LAZIO

# Introducing Rome and Lazio

The first settlements in the region can be traced back to the early Etruscan civilization in northern Lazio. Rome grew to rule a vast empire, and as the empire began to divide, the region became the center of the Christian world. Artists and architects flocked to work for the popes and their families, notably in the Renaissance and Baroque periods, when some magnificent architectural works were created. The legacy of this uninterrupted history can be seen all over the city and the surrounding area.

**St. Peter's**, with its majestic dome by Michelangelo, is a magnificent and sumptuous 16th-century basilica *(see pp422–3)*.

**Piazza Navona**, flanked by cafés, contains three Baroque fountains, including the colossal Fontana dei Quattro Fiumi, one of Bernini's finest works *(see p403)*.

**Santa Maria in Trastevere**, probably the first Christian church in Rome, holds some remarkable mosaics, such as this detail from Cavallini's *Life of the Virgin* that dates from 1291 *(see pp432–3)*.

THE VATICAN AND TRASTEVERE
*(See pp418–33)*

AR
PI
NA
*(See*

## Lazio
*(See pp464–75)*

Viterbo

Rieti

Tarquinia

Magliano Sabina

Civitavecchia

Tivoli

ROME
*(See main map)*

Velletri

Anagni

Sermoneta

Anzio

Terracina

Sperlonga

0 kilometers 15

0 miles 10

**Cerveteri** is one of the many necropolises left by the Etruscan civilization in northern Lazio. The larger tumulus tombs often contained frescoes and utensils useful for the afterlife *(see p470)*.

◀ The famous Trevi Fountain, designed by Nicola Salvi

**The Pantheon**, built between AD 118 and 125, is a marvel of Roman engineering with its huge dome hidden behind the Classical portico *(see p408)*.

**Locator Map**

**Santa Maria Maggiore's** richly decorated interior blends different architectural styles, such as this baldacchino from the 18th century *(see p417)*.

**NORTHEAST ROME**
*(See pp410–17)*

**THE ANCIENT CENTRE**
*(See pp386–99)*

**San Giovanni in Laterano**, the Cathedral of Rome, incorporates the elaborate Corsini Chapel built in the 1730s *(see p440)*.

**AVENTINE AND LATERAN**
*(See pp434–41)*

**The Capitoline Museums** have held treasures of the Classical world since the Renaissance, including this colossal 4th-century head of Constantine *(see pp390–91)*.

| 0 meters | 750 |
| 0 yards | 750 |

**The Colosseum** was constructed in AD 80 by Emperor Vespasian. His aim was to gain popularity by staging deadly gladiatorial combats and wild animal fights for public viewing *(see p397)*.

# The Flavors of Rome and Lazio

The countryside of Lazio varies from gently rolling hills to mountains to shimmering coast. Olive groves and vineyards cloak this fertile area, where wild boar roam and many other kinds of game find their way onto the table. But authentic Roman cuisine takes its origins from organ meats, and slow, inventive cooking transforms these traditionally "poor" cuts into flavorsome dishes. Pasta is still the vital ingredient in any meal, and several well-known dishes originate from Rome. Many of the capital's top restaurants are dedicated to seafood and, as home of *la dolce vita*, there is a long tradition of delicious pastries, cakes, and ice cream.

Globe artichokes

A stand of Lazio vegetables, fresh from field to market

Traditional Roman cuisine originated in the Testaccio area, near the old slaughterhouse. The butchers *(vaccinari)* there were paid partly in meat, usually organ meat. The "fifth quarter" *(quinto quarto)* included head, feet, tail, intestines, brain, and other bits of the beast that were not for the squeamish, but which, when cooked slowly and flavored with herbs and spices, became a culinary delight.

These robust dishes, such as the signature dish *coda alla vaccinara* (literally, "oxtail in the style of the slaughterhouse butcher") still appear on many menus.

## Cucina Romana

Authentic *cucina romana* also has its roots in Jewish cuisine of the atmospheric Ghetto area, whose origins date back over 400 years. Plump, locally grown globe artichokes are fried whole in olive oil *(carciofi alla giudia)* or served *alla romana*, with oil, garlic and Roman mint. Just as popular are salt cod fillets *(filetti di baccalà)* deep-fried, Jewish-style.

Seafood restaurants are among the best in Rome and, while not cheap, many are temples of gastronomy. It was in response to the launch of

Fusilli   Tagliatelle   Spaghettini   Lumaconi   Ravioli   Tortellini   Orecchiette
Just a few of the hundreds of types of pasta available in Italy

## Regional Dishes and Specialties

Crispy fried vegetables, especially artichokes and zucchini flowers, are often served as an *antipasto*. For the *primo* course, pasta dishes include *bucatini all'amatriciana* – long, thin pasta tubes in a delicious spicy tomato and bacon sauce, sprinkled with grated pecorino cheese made from tangy ewe's milk. Veal is a great favorite and features on many restaurant menus; look for *rigatoni alla pajata* (pasta with milk-fed veal intestines). Lamb is also very popular, with dishes such as *abbacchio al forno* (roasted milk-fed lamb) or *alla cacciatore* ("huntsman's style" with anchovy sauce). Organ meats are very common in traditional trattorias, and delicacies include *cervello* (calves' brains), *ossobuco* (beef shins with marrow jelly), *pajata* (veal intestines), and *trippa* (tripe).

Bruschetta

**Gnocchi alla romana** Little dumplings, made with semolina flour, are usually served with a tomato or meat *ragù*.

Sumptuous Roman pizzas, sizzling hot from the wood-fired oven

the first McDonald's in Rome in 1986 that the Slow Food movement started in Piedmont *(see p178)*, but more typical Roman fast food includes *bruschetta* ("lightly burned bread" in Roman dialect) rubbed with garlic, sea salt, and olive oil and topped with a selection of intense flavors. There's also authentic thin and crispy *pizza romana* from wood-fired ovens, often served *al taglio* – by the slice.

## Pasta, Pasta

Pasta is still the mainstay of the Roman meal, especially spaghetti. *Spaghetti alla carbonara*, made with *pancetta* (cured bacon) or *guanciale* (pig's cheek), egg yolks, and cheese, is a classic Roman dish, as is *spaghetti alle vongole*, with garlic and clams. At a

conservative estimate, there is one type of pasta for every day of the year. Many varieties have wonderfully descriptive or poetic names, such as *capelli d'angelo* (angel's hair) or *ziti* (bridegrooms), whose shape is best left to the imagination.

An array of mouthwatering *gelati* in a Roman ice-cream parlor

## La Dolce Vita

For those with a taste for "the sweet life," nuts, fruits, and versatile ricotta cheese are often combined in mouth-wateringly delicious desserts.

Ice cream is an art form in Rome, where some parlors offer over 100 flavors of homemade *gelati*. Types vary from the classic *crema* and *frutta* to *grattachecca* (water ice), from *semifreddo* (a half-frozen sponge pudding, similar to *tiramisù* in consistency) to *granita* (ice shavings flavored with fruit syrups). Glorious *gelato* is one of the great pleasures here, to be enjoyed at any time of the day – or night.

### ON THE MENU

**Abbacchio alla cacciatora** Lamb cooked with anchovies, garlic, Castelli Romani wine, rosemary, and olive oil.

**Coda alla vaccinara** Oxtail braised in herbs, tomatoes, and celery.

**Fave al guanciale** Young spring fava beans simmered in olive oil with pig's cheek and onion.

**Filetti di baccalà** Salt cod fillets in batter – once a Jewish specialty, now a feature of Roman cuisine.

**Spigola alla romana** Sea bass with porcini mushrooms (cèpes), Roman-style.

**Spaghetti alle vongole** The classic Italian pasta is here served with a sauce made of baby clams and tomatoes.

**Saltimbocca alla romana** Veal slices are rolled with prosciutto and sage. *Saltimbocca* means "jump in the mouth."

**Torta di ricotta** Ricotta cheese is baked in a tart with sugar, lemon, brandy, eggs, and cinnamon.

# Understanding Architecture in Rome and Lazio

The architecture of Imperial Rome, a combination of Etruscan and Classical Greek styles, gradually developed new and uniquely Roman forms based on the arch, the vault, and the dome. During the early Christian period, simple, rectangular basilicas were built, forms that by the 12th century had been incorporated into the stark Romanesque style. The Renaissance, inspired by the example of Florence, saw a return to Classical ideals of simplicity and harmonious proportions, though it was in the flamboyance of the 17th-century Baroque that Rome once again found great architectural expression.

The extravagant Baroque style of the Fontana di Trevi, Rome

## From Etruscan to Classical Rome

**The podium** made the temple more prominent.

**A portico** was a porch with columns.

**Etruscan temples**, based on Greek models, inspired early Roman architecture. A front portico was the only entrance.

**The arch** became a feature of Roman architecture.

**Reliefs** were scavenged from earlier monuments.

**The Arch of Constantine** (AD 315) is typical of triumphant Imperial Roman architecture *(see p393)*. It stands at a colossal 82 ft (25 m).

**Three naves** divided the interior of the basilica.

**Early Christian basilicas** (4th century) were based on a rectangular floorplan.

## From Renaissance to Baroque

**Doric columns** recall Classical architecture.

**Bramante** adopted the circular form of ancient temples.

**The Tempietto** (1502–10) at San Pietro in Montorio, Rome is a model of Renaissance architecture: simple and perfectly proportioned *(see p433)*.

**Rustication**, massive blocks divided by deep joints, was used for palazzi.

**Ionic pilasters** lend an air of elegance to the imposing upper stories.

**The elliptical staircase** was a typical feature of Mannerist houses.

**Palazzo Farnese** at Caprarola, a pentagonal building completed in 1575 *(see p469)*, combines some Mannerist tricks of architecture with the strict geometric proportions characteristic of the Renaissance.

## Where to See the Architecture

A walk through the backstreets of the center of Rome will reveal masterpieces of virtually every architectural age. The most ancient treasures are seven obelisks stolen from Egypt. One stands on the back of Bernini's elephant *(see p408)*. Highlights from ancient Rome include triumphal arches and temples such as the Pantheon *(see p408)*. Romanesque elements survive in the church of San Clemente *(see p439)*, while the Renaissance finds expression in the dome of St. Peter's *(see pp422–3)*. Magnificent Baroque treasures dot the entire city, in particular flamboyant fountains that adorn the squares. Outside the city, the outstanding sights are the late Renaissance villas such as Caprarola *(see p469)*.

Part of Bernini's elephant supporting an ancient Egyptian obelisk

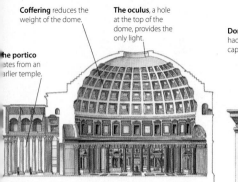

**Coffering** reduces the weight of the dome.

**The oculus**, a hole at the top of the dome, provides the only light.

**The portico** dates from an earlier temple.

**The Pantheon** *(see p408)* is one of the cardinal buildings of late Roman architecture. Completed around AD 126, it reveals how the form of the Greek temple was elaborated upon to create a masterpiece of perfect proportions.

**Corinthian capitals** were decorated with acanthus leaves.

**Doric columns** had straight capitals.

**Ionic columns** had scrolled capitals.

**The orders** of Classical architecture were building styles based on ancient Greek models, identified by the column capitals.

**Columns** around the altar draw attention away from the prominent lateral axis.

**The concave portico** reflects the oval body of the church.

**The oval floorplan** of the Baroque Sant'Andrea al Quirinale *(see p415)* makes ingenious use of restricted space.

**Engaged pillars** replace the flat pilasters of the Renaissance.

**The Gesù** facade (1584) epitomizes Counter-Reformation architecture and has been imitated throughout the Catholic world *(see p407)*.

**Deep recesses** create complex effects of light and shade.

**Two superimposed** equilateral triangles form the complex hexagonal floorplan.

**Sant'Ivo alla Sapienza's** floorplan (1642) favored grandiose design over Classical form *(see p404)*.

# THE ANCIENT CENTER

The Capitol, the southern summit of the Capitoline Hill, was the symbolic center of the Roman world and home to the city's three most important temples. These were dedicated to the god Jupiter Optimus Maximus, protector of Rome; Minerva, goddess of wisdom and war; and Juno Moneta, a guardian goddess. Below the Capitol lies the Forum, once the focus of political, social, legal, and commercial life; the Imperial Fora, built when Rome's population grew; and the Colosseum, the center of entertainment. Overlooking the Forum is the Palatine Hill, where Romulus is said to have founded Rome in the 8th century BC and emperors made their home for over 400 years.

## Sights at a Glance

### Churches
❸ Santa Maria in Aracoeli

### Museums and Galleries
❸ Capitoline Museums pp390–91

### Historic Piazzas
❷ Piazza del Campidoglio

### Ancient Sites and Buildings
❹ Trajan's Forum and Markets
❺ Forum of Augustus

❻ Mamertine Prison
❼ Forum of Caesar
❽ Roman Forum pp394–6
❾ Colosseum p397
❿ Arch of Constantine
⓫ Palatine pp398–9

See also Rome Street Finder
maps 3, 6, 7, 10

0 meters 250
0 yards 250

◄ The Colosseum's Ionic and Corinthian tiers, bathed in sunlight

**For keys to symbols** see back flap

# Street by Street: The Capitoline Hill

The Capitol, citadel of ancient Rome, was redesigned by Michelangelo in the 16th century. He was responsible for the trapezoid Piazza del Campidoglio as well as the Cordonata, the broad flight of steps leading up to it. The piazza is flanked by Palazzo Nuovo and Palazzo dei Conservatori, housing the Capitoline Museums, with their fine collections of sculpture and paintings. It is also well worth walking behind the museums to the Tarpeian Rock, for a fine view of the Forum lying below.

**The Victor Emmanuel Monument** was begun in 1885 and inaugurated in 1911 in honor of Victor Emmanuel II, the first king of unified Italy.

**San Marco**, dedicated to the patron saint of Venice, has splendid 9th-century mosaics in the apse.

PIAZZA VENEZIA

**Palazzo Venezia**, once the home of Mussolini, now holds a museum of fine and decorative arts. Exhibits include this medieval gilt and enamel angel.

**The Aracoeli Steps** were completed in 1348 to commemorate the end of the plague.

**The Cordonata** is presided over by the colossal statues of Castor and Pollux.

VIA DEL TEATRO DI MARCELLO

**❶ ★ Capitoline Museums**
The collections of art and ancient sculpture include this statue of the Emperor Marcus Aurelius, a replica of which stands in the center of the piazza.

**Key**

— Suggested route

| 0 meters | | 75 |
| 0 yards | | 75 |

**❸ Santa Maria in Aracoeli**
The brick facade hides treasures such as this 15th-century fresco of *The Funeral of San Bernardino* by Pinturicchio.

**Locator Map**
*See Rome Street Finder map 3*

**Palazzo Nuovo**
was made into a public museum in 1734.

**Palazzo Senatorio**, the splendid Renaissance seat of the city government, is built on the ruins of the ancient Tabularium.

**❷ Piazza del Campidoglio**
Michelangelo designed the geometric paving and the facades of the buildings.

Palazzo dei Conservatori

**The Temple of Jupiter**, represented on this coin, was dedicated to Jupiter Optimus Maximus, the most important of the Roman gods. He was believed to have the power to protect or destroy the city.

**The Tarpeian Rock** is a cliff from which traitors were believed to have been thrown to their death in ancient Rome.

Steps to the Capitoline

# ❶ Capitoline Museums

*See pp390–91.*

# ❷ Piazza del Campidoglio

**Map** 3 A5. 🚌 40, 63, 70, 81.

When Emperor Charles V announced he was to visit Rome in 1536, Pope Paul III Farnese asked Michelangelo to give the Capitoline a facelift. He redesigned the piazza, renovated the facades of its palaces, and built a new flight of steps, the Cordonata. This gently rising ramp is now crowned with the massive statues of Castor and Pollux.

# ❸ Santa Maria in Aracoeli

Scala dell'Arce Capitolina 14.
**Map** 3 A5. **Tel** 06 69 76 38 39.
🚌 63, 70, 81. **Open** 9am–6:30pm daily (9:30am–5:30pm in winter).

This church stands on the site of the temple of Juno on the northern summit of the Capitoline Hill, and dates back to at least the 6th century. The church is famous for its ornate gilded ceiling and a very fine series of frescoes by Pinturicchio, dating from the 1480s. They depict scenes from the life of San Bernardino of Siena. The miracle-working *Santo Bambino* figure, stolen in 1994, has been replaced by a replica.

The marble steps and austere facade of Santa Maria in Aracoeli

# ❶ Capitoline Museums:
## Palazzo Nuovo

A collection of Classical sculptures has been kept on the Capitoline Hill since Pope Sixtus IV donated a group of bronze statues to the city in 1471. Paintings as well as sculpture are now housed in two palaces designed by Michelangelo. The Palazzo Nuovo contains a fine selection of Greek and Roman sculptures. Access is via the Palazzo dei Conservatori *(opposite)*.

**Locator Map**
*See Rome Street Finder map 10*

**Discobolus**
The twisted torso was part of a Greek statue of a discus thrower. An 18th-century sculptor turned him into a wounded warrior.

**Mosaic of the Doves**
This 1st-century-AD naturalistic mosaic once decorated the floor of Hadrian's Villa at Tivoli *(see p472)*.

**Alexander Severus as Hunter**
In this marble of the 3rd century AD, the emperor's pose is a pastiche of the mythical hero, Perseus, holding up the head of Medusa the Gorgon after he had killed her.

Stairs to first floor

Stairs to second floor

Courtyard

**Hall of the Philosophers**
The hall contains Roman copies of portrait busts of Greek politicians, scientists, and poets. These adorned the homes of wealthy Romans.

Exit

**Dying Galatian**
Great compassion is conveyed in this Roman copy of a Greek work of the 3rd century BC.

**Key to Floorplan**
☐ First floor
☐ Second floor

# Palazzo dei Conservatori

The Palazzo dei Conservatori was the seat of the city's magistrates during the late Middle Ages. Its frescoed halls are still used occasionally for political meetings and the first floor houses the municipal registry office. While much of the palazzo is given over to sculpture, including fragments of a huge sculpture of Constantine, the art galleries on the second floor hold works by Veronese, Tintoretto, Caravaggio, Van Dyck, and Titian.

**St. John the Baptist**
Caravaggio's sensual portrait (1595–6) of the young saint caressing a sheep is a highly unorthodox image of Christ's forerunner.

**The Rape of the Sabine Women**
Pietro da Cortona glamorized the mass abduction of Sabine women by the Romans in this painting of 1629.

To temporary exhibition space

Portico of Marcus Aurelius

Second floor art gallery

**Medusa**
This bust by Bernini of the mythological Medusa is in Room 8.

**First floor**

Main entrance

Tickets

**Spinario**
This is a charming bronze sculpture from the 1st century BC of a boy trying to remove a thorn from his foot.

**Key to Floorplan**
- Exhibition space
- Non-exhibition space

Courtyard

# ❹ Trajan's Forum and Markets

**Map** 3 B4. Trajan's Forum, Via dei Fori Imperiali. **Closed** to the public. Trajan's Markets, Via IV Novembre. **Tel** 06 06 08. **Open** 9:30am–7:30pm daily (last adm: 6:30pm). 🏛 🗓 ♿

Trajan began to build his forum in AD 107 to commemorate his final conquest of Dacia (present-day Romania) after the campaigns in AD 101–2 and 105–6. His new forum was the most ambitious yet, with a vast colonnaded open space centering on an equestrian statue of the emperor, a huge basilica, and two big libraries. Dominating the ruins today is **Trajan's Column**, which originally stood

**Trajan's Column**

between the two libraries. Spiraling up its 98 ft- (30 m-) high stem are minutely detailed scenes from the Dacian campaigns, beginning with the Romans preparing for war and ending with the Dacians being ousted from their homeland. The subtly modeled reliefs were designed to be seen from viewing platforms on the libraries, and are consequently difficult to interpret from ground level. If you want to examine the scenes in detail there are casts in the Museo della Civiltà Romana *(see p446)*. The **market** complex, which is located directly behind the Forum, was begun slightly earlier. Like the Forum it was probably designed by Apollodorus of Damascus, and was the ancient Roman equivalent of the

**Via Biberatica, the main street through Trajan's Markets**

shopping mall. There were around 150 vendors selling everything from oriental silks and spices to fruit, fresh fish, and flowers. It was also here that the *annone*, or corn dole, was distributed. This was a free ration of corn given to Roman men, a practice introduced in the Republic by politicians who wanted to buy votes and prevent unrest during periods of famine. The markets now host contemporary art exhibitions.

## Reconstruction of Trajan's Markets

**Cross vaulting**

**The main hall** had 12 stores on two stories. The corn ration was distributed from the upper floor.

**Amphorae,** used for storing wine and oil, were discovered on the upper corridor.

**The terrace** has a good view of Trajan's Forum.

**The shops** on the first floor were cool, and probably sold vegetables, fruit, and flowers.

**Staircase**

**Via Biberatica** is named after the drinking inns that once lined it.

**Large hall with semidomed ceiling**

# Forum of Augustus

Piazza del Grillo 1. **Map** 3 B5. **Tel** 06 06
08. 87, 186. **Closed** to public, but
viewable from above.

The Forum of Augustus, which
once stretched from the foot
of sleazy Suburra to the edge
of Caesar's Forum, was built to
celebrate Augustus's victory in
42 BC over Brutus and Cassius,
the assassins of Julius Caesar.
Consequentially, the temple in
its center was dedicated to
Mars the Avenger. The temple,
with its cracked steps and four
Corinthian columns, is easily
identified. Originally it had a
statue of Mars that looked very
like Augustus, but in case anyone
failed to notice the resemblance,
a colossal statue of the emperor
himself was placed against the
wall of the Suburra quarter.

**19th-century engraving of the
Mamertine Prison**

# Mamertine Prison

Clivo Argentario 1. **Map** 3 A5.
**Tel** 06 69 89 61. 80, 85, 87, 175,
186. **Open** 9am–7pm daily (to 5pm in
winter). every 20 mins.

Below the 16th-century church
of San Giuseppe dei Falegnami
is a dank dungeon in which,
according to Christian legend,
St. Peter and St. Paul were imprisoned. They are said to have
caused a spring to bubble up

**Podium of the Temple of Mars the Avenger,
Forum of Augustus**

into the cell, and to have used
the water to baptize two prison
guards. The prison was in an old
cistern which was the city's
main sewer (the Cloaca Maxima).
The lower cell was used for
executions, and corpses were
thrown into the sewer. However,
the inmates, who received no
food, often died of starvation.

# Forum of Caesar

Clivo Argentario. **Map** 3 A5.
**Tel** 06 06 08. 80, 85, 87, 175, 186,
810. **Open** to research scholars by
appointment only.

The first of Rome's Imperial fora
was built by Julius Caesar to
relieve congestion in the Roman
Forum when Rome's population
boomed. He spent a fortune –
most of it booty from his recent
conquest of Gaul – buying up
and demolishing houses on the
site. Pride of place went to a
temple dedicated in 46 BC to
Venus Genetrix (Venus the Ances-
tor), as Caesar claimed to be
descended from the goddess.
The temple contained statues
of Caesar and Cleopatra as well
as of Venus, but all that remains
today is a platform and three
Corinthian columns. The forum
was once enclosed by
a double
colonnade,
under which
was sheltered
a row of
stores.
However, this
burned down
in AD 80 and
was rebuilt by
Domitian and
Trajan. The
latter also
added the
Basilica
Argentaria –

which became an important
financial exchange – as well
as stores and a heated
public restroom.

# Roman Forum

*See pp394–6.*

# Colosseum

*See p397.*

# Arch of Constantine

Between Via di San Gregorio and
Piazza del Colosseo. **Map** 6 F1.
75, 85, 87, 175, 673, 810. 3.
Colosseo.

This triumphal arch is one of
Imperial Rome's last monuments, built in AD 315, a few
years before Constantine
moved the capital of the Empire
to Byzantium. It was built to
celebrate Constantine's victory
in AD 312 over his co-emperor
Maxentius at the Battle of the
Milvian Bridge. Constantine
attributed the victory to a
dream in which he was told
to mark his men's shields with
*chi-rho*, the first two Greek
letters of Christ's name. Christian
tradition prefers a version in
which the emperor has a
vision of the Cross, mid-battle.
There is nothing Christian
about the arch: most of the
reliefs were from earlier
pagan monuments.

# Palatine

*See pp398–9.*

**The north side of the Arch of Constantine**

# Roman Forum

In the early Republic, the Forum was a chaotic place, containing food stands and brothels as well as temples and the Senate House. By the 2nd century BC it was decided that Rome required a more salubrious center, and the food stores were replaced by business centers and law courts. The Forum remained the ceremonial center of the city under the Empire, with emperors renovating old buildings and erecting new temples and monuments.

**Arch of Septimius Severus**
This triumphal arch was erected in AD 203, the 10th anniversary of Emperor Septimius Severus' accession.

**The Temple** of **Antoninus a** **Faustina** is n incorporat into the church San Loren in Miran

**Temple of Saturn**

**The Rostra** was the orator's tribune from which speeches were made.

*VIA DELLA CURIA*

*VIA SACRA*

**The Curia**, or ancient Roman Senate House, has been reconstructed.

**Basilica Julia**
Named after Julius Caesar, who began its construction in 54 BC, this was the seat of the civil magistrates court.

**Basilica Aemilia**
was a meeting hall for business and money exchange.

**Temple of Vesta**

**Temple of Castor and Pollux**
Although there has been a temple here since the 5th century BC, the columns and elaborate cornice date from AD 6, when the temple was rebuilt.

0 meters          500

0 yards          500

★ **House of the Vestal Virgins**
The priestesses who tended the sacred flame in the Temple of Vesta lived here. The house was a large rectangular building around a central garden.

*For hotels and restaurants in this region see pp573–6 and pp596–600*

### ★ Basilica of Constantine and Maxentius

The basilica's three vast barrel vaults are all that remain of the Forum's largest building. Like other basilicas, it was used for the administration of justice and conducting business.

**The Temple of Romulus**, now part of the church of Santi Cosma e Damiano, which stands behind it, retains its original 4th-century bronze doors.

**Arch of Titus**

This arch was erected by Emperor Domitian in AD 81 to commemorate the sack of Jerusalem by his father Vespasian and brother Titus, 13 years earlier.

**VISITORS' CHECKLIST**

**Practical Information**
Entrance: Via della Salara Vecchia 5/6.
**Map** 3 B5. **Tel** 06 39 96 77 00.
**Open** 8:30am–1 hour before sunset. **Closed** Jan 1, Dec 25.
🔊 includes entry to the Colosseum and the Palatine.
🏛🖼🚻

**Transportation**
🚌 85, 87, 117, 175, 186, 810.
Ⓜ Colosseo. 🚋 3.

**Antiquarium Forense**
This small museum contains finds from the Forum. Exhibits range from Iron Age burial urns to this frieze of Aeneas from the Basilica Aemilia.

VIA DEI FORI IMPERIALI

VIA SACRA

VIA SACRA

Colosseum

Palatine

**The Temple of Venus and Rome**
was built in AD 135, and was largely designed by Hadrian.

**Santa Francesca Romana**
The Romanesque bell tower of Santa Francesca Romana towers over one of a number of churches built among the ruins of the Forum.

### The Vestal Virgins

The cult of Vesta, the goddess of fire, dates back to at least the 8th century BC. Romulus and Remus were allegedly born of the Vestal priestess Rhea and the god Mars. Six virgins kept the sacred flame of Vesta burning in her circular temple. The girls, who came from noble families, were selected when they were between 6 and 10 years old, and served for 30 years. They had high status and financial security, but were buried alive if they lost their virginity and whipped by the high priest if the sacred flame died out. Although they were permitted to marry after finishing their service, few did so.

**Honorary statue of a Vestal Virgin**

# Exploring the Roman Forum

To appreciate the layout of the Roman Forum before wandering through its confusing patchwork of ruined temples, triumphal arches, and basilicas, it is best to view the whole area from the Capitoline Hill above. From there you can make out the more substantial ruins, and the course of the Via Sacra (Sacred Way), the route followed through the Forum by religious and triumphal processions making their way up to the Capitol to give thanks at the Temple of Jupiter *(see p389)*.

Corinthian columns of the Temple of Castor and Pollux

### The Main Sights

The first building you come to on entering the Forum is the **Basilica Aemilia**. A rectangular hall built in 179 BC, it was a meeting place for moneylenders, businessmen, and tax collectors. Although little more remains of it than a pastel marble pavement fringed with column stumps, you can still find splashes of verdigrised bronze, reputedly the remains of coins that melted when the Visigoths invaded Rome and burned down the basilica in the 5th century.

Inside the Curia – the stark brick building next to the Basilica – are the **Plutei of Trajan**, relief panels commissioned by either Trajan or Hadrian to decorate the Rostra, the public oratory platform. On one panel are piles of books holding tax records, which Trajan had destroyed in order to free citizens from debts. The **Arch of Septimius Severus** is the best preserved of the Forum's monuments. The marble relief panels depict the military triumphs of the emperor in Parthia (modern-day Iran and Iraq) and Arabia. The **Temple of Saturn** was the

focus of the annual Saturnalia celebrations, when, for up to a week in December, schools closed, slaves dined with their masters, presents were exchanged, and a fair and market were held.

Soaring above the remains of the Basilica Julia are three delicately fluted columns and a finely carved slab of entablature taken from the **Temple of Castor and Pollux**. This striking relic is dedicated to the twin brothers of Helen of Troy, who were supposed to have appeared at the battle of Lake Regillus in 499 BC, aiding the Romans in their defeat of the Etruscans.

Restored section of Temple of Vesta

The elegant circular **Temple of Vesta** was one of ancient Rome's most sacred shrines and was dedicated to the goddess of the hearth. The flame, kept alive by the Vestal Virgins, symbolized the perpetuity of the State and its extinction prophesied doom for the city. The building was partly reconstructed in 1930, but the circular form goes back to the

Latin mud huts which originally occupied the site. Just behind is the **House of the Vestal Virgins** the living quarters of the priestess and the Vestals. This enormous complex of 50 rooms was once annexed to the Temple. Best preserved are the rooms overlooking a pretty courtyard, ornamented with statues of Vestals, ponds of waterlilies and rose trees.

On the other side of the Forum lie the impressive remains of the **Basilica of Constantine**. It was begun in AD 308 by Maxentius, and is therefore also known as the Basilica of Maxentius. Constantine completed it after he defeated his rival at the battle of Milvio in AD 312. The stark remains of the huge arches and ceilings give an indication of the original scale and grandeur of the forum's public buildings. Three enormous coffered vaults remain, which originally measured up to 115 ft (35 m) and were faced with marble. The interior walls, which held niches for statues, were also covered with marble below and stucco above. Remains of a spiral staircase that once led to the roof can be found scattered on the ground.

The basilica's apse and hexagonal arches were often used as models by Renaissance architects striving to recreate a Classical symmetry and nobility in their work. They include Michelangelo, who allegedly studied the Basilica's architecture when working on the dome of St. Peter's.

Central courtyard of the House of the Vestal Virgins

# ❾ Colosseum

Rome's greatest amphitheater was commissioned by Emperor Vespasian in AD 72. Deadly gladiatorial combats and wild animal fights were staged by emperors and wealthy citizens, largely to gain popularity. Slaughter was on a huge scale: at the inaugural games in AD 80, more than 9,000 wild animals were killed. The Colosseum could hold up to 55,000 people, who were seated according to rank.

## VISITORS' CHECKLIST

**Practical Information**
Piazza del Colosseo. **Map** 7 A1.
**Tel** 06 39 96 77 00.
**Open** 8:30am–1 hour before sunset. **Closed** Jan 1, Dec 25. 🎫 includes entry to the Forum and Palatine. 🏛 📷 ♿ limited.

**Transportation**
🚌 75, 80, 85, 87, 117, 175, 810.
Ⓜ Colosseo. 🚊 3 to Piazza del Colosseo.

**Internal Corridors**
These allowed the large and often unruly crowd to move freely and be seated quickly.

**The Velarium**, a huge sailcloth awning that sheltered spectators from the sun, was supported by poles on the upper story.

**The Colossus of Nero**
This gilt bronze statue from Nero's palace, over which the Colosseum was built, may have given the amphitheater its name.

**Entry routes**
and stairs led to seats at the various levels. The emperor and consul had their own, separate entrances.

Corinthian columns

Ionic columns

Doric columns

**The arena floor** covered a network of elevators and cages for wild beasts.

Entrances

**Doric, Ionic, and Corinthian Tiers**
The tiers inspired many Renaissance architects, who also plundered the building, using its travertine to build palaces and part of St. Peter's.

**Roman Gladiators**
These were originally soldiers in training. Their combat became a sport, and slaves, prisoners of war, or criminals were forced to fight men or wild animals to the death.

**Emperor Vespasian**
He ordered the Colosseum to be built on the site of Nero's palace, to dissociate himself from the hated tyrant.

# ⓫ Palatine

The Palatine, once the residence of emperors and aristocrats, is the most pleasant of Rome's ancient sites. The ruins range from the simple house in which Augustus is thought to have lived, to the Domus Flavia and Domus Augustana, the public and private wings of a luxurious palace built by Domitian.

Cryptoporticus

**★ House of Augustus**
This building boasts four rooms with magnificent frescoes.

**★ House of Livia**
Many of the wall paintings have survived in the private quarters of the house where Augustus is believed to have lived with his wife Livia.

## KEY

① **Domus Augustana** was the private home of the emperors.

② **The Huts of Romulus**, indicated by holes left by the supporting posts, were reputedly founded by Romulus in the 9th century BC.

③ **Temple of Cybele**, goddess of fertility.

④ **The courtyard** of the Domus Flavia was lined by Domitian with mirror-like marble, so he could spot would-be assassins.

⑤ **The exedra** of the stadium may have housed a balcony.

**★ Domus Flavia**
The courtyard of the Domus Flavia was lavishly paved with colored marble. The Roman poets praised this villa as the most splendid.

**Emperor Septimius Severus**
During his reign (AD 193–211), he extended the Domus Augustana and built an impressive bath complex.

**Cryptoporticus**
This underground gallery, elaborately decorated with stuccoed walls, was built by Emperor Nero.

**VISITORS' CHECKLIST**

**Practical Information**
Via di San Gregorio 30.
**Map** 6 F1. **Tel** 06 39 96 77 00.
**Open** 8:30am–1 hour before sunset. **Closed** Jan 1, Dec 25.
includes entry to the Forum, the Colosseum and the Palatine Museum.

**Transportation**
75, 80, 81, 175, 673, 850.
Colosseo. 3.

## A History of the Palatine Hill

*Romans of the Decadence* by Thomas Couture (1815–79)

### The Founding of Rome
According to legend the twins Romulus and Remus were brought up on the Palatine by a wolf. Here Romulus, having killed his brother, is said to have founded the village that was destined to become Rome. Traces of mud huts dating back to the 8th century BC have been found on the hill, lending archaeological support to the legend.

### The Republic
By the 1st century BC the Palatine was the most desirable address in Rome and home to the leading citizens of the Republic. Its residents, including the erotic poet Catullus and the orator Cicero, were notoriously indulgent, and their villas were magnificent dwellings with doors of ivory, floors of bronze, and frescoed walls.

### The Empire
Augustus was born on the Palatine in 63 BC, and lived there in a modest house after becoming emperor. The hill was therefore an obvious choice of abode for future emperors. Domitian's ambitious house, the Domus Flavia (1st century AD), and its private quarters, the Domus Augustana, remained the official residence of future emperors (who were referred to as *Augustus*) for more than 300 years.

**↗ Forum entrance**

**The Palace of Septimius Severus**
This extension of the Domus Augustana projected beyond the hillside, supported on giant arches.

0 metres 75
0 yards 75

**Stadium**
Part of the Imperial palace, this enclosure may have been used by the emperors as a private garden.

# AROUND PIAZZA NAVONA

The area around Piazza Navona, known as the *centro storico*, has been inhabited for at least 2,000 years. Piazza Navona stands above an ancient stadium; the Pantheon has been a temple since AD 27; and the Theater of Marcellus in the Ghetto has been converted into exclusive apartments. The area's heyday began in the 15th century, when the papacy returned to Rome. Throughout the Renaissance and Baroque eras, princes, popes, and cardinals settled here, as did the artists and artisans they commissioned to build and adorn lavish palaces, churches, and fountains.

## Sights at a Glance

### Churches and Temples

2 Sant'Ivo alla Sapienza
3 San Luigi dei Francesi
5 Santa Maria della Pace
6 Chiesa Nuova
13 Gesù
15 Santa Maria sopra Minerva
17 Sant'Ignazio di Loyola
20 La Maddalena

### Ancient Sites and Buildings

4 Palazzo Altemps
7 Palazzo della Cancelleria
9 Palazzo Farnese
12 Area Sacra di Largo Argentina
16 Pantheon

### Museums and Galleries

10 Palazzo Spada
14 Palazzo Doria Pamphilj

### Historic Piazzas and Areas

1 Piazza Navona
8 Campo de' Fiori
11 Ghetto and Tiber Island
18 Piazza Colonna
19 Piazza di Montecitorio

| 0 meters | 250 |
| 0 yards | 250 |

*See also Rome Street Finder maps 9, 10*

◀ The starry blue vault of the nave in Santa Maria sopra Minerva, Piazza della Minerva

**For keys to symbols** *see back flap*

# Street by Street: Around Piazza Navona

No other piazza in Rome can rival the theatricality of
Piazza Navona. The luxurious cafés are the social center
of the city, and day and night there is always something
going on in the pedestrian area around the three
flamboyant Baroque fountains. The Baroque is also
represented in many of the area's churches.
To discover an older Rome, walk along
Via del Governo Vecchio to admire
the facades of Renaissance
buildings, browse in the
fascinating antiques shops,
and eat lunch in one of
the many trattorias.

**The Torre dell'Orologio** by
Borromini (1648) formed part of
the Oratorio dei Filippini.

**6 Chiesa Nuova**
This church was rebuilt in
1575 for the order founded
by San Filippo Neri.

↖ The Vatican

VIA DEL CORALLO

VIA DEL GOVERNO VECCHIO

VIA DI PARIONE

**At the
Oratorio
dei Filippini**
(1637), biblical
stories were
sung and the
congregation
responded with a
chorus – the origin
of the oratorio.

**Via del Governo
Vecchio** preserves a
large number of fine
Renaissance houses.

CORSO VITTORIO EMANUELE II

VIA DI S

PIAZZA DI
PASQUINO

**5 Santa Maria della Pace**
This Renaissance church has
frescoes of the Four Sibyls
by Raphael and a refined
courtyard by Bramante.
The Baroque
portico is by
Pietro da Cortona.

**Pasquino** is a 3rd-century-BC
Hellenistic statue of Menelaus.
Romans have been hanging
satirical verses at its feet since
the 16th century.

Palazzo
Pamphilj

**Palazzo Braschi**, a late 18th-century
building designed by Cosimo Morelli, has a
splendid balcony overlooking the piazza.

Fontana del
Moro

Campo de'
↙ Fiori

| 0 meters | 75 |
|---|---|
| 0 yards | 75 |

**Key**

— Suggested route

**Sant'Andrea della Valle**, begun
in 1591, has a flamboyant
Baroque facade flanked by
angels with outstretched wings
by Ercole Ferrata. The church is
the setting of the first act of
Puccini's *Tosca*.

*For hotels and restaurants in this region see pp573–6 and pp596–600*

**Sant'Agnese in Agone**
by Borromini (1657) is
allegedly built on
the site where, in
AD 304, the
young St. Agnes
was publicly
stripped to
force her to
renounce
her faith.

**Locator Map**
See Rome Street Finder map 2

Fontana dei
Quattro Fiumi

**③ San Luigi dei Francesi**
This church, which was
completed in 1589, is best
known for three paintings
by Caravaggio.

**Palazzo Madama**, the
seat of the Italian Senate,
was originally built for
the Medici family in the
16th century, on the site
of one of their banks.

**② Sant'Ivo alla
Sapienza**
This tiny domed church
is one of Borromini's
most original creations.
He worked on it
between 1642 and 1650.

Largo di Torre
Argentina

**① ★ Piazza Navona**
The piazza is lined with palaces and sidewalk cafés, and
punctuated by flamboyant Baroque fountains.

# ① Piazza Navona

**Map** 2 E4. 🚌 30, 70, 81, 87, 130, 186,
492, 628.

Rome's most beautiful Baroque
piazza follows the shape of a
1st-century-AD stadium built
by Domitian, which was used
for athletic contests (agones),
chariot races, and other sports.
Traces of the stadium are still
visible below the church of
Sant'Agnese in Agone, which is
dedicated to a virgin martyred
on the site for refusing to marry
a pagan.

The piazza began to take on
its present appearance in the
17th century, when Pope
Innocent X, whose family
palazzo was on the piazza,
commissioned a new church,
palace, and fountain. The
fountain, the Fontana dei
Quattro Fiumi, is Bernini's most
magnificent, with statues of the
four great rivers of the world at
that time (the Nile, the Plate,
the Ganges, and the Danube)
sitting on rocks below an
obelisk. Bernini also designed
the musclebound Moor in the
Fontana del Moro, though the
present statue is a copy. Until
the 19th century, the piazza
was flooded in August by
stopping the fountain outlets.
The rich would splash around
in carriages, while street
urchins paddled. Even today
the piazza remains the social
center of the city.

Symbolic figure of the Nile River on
Bernini's Fontana dei Quattro Fiumi

## ❷ Sant'Ivo alla Sapienza

Corso del Rinascimento 40. **Map** 2 F4.
**Tel** 06 06 08 (tourist information).
🚌 30, 70, 81, 87, 116, 186, 492, 628.
**Open** 9am–noon Sun. ♿

Hidden in the courtyard of Palazzo della Sapienza, seat of the old University of Rome, Sant'Ivo's spiral belfry is nevertheless a distinctive landmark on Rome's skyline. Built by Borromini in 1642–60, the church is astonishingly complex, an ingenious combination of concave and convex surfaces. The work spanned the reigns of three popes, and incorporated in the design are their emblems: Urban VIII's bee, Innocent X's dove and olive branch, and the star and hills of Alexander VII.

## ❸ San Luigi dei Francesi

Piazza di San Luigi de' Francesi 5.
**Map** 2 F4 & 10 D2. **Tel** 06 68 82 71.
🚌 70, 81, 87, 116, 186, 492, 628.
**Open** 10am–12:30pm & 3–7pm daily
(Thu: am only). 🎥

The French national church in Rome, San Luigi is a 16th-century building, best known for three magnificent canvases by Caravaggio in the Cerasi chapel. Painted between 1597 and 1602, these were Caravaggio's first significant religious works: *The Calling of St. Matthew*, *Martyrdom of St. Matthew*, and *St. Matthew and the Angel*. The first version of this last was initially rejected because it depicted the saint as an old man with dirty feet.

Detail from Caravaggio's *The Calling of St. Matthew* (1597–1602) in San Luigi dei Francesi

Side relief of the Ludovisi Throne, on display in the Palazzo Altemps

## ❹ Palazzo Altemps

Via di Sant'Apollinare 46. **Map** 2 E3.
**Tel** 06 39 96 77 00. 🚌 70, 81, 87, 115, 280, 628. **Open** 9am–7:45pm Tue–Sun. **Closed** Jan 1, Dec 25. 🎥 📷 📷 ♿

An extraordinary collection of Classical sculpture is housed in this branch of the Museo Nazionale Romano (*see p416*). Restored as a museum during the 1990s, the palazzo was originally built for Girolamo Riario, nephew of Pope Sixtus IV, in 1480. In the popular uprising that followed the pope's death in 1484, the building was sacked and Girolamo fled the city. In 1568 Cardinal Marco Sittico Altemps bought the palazzo; it was renovated in the 1570s by Martino Longhi the Elder, who added the obelisk-crowned belvedere and marble unicorn.

The Altemps family were avid collectors; the court-yard and its staircase are lined with ancient sculptures, which complement the Ludovisi sculptures. One of the highlights is the marble statue *Galata's Suicide*, a copy of the original in the Salone del Camino. On the first floor is the Greek, 5th-century-BC Ludovisi Throne, with a panel depicting Aphrodite.

*Galata's Suicide* in the Palazzo Altemps

## ❺ Santa Maria della Pace

Vicolo del Arco della Pace 5. **Map** 2 E3.
🚌 70, 81, 87, 116, 492, 628. **Open** 9–11:45am Mon, Wed, & Sat. ♿

Named by Pope Sixtus IV to celebrate the peace he hoped to bring to Italy, this church dates from the 1480s and contains a beautiful fresco by Raphael. Bramante's refined cloister was added in 1504, while the facade was designed in 1656 by Pietro da Cortona.

## ❻ Chiesa Nuova

Via del Governo Vecchio 134.
**Map** 2 E4. **Tel** 06 687 52 89. 🚌 46, 64. **Open** 7:30am–noon & 4:30–7pm daily. ♿

San Filippo Neri commissioned this church in 1575 to replace the dilapidated one given to his Order by Pope Gregory XIII. Neri required his followers to humble themselves, and set aristocratic young men to work as laborers on the church.

Against his wishes, the nave, apse, and dome were richly frescoed after his death by Pietro da Cortona. Three paintings by Rubens surround the altar. The initial versions were rejected, so he repainted them on slate, placing the originals above his mother's tomb.

## ❼ Palazzo della Cancelleria

Piazza della Cancelleria. **Map** 2 E4.
**Tel** 06 69 88 75 66. 🚌 46, 62, 64, 116, 916. **Open** 7:30am–8pm Mon–Sat, 9:30am–7:30pm Sun and public hols.

A supreme example of the confident delicacy of early Renaissance architecture, this palazzo was begun in 1485, and was allegedly financed by the gambling proceeds of Raffaele

Riario, a nephew of Pope Sixtus I. In 1478 Riario was involved in the Pazzi conspiracy against the Medici, and when Giovanni de' Medici became Pope Leo XIII in 1513, he took belated revenge, seizing the palace and turning it into the papal chancellery.

## ❽ Campo de' Fiori

**Map** 2 E4. 🚍 116 & routes to Corso Vittorio Emanuele II.

Campo de' Fiori (Field of Flowers) was one of the liveliest and roughest areas of medieval and Renaissance Rome. Cardinals and nobles mingled with fishmongers and foreigners in the piazza's market; Caravaggio killed his opponent after losing a game of tennis on the square; and the goldsmith Cellini murdered a business rival nearby. Today, the area continues to be a hub of secular activity. The colorful market, trattorias, and down-to-earth bars retain the original animated atmosphere.

In the Renaissance the piazza was surrounded by inns, many of which were owned by the 15th-century courtesan Vannozza Catanei, mistress of Pope Alexander VI.

The square was also a place of execution. The statue in its center is the philosopher Giordano Bruno, burned at

Tiber Island, with Ponte Cestio, built in 46 BC, linking it to Trastevere

the stake for heresy on this spot in 1600 for suggesting the earth moved around the sun.

## ❾ Palazzo Farnese

Piazza Farnese. **Map** 2 E5. Tel 06 68 60 11. 🚍 23, 116, 280, & routes to Corso Vittorio Emanuele II. 📷 only (3pm, 4pm, & 5pm on Mon, Wed, & Fri. Reserve. 🖥 **ambafrance-it.org**

Originally constructed for Cardinal Alessandro Farnese, who became Pope Paul III in 1534, this palazzo was started by Antonio da Sangallo the Younger, and continued after his death by Michelangelo, who created the cornice on the facade and the courtyard's third story.

The palace, now the French Embassy, is closed to the public, but when the chandeliers are lit at night you may be able to glimpse the ceiling of the Galleria, an illusionistic masterpiece (1597–1603) by Annibale Carracci based on Ovid's *Metamorphoses*.

## ❿ Palazzo Spada

Piazza Capo di Ferro 13. **Map** 2 E5. **Tel** 06 683 24 09. 🚍 23, 116, 280 & routes to Largo di Torre Argentina. **Open** 8:30am–7:30pm daily (last adm: 7pm). **Closed** Jan 1, Dec 25.

A stucco extravaganza studded with reliefs of illustrious Romans, this palazzo was built in 1550, but bought in 1637 by Cardinal Bernardino Spada. A patron of the arts, Spada commissioned Borromini to create an illusionistic tunnel that appears four times longer than it is. The cardinal's art collection, located in the Galleria Spada, includes works by Guercino, Dürer, and Artemisia Gentileschi.

## ⓫ Ghetto and Tiber Island

**Map** 2 F5 & 6 D1. 🚍 23, 63, 280, 780 and routes to Largo di Torre Argentina.

The first Jews came to Rome as traders in the 2nd century BC and were greatly appreciated for their financial and medical skills during the Roman Empire. Persecution began in the 16th century, when Pope Paul IV forced all of the Jews to live within a walled enclosure, an area later to form the hub of the present-day Ghetto.

Today Via del Portico d'Ottavia, the district's main street, leads to Rome's central synagogue, passing restaurants and stores selling Roman Jewish food. Ponte Fabricio links the Ghetto with Tiber Island, a center of healing since 293 BC, when a Temple to Aesculapius was founded. The island is now home to a hospital.

Fruit stands at Campo de' Fiori's lively morning market

# Street by Street: Around the Pantheon

The maze of narrow streets around the Pantheon is a mixture of lively restaurants and cafés, and some of Rome's finest sights. This is also the city's financial and political district, home to Parliament, government offices, and the Stock Exchange. The Pantheon itself, with its awe-inspiring domed interior, has long been a symbol of the city.

**⓮ ★ Palazzo Doria Pamphilj**
Among the masterpieces in the art gallery of this vast family palazzo is *Salomé* by Titian *(above)*, painted in 1516.

**⓱ Sant'Ignazio di Loyola**
This church has a superb illusionistic ceiling painted by Andrea Pozzo in 1685.

**The Temple of Hadrian** now forms the facade of the Stock Exchange.

Via della Gatta

**Piazza della Minerva** centers on Bernini's outlandish sculpture of an elephant supporting an Egyptian obelisk.

PIAZZA DI SANT'IGNAZIO

VIA DI SANT' IGNAZIO

PIAZZA DEL COLLEGIO ROMANO

VIA DELLA GATTA

PIAZZA DELLA ROTONDA

VIA DEL SEMINARIO

VIA DEL PIE DI MARMO

PIAZZA DELLA MINERVA

VIA DEL GESÙ

VIA DEL PLEB

The Pie' di Marmo

Santa Maria Sopra Minerva

**Palazzo Altieri** incorporates the hovel of an old woman who refused to allow her house to be demolished when this palace was built in the 17th century.

**⓰ ★ Pantheon**
The Pantheon, a temple to "all the gods," is Rome's best-preserved ancient building. It was built in the 1st century AD, probably to a design by Emperor Hadrian.

**⓭ Gesù**
Built in the late 16th century, this Jesuit church served as a model for the Order's churches throughout the world.

*For hotels and restaurants in this region see pp573–6 and pp596–600*

**Locator Map**
*See Rome Street Finder map 3*

**Via della Gatta** is overlooked by this marble statue of a cat *(gatta)* that gives the narrow street its name.

**The Pie' di Marmo**, an ancient marble foot, is probably part of a giant statue from the temple to the Egyptian goddess Isis.

**⑮ Santa Maria sopra Minerva**
This is one of Rome's few Gothic churches, with works by Michelangelo, Bernini, and Filippino Lippi.

**Key**

— Suggested route

| 0 meters | 75 |
| 0 yards | 75 |

## ⑫ Area Sacra di Largo Argentina

Largo di Torre Argentina. **Map** 2 F5.
🚌 40, 46, 62, 64, 70, 81, 87, 186, 492.
**Closed** to the public.

The remains of four temples were discovered in the 1920s at the center of Largo Argentina, now a busy bus terminal and traffic intersection. They date from the era of the Republic, and are among the oldest found in Rome. For the purpose of identification, they are known as A, B, C, and D. The oldest (temple C) dates from the early 3rd century BC. It was placed on a high platform preceded by an altar and is typical of Italic temple plans as opposed to the Greek model. Temple A is from the 3rd century BC, but in medieval times the small church of San Nicola di Cesarini was built over its podium, and the remains of its two apses are still visible. The column stumps to the north belonged to a great portico, known as the Hecatostylum (portico of 100 columns). In Imperial times two marble latrines were built here – the remains of one are visible behind temple A. Behind temples B and C, near Via di Torre Argentina, are the remains of a great platform of tufa blocks. These have been identified as part of the Curia of Pompey, a rectangular building where the Senate met, and where Julius Caesar was assassinated by Brutus, Cassius, and their followers on March 15, 44 BC.

Area Sacra, with the ruins of circular temple B

Baroque *Triumph of Faith over Idolatry* by Pierre Legros, Gesù

## ⑬ Gesù

Piazza del Gesù. **Map** 3 A4. **Tel** 06 69 70 01. 🚌 H, 46, 62, 64, 70, 81, 87, 186, 492, 628, & other routes.
**Open** 7am–12:30pm & 4–7:45pm daily.

Built between 1568 and 1584, the Gesù was Rome's first Jesuit church. The Jesuit order was founded in Rome in 1537 by a Basque soldier, Ignatius Loyola, who became a Christian after he was wounded in battle. The order was austere, intellectual, and heavily engaged in missionary activity and religious wars.

The much-imitated design of the Gesù typifies Counter-Reformation architecture, with a large nave with side pulpits for preaching to crowds, and a main altar as the centerpiece for the Mass. The illusionistic decoration on the nave ceiling and dome was added by Il Baciccia in the 17th century.

The nave depicts the *Triumph of the Name of Jesus* and its message is clear: faithful Catholic worshipers will be joyfully uplifted to Heaven while Protestants and heretics are flung into the fires of Hell. The message is reiterated in the Cappella di Sant'Ignazio, a rich display of lapis lazuli, serpentine, silver, and gold. The Baroque marble by Legros, *Triumph of Faith over Idolatry*, shows a female "Religion" trampling on the head of the serpent Idolatry, while in Théudon's *Barbarians Adoring the Faith*, an angel aims a kick toward a decrepit old barbarian couple entangled with a snake.

## ⓮ Palazzo Doria Pamphilj

Via del Corso 305. **Map** 3 A4.
**Tel** 06 679 73 23. 🚍 64, 81, 119, 492.
**Open** 9am–7pm daily. **Closed** Jan 1,
Easter Sun, May 1, Dec 25. 🅰️ ♿ 🖥️ 📷
📷 📷 by appt for private apartments.
**W** doriapamphilj.it

Palazzo Doria Pamphilj is a vast
edifice whose oldest parts date
from 1435. When the Pamphilj
family took over in 1647, they
built a new wing, a splendid
chapel, and a theater.

The family art collection has
over 400 paintings dating
from the 15th to 18th centuries,
including a portrait of Pope
Innocent X by Velázquez and
works by Titian, Guercino,
Caravaggio, and Claude Lorrain.
The opulent private apartments
retain many of their original
furnishings, including Brussels
and Gobelins tapestries, Murano
chandeliers, and a gilded crib.

Velázquez's *Pope Innocent X* (1650)

## ⓯ Santa Maria sopra Minerva

Piazza della Minerva 42. **Map** 2 F4.
**Tel** 06 679 39 26. 🚍 116 & many
other routes. **Open** 7am–7pm Mon–
Fri; 7:30am–12:30pm & 3:30–7pm Sat;
8am–noon & 3:30–7pm Sun.

One of Rome's rare Gothic
buildings, this church was built
in the 13th century over what
were thought to be the ruins of
a Temple of Minerva. It was a
stronghold of the Dominicans,
who produced some of the
Church's most infamous inquisitors and tried the scientist
Galileo in the adjoining monastery.

Inside, the church has a superb
collection of art and sculpture,
ranging from 13th-century

Cosmatesque tombs to a bust
by Bernini. Highlights include
Antoniazzo Romano's
*Annunciation* featuring Cardinal
Juan de Torquemada, uncle of
the vicious Spanish Inquisitor,
and the Carafa Chapel's frescoes
by Filippino Lippi.

In the Aldobrandini Chapel are
the tombs of the 16th- century
Medici popes, Leo X and his
cousin Clement VII, and near the
steps of the choir is a stocky *Risen
Christ*, begun by Michelangelo.

The church also contains the
tombs of many famous Italians,
such as St. Catherine of Siena,
who died in 1380, and Fra
Angelico, the Dominican friar
and painter, who died in 1455.
Outside, Bernini's spectacular
sculpture of an elephant holds
an obelisk on its back.

Simple vaulted nave of Santa Maria
sopra Minerva

Interior of the Pantheon, burial place for Italian monarchs

## ⓰ Pantheon

Piazza della Rotonda. **Map** 2 F4.
**Tel** 06 68 30 02 30. 🚍 116 & many
routes. **Open** 9am–7:30pm daily
(9am–6pm Sun). **Closed** Jan 1,
May 1, Dec 25. ♿

The Pantheon, the Roman
"temple of all the gods," is the
most extraordinary and best-
preserved ancient building in
Rome. The first temple on the
site was a conventional
rectangular affair erected by
Agrippa between 27 and 25 BC;
the present structure was built
and possibly designed by
Emperor Hadrian in AD 118.

The temple is fronted by a
massive pedimented portico
screening what appears to be a
cylinder fused to a shallow
dome. Only from the inside can
the true scale and beauty of this
building be appreciated: a vast
hemispherical dome equal in
radius to the height of the
cylinder, giving perfectly
harmonious proportions to the
building. A circular opening, the
*oculus*, lets in the only light.

In the 7th century, Christians
claimed to be plagued by
demons as they passed by, and
permission was given to make
the Pantheon a church. Today it
is lined with tombs, ranging
from a restrained monument to
Raphael to huge marble and
porphyry sarcophagi holding
the bodies of Italian monarchs.

## ⓱ Sant'Ignazio di Loyola

Piazza di Sant'Ignazio. **Map** 2 F4.
**Tel** 06 679 44 06. 🚌 117, 119,
492. **Open** 7:30am–7pm daily (from
9am Sun). 🚹

This church was built by Pope
Gregory XV in 1626 in honor
of St. Ignatius of Loyola, founder
of the Society of Jesus (Jesuits)
and the man who most
embodied the zeal of the
Counter-Reformation.

Together with the Gesù *(see
p407)*, Sant'Ignazio forms the
nucleus of the Jesuit area of
Rome. It is one of the most
extravagant Baroque churches,
and its vast interior is plated with
precious stones, marble, stucco,
and gilt, creating a thrilling sense
of theater. The church has a Latin-
cross plan, with an apse and
many side chapels. A cupola
was planned but never built, as
the nuns from a nearby convent
objected that it would obscure
the view from their roof garden.
Instead, the space was filled by
a perspective painting of a
dome on a flat disc.

Even more striking is the
illusionistic ceiling created by
the Jesuit artist Andrea Pozzo
in 1685, a propagandist extravaganza extolling the success of
Jesuit missionaries throughout
the world. Above four women,
representing Asia, Europe,
America, and Africa, lithe angels
and beautiful youths are sucked
into a heaven of fluffy clouds.

Detail from the AD 180 Column of Marcus
Aurelius, Piazza Colonna

## ⓲ Piazza Colonna

**Map** 3 A3. 🚌 116, 117, 492.

Home to Palazzo Chigi, official
residence of the prime minister,
Piazza Colonna is dominated by
and named after the majestic
Column of Marcus Aurelius.
This was erected after the death
of Marcus Aurelius in AD 180 to
commemorate his victories
over the barbarian tribes of the
Danube. It is clearly an imitation
of Trajan's Column *(see p392)*,
with scenes from the emperor's
wars spiraling in reliefs up the
column. The 80-year lapse
between the two works
produced a great artistic
change: the wars of Marcus
Aurelius are rendered with
simplified pictures in stronger
relief, sacrificing Classical
proportions for the sake of
clarity and immediacy.

## ⓳ Piazza di Montecitorio

**Map** 2 F3. Palazzo di Montecitorio
**Tel** 06 676 01. 🚌 116. **Open** 10am–
3:30pm 1st Sun of month (except Jul,
Aug & 1st week of Sep).

The obelisk in the center of
Piazza di Montecitorio formed
the spine of a giant sundial
brought back from Egypt by
Augustus. It vanished in the 9th
century, and was rediscovered
under medieval houses during
the reign of Julius II (1503–13).

The piazza is dominated by the
Palazzo di Montecitorio, designed
by Bernini and completed in
1697, after his death, by Carlo
Fontana. It has been the seat of
Italy's Chamber of Deputies
since the late 19th century.

La Maddalena's stuccoed facade

## ⓴ La Maddalena

Piazza della Maddalena 53. **Map** 2 F3.
**Tel** 06 899 281. 🚌 116 & many other
routes. **Open** 8:30–11:30am &
5–6:30pm daily (9–11:30am Sat).

Located in a small piazza near
the Pantheon, the Maddalena's
Rococo facade, built in 1735,
epitomizes the love of light and
movement of the late Baroque.
The facade has been restored,
despite the protests of Neo-
Classicists who dismissed its
painted stucco as icing sugar.

The diminutive dimensions
of the church did not deter
17th- and 18th-century
decorators from filling the
interior with paintings and
ornaments from the floor to
the top of the elegant cupola.

Baroque illusionistic ceiling by Andrea Pozzo in Sant'Ignazio di Loyola

# NORTHEAST ROME

This area stretches from the exclusive shopping streets around Piazza di Spagna to the Esquiline Hill, once bourgeois, but now a poor, often seedy area full of early Christian churches. The Piazza di Spagna and Piazza del Popolo district grew up in the 16th century, when the increase in the influx of pilgrims was such that a road was built to channel them as quickly as possible to the Vatican. Around the same time, the Quirinal Hill became the site of a papal palace. When Rome became capital of Italy in 1870, Via Veneto became a lavish residential area, and the Esquiline was covered with apartments for the new civil servants.

## Sights at a Glance

### Churches
❸ Santa Maria del Popolo
❼ Sant'Andrea al Quirinale
❽ San Carlo alle Quattro Fontane
❿ Santa Maria della Concezione
⓫ Santa Maria della Vittoria
⓭ Santa Prassede
⓮ San Pietro in Vincoli
⓯ *Santa Maria Maggiore p417*

### Museums and Galleries
❾ Galleria Nazionale di Arte Antica: Palazzo Barberini
⓬ Museo Nazionale Romano Palazzo Massimo

### Ancient Sites and Buildings
❹ Ara Pacis
❺ Mausoleum of Augustus

### Historic Buildings
❷ Villa Medici

### Piazzas and Fountains
❶ Piazza di Spagna and the Spanish Steps
❻ Trevi Fountain

0 metres 250

0 yards 250

*See also Rome Street Finder maps 2, 3, 4, 7*

◀ The Spanish Steps leading up to the church of the Santissima Trinità dei Monti

**For keys to symbols** *see back flap*

# Street by Street: Piazza di Spagna

The network of narrow streets around Piazza di Spagna forms one of the most exclusive areas in Rome, drawing droves of tourists and Romans to the elegant stores around Via Condotti. The square and its nearby coffeehouses have long attracted those who want to see and be seen. In the 18th century the area was full of hotels for frivolous aristocrats doing the Grand Tour, as well as artists, writers, and composers, who took the city's history and culture more seriously.

**Caffé Greco** is an 18th-century café once frequented by writers and musicians such as Keats, Goethe, Byron, Liszt, and Wagner.

Spagna

**VIALE TRINITA DEI MONTI**

**Trinità dei Monti** is a 16th-century church at the top of the Spanish Steps. There are fine views of Rome from the stairway.

**Babington's Tea Rooms**, founded by two English spinsters in 1896, still serves English teas.

**PIAZZA DI SPAGNA**

**VIA CONDOTTI**

**PIAZZA MIGNANELLI**

**VIA DI PROPAGANDA**

**The Keats-Shelley Memorial House**, where the poet Keats died in 1821, is now a museum honoring English Romantic poets.

**❶ ★ Piazza di Spagna and the Spanish Steps**
These have been at the heart of tourist Rome since the 18th century.

**The Colonna dell' Immacolata**, erected in 1857, commemorates Pope Pius IX's doctrine of the Immaculate Conception.

**The Collegio di Propaganda Fide**, built for the Jesuits in 1662, has a superb facade designed by Francesco Borromini.

*For hotels and restaurants in this region see pp573–6 and pp596–600*

**Locator Map**
*See Rome Street Finder map 3*

**Sant'Andrea delle Fratte**
contains two angels by Bernini (1669) made for Ponte Sant'Angelo, which Pope Clement X thought too lovely to expose to the weather.

0 meters          75
0 yards          75

**Key**
— Suggested route

The Fontana della Barcaccia at the foot of the Spanish Steps

# ❶ Piazza di Spagna and the Spanish Steps

**Map** 3 A2. 🚌 116, 117. Ⓜ Spagna.

Shaped like a crooked bow tie, and surrounded by muted, shuttered facades, Piazza di Spagna is crowded all day and (in summer) most of the night. The most famous square in Rome, it takes its name from the Palazzo di Spagna, built in the 17th century to house the Spanish Embassy to the Holy See.

The piazza has long been the haunt of foreign visitors and expatriates. In the 18th and 19th centuries the square stood at the heart of the city's main hotel district. Some of the travelers came in search of knowledge and inspiration, although most were more interested in collecting statues to adorn their family homes.

When the Victorian novelist Charles Dickens visited, he reported that the Spanish Steps were crowded with models dressed as Madonnas, saints, and emperors, hoping to attract the attention of foreign artists.

The steps were built in the 1720s to link the square with the French church of Trinità dei Monti above. The French wanted to place a statue of Louis XIV at the top, but the pope objected, and it was not until the 1720s that the Italian architect Francesco de Sanctis produced the voluptuous Rococo design that satisfied both camps. The Fontana Barcaccia, sunk into the paving at the foot of the steps due to low water pressure, was designed by Bernini's less famous father, Pietro.

# ❷ Villa Medici

Accademia di Francia a Roma, Viale Trinità dei Monti 1. **Map** 3 A2.
**Tel** 06 676 12 23. 🚌 117. Ⓜ Spagna.
**Open** for tours only. 🎟 Gardens: in English at noon & 4:30pm Tue–Sun (4pm in winter), but call to confirm; Cardinal's apartments: Wed only. 🅿 💻

Superbly positioned on the Pincio Hill, this 16th-century villa retains the name it assumed when Cardinal Ferdinando de' Medici bought it in 1576. It is now home to the French Academy, founded in 1666 to enable artists to study in Rome. From 1803, musicians were also allowed to study here: Berlioz and Debussy were students.

The villa is only open for exhibitions, but the formal gardens, with a gorgeously frescoed pavilion and copies of ancient statues, can be visited in certain months.

19th-century engraving of the inner facade of the Villa Medici

Pinturicchio's fresco of the *Delphic Sibyl* (1509) in Santa Maria del Popolo

### ❸ Santa Maria del Popolo

Piazza del Popolo 12. **Map** 2 F1. **Tel** 06 361 08 36. 🚌 117, 119, 490, 495, 926. Ⓜ Flaminio. **Open** 7:30am–12:30pm & 4–7pm Sun–Thu; 7:30am–7pm Fri & Sat.

Santa Maria del Popolo was one of the first Renaissance churches in Rome, commissioned by Pope Sixtus IV della Rovere in 1472. Lavish endowments by Sixtus's descendants and other powerful families have made it one of Rome's greatest artistic treasures.

Shortly after Sixtus died in 1484, Pinturicchio and his pupils frescoed two chapels (first and third right) for the della Rovere family. On the altar of the first chapel there is a lovely *Nativity* from 1490 that depicts a stable at the foot of a Classical column.

In 1503 Sixtus IV's nephew Giuliano became Pope Julius II and had Bramante build a new apse. Pinturicchio was called in again to paint its vaults with Sibyls and Apostles framed in an intricate tracery of freakish beasts.

In 1513 Raphael created the Chigi chapel (second left) for the wealthy banker Agostino Chigi. The design is an audacious Renaissance fusion of the sacred and profane; there are pyramid-like tombs and a ceiling mosaic of God holding the signs of the zodiac describing Chigi's horoscope. Raphael died before the chapel was finished, and it was completed by Bernini, who added the dynamic statues of Daniel and Habakkuk. In the Cerasi chapel, left of the altar, there are two realistic works

painted by Caravaggio in 1601: the *Conversion of St. Paul* and the *Crucifixion of St. Peter*. The artist uses daringly exaggerated lighting effects and foreshortening techniques to intensify the dramatic effect.

Detail of the Ara Pacis frieze

### ❹ Ara Pacis

Lungotevere in Augusta. **Map** 2 F2. **Tel** 06 06 08. 🚌 70, 81, 117, 119, 186, 628. **Open** 9am–7:30pm daily (last adm: 6:30pm). **Closed** Jan 1, Dec 25. ♿ 🅦 arapacis.it

Painstakingly reconstructed over many years from scattered fragments, the exquisitely carved Ara Pacis (Altar of Peace) celebrates the peace created by Emperor Augustus throughout the Mediterranean. Commissioned by the Senate in 13 BC and completed four years later, the altar stands in a square enclosure of Carrara marble, carved with realistic reliefs of such quality that experts think the craftsmen may have been Greek.

The reliefs on the north and south walls depict a procession that took place on July 4, 13 BC, in which the members

of the emperor's family can be identified, including Augustus's grandson, Lucius, clutching at the skirt of his mother, Antonia. The site is housed in a building by architect Richard Meier.

### ❺ Mausoleum of Augustus

Piazza Augusto Imperatore. **Map** 2 F2. **Tel** 06 06 08. 🚌 81, 117, 492, 628, 926. **Open** for events; call for info. 🚼 ♿

Now just a weedy mound ringed with cypresses and strewn with garbage, this was once the most prestigious burial place in Rome. Augustus had the mausoleum built in 28 BC, the year before he became sole ruler, as a tomb for himself and his descendants. The circular building was 270 ft (87 m) in diameter with two obelisks (now in Piazza del Quirinale and Piazza dell'Esquilino) at the entrance. Inside were four concentric passageways linked by corridors where urns holding the ashes of the Imperial family were placed, including those of Augustus, who died in AD 14.

### ❻ Trevi Fountain

Piazza di Trevi. **Map** 3 B3. 🚌 116 & many other routes.

Nicola Salvi's theatrical design for Rome's largest and most famous fountain was completed in 1762. The central figures are Neptune, flanked by two Tritons, one trying to master an unruly "sea horse," the other leading

Rome's largest and most famous fountain, the Trevi

*For hotels and restaurants in this region see pp573–6 and pp596–600*

a quieter beast, symbolizing the two contrasting moods of the sea.

The site originally marked the terminal of the Aqua Virgo aqueduct, built by Augustus's right-hand man and son-in-law, Agrippa, in 19 BC to channel water to Rome's new bath complexes. One of the reliefs on the first story shows a young girl, Trivia, after whom the fountain may have been named. She is said to have first shown the spring, 14 miles (22 km) from the city, to thirsty Roman soldiers.

Interior of the Sant'Andrea al Quirinale

## ⊘ Sant'Andrea al Quirinale

Via del Quirinale 29. **Map** 3 B3. **Tel** 06 487 45 65. 116, 117. **Open** 8:30am–noon & 2:30–7pm Tue–Sat; 9am–noon & 2:30–6pm Sun.

Sant'Andrea was designed for the Jesuits by Bernini and executed by his assistants between 1658 and 1670. The site was wide but shallow, so Bernini took the radical step of pointing the long axis of his oval plan toward the sides, and leading the eye around to the altar by means of a strong horizontal cornice. At the altar he combined sculpture and painting to create a theatrical crucifixion of Sant'Andrea (St. Andrew); the diagonally crucified saint on the altarpiece looks up at a stucco effigy of himself ascending to the lantern, where the Holy Spirit and cherubs await him in heaven.

The dome of San Carlo alle Quattro Fontane, by Borromini

## ⊘ San Carlo alle Quattro Fontane

Via del Quirinale 23. **Map** 3 B3. **Tel** 06 488 32 61. 116 & routes to Piazza Barberini. Barberini. **Open** 10am–1pm & 3–6pm daily (only am Sat & Sun).

In 1638, Borromini was commissioned by the Trinitarians to design a church and convent on a tiny cramped site at the Quattro Fontane crossroads. The church, so small that it is said it would fit inside one of the piers of St. Peter's, is designed with bold, fluid curves on both facade and interior to give light and life to the diminutive building. The dome, with its concealed windows, illusionistic coffering, and tiny lantern designed to make it look higher than it really is, is a clever feature.

Ceiling fresco detail in Palazzo Barberini (1633–9)

## ⊘ Galleria Nazionale di Arte Antica: Palazzo Barberini

Via delle Quattro Fontane 13. **Map** 3 B3. **Tel** 06 482 41 84. 52, 53, 61, 62, 63, 80, 116, 175, 492, 590. Barberini. **Open** 8:30am–7pm Tue–Sun (last adm: 6:30pm). **Closed** Jan 1, Dec 25. **W galleriabarberini.beniculturali.it**

When Maffeo Barberini became Pope Urban VIII in 1623, he decided to build a grand family palazzo. Designed by Carlo Maderno as a typical country villa on the fringes of the city, it now overlooks Piazza Barberini, where traffic hurtles around Bernini's Triton fountain. Maderno died shortly after the foundations had been laid, and Bernini and Borromini took over. The most dazzling room is the Gran Salone, with an illusionistic ceiling frescoed by Pietro da Cortona in 1633–9. The palazzo also houses part of the Galleria Nazionale d'Arte Antica with works by Titian, Filippo Lippi, Caravaggio, and Artemisia Gentileschi. The most famous is a portrait of a courtesan, reputedly Raphael's lover, *La Fornarina*, although not painted by the artist himself.

## ⊘ Santa Maria della Concezione

Via Veneto 27. **Map** 3 B2. **Tel** 06 88 80 36 95. 52, 53, 61, 62, 63, 80, 116, 175. Barberini. **Open** Capuchin Museum: 9am–7pm daily; Church: 7am–1pm & 3–6pm daily.

Below this unassuming church is a crypt decked with the dismembered skeletons of 4,000 Capuchin monks. They form a macabre reminder of the transience of life, with vertebrae wired together to make sacred hearts and crowns of thorns, and, in one chapel, the skeleton of a tiny Barberini princess.

## ⓫ Santa Maria della Vittoria

Via XX Settembre 17. **Map** 3 C2.
**Tel** 06 42 74 05 71. 🚌 61, 62, 175, 910.
Ⓜ **Repubblica. Open** 8:30am–noon
& 3:30–6pm daily.

Santa Maria della Vittoria is an intimate Baroque church with a lavish, candlelit interior. Inside the Cornaro chapel is one of Bernini's most ambitious sculptures, the *Ecstasy of St. Teresa* (1646). The physical nature of St. Teresa's ecstasy is apparent as she appears collapsed on a cloud with her mouth half open and eyes closed, struck by the arrow of a smiling angel. Past and present ecclesiastical members of the Venetian Cornaro family, who commissioned the chapel, sit in boxes as if watching and discussing the scene being played out in front of them.

Bernini's *Ecstasy of St. Teresa* (1646) in Santa Maria della Vittoria

## ⓬ Museo Nazionale Romano Palazzo Massimo

Palazzo Massimo, Largo di Villa Peretti
1 (1 of 5 sites). **Map** 4 D3. **Tel** 06 39 96
77 00. 🚌 all routes to Termini.
Ⓜ **Repubblica. Open** 9am–7:45pm
Tue–Sun. 🎫 ticket valid for all sites.
🏛 ♿ 📷 📋

Founded in 1899, the Museo Nazionale Romano – one of the world's leading museums of Classical art – houses most of the antiquities found in Rome since 1870, as well as important

older collections. During the 1990s it underwent a major reorganization and now has five branches: the Palazzo Altemps *(see p404)*; the Baths of Diocletian; the Aula Ottagona, the Crypta; Balbi; and the Palazzo Massimo. In the latter, exhibits dating from the 2nd century BC to the late 4th century AD are displayed in a series of rooms over three floors. Highlights include the *Quattro Aurighe* mosaics from a villa in northern Rome, the breathtaking series of frescoes from Livia's summer villa, and the famous statue of her husband, the Emperor Augustus.

One of the finely detailed *Quattro Aurighe* mosaics on display at the Museo Nazionale Romano Palazzo Massimo

## ⓭ Santa Prassede

Via Santa Prassede 9a. **Map** 4 D4.
**Tel** 06 488 24 56. 🚌 16, 70, 71, 75,
714. Ⓜ Vittorio Emanuele. **Open**
7:30am–noon & 4–7pm daily. ♿

The church was founded by Pope Paschal II in the 9th century and decorated by Byzantine artists with the most important glittering mosaics in Rome. In the apse Christ stands between Santa Prassede and her sister, dressed as Byzantine empresses, among white-robed elders, lambs, feather-mop palms, and bright red poppies. The Cappella di San Zeno is even lovelier, a jewel box of a

9th-century mosaic, Santa Prassede

mausoleum, built by Pope Paschal II for his mother, Theodora. Her square halo shows that she was still alive when the mosaic was created.

## ⓮ San Pietro in Vincoli

Piazza di San Pietro in Vincoli. **Map** 3
C5. **Tel** 06 97 84 49 50. 🚌 75, 85, 117.
Ⓜ Colosseo. **Open** 8am–12:30pm &
3–7pm daily (Oct–Mar: to 6pm). ♿

The church's name means "St. Peter in Chains," so called because it houses what are said to be the chains with which St. Peter was shackled in the Mamertine Prison *(see p393)*. According to tradition, one set of chains was sent to Constantinople by Empress Eudoxia; when it was returned to Rome some years later, it miraculously fused with its partner.

San Pietro is now best known for the Tomb of Julius II, commissioned from Michelangelo by the pope in 1505. Much to the artist's chagrin, Julius soon became more interested in the building of a new St. Peter's, and the tomb project was laid to one side. After the pope died in 1513, Michelangelo resumed work on the tomb, but had only completed the statues of the *Dying Slaves* (now found in Paris and Florence) and *Moses* when he was called away to paint *The Last Judgment* in the Sistine Chapel.

# ⓯ Santa Maria Maggiore

A confident blend of architectural styles, ranging from Early Christian to late Baroque, Santa Maria is also famous for its superb mosaics. Founded in about AD 420, it retains the original colonnaded triple nave, lined with panels of rare 5th-century mosaics. The Cosmatesque marble floor and bell tower are medieval, as are the spectacular mosaics on the triumphal arch and in the loggia. The lavish coffered ceiling is Renaissance; the facades, domes, and chapels, Baroque.

### VISITORS' CHECKLIST

**Practical Information**
Piazza di Santa Maria Maggiore.
**Map** 4 D4.
**Tel** 06 69 88 68 00.
**Open** 7am–6:45pm daily. 🕆 ♿

**Transportation**
🚌 16, 70, 71, 714. 🚃 14. Ⓜ
Termini, Cavour.

**Coronation of the Virgin**
This is one of the wonderful 13th-century mosaics in the apse by Jacopo Torriti.

**Bell tower**

**Tomb of Cardinal Rodriguez**
This Gothic tomb, which dates from 1299, contains magnificent marblework by the Cosmati.

**5th-century mosaics**

**18th-century facade by Ferdinando Fuga**

**13th-century mosaics**

**Cappella Paolina**
Flaminio Ponzio, architect of the Villa Borghese, designed this sumptuous chapel in 1611 for Pope Paul V, who is buried here.

**Column in Piazza Santa Maria Maggiore**
In 1611, a bronze of the Virgin and Child was added to this ancient marble column, which came from the Basilica of Constantine.

**Cappella Sistina**
This chapel was built for Pope Sixtus V (1584–7) by Domenico Fontana and was opulently covered with ancient marble. It houses the pope's tomb.

# THE VATICAN AND TRASTEVERE

Vatican City, the world capital of Catholicism, is the world's smallest state. It occupies 106 acres (43 ha) within high walls watched over by the Vatican guard. It was the site where St. Peter was martyred (c.AD 64) and buried, and it became the residence of the popes who succeeded him. The papal palaces, next to the great basilica of St. Peter's, are home to the Sistine Chapel

and the eclectic collections of the Vatican Museums, as well as being the residence of the pope. Neighboring Trastevere is quite different, a picturesque old quarter whose inhabitants consider themselves to be the only true Romans. The proletarian identity of the place is in danger of being destroyed by the proliferation of trendy restaurants, clubs, and stores.

## Sights at a Glance

### Churches

2 St. Peter's pp422–3
7 Santa Maria in Trastevere
8 Santa Cecilia in Trastevere
9 San Francesco a Ripa
10 San Pietro in Montorio and the Tempietto

### Museums and Galleries

3 Vatican Museums pp424–31
5 Palazzo Corsini and Galleria Nazionale d'Arte Antica

### Historic Buildings

1 Castel Sant'Angelo
4 Villa Farnesina

### Parks and Gardens

6 Botanical Gardens

See Rome Street Finder maps 1, 2, 5, 6, 9

◀ St. Peter's with the Ponte Sant'Angelo in the foreground

For keys to symbols see back flap

# A Tour of the Vatican

The Vatican, a sovereign state since February 1929, is ruled by the pope, Europe's only absolute monarch. About 500 people live here, and in addition to accommodations for staff and ecclesiasts, the city has its own post office, banks, currency, judicial system, radio station, stores, and a daily newspaper, *L'Osservatore Romano*.

★ **St. Peter's**
Most of the great architects of the Renaissance and Baroque periods had a hand in the design of the Basilica of St. Peter's, the most famous church in Christendom
*(see pp422–3)*.

★ **Sistine Chapel**
Michelangelo frescoed the ceiling with scenes from Genesis (1508–12), and the altar wall with *The Last Judgment* (1534–41). The chapel is used by cardinals when electing a new pope *(see p428)*.

0 meters 75
0 yards 75

Raphael Rooms

## KEY

① **Piazza San Pietro** was laid out by Bernini between 1656 and 1667.

② **Information office**

③ **The Papal Audience Chamber**

④ **Vatican Radio** broadcasts throughout the world in 20 languages from this tower, part of the 9th-century Leonine Wall.

⑤ **The Vatican Gardens**, open for guided tours, make up one third of the Vatican's territory.

PIAZZA DEL SANT'UFFIZIO

PIAZZA SAN PIET

PIAZ PIO

To Via della Conciliazione

**This staircase** leading down from the museums, designed in 1932 by Giuseppe Momo, is in the form of a double helix, consisting of two spirals: one to walk up and one to walk down.

**Locator Map**
*See Rome Street Finder map 1*

Entrance to Vatican Museums

★ **Vatican Museums**
The marble group of the *Laocoön* (AD 1) is one of many prestigious works of art in the Vatican *(see p426)*.

**The Cortile della Pigna** is named after a bronze pine cone from an ancient fountain.

★ **Raphael Rooms**
Raphael frescoed this suite in the early 16th century. Works like *The School of Athens* established his reputation, which soon equalled that of his contemporary Michelangelo *(see p431)*.

---

# ❶ Castel Sant'Angelo

Lungotevere Castello. **Map** 2 D3.
**Tel** 06 681 91 11. 🚌 34, 280.
**Open** 9am–7:30pm daily (last entry 6:30pm). **Closed** Jan 1, Dec 25. ♿
🏛 🖼 📷 ♿ 🚻 **W** castelsantangelo.
beniculturali.it

This massive fortress takes its name from the vision of the Archangel Michael by Pope Gregory the Great in the 6th century as he led a procession across the bridge, praying for the end of the plague.

The castle began life in AD 139 as the Emperor Hadrian's mausoleum. Since then it has been a bridgehead in the Emperor Aurelian's city wall, a medieval citadel and prison, and a place of safety for popes during times of political unrest. A corridor links it with the Vatican Palace, providing an escape route for the pope. From dank cells to fine apartments of Renaissance popes, the museums cover all aspects of the castle's history, including the Sala Paolina, with illusionistic frescoes (1546–8) by Pellegrino Tibaldi and Perin del Vaga and the Courtyard of Honor.

Illusionistic frescoes by Pellegrino Tibaldi

Castel Sant'Angelo viewed from the Ponte Sant'Angelo

# ❷ St. Peter's

Catholicism's most sacred shrine, the sumptuous, marble-caked basilica of St. Peter's draws pilgrims and tourists from all over the world. It holds hundreds of precious works of art, some salvaged from the original 4th-century basilica built by Constantine, others commissioned from Renaissance and Baroque artists. The dominant tone is set by Bernini, who created the baldacchino twisting up below Michelangelo's huge dome. He also created the Cathedra in the apse, with four saints supporting a throne that contains fragments once thought to be relics of the chair from which St. Peter delivered his first sermon.

**Dome of St. Peter's**
The 448-ft- (136.5-m-) high dome, designed by Michelangelo, was not completed in his lifetime.

## KEY

① **Entrance to Historical Artistic Museum and Sacristy**

② **The Monument to Pope Alexander VII** was Bernini's last work in St. Peter's. Completed in 1678, it shows the Chigi Pope among figures of Truth, Justice, Charity, and Prudence.

③ **A staircase** of 537 steps leads to the summit of the dome.

④ **The Baldacchino** was commissioned by Pope Urban VIII in 1624; Bernini's extravagant Baroque canopy stands above St. Peter's tomb.

⑤ **The Papal Altar** stands over the crypt where St. Peter is reputedly buried.

⑥ **The church** is 615 ft (186 m) long.

⑦ **The foot of St. Peter**, sculpted by Arnolfo di Cambio in the 13th century, has worn thin from the touch of pilgrims over the centuries.

⑧ **Two minor cupolas by Vignola (1507–73)**

⑨ **Markings on** the floor of the nave show how other churches compare in length.

⑩ **Facade by Carlo Maderno (1614)**

⑪ **From this Library window**, the pope blesses the faithful gathered in the piazza below.

⑫ **The Holy Door** is used only in Holy Years.

⑬ **Atrium by Carlo Maderno**

## Historical Plan of the Basilica of St. Peter's

St. Peter was buried in AD 64 in a necropolis near the site of his crucifixion in the Circus of Nero. In AD 324 Constantine constructed a basilica over the tomb. The old church was rebuilt in the 15th century, and throughout the 16th and 17th centuries various architects developed the existing structure. The new church was inaugurated in 1626.

### Key

▨ Circus of Nero

▨ Constantinian

▨ Renaissance

▨ Baroque

### The Grottoes
A fragment of this 13th-century mosaic by Giotto, salvaged from the old basilica, is now in the Grottoes, where many popes are buried.

### Michelangelo's Pietà
Protected by glass since an attack in 1972, the *Pietà* was created in 1499 when Michelangelo was only 25.

## VISITORS' CHECKLIST

**Practical Information**
Piazza San Pietro.
**Map** 1 B3.
**Tel** 06 69 88 37 12 (Sacristy);
06 69 88 16 62 (tourist info).
Basilica: **Open** Apr–Sep:
7am–7pm daily (mid-Oct–Mar:
to 6:30pm). 🚻 ♿ 📷
Treasury: **Open** Apr–Sep:
8am–7pm daily (Oct–Mar:
to 6:15pm). 📷
Grottoes: **Open** Apr–Sep: 8am–
6pm daily (Oct–Mar: to 5:30pm).
Dome: **Open** 8am–6pm daily
(Oct–Mar: to 5pm). 📷
Papal audiences: usually Wed at
10:30am in Piazza San Pietro or in
the Papal Audience Chamber.
Tickets (free) from Prefecture of
the Pontifical Household. Call 06
69 88 31 14 or check availability
at office through the bronze doors
on the right of the colonnade
(9am–1pm). The pope appears
at noon Sun to bless the crowd
in Piazza San Pietro.

**Transportation**
🚌 23, 49, 70, 180, 492.
Ⓜ Ottaviano San Pietro.

### Filarete Doors
These bronze doors from the old basilica were decorated with biblical reliefs by Filarete between 1439 and 1445.

**Entrance**

### Piazza San Pietro
On Sundays, religious festivals, and special occasions such as canonizations, the pope blesses the crowds from a balcony.

# ❸ Vatican Museums

Home to the Sistine Chapel and Raphael Rooms as well as to one of the world's most important art collections, the Vatican Museums are housed in palaces originally built for Renaissance popes Julius II, Innocent VIII, and Sixtus IV. Most of the later additions were made in the 18th century, when priceless works of art accumulated by earlier popes were first put on show.

**Etruscan Museum**
The Etruscan collection includes a woman's gold clasp *(fibula)* from the 7th-century-BC Regolini-Galassi tomb at Cerveteri, north of Rome.

**Gallery of Maps**
The *Siege of Malta* is one of 40 maps of the Church's territories, frescoed by the 16th-century cartographer Ignazio Danti on the gallery's walls.

**Gallery of the Candelabra**

**Raphael Rooms**
This is a detail of the *Expulsion of Heliodorus from the Temple*, one of many frescoes painted by Raphael and his pupils for Julius II's private apartments *(see p431)*.

**Gallery of Tapestries**

Sta
do

**Upper floor**

Sala dei Chiaroscuri

Raphael Loggia

Sistine Chapel
*(see p428-30)*

## Gallery Guide

*The museum complex is vast: the Sistine Chapel is 20 to 30 minutes' walk from the entrance, so allow plenty of time. There is a strict one-way system, and it is best to be selective or choose one of four color-coded itineraries, which vary from 90 minutes to a 5-hour marathon.*

**Borgia Apartment**
Pinturicchio and his assistants frescoed these rooms for Alexander VI in 1492–5.

**Modern religious art** on view here was sent to the popes by artists worldwide, such as Bacon, Ernst, and Carrà

**Gregorian Profane Museum**

**Pio-Clementine Museum**
The finest of the Vatican's Classical statues are on display here, like the *Apollo Belvedere*, a Roman copy in marble of a 4th-century-BC Greek bronze.

**Stairs up to Etruscan Museum**

**Entrance**

**Lower floor**

**Braccio Nuovo**

**Chiaramonti Museum**

**The Lapidary Gallery**
contains inscriptions from pagan and Christian catacombs, but is closed to the public.

**Cortile Ottagonale**

**Egyptian Museum**
The collection of Egyptian artifacts includes this painted bas-relief from a 2400 BC tomb. The museum was organized by Father Ungarelli, a 19th-century Egyptologist.

**Pio-Christian Museum**
Early Christianity adopted Classical images so that its doctrines could be more easily understood. This 4th-century statue of Christ as the Good Shepherd derives from the pastoral figure of the shepherd.

**Pinacoteca**
The Vatican's art gallery has 15th- to 19th-century works, and is particularly strong on the Renaissance. This unfinished painting of *St. Jerome* by Leonardo da Vinci reveals his mastery of anatomy.

**Key to Floorplan**

- ▪ Egyptian and Assyrian art
- ▫ Greek and Roman art
- ▪ Etruscan art
- ▫ Early Christian and Medieval art
- ▪ 15th- to 19th-century art
- ▪ Modern religious art
- ▪ Lapidary Gallery
- ▫ Non-exhibition space

# Exploring the Vatican's Collections

The Vatican's greatest treasures are its superlative Greek and Roman antiquities, together with the magnificent artifacts excavated from Egyptian and Etruscan tombs during the 19th century. Some of Italy's greatest artists, such as Raphael, Michelangelo, and Leonardo da Vinci, are represented in the Pinacoteca (art gallery) and parts of the former palaces, where the artists were employed by popes to decorate sumptuous apartments and galleries.

Head of an athlete in mosaic from the Baths of Caracalla, AD 217

### Egyptian and Assyrian Art

The Egyptian collection contains finds from 19th- and 20th-century excavations in Egypt, as well as statues that were brought to Rome in Imperial times. There are also Roman imitations of Egyptian art from Hadrian's Villa *(see p472)* and from temples in Rome devoted to Egyptian gods and goddesses, such as Isis and Serapis.

The genuine Egyptian works, displayed on the lower floor next to the Pio-Clementine Museum, include statues, mummies, mummy cases, and a Book of the Dead. One of the main treasures is a colossal 13th-century granite statue of Queen Mutuy, the mother of Rameses II, which was found on the site of the Horti Sallustiani gardens near Via Veneto. Also noteworthy are the head of a statue of Montuhotep IV (20th century BC), the beautiful mummy case of Queen Hetepheres, and the tomb of Iri, who was the guardian of the Pyramid of Cheops. This dates back to the 22nd century BC.

**Roman copy of the Greek *Doryphoros***

### Greek, Etruscan, and Roman Art

The greater part of the Vatican Museums is dedicated to Greek and Roman art. However, the Etruscan Museum houses a superb collection of Etruscan *(see p48)* and pre-Roman artifacts from Etruria and the Greek colonies of southern Italy.

Here, the most famous exhibits are the gold jewelry and bronze throne, bed, and funeral cart, found in the 650 BC Regolini-Galassi tomb in Cerveteri *(see p470).*

Prize Greek and Roman pieces form the nucleus of the Pio-Clementine Museum. These include high-quality Roman copies of 4th-century-BC Greek statues, such as the *Apoxyomenos* (an athlete wiping his body after a race) and the *Apollo del Belvedere.* The splendid *Laocoön* (1st century AD), originally from Rhodes, was found in 1506 in the ruins of Nero's Golden House. Works such as these inspired Michelangelo and other Renaissance artists. The much smaller Chiaramonti Museum is lined with ancient busts, and its extension, the Braccio Nuovo, has a 1st-century-BC statue of Augustus from the villa of his wife Livia. It is based on the *Doryphoros* (spear-carrier) by

the 5th-century BC Greek sculptor Polyclitus. There is also a Roman copy of this on display opposite. The Museo Gregoriano Profano, housed in a separate wing, follows the evolution of Roman art from reliance on Greek models to a recognizably Roman style.

In this museum, original Greek works include large marble fragments from the Parthenon in Athens. Among the Roman pieces are two reliefs, the *Rilievi della Cancelleria,* commissioned by Domitian in AD 81 to glorify the military parades of his father, Emperor Vespasian. There are also fine Roman floor mosaics, two from the Baths of Caracalla *(see p441),* and one, in the Round Room, dated 3rd century AD, from the Baths of Otricoli in Umbria.

In the Vatican Library is the 1st-century-AD *Aldobrandini Wedding,* a beautiful Roman fresco depicting a bride being prepared for her marriage.

Roman mosaic from the Baths of Otricoli, Umbria, in the Round Room

## Early Christian and Medieval Art

The main collection of early Christian antiquities is in the Pio-Christian Museum, which contains inscriptions and sculpture from catacombs and early Christian basilicas. The sculpture consists chiefly of reliefs from sarcophagi, though the most striking work is a freestanding 4th-century statue of the *Good Shepherd*. The sculpture's chief interest lies in the way it blends biblical episodes with pagan mythology. The idealized pastoral figure of the shepherd became Christ himself, while bearded philosophers turned into the Apostles.

The first two rooms of the Pinacoteca are dedicated to late medieval art, mostly wooden altarpieces painted in tempera. The outstanding work is Giotto's *Stefaneschi Triptych* of about 1300, which decorated the main altar of the old St. Peter's.

The Vatican Library has a number of medieval treasures, including reliquaries, textiles, enamels, and icons.

*Pietà (c. 1471–4) by the Venetian artist Giovanni Bellini in the Pinacoteca*

*Detail of Giotto's Stefaneschi Triptych (1330) in the Pinacoteca*

## 15th- to 19th-Century Art

Many Renaissance popes were connoisseurs of the arts who considered it their duty to sponsor the leading painters, sculptors, and goldsmiths of the age. The galleries around the Cortile del Belvedere were decorated by great artists between the 16th and the 19th centuries.

The Gallery of Tapestries is hung with tapestries woven in Brussels to designs by students of Raphael. The Apartment of Pope Pius V has beautiful 15th-century Flemish tapestries, and the Gallery of Maps is frescoed with 16th-century maps of ancient and contemporary Italy.

Alongside the Raphael Rooms *(see p431)* are the Room of the Chiaroscuri and Pope Nicholas V's private chapel. This was frescoed between 1447 and 1451 by Fra Angelico. Also worth seeing is the Borgia Apartment, decorated in the 1490s by Pinturicchio and his pupils for the Borgia pope, Alexander VI. Another set of fascinating

*Pinturicchio's Adoration of the Magi (1490s), Borgia Apartment*

frescoes can be found in the Loggia of Raphael, but a visit here requires special permission.

The Pinacoteca has many important Renaissance works. Highlights from the 15th century are a fine *Pietà* by Giovanni Bellini, part of his *Coronation of the Virgin* altarpiece in Pèsaro *(see p372)*; and Leonardo da Vinci's unfinished *St. Jerome*, discovered, after being long lost, in two halves. One was being used as a coffer lid in an antiques shop, the other as the seat of a stool in a shoemaker's. Exceptional pieces from the 16th century include eight tapestry cartoons, the *Transfiguration*, and *Madonna of Foligno* by Raphael, in a room devoted to the artist; a *Deposition* by Caravaggio; an altarpiece by Titian; and *St. Helen* by Veronese, which shows the saint as a gorgeously dressed aristocrat.

# Sistine Chapel: The Ceiling

Michelangelo frescoed the ceiling for Pope Julius II between 1508 and 1512, working on specially designed scaffolding. The main panels, which chart the Creation of the World and Fall of Man, are surrounded by subjects from the Old and New Testaments – except for the Classical Sibyls, who are said to have foreseen the birth of Christ. In the 1980s the ceiling was restored, revealing colors of an unsuspected vibrancy.

**Libyan Sibyl**
The pagan prophetess reaches for the Book of Knowledge. Like most female figures Michelangelo painted, the beautiful Libyan Sibyl was probably modeled on a man.

Creation of the Sun and Moon

## KEY

① **Illusionistic architecture**

② **The lunettes** are devoted to frescoes of the ancestors of Christ, like Hezekiah.

③ **The Ignudi** are athletic male nudes whose significance is uncertain.

### Key to Ceiling Panels

**Genesis: 1** God Dividing Light from Darkness;
**2** Creation of the Sun and Moon; **3** Separating Waters from Land; **4** Creation of Adam; **5** Creation of Eve; **6** Original Sin; **7** Sacrifice of Noah; **8** The Deluge; **9** Drunkenness of Noah.

**Ancestors of Christ: 10** Solomon with his Mother; **11** Parents of Jesse; **12** Rehoboam with Mother; **13** Asa with Parents; **14** Uzziah with Parents; **15** Hezekiah with Parents; **16** Zerubbabel with Parents; **17** Josiah with Parents.

**Prophets: 18** Jonah; **19** Jeremiah; **20** Daniel; **21** Ezekiel; **22** Isaiah; **23** Joel; **24** Zechariah.

**Sibyls: 25** Libyan Sibyl; **26** Persian Sibyl; **27** Cumaean Sibyl; **28** Erythrean Sibyl; **29** Delphic Sibyl.

**Old Testament scenes of salvation: 30** Punishment of Haman; **31** Moses and the Brazen Serpent; **32** David and Goliath; **33** Judith and Holofernes.

**Original Sin**
This shows Adam and Eve tasting the forbidden fruit from the Tree of Knowledge, and their expulsion from Paradise. Michelangelo represents Satan as a snake with the body of a woman.

**Creation of the Sun and Moon**
Michelangelo depicts God as a dynamic but terrifying figure commanding the sun to shed light on the earth.

## Restoration of the Sistine Ceiling

The restorers of the Sistine Chapel used computers, photography, and spectrum technology to analyze the fresco before cleaning began. They separated Michelangelo's work from that of later restorers and discovered that the restorers had attempted to clean the ceiling with materials ranging from bread to retsina wine. The new restoration revealed the familiarly dusky, eggshell-cracked figures to have creamy skins, lustrous hair, and brightly colored, luscious robes: "a Benetton Michelangelo," mocked one critic, claiming that a layer of varnish that the artist had added to darken the colors had been removed. However, after examining the work, most experts agreed that the new colors probably matched those painted by Michelangelo.

A restorer cleaning the Libyan Sibyl

# Sistine Chapel: The Walls

The massive walls of the Sistine Chapel, the main chapel in the Vatican Palace, were frescoed by some of the finest artists of the 15th and 16th centuries. The 12 paintings on the side walls, by artists including Perugino, Ghirlandaio, Rosselli, Botticelli, and Signorelli, show parallel episodes from the lives of Moses and Christ. The decoration of the chapel walls was completed between 1534 and 1541 by Michelangelo, who added the great altar wall fresco, *The Last Judgment*.

**Key to the Frescoes: Artists and Subjects**

*The Last Judgment*

☐ Perugino ☐ Botticelli ☐ Ghirlandaio
☐ Rosselli ☐ Signorelli ☐ Michelangelo

**1** Baptism of Christ in the Jordan
**2** Temptations of Christ
**3** Calling of St. Peter and St. Andrew
**4** Sermon on the Mount
**5** Handing over the Keys to St. Peter
**6** Last Supper
**7** Moses's Journey into Egypt
**8** Moses Receiving the Call
**9** Crossing of the Red Sea
**10** Adoration of the Golden Calf
**11** Punishment of the Rebels
**12** Last Days of Moses

## The Last Judgment by Michelangelo

Revealed in 1993 after a year's restoration, *The Last Judgment* is considered to be the masterpiece of Michelangelo's mature years. It was commissioned by Pope Paul III Farnese, and required the removal of some earlier frescoes and two windows over the altar. A new wall was erected, slanting inward to stop dust from settling on it. Michelangelo worked alone on the fresco for seven years, until its completion in 1541.

The painting depicts the souls of the dead rising up to face the wrath of God, a subject that is rarely used for an altar decoration. The pope chose it as a warning to Catholics to adhere to their faith in the turmoil of the Reformation. In fact, the work conveys the artist's own tormented attitude to his faith. It offers neither the certainties of Christian orthodoxy nor the ordered view of Classicism.

In a dynamic, emotional composition, the figures are caught in a vortex of motion. The dead are torn from their graves and hauled up to face Christ the Judge, whose athletic, muscular figure is the focus of all the painting's movement.

Christ shows little sympathy for the agitated saints around him, clutching the instruments of their martyrdom. Neither is any pity shown for the damned, hurled down to the demons in hell. Here Charon, pushing people off his boat into the depths of Hades, and the infernal judge Minos, are taken from Dante's *Inferno*. Minos has ass's ears, and is a portrait of courtier Biagio da Cesena, who had objected to the nude figures in the fresco. Michelangelo's self-portrait is on the skin held by the martyr St. Bartholomew.

Souls meeting the wrath of Christ in Michelangelo's *The Last Judgment*

# Raphael Rooms

Pope Julius II's private apartments were built above those of his hated predecessor, Alexander VI, who died in 1503. Julius was impressed with Raphael's work and chose him to redecorate the four rooms *(stanze)*. Raphael and his pupils began in 1508, replacing works by better-known artists, including Raphael's teacher, Perugino. The new frescoes quickly established the young artist's reputation in Rome, but the project took 16 years to complete and he died before it was finished.

**Key to Floorplan**

① Hall of Constantine
② Room of Heliodorus
③ Room of the Segnatura
④ Room of The Fire in the Borgo

Detail from Raphael's *The Mass of Bolsena* (1512)

## Hall of Constantine

The frescoes in this room were started in 1517 and completed in 1525, five years after Raphael's death, and are largely the work of the artist's pupils. The theme of the decoration is the triumph of Christianity over paganism, and the four major frescoes show scenes from the life of Constantine, the first Christian emperor. These include the *Vision of the Cross* and the emperor's victory over his rival, Maxentius, at *The Battle of the Milvian Bridge*, for which Raphael had provided a preparatory sketch.

## Room of Heliodorus

Raphael decorated this private antechamber between 1512 and 1514. The main frescoes all contain thinly veiled references to the protective powers of the papacy. The room's name refers to the fresco on the right, *The Expulsion of Heliodorus from the Temple*, showing Heliodorus felled by a horseman as he tries to rob the Temple in Jerusalem. It alludes to Pope Julius II's victory over foreign armies in Italy. *The Mass of Bolsena* on the left wall refers to a miracle that occurred in 1263, in which a priest who doubted the doctrine of the Holy Host was said to have seen blood issue from it at the moment of sacrifice.

## Room of the Segnatura

Completed between 1508 and 1511, the frescoes here are the most harmonious in the series. The scheme followed by Raphael, dictated by Pope Julius II, reflected the Humanist belief that there could be perfect harmony between Classical culture and Christianity in the search for truth. The most famous work, *The School of Athens*, centers on the debate about truth between the Greek philosophers Plato and Aristotle. Raphael depicted some of his contemporaries as philosophers, including Leonardo da Vinci, Bramante, and Michelangelo.

## Room of The Fire in the Borgo

This was originally the dining room, but when the decoration was completed under Pope Leo X it became a music room. All the frescoes exalt the reigning pope by depicting events in the lives of his 9th-century namesakes, Leo III and IV. The main frescoes were designed by Raphael, but finished by his assistants between 1514 and 1517. The most famous, *The Fire in the Borgo*, shows a miracle of 847, when Pope Leo IV put out a fire by making the sign of the cross. Raphael draws a parallel between this and the legendary flight of Aeneas from Troy, recounted by Virgil. Aeneas appears in the fore-ground, carrying his father, Anchises, on his back.

*The School of Athens* (1511) showing philosophers and scholars

## ❹ Villa Farnesina

Via della Lungara 230. **Map** 2 D5.
**Tel** 06 68 02 72 68. 🚌 23, 280.
**Open** 9am–2pm Mon–Sat and
every 2nd Sun of the month. 🎫
🕐 10am Sat (English). 📧

The fabulously wealthy Sienese
banker Agostino Chigi commissioned this villa in 1508 from his
fellow Sienese Baldassare Peruzzi.
Chigi's main home was across the
Tiber, and the villa was designed
purely for lavish banquets.
Artists, poets, cardinals, princes,
and the pope himself were
entertained here in magnificent
style. Chigi also used the villa
for sojourns with the courtesan
Imperia, who allegedly inspired
one of the *Three Graces* painted
by Raphael in the Loggia of
Cupid and Psyche.

The simple, harmonious
design of the Farnesina, with a
central block and projecting
wings, made it one of the first
true villas of the Renaissance.
Peruzzi decorated some of
the interiors himself, such as
the Sala della Prospettiva
upstairs, in which the illusionistic frescoes create the
impression of looking out over
16th-century Rome through
a marble colonnade.

Other frescoes, by Sebastiano
del Piombo and Raphael and his
pupils, illustrate Classical myths,
while the vault of the main hall,
the Sala di Galatea, is adorned
with scenes showing the
position of the stars at the time
of Chigi's birth. After his death
the business collapsed, and in
1577 the villa was sold off to
the Farnese family.

Raphael's *Three Graces* in the Villa Farnesina

Queen Christina of Sweden's bedroom in
the Palazzo Corsini

## ❺ Palazzo Corsini and Galleria Nazionale d'Arte Antica

Via della Lungara 10. **Map** 2 D5.
**Tel** 06 68 80 23 23. 🚌 23, 280. **Open**
8:30am–7:30pm Wed–Mon. **Closed**
Jan 1, Dec 25 & 31. 🎫 🕐 ♿ 📧 📷
🌐 **galleriacorsini. beniculturali.it**

Built for Cardinal Domenico
Riario in 1510–12, the Palazzo
Corsini has welcomed Bramante,
the young Michelangelo,
Erasmus, and the mother of
Napoleon among its guests.
Queen Christina of Sweden died
here in 1689. The palazzo was
rebuilt by Ferdinando Fuga,
who planned the facade to
be viewed from an angle, as
Via della Lungara is too narrow
for a full-frontal view.

When the palazzo was
bought by the state in 1893,
the Corsini family donated their
collection of paintings, which
formed the core of the national
art collection and was soon
augmented. The collection is
now split between Palazzo
Barberini and Palazzo Corsini.
Although the best works are
in the Barberini, there are
paintings by Van Dyck, Rubens,
Murillo, and, notably, an
androgynous *St. John the
Baptist* (c.1604) by Caravaggio
and a *Salome* (1638) by Reni.
The strangest work is a portrait
of the rotund Queen Christina
as the goddess Diana by
J. Van Egmont.

## ❻ Botanical Gardens

Largo Cristina di Svezia 24. **Map** 2 D5.
**Tel** 06 49 91 71 07. 🚌 23, 280. **Open**
9:30am–6:30pm (Oct–Mar: 5:30pm)
Mon–Sat. **Closed** public hols. 🎫 🕐

Sequoias, palm trees, orchids,
and bromeliads are among
the 7,000 plants from all over
the world represented in the
Botanical Gardens (Orto
Botanico). Indigenous and
exotic species are grouped
to illustrate their botanical
families and their adaptation
to different climates and eco-
systems. There are also some
curious plants like the ginkgo
that have survived almost
unchanged from earlier eras.

Palm trees in the Botanical
Gardens, Trastevere

## ❼ Santa Maria in Trastevere

Piazza Santa Maria in Trastevere.
**Map** 5 C1. **Tel** 06 581 48 02. 🚌 H, 23,
280. **Open** 7:30am–9pm daily. ♿ 📷

Santa Maria in Trastevere was
probably the first Christian
place of worship in Rome,
founded by Pope Callixtus I in
the 3rd century, when emperors
were still pagan and Christianity
a minority cult. According to
legend, it was built on the site
where a fountain of oil had
miraculously sprung up on the
day that Christ was born. The
basilica became the focus of
devotion to the Madonna, and
although today's church and
its remarkable mosaics date
largely from the 12th and 13th
centuries, images of the Virgin
continue to dominate. The
facade mosaics probably date

Apse mosaic of the *Coronation of the Virgin*, Santa Maria in Trastevere

from the 12th century, and show Mary, Christ, and ten lamp-bearing women. Inside in the apse is a stylized 12th-century *Coronation of the Virgin* and, below, a series of realistic scenes from the life of the Virgin by the 13th-century artist Pietro Cavallini. The oldest image of the Virgin is a 7th-century icon, the *Madonna di Clemenza*, which depicts her as a Byzantine empress flanked by a guard of angels. It sits above the altar in the Cappella Altemps.

## 8 Santa Cecilia in Trastevere

Piazza di Santa Cecilia. **Map** 6 D1. **Tel** 06 589 92 89. 🚌 H, 23, 44, 280. **Open** 10am–1pm & 4–7pm daily. Cavallini fresco: **Open** 10am–12:30pm Mon–Sat.

St. Cecilia, aristocrat and patron saint of music, was martyred here in AD 230. After an unsuccessful attempt to suffocate her by locking her in the hot steam bath of her house for three days, she was beheaded. A church was built, possibly in the 4th century, on the site of her house (still to be seen beneath the church, along with the remains of a tannery). Her body was lost, but it turned up again in the Catacombs of San Callisto *(see p446).* In the 9th century it was reburied here by Pope Paschal I, who rebuilt the church.

A fine apse mosaic survives from this period. The altar canopy by Arnolfo di Cambio and the fresco of *The Last Judgment* by Pietro Cavallini can be reached through the adjoining convent; they date from the 13th century, one of the few periods when Rome had a distinctive artistic style.

In front of the altar is a delicate statue of St. Cecilia by Stefano Maderno, which is based on sketches made of her perfectly preserved relics when they were briefly disinterred in 1599.

## 9 San Francesco a Ripa

Piazza San Francesco d'Assisi 88. **Map** 5 C2. **Tel** 06 581 90 20. 🚌 H, 23, 44, 75, 280. **Open** 7:30am–1pm & 2–7:30pm daily. ♿

St. Francis of Assisi lived here in a hospice when he visited Rome in 1219, and his stone pillow and crucifix are preserved in his cell. The church was built by a follower, a local nobleman called Rodolfo Anguillara, who is portrayed on his tombstone wearing the Franciscan habit.

Entirely rebuilt in the 1680s by Cardinal Pallavicini, the church is rich in 17th- and 18th-century sculptures. Not to be missed in the Altieri chapel (fourth left, along the nave) is Bernini's exquisite late work, the *Ecstasy of Beata Ludovica Albertoni* (1674).

Bramante's circular Tempietto at San Pietro in Montorio

## 10 San Pietro in Montorio and the Tempietto

Piazza di San Pietro in Montorio 2. **Map** 5 B1. **Tel** 06 581 39 40. 🚌 44, 75, 115. **Open** 8am–noon & 3–4pm daily. Tempietto: **Tel** 06 581 28 06. **Open** 10am–6pm Tue–Sun.

The Tempietto, a diminutive masterpiece of Renaissance architecture completed by Bramante in 1502, stands in the courtyard of San Pietro in Montorio. The name means "little temple," and its circular shape echoes early Christian *martyria*, chapels built on the site of a saint's martyrdom. This was erroneously thought to be the spot in Nero's Circus where St. Peter was crucified. Bramante ringed the chapel with Doric columns, a Classical frieze, and a fine balustrade.

Bernini's *Ecstasy of Beata Ludovica Albertoni*, San Francesco a Ripa

# AVENTINE AND LATERAN

This is one of the greenest parts of the city, taking in the Celian and Aventine Hills, as well as the very congested area around San Giovanni in Laterano. The Celian, now scattered with churches, was a fashionable place to live in Imperial Rome. Some of the era's splendor is still apparent in the ruins of the Baths of Caracalla. Behind the Baths rises

the Aventine Hill, a peaceful, leafy area, with the superb basilica of Santa Sabina, and lovely views across the river to Trastevere and St. Peter's. In the valley below, cars and Vespas skim around the Circus Maximus, following the ancient charioteering track, while to the south lies Testaccio, a lively working-class district.

## Sights at a Glance

### Churches
2 Santa Maria in Cosmedin
3 Santa Maria in Domnica
4 Santo Stefano Rotondo
5 Santi Quattro Coronati
6 San Clemente *p439*
7 San Giovanni in Laterano *p440*
11 Santa Sabina

### Ancient Sites and Buildings
1 Temples of the Forum Boarium
8 Baths of Caracalla

### Monuments and Tombs
9 Pyramid of Caius Cestius
10 Protestant Cemetery

*See Rome Street Finder maps 6, 7, 8*

0 metres   250
0 yards    250

◀ The majestic interior of the cathedral of San Giovanni in Laterano

**For keys to symbols** *see back flap*

# Street by Street: Piazza della Bocca della Verità

The site of Rome's first port and its busy cattle market, this is an odd little corner of the city, stretching from the heavily trafficked road running along the Tiber to the southern spur of the Capitoline Hill, a place of execution from ancient times until the Middle Ages. Although best known for the Bocca della Verità (Mouth of Truth) in Santa Maria in Cosmedin, which is supposed to snap shut on the hands of liars, there are many other sites in the area, notably two temples from the Republican era. In the 6th century the area became home to a Greek community

**The Casa dei Crescenzi**, studded with ancient fragments, incorporates the ruins of a 10th-century tower built by the powerful Crescenzi family to guard the Tiber River.

that founded the churches of San Giorgio in Velabro and Santa Maria in Cosmedin.

**❶ ★ Temples of the Forum Boarium**
These two buildings are the best preserved of Rome's Republican temples.

**Sant'Omobono** stands on an archaeological site where finds date back to the 6th century.

**Ponte Rotto**, as this forlorn ruined arch in the Tiber is called, simply means "broken bridge." Built in the 2nd century BC, its original name was the Pons Aemilius.

**The Fontana dei Tritoni**, built by Carlo Bizzaccheri in 1715, shows the strong influence of Bernini.

**❷ ★ Santa Maria in Cosmedin**
The *Bocca della Verità*, a medieval drain cover, is set into the portico.

LUNGOTEVERE DEI PIERLEONI

TEVERE

PONTE PALATINO

PIAZZA DELLA BOCCA DELLA VERITÀ

VIA DI SAN GIOVANNI DECOLLATO

VIA DELLA G

**San Giovanni Decollato**
belonged to a confraternity that encouraged condemned prisoners to repent.

**Key**

— Suggested route

0 meters 75
0 yards 75

**Santa Maria della Consolazione** was named after an image of the Virgin placed here in 1385 to give consolation to the condemned.

**Locator Map**
*See Rome Street Finder map 6*

**San Teodoro** is a circular church on the edge of the Palatine with exceptional 6th-century apse mosaics.

**San Giorgio in Velabro**, a 7th-century basilica, was damaged in an explosion in 1994, and has now been restored.

**Arco degli Argentari**

DEI FIENILI

VIA DI SAN TEODORO

DEI CERCHI

**The 4th-century Arch of Janus**, a four-faced marble-plated arch at the edge of the Forum Boarium market, was an ideal place for merchants and customers to do business in the shade.

## ❶ Temples of the Forum Boarium

Piazza della Bocca della Verità. **Map** 6 E1. 🚌 23, 44, 81, 160, 170, 280, 628, 715, 716. **Open** 1st & 3rd Sun of month for guided tours only (**Tel** 06 3996 7700).

These wonderfully preserved Republican-era temples are at their best in moonlight, standing in their grassy enclave beside the Tiber, sheltered by umbrella pines. During the day, they look less romantic, stranded in a sea of traffic. They date from the 2nd century BC, and were saved from ruin by being consecrated as Christian churches in the Middle Ages by the Greek community then living in the area. The rectangular temple, formerly known as the Temple of Fortuna Virilis, was probably dedicated to Portunus, the god of rivers and ports. Set on a podium, it has four Ionic travertine columns fluted at the front and 12 half-columns embedded in the tufa wall of the *cella* – the room that housed the image of the god. In the 9th century the Temple was converted into the church of Santa Maria Egiziaca, after a 5th-century prostitute who reformed and became a hermit.

The smaller circular Temple, made of solid marble and surrounded by 20 fluted columns, was dedicated to Hercules, but long thought to be a Temple of Vesta because of its similarity to the one in the Forum.

The Ionic facade of the Republican-era Temple of Portunus

Apse mosaic from the 9th century of the Virgin and Child in Santa Maria in Domnica

## ❷ Santa Maria in Cosmedin

Piazza della Bocca della Verità. **Map** 6 E1. **Tel** 06 678 77 59. 🚌 23, 44, 81, 160, 170, 280, 628, 715, 716. **Open** 9:30am–6pm daily (5pm in winter). 🕇 👍 📷

This beautiful church was built in the 6th century on the site of the ancient city's food market. The Romanesque bell tower and portico were added during the 12th century. In the 19th century a Baroque facade was removed and the church was restored to its original simplicity. It contains many fine examples of Cosmati work, in particular the mosaic sidewalk, the raised choir, the bishop's throne, and the canopy over the main altar.

Set into the wall of the portico is the Bocca della Verità (Mouth of Truth), a grotesque marble face, thought to have been an ancient drain cover.

The nave of Santa Maria in Cosmedin with its Cosmati floor

Medieval tradition had it that the jaws would snap shut on liars – a useful way of testing the faithfulness of spouses.

## ❸ Santa Maria in Domnica

Piazza della Navicella 12. **Map** 7 A2. **Tel** 06 772 02 685. 🚌 81, 117, 673. Ⓜ Colosseo. **Open** 9am–noon, 3:30–7pm daily (until 6pm in winter). 👍

Santa Maria in Domnica was probably founded in the 7th century, and renovated in the 9th century. By this time the Romans had lost the art of making mosaics, so Pope Paschal I imported mosaicists from Byzantium. They created an exquisite apse mosaic showing the Virgin, Child, and angels in a delicate garden of paradise. Paschal I is kneeling at the Virgin's feet wearing a square halo, indicating that he was alive when it was made.

In 1513 Andrea Sansovino added a portico decorated with lions' heads, a punning homage to Pope Leo X.

## ❹ Santo Stefano Rotondo

Via di Santo Stefano Rotondo 7. **Map** 7 B2. **Tel** 06 42 11 99. 🚌 81, 117, 673. **Open** 9:30am–12:30pm & 3–6pm (2–5pm in winter) Tue–Sat; 9:30am–noon Sun. 📷

Santo Stefano Rotondo was built between 468 and 483 on a circular plan with four chapels in a cruciform shape. Its circular inner area is enclosed by two

concentric corridors. A third, outer corridor was demolished on the orders of Leon Battista Alberti in 1453. In the 1500s Niccolò Pomarancio, Antonio Tempesta, and others covered the walls with 34 frescoes of the martyrdoms of saints.

Cloister of Santi Quattro Coronati

## ❺ Santi Quattro Coronati

Via dei Santi Quattro Coronati 20. **Map** 7 B1. **Tel** 06 70 47 54 27. 🚌 85, 117, 810. 🚊 3. Basilica, Cloister, & Chapel of St. Sylvester: **Open** 10–11:45am & 4–5:45pm daily (Sun pm only). 👍

This fortified convent was built in the 4th century to house the relics of four Persian stonemasons, martyred after they refused to make a statue of the pagan god Aesculapius. It was rebuilt after invading Normans set fire to it in 1084.

Highlights are a delightful garden cloister and the Chapel of St. Sylvester, where 12th-century frescoes recount the legend of Emperor Constantine's conversion to Christianity.

# **San Clemente**

In 1857 Father Mullooly, the Irish Dominican prior of
San Clemente, began excavations beneath the existing
12th-century basilica. Directly underneath, he and his
successors discovered a 4th-century church, and below
that a number of ancient Roman buildings. Both basilicas
are dedicated to St. Clement, the fourth pope. On the
lowest level is a temple devoted to the cult of Mithras,
a mystical all-male religion imported from Persia which
rivaled Christianity for popularity.

**VISITORS' CHECKLIST**

**Practical Information**
Via di Labicana 95. **Map** 7 B1.
**Tel** 06 774 00 21.
**Open** 9am–12:30pm & 3–6pm
Mon–Sat (from noon Sun &
public hols). Last adm: 20 mins
before closing. 🖈 excavations.
🕇 🖾 🖼

**Transportation**
🚌 85, 87, 117, 186, 810.
Ⓜ Colosseo. 🚊 3.

**Cappella di Santa Caterina**
Restored frescoes by the
15th-century artist Masolino
da Panicale show scenes from
the life of St. Catherine of
Alexandria.

Entrance

**Apse Mosaic**
The 12th-century *Triumph
of the Cross* includes
finely detailed animals
and acanthus leaves.

**Paschal Candlestick**
This splendid 12th-
century spiraling
candlestick, striped
with glittering
multi-
colored
mosaic, is
the work of
the Cosmati.

12th-century
basilica

18th-century
facade

Piscina

Schola
Cantorum

4th-century basilica

Temple of
Mithras

**Life of San Clemente**
Faded frescoed episodes from
the life of the fourth pope
decorate the lower church.
This one tells the story of a
boy found alive in his tomb
under the sea.

**Triclinium**
An altar to the god
Mithras, showing him
slaying a bull, stands in the
dank triclinium, a room used
for ritual banquets by
cult members.

# ❼ San Giovanni in Laterano

San Giovanni, the cathedral of Rome, was founded by Emperor Constantine in the early 4th century. It has been rebuilt several times, notably in 1646, when Borromini restyled the interior, but retains its original basilica form. Before the papacy moved to Avignon in 1309, the adjoining Lateran Palace was the official papal residence. The present structure dates from 1589, but older parts survive, like the Scala Santa (Holy Staircase), which Christ is said to have climbed at his trial.

**VISITORS' CHECKLIST**

**Practical Information**
Piazza di San Giovanni in Laterano. **Map** 7 C2. **Tel** 06 69 88 64 93. Cathedral: **Open** 7am–6:30pm daily. Cloisters: **Open** 9am–6pm daily. Museum: **Open** 10am–5:30pm daily. Baptistery: **Open** 7am–12:30pm & 4–6:30pm daily.

**Transportation**
🚌 16, 81, 85, 87, 650. 🚊 3. Ⓜ San Giovanni.

**Baptistery**
Though much restored, the octagonal baptistery contains some beautiful 5th-century mosaics.

North facade

**East Facade**
The main entrance, on the east facade (1735), is adorned with statues of Christ and the Apostles.

Museum entrance

Apse

Lateran Palace

**Papal Altar**
The Gothic baldacchino, which rises over the papal altar, is decorated with 14th-century frescoes.

**On Maundy Thursday** the pope as Bishop of Rome gives a blessing the loggia of the city's main cathe

**The Corsini Chapel** was built in the 1730s for Pope Clement XII Corsini, who lies buried in a porphyry tomb from the Pantheon.

Main entrance

**Boniface VIII Fresco**
Possibly by Giotto, this fragment shows the pope announcing the Holy Year of 1300, which attracted around two million pilgrims.

**Cloisters**
Built by the Vassalletto family in about 1220, the cloisters are remarkable for their twisted columns and inlaid marble mosaics.

Part of one of the gymnasia in the Baths of Caracalla

## ❽ Baths of Caracalla

Viale delle Terme di Caracalla 52. **Map** 7 A3. **Tel** 06 39 96 77 00. 🚌 160, 628. 🚋 3. **Open** 9am–1 hour before sunset Tue–Sun, 9am–2pm Mon. **Closed** Jan 1, Dec 25. 🛇 🏛 🄋

Rearing up at the foot of the Aventine Hill are the monolithic red-brick ruins of the Baths of Caracalla. Begun by Emperor Septimius Severus in AD 206, and completed by his son Caracalla in AD 217, they remained in use until the 6th century, when the Goths sabotaged the city's aqueducts.

Going for a bath was one of the social events of the day in ancient Rome. Large complexes such as Caracalla, with a capacity for 1,600 bathers, were not simply places to have a chat and get washed, but also areas which offered an impressive array of amenities: art galleries, gymnasia, gardens, libraries, conference rooms, lecture rooms, and stores selling food and drink.

A Roman bath was a long and complicated business, beginning with a form of Turkish bath, followed by a spell in the *caldarium*, a large hot room with pools of water to moisten the atmosphere. Then came the lukewarm *tepidarium*, followed by a visit to the large central meeting place known as the *frigidarium*, and finally a plunge into the *natatio*, an outdoor swimming pool. For the rich, this was followed by a rubdown with scented woolen cloth.

Most of the rich marble decorations of the baths were scavenged by the Farnese family in the 16th century to adorn the rooms of Palazzo Farnese *(see p405)*. There are, however, statues and mosaics from the Baths in the Museo Archeologico Nazionale in Naples *(see pp494–5)* and in the Vatican's Gregorian Profane Museum *(see p426)*.

So dramatic is the setting that it is the regular venue for the outdoor summer opera season.

## ❾ Pyramid of Caius Cestius

Piazzale Ostiense. **Map** 6 E4. 🚌 23, 280. 🚋 3. Ⓜ Piramide. 🗝 only on 1st & 3rd Sat; call 06 574 31 93.

Caius Cestius was a wealthy but unimportant 1st-century BC *praetor*, or senior magistrate. At the time, inspired by the Cleopatra scandals, there was a craze for all things Egyptian, and Caius decided to commission himself a pyramid as a tomb. Set into the Aurelian Wall near Porta San Paolo, it is built of brick and faced with white marble; according to an inscription, it took just 330 days to build in 12 BC.

The Pyramid of Caius Cestius on Piazzale Ostiense

## ❿ Protestant Cemetery

Cimitero Acattolico, Via di Caio Cestio. **Map** 6 D4. **Tel** 06 574 19 00. 🚌 23, 280. 🚋 3. **Open** 9am–5pm Mon–Sat, 9am–1pm Sun. Last adm: 30 mins before closing. Donation.

Non-Catholics have been buried in this cemetery behind the Aurelian Wall since 1738. In the oldest part (on the left as you enter) is the grave of the poet John Keats, who died in 1821 in a house on Piazza di Spagna *(see p412)*. He wrote his own epitaph: "Here lies one whose name was writ in water." Close by rest the ashes of Percy Bysshe Shelley, who drowned in 1822.

The interior of Santa Sabina

## ⓫ Santa Sabina

Piazza Pietro d'Illiria 1. **Map** 6 D2. **Tel** 06 57 94 01. 🚌 23, 44, 170, 781. **Open** 8:15am–12:30pm & 3:30–6pm daily. ♿

High on the Aventine stands an early Christian basilica, founded by Peter of Illyria in AD 425 and later given to the Dominican order. It was restored to its original simplicity in the early 20th century. Light filters through 9th-century windows onto a nave framed by pale Corinthian columns. Above the main door is a blue and gold 5th-century mosaic inscription to Peter. In the side portico outside is a 5th-century paneled door carved with biblical scenes, notably one of the oldest images of the Crucifixion (top left-hand corner).

# Farther Afield

It is well worth making the effort to see some of Rome's outlying sights. Highlights are the Villa Giulia, home to a magnificent Etruscan museum, and the Museo Borghese on the splendid Villa Borghese estate, with its extraordinary collection of virtuoso statues by Bernini. Other sights range from ancient churches and catacombs to the more modern suburb of EUR, a strange architectural medley begun by Mussolini in the 1930s.

## Sights at a Glance

**Churches and Temples**
⑤ Sant'Agnese fuori le Mura
⑥ Santa Costanza
⑩ San Paolo fuori le Mura

**Museums and Galleries**
② Museo e Galleria Borghese
③ Villa Giulia
④ MAXXI

**Parks and Gardens**
① Villa Borghese

**Ancient Roads and Sites**
⑦ Via Appia Antica
⑧ Catacombs

**City Districts**
⑨ EUR

**Key**
▨ Central Rome
▢ Suburbs
▬ Highway
▬ Major road
▭ Minor road
— City walls

0 kilometers        3
0 miles             3

# ① Villa Borghese

**Map** 3 B1. 🚌 52, 53, 88, 116, 490. 🚋 3, 19. Park **Open** dawn–dusk daily.

The villa and its park were designed in 1605 for Cardinal Scipione Borghese, the sybaritic nephew of Pope Paul V. An extravagant patron of the arts, he amassed one of Europe's finest collections of paintings, statues, and antiquities, many of which are still displayed in the villa, which he built especially to house his antique sculptures.

The **park** was one of the first of its kind in Rome, its formal gardens divided by avenues and graced with statues. It contained 400 newly planted trees and garden sculpture by Bernini's father, Pietro, along with many ingenious fountains, "secret" flower gardens, enclosures of exotic animals and birds, and even a grotto with artificial rain. There was also a speaking robot and a trick chair, which trapped anyone who sat in it. At first the grounds were

open to the public, but after a visitor was shocked by the collection of erotic paintings, Paul V decided to keep the park private.

In 1773 work began on redesigning the park in the wilder, Romantic style made fashionable by landscape artists like Claude Lorrain and Poussin. Over the next few years, mock-Classical temples, fountains,

Temple of Aesculapius, an 18th-century folly, at the Villa Borghese

and *casine* (summerhouses) were added. In 1901, the park and villa were acquired by the state, and in 1911 the area was chosen as the site for the International Exhibition. Pavilions were built by many of the world's nations, the most impressive of which is the **British School at Rome** by Edwin Lutyens. In the north-eastern corner of the park lie the Museo Zoologico and a small redeveloped zoo, known as the Bioparco, where the emphasis is on conservation. Today the estates of the Villa Borghese, Villa Giulia, and the Pincio gardens form one vast park, with the **Giardino del Lago**, at its center, named after an artificial boating lake. Its main entrance is marked by an 18th-century copy of the Arch of Septimius Severus, while on the lake's island is a fake Ionic temple to the Greek god of health, Aesculapius, designed by the 18th-century architect Antonis Aspurucci.

A circular Temple of Diana folly lies between the Porta Pinciana, at the top of Via Veneto, and Piazza di Siena, a grassy amphitheater that hosts Rome's international horse show in May. Its umbrella pines inspired the composer Ottorino Respighi to write *The Pines of Rome* (1924). The outdoor opera season is also held in the park.

To the northwest of the park is the Galleria Nazionale d'Arte Moderna, and the Orangery is now home to the Carlo Bilotti Museum.

*Sacred and Profane Love* by Titian (1514), in the Galleria Borghese

# ❷ Museo e Galleria Borghese

Villa Borghese, Piazzale Scipione Borghese 5. **Tel** 06 328 10. 🚌 52, 53, 116, 910. 🚊 3, 19. **Open** 9am–7pm Tue–Sun (reservations required). **Closed** Jan 1, Dec 25. 🎫 (free 1st Sun of month). 🖼🔲📷🛍🎧♿ 🌐 **galleriaborghese.beniculturali.it**

Cardinal Scipione Borghese's villa was designed in 1605 as a typical Roman country house, with its wings projecting into the surrounding gardens. It was built by Flaminio Ponzio, Pope Paul V's architect, and was used by Scipione for entertaining guests and for displaying his impressive collection of paintings and sculpture. Between 1801 and 1809 Prince Camillo

Borghese, husband to Napoleon's sister Pauline, unfortunately sold many of the family paintings to his brother-in-law, and swapped 200 of Scipione's Classical statues for an estate in Piedmont. These statues are still in the Louvre and, as a consequence, the remaining antique Classical collection is less interesting than it might once have been. However, the hedonistic cardinal was an enthusiastic patron of the arts, and the sculptures he commissioned from artists such as the young Bernini now rank among their most famous works.

The eight rooms of the first floor of the Villa Borghese are set around a central hall, the Salone. The most famous statue, in room 3, is one of Bernini's finest works: *Apollo and Daphne* (1624) shows the nymph Daphne with bay leaves sprouting from her outstretched fingers, roots growing from her toes, and rough bark enfolding her smooth body, as she begins to metamorphose into a laurel tree to escape being abducted by the god Apollo. Abduction is also the theme of *The Rape of Proserpina*, again by Bernini, in room 4. Depicting Pluto, the god of the Underworld, carrying Proserpina, daughter of Ceres, off to be his bride, the sculpture is a virtuoso piece in which Bernini contrasts the taut musculature of Pluto with the soft, yielding flesh of Proserpina, whose thigh dimples in his iron grip.

The third famous Bernini piece, which dates from 1623, is *David* in room 2. The artist captures the tensed, grimacing youth the moment before he releases the stone that slew Goliath. It is said that Pope Urban VIII held a mirror up to Bernini so that the sculptor could model David's face on his own. In the next

Detail of *Rape of Proserpina* by Bernini (1622), Museo Borghese

alcove is the Villa Borghese's most infamous work – a sculpture, executed in 1805 by Canova, of Pauline Borghese as *Venus Victrix* (Venus the Conqueror). The semi-naked Pauline reclining on a chaise longue shocked those who saw it, and Pauline's husband kept the statue locked away, even denying Canova access to it. The next room holds a selection of antiquities, notably a Roman copy of a plump *Bacchus* by the 4th-century BC Greek sculptor Praxiteles, and fragments of a 3rd-century AD mosaic found on one of the Borghese estates in Torrenova, showing gladiators battling with wild animals.

The Galleria Borghese, on the upper floor, houses some magnificent Baroque and Renaissance paintings. Works on display include Raphael's masterpiece, the *Deposition*, various works by Caravaggio, the graceful *Danäe* by the 16th-century artist Correggio, as well as works by Pinturicchio, Barocci, Rubens, and Titian.

Bernini's *Apollo and Daphne* (1624)

# ❸ Villa Giulia

This villa was built in 1550 as a country retreat for Pope Julius III. Designed by Vignola and Ammannati, with contributions by Michelangelo and Vasari, it was intended for entertaining guests of the Vatican, such as Queen Christina of Sweden, rather than as a permanent home. The gardens were planted with 36,000 trees and peppered with pavilions and fountains. Villa Giulia also used to house an outstanding collection of sculptures: 160 boats filled with statues and ornaments were sent to the Vatican after the death of Pope Julius III in 1555.

Since 1889 the villa has been home to the Museo Nazionale Etrusco, an impressive collection of pre-Roman antiquities from central Italy.

**VISITORS' CHECKLIST**

**Practical Information**
Piazzale di Villa Giulia 9.
**Tel** 06 322 65 71.
**Open** 8:30am–7:30pm Tue–Sun (last adm: 6:30pm).
**Closed** Jan 1, Dec 25.
📷 with 7 days' notice.
🔲 ♿ 📷

**Transportation**
🚌 52. 🚊 3, 19.

**Rooms 31–36** contain finds from the Ager Faliscus, an area between the Tiber and Lake Bracciano.

**Rooms 14–21**, the Antiquarium collection, display domestic and votive objects and ceramics, including the Cima-Pesciotti collection.

**Ficoroni Cist**
Engraved and beautifully illustrated, this 4th-century-BC bronze marriage coffer held mirrors and other body care implements.

**Rooms 22–24** exhibit finds from the Castellani collection, including early 6th-century ceramics and bronzes.

**Spiraled Faliscan Crater**
Painted in the free style of the 4th century BC, this spiral-handled vase was used to hold wines or oil. The Falisci were an Italic tribe influenced by the Etruscans.

**Husband and Wife Sarcophagus**
This 6th-century-BC tomb from Cerveteri shows a deceased couple banqueting in the afterlife. Their tender expression bears witness to the skill of Etruscan artists.

Ninfeo
(Nympheum)

**Rooms 1–13b** are arranged by site, starting with Vulci (most importantly, articles from the Warrior's Tomb) and including finds from Cerveteri.

**Key to Floorplan**
- ▢ Lower ground floor
- ▢ First floor
- ▢ Second floor
- ▢ Nonexhibition space

**Rooms 37–40** exhibit finds from Veio, including the stunning Etruscan statue Apollo of Veii.

Entrance

MAXXI, the National Museum of 21st Century Arts, designed by Zaha Hadid

## ❹ MAXXI (National Museum of 21st Century Arts)

Villa Guido Reni 4A. **Tel** 06 320 19 54.
🚌 53, 217, 910. 🚋 2. **Open** 11am–7pm Tue–Sun (to 10pm Sat).
**Closed** May 1, Dec 25. ♿ ❒ ▣ 📷
🎦 (free up to age 14). 📖
**W** fondazionemaxxi.it

Along with the nearby Parco della Musica (see p449), MAXXI, the National Museum of 21st Century Arts, has put Rome on the contemporary arts map. Completed in 2009, it is located in a stunning building designed by architect Zaha Hadid. The museum showcases emerging Italian and international artists. An impressive amount of space is also given over to architecture.

## ❺ Sant'Agnese fuori le Mura

Via Nomentana 349. **Tel** 06 862 054 56.
🚌 60, 82, 90. **Open** 8am–7pm daily.
**Closed** late Oct–late Nov. 🎦 to catacombs. ♿ 📷

Sant'Agnese fuori le Mura was built in the 4th century above the crypt of the 13-year-old martyr St. Agnes, and although much altered it retains the form of the original basilica. According to legend it was founded by Constantine's daughter Constantia, who was cured from leprosy after sleeping beside Agnes's tomb.

In the 7th-century apse mosaic, St. Agnes appears as a bejeweled Byzantine empress in a stole of gold and a violet robe. Tradition has it that she appeared like this eight days after her death, holding a white lamb. On January 21, two lambs are blessed in the church and a vestment called a *pallium* is woven from their wool, to be given to a new archbishop.

Apse mosaic in Sant'Agnese, showing the saint flanked by popes

## ❻ Santa Costanza

Via Nomentana 349. **Tel** 06 862 054 56. 🚌 60, 82, 90. **Open** 9am–noon & 3–6pm daily (Sun pm only). **Closed** late Oct–late Nov. 🎦 ♿ 📷

This circular church was built in the early 4th century as a mausoleum for Emperor Constantine's daughters, Constantia and Helena. The dome and its drum are supported by an arcade that rests on 12 magnificent pairs of granite columns. The encircling ambulatory has a barrel-vaulted ceiling decorated with the world's earliest surviving Christian mosaics, which date from the 4th century.

In a niche on the far side of the church is a replica of Constantia's ornate porphyry sarcophagus, carved with cherubs crushing grapes.

The original was moved to the Vatican Museums in 1790. The sanctity of Constantia is somewhat debatable. Described by the historian Marcellinus as a fury incarnate, constantly goading her equally unpleasant husband, Hannibalianus, to violence, her canonization was probably the result of some confusion with a saintly nun of the same name.

## ❼ Via Appia Antica

🚌 118, 218.

The first part of the Via Appia was built in 312 BC by Appius Claudius Caecus. In 190 BC, when it was extended to the ports of Taranto and Brindisi, the road became Rome's link with its empire in the East. It was the route taken by the funeral processions of the dictator Sulla (78 BC) and Emperor Augustus (AD 14), and it was along this road that St. Paul was led as a prisoner to Rome in AD 56. The church of Domine Quo Vadis marks the spot where St. Peter is said to have met Christ when fleeing Rome. The road is lined with ruined family tombs, decaying monuments, and collective burial places (columbaria). Beneath the fields on either side lies a maze of catacombs, including those of San Callisto and San Sebastiano.

Cypresses lining the Roman road, Via Appia

## ❽ Catacombs

Via Appia Antica 126. 🚌 118, 218. San
Callisto: **Tel** 06 513 01 580. **Open** 9am–
noon & 2–5pm Thu–Tue. **Closed** Jan 1,
late Jan–late Feb, Easter Sun, Dec 25.
🅿️ ⛪ 📷 🎞️ ➰

In burying their dead in
underground cemeteries
outside the city walls, the early
Christians were simply obeying
the laws of the time. They were
not forced to use them because
of persecution, as later popular
myth has suggested. Many
saints were buried here, and the
catacombs later became shrines
and places of pilgrimage.

Today several catacombs are
open to the public. The vast
Catacombs of San Callisto,
hewn from volcanic tufa,
contain niches, or *loculi*, which
held two or three bodies, as
well as the burial places of
several early popes. Close by,
walls in the Catacombs of San
Sebastiano are covered in
graffiti invoking St. Peter and
St. Paul, whose remains may
once have been moved here.

Engraving of Christian ceremony in
Catacombs of San Callisto (AD 50)

## ❾ EUR

🚌 170, 671, 714. Ⓜ EUR Fermi, EUR
Palasport. Museo della Civiltà Romana,
Piazza G. Agnelli 10. **Tel** 06 06 08.
Museo della Civiltà Romana: closed for
restoration – call for details. 🅿️

The Esposizione Universale di
Roma (EUR), a suburb to the
south of the city, was originally
built for an international
exhibition, a kind of "Work
Olympics," that was planned
for 1942, but never took place

EUR's Palazzo della Civiltà del Lavoro, the
"Square Colosseum"

because of the outbreak of war.
The architecture was intended
to glorify Fascism, and as a
result the bombastic style of the
buildings can look overblown
and rhetorical to modern eyes.
Of all the buildings the best
known is probably the Palazzo
della Civiltà del Lavoro (the
Palace of the Civilization
of Work), an unmistakable
landmark for people arriving
from Fiumicino airport.

The scheme was eventually
completed in the 1950s.
Despite the area's dubious
architecture, EUR has been a
planning success, and people
are still keen to live here. As
well as residential housing, the
vast marble halls along the
wide boulevards are also home
to a number of government
offices and museums. Best
among the latter is the Museo
della Civiltà Romana, famous
for its casts of the reliefs from
the Column of Trajan, and for
a large-scale model
depicting

4th-century Rome with all
the buildings which then
stood within the Aurelian
walls. The south of the suburb
features a lake and shady park,
and the huge domed Palazzo
dello Sport, built for the
1960 Olympics.

## ❿ San Paolo fuori
le Mura

Via Ostiense 186. 🚌 23, 128, 170, 670,
761, 766, 769. Ⓜ San Paolo. **Tel** 06
4543 4185. **Open** 7am–6:30pm daily.
Cloister **Open** 8am–6:15pm daily. ⛪
♿ 📷

Today's church is a faithful if
soulless reconstruction of
the great 4th-century basilica
destroyed by fire in 1823. Only
a few fragments of the earlier
church survived, most notably
the cloister (1241), with its pairs
of colorful inlaid columns,
considered one of the most
beautiful in Rome.

Elsewhere, the triumphal arch
is decorated on one side with
heavily restored 5th-century
mosaics, and on the other with
mosaics by Pietro Cavallini. The
equally fine mosaics (1220) in
the apse represent the figures
of Christ with saints Peter, Paul,
Andrew, and Luke.

The most outstanding work
of art is the fine marble canopy
over the high altar, by Arnolfo di
Cambio (1285), with the possible
assistance of Pietro Cavallini.
Below the altar is the *confessio*
where it is alleged St. Paul was
once buried. To its right is an
impressive Paschal candlestick dating from the 12th
century by Nicolò di Angelo
and Pietro Vassalletto.

19th-century mosaic on facade of San Paolo fuori le Mura

# Shopping in Rome

Rome has always been a thriving center for design and shopping. In ancient times, the finest craftsmen were drawn to the city, and artifacts and products of all kinds, including gold, furs, and wine, were imported from far-flung corners of the empire to satisfy the needs of the wealthy local population. Shopping in Rome today in many ways reflects this diverse tradition. Italian designers have a well-deserved reputation for their luxuriously chic style in fashion, knitwear, and leather goods (especially shoes and purses), as well as in interior design, fabrics, ceramics, and glass. The artisan tradition is strong, and the love of good design filters through into the smallest items. Rome is not a city for bargains (although it is often better value than Florence or Milan), but the joys of window shopping here will offer plenty of compensation.

## Fashion

Italy is one of the leading lights in high fashion, or *alta moda*. Many famous designers may be based in Milan, but Rome is home to a cluster of sophisticated and internationally distinguished fashion houses. The most notable among them are probably **Fendi**, **Laura Biagiotti**, **Prada**, and **Valentino**, whose studio dominates Piazza Mignanelli.

But even for those unable to splash out on genuine designer gear, much fun can be gained from a stroll down the streets that radiate out from the Piazza di Spagna: some of the window displays here are truly spectacular.

Rome is not a good place to buy everyday wear, since there is a distinct lack of mid-price stores that bridge the gap between the dazzlingly priced *alta moda* designer exclusives and the ultracheap goods sold in markets. However, at **Discount dell'Alta Moda** you can find end-of-season designer labels at 50 percent less than the boutique prices.

## Books and Gifts

Rome offers huge scope for gift buying, both in the well-established tourist stores in the historic center and in smaller stores located in less frequented parts of the city that might not feature in your planned itinerary.

The central Via del Pellegrino is a street crammed with small specialty outlets, such as **Le Tre Ghinee**, which sells ceramics and glass objects. If you are more interested in contemporary design, visit the **Palazzo delle Esposizioni Arion**, where a wide range of objects by famous designers are available.

The **Feltrinelli International** bookstore has an excellent range of foreign-language fiction, as well as nonfiction covering various subjects, including Italian art and architecture, cooking, travel, and history. It also stocks some superb photographic, art, and film posters. For discount prices on books, try the secondhand stands in Via delle Terme di Diocleziano and in Largo della Fontanella di Borghese.

Near the Pantheon, the Florentine **Il Papiro** sells a great range of illustrious paper-based products, including diaries, notebooks, envelopes, and beautiful seal-and-wax sets that make ideal gifts.

Religious artifacts are readily available in bookstores near the main basilicas, such as the **Libreria Belardetti** near St. Peter's. Other stores specialize in religious items for both the clergy and the layperson. Facing the Vatican gates, in Via di Porta Angelica, there are several stores, including **Al Pellegrino Cattolico**, that sell mementos to visiting pilgrims.

## Food and Drink

If you are tempted to take home some irresistible Italian delicacies, such as pecorino romano cheese, Parma ham, extra virgin olive oil, dried porcini mushrooms, sun-dried tomatoes, olives, and grappa, as well as superb wines from Lazio and elsewhere, then the traditional food stores, *alimentari*, are a great place to start. Try the well-stocked **Fratelli Fabbi**, near Piazza di Spagna, with its exceptional selection of delicious cold meats and cheeses from every corner of Italy, as well as quality wines and champagnes. A few doors down on the same street is **Focacci**, with its wonderful array of Italian delicacies. The historic but expensive **Volpetti** in Testaccio is synonymous with great service and uncompromising quality. Aside from specializing in unusual cheeses, olive oils, vinegars, and a fabulous selection of food baskets, Volpetti also stocks a variety of Italian lard and caviar – you can even try before you buy.

In Pinciano, **Casa dei Latticini Micocci** sells a comprehensive range of cheeses from even the most remote regions of Italy, while in Trastevere, the family-run **Antica Caciara Trasteverina** has a vast assortment of local and regional dairy products, which include sheep's ricotta and the Piedmontese *toma del fen*. More local, reasonably priced cheeses are available at **Cisternino**.

If cakes and chocolate feature on your list, then there is plenty of opportunity to satisfy those cravings too. **Il Mondo di Laura**, in the Jewish ghetto, sells delicious homemade cookies, and cakes. The dark chocolate "Pepita" cookie is spectacular. **Moriondo e Gariglio** specializes in chocolate delights made to traditional Piedmontese recipes.

To find all of the above and more under one roof, head to **Eataly**, a temple to Italian food. Occupying an entire section of the Ostiense train station, Eataly is filled with the finest Italian food products available on the market. Do check importing restrictions before purchasing.

## Markets

Rome's outdoor markets are quintessential examples of the bubbling exuberance and earthiness for which Romans are renowned. They are wonderfully vivid experiences, too, since Italian vendors have raised the display of even the humblest vegetable to an art form.

The city is dotted with small local food markets, and there are several fascinating well-established markets near the center. These include **Campo de' Fiori** for foodstuffs, the **Mercato delle Stampe** for old prints, books, and magazines, and the **Nuovo Mercato Esquilino** for international foods.

Trastevere's famous flea market, **Porta Portese**, was established shortly after the end of World War II and is said to have grown out of the thriving black market that operated at

Tor di Nona, opposite Castel Sant'Angelo, during those lean years. Anything and everything seems to be for sale, piled high on stands in carefully arranged disorder – clothes, shoes, bags, linen, luggage, camping equipment, towels, pots, pans, kitchen utensils, plants, pets, cassettes and CDs, old LPs, and 78s.

If you are looking for a traditional food market in the heart of the old city, Rome's most picturesque market is also its most historical. Its name, Campo de' Fiori *(see p405)*, which translates as "field of flowers," sometimes misleads people into expecting a flower market. In fact, the name is said to derive from *Campus Florae* ("Flora's Square") – Flora being the lover of the great Roman general Pompey. A market has been held in this beautiful

central piazza for many centuries. Every morning, except Sunday, the piazza is transformed by an array of stands selling fruit and vegetables, meat, poultry, and fish. One or two stands also specialize in legumes, rice, and dried fruits and nuts.

Throughout the year Rome also plays host to many street fairs. If they coincide with your visit, these are fun to go to, because they normally sell a good variety of local produce, handicrafts, and clothes. Seasonal fairs also occur, especially around Christmas; among them is **Mercatino di Natale** in Piazza Navona, where you can stock up on toys and Nativity figurines.

Be sure to keep your wits about you at markets: pickpockets work with lightning speed in the bustling crowds.

# DIRECTORY

## Fashion

### Discount dell'Alta Moda
Via di Gesù e Maria 14 & 16A. **Map** 2 F2.
**Tel** 06 322 50 06.

### Fendi
Largo Goldoni 419.
**Map** 10 E3.
**Tel** 06 33 45 01.

### Laura Biagiotti
Via Mario de' Fiori 26.
**Map** 10 F1.
**Tel** 06 679 12 05.

### Prada
Via Condotti 88.
**Map** 3 A2.
**Tel** 06 679 08 97.

### Valentino
Piazza di Spagna 38.
**Map** 3 A2.
**Tel** 06 945 157 10.

## Books and Gifts

### Feltrinelli International
Via VE Orlando 84–6.
**Map** 3 C3.
**Tel** 06 482 78 78.

### Libreria Belardetti
Via della Conciliazione 4A.
**Map** 1 C3.
**Tel** 06 686 55 02.

### Il Mondo di Laura
Via del Portico d'Ottavia 6.
**Map** 2 F5.
**Tel** 06 68 80 61 29.

### Palazzo delle Esposizioni Arion
Via Milano 15–17.
**Map** 3 B4.
**Tel** 06 48 91 33 61.

### Il Papiro
Via del Pantheon 50 (leading to Via degli Orfani).
**Map** 10 D2.
**Tel** 06 679 55 97.

### Al Pellegrino Cattolico
Via di Porta Angelica 83.
**Map** 1 C2.
**Tel** 06 68 80 23 51.

### Le Tre Ghinee
Via del Pellegrino 90.
**Map** 2 E4.
**Tel** 06 687 27 39.

## Food and Drink

### Antica Caciara Trasteverina
Via San Francesco a Ripa 140A/B.
**Map** 5 C1.
**Tel** 06 581 28 15.

### Casa dei Latticini Micocci
Via Collina 14. **Map** 4 D2.
**Tel** 06 474 17 84.

### Cisternino
Vicolo del Gallo 18–19.
**Map** 9 C4.
**Tel** 06 687 28 75.

### Eataly
Piazzale XII Ottobre.
**Map** 6 F5.
**Tel** 06 90 27 92 01.

### Focacci
Via della Croce 43.
**Map** 2 F2.
**Tel** 06 679 12 28.

### Fratelli Fabbi
Via della Croce 27.
**Map** 2 F2.
**Tel** 06 679 06 12.

### Moriondo e Gariglio
Via del Piè di Marmo 21.
**Map** 10 E3.
**Tel** 06 699 08 56.

### Volpetti
Via Marmorata 47.
**Map** 6 D2.
**Tel** 06 574 23 52.

## Markets

### Campo de' Fiori
Piazza Campo de' Fiori.

**Map** 2 E4 & 9 C4.
**Open** 7am–1:30pm Mon–Sat.

### Mercatino di Natale
Piazza Navona.
**Map** 9 C4.
**Open** end Nov–early Jan: daily.

### Mercato delle Stampe
Largo della Fontanella di Borghese.
**Map** 2 F3 & 10 D1.
**Open** 9am–1pm Mon–Sat.

### Nuovo Mercato Esquilino
Via Principe Amedeo.
**Map** 4 E4.
**Open** 9am–2pm Mon–Fri.

### Porta Portese
Via Portuense & Via Ippolito Nievo.
**Map** 5 C3.
**Open** 6:30am–2pm Sun.

# Entertainment in Rome

There's a particular excitement attached to entertainment in Rome. Soccer and opera, for example, are worth experiencing for sheer atmosphere alone, whether or not you are a fan. There is also a good jazz scene, with international stars appearing alongside local talent. Unexpectedly, given the general shutdown among stores and restaurants, the summer is Rome's liveliest time in terms of entertainment and cultural events, with the city's Renaissance squares, vast parks, villa gardens, Classical ruins, and other open spaces hosting various arts festivals. Concerts and movies take on an added dimension when performances take place beneath the stars in the many outdoor arenas across the city. Rome also has plenty of nightclubs to choose from.

## Practical Information

Good sources of information about what's happening are the listings magazine WHERE Rome and Trovaroma, the weekly Thursday supplement to La Repubblica newspaper. Also worth getting hold of is L'Evento, available from the Rome Tourist Office (see p617), which gives details in English for cultural events in the city.

## Buying Tickets

Among the ticket agencies that will book seats for some performances for you (for a small fee) are **Orbis** and **Box Office**. Many theaters do not accept telephone reservations – you have to visit the box office in person. They will charge you a prevendita supplement (about 10 percent of the normal price) for any tickets sold in advance. The **Teatro dell'Opera** box office handles sales for both summer and winter seasons. Tickets for most big rock and jazz events can be bought at Orbis and at larger record stores, such as **Ricordi Media Store**. Look out for due per uno coupons in local bars – these allow two people entrance for the price of one.

## Outdoor Entertainment

Outdoor opera, movies, classical music, and jazz concerts fill the Roman calendar from late June through the end of September. Both the **Cineporto**, a festival held along the Tiber, at the

Ponte Milvio, and the **Festival di Massenzio**, at the Forum, offer movies, live music, food, and small exhibitions in July and August. The summer months also bring excellent outdoor rock, jazz, and world-music festivals, while Rome's main autumn performing-arts festival, **RomaEuropa**, has occasional performances on the grounds of the Villa Medici. Theater also moves outside in the summer months, and some movie theaters roll back their ceilings for open-air screenings.

More traditional is Trastevere's community festival, the **Festa de Noantri** (see p71), with music, processions, and fireworks. This religious festival begins on the Saturday after July 16, and celebrations continue until the end of the month.

## Classical Music and Dance

Classical concerts take place in a surprising number of venues. Tickets for opera premieres may be hard to find, but soloists, groups, or orchestras playing in gardens, churches, villas, or ancient ruins are more accessible.

World-renowned soloists and orchestras make appearances throughout the year in venues such as the Renzo Piano-designed **Parco della Musica** and the **Accademia Filarmonica Romana**. Past visitors have included Luciano Pavarotti and Placido Domingo, the Berlin Philharmonic, and prima ballerina

Sylvie Guillem. One of the most innovative programs of classical and contemporary music is provided by the **Aula Magna dell'Università La Sapienza**. The opera season starts late at the **Teatro dell'Opera**, between November and January. The great ballet classics are also staged at this venue. The **Equilibrio Festival** in February brings contemporary dance to the city; performances take place mainly at the Parco della Musica.

## Rock, Jazz, and World Music

Rome's nonclassical music scene is unpredictable and subject to vast seasonal changes. However, there is a huge variety of music at the many clubs and stadiums, such as the **Palalottomatica** and the **Stadio Olimpico**, which attract foreign and homegrown stars. The best jazz musicians play at the splendid **Casa del Jazz**, and at **Alexanderplatz**. Trastevere's **Big Mama** is one of the city's legendary addresses for important jazz names, while world music is well served at the aptly named **Rome Meets the World** summer festival in Villa Ada.

For smaller venues you might need to buy a monthly or annual membership card (between €2 and €11), which often includes the entrance fee for smaller bands.

## Film and Theater

Moviegoing is a popular pastime in Rome, with around 40 movies showing on an average weekday. Most Roman movie theaters are prima visione (first run) and show the latest international releases in dubbed versions. The best theaters for decor and comfort are the **Fiamma** (two screens) and the **Barberini** (three screens). Movies in their original language are often shown at the excellent **Casa del Cinema** and at the **Nuovo Olimpia**. Smaller art movie theaters, such as the **Azzurro Scipioni**, are more likely to show subtitled versions of foreign movies.

Theater productions are performed in Italian whether the plays are national classics or by foreign playwrights. The main theaters – **Teatro Argentina**, **Teatro Quirino**, and the **Eliseo** – offer a selection by great Italian playwrights. There are also performances of traditional cabaret, dance, and avant-garde theater at the **Teatro India**. Theater tickets cost between €8 and €50 and can generally be reserved only in advance, by visiting the theater box office in person or through agencies such as Box Office.

## Nightlife

Rome's nightlife has never been as vibrant as it is today, with a sharp rise in the number of bars and clubs, all catering to an ever more demanding clientele.

Once the choice was limited to a few well-established bars in the center and the hugely popular clubs in the Ostiense area and in San Lorenzo, such as the unashamedly commercial **Goa** or the more cutting-edge **Locanda Atlantide**, which hosts a whole range of DJs from funk to reggae. Now, though, the capital offers a wide range of options designed to satisfy all tastes and budgets.

Head first to a stylish pre-clubbing venue such as **'Gusto**, where you can rub shoulders with out-on-the-town locals taking advantage of the range of amenities – on three sites there is a restaurant, a pizzeria, a wine bar, and live music. Or, for a more leisurely start to your evening, simply relax in a wine bar on one of the historic center's breathtaking squares.

If you are looking for a gay venue, **Coming Out**, near the Colosseum, attracts both gay and straight drinkers, and **Planet Roma** just off Via Ostiense regularly hosts gay nights.

For an alternative edge to Rome's vivacious nightlife, try out the *centri sociali*, illegally occupied buildings that have been converted into arts and entertainment centers. Top billing goes to **Brancaleone**, which features Italian and international DJs for the best in electronic and house spins.

A night out in Rome can be expensive – you can be charged as much as €10 for a cocktail in the bars around the central parts of Rome. For a cheaper alternative, visit one of the many bars in the area around San Lorenzo.

# DIRECTORY

## Buying Tickets

**Box Office**
Largo di Torre Argentina 11 (inside Feltrinelli bookstore). **Map** 10 D4.
**Tel** 06 94 36 47 67.

**Orbis**
Piazza dell'Esquilino 37.
**Map** 4 D4. **Tel** 06 482 74 03. **W** boxofficelazio.it

**Ticketeria**
**W** ticketeria.it

## Classical Music and Dance

**Accademia Filarmonica Romana**
Via Flaminia 118.
**Tel** 06 320 17 52.
**W** filarmonica romana.org

**Aula Magna dell'Università La Sapienza**
Piazzale Aldo Moro 5.
**Map** 4 F3. **Tel** 06 361 00 51. **W** concertiiuc.it

**Parco della Musica**
Viale de Coubertin 30.
**Tel** 06 80 24 12 81 (info); 89 29 82 (credit card sales).
**W** auditorium.com

**RomaEuropa**
Via dei Magazzini Generali 20a (and other locations).
**Tel** 06 45 55 30 50.
**W** romaeuropa.net

**Teatro dell'Opera**
Piazza Beniamino Gigli 1.
**Map** 3 C3.
**Tel** 06 48 16 01.
**W** operaroma.it

## Rock, Jazz, and World Music

**Alexanderplatz**
Via Ostia 9. **Map** 1 B1.
**Tel** 06 83 77 56 04.

**Big Mama**
Vicolo San Francesco a Ripa 18. **Map** 5 C2.
**Tel** 06 581 25 51.

**Casa del Jazz**
Viale di Porta Ardeatina 55.
**Map** 7 A4.
**Tel** 06 06 08.
**W** casajazz.it

**Palalottomatica**
Piazzale Plerluigi Nervi.
**Tel** 06 54 09 01.

**Rome Meets the World**
Villa Ada, Via Salaria.
**W** villaada.org

**Stadio Olimpico**
Viale dei Gladiatori (north-west of city center, across the Tiber by Monte Mario).

## Film and Theater

**Azzurro Scipioni**
Via degli Scipioni 82.
**Map** 1 C2.
**Tel** 06 39 73 71 61.

**Barberini**
Piazza Barberini 24.
**Map** 3 B3.
**Tel** 06 86 39 13 61.

**Casa del Cinema**
Largo Mastroianni 1.
**Map** 3 B1. **Tel** 06 423 601.
**W** casadelcinema.it

**Eliseo**
Via Nazionale 183. **Map** 3 B4. **Tel** 06 88 80 12 84.

**Fiamma**
Via Bissolati 47. **Map** 3 C2.
**Tel** 06 48 55 26.

**Nuovo Olimpia**
Via in Lucina 16.
**Map** 10 E1.
**Tel** 06 88 80 12 83.

**Teatro Argentina**
Largo di Torre Argentina 56. **Map** 2 F4.
**Tel** 06 684 00 03 11.
**W** teatrodiroma.net

**Teatro India**
Lungotevere Vittorio Gassman 1. **Map** 5 C5.
**Tel** 06 684 00 03 11.

**Teatro Quirino**
Via delle Vergini 7.
**Map** 3 B3 & 10 F2.
**Tel** 06 679 45 85.
**W** teatroquirino.it

## Nightlife

**Brancaleone**
Via Levanna 13
(in Montesacro).
**Tel** 06 82 00 43 82.

**Coming Out**
Via San Giovanni in Laterano 8. **Map** 7 B1.
**Tel** 06 700 98 71.

**Goa**
Via Libetta 13 (in Ostiense)
**Tel** 06 574 82 77.
**W** goaclub.com

**'Gusto**
Piazza Augusto Imperatore 9. **Map** 2 F2.
**Tel** 06 6813 4221.

**Locanda Atlantide**
Via dei Lucani 22b (San Lorenzo district).
**Tel** 06 96 04 58 75.

**Planet Roma**
Via del Commercio 36–8.
**Map** 6 D5. **Tel** 06 574 78 26.

# ROME STREET FINDER

Map references given with sights described in the Rome chapters relate to the maps on the following pages. Map references are also given for hotels *(see pp573–6)* and restaurants *(see pp596–600)* and for useful addresses in the *Travelers' Needs* and *Survival Guide* sections at the back of the book. The first figure in the map reference tells you which Street Finder map to turn to,

and the letter and number that follow refer to the grid reference on that map. The small map below shows the area of Rome covered by each of the eight maps, and the corresponding map number is given in black. All the major sights are sketched out on the maps, and symbols, listed in the key below, are used to indicate the location of other important buildings.

0 kilometers               2

0 miles                  1

**Key and Scale for Street Finder Pages**

| | |
|---|---|
| Major sight | Synagogue |
| Place of interest | Railroad track |
| **FS** Train station | City walls |
| **M** Metro station | Pedestrian-only street |
| Streetcar stop | |
| **i** Tourist information | |
| Hospital with emergency room | |
| Police station | |
| Church | |

**Scale of Maps 1–8**

0 meters         250

0 yards          250

1:12,000

**Scale of Maps 9–10**

0 meters         150

0 yards          150

1:7,600

# Rome Bus Routes

# LAZIO

Lying between the Apennines and the Tyrrhenian Sea, Lazio is a varied region of volcanic lakes, mountains, ravines, vineyards, and olive groves. Before the rise of Rome, it was populated by the Etruscans and various Italic tribes, including the Latins, after whom the region is named. Besides its archaeological sites, Lazio also offers skiing, and swimming and water sports in the lakes and sea.

Lazio was inhabited at least 60,000 years ago, although the first signs of a substantial civilization date back to the 10th century BC. By the 7th century BC a flourishing Etruscan and Sabine civilization based on trade and agriculture existed in the north, while the region's southern margins were colonized by the Latins, Volsci, and Hernici. History mingles with myth in the writings of Virgil, who describes how Aeneas landed in Lazio, where he married the daughter of the king of the Latins. Romulus and Remus (legendary founders of Rome) were descendants of this alliance.

With the rise of Rome as a power, the Etruscan and Latin peoples were, in time, overwhelmed and the focus of the region turned to the city of Rome. Great roads and aqueducts extended out of the city like spokes of a wheel, and wealthy patricians built lavish villas in the surrounding countryside.

The early Middle Ages saw the rise of the Church's temporal power and, with the foundation of monasteries at Subiaco and Montecassino, Lazio became the cradle of western monasticism, and eventually part of the Papal States. In the 16th and 17th centuries, wealthy papal families competed with one another to build luxurious villas and gardens, hiring some of the best architects of the Renaissance and Baroque.

Throughout its history, however, Lazio has been eclipsed and neglected by Rome. The Pontine marshes were a malaria-ridden swamp until the 1920s, when Mussolini had them drained and brought new highways and agricultural improvements to the area.

The courtyard at the Benedictine Abbey of Montecassino

◄ Civita di Bagnoregio, a small hill-town in Viterbo

# Exploring Lazio

Much of Lazio's landscape was formed by the eruption of four volcanoes, which showered the area with lava. Lakes formed in the craters, and the soil, rendered fertile by the lava, nourished vines, olives, fruit, and nut trees. The volcanic activity also left Lazio with hot springs, notably around Tivoli, Viterbo, and Fiuggi. Rome dominates the area, dividing the wooded hills of the north from the reclaimed Pontine marshes in the south. Swimming and sailing are possible in lakes Bracciano, Bolsena, and Albano, while Lazio's best beaches lie between Gaeta and Sabaudia in the Parco Nazionale del Circeo.

## Sights at a Glance

1. Tuscania
2. Viterbo
3. Montefiascone
4. Bomarzo
5. Caprarola
6. Tarquinia
7. Cerveteri
8. Lake Bracciano
9. Ostia Antica
10. Frascati and the Castelli Romani
11. Tivoli
12. Palestrina
13. Subiaco
14. Montecassino
15. Anagni
16. Sermoneta and Ninfa
17. Terracina
18. Sperlonga
19. Gaeta

The Tolfa hills southwest of Lake Bracciano

## Key

═══ Freeway
═══ Major highway
═ ═ Road under construction
─── Secondary road
∷∷∷ Minor road
─── Scenic route
╍╍╍ Main railroad line
─── Minor railroad line
╍╍╍ Regional border
△ Summit

**For additional map symbols** *see back flap*

Whitewashed houses in Sperlonga's Old Town

## Getting Around

Rome's two international airports at Fiumicino and Ciampino serve the region. The main freeways are the *Autostrada del Sole* Firenze–Roma (A1) and Roma–Napoli (A1–E45), and the Roma–L'Aquila (A24–E80). The beltway *(raccordo anulare)* around Rome connects the freeways and main highways.

The Lazio bus service, COTRAL, serves all the main towns with changeover points for the smaller locations in Rome and at Latina, Frosinone, Viterbo, and Rieti. Train routes into the region from other Italian cities are efficient, although within Lazio the services are slower and less frequent.

The medieval Porta del Sole (Sun Gate), at the entrance of Palestrina

Ascoli Piceno
Accumoli
Cittareále
Amatrice
Leonessa S4
*Monti Reatini*
Posta
Monte Terminillo △ 2216m
cio
Rieti
Antrodoco
S17
L'Aquila
Monte Nuria △ 1888m
Concerviano
*Lago del Salto*
Fiamignano
*Lago di Turano*
Borgorose
telibretti
ricone Orvinio
S4
*Salto*
Licenza
A24 S5
a Cervara di Roma
*Monti Simbruini*
Avezzano
TIVOLI
a Adriana
**13** SUBIACO
Avezzano
Arcinazzo Romano
L A Z I O
**12** PALESTRINA
CATI
*Monti Ernici*
Guarcino
*Crociaria*
S155
Alatri
ANAGNI **15**
Segni
Ferentino
Sora
S6
Monte Petroso △ 2247m
elletri
*Monti Lepini*
S214
Arpino
Picinisco
Frosinone
S6
Arce
Atina
Cardito
Ninfa
Pofi
Ceprano
Monte Cairo 1669m
**16** SERMONETA
Prossedi
**14** MONTECASSINO
tina
Priverno
*Liri*
S156
Pontecorvo
S6 A1
*Pontino*
Pontinia
Sonnino
Pico
*Gariglano*
Lago gliano
S148 S7
*Sisto*
Fondi
Esperia
S630
Napoli
Sabaudia
*Monti Ausoni*
*Monti Aurunci*
Lago di Sabaudia
**17** TERRACINA
Itri
Formia
Minturno
Capo Circeo
**18** S213
Pozzuoli
SPERLONGA
**19** GAETA
*Golfo di Gaeta*
sola marola
Isola Zannone
*Isole Ponziane*

0 kilometres 15
0 miles 10

Carved loggia of the Palazzo Papale, Viterbo

# ❶ Tuscania

Viterbo. 🚗 8,200. 🚌 ℹ️ Piazzale Trieste (0761 445 42 59). 🕐 Fri am.

Tuscania's trim walls and towers are visible from afar on the empty low-lying plains between Viterbo and Tarquinia. Although shaken by an earthquake in 1971, its medieval and Renaissance buildings have since been carefully reconstructed. Just outside the city walls, on the rocky Colle San Pietro, two remarkable churches dating from the Lombard-Romanesque period occupy the site of Tuscana, a major Etruscan center conquered by Rome in 300 BC.

**Santa Maria Maggiore**, at the foot of the hill, has a typically Lombard-Romanesque asymmetric facade with blind arcades and a bold rose window. Over the central door lies a simple marble Madonna and Child, framed by abstract motifs and biblical scenes. Inside, a rare 12th-century full-immersion baptism font stands in the aisle. The Lombard-Romanesque church of **San Pietro**, on top of the hill, is a striking building of ochre-hued tufa and white marble details. It stands on a grassy piazza, along with two medieval towers and a bishop's palace. The facade features an intricately inlaid rose window flanked by strange reliefs, including three-headed bearded demons. The interior is true to its 8th-century form, with squat columns, toothed arches, capitals carved with stylized plants, and a Cosmati floor. Below the church lies a strange mosque-like crypt.

Facade of San Pietro, Tuscania

# ❷ Viterbo

🚗 63,000. 🚆 🚌 ℹ️ Via Ascenzi 1 (0761 32 59 92). 🕐 Sat. 🌐 **visit. viterbo.it**

Viterbo was an important Etruscan center before falling to the Romans in the 4th century BC. Its heyday, however, came in the 13th century, when it briefly became the papal seat (1257–81). During World War II it was devastated, but the austere gray-stone medieval core and many of the town's churches, have been carefully restored.

In **San Pellegrino**, Viterbo's oldest and best-preserved quarter, medieval houses with towers, arches and external staircases line narrow streets running between little piazzas decorated with fountains.

On Piazza San Lorenzo the 12th-century **Duomo** boasts an elegant black-and-white-striped bell tower, a solemn 16th-century facade and a stark Romanesque interior. The adjacent 13th-century **Palazzo Papale**, with a finely carved loggia, was built for popes on their visits to the city.

The town's civic buildings border the main square, Piazza del Plebiscito. The most interesting is the 15th-century **Palazzo dei Priori**, frescoed inside by Baldassare Croce with scenes from the town's history and mythological past.

Outside the city walls, on Viale Capocci, the Romanesque **Santa Maria della Verità** has wonderful 15th-century frescoes by Lorenzo da Viterbo.

Villa Lante's small but splendid Renaissance gardens, considered Vignola's masterpiece

## Environs

The **Villa Lante**, northeast of Viterbo, was begun in 1562 by Vignola for Cardinal Gambara. The main attractions are the Renaissance gardens and fountains. Be careful not to fall victim to a 16th-century practical joke: many of the fountains will sprinkle people without warning.

**Palazzo dei Priori**
Piazza Plebiscito. **Tel** 0761 30 47 95.
**Open** daily.

**Villa Lante**
Bagnaia. **Tel** 0761 28 80 08. **Open** 8:30am to 1 hour before sunset Tue–Sun. **Closed** Jan 1, May 1, Dec 25.
to gardens.

Carved 11th-century capital in San Flaviano, Montefiascone

## ❸ Montefiascone

Viterbo. 13,000. Piazza V. Emanuele (0761 83 20 60). Wed.

This pretty town is perched on the edge of a defunct volcanic crater between the shores of Lake Bolsena, over which there are splendid views, and the Via Cassia. It is dominated by the octagonal bulk of its cathedral, **Santa Margherita**, whose dome, created in the 1670s by Carlo Fontana, is second only in size to St. Peter's.

On the town's outskirts, along the Via Cassia toward Orvieto, lies **San Flaviano**, a lovely two-level building with a 12th-century church oriented east over an 11th-century church pointing west. Inside are some fine 14th-century frescoes and freely carved capitals, thought to have been inspired by the traditions of Etruscan art.

The main facade of the pentagonal Palazzo Farnese at Caprarola

## Environs

The popular lakeside beach resort of **Bolsena**, 9 miles (15 km) north on Lake Bolsena, has a medieval castle, as well as boats to the islands of Bisentina and Martana.

## ❹ Bomarzo

Parco dei Mostri, Bomarzo.
**Tel** 0761 92 40 29. to Viterbo.
from Viterbo (not Sun or public hols). **Open** 8:30am–sunset in winter (8:30am–7pm in summer).
**sacrobosco.it**

The Sacro Bosco beneath the town of Bomarzo was created between 1522 and 1580 by Duke Vicino Orsini as a bizarre memorial to his late wife. Far from a simple monument, Orsini embraced the artificiality and distortion of the Mannerist period by creating lopsided buildings and sculpting huge boulders of stone into fantastic creatures and vast allegorical monsters.

One of the bizarre stone monsters in Bomarzo's Sacro Bosco

## ❺ Caprarola

Viterbo. 5,700. Via Filippo Nicolai 2 (0761 64 79 41). Tue.

Perhaps the grandest of the country villas created during the 17th century by the wealthy families of Rome, **Palazzo Farnese** (see p384) is the focal point of the medieval village of Caprarola. Designed by Vignola, it was built between 1559 and 1575 and takes its star shape from the foundations of a large pentagonal fortress designed by Antonio da Sangallo the Younger half a century earlier. On the main floor, reached by an elaborately stuccoed spiral staircase, the rooms were frescoed, largely by the Zuccari brothers in 1560, with scenes depicting heroic episodes from the life of Hercules and the Farnese family.

## Environs

Created, according to legend, by the god Hercules ramming his club into the ground, **Lago di Vico**, 3 miles (5 km) west of Caprarola, in fact occupies the remnants of a volcanic crater. An idyllic enclave, the lake is encircled by the wooded slopes of the Cimini Hills (much of which is a nature preserve). A scenic road runs around the lake, and the best place for swimming is on the southeast shore.

**Palazzo Farnese**
Caprarola. **Tel** 0761 64 60 52. **Open** Tue–Sun. **Closed** Jan 1, Dec 25.

Etruscan tumulus tombs from the necropolis at Cerveteri

## ❻ Tarquinia

Viterbo. 🚗 15,000. 🚉 🚌 ℹ️ Barriera di San Giusto (0766 84 92 82). 🛒 Wed.

Ancient Tarquinia (Tarxuna) was one of Etruria's most important centers. It occupied a strategic position to the northeast of the present town, on a ridge dominating the coastal plain, until the 4th century BC, when it fell to Rome.

Tarquinia itself is worth a wander for its crumbling medieval churches and spacious main square, though the main reason to visit is the **Museo Archeologico e Necropoli**, which has one of Italy's better collections of Etruscan finds. Reclining statues of the deceased adorn the sarcophagi on the first floor, but the star attraction is a group of terra-cotta winged horses dating from the 4th century BC.

On a hilltop 1 mile (2 km) southeast of town are the frescoed tombs of the **necropolis** dug into the soft volcanic tufa. There are almost 6,000 tombs, but only about 15 can be visited at a time.

Dancers from the 4th-century-BC frescoed Tomba del Triclinio in the Museo Archeologico, Tarquinia

The frescoes that decorate them, designed to remind the dead of life, range from frenetic dancing figures in the Tomba delle Leonesse to the diners reclining in the Tomba dei Leopardi.

### 🏛️ Museo Archeologico e Necropoli

Piazza Cavour. **Tel** 0766 85 00 80 or 0766 84 00 00 (necropolis). **Open** Tue–Sun. **Closed** Jan 1, May 1, Dec 25. 🖼️ ♿

## ❼ Cerveteri

Roma. 🚗 36,000. 🚉 🚌 ℹ️ Piazza Risorgimento 19 (06 99 55 19 71). 🛒 Fri.

In the 6th century BC Cerveteri (ancient Kysry) was one of the largest and most culturally rich towns of the Mediterranean, trading with Greece and controlling a large area along the coast. The **necropolis**, a city of the dead 1 mile (2 km) outside town, is a network of streets lined with tombs dating from the 7th to the 1st century BC. Some of the larger tumulus tombs, like the Tomba degli Scudi e delle Sedie, are arranged like houses, with rooms, doors, and corridors. The Tomba dei Rilievi is decorated with plaster reliefs of tools, pets, and mythological figures. Although the best finds from the necropolis are in museums such as the Vatican Museums, Villa Giulia, and the British Museum in London, some can be seen in the small **Museo Nazionale Cerite** in the center of town.

#### Environs

There are more traces of the Etruscans to be seen at **Norchia**, where the tombs are carved out of a rock face, and **Sutri**, whose amphitheater is one of the few relics of the living Etruscans.

### 🏛️ Necropolis

Via Necropoli. **Tel** 06 994 00 01. **Open** Tue–Sun. **Closed** some pub hols. 🖼️

### 🏛️ Museo Nazionale Cerite

Piazza Santa Maria. **Tel** 06 994 13 54. **Open** Tue–Sun. **Closed** pub hols. 🖼️

Medieval Anguillara on Lake Bracciano

## ❽ Lake Bracciano

Roma. 🚉 🚌 Bracciano. ℹ️ Piazza Mazzini 5, Bracciano (06 60 65 78 83).

Bracciano is a large lake famous for its fish and popular for water sports and lakeside lunches.

Medieval **Anguillara**, to the south, is the prettiest of the lakeside towns, with romantic views over the water. The main town, **Bracciano**, on the east shore, is dominated by **Castello Orsini-Odescalchi**, a pentagonal 15th-century structure with frescoes by Antoniazzo Romano and other Tuscan and Umbrian artists.

### 🏰 Castello Orsini-Odescalchi

Piazza Mazzini 14. **Tel** 06 99 80 23 79. **Open** Tue–Sun. **Closed** Jan 1, Dec 25. 🖼️ 🏛️

# ❾ Ostia Antica

Viale dei Romagnoli 717, Ostia.
**Tel** 06 56 35 80 03. 🅜 Piramide, then
🄵🅂 from Porta San Paolo to Ostia
Antica. Excavations & Museum: **Open**
8:30am–1 hour before sunset Tue–
Sun. **Closed** Jan 1, May 1, Dec 25. ▨

For over 600 years Ostia
was Rome's main port
and a busy trading
center, until the 5th
century AD, when a
disastrous combination
of malaria and com-
mercial competition
brought the town into
decline. Silt preserved
its buildings, and it
now lies 3 miles
(5 km) inland.

The ruins of Ostia give a
vivid idea of life in Classical
times. The main thoroughfare,
the **Decumanus Maximus**,
runs through the Forum,
which houses Ostia's largest
temple, the **Capitol**, and past
the restored **theater**, still used
for concerts in summer. The
road is lined with baths, stores,
and multistory buildings, and
even a **Thermopolium**, or bar,
with a marble counter and
paintings advertising food
and drink.

**The building material** for the houses was brick, left plain or covered in mural decoration.

**The internal courtyard** has remained a feature of Italian housing.

Ruins of stores and offices along the Decumanus Maximus

Balcony

**Apartments** or single rooms were rented out.

## Ostia Apartments

*Much of Ostia's population lived in apartment blocks, such as this building, based on the Casa di Diana (2nd century AD).*

**Stores** occupied the first floor of the block.

**The bar** served wine and snacks.

# ❿ Frascati and the Castelli Romani

Roma. 🄵🅂 🚌 Frascati. Villa
Aldobrandini Gardens: **Tel** 06 94 18 41.
**Open** Mon–Fri. ▨

The Alban hills have long been
a country retreat for Romans. In
Classical times they were scattered with villas; in the Middle
Ages with fortified castles
(hence the name); and in the
16th and 17th centuries with
luxurious residences and their
spectacular parks. During World
War II, German defenses were
based in the Alban hills and
many Castelli towns were
damaged by Allied bombs.
Although partly protected by
a nature preserve, the hilltop
towns are popular day-trip
destinations as well as being
famous for their white wine.
**Frascati**'s central piazza is a
belvedere overlooked by the

Villa Aldobrandini, a majestic
17th-century building set in a
splendid park of secret grottoes,
fountains, and statues.

The fortified Abbazia di San
Nilo in **Grottaferrata**, 2 miles
(3 km) south, was founded in
1004 and contains some lovely
17th-century frescoes by
Domenichino in the chapel.
Overlooking Lake Albano,

4 miles (6 km) south, **Castel
Gandolfo** is the site of the
pope's summer palace. When in
residence, the pope addresses
the crowd from the balcony.

Gathered around a sturdy
9th-century castle, and famed
for its strawberries, **Nemi**, 6 miles
(10 km) southeast, looks down
onto the glassy dark blue waters
of Lake Nemi.

The forested shores around the small, volcanic Lake Nemi

Tivoli, a favorite place to escape the heat of the Roman summer

# ⓫ Tivoli

Roma. 🚗 57,000. 🚆 🚌 🅸 Piazzale
Nazioni Unite (0774 313 35 36). 🍴
Wed.

A popular excursion from Rome,
Tivoli was a favored resort of the
ancient Romans, attracted by its
fresh water and sulfur springs
and its beautiful countryside.
The temples that once covered
Tivoli's hilltop are still visible in
places. Some are half buried in
medieval buildings; others, such
as the temples of Sibyl and
Vesta, inside the gardens of the
Sibilla restaurant (on Via Sibilla),
are relatively intact.

The town's most famous sight
is the **Villa d'Este**, a sumptuous

Splendors from around the world
reproduced in Hadrian's Villa

country residence created in the
16th century by Pirro Ligorio
for Cardinal Ippolito d'Este from
the shell of a Benedictine
monastery. It is known primarily
for its gardens, steeply raked
on terraces, and studded with
spectacular, if somewhat faded
and moss-hung, fountains.
Although suffering from
reduced water pressure and
polluted water due to centuries
of neglect, the gardens give a
vivid impression of the frivolous
luxury enjoyed by the papal
families. Highlights include the
Viale delle Cento Fontane and
the Fontana dell'Organo
Idraulico, which, thanks to a
hydraulic system, can play
music. At the other end of town,
the **Villa Gregoriana**, now a
hotel, is set in a lush wooded
valley where paths wind down
into a deep ravine.

**Environs**
About 3 miles (5 km) west of
Tivoli are the ruins of **Hadrian's
Villa**. Easily seen in conjunction
with a visit to the town, this is
one of the largest and most
spectacular villas ever built in
the Roman Empire (it once
covered an area greater than
the center of Imperial Rome).

Hadrian was an inveterate
traveler and his aim in creating
the villa was to reproduce
some of the wonders he had
seen around the world. The
Stoa Poikile, for example, a
walkway around a rectangular
pool and garden, recalls the
painted colonnade of the
Stoic philosophers in Athens,
while the Canopus evokes the
grand sanctuary of Serapis in

Alexandria. There are also ruins
of two bath complexes, a Latin
and a Greek library, a Greek
theater, and a private study
on a little island known as the
Teatro Marittimo.

Today the rambling ruins, full
of shady nooks and hidden
corners, make a lovely place to
relax, picnic, or explore.

🏛 **Villa d'Este**
Piazza Trento 1. **Tel** 0774 33 29 20. **Open**
Tue–Sun. **Closed** Jan 1, Dec 25. 🖼

🏛 **Villa Gregoriana**
Largo Sant'Angelo. **Tel** 0774 33 26 50.
**Open** daily. **Closed** Nov–Mar: Mon.

🏛 **Hadrian's Villa**
**Tel** 0774 53 02 03. **Closed** pub hols. 🖼

Mosaic fragment of Nile in flood, Museo
Nazionale Prenestino, Palestrina

# ⓬ Palestrina

Roma. 🚗 18,000. 🚌 🍴 Sat.

Medieval Palestrina grew up
over the terraces of a huge
temple dedicated to the
goddess Fortuna Primigenia,
the mother of all gods. The
temple, founded in the 8th
century BC and rebuilt in
the 2nd century BC by Sulla,
housed one of the most
important oracles of ancient
times. The terraces of the
sanctuary, littered with
fragments of columns and
porticoes, lead up to the
curved **Palazzo Barberini**.
Built over the site of a circular
temple, the Palazzo now
houses the **Museo Nazionale
Prenestino**, best known for a
1st-century-BC mosaic of the
Nile in flood. This museum also
boasts a famous sculpture of
the Capitoline Triad.

🏛 **Museo Nazionale Prenestino**
Via Barberini. **Tel** 06 953 81 00. **Open**
daily. **Closed** Jan 1, May 1, Dec 25. 🖼

## ⓭ Subiaco

Roma. 🚐 9,000. 🚌 ℹ️ Town
Library, Viale della Repubblica 26
(0774 85 050). 🛍️ Sat.

In the 6th century, weary of the
decadence of Rome, St. Benedict
left the city to become a hermit
in a cave above Subiaco. Others
joined him, and eventually there
were 12 monasteries in the area.

Only two now survive: **Santa
Scolastica**, dedicated to
Benedict's sister, is organized
around three cloisters, one
Renaissance, one early Gothic,
and the third Cosmatesque.
Higher up, the 12th-century
**San Benedetto** is a more
rewarding destination.
Overhanging a deep gorge, it
comprises two churches built
on top of each other. The upper
is decorated with 14th-century
Sienese frescoes; the lower,
built over several levels,
incorporates the original cave
where Benedict spent three
years after fleeing Rome.

🏛️ **Santa Scolastica**
2 miles (3 km) E of Subiaco.
**Tel** 0774 824 21. **Open** daily. 📷

🏛️ **San Benedetto**
2 miles (3 km) E of Subiaco.
**Tel** 0774 85 039. **Open** daily. 📷
♿ (upper church only).

## ⓮ Montecassino

Cassino. **Tel** 0776 31 15 29. 🚆 Cassino,
then bus. **Open** 9am–12:30pm &
3:30–6pm daily (Nov–Mar: to 5pm).

The Abbey of Montecassino,
mother church of the Benedictine
Order and a center of medieval
art, was founded in 529 by
St. Benedict. By the 8th century
it was an important center of
learning, and by the 11th century
it had become one of the
richest monasteries in Europe.

In 1944 it was a German
stronghold and a target for
Allied bombs. Most of the
complex was devastated,
including the lavish Baroque
church, but the walls remained
intact and the abbey stood for
three months before falling
to the Allies. The adjoining war
cemeteries commemorate the
30,000 soldiers killed.

### The Monasteries of Lazio

Rose
window,
Fossanova

St. Benedict founded the Abbey of Montecassino
around 529 and there wrote his famous Rule. Based
on the principles of prayer, study, and manual labor,
it became the fundamental monastic code of western
Europe. The Cistercian Order, an offshoot of the
Benedictines, came to Italy from Burgundy in the
12th century. The Cistercians were followers of St. Bernard,
whose creed was based on austerity and self-sufficiency,
qualities that were reflected in the simple, early Gothic architecture
of their monasteries. Their first
abbey was at Fossanova. Other
Cistercian abbeys in Lazio include
Valvisciolo (northeast of
Sermoneta) and San Martino in
Cimino (near Lago di Vico).

**The Abbey of Montecassino**,
destroyed during World War II,
was rebuilt as a replica of its
17th-century predecessor.

**The Abbey of San Benedetto**,
Subiaco, was founded in the
11th century over St. Benedict's
cave. A staircase carved in the
rock leads to the grotto where
he preached to shepherds.

**The Abbey of Casamari**, 8 miles
(13 km) east of Frosinone, was
founded by Benedictine monks in
1035 and handed over to the
Cistercians, who rebuilt it in 1203.

The abandoned medieval village of Ninfa, now a beautiful garden

## ⓯ Anagni

Frosinone. 🚗 20,000. 🚆 🚌
ℹ️ Piazza Innocenzo III (0775 72 78 52 or 0775 21 14 17). 🅿️ Wed.

According to legend, Saturn founded five towns in southeast Lazio, including Anagni, Alatri, and Arpino. This area is now known as La Ciociaria, from *ciocie*, the bark clogs worn in the area until about 30 years ago.

Before the Romans conquered this part of Lazio, it was inhabited by several different tribes: the Volsci, the Sanniti, and the Hernici. Little is known of them, aside from the extraordinary walls with which they protected their settlements. In later years these were believed to have been built by the Cyclops, a mythical giant, which gave them their present name of Cyclopean walls.

**Anagni** was the most sacred Hernician center until its destruction by the Romans in 306 BC. In the Middle Ages it was the birthplace and family seat of several popes, an era from which many buildings survive, most notably Boniface VIII's 13th-century mullion-windowed palace.

The beautiful Romanesque **Duomo**, Santa Maria, built over the ancient Hernician acropolis, boasts a fine Cosmati mosaic floor from the 13th century as

well as 14th-century Sienese frescoes. The crypt of San Magno is frescoed with one of the most complete surviving cycles of the 12th and 13th centuries.

**Environs**
**Alatri**, perched on an olive-covered slope 17 miles (28 km) east of Anagni, was an important Hernician town. It preserves an impressive double set of Cyclopean walls, 1 mile (2 km) long and 10 ft (3 m) high, from its 7th-century-BC acropolis. In the medieval town below the walls is the Romanesque church of Santa Maria Maggiore, greatly restored in the 13th century.

**Arpino**, 25 miles (40 km) east of Alatri, is a bustling town with a medieval core, and was the birthplace of the Roman orator

An unusual pointed arch in the Cyclopean walls at Arpino

Cicero. About 2 miles (3 km) above Arpino, at the site of the ancient town of Civitavecchia, is a tremendous stretch of Cyclopean walls that includes a rare gateway with a pointed arch.

## ⓰ Sermoneta and Ninfa

Latina. 🚆 Latina Scalo. 🚌 from Latina. ℹ️ Via Varsavia, Latina (0773 48 06 72). Sermoneta: Loggia dei Mercanti (0773 30 312). Ninfa: **Tel** 0773 35 42 41 (call for group reservations). **Open** Apr–Nov: 1st Sat & Sun of the month. 🅿️

Sermoneta is a lovely hilltop town overlooking the Pontine Plains, with narrow cobblestone streets winding around medieval houses, palaces, and churches. The **Duomo** has a fine 15th-century panel by Benozzo Gozzoli showing the Virgin cradling Sermoneta in her hands. At the top of the town rises the moated fairy-tale Castello Caetani, frescoed with mythological scenes by a pupil of Pinturicchio.

In the valley below lies the abandoned medieval village of **Ninfa**, converted into lush gardens by the Caetani family in 1921. Streams and waterfalls punctuate the picturesque garden laid out among the crumbling buildings.

# ⑰ Terracina

Latina. 🚶 44,000. 🚆 🚌 ℹ️ Viale Europa 204 (0773 70 77 02). 🗓️ Thu.

Roman Terracina was an important commercial center on the Via Appia (the Appian Way). Today it is a popular beach resort, with a fascinating collage of medieval buildings and Roman ruins in its historic center, perched on the slopes of the Ausonian Hills. The more modern part of town by the sea is full of restaurants, bars, and hotels.

Bombing during World War II uncovered many of the town's ancient structures, notably a stretch of the Appian Way and the original paving of the Roman Forum in Piazza del Municipio. The 11th-century **Duomo** was built in the shell of a Roman temple, and is still entered by the temple's steps. The medieval portico is adorned with a lovely 12th-century mosaic and the interior preserves the 13th-century mosaic pavement. Next door, the modern town hall houses the **Museo Archeologico**, devoted to local Greek and Roman finds.

Duomo at Terracina with original Roman steps

About 2 miles (3 km) above the town are the podium and foundations that once supported the Temple of Jove Anxur, dating back to the 1st century BC. This huge arcaded platform is illuminated at night and offers vertiginous views of Terracina and its bay.

**🏛️ Museo Archeologico**
Piazza Municipio. **Tel** 0773 70 73 13. **Open** daily. **Closed** Mon pm, some public hols. 📷

# ⑱ Sperlonga

Latina. 🚶 4,000. 🚌 ℹ️ Corso San Leone 22 (0771 55 70 00). 🗓️ Sat.

Sperlonga is a seaside resort surrounded by sandy beaches. The old town sits on a rocky promontory, a picturesque labyrinth of whitewashed buildings, narrow alleyways, piazzettas, and balconies offering an occasional glimpse of the sea below. It is now full of bars, restaurants, and boutiques. The modern part of town lies down on the seafront.

The area around Sperlonga was a favorite retreat for the ancient Romans during the summer months. They built villas along the coast, and converted the natural caves in the nearby cliffs into places to dine and relax.

In 1957, archaeologists excavating the complex of Tiberius's luxury villa, a half-mile (1 km) from the southern outskirts of town, found some marvelous 2nd-century-BC Hellenistic sculptures in a large cave open to the sea. These sculptures, representing incid-

12th-century bell tower at Gaeta

ents from Homer's *Odyssey*, are thought to be by the same artists from Rhodes (where the Emperor Tiberius once lived) who were responsible for the Laocoön (see p421). They are displayed, along with other local finds, in the **Museo Archeologico Nazionale**, which is part of the Archaeological Zone.

**🏛️ Zona Archeologica**
Via Flacca. **Tel** 0771 54 80 28. **Open** daily. **Closed** Jan 1, Dec 25. 📷

# ⑲ Gaeta

Latina. 🚶 22,000. 🚌 ℹ️ Piazza XIX Maggio (0771 46 91). 🗓️ Wed.

According to Virgil, Gaeta was named after Aeneas's wet nurse Caieta, who was allegedly buried here. The town sits on the southern headland of the gulf of Gaeta, under Monte Orlando. The historic center is dominated by a mighty Aragonese castle and the pinnacles of mock-Gothic San Francesco. To the north, the modern quarter links Gaeta to the bay of Serapo, a picturesque beach resort.

Gaeta's most beautiful feature is the **Duomo**'s elegant late Romanesque bell tower, its lofty summit topped by a roof of colored ceramic tiles. On the seafront lies the tiny 10th-century church of **San Giovanni a Mare**, with faded frescoes, a hemispherical dome, and a sloping floor to let the sea flow out after flooding.

Stretches of sandy beach along the coast between Gaeta and Terracina

# SOUTHERN ITALY

# Introducing Southern Italy

Visitors to southern Italy find a rich array of archaeological remains. Although those of the Romans at Pompeii are high on everyone's list, Greek ruins are found in Sicily and the southern coast, and there are mysterious ancient structures, called *nuraghi*, in Sardinia. Campania, Puglia, and Sicily are famed for their architecture, while across the south there are magnificent landscapes, abundant wildlife, and endless opportunities for outdoor activities. The cuisine alone, with its eclectic heritage and diversity of tastes, provides the excuse to dawdle on the coast or in the mountain villages.

**The Parco Nazionale d'Abruzzo**, a vast, unspoiled wilderness, is home to wolves, bears, and many species of birds *(see pp510–11)*.

**Su Nuraxi at Barumini**, built around 1500 BC, is the most celebrated of Sardinia's mysterious stone *nuraghi* sites *(see p553)*.

SARDINIA
*(See pp548–55)*

Porto Torres
Olbia
Alghero
Nuoro
Macomer
Oristano
Arbatax
Cagliari

**The cloister decoration** at Monreale cathedral is a legacy of Sicily's Arabic past, with elaborate columns adorned with fine mosaics and splendid sculpted capitals *(see pp534–5)*.

Trapani
Marsala
Sciacca
Pale
SIC
*(See pp5*

**Sicily's Valley of the Temples at Agrigento** contains some of the best-preserved Greek ruins outside Greece. Mostly Doric in style, they date from the 5th and 6th centuries BC *(see p540)*.

◀ Colorful terraced villas scaling down to the beach in Positano on the Amalfi Coast

**The Museo Archeologico Nazionale** in Naples is one of Italy's most important museums. It houses the treasures of Pompeii, including sculptures, vases, and everyday artifacts that provide a detailed glimpse of Roman life *(see pp494–5)*.

**Locator Map**

Pescara

ieti

UZZO

Termoli

MOLISE

basso

Foggia

ABRUZZO, MOLISE AND PUGLIA
*(See pp504–17)*

Bari

NAPLES AND CAMPANIA
*(See pp486–503)*

Naples

Pompeii

PUGLIA

Fasano

Potenza

Matera

Taranto

Brindisi

BASILICATA

Lecce

Otranto

Cassano allo Ionio

Rossano

BASILICATA AND CALABRIA
*(See pp518–25)*

ometers                    100

les                50

Crotone

Catanzaro

Tropea

Vibo Valentia

Isole Eolie

CALABRIA

Messina

Reggio di Calabria

Catania

Siracusa

Scicli

**Pompeii's Roman ruins** include streets, houses, and an amphitheater *(see pp498–9)*.

**The church of Santa Croce** in Lecce is an excellent example of the exuberant Lecce Baroque style, from its elaborate rose window to the intricately carved capitals *(see pp516–17)*.

**Mount Etna,** one of the world's largest volcanoes, is still active, with lava erupting from fissures that dot its flanks. The nearby city of Catania has suffered repeatedly from volcanic damage *(see p543)*.

# The Flavors of Southern Italy

The "land of the midday sun," the *Mezzogiorno* is majestic and fertile, yet in places barren and achingly poor. This is the land of the Mediterranean diet, which relies heavily on bright vegetables, fresh seafood, aromatic herbs, and fruity olive oil. Puglia produces more grapes and olives than any other region in Italy, while the fertile volcanic soil around Vesuvius and Etna is ideal for growing plump vegetables, juicy fruits, and vines. Naples is the birthplace of the pizza, and the region of Campania also produces the best buffalo mozzarella in the country.

Mixed herbs

Sicilian cheesemaker with a basket of fresh ricotta

## Campania

Naples is famous for pizza, but it's also the home of the tomato-based pasta sauce. Especially prized are the distinctive long, tapered tomatoes from San Marzano in Salerno. The tradition of combining mozzarella and tomato originates here. Pasta is generally tubular (in the north it tends to be ribbonlike).

Other staple Campanian ingredients are olive oil, garlic, basil, chilies, and lemons. Excellent seafood includes octopus and squid, anchovies, mussels, and clams, most of which are prepared simply, using lemon, garlic, and pepper. Lamb, kid, and buffalo are the most popular meats. There is also a long tradition of making pastries and ice cream.

## Puglia

This region is responsible for producing 80 percent of Italy's pasta, as well as being the source of most of the country's fish. As in the rest of southern Italy, meats such as poultry, pork, and kid are often roasted over aromatic herbs. The distinctive local ear-shaped pasta, *orecchiette*, is popular, and fruits and vegetables,

Tuna    Lobster    Squid    Sardines

Mussels    Clams

Display of the superb seafood caught along the coastline of the south

## Regional Dishes and Specialties

Some of Italy's classic sauces originated in the south, such as the powerful *puttanesca* with tomatoes, anchovies, chilies, capers, and olives. Along the Campanian coast, *zuppa di cozze* (mussels in hot pepper sauce) is a specialty. Octopus is particularly good served in dishes such as *polpo alla luciana*, where it is gently cooked in tomatoes and olive oil with parsley and garlic. *Orecchiette con cime di rapa* (ear-shaped pasta with turnip tops) is a signature dish from Puglia, as is *agnello allo squero* – lamb, spit-roasted over a fire scented with thyme and herbs. For those with a sweet tooth, mouthwatering *cassata Siciliana* is a rich sponge cake layered with ricotta cheese, liqueur, candied fruits, and pistachio nuts.

Figs

**Maccheroncini con le sarde**
Sicilian macaroni with sardines, fennel, pine nuts, raisins, breadcrumbs, and saffron.

Tresses of vine-ripened tomatoes hanging on a southern market stand

especially figs and quinces, are abundant.

A bounty of fish and shellfish is caught along the 250 mile (400 km) coastline. As well as mozzarella, other good cheeses include ricotta, goat's, and smoked cheeses.

## Sicily

The island's long list of invasions is reflected in its varied cuisine. Greek colonists in the 8th century BC were amazed at the fertility of the volcanic soil. Rice was introduced to the area by the Arabs, while the influence of North African cuisine is shown in *cuscus* (couscous) and other Arab flavors that appear in sweet and spicy dishes.

The lamb and pork raised in mountain pastures and oak forests is exceptional. Fish is excellent, especially sardines, tuna, anchovies, and swordfish. Vegetables are plump and delicious and eggplant (aubergine) is a firm favorite. Sheep's milk ricotta cheese features in many delicious

Newly harvested olives, ready to be pressed into olive oil

pastries and puddings, such as the sinfully rich Sicilian *cassata*.

## Other Regions

Mountainous Abruzzo and Molise are good sheep-rearing territory, so lamb is a specialty here, as is the pasta *(maccheroni alla chitarra)*. Food in Calabria and Basilicata is strong on spices, especially chili peppers, considered a cure-all. Sardinia bakes wafer-thin unleavened bread – *pane carasau* (known by its local name even outside Sardinia). Honey, wild boar ham, and thrushes are popular, as is *torrone*, a delicious almond nougat.

### ON THE MENU

**Arancini** Sicilian rice balls, usually stuffed with a meat, cheese, or vegetable filling.

**Caciocavallo** Spun cow's milk cheese, especially good from Avellino in Campania.

**Insalata caprese** Salad from Campania with mozzarella, tomato, basil, olives, and oregano.

**Maccheroni di fuoco** Pasta dish from Basilicata with large quantities of garlic and chili.

**Seadas** A kind of doughnut from Sardinia, fried and covered with honey.

**Soppressata** A spicy, dry-cured salami from Calabria.

**Pizza napoletana alla marinara** This thin-crusted pizza is topped simply with tomato, garlic, oregano, basil, and anchovies.

**Pesce spada** In Campania, Puglia, Calabria, and Sicily, swordfish steak is grilled with lemon and oregano.

**Sfogliatella** Paper-thin layers of pastry ooze with butter, sugar, cinnamon, orange peel, and ricotta.

# Understanding the Architecture of Southern Italy

The Romanesque style of southern Italy owes much to the Normans, who in the 11th century brought from France both form and style in architecture and sculpture. In the southeast, the style has hefty Byzantine overtones; in Sicily it is characterized by strong traditional Islamic motifs and a love of rich color, pattern, and ornamentation. These

Baroque carving on Bagheria's Villa Palagonia

elements surface later in Sicily's Baroque style and are allied to a dynamism that originates in the Baroque of Rome – though in Sicily it is more vivacious. Neapolitan Baroque is more sophisticated and displays a greater interest in the creative use of space.

## Byzantine and Romanesque Features

Lateral towers

Interlacing arches

**Cefalù**, begun in 1131 by Roger II, is one of Sicily's great Norman cathedrals (see p539). Its west front exhibits many northern Romanesque features, such as the massive towers.

Multicolored marble

Glass and plaster mosaics on gold

**Christ Pantocrator**, a Byzantine apse mosaic (c.1140), adorns the Cappella Palatina (see p530).

Rich ornamentation

Interlacing arches

**The east end** of the Norman cathedral of Monreale, founded in 1172 by William II, is built of multicolored materials with interlacing arches (see pp534–5).

## Baroque Features

Massive scale of stairway

Sweeping view down corridor

Bold statue of lion

**Caserta's Palazzo Reale**, a sumptuous royal palace begun by Charles III in 1752, is characterized by its monumental scale (see p500). The richly decorated interior is prefaced by several huge entrances and impressive staircases offering views. The enormous building was designed by Luigi Vanvitelli.

Lifelike putti

Brilliant realism of drapery

**Giacomo Serpotta's** stucco reliefs (after 1688) in Palermo's Oratorio di Santa Zita illustrate Sicilians' love of exuberant decoration (see p533).

## Where to See the Architecture

The best places to see Romanesque architecture are Puglia and the cathedral cities of northwestern Sicily. Puglia's best churches are those at Trani *(see p513)* and nearby Canosa, Molfetta, and Bitonto, Ruvo di Puglia *(p514)*, San Leonardo di Siponto on the Gargano Peninsula, and Martina Franca, near Alberobello. The Baroque style of the south is epitomized by the villas, palaces,

The Duomo portal in Ruvo di Puglia

and churches of Naples and Sicily, and by the deeply encrusted ornamentation found on church facades in Lecce *(pp516–17)*, in Puglia. In Sicily, the Baroque of Palermo *(pp530–31)*, Bagheria *(p536)*, Noto, Modica, and Ragusa *(p547)* and Siracusa *(pp546–7)* is well-known. Less so are churches at Piazza Armerina *(p541)*, Trapani *(p536)*, Palazzolo Acreide, close to Siracusa, and Acireale, near Catania.

**Bari's Basilica di San Nicola** (founded 1087) was the model for subsequent churches in Puglia *(see p514)*. Based on Norman architecture, its facade is flanked by towers and divided vertically into three, reflecting the tripartite nature of its plan.

**The facade of Troia cathedral** (1093–1125) owes its design to Pisan architecture and its rich ornamentation to Byzantine and Arab models *(see pp512–13)*.

**The facade** of Siracusa's Duomo, begun in 1728 by Andrea Palma, is animated by broken or curved elements *(see p546)*.

**San Giorgio in Ragusa** *(c.1746)* has a facade by Gagliardi with layers of ornamentation culminating in the tower *(see p547)*.

**Lecce's Chiesa del Rosario** (begun 1691) was built by Lo Zingarello of soft local sandstone in the Lecce Baroque style of profuse carving *(see pp516–17)*.

# The Ancient Greeks in Southern Italy

Some of the best ruins of the ancient Greek world are in southern Italy. Syracuse, Selinunte, Segesta, and Gela are among the better-known Sicilian sites, while those on the mainland include Crotone, Locri, and Paestum. Magna Graecia is the collective name given to these scattered colonies of ancient Greece, the earliest of which were founded in the Naples area between the 8th and 6th centuries BC. Many great figures of the age – including Pythagoras, Archimedes, and Aeschylus – lived in these settlements, and it was here that wine-making flourished. Artifacts from this age are exhibited in the excellent archaeological museums of Naples, Syracuse, and Taranto.

KYME
Cuma

NEAPOLIS
Napoli

HERA
Ercola

**Ancient Herakleia** (Herculaneum) was named after its patron deity, the mighty Hercules. It was buried by the eruption of Mount Vesuvius in AD 79 *(see p499)*.

POSEIDONIA
Paestum

**Poseidonia** (today's Paestum) was the city of Poseidon, God of the Sea. Its ruins, dating from the 6th century BC, include the hulks of two of the finest Doric temples in Europe *(see pp502–3)*.

**Mount Etna** was believed to be the forge of Hephaistos (Vulcan) – God of Fire – and the Cyclops, the one-eyed giant *(see p543)*.

**Tyndaris** was one of the last Greek cities founded on Sicily.

LIPA
Lip

TYNI
Tin

PANORMOS
Palermo

SOLUS
Soluto

ERYX
Erice

EGESTA
Segesta

HIMERA
Himera

**Eryx,** founder of the town, was the son of Aphrodite and Poseidon.

Valley
of the
Temples

SELINUS
Selinunte

HENNA
Enna

KA
G.

MEGARA HYB
Megara

**The legendary** founder of Agrigento was Daedalus, who created wings for himself and his son, Icarus, so they could fly.

AKRAGAS
Agrigento

GELA
Gela

Archeo
Reg
Pao

**Gela** was prosperous under the rule of Hippocrates in the 5th century BC.

**Egesta** (built 426–416 BC) was colonized by the Elymians, who may have originated at Troy. Among the ruins of this town are a half-completed temple and a theater *(see p538)*. Ancient Greeks used theaters for plays and cultural entertainment rather than combat.

**Aeschylus**, the dramatist, died in Gela in 456. Considered the father of Greek tragedy, his plays include *Seven Against Thebes*, *Women of Aetna*, and *Prometheus Bound*.

| 0 kilometers | 100 |
|---|---|
| 0 miles | 50 |

**Metapontion** was home to Pythagoras after his expulsion from Crotone. Its ruins include Doric temples, the Tavole Palatine, and a theater *(see p523)*.

**Taras** was home to the philosopher and scientist Archytas, and to Aristoxenes, author of the earliest treatise on music.

**Founded by** Spartan Greeks (8th century BC), Taras was a rich and powerful city.

**Greece and its Colonies**
7th–5th century BC

Museo Archeologico Nazionale

Museo azionale di Metaponto

*asento*

• TARAS
Taranto

METAPONTION •
Metaponto

SIRIS •
Nova Siri

SYBARIS •
Sibari   THURII
         Thuri

**The Sybarites** were famed for their luxurious lifestyle, hence the word *sybaritic*. The wealth of Sybaris resulted from trade with the Etruscans.

KROTON
Crotone •

**In about 540 BC**, Crotone became the chief school of Pythagoras's philosophy. Here the great thinker and mathematician remained for 30 years, until the government (which he supported) was overthrown, and he was expelled.

**Locri Epizefiri** was the first Greek city to have a written code of law.

ANKLE-
ESSENE
essina

• LOKROI
Locri Epizefiri

RHEGION
Reggio di Calabria

ai Naxos

**The Strait of Messina** vexed Odysseus, the hero of Homer's *Odyssey*. Here, at the meeting of two seas, the currents created a "whirlpool" – Charybdis – which posed a threat to safe entry of Messina *(see p542)*. Another threat were the Sirens, who lured voyagers onto rocks with their singing. Odysseus is seen here tied to a mast, so he can hear their song but resist its call.

**Plato the philosopher** visited Syracuse and advised the ruler Dionysius II how to govern.

OUSAI
sa

**The mathematician** and inventor Archimedes was born in Syracuse c.287 BC. His inventions included the famous Archimedean screw, and various weapons to stave off the Romans *(see pp546–7)*.

## Demeter and Persephone

The complex web of Greek mythology was part of the daily life of the ancients. Enna was once the seat of the cult of Demeter, the earth goddess, and between 480 and 460 BC a temple was erected there in her honor. According to the legend, Persephone, the daughter of Demeter and Zeus, was abducted in the nearby fields by Hades, who carried her off into the Underworld. Demeter then left Olympus and wandered the world searching in vain for her daughter. Discovering that Zeus had allowed the abduction to happen, Demeter put a blight on Sicily: it would remain barren until Persephone returned. Finally, Hades allowed her return from the Underworld, but only for a few months of each year – from spring to fall. Demeter, satisfied with the result, ensured that Sicily became the most fertile place on earth.

Sculpture of Persephone

# NAPLES AND CAMPANIA

The capital of Campania, Naples is one of the few European cities of the ancient world that has never been completely extinguished. Founded by Greeks, it was embellished and enlarged by the Romans and in subsequent centuries was the much-prized booty of foreign invaders and Imperialists – most prominently the Normans, Hohenstaufen, French, and Spanish.

Naples today is a chaotic yet spectacular metropolis sprawling noisily and dirtily around the edge of the Bay of Naples. To one side is Mount Vesuvius; facing from the sea are the islands of Capri, Ischia, and Procida. Pompeii and Herculaneum, lying in the shadow of the volcano that destroyed them, contain the most revealing Roman ruins in Italy.

For centuries Naples dominated the Italian south, or *Mezzogiorno* (land of the midday sun). Unemployment and crime are a problem – the Camorra is as deep-seated here as the Mafia is in Sicily – but there is also an attractive, rude ebullience to the city.

The ancient history of Campania is linked to the Etruscans and the Greeks, whose massive ruins can be seen at Paestum. Next came a time of great prosperity under the Romans; archaeological evidence of this still exists at Benevento, Santa Maria Capua Vetere, and Pozzuoli.

The hinterland, with its rich, well-cultivated plains, is eclipsed by the Amalfi coastline with its breathtaking views and the terrific seaboard of the Cilento. The mountainous interior, remote and unvisited, contains small towns that were settled by the Greeks, developed by the Romans and often abandoned in the wake of malaria and Saracen attacks.

Tall buildings lining a typical street in the historic center of Naples

◀ Picturesque beach and town of Amalfi, the largest town on the Amalfi Coast

# Exploring Naples and Campania

The main center from which to explore Campania is the city of
Naples (Napoli). To the north, verdant plains sweep down to Santa
Maria Capua Vetere. To the east, the mountainous
province of Benevento overlooks the valley, while
earthquake-ravaged Avellino and its
province lurk on a plain beyond
Vesuvius. The Campi Flegrei area,
west of Naples, is famous for the
Roman ruins at Cuma. Farther
south is the splendid, rugged
Amalfi Coast. Clean sandy
beaches lie beyond the tip
of the Sorrentine Peninsula
and along the Cilento coast
as well as on Capri, Ischia, and
Procida in the Gulf of Naples.

## Sights at a Glance

1. Naples (Napoli) pp490–97
2. Pompeii pp498–9
3. Santa Maria Capua Vetere
4. Caserta
5. Benevento
6. Amalfi Coast
7. Salerno
8. Paestum
9. Capri
10. Ischia and Procida

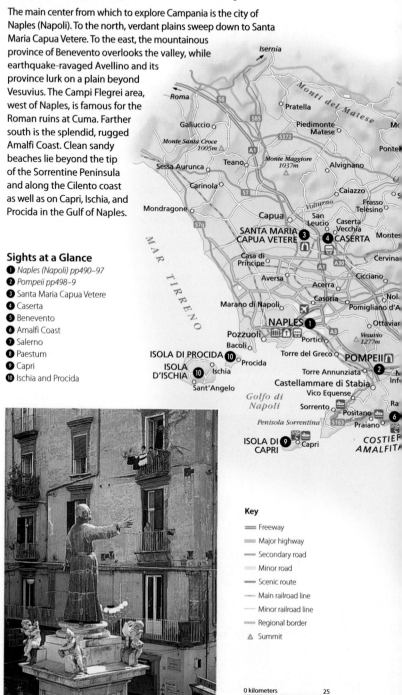

Typical Naples street viewed from San Lorenzo Maggiore

**For additional map symbols** see back flap

### Key

═══ Freeway
─── Major highway
─── Secondary road
····· Minor road
─── Scenic route
─── Main railroad line
─── Minor railroad line
═══ Regional border
△ Summit

0 kilometers        25
0 miles          20

The stunning Amalfi Coast viewed from the hill-town of Ravello

## Getting Around

Northern Campania is easily accessible from Naples on the A1. The A16 heads east toward Puglia. Salerno and the Cilento can be reached on the A3. Branching off the A3, the S18 heads deep into the Cilento. To reach its coast, take the S267. The villages of the Amalfi Coast (Costiera Amalfitana) lie along the scenic S163, accessed via the S145. The islands of Capri, Ischia, and Procida are accessible by boat from Mergellina, Porto di Massa, Pozzuoli and Molo Beverello in Naples, Sorrento, Positano, Amalfi, and Salerno. Campania's main towns and sights are linked by trains. The bus service is comprehensive but infrequent in the interior of the Cilento.

Baselice
Colle Sannita
Castelfranco in Miscano    *Foggia*
Pesco Sannita    S90
Savignano Irpino
S90b
Paduli    Ariano Irpino    Cerignola
BENEVENTO    S90
Apice
Grottaminarda    A16    Lacedonia
Itavilla    Sturno    *Lago di San Pietro*
Monteverde
A M P A N I A    *I r p i n i a*
Paternopoli    Andretta
S400    Calitri
vellino    Volturara    Lioni
Montella    57
*nte Terminio 1607m*    Bagnoli Irpino
*Monte Cerviallo 1809m*    Calabritto
*Monti Picentini*    △ *Monte Eremita 1579m*
ei Tirreni    Montecorvino Rovella
SALERNO    Bagni di Contursi
Eboli    Contursi    Buccino    *Potenza*
Battipaglia    A3
S18    Serre    Auletta
Altavilla Silentina    S19    Polla
*Monti Alburni*
Castelcivita
*fo di*    Roccadaspide    San Rufo
*erno*    Capaccio
PAESTUM ❽    Teggiano    Sala Consilina
Agropoli    Laurino    Padula
Campora    *Monte Cervati 1898m* △
Castellabate    *C i l e n t o*    Sanza    Montesano sulla Marcellana
ta Licosa    Rofrano    S19
astro Marina    *Monte Sacro 1705m* △    A3
Pollica    S18    Caselle in Pittari
Castellamare di Velia    Ascea    Futani    Torre Orsaia
Pisciotta    Torraca    *Castrovillari*
Palinuro    Scario    Sapri
*MAR*    *Punta degli Infreschi*
*TIRRENO*    Marina di Camerota    Cetraro

# ❶ Naples

The compact center of Naples, filled with palaces and churches, revolves around just a few streets. From the Piazza del Plebiscito, Via Toledo (also called Via Roma) proceeds north toward Piazza Dante. To the east, narrow Via Benedetto Croce and Via San Biagio dei Librai cut through the historic and noisy heart of the city in a straight line and are known as the *Spaccanapoli* (Naples-splitter). South of Palazzo Reale is the Santa Lucia district. To the west is the port of Mergellina and overlooking the city is the Vomero district.

The Bay of Naples with Mount Vesuvius in the background

## Exploring Northeast Naples

Much of the city's most interesting art and architecture can be found here, including the Museo Archeologico Nazionale and its Roman treasures from Herculaneum and Pompeii. The buildings provide a wide range of architectural styles from the French-Gothic of the Duomo to the Florentine-Renaissance style of the Porta Capuana.

### 🏛 MADRE

Via Settembrini 79. **Tel** 081 193 13 016. **Open** 10am–7:30pm Mon & Wed–Sat, 10am–8pm Sun. 🕙 (free Mon). ▢ 📷 W madrenapoli.it

Opened in 2005, the Museo d'Arte Contemporanea Donna Regina Napoli (MADRE) is located in the Palazzo Donnaregina, from which it gets its name. The museum houses a remarkable collection by well-known artists such as Andy Warhol, Robert Rauschenberg, Mimmo Paladino, Claes Oldenburg,

Robert Mapplethorpe, and Roy Lichtenstein among others. On the first floor is a library and a children's area, while the third floor is used for temporary exhibitions. The museum often hosts special events such as movie screenings, concerts, and theatrical performances. The church of Santa Maria Donnaregina, at the back of the museum, provides additional exhibition space in a beautiful setting.

### 🏛 Castel Capuano and Porta Capuana

Piazza Enrico de Nicola.
Begun by Norman King William I and completed by Frederick II, Castel Capuano was a royal palace until 1540, when it became the Court of Justice. Today it is a courthouse.

Nearby, between the Aragonese towers of the Capua Gate and facing a market, is a rare sculpture in the Florentine-Renaissance manner. Created by Giuliano da Maiano (and finished in 1490 by Luca Fancelli) as a defensive gate, Porta Capuana is perhaps Italy's finest Renaissance gateway.

The beautiful Renaissance gate of Porta Capuana

| 0 metres | 250 |
| 0 yards | 250 |

*For hotels and restaurants in this region see p576–7 and pp600–605*

## Sights at a Glance

Interior of the Duomo

### 🏛 Duomo

Via Duomo 147. **Tel** 081 44 90 97.
**Open** 8:30am–12:30pm & 4:30–
7pm Mon–Sat; 8am–1:30pm &
5–7:30pm Sun. **Closed** public
hols. ♿

Built between 1294 and
1323, the Cattedrale di
Santa Maria Assunta, or
Duomo, lies behind a mostly
19th-century facade. The nave is
lined with ancient columns, and
there is an array of monuments
to past rulers, and paintings by
Lanfranco and Domenichino.

The Duomo houses the relics
of San Gennaro, Naples' patron
saint (martyred AD 305). The
Cappella San Gennaro holds
phials of his congealed blood,
which miraculously liquefies
three times a year (the Saturday
before the first Sunday in May,
19 Sep and 16 Dec). The Cappella
Carafa, a Renaissance masterpiece built from 1497 to 1506,
contains the saint's tomb.

Accessible from the Duomo's
north aisle is the Cappella di
Santa Restituta, founded in the
4th century on the site of a
former Temple of Apollo, and
rebuilt in the 1300s. It has ceiling
paintings by Luca Giordano
(1632–1705) and a 5th-century
baptistery. The nearby Museo del
Tesoro di San Gennaro (tel: 081 29
49 80) exhibits a range of gold,
silverware, jewels, statues, and art.

### 🏛 Pio Monte della Misericordia

Via dei Tribunali 253. **Tel** 081 44 69 44.
Church & gallery: **Open** 9am–6pm
daily (to 2:30pm Sun). **Closed** public
hols. 📷 Gallery only.

The octagonal church that
belongs to this charitable
foundation houses Caravaggio's
*Seven Acts of Mercy* (1607).
The art gallery has paintings by
Luca Giordano and Mattia Preti.

### 🏛 Cappella Sansevero

Via F. de Santis 19. **Tel** 081 551 84 70.
**Open** 9:30am–6:30pm Wed–Mon.
📷 ✉ ♿ (church).
🌐 museosansevero.it

This tiny 16th-century chapel
is the burial sepulchre of the
Princes of Sangro di Sansevero.
Featuring both Christian and
Masonic symbolism, the chapel
has an unusual character.

Remarkable 18th-century
sculpture fills the chapel. *The
Resurrection of the Prince*, by an
unknown artist, is mirrored by
that of Christ, above the altar.
Giuseppe Sammartino's *Veiled
Christ* is an alabaster figure
beneath a marble veil, and is
a work of technical virtuosity.

Prince Raimondo, an 18th-
century alchemist, is associated
with the chapel. He performed
gruesome experiments on
human bodies, for which he was
excommunicated. The results
of some of his experiments
can be seen in the crypt.

Sammartino's Veiled Christ (1753) in the Cappella Sansevero

For keys to symbols *see back flap*

# Exploring Central Naples

The part of Naples bordered by Via Duomo to the east, Via Tribunali to the north, Via Toledo (Roma) to the west, and the water to the south is the old heart of the city. Especially rich in 14th- and 15th-century churches, the area offers visitors an abundance of sights.

Interior of San Gregorio Armeno

### ⛪ San Lorenzo Maggiore

Via dei Tribunali 316. **Tel** 081 45 49 48 (church), 081 211 08 60 (excavations). **Open** 9:30am–5:30pm Mon–Sat; 9:30am–1:30pm Sun. 🎟 excavations. ♿ church.

This Franciscan church is mainly 14th-century (with an 18th-century facade) and was built during the reign of Robert the Wise of Anjou. The storyteller Giovanni Boccaccio (1313–75) reputedly based the character Fiammetta on King Robert's daughter Maria, whom he saw here on Easter Eve 1334. For Naples, San Lorenzo Maggiore is a rare Gothic edifice. Its nave and the apse ambulatory have a magnificent period simplicity. The church houses medieval tombs, including the Gothic tomb of Catherine of Austria, who died in 1323, by a pupil of Giovanni Pisano. Excavations in the monastic cloister, where Petrarch (see p163) once stayed, have found remains of a Roman basilica. There are also important Greek and medieval excavations.

### ⛪ San Gregorio Armeno

Piazza San Gaetano 1. **Tel** 081 552 01 86. **Open** am daily. 🎟 cloister.

Benedictine nuns still preside over this church. The attached convent earned a reputation for luxury since the nuns, traditionally from noble families, were accustomed to lavish living.

The sumptuous Baroque interior of the church sports frescoes by Luca Giordano. Via San Gregorio Armeno is lined with the workshops of vendors of Nativity figures (presepi).

### 🏛 Museo Filangieri

Palazzo Cuomo, Via Duomo 288. **Tel** 081 20 31 75. **Open** 10am–4pm Tue–Sat, 10am–2pm Sun and public hols. 🎟

The 15th-century Renaissance Palazzo Cuomo houses the Museo Filangieri. Founded in 1881, the original museum collections put together by Prince Gaetano Filangieri were destroyed during World War II. The current collection contains interesting and varied objects, including porcelain, embroidery, manuscripts, Italian and Spanish arms, objects from local archaeological excavations, and paintings by such artists as Luca Giordano, Ribera, and Mattia Preti. There is also an important bust by Antonio Canova.

Renaissance tomb of Cardinal Brancaccio, Sant'Angelo a Nilo

### ⛪ Sant'Angelo a Nilo

Piazzetta Nilo. **Tel** 081 211 08 60. **Open** 9am–1pm & 4:30–7pm Mon–Sat; 9am–1pm Sun & public hols. ♿

This 14th-century church holds a fine Renaissance work: the Tomb of Cardinal Rinaldo Brancaccio. Designed by Michelozzo, it was sculpted in Pisa, and shipped to Naples upon completion in 1428. Donatello reputedly carved the right-hand angel drawing back the curtain, the Assumption, and the cardinal's head.

The simple Gothic interior of San Lorenzo Maggiore, looking down the nave to the apse

## 🏛 San Domenico Maggiore

Piazza San Domenico Maggiore. **Tel** 081 442 00 39. **Open** 10am–7pm daily. ♿ Treasury: **Open** same as church. 📷

This Gothic church (1289–1324) contains some of the finest Renaissance monuments and sculpture in Naples. The tomb slab of John of Durazzo (died 1335), by Tino da Camaino, is in the south transept. In the sacristy are the *Apotheosis of Faith* ceiling frescoes by Solimena (18th century). The choir features a paschal candlestick (1585) supported by figures by da Camaino. The Cappellone del Crocifisso contains a medieval painting of the *Crucifixion*, which supposedly spoke to St. Thomas Aquinas. The grand Brancaccio tomb by Jacopo della Pila (1492) is in the Chiesa Antica.

Detail of the embossed facade of Gesù Nuovo

## 🏛 Santa Chiara

Via Benedetto Croce. Church: **Tel** 081 797 12 31. **Open** 7:30am–1pm, 4:30–8pm daily. ♿ 📷 Cloister: **Tel** 081 797 12 24 or 081 551 66 73. **Open** 9:30am–5:30pm Mon–Sat, 10am–2:30pm Sun & public hols.

This 14th-century church was bombed in World War II, but a reconstruction uncovered the original Provençal-Gothic structure. The tombs of the Angevin rulers are housed here. The tomb of Robert the Wise (died 1343) is by Giovanni and Pacio Bertini; that of his son, Charles of Calabria (died 1328), is by Tino da Camaino; and the tomb of Charles's wife, Mary of Valois (died 1331), is by da Camaino and his followers. Adjacent is a convent with a cloister designed by Vaccaro (1742). There is also a museum and a Roman bathhouse (AD 1).

## 🏛 Gesù Nuovo

Piazza del Gesù Nuovo 2. **Tel** 081 557 81 11. **Open** daily.

The 16th-century Jesuit church was built by Valeriano (and later Fanzago and Fuga) from the Severini palace (15th century), of which only a facade survives. The interior decoration (1600s) is in accordance with the needs of the Jesuits, who used drama and an appeal to the emotions to draw the faithful. It is resplendent with colored marble and paintings, including works by Ribera and Solimena. In 1688 an earthquake destroyed the dome – the present one is 18th-century.

## 🏛 Sant'Anna e San Bartolomeo dei Lombardi

Via Monteoliveto. **Tel** 081 551 33 33. **Open** 10am–1pm & 4–6pm Mon–Sat; 10am–noon Sun & public hols.

Mazzoni's *Pietà* (1492) in Sant'Anna e San Bartolomeo dei Lombardi

Also known as Santa Maria di Monteoliveto, this church was built in 1411 and restored after World War II. It is a repository of Renaissance art. Entering, past the tomb (1627) of Domenico Fontana (who completed the dome of St. Peter's in Rome after Michelangelo's death), the richness of the interior unfolds.

The Cappella Mastrogiudice contains an *Annunciation* panel by Florentine sculptor Benedetto da Maiano (1489). In the Cappella Piccolomini is Antonio Rossellino's monument (c.1475) to Maria d'Aragona (completed by da Maiano). The Cappella del Santo Sepolcro houses a *Pietà* by Guido Mazzoni (1492). Its eight terra-cotta figures are considered life-size portraits of the artist's contemporaries. The old Sacristy, frescoed by Vasari (1544), has inlaid stalls by Giovanni da Verona (1510).

Majolica tiles decorated with scenes of rural life in the cloisters of Santa Chiara

# Naples: Museo Archeologico Nazionale

This building, housing one of the world's most important archaeological museums, started out in the late 1500s as the home of the royal cavalry and was rebuilt in the early 17th century as the seat of Naples university. In 1777, when Ferdinand IV transferred the university to the former monastery of Gesù Vecchio, the building was again adapted to house the Real Museo Borbonico and library. In 1860 it became public property. The 1980 earthquake caused much damage to the collections. Major restoration and reorganization of exhibits continue but most areas of the museum are open.

**Spring Fresco**
The fresco removed from the Villa Stabia in the Varano plain is a masterpiece of grace and elegance; the female figure rendered with soft, delicate colors.

Villa of the Papyri

**Bust of "Seneca"**
Found in the Villa dei Papiri in Herculaneum, this 1st-century BC bronze head was long thought to represent the philosopher Seneca the Elder (c.55 BC–AD 39). Today, however, its identity is less certain.

**★ The Battle of Alexander**
The splendid mosaic from the House of the Faun in Pompeii (see p498) depicts Alexander the Great's victory over Persian Emperor Darius III (333 BC).

**Key**

- ▢ Epigraphs
- ▢ Egyptian collection
- ▢ Engraved gems
- ▢ Sculptures
- ▢ Mosaics
- ▢ Numismatics
- ▢ Didactics
- ▢ Herculaneum and Pompeii
- ▢ Hall of the Sundial
- ▢ Prehistoric, Greek, and Etruscan collections
- ▢ Non-exhibition space

**The Secret Cabinet**
The erotic works from Pompeii and Herculaneum housed here caused embarrassment at the time of the Bourbons. Today, however, they are available for public viewing (by reservation).

**Blue Vase**
This wine vessel found in a Pompeii tomb was made with the so-called glass-cameo technique: a layer of opaque white paste was placed over colored glass and then engraved with decorative motifs.

Temple of Isis

**Sacrifice of Iphigenia**
In this Pompeiian fresco, Iphigenia, daughter of Agamemnon, is about to be sacrificed to Artemis, who saves her by taking a deer instead.

★ **Farnese Hercules**
Made by Glykon of Athens, this statue is an enlarged copy of a sculpture by the Greek master Lysippus. Napoleon is said to have regretted leaving it behind when he removed his spoils from Italy in 1797.

Entrance

Stairs down to Egyptian Collection

★ **Farnese Bull**
Excavated in the Baths of Caracalla in Rome *(see p441)*, this is the largest sculptural group (c.150 BC) to have survived from antiquity. The best-known piece in the Farnese Collection, it shows the punishment of Dirce, who, having ill-treated Antiope, was tied to an enraged bull by the latter's sons.

# Exploring Southeast Naples

The area south of Via Armando Diaz is home to Naples' castles and royal palace as well as the densely populated Spanish Quarter. On the outskirts of the old town are a number of museums in historic buildings.

### ⊞ Castel Nuovo

Piazza Municipio. **Tel** 081 795 58 77.
**Open** 9am– 7pm Mon–Sat (last adm:
6pm). **Closed** some public hols. ♿
Museo Civico: **Tel** 081 795 58 77.
**Open** 9am–6pm Mon–Sat. 📷

Also known as the Maschio Angioino, this Angevin fortress was built for Charles of Anjou in 1279–82. However, aside from the squat towers and the Cappella Palatina (with Francesco Laurana's *Madonna* of 1474 above the portal), most of the structure is Aragonese.

The castle was the main royal residence. In the Sala dei Baroni, Ferdinand I of Aragon brutally suppressed the ringleaders of the Barons' revolt of 1486. The Aragonese were capable of violence, but they were also patrons of the arts.

The triumphal arch of the castle's entrance (begun 1454) is theirs. Commemorating Alfonso of Aragon's entry to Naples in 1443, this ingenious application of the ancient triumphal arch design was worked on, in part, by Laurana. The original bronze doors by Guillaume le Moine (1468) are in the Palazzo Reale. Part of the castle houses the **Museo Civico**.

The colorful and compact
Quartieri Spagnoli

### ⊞ Quartieri Spagnoli

Via Toledo (Roma) to Via Chiaia.
The Spanish Quarter – west of Via Toledo, sloping up to San Martino and Vomero – is one of the city's most densely populated areas. It was named after the Spanish troops who laid out its narrow streets in the 1600s. While lively, the area is strongly linked to the Camorra, the local mafia, and outsiders soon realize

they are not welcome. Stick to side streets near Via Toledo, and avoid the rest of the area, especially at night.

### ⊞ Museo Nazionale di San Martino

Largo di San Martino 5. **Tel** 081 229 45 02/68. Museo: **Open** 8:30am–7:30pm Thu–Tue. 📷 ♿ Castel Sant'Elmo: **Open** 8:30am–6:30pm Wed–Mon.

High above Santa Lucia, the Baroque Certosa di San Martino, founded in the 1300s as a Carthusian monastery, has great views of the Bay of Naples. It houses a museum featuring a variety of *presepi*, Christmas cribs of Neapolitan tradition. The cloister was completed in 1623–9 by Cosimo Fanzago (the creator of Neapolitan Baroque) to the 16th-century designs of Dosio. The church and choir are other examples of his virtuosity.

Next to the Certosa, **Castel Sant'Elmo**, built from 1329–43 and rebuilt in the 1500s, offers stunning views over the bay.

### ⊞ Museo Diego di Aragona Pignatelli Cortes

Riviera di Chiaia 200. **Tel** 081 66 96 75 or 081 761 23 56. **Open** 8:30am–7pm Wed–Mon (last adm: 6pm). **Closed** Jan 1, May 1, 15 Aug. 📷

The Neo-Classical Villa Pignatelli, once home to the Rothschilds, houses an interesting collection of porcelain, period furniture, paintings, and sculpture.

The bold Castel Nuovo, with the triumphal arch entrance

### 🚇 Galleria Umberto I
Via Toledo. **Open** daily. Teatro San Carlo: **Tel** 081 797 23 31. **Open** Aug, rehearsals and performances. 🎟 9am–5:30pm daily (081 66 45 45 to book). 🅿 ♿ 🌐 **teatrosancarlo.it**

Once a focus for fashionable Neapolitans, the handsome arcades of the Galleria Umberto I were built in 1887 and rebuilt after World War II. They face Italy's largest and oldest opera house: the **Teatro San Carlo**. Built for Charles of Bourbon in 1737, and later rebuilt, its fine auditorium once aroused envy in the courts of Europe.

Magnificent glass-roofed interior of the Galleria Umberto I

### 🚇 Palazzo Reale
Piazza Plebiscito. Museo: **Tel** 081 40 05 47. **Open** 9am–8pm Thu–Tue (last adm: 1 hr before closing). **Closed** Jan 1, May 1, Dec 25. 🅿 🎟 Biblioteca: **Tel** 081 781 92 31. **Open** 8:30am–7pm Mon–Fri; 8:30am–1:30pm Sat. Bring ID. 🌐 **palazzorealenapoli.it**

Begun by Domenico Fontana for the Spanish Viceroys in 1600, and expanded by subsequent residents, Naples' royal palace is a handsome edifice with great halls filled with furniture, tapestries, paintings, and porcelain. The small private Teatro di Corte (1768) was built by Ferdinando

*Danaë and the Shower of Gold* by Titian in the Museo di Capodimonte

Fuga. The building houses the Biblioteca Nazionale (library). The exterior has been partly restored and Piazza del Plebiscito has been cleaned up. The great colonnades sweep toward 19th-century **San Francesco di Paola**, modeled on Rome's Pantheon.

### 🚇 Villa Floridiana
Via Aniello Falcone 171. **Tel** 081 578 84 18. **Open** 8:30am–4pm Wed–Mon. 🎟 ♿ Park: **Open** daily. **Closed** Jan 1, May 1, Aug 15, Dec 25. 🅿 Museum: **Open** 9am–1pm Wed–Mon.

Set in handsome gardens, this Neo-Classical villa houses the **Museo Nazionale della Ceramica Duca di Martina**, famous for its ceramics collection, including porcelain and majolica.

### 🏛 Museo di Capodimonte
Parco di Capodimonte. **Tel** 081 749 91 11. **Open** 8:30am–7:30pm Thu–Tue. 🅿 🌐 **museo-capodimonte. beniculturali.it**

Begun in 1738 by the Bourbon king Charles III as a hunting lodge, the **Palazzo Reale di Capodimonte** houses this museum and its magnificent collections of Italian paintings.

Many works by Titian, Botticelli, Raphael, and Perugino are from the Farnese family collections. The 19th-century art is largely from southern Italy.

### 🏛 Catacombs of San Gennaro
Via di Capodimonte 13. **Tel** 081 744 37 14. **Open** 10am–5pm Mon–Sat; 10am–2pm Sun. 🎟 call to arrange visit. 🅿 🌐 **catacombedinapoli.it**

These catacombs – the original burial place of San Gennaro – are near the church of San Gennaro in Moenia. The small church, founded in the 8th century, is adjoined by a 17th-century workhouse. Catacombs dating from the 2nd century penetrate the tufa, and there are mosaics and early Christian frescoes. Farther along the street, the Catacombs of San Gaudioso honor the 5th-century saint who founded a monastery here. Above is the 17th-century church of Santa Maria della Sanità.

### 🏰 Castel dell'Ovo
Borgo Marinari. **Tel** 081 795 45 93. **Open** 9am–6:30pm daily (to 7:30pm in summer). 🅿 for exhibitions.

This castle, begun in 1154, is on a small island facing, and joining, the Santa Lucia district – once the site of the city's shellfish market. A royal residence under the Normans and Hohenstaufen, today it belongs to the army and hosts interesting exhibitions.

Beneath its ramparts, tiny Porta Santa Lucia is filled with seafood restaurants, and the Via Partenope running past it is a lovely promenade.

The facade of the Palazzo Reale, Naples' royal palace

# ❷ Pompeii

An earthquake in AD 62, which shook Pompeii and damaged many buildings, was merely a prelude to the tragic day in AD 79 when Mount Vesuvius erupted, burying the town in 20 ft (6 m) of pumice and ash. Although it was discovered in the 16th century, serious excavation began only in 1748, revealing a city petrified in time. In some buildings paintings and sculpture have survived, and graffiti is still visible on street walls.

★ **House of the Ve...**
The villa of the wealthy merchants Au... Vettius Conviva and Aulus Vetti... Restitutus contains frescoes *(see pp48–...* It is currently closed for renovati...

Villa of the Mysteries

VICOLO DEI VETTI

VIA DELLA FORTUNA

VIA STABIANA

VIA DEGLI AUGUSTALI

VICOLO DEL

VIA DELL'ABBOND...

Forum Baths

★ **House of the Faun**
This famous villa of the wealthy patrician Casii is named after its bronze statuette.

VIA DEL FORO

| 0 meters | 100 |
| 0 yards | 100 |

\ In the bakery
of Modestus, carbonized loaves of bread were found.

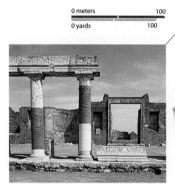

**Sacrarium of the Lares**
Close to the Temple of Vespasian, this building housed the statues of Pompeii's guardian deities, the Lares Publici.

Forum

**Macellum**
Pompeii's market-place was fronted by a portico with two money-changers' kiosks.

*For hotels and restaurants in this region see pp576–7 and pp600–605*

## Plan of Pompeii

VIA DI NOLA

VIA DELL'ABBONDANZA

WESTERN POMPEII

Porta Marina entrance

Piazza Esedra entrance

Piazza Anfiteatro entrance

▨ Area illustrated below

### VISITORS' CHECKLIST

**Practical Information**
Piazza Esedra 5. **Tel** 081 857 53 47.
**Open** 9am–7:30pm daily (last adm: 6pm) (Nov–Mar: to 5pm, last adm: 3:30pm). **Closed** Jan 1, Dec 25.
▨ ▨ ▨ ▨ ▨ pompeii sites.org ▨ www.ticket4art.it

**Transportation**
▨ FS Naples–Salerno: station Pompei Scavi; Circumvesuviana Naples–Sorrento: station Pompei Villa dei Misteri.

## Western Pompeii

*This detailed illustration is of the western area, where the most impressive and intact Roman ruins are located. There are several large patrician villas in the eastern section, as wealthy residents built their homes outside the town center. However, much of eastern Pompeii awaits excavation.*

Amphitheater and sports ground

Teatro Grande

**Via dell'Abbondanza**
This was one of the original and most important roads through ancient Pompeii. Many inns lined the route.

### Vesuvius and the Campanian Towns

Nearly 2,000 years after the eruption of Mount Vesuvius, the Roman towns in its shadow are still being released from the petrification that engulfed them. Both Pompeii and Stabiae (Castellammare di Stabia), to the southeast of Naples and the volcano, were smothered by hot ash and pumice stone blown there by the wind. The roofs of the buildings collapsed under the weight of the volcanic debris. To the west, Herculaneum (Ercolano) vanished under a sea of mud. A large number of its buildings have survived, their roofs intact, and many domestic items were preserved by the mud. In all, about 2,000 Pompeiians perished, but few, if any, of the residents of Herculaneum died.

In AD 79, Pliny the Elder, the Roman soldier, writer, and naturalist, was the commander of a fleet stationed off Misenum (present-day Miseno, west of Naples), and with his nephew, Pliny the Younger, observed the impending eruption from afar. Eager to see this natural catastrophe closer at hand, Pliny the Elder proceeded to Stabiae, but was overcome by fumes and died. Based on reports by survivors,

**Pompeiian vase in Museo Nazionale Archeologico**

Pliny the Younger related the first hours of the eruption and his uncle's death in detail in two letters to the Roman historian Tacitus.

Much of our knowledge of the daily lives of the ancient Romans derives from the excavations of Pompeii and Herculaneum. Most of the artifacts from them, as well as Stabiae, are now in Naples' Museo Archeologico Nazionale (*see pp494–5*), creating an outstanding collection.

Mount Vesuvius has not erupted since 1944, but occasional rumbles have caused minor earthquakes. Visitors can reach it by train to Castellammare di Stabia, or by car. A useful website is www.guidevesuvio.it.

Casts of a dying mother and child seen at Pompeii

## ❸ Santa Maria Capua Vetere

Caserta. 🔼 34,000. 🚇 🚌 ℹ️ Palazzo Reale, Caserta (0823 32 22 33). 🗓️ Thu & Sun.

The 1st-century-AD Roman **amphitheater** here, once Italy's largest after the Colosseum, has well-preserved tunnels beneath it. The town occupies the site of ancient Capua, an Etruscan city and then a flourishing center during the Roman Empire. It was the scene of the revolt of the gladiators, led by Spartacus in 73 BC. The on-site **Gladiator Museum** re-creates the history of the gladiators. Nearby is a **Mithraeum** (2nd–3rd century) with well-preserved frescoes. Finds from the sites are shown in the **Museo Archeologico dell'Antica Capua** in Capua.

🏛️ **Amphitheater**
Piazza 1 Ottobre. **Tel** 0823 79 88 64.
**Open** 9am–1 hr before sunset Tue–Sun. 🗝️ valid for Mithraeum: **Open** Tue–Sun on request.

🏛️ **Museo Archeologico dell'Antica Capua**
Via Roberto d'Angio 48, Capua. **Tel** 0823 84 42 06. **Open** 9am–7:30pm Tue–Sun. 🗝️

Tunnels under the amphitheater in Santa Maria Capua Vetere

## ❹ Caserta

🔼 79,000. 🚇 🚌 ℹ️ Palazzo Reale (0823 44 80 84 or 0823 27 73 80). 🗓️ Wed & Sat. 🌐 **reggiadicaserta. beniculturali.it**

Magnificently opulent, the vast **Palazzo Reale** dominates Caserta. Built for the Bourbon King Charles III, Italy's largest royal palace has over 1,000 rooms and richly

A fountain in the gardens of the Palazzo Reale at Caserta

adorned apartments. It was designed by Luigi Vanvitelli and construction started in 1752. The park has fountains, ornamental waterworks, statuary, and an English Garden. Sound and light shows, in English and Italian, take place in summer.

### Environs

The medieval town of **Caserta Vecchia** lies 6 miles (10 km) to the northeast. Its 12th-century cathedral is a fine example of southern Norman architecture. **San Leucio**, 2 miles (3 km) northwest of Caserta, is a model town built by Ferdinand IV, who also founded its silk industry.

🏛️ **Palazzo Reale**
Piazza Carlo III. **Tel** 0823 44 80 84. **Open** 8:30am–7:30pm Wed–Mon. **Closed** public hols. 🗝️ 🅿️ Park: **Open** 8:30am to 1 hr before sunset daily.

## ❺ Benevento

🔼 62,000. 🚇 🚌 ℹ️ Via Sala 31 (0824 31 99 11). 🗓️ Mon & Wed–Sat. 🌐 **comune.benevento.it**

Benevento, set in a lonely, mountainous province, is home to one of southern Italy's most interesting ancient Roman monuments: the **Arch of Trajan** on Via Traiano. The Roman city, Beneventum, was an important center. It stood at the end of the first extension of the Via Appia from Capua, and the Arch was erected across the old road in honor of Trajan. Built of marble in AD 114–166, it is extremely well preserved. The relief sculpture adorning it – scenes from the life of Trajan and mythological subjects – is in excellent condition.

Elsewhere, evidence of the Romans is to be found in the ruined **Roman theater**, built during Hadrian's reign, and in the **Museo del Sannio**, which contains artifacts from the region, from ancient Greek finds to modern art.

During World War II, the city stood directly in the way of the Allied advance from the south. It was heavily bombed, hence its largely modern appearance. The Duomo, a 13th-century building that was reconstructed after the war, has a sculpted facade that, though badly damaged, has since been restored. The remains of its Byzantine bronze doors are

The ornate 2nd-century Roman arch in Benevento, built to honor Trajan

within. The town has centuries-old associations with pagan worship, and a liqueur called *Strega* (witch) is made here.

### ⌂ Roman Theater
Piazza Caio Ponzio Telesino. **Tel** 089 25 20 75. **Open** 9am–1 hr before sunset daily. **Closed** public hols. 🄰 ♿

### ⤶ Museo del Sannio
Piazza Santa Sofia. **Tel** 0824 77 47 63. **Open** 9am–7pm Tue–Sun. **Closed** Jan 1, Dec 25. 🄰 ♿

## ❻ Amalfi Coast
Salerno. 🚍 ⛴ Amalfi. 🛈 Corso delle Repubbliche Marinare 27, Amalfi (089 87 11 07). 🖳 **amalfitourist office.it**; 🖳 **ravellotime.it**; 🖳 **aziendaturismopositano.it**

The small town of Atrani on the Amalfi Coast

The most enchanting route in Campania is that skirting the southern flank of Sorrento's peninsula: the Amalfi Coast (Costiera Amalfitana). Popular pleasures here include dining on grilled fish and sipping Lacrima Christi from the vineyards on the slopes of Vesuvius, beach-hopping, and trips to coastal summits to admire the breathtaking views.

From **Sorrento**, a well-developed holiday resort, the road winds down to **Positano**, a village clambering down a vertiginous slope to the sea. A top spot for the jet set, it is nonetheless a good place to swim, or to catch the hydrofoil or ferry to Capri. Farther on, **Praiano** is just as fashionable.

**Amalfi** is the coast's largest town and a popular resort. It was a maritime power before being subdued in 1131 by King Roger of Naples. The world's oldest maritime code, the *Tavole Amalfitane*, originated here. The 13th-century Chiostro del Paradiso flanks the Duomo, a magnificent 9th-century structure fronted by a rich 13th-century facade, and facing the town from the top of a long flight of steps. The style is Lombard-Norman, though the cloisters have a Saracenic-inspired appearance.

**Ravello** has the best views on this coast, the prime vantage points being the gardens of Villa Cimbrone and Villa Rufolo. Views from the latter provided inspiration for Wagner's *Parsifal*. The 11th-century Duomo has entrance doors by Barisano da Trani (1179) and an ornate 13th-century ambo (pulpit) held aloft by six spiral columns. The chapel of San Pantaleone contains the blood of its 4th-century namesake, which liquefies annually in May and August.

Beyond **Atrani**, the ruins of a Roman villa at **Minori** show that this coastline has always been a popular vacation spot.

A breathtaking view of the steep village of Positano on the Amalfi Coast

## ❼ Salerno

Salerno. 🚆 🚌 🚢 Salerno. 🛈 Piazza
Vittorio Veneto 1 (089 23 14 32).

Salerno is a big, busy port. Here
the Allies landed in 1943, leaving
in their wake a much-bombed
city. Once famous for its School
of Medicine (12th century), it is
visited today for its **Duomo**, an
11th-century structure built on an
earlier foundation. Its best feature
is the Atrium, whose columns
came from nearby Paestum. In
the crypt is the Tomb of St.
Matthew, brought here in 954.
   The **Museo Diocesano** is
home to most of the cathedral
treasures, including an 11th-
century ivory altar-front called
the Paliotto. Before wandering
off down the bustling Corso
Vittorio Emanuele, visit the
**Museo Provinciale** for local
archaeological finds.

### Environs

The **Cilento** is a mountainous
region south of Salerno with a
remote interior and a lovely,
quiet coastline that is only
slightly more populous. Among
the towns along the coast,
**Agropoli** is a busy little seaside
resort 25 miles (42 km) south of
Salerno. Outside Castellammare
di Velia, a further 17 miles
(28 km) to the southeast, are
the ruins of the Greek town of
**Elea** (founded 6th century BC).
It was much visited by the
Romans – Cicero visited
and Horace came on his
doctor's orders to undergo a
treatment of sea bathing.
Excavations have revealed a

The busy port of Salerno

The Temple of Hera I (left) and the Temple of Neptune at Paestum

magnificent 4th-century
Roman gateway: the Porta
Rosa, Roman baths, the
foundations of a temple, and
the remains of the acropolis.

🏛 **Museo Diocesano**
Largo Plebiscito. **Tel** 089 23 91 26.
**Open** 9:30am–1pm & 3–7pm
Thu–Tue.

🏛 **Museo Provinciale**
Via San Benedetto. **Tel** 089 23 11 35.
**Open** 9am–7:30pm Tue–Sun.

## ❾ Capri

Napoli. 🚢 Capri. 🛈 Piazza Umberto I,
Capri (081 837 06 86). Grotta Azzurra
🚢 from Marina Grande; 🚌 from
Anacapri. **Open** in calm sea. Certosa:
Via Certosa, Capri. **Tel** 081 837 62 18.
**Open** May–Dec: Tue–Sun; times vary,
so call first. 🚹 Villa Jovis: Via Tiberio.
**Open** daily. **Closed** 1st two Tue and
last two Sun of month 🚹
**ⓦ** capritourism.com

Capri's reputation as a sybaritic
paradise is nearly eclipsed by
its notoriety as a tourist

## ❽ Paestum

Zona Archeologica. 🛈 Via Magna
Grecia 887. **Tel** 0828 81 10 16. 🚌 from
Salerno. 🚆 Paestum. **Open** 8:30am to
1hr before sunset daily. Museum: **Tel**
0828 81 10 23. **Open** 8:30am–6:45pm
Tue–Sun. **Closed** 1st & 3rd Mon of
month, Jan 1, Dec 25. 🚹 🚹

This is the most important
ancient Greek site south of Naples
in Campania. The Greeks founded
this city on the edge of the Piana

trap. However, the views are
unmarred by the throng. Home
to emperors, monasteries, and
exiles, its fortunes changed
during the 19th century, when
English and German expats
discovered it. Now it barely has
a "low season"; farmers run little
hotels, and fishermen rent
pleasure boats. Capri enjoys its
well-deserved reputation as a
Garden of Eden.

**The Grotta Azzurra**,
or the Blue Grotto,
is a cave bathed in
iridescent blue light,
which can be reached
by tour boat from
Marina Grande.

**Anacapri** is Capri's
second town.

0 kilometers          1

0 miles          0.5

del Sele in the 6th century BC and called it Poseidonia, the City of Poseidon. The Romans renamed it in 273 BC. It fell into decline and was abandoned in the 9th century due to malaria and a Saracen assault, and was rediscovered in the 18th century.

Paestum has three massive Doric temples in an excellent state of repair: the **Basilica** or **Temple of Hera I** (mid-6th century BC); the **Temple of Neptune** (5th century BC), the largest and most complete at Paestum; and the **Temple of Ceres**, thought to date between its two neighbors.

Excavations have revealed the remains of the ancient city, its public and religious buildings, roads and protective walls. A **museum** contains the extensive finds from the site, including tomb paintings, tomb treasures, terra-cotta votive offerings, architectural fragments, and sculpture.

A view from the highest point of Procida, called Terra Murata

## ⓾ Ischia and Procida

Napoli. 🚢 Ischia & Procida. 🛈 Via Sogliuzzo 72, Ischia (081 507 42 11), Via V. Emanuele 168 (081 810 19 68). La Mortella: **Tel** 081 98 62 20. **Open** Apr–Oct: 9am–7pm Tue, Thu, Sat, & Sun. 🚗 🆆 **infoischiaprocida.it**

Ischia is the biggest island in the Bay of Naples and, with its beach resorts, thermal springs, and therapeutic mudbaths, it is nearly as popular as Capri. Ferries dock at **Ischia Porto**, the harbor and modern part of the main town, **Ischia**. **Ischia Ponte**, the older part, is a short walk away. The northern and western shores are developed; the southern flank of the island is the quietest. Here, the village of **Sant'Angelo** is dominated by a long-extinct volcano, **Monte Epomeo**, whose summit of 2,585 ft (788 m) offers terrific views across the bay. Also worth a visit are the gardens of **La Mortella** in Forio.

The tiny, picturesque island of Procida is less visited and very tranquil. The swimming is good at **Chiaiolella**, and, as at Ischia, there are inexpensive places to stay. The main town, also called **Procida**, is home to the main ferry port – the **Marina Grande**.

**There are views** toward Vesuvius and the Bay of Naples from the north of the island.

**Capri** is the main town on the island.

**Marina Grande**
This is Capri's main port of call for ferries from Naples and other ports on the Tyrrhenian coast. An array of colorful houses overlooks the harbor.

**I Faraglioni**

**Marina Piccola** is reached by dramatic Via Krupp.

**Villa Jovis**
Covering an enormous area, this was the Imperial villa from which Tiberius ruled the Roman Empire during his final years.

**Certosa di San Giacomo**
Founded in 1371 on the site of one of Tiberius's villas, this Carthusian monastery was suppressed in 1808 and is now in part a school. The distant rocks are I Faraglioni.

# ABRUZZO, MOLISE, AND PUGLIA

Puglia is the "heel" of the Italian boot, the Gargano Peninsula is its "spur," and Abruzzo and Molise together form the "ankle." Hugging the southeastern seaboard of Italy and looking toward the Balkans, the mountainous regions of Abruzzo and Molise, united until 1963, differ considerably from Puglia, the richest of the three.

Abruzzo and Molise are sparsely populated, quiet places where the wild landscape exerts a strong influence. Settled by various Apennine tribes in the Middle Bronze Age, the areas were later subdued by the Romans, united under the Normans in the 12th century, and thereafter ruled by a succession of dynasties based in Naples. Abruzzo, dominated by the Apennines, is a brooding, introspective land of shepherds. Vertiginous drops preface the ascent to ramshackle hill-towns clinging to the sides of high mountains, semi-abandoned and poor. Molise's landscape is less dramatic. Legends of witches persist in both regions, as do strange fertility rites and rituals celebrating the changing seasons.

Puglia's advantage over its poverty-stricken neighbors is that it is nearly all flat and highly fertile. It produces the largest amount of olive oil in Italy, and its big cities – Lecce, Bari, and Taranto – are lively commercial centers. The region experienced a long-lasting Greek influence, though the golden age of Puglia's past was under the rule of the Normans, followed by Frederick II, who, between his return from Germany as emperor in 1220 and his death 30 years later, spent only four years away from here.

Puglia has glorious architecture, particularly in the churches and castles of the north. The curious *trulli* houses in central Puglia, the florid Baroque of Lecce, and the Levantine atmosphere of its merchant cities complete the picture of an ancient land subject to more influences from outside the Italian peninsula than from within it.

Traditional dress worn in the town of Scanno in Abruzzo

◀ A row of *trulli* houses in the town of Alberobello, Puglia

# Exploring Abruzzo, Molise, and Puglia

Dominated by the Apennine mountain range, the hinterland of Abruzzo and Molise forms one of Italy's last wildernesses. At 9,554 ft (2,912 m), the highest peak is the Gran Sasso. Parts of Abruzzo are covered in tracts of forest, while Molise features high plains, gentle valleys, and lonely peaks. The coastline of the Gargano Peninsula in Puglia (Apulia) is packed with cliffs, caves, and islets. Reaching south is the fertile Tavoliere plain, and farther south a series of upland plateaus (the Murge) descends toward the dry Salentine Peninsula and the Adriatic.

The picturesque medieval hill-town o Scanno, in Abruzzo

## Getting Around

Northern Abruzzo is well served by the A24 and A25–E80, and the S17 traverses the interior of Abruzzo and Molise. The coastal highway (A14–E55) heads south through Abruzzo and Molise into Puglia. Beyond Foggia, it joins the S16 to Taranto. Brindisi, the main port for Greece, is accessible from Bari or Taranto. The roads throughout are good. Train and bus services go to the major centers, with buses only to more remote parts.

Isola-la-Chianca beach on the beautiful Gargano Peninsula

**For additional map symbols** *see back flap*

## Key

- ▬▬ Freeway
- ▬▬ Major highway
- ▬▬ Secondary road
- ▬ ▬ Road under construction
- ▬▬ Minor road
- ▬▬ Scenic route
- ▬▬ Main railroad line
- ▬▬ Minor railroad line
- ▬▬ Regional border
- △ Summit

## Sights at a Glance

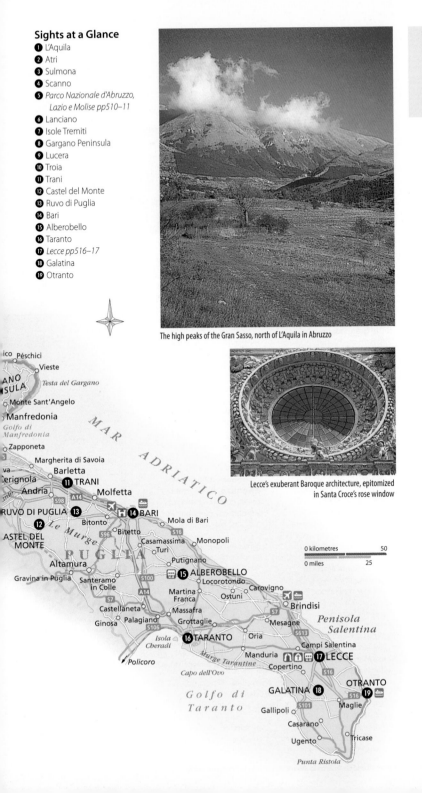

The high peaks of the Gran Sasso, north of L'Aquila in Abruzzo

Lecce's exuberant Baroque architecture, epitomized in Santa Croce's rose window

The pink-and-white stone facade of Santa Maria di Collemaggio in L'Aquila

# ❶ L'Aquila

🗺 73,000. 🚉 🚌 ℹ Via XX Settembre 10 (800 502 520). 🏛 daily.
🌐 abruzzoturismo.it

Abruzzo's capital lies at the foot of the **Gran Sasso**, at 9,554 ft (2,912 m) the highest point of the Italian mainland south of the Alps (and good for skiing). Its ancient streets are peppered with churches. In April 2009 an earthquake, measuring 6.3 in magnitude, struck central Italy with the epicenter close to L'Aquila. Many of the historical churches and buildings described below have been seriously damaged by the quake. Restoration work is being carried out on many buildings, so check with the tourist office before visiting.

The domed **Santa Giusta** (1257), off Via Santa Giusta, has a rose window and a *Martyrdom of St. Stephen* (1615) by Cavalier d'Arpino. **Santa Maria di Paganica**, off Via Paganica, has a 14th-century facade and a carved portal. The **Duomo** (1257) in Piazza del Duomo was rebuilt in the 18th century. The massive church of **Santa Maria di Collemaggio**, on Piazza di Collemaggio, has a facade of pink and white stone. It was built in the 13th century by Pietro dal Morrone, who later became Pope Celestine V.

**San Bernardino**, on Via di San Bernardino, houses the tomb (1505) of San Bernardino of Siena. The church (built 1454–72), has a facade (1527) by Cola dell'Amatrice and an 18th-century carved ceiling by Ferdinando Mosca. The bell tower collapsed in the 2009 earthquake. The second chapel in the south aisle has an altarpiece by Renaissance artist Andrea della Robbia.

The medieval **Fontanelle delle Novantanove Cannelle** at the end of Via San Iacopo is a fountain commemorating the 99 villages that Frederick II supposedly united when he founded L'Aquila in 1240.

The **Museo Nazionale d'Abruzzo**, in the 16th-century castle, contains the remains of a prehistoric elephant, Roman artifacts, and religious works.

🏛 **Museo Nazionale d'Abruzzo**
Temporarily housed in front of the Novantanove Cannelle. **Tel** 0862 487 42 97. **Open** 9am–7pm Tue–Sun. 🔲 🔲

Detail of Fontanelle delle Novantanove Cannelle in L'Aquila

# ❷ Atri

Teramo. 🗺 12,000. 🚌
ℹ 0861 24 42 22. 🏛 Mon.
🌐 comune.atri.te.it

The prettiest in a series of small hill-towns in Abruzzo, Atri is a warren of stepped streets, alleys, and passages bound by mostly brick and stone churches and houses.

The 13th-century **Duomo** occupies the site of a Roman bath; the crypt was once a swimming pool; and fragments of the original mosaic floor are visible in the apse. Also in the apse is Andrea Delitio's beautiful 15th-century fresco cycle, in which he combined landscape and architecture in a variety of religious scenes from the Old and New Testaments. The cloister has views of the 15th-century brick campanile.

**Environs**
South of Atri is the hill-town of **Penne**, with its homogeneous buildings of reddish brick, which give it a wonderful, warm glow. East of Atri, **Loreto Aprutino** is known for *The Last Judgment* fresco (14th century) in Santa Maria in Piano.

Detail from 15th-century fresco by Andrea Delitio in Atri's Duomo

# ❸ Sulmona

L'Aquila. 🗺 26,000. 🚉 🚌 ℹ Corso Ovidio 208 (0864 532 76). 🏛 Wed & Sat. 🎭 Sep: International Exhibition of Contemporary Art.
🌐 comune.sulmona.aq.it

This town is famous as the home of both Ovid and *confetti* (sugared almonds). At weddings, guests are given *confetti* for good luck. Sulmona is filled with ancient buildings, especially along medieval **Via dell'Ospedale**. The **Palazzo dell'Annunziata**, founded in 1320, combines Gothic and Renaissance styles.

The **Museo Civico** holds a collection of local antiquities, costumes, paintings, and the work of goldsmiths formerly housed in the palace. The adjacent church of the **Annunziata**, with a Baroque facade, was rebuilt in the 18th century. Behind the church are 1 BC–AD 2 ruins of a Roman house.

At the end of Viale Matteotti is the cathedral of **San Panfilo**, built over a Roman temple. **San Francesco della Scarpa**, in Piazza del Carmine, has a 13th-century portal. Winding past it to the **Fontana del Vecchio** (1474) is an aqueduct that once fueled local industry.

#### Environs
East of Sulmona is the Maiella National Park, a massif of 61 peaks and forested valleys offering walking, bird-watching, climbing, and skiing. To the west, Cocullo hosts the May Processione dei Serpari (Festival of Snakes) in which a statue of the patron saint, Domenico Abate, is draped with snakes and carried through the town. In the 11th century he is said to have rid the area of venomous snakes.

🏛 **Museo Civico**
Palazzo dell'Annunziata, Corso Ovidio.
**Tel** 0864 21 02 16. **Open** 9am–1pm & 4–6:30pm daily.

### Ovid, the Latin Poet

Born in 43 BC, Ovid (Publius Ovidius Naso) was Sulmona's most illustrious inhabitant. Not much survives here to remind you of his presence, however, aside from a **Corso Ovidio**, a 20th-century statue of him in Piazza XX Settembre, and, just outside the town, a ruin traditionally known as **Ovid's Villa**. Known as one of the greatest poets of Classical Rome, his subjects included love (*Ars Amatoria*) and mythology (*Metamorphoses*). In AD 8 he was banished into exile on the Black Sea, the far edge of the Roman Empire, after being implicated in a scandal of adultery with Julia, the granddaughter of Emperor Augustus (*see pp52–3*). Ovid continued to write of his hardships, and died in exile in AD 17.

## ❹ Scanno

L'Aquila. 👥 2,400. 🚌 ℹ️ Piazza Santa Maria della Valle 12 (0864 743 17).
🗓 Tue. 🔲 scanno.org

Wonderfully well-preserved, this medieval hill-town set in beautiful, wild countryside is one of Abruzzo's most popular attractions. There are alleys and narrow flights of steps, oddly shaped courtyards into which small churches have been pressed, and ancient mansions in whose windows women can be seen making lace or embroidering.

*Traditional costume still worn in Scanno*

In the shadow of Apennine peaks and beside lovely **Lago di Scanno**, the town is also a favored stop on the way to the Parco Nazionale d'Abruzzo (*see pp510–11*). The summer months are the busiest, with a variety of activities from horseback riding, boating, and camping by the lake, to the August classical music festival. During the January Festa di Sant' Antonio Abate, a large lasagna is cooked outside **Santa Maria della Valle**, which is built on the remains of a pagan temple. The food is doled out on a first-come, first-served basis.

High Apennine peaks looming above the medieval hill-town of Scanno in Abruzzo

# ❺ Parco Nazionale d'Abruzzo, Lazio, e Molise

This vast park, inaugurated in 1922, has a rich landscape of high peaks, rivers, lakes, and forests, and is one of Europe's most important nature preserves. Part of a royal hunting preserve until 1877, today it provides refuge for 66 species of mammal, 52 types of reptile, amphibian, and fish, and 230 species of bird, including the golden eagle and white-backed woodpecker, as well as over 2,000 varieties of flora. The park offers an extensive network of paths, and there are opportunities for horseback riding, trekking, and climbing.

Pescina
Avezzano

**Golden eagles**
may be seen near
the Sangro River.

S83

ℹ **Pescasseroli**

**Opi**

Sangro

S509

Cassino ↓

**Young Chamois**
Dense forests of beech and maple hide the Apennine chamois. There are also red and roe deer in the park.

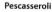

**Forests of beech**
and black pine provide beautiful scenery.

**Pescasseroli**
This town is a major center for information on the area. It has good tourist amenities and a small zoological garden with animals living in the region, such as bears and wolves.

**Apennine Wolves**
The park guarantees protection for the Apennine wolf, and about 60 wolves survive here. The chances of seeing one, however, are fairly remote.

**Marsican Brown Bear**
Once hunted almost to extinction, between 80 and 100 brown bears now roam in the park.

*For hotels and restaurants in this region see pp576–7 and pp600–605*

**Horseback Riding** is an excellent way to explore more remote areas of the park.

**Lake Barrea**
Created by the artificial damming of the River Sangro, this lake is surrounded by valleys and forests offering walking and pony trekking.

**The Camosciara** is a spectacular area, home to many wild animals.

**Dense Forests**
Beech and maple forests, dotted with black hornbeam, ash, hawthorn, cherry, wild apple, and pear, protect the once persecuted bears and wolves.

**Key**

▬▬ Major highway

▬▬ Minor road

▬ ▬ Walking path

0 kilometers    5

0 miles    5

## ❻ Lanciano

Chieti. 🚹 35,000. 🚆 🚌 ℹ️ Piazza Plebiscito 50 (0872 71 91 27). 🛒 Wed & Sat. 🌐 **lanciano.eu**

Large parts of Lanciano's old nucleus remain from the Middle Ages. In the crumbling Civitanova quarter is the 13th-century church of **Santa Maria Maggiore**, with a magnificent 14th-century portal and a silver processional cross (1422). Also in this area is the now disused **San Biagio** (begun c.1059), near the 11th-century **Porta San Biagio** – a rare surviving town gate. The **Duomo** stands on the remains of a Roman bridge dating from the time of Diocletian. An underground passage links the bridge to the **Sanctuary of the Eucharistic Miracle**, where a host and wine that turned into live Flesh and Blood in the 8th century are kept. The Ripa Sacca (Jewish ghetto) was a busy commercial center in the Middle Ages – the period of Lanciano's greatest prosperity. The hefty walls of the **Torri Montanara** were built then by the Aragonese as a bulwark against attack.

## ❼ Isole Tremiti

Foggia. 🚹 400. ⛴️ San Nicola. ℹ️ Via Perrone 17, Foggia (0881 72 31 41); Via Sant'Antonio Abate 21, Monte Sant'Angelo (0884 56 89 11). 🌐 **lecinqueisole.it**

Off the Gargano coast, the Tremiti are the Italian islands least visited by foreigners. **San Domino** is the largest, with a sandy beach and coves. Julia, granddaughter of Augustus, was exiled here for adultery from AD 8 until her death in AD 28. The poet Ovid was allegedly involved (see p509).

**Santa Maria a Mare**, in **San Nicola**, the administrative center of the islands, is an abbey fortress founded in the 8th century. It was turned into a prison in the late 1700s, a role it maintained until 1945.

Both the islands of San Domino and Santa Maria a Mare are popular with Italians. The swimming is good, though the coastline of San Nicola is rocky.

The coast near Peschici on the Gargano Peninsula

## ❽ Gargano Peninsula

Foggia. **FS** 🚌 **ℹ** Piazza del Popolo 10, Manfredonia (0884 58 19 98); Via Sant'Antonio Abate 21, Monte Sant'Angelo (0884 56 89 11).
**W** parcogargano.it

A rocky spur jutting into the Adriatic Sea, the Gargano is dotted with coves and cliffs. Its coastal towns of **Manfredonia**, **Rodi Garganico**, **Peschici**, and **Vieste** are popular with vacationers. To the east lies the **Foresta Umbra**, a vast woodland of beech, oak, yew, and pine, and to the north the salt lakes

Typical street scene in the town of Vieste on the Gargano Peninsula

of **Lesina** and **Varano**, havens for waterfowl. Plunging through the Gargano is an old pilgrim route (S272) from **San Severo** in the west to the shrine at **Monte Sant'Angelo** in the east. The first stop is **San Marco in Lamis**, dominated by a huge 16th-century convent. Farther along, **San Giovanni Rotondo** is a focus for pilgrims visiting the tomb of Padre Pio (1887–1968), a beatified miracle worker. The last stop is **Monte Sant'Angelo**, with its grotto where the Archangel Michael is said to have appeared to the Bishop of Sipontum in 493.

To the south of Manfredonia, beside the ruins of ancient Siponto, is the oriental-inspired 12th-century church of **Santa Maria di Siponto**.

## ❾ Lucera

Foggia. 🅰 35,000. 🚌 **ℹ** Piazza Nocelli 6 (0881 52 27 62). 🛒 Wed.
**W** www.comune.lucera.fg.it

On the northeast edge of town, once a prosperous Roman colony, are the ruins of a Roman **amphitheater**. Lucera was rebuilt in the 13th century by Frederick II, who peopled it with 20,000 Sicilian Muslims. It became one of the strongest fortresses in southern Italy, and its **castle** is one of Puglia's most magnificent. Built in 1233 by Frederick II, and enlarged after

1269, its fortified wall of 2,953 ft (900 m) is interspersed with 24 towers. Of Frederick's original palace, only the base and some vaulting remains.

In 1300, Charles II, who killed most of Lucera's Muslim population, began the **Duomo** on the site of their main mosque. The high, soaring nave is filled with 15th- and 16th-century frescoes and carvings.

The **Museo Civico Fiorelli** has displays of episodes from throughout Lucera's history.

🏛 **Museo Civico Fiorelli**
Via de Nicastri 44. **Tel** 0881 54 70 41. **Open** 10am–1pm & 3–7pm Tue–Sun.

The remains of Lucera castle

## ❿ Troia

Foggia. 🅰 33,000. 🚌 **ℹ** 0881 97 82 41. 🛒 1st & 3rd Sat of month.
**W** www.comune.troia.fg.it

Founded in 1017 as a Byzantine fortress against the Lombards, Troia fell to the Normans in 1066. Until Frederick II destroyed it in 1229, the town had been ruled by a succession of powerful bishops who were responsible for producing many remarkable buildings, including Troia's **Duomo** (see pp482–3).

Begun in 1093 and constructed over the following 30 years, it exhibits an extraordinary diversity of styles. It successfully blends elements of Lombard, Saracenic, and Byzantine style with that of the Pisan-Romanesque.

Elegant blind arcading distinguishes the Duomo's lower story. The upper sections are characterized by powerfully carved sculpture – projecting lions and bulls. The upper facade displays a rose window with Saracenic-style detailing.

The main entrance, with bronze doors by Oderisio da Beneventano (1119), is dominated by carved capitals and an architrave, both Byzantine in style. Within the Duomo is a Romanesque pulpit (1169).

## ⑪ Trani

Bari. 🔼 55,000. 🚇 🚌 ℹ️ Piazza Sacra Regia Udienza II (0883 58 88 30). 🗓️ Tue. 🌐 **traniviva.it**

During the Middle Ages, this small, lively whitewashed port bustled with mercantile activity and was filled with merchants and traders from Genoa, Amalfi, and Pisa. It reached its peak of prosperity under Frederick II.

Today it is visited for its Norman **Duomo** in Piazza Duomo, built mainly from 1159 to 1186 over an earlier church

The facade of Trani's Duomo

whose predecessor, the Ipogei di San Leucio, dates from the 7th century. It is dedicated to St. Nicholas the Pilgrim, a little-remembered miracle worker (died 1094) who was canonized as an act of rivalry against the town of Bari, which possessed the bones of another, more memorable St. Nicholas. The Duomo's most notable external

features are its sculptures, particularly surrounding the rose window and the arched window below it, and the entrance portal with bronze doors (1175–9) by Barisano da Trani. The vigor of the interior has been revealed following restoration.

Next to the Duomo is the **castle** (1233–49), which was founded by Frederick II. Rebuilt in the 14th and 15th centuries, it is a well-preserved edifice with one wall dropping sheer into the sea.

The 15th-century Gothic-Renaissance **Palazzo Caccetta**, in Piazza Trieste, is a rare survivor. Nearby, on Via Ognissanti, the 12th-century Romanesque church of the **Ognissanti**, the chapel of the Knights Templar erected in the courtyard of their hospital, is notable for its original portico. Other churches worth a visit are Santa Teresa and the monastery of La Colonna.

## ⑫ Castel del Monte

Località Andria, Bari. ℹ️ Beni Culturali (0883 56 99 97). **Open** Apr–Sep: 10:15am–7:15pm daily; Oct–Mar: 9am–6:30pm daily. **Closed** Jan 1, Dec 25. 🅿️ 🌐 **casteldel monte.beniculturali.it**

**Frederick II**

Remote in the endless plains near Ruvo di Puglia, Castel del Monte, built in the mid-13th century, out-classes every other castle associated with Frederick II. It is also one of the most sophisticated secular buildings of the Middle Ages. The emperor had broad intellectual

interests, and he used his castles as hunting lodges where he could retire from court life with his falcons and books. Inside there are two floors, each with eight rib-vaulted rooms, some still lined with marble. This, and the marble moldings on the entrance and the upper floor, as well as sophisticated restroom arrangements, mark the castle as a palace.

**Thick and impenetrable walls**

**Octagonal satellite tower**

**Graceful, arched windows**

**Octagonal courtyard**

**The main entrance portal** is in the style of a Roman triumphal arch.

### Floorplan of the Castle

The building is a harmonious geometrical study with two stories of eight rooms each. The reasons for such precise planning of this giant octagon remain a mystery to this day.

Castel del Monte standing alone on the summit of a low hill

## ⑬ Ruvo di Puglia

Bari. 🗺 24,000. 🚆 🚌 ℹ️ Piazza Matteotti 31 (080 950 71 11). 🛒 Sat.

Once celebrated for its vases, Ruvo di Puglia's ceramics industry, producing "Apulian" ware, flourished until the 2nd century BC. The style was inspired by the striking red and black colors of Attic and Corinthian models. The **Museo Archeologico Nazionale Jatta** has a good overview.

The 13th-century **Cattedrale** is a bold example of Apulian-Romanesque architecture, with a portal that incorporates Byzantine, Saracenic, and Classical motifs.

### 🏛 Museo Archeologico Nazionale Jatta

Piazza Bovio 35. **Tel** 080 361 28 48. **Open** 8:30am–7:30pm Thu–Sat; 8:30am–1:30pm Sun–Wed. **Closed** Jan 1, May 1, Dec 25. 📷 ♿ 🌐 palazzojatta.org

## ⑭ Bari

🗺 321,000. ✈️ 🚆 🚌 🚢 ℹ️ Piazza Aldo Moro 33a (080 524 23 61). 🛒 daily. 🌐 www.comune.bari.it

Roman Barium was simply a commercial center, but the city became the regional capital under the Saracens in 847, and was later the seat of the *catapan*, the Byzantine governor of southern Italy. Under the Normans, to whom it fell in 1071, Bari became a center of maritime significance. Today it is Puglia's lively capital and an important port with ferries to and from Croatia and Greece.

The **Basilica di San Nicola**, one of Puglia's first great Norman churches (begun 1087), has a plain exterior with a tall gabled section flanked by towers. The Apulian-Romanesque portal has carving on the doorjambs and arch in Arabic, Byzantine, and Classical styles. Beyond the choir screen is a fine 12th-century altar canopy and an episcopal throne (c.11th century). The relics of St. Nicholas – patron saint of the city (and also of Russia) – are buried in the crypt.

The late 12th-century Apulian-Romanesque **Cattedrale** is based on San Nicola, with a dome and one surviving tower (the other one collapsed in 1613). The Baroque portals on the facade incorporate 12th-century doorways. The interior has been restored to its medieval simplicity. The canopy over the high altar, the pulpit, and the episcopal throne are reconstructions from fragments of the originals. The sacristy, built as a baptistery, is known as the *Trulla*. The crypt houses the remains of San Sabino, Bari's original patron saint.

The city's **castle**, founded by Roger II, was adapted by Frederick II in 1233–9. In the vaulted hall is a collection of plaster casts of sculpture and architectural fragments from various Romanesque monuments in the region.

Portal detail of Ruvo di Puglia's Cattedrale

Sculpture at Bari castle

Bari castle, in the old district known as Città Vecchia

# ⑮ Alberobello

Bari. 🚂 11,000. 🚆 to Alberobello & Ostuni. *i* Piazza Ferdinando IV (080 432 51 71). 📷 in English, French, and German offered by Trulli e Natura. 📷 Oct/Nov: Frantoi Aperti (visits to the major olive-pressing factories).

The parched landscape of the **Murge dei Trulli** features olive groves, vineyards, and *trulli*. Strange circular buildings with conical roofs and domed within, *trulli* are built from local limestone stacked without using mortar. The walls and openings are generally whitewashed, while the stone roof tiles often have religious, pagan, or magical symbols painted on them. The origins of *trulli* are obscure, though the name is traditionally applied to ancient round tombs found in the Roman countryside. Most *trulli* are souvenir shops.

Alberobello is a UNESCO World Heritage Site and the *trulli* capital. Here the strange white buildings crowd the narrow streets, and there are *trulli* restaurants, stores, and even a *trulli* cathedral.

### Environs

The pretty white-washed hill-town of **Locorotondo** is an important wine center. The elegant streets of **Martina Franca** are enlivened by Rococo balconies. The spectacular **Grotte di Castellana** are caves estimated to be 50 million years old.

Whitewashed and sun-baked *trulli* in Alberobello

# ⑯ Taranto

🚂 200,000. 🚆 📷 *i* Corso Umberto I (099 453 23 92). 📷 Wed, Fri, & Sat. 🌐 **www.comune.taranto.it**

Little remains of the old city of Taras, founded by Spartans in 708 BC and at its most prosperous in the mid-4th century BC. The **Museo Archeologico Nazionale**, founded in 1887, has artifacts that shed light on the region's history. The museum has since

*Aphrodite* in museum in Taranto

been expanded to allow for a growing collection of historically significant pieces. Taranto was heavily bombed in World War II and is garlanded by factories. The rundown but picturesque **Città Vecchia**, an island dividing the Mare Grande from the Mare Piccolo, was the site of the Roman citadel of Tarentum. A lively fish market offering the shellfish for which the city is famous, is housed in an Art Nouveau building. Here, too, is the **Duomo**. Founded in 1071, it was subsequently rebuilt. The most interesting features include the catacomb-like crypt, with its sarcophagi and fragmented frescoes, and the antique marble columns of the nave. Behind it is the 11th-century **San Domenico Maggiore**, which later gained a high double-approach Baroque staircase. The huge **castle** built by Frederick of Aragon (15th century) covers the eastern corner of the Città Vecchia. Now a military area, the castle can only be visited on daily guided tours (free of charge).

🏛 **Museo Archeologico Nazionale**
Via Cavour 10. **Tel** 0994 53 21 12. **Open** 8:30am–7:30pm daily. 📷

## The Tarantella

Italy's lively and graceful folk dance, the Tarantella, grew out of tarantism – the hysteria that appeared in 15th- to 17th-century Italy, and was prevalent in Galatina (*see p517*). Alleged victims of the tarantula spider's bite could supposedly cure themselves through frenzied dancing, which sweated out the poison. The dance is characterized by light, quick steps and a "teasing" flirt. The strange, private ritual takes place annually on June 29 at 6am at the celebrations for the Feast of Saints Peter and Paul in Galatina, the only place on the Salentine Peninsula where tarantism has survived.

# ⑰ Street by Street: Lecce

Lecce was the site of the Greek Messapi settlement. It became an important center of the Roman Empire, and in the Middle Ages developed a strong tradition of scholarship. Much of the architecture is in the highly decorative Lecce Baroque style, which flourished in the 1600s and earned the city the name of Florence of the South. This style was possible due to the *pietra di Lecce*, an easily carved stone. Giuseppe Zimbalo (Lo Zingarello) was its greatest master. Lecce is also famed for its papier-mâché workshops.

★ **Palazzo Vescovile and Duomo**
The bishop's palace (rebuilt in 1632), the adjoining Duomo by Lo Zingarello (after 1659), and a seminary (1709) enclose the Piazza Duomo.

**Key**

– – – Suggested route

0 meters    100
0 yards     100

**Chiesa del Rosario**
Said to be the finest work by Lo Zingarello (begun 1691), the exterior is ornate and idiosyncratic in its detail.

**Porta Rudiae**
This 18th-century city gate leads to the suburbs and to the ruins of Roman Rudiae.

Tourist information

VIA UMBERTO

PIAZZA CASTROMEDIANO

VIA RUBICHI

PIAZZA SANT'ORONZO

VIA VITTORIO EMANUELE

PIAZZA DUOMO

VIA PALADINI

VIA GIUSEPPE LIBERTINI

VICOLO SANTA VENERA

VIA MARCO BASSEO

VIA MORELLI

Famous papier-mâché (*carta pesta*) workshops

**The Seminary** once supplied the Vatican with *castrato* singers – eunuchs noted for their high voices.

VIA G CINO

VIA R CARACCIO

Chiesa del Carmine

**★ Santa Croce**
Built 1549–1679, this church was begun by Gabriele Riccardi; the rose window is by Lo Zingarello. Next door is the ex-convent of the Celestines.

**VISITORS' CHECKLIST**

**Practical Information**
🗺 105,000. ℹ️ Via Vittorio Emanuele 23 (0832 68 29 85), Via Monte San Michele 20 (0832 31 41 17). 🎭 Aug 24–26: Sant' Oronzo; Dec 13–24: Fiera dei Pupi e Pastori. 🅦 **ilecce.it**

**Transportation**
🚉 Viale Oronzo Quarta.
🚌 Via Boito & Via Adua.

Detail of a 15th-century fresco in Santa Caterina d'Alessandria

**The 16th-century Castello** lies between ancient city and modern suburbs. A 12th-century construction is enclosed by a wall built later by Charles V. Only one floor is open to the public.

VIALE XXV LUGLIO

VIA A GRANDI

VIA D'ARAGONA

ECCE

**Church of San Matteo**

**Colonna di Sant'Oronzo**
St. Oronzo was appointed Bishop of Lecce by St. Paul in AD 57, and later martyred by the Roman emperor Nero. This bronze statue dates from 1739.

**A Roman theater**
was excavated virtually intact with its orchestra and seats.

**Roman Amphitheater**
Excavated in 1938, only part of this 1st-century-BC amphitheater is visible.

## ⑱ Galatina

Lecce. 🗺 28,000. 🚉 🚌 ℹ️ Sala dell'Orologio (0836 56 99 84). 🛒 Thu. 🎭 Jun 29: Feast of Saints Peter & Paul. 🅦 www.comune.galatina.le.it

An important Greek colony in the Middle Ages, this *città d'arte* (city of art, a status given by the region) retains its Greek flavor. It is the center of one of Puglia's chief wine-producing regions, although it is more famous for the ritual of tarantism *(see p515)*.

The Gothic church of **Santa Caterina d'Alessandria** (begun 1384) on Piazza Orsini contains early 15th-century frescoes with scenes from the Old and New Testaments that glorify the Orsini, who were feudal lords.

## ⑲ Otranto

Lecce. 🗺 5,500. 🚉 🚌 🚌 ℹ️ Piazza Castello (0836 84 14 36). 🛒 Wed. 🅦 www.comune.otranto.le.it

Otranto was one of Republican Rome's leading ports for trade with Asia Minor and Greece, and under the Byzantines was an important toehold of the Eastern Empire in Italy. In 1070 it fell to the Normans. Turks attacked in 1480 and slaughtered its inhabitants. The 800 survivors were promised their lives if they re-nounced Christianity: all refused.

The Norman **Duomo** (founded 1080) on Via Duomo houses the bones of the martyrs. There is a 12th-century mosaic floor and a fine crypt. A **castle** (1485–98) built by the Aragonese at the center of town adds to Otranto's charm, and there are some fine beaches close by.

# BASILICATA AND CALABRIA

Remote and wild, Basilicata is one of the poorest regions in Italy. It is underdeveloped and undervisited, and rural areas remain unspoiled. Neighboring Calabria has been immortalized in the drawings of Edward Lear, who, traveling through on a donkey in 1847, was transfixed by the "horror and magnificence" of its savage landscape.

Today these regions are distinctly separate, but they share a common history and, along with Sicily and Puglia, were part of Magna Graecia. Ancient Metaponto in Basilicata was an important center, as were Crotone and Locri Epizephiri in Calabria. Their ruins evoke an illustrious past.

After the Greeks came the Romans, followed by Basilian monks. These were members of the Greek-Byzantine church who were fleeing their territories that had been invaded by Muslims. Their religious establishments make up a core of interesting monuments, such as the Cattolica at Stilo and Matera, where the monks took refuge in caves.

Many of the historic remains are Norman, but sporadic evidence of Swabian, Angevin, Aragonese, and Spanish occupation still exists.

Centuries of rule by Naples led to the marginalization of Basilicata and Calabria. Nowadays Calabria has an infamous reputation due to the 'Ndrangheta, the ferocious first cousin to the Mafia, whose activities are a constant menace. Banditry exists, but the sensible traveler should have little to fear.

Owing to emigration, Basilicata and Calabria are sparsely populated and have as much to offer in unspoiled countryside as in historic centers. The vast coastline boasts fine beaches, while the interior features the Aspromonte and Sila mountain ranges.

The remote landscape has kept change at bay. Isolated Pentedattilo, for example, preserves customs of Byzantine origin, while around San Giorgio Albanese there live close-knit communities of Albanians, descended from 15th-century refugees.

Sparsely populated, rugged countryside surrounding Stilo in southern Calabria

◄ Traditional white houses nestled among the hills of il Dirupo, Pisticci

# Exploring Basilicata and Calabria

Mostly upland country, Basilicata (or Lucania, as it is also known) is scattered with Greek ruins (like those at Metaponto), medieval abbeys, and Norman castles (such as Melfi's). Matera, its most interesting city, stands amid an arid lunar landscape of denuded valleys. Calabria is often described as the land between two seas. The lovely beaches and virgin landscape between Tropea and Maratea attract many visitors. The Ionian coast's chief attractions are its Greek ruins, such as Locri Epizephiri, and the hill-towns, like Stilo and Gerace.

**Key**

━━ Highway
━━ Major road
━━ Secondary road
━━ Minor road
━━ Scenic route
━━ Main railroad line
━━ Minor railroad line
━━ Regional border
△ Summit

Repairing nets in the town of Pizzo, northeast of Tropea

The picturesque hill town of Rivello, north of Maratea in Basilicata

## Sights at a Glance

❶ Melfi
❷ Venosa
❸ Lagopesole
❹ Matera
❺ Metaponto
❻ Maratea
❼ Rossano
❽ Tropea
❾ Stilo
❿ Gerace
⓫ Reggio di Calabria

**For additional map symbols** *see back flap*

The port of Maratea on the Tyrrhenian coast of Basilicata

## Getting Around

Calabria's Tyrrhenian coast is well served by the A3–E45, a spur of which extends to Potenza in Basilicata. To reach the Ionian coast, it is best to skirt the Aspromonte via the S106–E90 from Reggio to Basilicata. Although the mountains can be crossed, namely on the S280–E848 to Catanzaro, the roads are narrow and pass through isolated countryside. Much of Basilicata is even less accessible, and Matera is more easily reached from Puglia. There are airports at Reggio di Calabria, Lamezia Terme (west of Catanzaro), Crotone, Bari, and Brindisi (Puglia). Trains connect the bigger centers and country buses serve the small towns.

The countryside near Miglionico, south of Matera

The impressive castle at Melfi, showing evidence of both Angevin and later construction

# ❶ Melfi

Potenza. 🏘 18,000. 🚆 🚌 ℹ️ Piazza Umberto I (0972 23 97 51). 🛒 Wed & Sat. 🌐 aptbasilicata.it

A brooding and now almost deserted medieval town, Melfi is crowned by the **castle** where Pope Nicholas II conducted Robert Guiscard's investiture in 1059, thus legitimizing the Normans in the south. Melfi later became the Norman capital. Here Frederick II proclaimed his *Constitutiones Augustales* (1231), which unified his kingdom as a state. In the castle is the **Museo Nazionale del Melfese**, with its collection of Byzantine jewelry. The **Duomo**, off Via Vittorio Emanuele, was begun in 1155 by William the Bad but rebuilt in the 18th century. Only the campanile survives.

**🏛 Museo Archeologico Nazionale del Melfese**
Castello di Melfi, Via Castello. **Tel** 0972 23 87 26. **Open** 9am–8pm daily (from 2pm Mon). **Closed** Jan 1, Dec 25. 🚫 ♿ 🎫 (Sat & Sun).

# ❷ Venosa

Potenza. 🏘 12,200. 🚆 🚌 ℹ️ Piazza Castello 47 (0972 316 09). 🛒 1st & 3rd Thu of month. 🌐 comune.venosa.pz.it

Venosa was one of the most important Roman colonies around 290 BC, and remains of **baths** and an **amphitheater**

survive in the archaeological zone along Via Vittorio Emanuele. It was also the birthplace of the Latin poet Horace (65 BC–8 BC) and the site where the Roman general Marcellus died at the hands of Hannibal in 208 BC. Marcellus' reputed **tomb** is in Via Melfi. For more treasures, visit the **Museo Archeologico Nazionale**.

The **Duomo**, also on Via Vittorio Emanuele, and the huge **castle** in Piazza Umberto I date from the 16th century.

An abbey complex formed by an older, possibly early Christian (5th–6th century) church, **La Trinità** is backed by an unfinished 11th-century construction, in which Robert Guiscard (died 1085) was buried with his half-brothers and Alberada, his first wife. Only her tomb has survived.

**🏛 Museo Archeologico Nazionale**
Piazza Castello. **Tel** 0972 360 95. **Open** 9am–8pm daily (from 2pm Tue). 🚫

# ❸ Lagopesole

Potenza. **Tel** 0971 860 83. 🚆 to Lagopesole Scalo, then bus to town. **Open** 9:30am–1pm & 4–7pm daily (3–5pm in winter). 🌐 aptbasilicata.it

Rising dramatically on a hill, Lagopesole's **castle** (1242–50) was the last castle built by Frederick II. The interesting carved heads above the portal of the keep are said to

represent Frederick Barbarossa (grandfather of Frederick II) and Barbarossa's wife, Beatrice. Inside, the royal apartments and chapel can be visited.

The Sassi district of Matera

# ❹ Matera

🏘 56,900. 🚆 🚌 ℹ️ Via de Viti de Marco 9 (0835 33 19 83). 📱 329 791 70 56. 🛒 Sat. 🌐 materaturismo.it

Perched on the edge of a deep ravine, this town consists of the bustling upper district and the silent, lower **Sassi** (caves) district, divided into the Sasso Barisano and the more picturesque Sasso Caveoso. The people of Matera once lived here in dwellings scooped out of the rock. The two parts are odd neighbors, making Matera a truly fascinating city.

For the best overview, walk along the **Strada Panoramica dei Sassi** and look down into the caves. From the 8th to the

13th centuries, such caves probably provided refuge for monks from the Byzantine empire. Many chapels, gouged out of the rock, were taken over in the 15th century by peasants. Later, a cave-dwelling Matera evolved and by the 18th century some buildings fronting the caves had become fairly grand mansions and convents. By the 1950s and 1960s, the Sassi were overtaken by squalor and poverty, and the inhabitants forcibly rehoused. Carlo Levi (1912–75) drew attention to their living conditions in his book *Christ Stopped at Eboli*, comparing the Sassi to Dante's *Inferno*. The area was made a UNESCO World Heritage Site in 1993.

Of the 120 *chiese rupestri* (rock-cut churches; www.parco murgia. it) in the Sassi and the Agri district outside the town, **Santa Maria di Idris** in the Monte Errone area and **Santa Lucia alle Malve** in the Albanian quarter both contain 13th-century frescoes.

The **Museo della Tortura** (torture), in Via San Biagio, has exhibits dating back to the time of the Inquisition, while the **Museo Nazionale Ridola** provides a background to Matera and the Sassi. The artifacts from many Neolithic trench villages, necropolises, and other ancient sites are displayed here.

The Apulian-Romanesque **Duomo** (13th century), in Piazza Duomo, has a 12th-century painting of the *Madonna della Bruna*, the patroness of Matera. Via Duomo leads toward **San Francesco d'Assisi** (13th century with Baroque overlay). Other churches to visit are **San Domenico** and **San Giovanni Battista** on Via San Biagio (both 13th century), and the **Purgatorio** (1770) on Via Ridola.

Matera is where Mel Gibson's *The Passion of the Christ* (2004) was largely filmed.

Church of San Francesco in Matera

🏛 **Museo Nazionale Ridola**
Via Ridola 24. **Tel** 0835 31 00 58. **Open** 9am–8pm daily (from 2pm Mon). **Closed** Jan 1, Dec 25. 🌣

The Tavole Palatine in Metaponto

## ❺ Metaponto

Metaponto Borgo. 🚌 **FS** to Metaponto. 𝑖 Via Apollo Licio. **Open** 9am–1 hr before sunset daily. **Closed** Mon am, Jan 1, Easter, Dec 25. 🌣 ♿ 🖥 aptbasilicata.it

Founded in the 7th century BC, ancient Metaponto was the center of a wealthy city-state with a philosophical tradition expounded by Pythagoras, who settled here after his expulsion from Croton. Its ruins include the **Tavole Palatine** (6th century BC) at the Bradano River bridge, 15 columns that are part of a Doric temple, probably dedicated to Hera. The **Museo Nazionale di Metaponto** displays artifacts from the site. The ruins of a theater and the Doric **Temple of Apollo Lycius** (6th century BC) are in the **Archaeological Zone**.

Farther south, modern **Policoro** occupies what was ancient Heraclea (founded 7th–5th century BC). Its **Museo Nazionale della Siritide** has finds from this and other sites.

🏛 **Museo Nazionale di Metaponto**
Via Aristea 21. **Tel** 0835 74 53 27. **Open** 9am–8pm daily (from 2pm Mon). **Closed** public hols. 🌣 includes Archaeological Zone.

🏛 **Museo Nazionale della Siritide**
Via Colombo 8, Policoro. **Tel** 0835 97 21 54. **Open** 9am–7pm daily (from 2pm Tue). **Closed** Jan 1, May 1, Dec 25. 🌣

## ❻ Maratea

Potenza. 🏔 5,200. **FS** 🚌 𝑖 Piazza del Gesù 32 (0973 87 69 08). 🎪 1st & 3rd Sat of month.

A tiny stretch of Basilicata meets the Tyrrhenian Sea in the Gulf of Policastro. This unblemished coast is home to Maratea. Its small port (Maratea Inferiore) is beneath the old center (Maratea Superiore), which straddles the flank of a hill. From here the road climbs Monte Biagio to a summit with breathtaking views, where a huge statue of the **Redeemer** stands.

**Environs**
Dramatically located **Rivello**, 14 miles (23 km) to the north, once had a largely Greek population. Byzantine influences can be seen in the churches of **Santa Maria del Poggio** and **Santa Barbara**.

The small port of Marina di Maratea with fishing boats

A page from the precious *Codex Purpureus Rossanensis*

## ❼ Rossano

Cosenza. 39,000. Piazza Steri (393 492 52 12 91); Lungomare di Sant'Angelo (390 983 03 07 60). 2nd & 4th Fri of month. rossanoturismo.it

This pretty hill-town, one of the main centers of Byzantine civilization in Calabria, assumed power when Reggio di Calabria fell to the Saracens (9th–11th centuries). The **Museo Diocesano** houses the *Codex Purpureus Rossanensis*, a rare 6th-century Greek Gospel with silver lettering and intricate miniatures.

In the Baroque **cathedral**, the *Madonna Achropita* fresco is a much-venerated Byzantine relic of the 8th or 9th century.

### Environs

On a hilltop to the southeast is the five-domed Greek church of **San Marco** (10th century). The 12th-century **Panaghia**, another Greek church, lies off Via Archivescovado. Both contain fragments of early frescoes.

**Santa Maria del Patire**, on a hilltop 11 miles (18 km) to the west, is magnificently adorned with colored brickwork, tile, and stone. It offers great views over the Piana di Sibari (Plain of Sibari), the alleged location of the fabled city of Sybaris, destroyed in 510 BC.

### 🏛 Museo Diocesano

Palazzo Arcivescovile, Via Arcivescovado 5. **Tel** 0983 52 52 63. **Open** 9:30am–12:30pm & 3–5pm Tue–Sun, 10am–noon & 4–6pm public hols.

## ❽ Tropea

Vibo Valentia. 6,700. Piazza Ercole (0963 614 75). Sat. tropea.biz

One of the most picturesque towns on Calabria's largely built-up Tyrrhenian coast, Tropea offers superb views of the sea and beaches. The old town hangs on to a cliffside facing a large rock, formerly an island. The rock is topped by **Santa Maria dell'Isola**, a former medieval Benedictine sanctuary. The **cathedral** at the end of Via Roma is of Norman origin, although it has been rebuilt several times. Inside is a 14th-century painting, the *Madonna di Romania*, by an unknown artist.

**Casa Trampo** (14th century) and **Palazzo Cesareo** (early 20th century) in Vicolo Manco are the most interesting of the small palaces in Tropea. The latter has a splendid balcony adorned with carvings.

Below the town are pretty beaches and a good choice of places to eat. Other seaside towns to visit are **Scilla** to the south and **Pizzo** to the north.

## ❾ Stilo

Reggio di Calabria. 3,000. Town hall (0964 77 60 06). Tue.

A short distance from the coast, Stilo is an earthquake-damaged town clamped to the side of Monte Consolino. Standing on a ledge looking out over the olive trees is the **Cattolica**, which has made Stilo a focus of pilgrimage for lovers of Byzantine architecture. Built in the 10th century by Basilian monks, the brick building with its terra-cotta-tiled roof is based on a Greek cross-in-a-square plan. Four antique, mis-matched marble columns divide the interior into nine sections. The capitals are placed at the base of the columns, instead of on top, to indicate the triumph of Christianity over paganism. The frescoes within, discovered and restored in 1927, date from the 11th century.

The Cattolica dominates the town, but on Via Tommaso Campanella there is a medieval **Duomo** as well as the 17th-century ruins of the **Convent of San Domenico**, where the philosopher and Dominican friar Tommaso Campanella (1568–1639) lived. The church of **San Francesco**, built around 1400, has an ornate carved wooden altar and a lovely 16th-century painting of the *Madonna del Borgo* (unknown origin). Bivongi, northwest of Stilo, has two churches dedicated to St. John: the Byzantine-Norman **San Giovanni Theristis**, and the Norman **San Giovanni Vecchio**.

### 🏛 Cattolica

1 mile (2 km) above Stilo on Via Cattolica. **Tel** 0965 81 22 56. **Open** Mon–Sat.

The beautiful and unspoiled coastline at Tropea

The distinctive five-domed Cattolica in Stilo

## ⑩ Gerace

Reggio di Calabria. 🏠 3,000. 🚌
🛈 Pro Loco, Via Regina Margherita
77, Locri (0964 23 27 60).
🌐 comune.gerace.rc.it

Occupying a crag on the north-eastern flank of the Aspromonte, Gerace was founded by refugees from **Locri Epizephiri** who fled in the 9th century to escape Saracen attack. Its defensive character is reinforced by the medieval town walls and the remains of the castle.

Aside from the slow pace of life here – where you are as likely to meet a flock of sheep in an alley as a FIAT 500 – the main attraction is Calabria's grandest **Duomo**. This large structure indicates the significance of Gerace at least up to the time of the Normans. Constructed around the early 12th century, rebuilt in the 13th century, and restored in the 18th century, the crypt is its chief treasure. Both crypt and church are simple, adorned by a series of antique colored marble and granite columns probably stolen from the site of ancient

Locri Epizephiri. At the end of Via Cavour is 12th-century **San Giovanello**, part Byzantine and part Norman. Nearby is the Gothic church of **San Francesco d'Assisi**, which contains a Baroque marble altar (1615) and the Pisan-style tomb of Niccolò Ruffo (died 1372), a member of a prominent Calabrian family.

**Environs**
The vast site of **Locri Epizephiri**, the first Greek city to have a written code of law (660 BC), was a famous center of the cult of Persephone. Remains of **temples**, a **theater**, and Greek and Roman **tombs** can be seen. The **Museo Nazionale** displays a ground plan of the site, as well as Greek and Roman votive statues, coins, and sculptural fragments.

**🏛 Locri Epizephiri**
Southwest of Locri on the SS 106, Contrada Marasà. **Open** 9am–7pm Tue–Sun. 🌐 locriantica.it

**🏛 Museo Nazionale**
Contrada Marasà, SS 106.
**Tel** 0964 39 00 23. **Open** Tue–Sun.
**Closed** May 1, Dec 25.

## ⑪ Reggio di Calabria

🏠 183,000. ✈ 🚊 🚌 ⛴
🛈 Station. 🛒 Fri.
🌐 turismo.reggiocal.it

One reason to visit Reggio di Calabria, which was heavily rebuilt after a major earthquake in 1908, is the **Museo Nazionale della Magna Grecia**. It houses a fine collection of artifacts from ancient Rhegion – a Greek city on the site of the present town – and from other Greek sites.

Chief among its treasures are the Greek bronzes, larger-than-life statues of warriors dredged from the sea off Riace Marina in 1972. Statue A (460 BC) is thought to be by Phidias, the Athenian sculptor and chief exponent of the idealizing, Classical style. If true, it is a rare survivor, because his works were hitherto known to us only from Roman copies. Statue B (430 BC) has been attributed to Polyclitus. It is possible that the statues origi-nated from an Athenian shrine at Delphi built to celebrate the victory in the Battle of Marathon in 490 BC.

**🏛 Museo Nazionale della Magna Grecia**
Piazza de Nava 26. **Tel** 0965 81 22 55.
**Open** 9am–7:30pm Tue–Sun. 🅿
♿ ♿

Riace bronzes (6th and 5th century BC) in Reggio's Museo Nazionale

# SICILY

On a crossroads in the Mediterranean, part of Europe and Africa, yet belonging to neither, Sicily was tramped across by half the ancient civilized world. As conquerors came and went, they left behind elements of their culture, resulting in the rich and varied mixture that typifies every aspect of Sicilian life, from language, customs, and cooking to art and, most notably, the architecture of the island.

During the 6th and 5th centuries BC, there cannot have been much difference between Athens and the Greek cities of Sicily. Their ruins are among the most spectacular of the ancient Greek world. The Romans took over in the 3rd century BC, followed by the Vandals, Ostrogoths, and Byzantines. Not much that is tangible has survived from the days of the Arabs, who ruled from the 9th to 11th centuries, though Palermo's Vucciria is more souk than market. The Norman era, beginning in 1061, spawned brilliant artistic achievements, such as the cathedrals of Monreale and Cefalù, while the eclecticism of that period's architecture is best seen at Santi Pietro e Paolo outside Taormina.

The Sicilian Baroque of the 17th and 18th centuries is just as individual. The palaces and churches of Palermo, reflecting the elaborate ritual of the Spanish Viceregal court, tend toward extravagant display. At Noto, Ragusa, Modica, Siracusa, and Catania the buildings are a useful vehicle for the Sicilians' love of ornamentation, itself a remnant from the island's early fling with the Arab world. The style is an expression of the nature of Sicilians, whose sense of pomp and pageantry is both magnificent and extreme.

Sicily is a curiosity, and the legacy of the past is redolent everywhere. The fact that it is an island has intensified the cultural impact of each successive occupier. They say that today there's as much Phoenician, Greek, Arabic, Norman, Spanish, or French blood in Sicilian veins as there is Italian. The resulting mixture – exotic, spicy, and highly inflammable – has created a distinct culture at the foot of Italy.

Detail of a 12th-century mosaic from the Palazzo dei Normanni in Palermo

◀ The fishing harbor in the town of Cefalù on a clear summer evening

# Exploring Sicily

The vast coastline of Sicily (Sicilia) provides hundreds of long, sandy beaches, particularly at Taormina and the Golfo di Castellammare by San Vito Lo Capo – part of a large nature preserve. Sicily's varied interior is characterized by remote hill-towns and plains punctuated by mountain ranges known for spring flowers and wildlife. Among the most famous sights is Mount Etna, an active volcano whose lava flows over the centuries have fertilized the land, which supports an abundance of walnut trees, citrus groves, and vineyards.

Fishermen at work in their boats at Siracusa

## Sights at a Glance

## Getting Around

The A19–E932 links Palermo and Catania, the A18–E45 Catania and Messina, and the A20–E90 Palermo and Messina. The west is accessible from Palermo on the A29–E90. Ferry routes run from Messina to Reggio di Calabria, and from Palermo to Genoa or Naples. Between the larger towns, train services are efficient, but for smaller towns the buses are better. Catania, Palermo, and Trapani have international airports.

The magnificent temple at Segesta

**For additional map symbols** see back flap

The Norman Duomo in Palermo

## Key

━━ Freeway

= = Road under construction

▭▭ Major highway

━━ Minor road

━━ Other road

━━ Scenic route

━━ Main railroad line

━━ Minor railroad line

△ Summit

0 kilometers            50

0 miles            25

# ❶ Palermo

Nestling on the protective flank of Monte Pellegrino, with Monte Alfano to the east, Palermo lies in a natural amphitheater called the Conca d'Oro (Golden Shell). The city is an eclectic mix of Oriental and old European influences, and it features architectural styles that range from Arabic to Norman, Baroque, and Art Nouveau. This cultural infusion is unmatched in Italy, making this exotic city an exciting place to explore.

### ⌂ Il Gesù

Piazza Casa Professa 21. **Tel** 091 607 62 23. **Open** 7–11:30am & 5–6:30pm Mon–Sat, 7am–12:30pm Sun (Aug: 7–10am only). **Closed** for Mass.

This Baroque church (1564–1633) is also known as the church of the Casa Professa. The interior is an example of the skill of Sicilian craftsmen in the treatment of marble carving and inlay. The oldest Jesuit church in Sicily, it was restored after World War II.

Ruined cloister with the red domes of San Giovanni degli Eremiti behind

### ⌂ San Giovanni degli Eremiti

Via dei Benedettini. **Tel** 091 651 50 19. **Open** 9am–7pm Tue–Sat, 9am–1pm Sun.

Reflecting Islamic architectural tradition with bulbous domes, corner arches, and filigreed windows, this deconsecrated Norman church (1132–48) was built on the grounds of a mosque. Beyond church and mosque, a ruined cloister from a 13th-century monastery encloses a garden.

### ⌂ Palazzo dei Normanni

Piazza Indipendenza. **Tel** 091 626 28 33. **Open** 8:15am–5:40pm Mon–Sat; 8:15am–1pm Sun & hols (last adm: 45 mins before closing). Cappella Palatina **Open** 9am–5pm Mon–Sat; 8:30am–9:40am & 11:15–1pm Sun & hols. **Closed** for Mass; Easter, Apr 25, May 1, Dec 26. Sun.

This site has been the focus of power since the days of Byzantine rule and is now home to Sicily's regional government. The nucleus of the structure was built by the Arabs, but after the Norman conquest of the city in 1072 it was enlarged for the Norman court. See the luxurious royal apartments, especially the Sala di Ruggero, and the splendid Cappella Palatina. Built by Roger II (1132–40), this dazzling chapel blends Byzantine, Islamic, and Norman styles. It is lavishly adorned with mosaics and marble inlaid with gold. Next to the palace is the eccentrically decorated Porta Nuova (1535).

Sumptuous interior of the Cappella Palatina, Palazzo dei Normanni

Duomo's exterior displaying a mixture of styles

## Sights at a Glance

① San Giovanni degli Eremiti
② Palazzo dei Normanni
③ Il Gesù
④ Duomo
⑤ Santa Caterina
⑥ La Martorana
⑦ Vucciria
⑧ Oratorio del Rosario di San Domenico
⑨ San Domenico
⑩ Museo Archeologico Regionale
⑪ Oratorio del Rosario di Santa Zita
⑫ Oratorio di San Lorenzo
⑬ Palazzo Abatellis and Galleria Regionale di Sicilia
⑭ La Magione
⑮ Villa Giulia

### 🏛 Santa Caterina

Piazza Bellini. **Tel** 091 616 24 88.
**Open** 9:30am–1pm daily (summer: also 5–7pm Mon–Sat).

Although begun in 1580, most of the internal decoration of this unique church dates from the 17th and 18th centuries. A powerful example of the Palermitan Baroque, it boasts sculpture, marble inlay, and illusionistic ceiling frescoes (18th century) – by Filippo Randazzo in the nave and by Vito d'Anna in the dome.

The church is flanked by Piazza Pretorio, which is dominated by the huge Mannerist Fontana Pretoria (1544).

### 🏛 Duomo

Corso Vittorio Emanuele. **Tel** 091 33 43 73. **Open** 7am–7pm Mon–Sat, 8am–1pm & 4–7pm Sun & hols. **Closed** for Mass. 💷 Treasury **Open** 9am–5pm Mon–Sat, 10am–1pm Sun & hols (only tombs). 📷 W cattedrale.palermo.it

Founded in 1184, the Duomo displays many architectural styles. The exterior shows the development of the Gothic style from the 13th to 14th centuries. The south porch (1453) is a masterpiece of the Catalan style, and, at the apse end, sturdy Norman work can be seen through an Islamic-inspired overlay. The dome is 18th century. Within the much-altered interior are the tombs of Sicily's kings. Squeezed into an enclosure by the south porch are the remains of Emperor Frederick II; his wife, Constance of Aragon; his mother, Constance, daughter of Roger II (also entombed here); and his father, Henry VI. The Treasury houses the 12th-century Imperial Diadem of Constance of Aragon, which was removed from her tomb in the 18th century.

Fontana Pretoria with Santa Caterina in the background

**For keys to symbols** *see back flap*

# Exploring Palermo

East of the Quattro Canti, where Via Maqueda and Corso Vittorio Emanuele meet, the city is sprinkled with ornate palaces and more churches. Squeezed behind them are labyrinthine medieval quarters where ancient, crumbling buildings still stand.

### ⬆ La Martorana
Piazza Bellini. **Tel** 345 828 82 31.
**Open** 8:30am–1pm & 3:30–5:30pm Mon–Sat; 9–10:30am Sun & public hols (to 7pm in summer).

Also called Santa Maria dell' Ammiraglio, this church was built around 1140 by George of Antioch, Roger II's admiral. The design derives from Norman and Islamic traditions, with mosaics possibly by Greek artisans. In the right aisle, King Roger receives the Imperial Diadem from Christ; in the left aisle, George of Antioch is portrayed.

A nearby convent, founded by Eloisa Martorana in 1193, was the site where the Sicilian Parliament met in 1295 and decided to hand the crown of Sicily to Frederick of Aragon. The church was given to the convent in 1433.

Mosaic of Christ with Four Angels in the dome of La Martorana

### ⬆ Vucciria
Via Roma. **Open** daily.
Nowhere is Palermo's Arabic past more apparent than in this medieval casbah-style market that burrows through the ruinous Loggia district below Via Roma. Merchants, hawkers, shoppers, and pickpockets crowd an area once the haunt of artisans. The alleys all around are named after their professions, such as silversmiths, dyers, and key-makers. This busy market, the largest in Palermo, offers the usual market wares, from household items to junk, as well as a wide selection of fresh fruit, vegetables, fish, and meat.

Stuccoed interior of the Oratorio del Rosario di San Domenico

### ⬆ Oratorio del Rosario di San Domenico
Via dei Bambinai 2. **Open** Apr–Oct: 9am–6pm Mon–Fri, 9am–3pm Sat; Nov–Mar: 9am–3pm Mon–Sat. 🅿 ♿

The interior of this tiny 16th-century chapel displays elegant Baroque decoration by master of stucco Giacomo Serpotta. Created around 1720–30, this was possibly his finest work. Serpotta's technical virtuosity and the sensory indulgence and whimsical fantasy in evidence here, is remarkable. The altar-piece is the famous *Madonna of the Rosary* (1624–8) by Anthony Van Dyck, and there are wall paintings by Luca Giordano and Pietro Novelli.

### ⬆ San Domenico
Piazza San Domenico. **Tel** 091 32 95 88. **Open** 8am–2pm Tue–Sun (cloister: from 9:30am). Risorgimento: **Tel** 091 58 27 74. **Open** 9am–1pm Mon–Fri. **Closed** Aug. 🆆 domenicani-palermo.it

Although the present building was begun in 1640, there has been a Dominican church on the site since the 14th century. Tommaso Maria Napoli, one of the masters of Sicilian Baroque, created the exuberant church facade (1726) and square in front (1724). Within, the most interesting feature is Antonello Gagini's bas-relief of *Santa Caterina* (1528) in the third chapel on the left. Next to the church is a 14th-century cloister that gives access to the Museo del Risorgimento.

### 🏛 Museo Archeologico Regionale
Piazza Olivella 24. **Tel** 091 68 06 07. **Open** 9:30am–7pm Tue–Fri, 9:30am–1pm Sat & Sun.

Housed in a former monastery of the Filippini, Sicily's most important museum contains sculpture, architectural fragments and ceramics, bronzes, glassware, jewelry, weapons, and terra-cottas. The collection is from the island's Phoenician, Greek, and Roman sites of antiquity – Tindari, Termini Imerese, Agrigento, Siracusa, Selinunte, and Mozia. The highlights are sculptures from the friezes of the ancient Greek temples at Selinunte.

Palermo's noisy, bustling Vucciria market, east of Via Roma

### 🏠 Oratorio del Rosario di Santa Zita

Via Valverde 3. **Tel** 091 33 27 79 or 091 843 16 05 (to book). **Open** Apr–Oct: 9am–6pm Mon–Fri, 9am–3pm Sat; Nov–Mar: 9am–3pm Mon–Sat. 🏠

This small chapel is dedicated to the Virgin of the Rosary after her miraculous intervention at the Battle of Lepanto (see pp62–3). The stucco relief decoration is the work of Giacomo Serpotta (after 1688): the panel on the rear wall depicts the battle, and other reliefs show scenes from the New Testament. The neighboring 16th-century church of Santa Zita, from which the oratory takes its name, is filled with sculptures (1517–27) by Antonello Gagini.

Ornate interior of the Oratorio di Santa Zita

### 🏠 Oratorio di San Lorenzo

Via Immacolatella 5. **Tel** 091 611 81 68. **Open** 10am–6pm daily. 🏠

Lining the walls of this tiny oratory are incredible stucco scenes from the lives of St. Francis and St. Lawrence, and allegorical figures and putti by Giacomo Serpotta (1699–1706). These remarkable works exhibit the virtuosity of their creator in the handling of his medium. Caravaggio's *Nativity with St. Francis and St. Lawrence* (1609) was stolen from above the altar in 1969. The oratory lies hidden next to the 13th-century church of San Francesco d'Assisi, which brims with great sculpture. The highlight of the church is the triumphal arch (1468) by Pietro da Bonitate and Francesco Laurana in the Cappella Mastrantonio.

The Palazzina Cinese (c.1799), set in the Parco della Favorita

### 🏛 Palazzo Abatellis and Galleria Regionale di Sicilia

Via Alloro 4. **Tel** 091 623 00 11. **Open** 9am–6pm Tue–Sat. 🏠

Matteo Carnelivari built this palace combining Spanish late-Gothic and Italian Renaissance styles in the 15th century. It is home to the Galleria Regionale di Sicilia, which houses Antonello da Messina's *Vergine Annunziata* (1476) and Francesco Laurana's marble head of Eleanor of Aragon (15th century). Nearby, the 15th-century church of Santa Maria degli Angeli (or La Gancia) contains works by Antonello Gagini and Giacomo Serpotta.

*Vergine Annunziata* (1476) by da Messina in the Galleria Regionale

### 🏠 La Magione

Via Magione 44. **Tel** 091 617 05 96 or 339 377 41 37 (cell). **Open** 9am–7pm daily (to 1pm Sun in winter). 🏠 **basilicalamagione. diocesipia.it**

Restorations have revealed the ancient structure of this church founded in 1191 by Roger II's chancellor, Matteo d'Aiello. A highlight of Norman architecture, it has a simple nave flanked by fine Gothic columns.

### 🌳 Villa Giulia

Via Lincoln. **Open** 9am–5pm daily. Orto Botanico: **Tel** 091 740 40 28. **Open** Nov–Mar: 8am–5pm Mon–Sat, 8am–2pm Sun; longer opening hours in summer. **Closed** public hols. 🌳

The villa's formal gardens were established in the 1700s. Once, with their statues and fountains, they evoked the antique world. Nowadays, their tropical flora and faded grandeur make them delightful for walks. There are splendid tropical plants in the adjacent Orto Botanico (botanical gardens), and plant specimens can be examined in Léon Dufourny's Neo-Classical Gymnasium (1789). Palermo's only central park, Villa Giulia has good children's amenities.

### 🌳 Parco della Favorita

Entrance on Piazza Leoni & Piazza Generale Cascino. **Open** daily. Museo Etnografico Siciliano Pitré: Via Duca degli Abruzzi 1. **Tel** 091 740 48 90. **Open** 9am–1pm Mon–Fri (Wed: also 3:30–5pm). **Closed** public hols. 🏠

This park, laid out as a hunting ground in 1799 by the Bourbon Ferdinand IV, was surrounded by the nobles' summer villas. One of these, the Palazzina Cinese (c.1799), was built in a Chinese style for Ferdinand III and Maria Carolina, the sister of Marie Antoinette. The Museo Etnografico Siciliano Pitré, in the stables of the Palazzina Cinese, has some fine Sicilian objects.

# ❷ Monreale

Magnificently adorned, and with a splendid view of the Conca d'Oro, the Duomo at Monreale is one of the great sights of Norman Sicily. Founded in 1172 by the Norman King William II, it flanks a monastery of the Benedictine Order. The interior of the cathedral glitters with mosaics carried out by Sicilian and Byzantine artists – the inspiration of a king who wanted to rival the power of the Archbishop of Palermo. Like Cefalù, and later Palermo, it was to serve as a royal sepulchre.

★ **Christ Pantocrator**
The cathedral's Latin-cross plan focuses on the imposing mosaic (12th to 13th century) of the all-powerful Christ.

**Apse Exterior**
With their rich multicolored ornamentation in tufa and marble, the three apses represent the apogee of Norman decoration.

**KEY**

① **Barisano da Trani's bronze door** (1179) on the north side is shielded by a portico designed by Gian Domenico and Fazio Gagini (1547–69).

② **Original Cosmati floor** in choir.

③ **Nave and aisles separated by Roman columns**

④ **The royal tomb** of William II, in white marble, flanks the porphyry tomb of William I in the corner of the transept.

⑤ **Magnificent gilded wood ceiling**

⑥ **The south wall and cloisters** survive as elements from the Benedictine monastery.

⑦ **Small Oriental-inspired fountain**

⑧ **The 18th-century porch** is surrounded by two squat towers.

**Entrance to Cappella del Crocifisso and Treasury**

★ **Mosaic Cycle**
Completed in 1182, the rich mosaics show scenes from the Old Testament (nave), Teachings of Christ (aisles, choir, and transepts) and the Gospels (side apses). The story of Noah's Ark is depicted here.

*For hotels and restaurants in this region see pp576–7 and pp600–605*

**★ Cloisters**
A masterpiece of Norman artistic expression from the time of William II, the columns – plain, carved, or inlaid with richly lustered tiles – support elaborate capitals from which spring Saracenic-style arches.

## VISITORS' CHECKLIST

**Practical Information**
Piazza Duomo.
🅆 monrealeduomo.it
Church: **Tel** 091 640 44 13.
**Open** Mar–Oct: 8:30am–12:30pm & 2:30–5pm daily; Nov–Feb: 8am–12:30pm & 3:30–6pm daily. 🚻 📷 Cloister: **Tel** 091 640 44 03. **Open** 9am–1pm Mon–Sat. 📷 Treasury: **Open** same as the church. 📷

**Transportation**
🚌 389, 809, 8/9 and many others going west.

**Column Detail**
Craftsmen from Campania, Puglia, Lombardy, and Sicily worked on the cloister columns. The detail here shows Adam and Eve.

**Bronze Door Panel**
Bonanno da Pisa's fine bronze door (1185), signed by him, depicts 42 scenes from the Bible, set within elaborate borders. The lion and griffin are symbols of the Norman kingdom.

# ❸ Bagheria

Palermo. 🏛 50,000. 🚉 🚌 ℹ Corso
Umberto I (091 90 90 20). 🛒 Wed.
🌐 comune.bagheria.pa.it

Today Bagheria is almost a
suburb of Palermo, though open
countryside with olive and
orange groves once separated
them. In the 17th century,
Giuseppe Branciforte, Prince of
Butera, built a summer retreat
here, starting a fashion that
was quickly followed by other
Palermitan aristocrats. The town's
core is sprinkled with their
Baroque and Neo-Classical villas.

The **Villa Palagonia** was
designed in 1705 by the architect
Tommaso Maria Napoli for
Ferdinando Gravina, the
Prince of Palagonia. It has
remarkable architectural
qualities: a complex
open-air staircase leads
to the first floor, and the
principal rooms, all with
unusual shapes, are
arranged around a
curved axis. A later
prince adorned the
perimeter wall with the
grotesque stone monsters
that amused the 18th-century
traveler Patrick Brydone, and

Stone figure on
Villa Palagonia

horrified Goethe, who also
traveled here and called this
the "Palagonian madhouse."
Across the piazza are **Villa
Valguarnera** (begun in 1713
by Napoli), set in its own park,
and **Villa Trabia** (mid-18th
century), but neither
is open to the
public. **Museo
Guttuso** (18th
century) houses a
modern art gallery.

🏛 **Villa Palagonia**
Piazza Garibaldi 3.
**Tel** 091 93 20 88.
**Open** daily (except
during functions). 🎫

🏛 **Museo Guttuso**
Via Rammacca 9. **Tel** 091 94 39 02.
**Open** daily. 🎫

Fishing and pleasure boats moored in the harbor of Trapani

# ❹ Trapani

🏛 70,000. 🚉 🚌 🚢 ℹ Piazza
Scarlatti 1. 🛒 daily. 🌐 apt.trapani.it

Old Trapani occupies a narrow
peninsula. The best buildings
in this lively quarter are the
churches, such as the **Cathedral
of San Lorenzo** (1635) and the
**Chiesa del Collegio dei Gesuiti**
(c.1614–40). The facades of both,
and that of the **Palazzo d'Ali**
(17th century) on Via Garibaldi,
display magnificently the
ebullience of west Sicilian
Baroque architecture.

The 17th-century **Purgatorio**
on Via San Francesco d'Assisi
contains 18th-century *Misteri* –
realistic, life-sized wooden
statues that are used annually
in the Good Friday procession.
**Santa Maria del Gesù** on
Via Sant' Agostino should be
visited for the *Madonna degli
Angeli* by Andrea della Robbia
(1435–1525) and Antonello
Gagini's canopy (1521). In
the Jewish quarter, to the west
of Via XXX Gennaio, the
**Palazzo della Giudecca** (16th
century) has a strangely
textured facade.

The **Museo Pepoli** has a
collection of local antiquities.
Of interest are the coral objects
and the Nativity scene figures
(*presepi*), modern versions of
which are made here. Next to
the museum, the **Santuario di
Maria Santissima Annunziata**
contains the *Madonna di Trapani*,
a statue that has long been
revered by fishermen and
mariners for its legendary
miraculous powers.

🏛 **Museo Pepoli**
Via Conte Agostino Pepoli. **Tel** 0923 55
32 69. **Open** 9am–5:30pm Tue–Sat,
9am–12:30pm Sun & hols. 🎫

Open-air staircase of the eccentric Villa Palagonia in Bagheria

## ❺ Erice

Trapani. 🚇 29,000. 🚌 ℹ️ Via Conte a Repoli 11 (0923 50 21 11). 🚪 Mon.

Poised on a crag overlooking Trapani, the medieval town of Erice was once the seat of the cult of the fertility goddess Venus Erycina. Her temple stood on the present site of the Norman castle (**Castello di Venere**), beyond the **Villa Balio** public gardens. On a clear day, you can see all the way to Tunisia from the castle. The ancient town of Eryx was renamed Gebel-Hamed by the Arabs, Monte San Giuliano by the Normans, and finally Erice in 1934 by Mussolini.

The **Duomo** (14th century) has a battlemented campanile and a 15th-century porch. Inside is a *Madonna and Child* (*c*.1469), attributed to either Francesco Laurana or Domenico Gagini. The deconsecrated 13th-century **San Giovanni Battista** on Viale Nunzio Nasi (now a hotel) contains Antonello Gagini's *St. John the Evangelist* (1531) and Antonino Gagini's *St. John the Baptist* (1539). **San Cataldo**, a plain 14th-century building on Via San Cataldo, houses a holy water stoup (*c*.1474) from Domenico Gagini's workshop. In the **Museo Cordici** are Antonello Gagini's *Annunciation* (1525), a variety of Classical remains, and an old library.

### 🏛️ Museo Cordici
Piazza Umberto I. **Tel** 346 577 35 50. **Open** times vary greatly; call in advance to check.

A typical medieval street in the small hill-town of Erice

## Sicilian Islands

Surrounding Sicily are several island groups. The Isole Eolie (Aeolian Islands), to which Panarea, Lipari, Vulcano, and Stromboli belong, are a mass of volcanoes (most of them nearly extinct) poking out of the sea off the coast of Milazzo. The Isole Egadi (Egadi Islands), off the coast of Trapani, have a distinctly Arabic flavor. They include Favignana, Levanzo (which has Paleolithic and Neolithic paintings and drawings), and Marettimo – the smallest and most unspoiled. Ustica, renowned for its marine life and popular among divers, lies north of Palermo. To the south are the remarkably tourist-free Isole Pelagie (Pelagic Islands), Lampedusa and Linosa, which are North African in character. Remote Pantelleria lies closer to Tunisia than to Sicily.

**The biggest and most popular** of the Isole Eolie is Lipari, which has a pretty port and a good range of bars, restaurants, and hotels. Nearby sulfur-smelling Vulcano offers hot mudbaths and black beaches.

**Favignana,** the largest and most populous of the Isole Egadi, is the scene of the traditional tuna slaughter – *la mattanza*. Although rare nowadays, this still sometimes takes place in May. These fishermen are bringing in the nets following the slaughter.

**Part of the Isole Pelagie,** Lampedusa was once owned by the family of Giuseppe Tomasi di Lampedusa, author of *The Leopard*, Sicily's most famous novel. The island is nearer to Malta than Sicily and has limpid water and white beaches.

Ustica

Isole Eolie (Lipari)

Palermo

Isole Egadi

Sicily

Pantelleria

Isole Pelagie

0 kilometers 100
0 miles 50

## ❻ Marsala

Trapani. 🔼 83,000. 🚆 🚌 🚢 ℹ️ Via XI Maggio 100 (0923 71 40 97). 🚢 Tue. 🔲 **consorziovinomarsala.it**

The port of Marsala is the home of a thick, strong, sweet wine that has been in production here since the 18th century. In 1798 Admiral Nelson ordered vast quantities of it after the Battle of the Nile. Its early manufacture was presided over by three British families living in Sicily. One of the old warehouses where the wine was produced is now the **Museo Archeologico Baglio Anselmi**, with important Phoenician artifacts.

The ruins of **Lily-baeum** are another attraction. Founded in 397 BC, this outpost of the Phoenician Empire was peopled by the survivors of the massacre by Dionysius I of Siracusa at Mozia (ancient Motya) – the island used by the Phoenicians as a commercial center. Best of all are the reconstructed remains of a Punic ship thought to have been active in the First Punic War (263–241 BC). The **Museo di Mozia** in the Whitaker villa has a remarkable early 5th-century BC statue of a Greek youth.

The excavations here are important; what we know of the Phoenicians today comes mostly from the Bible, and from Mozia. The **Duomo**, begun in the 17th century, was built on the site of an earlier church; both were dedicated to Marsala's patron saint, Thomas à Becket of Canterbury. Its interior is full of sculptures by members of the Gagini family. The small **Museo degli Arazzi**, behind the Duomo, has several superb 16th-century Brussels tapestries.

**Statue of a Greek youth in Museo di Mozia**

### 🏛 Museo Archeologico Baglio Anselmi

Via Lungomare. **Tel** 0923 95 25 35. **Open** 9am–6:30pm Tue–Sat & 1st Sun of month; 9am–12:30pm Mon, Sun, & hols. ♿♿

### 🏛 Museo di Mozia

Isola di Mozia. **Tel** 0923 71 25 98. **Open** Apr–Oct: 9:30am–6:30pm daily; Nov–Mar: 9am–3pm daily. ♿♿

### 🏛 Museo degli Arazzi

Via Garaffa 57. **Tel** 0923 71 13 27. **Open** 9am–1pm & 4–6pm Tue–Sat; 9am–1pm Sun & Mon. ♿

## ❼ Segesta

Trapani. 🔼 7,500. 🚌 from Trapani & Palermo. **Tel** 0924 95 58 41. **Open** 9am–6:30pm daily (to 4pm in winter).

According to legend, the ancient town of Segesta – still largely unexcavated – was founded by Trojan followers of Aeneas. It presents one of the most spectacular sights on the island: a massive unfinished **temple** stranded on a remote hillside. Its construction was started between 426 and 416 BC, and it was left incomplete following the devastation of Selinunte by the Carthaginians in 409 BC. Archaeologists regard the temple as a good example of "work in progress." Nearby, close to the summit of Monte Barbaro, the ruins of an ancient theater (3rd century BC) can be visited. Summer concerts are now held here.

## ❽ Selinunte

Trapani. **Tel** 0924 462 77. 🚆 Castelvetrano then bus. **Open** 9am–6pm daily (to 4pm in winter). ♿

Founded in 651 BC, Selinunte became one of the great cities of Magna Graecia – the part of southern Italy that was colonized by ancient Greece – and its toppled ruins are among Sicily's most important historic sites. Its ancient name, Selinus, derives from the wild celery that still grows here. The city was an important port, and its wall defenses can still be seen around the Acropolis. The Carthaginians, under Hannibal, completely destroyed the city in 409 BC in a battle famous for its epic and spectacularly savage proportions.

While the city itself has virtually disappeared, eight of its temples are distinguishable, particularly the so-called **Eastern Temples** (E, F, and G). Of these, the columns of huge Doric **Temple E** (490–480 BC) have been partially re-erected. **Temple F** (c.560–540 BC) is in ruins. **Temple G** (late 6th century BC), which had 17 massive side columns, was one of the greatest Greek temples ever built.

Higher on the Acropolis lie the remains of **Temples A, B, C, D,** and **O**. Metope sculpture from **Temple C** (early 6th century), originally located on the frieze between the triglyphs, can be seen in the Museo Archeologico Regionale in Palermo (*see p532*), along with ceramics, jewelry, and other artifacts excavated here. A small **museum** on site houses less important finds, as does one in Castelvetrano, 8.5 miles (14 km) north of Selinunte. The ancient city is still being excavated; its **North Gate** entrance is well preserved and farther north there is also a **necropolis**.

The spectacularly located, unfinished Doric temple at Segesta

## ❾ Cefalù

Palermo. 🗺 14,000. 🚆 🚌 ℹ️ Corso Ruggero 77 (0921 42 10 50). 🛒 Sat.
🌐 **cefalu.it**

This pretty seaside town, with sandy beaches, restaurants, and hotels, is dominated by a huge rock known as **La Rocca** – once the site of a Temple of Diana – and by one of the finest Norman cathedrals in Sicily. Begun in 1131 by Roger II, the **Duomo** was intended as the main religious seat in Sicily. Though it failed to fulfill this function, the building's magnificence has never been eclipsed. Its splendid mosaics (1148), which feature an image of Christ Pantocrator in the apse, are remarkable and often celebrated as purely Byzantine works of art on Sicilian soil.

The **Museo Mandralisca** houses a fine *Portrait of a Man* (c.1465) by Antonello da Messina and a collection of coins, ceramics, vases, and minerals.

🏛 **Museo Mandralisca**
Via Mandralisca. **Tel** 0921 42 15 47. **Open** 9am–7pm daily (later in summer). 🖼

The lavish apse of Cefalù's Duomo

## ❿ Agrigento

🗺 59,000. 🚆 🚌 🚌 ℹ️ Via Empedocle 73 (0922 203 91); Piazzale Aldo Moro (0922 59 36 78). 🛒 Fri.
🌐 **www.comune.agrigento.it**

Modern Agrigento occupies the site of Akragas, an important city of the ancient Greek world. Founded by Daedalus, according to legend, it was famed for the luxurious lifestyle of its

The twin-towered facade of the Norman Duomo in Cefalù

inhabitants, and was a great power and rival to Siracusa. In 406 BC it fell to the Carthaginians, who sacked and burned it.

The historic core of the city, with its medieval streets, focuses on the Via Atenea. **Santo Spirito** (13th century) houses stuccoes by Giacomo Serpotta (1695). **Santa Maria dei Greci** was built on the remains of a 5th-century BC temple – see the flattened columns in the nave. The **Duomo**, founded in the 14th century and altered in the 16th and 17th centuries, exhibits a unique mixture of Arab, Norman, and Catalan detailing.

### Environs

The main reason to visit Agrigento is to see the archaeological zone known as the Valley of the Temples *(see p540)*. The **Museo Regionale Archeologico** houses an interesting display of artifacts from the temples and the city, including vases, coins, and Greek and Roman sculpture.

🏛 **Museo Regionale Archeologico**
Contrada San Nicola, Viale Panoramica. **Tel** 0922 40 15 65. **Open** 9am–7:30pm Tue–Sat, 9am–1:30pm Mon & Sun. 🖼 ♿

## The Mafia

An international organization founded in Sicily, the Mafia developed as a result of the cruel State and severe poverty. By the late 19th century it had become a criminal organization thriving on property speculation and drug trafficking. Since the "singing" of Tommaso Buscetta and the capture of Toto Riina, the Mafia has been on the defensive against a State that has doubled its efforts against it. The "Boss of Bosses," Bernardo Provenzano, was arrested in 2006 after 43 years on the run. Violence is common in Sicily, but it is not directed at tourists.

Mafia assassination depicted in this scene from the movie *The Godfather Part III* (1990)

# Valley of the Temples

Straddling a low ridge to the south of Agrigento, the Valley of the Temples (Valle dei Templi) is one of the most impressive complexes of ancient Greek buildings outside Greece. Its Doric temples, dating from the 5th century BC, were destroyed in part by the Carthaginians in 406 BC, and in part by Christians, who believed the temples to be pagan, in the 6th century. Earthquakes wreaked further havoc. Nine of the original ten temples are still visible, and the whole area can be covered in a day. To avoid crowds, visit early in the morning (some temples open as early as 8:30am) or late afternoon.

### ① Temple of Hephaestus
Aside from a couple of incomplete columns still standing, very little remains of this temple, built c.430 BC. It is also called the Temple of Vulcan.

### ② Sanctuary of the Chthonic Divinities
At this group of shrines, the forces of nature were worshipped.

Telamone from the Temple of Olympian Zeus

San Biagio

Rock Sanctuary of Demeter →

(see p539)
Museo Regionale Archeologico

San Nicola

Via dei Templi

Via dei Templi

Strada Panoramica

Hellenistic and Roman Quarter

Catacombs

S115

P

Via Sacra

Temple of Asklepios

S115

### ④ Temple of Olympian Zeus
Begun c.480 BC, this was the biggest Doric temple ever built. Unfinished at the time of the Carthaginian attack, it is now a toppled ruin. Giant figures known as telamones were used in its construction.

### ⑤ Tomb of Theron
Here are the ruins of a Roman tomb (1st century AD).

### ⑥ Temple of Herakles
This is the oldest temple in the valley (late 6th century BC).

### ⑧ Temple of Juno
Built around 450 BC, this temple still has many intact columns.

### ③ Temple of Castor and Pollux
This is a controversial assemblage of pieces from other buildings, erected in the 19th century. Modern Agrigento (see p539) is in the background.

**Key**

━ Suggested route

─ Ancient walls

| 0 metres | 500 |
|---|---|
| 0 yards | 500 |

### ⑦ Temple of Concord
This beautifully preserved temple (c.430 BC) was converted into a Christian church in the 4th century AD, thus saved from destruction.

# ⓫ Piazza Armerina

Enna. 🚠 21,000. 🚌 𝒊 Via Generale
Muscara (0935 68 02 01). 🕭 Thu.
🌐 **piazzaarmerina.org**

This active town is half medieval
and half Baroque. The 17th-
century **Duomo**, at its highest
point, is the most interesting of
the Baroque buildings.

In August, the lively Palio dei
Normanni festival attracts many
visitors, but the real draw are
the mosaics in the UNESCO-
listed **Villa Romana del Casale**,
3 miles (5 km) southwest of the
town. The mosaics were only
excavated in the 20th century.

It is thought that this huge,
once sumptuous villa, with its
public halls, private quarters,
baths, and courtyards, belonged
to Maximianus Herculeus,
Diocletian's co-emperor, from
AD 286 to 305. His son and
successor, Maxentius, probably
continued its decoration, with
Constantine taking over on
Maxentius's death in 312.

Although little remains of the
building fabric, the floors have
some of the finest surviving
mosaics from Roman antiquity.
The hunting, mythological and
domestic scenes, and exotic
landscapes, all exhibit realistic
attention to detail.

🏛 **Villa Romana del Casale**
Contrada Casale. **Tel** 0935 68 00 36.
**Open** 9am–6pm (winter: to 4pm). 🖼

Roman *Girls in Bikinis* mosaic from the Villa Romana del Casale

# ⓬ Enna

🚠 28,000. 🚆 🚌 𝒊 Piazza
Colaianni 6 (0935 50 08 75). 🕭 Tue.
🌐 **culturasicilia.it**

Impregnable on a crag above
a fertile landscape where Persephone, mythological daughter
of Demeter, once played, Sicily's
highest town (3,090 ft /942 m)
has been coveted by successive
invaders since its earliest days.
The venerated seat of the
Cult of Demeter (goddess of
fertility) was at Enna. Her temple
stood on the **Rocca Cerere**, not
far from the huge **Castello di
Lombardia** (13th century) built
by Frederick II.

Most sights are clustered in the
old town, among the ancient
streets that open out of the
Via Roma. The church of **San**
**Francesco** has a 16th-century
tower. **Piazza Crispi**, with its
fine views to nearby Calas-
cibetta, is dominated by a copy
of Bernini's *Rape of Persephone*.
The 14th-century **Duomo**, altered
in later centuries, contains parts
of Demeter's temple, an arch
of which is still visible in the
exterior of the Apse. Its facade
is rich in Gothic decorations.
Inside, don't miss the original
wooden ceiling and the
restored sacristy.

The **Museo Varisano** has
exhibits on the area's history,
from Neolithic to Roman. Away
from the center, the octagonal
**Torre di Federico II** (13th century)
is a former watchtower.

### Environs

The ancient hill-town of **Nicosia**,
northeast of Enna, was damaged
in the 1967 earthquake, but
still contains a smattering of
churches. San Nicola, built in the
14th century, has a magnificent,
carved entrance portal. Inside
there is a much venerated
wooden crucifix (17th century)
by Fra Umile di Petralia. Santa
Maria Maggiore houses a 16th-
century marble polyptych by
Antonello Gagini and a throne
reputedly used by Charles V in
1535. Farther east is **Troina**.
It was captured in 1062 by the
Normans, whose work survives
in the Chiesa Matrice. Southeast
of Enna, **Vizzini** commands fine
views of the countryside.

🏛 **Museo Varisano**
Piazza Mazzini. **Tel** 0935 52 81 00.
**Open** 9am–7pm Mon–Sat.

An aerial view of the small town of Troina

Taormina's magnificently located Greek theater, with Mount Etna in the distance

## ⑬ Tindari

Messina. 🛈 **Tel** 0941 24 11 36. 🚈
Patti or Oliveri, then bus. **Open** 9am–
6:30pm daily (to 4pm in winter). ♿ 🅿

Poised on the edge of a cliff
overlooking the Golfo di Patti
are the ruins of **Tyndaris**, one
of the last Greek cities to have
been founded in Sicily (395 BC).
Aside from the city walls, the
ruins are mostly Roman,
including the **basilica** and
**theater**. An **antiquarium**
houses artifacts from the site.
A combined ticket allows entry
at the massive 2nd-century
**Villa Romana** in Patti Marina.
Tindari is also known for
its shrine to a Byzantine icon,
the **Black Madonna** on
Piazzale Belvedere.

## ⑭ Messina

🛆 250,000. 🚈 🚌 ⛴ 🛈 Piazza
Cairoli 45 (090 293 52 92). 🛒 daily.
🌐 www.comune.messina.it

Messina has been the victim of
earthquakes and World War II
bombing. The **Museo Regionale**
houses treasures including works
by Antonello da Messina and
Caravaggio. In Piazza Catalani
**Santissima Annunziata dei
Catalani** displays the eclecticism
of 12th-century Norman archi-

tecture, with rich decoration. To
visit, ask at the tourist office.
Outside, G. A. Montorsoli's
**Fontana d'Orione** (1547) is the
finest fountain of its kind from
16th-century Sicily. His **Fontana
di Nettuno** (1557) celebrates
Messina's foundation and
position in the world as a
principal commercial port.

### 🏛 Museo Regionale
Via Libertà 465. **Tel** 090 36 12 92.
**Open** 9am–7pm Tue–Sat, 9am–1pm
Sun (last adm: 30 mins before closing).
🅿 ♿

Antonello da Messina's *Madonna and Child*
(1473), Museo Regionale

## ⑮ Taormina

Messina. 🛆 10,000. 🚈 🚌
🛈 Palazzo Corvaja, Piazza Santa
Caterina (0942 232 43). 🛒 Wed.

Splendidly located, Taormina
is Sicily's best-known resort.
It retains an air of exclusivity
while being on the tourist trail,
with sandy beaches and a wide
range of restaurants and hotels.
The most illustrious relic of
the past is the **theater**. Begun in
the 3rd century BC by the Greeks,
it was subsequently rebuilt by the
Romans. Among other Classical
remains are the ruins of the
**odeon** (for musical performances)
and the **naumachia** (an artificial
lake for mock battles). On Piazza
Vittorio Emanuele (site of the
Roman Forum), **Palazzo Corvaia**
(14th century) was built using
stone from a temple that once
stood here. The 13th-century
**Duomo** (renovated in 1636) is
a fortresslike building.

### Environs
Taormina's main beach,
**Mazzarò**, boasts clear waters
and is easily reached from the
town. South of Taormina at
**Capo Schisò** are the ruins of
ancient **Naxos**. To the west is
**Gole dell'Alcantara**, a 66 ft-
(20 m-) deep gorge of basalt
rock, a river, and waterfalls.

*For hotels and restaurants in this region see pp576–7 and pp600–605*

## ⑯ Mount Etna

Catania. **FS** Linguaglossa or Randazzo; Circumetnea train from Catania to Riposto. 🚌 to Nicolosi. 🛈 Via G. Garibaldi 63, Nicolosi (095 91 15 05). To hire a guide: 095 791 47 55. **W** turismo.provincia.ct.it

Europe's highest (11,050 ft/ 3,370 m) and most active volcano, Mount Etna was thought by the Romans to have been the forge of Vulcan (god of fire). The climb to the summit should be made only with an experienced guide. The Circumetnea train runs around the base, offering an alternative to hiking and good views.

## ⑰ Catania

🏛 315,000. ✈ **FS** 🚌 🛈 Via Cimarosa 10 (095 401 40 40). 🗓 Mon–Sat (general); Sun (antiques & bric-a-brac). **W** apt-catania.com

Having been decimated by the earthquake of 1693, Catania was comprehensively rebuilt. While it is not immediately beautiful, it

The facade of Catania's Duomo

contains some of the most imaginative lava-built Baroque buildings in Sicily. **Piazza del Duomo**, featuring a lava elephant (Catania's symbol) carrying an Egyptian obelisk, offers a dramatic vista to Mount Etna. In 1736, the Norman **Duomo** was given a new facade by Vaccarini, who also worked on the **Municipio** (finished 1741), on the facade of **Sant'Agata** (1748), on the designs of **Collegio Cutelli**,

built around 1779, and on **Palazzo Valle** (c.1740–50).

Carrying on the Vaccarini tradition is Stefano Ittar's **San Placido** (around 1768). The frenzied stone carving on the **Palazzo Biscari** (early 18th century) is exceeded by Antonino Amato's unrestrained decoration of the vast Benedictine **convent** (1704) and the adjacent huge church of **San Niccolò** (1730).

On Via Vittorio Emanuele is the **Museo Belliniano**, birthplace of composer Vincenzo Bellini (1801–35). The lava ruins of the **Teatro Romano** (21 BC) are at Piazza Stesicono. **Verga's House**, home of the great Sicilian novelist Giovanni Verga (1840–1922), is on Via Sant'Anna. Via Crociferi is home to 18th-century churches **San Francesco Borgia**, **San Benedetto**, and **San Giuliano**, whose interior is Vaccarini's masterpiece (1760). Farther along Via Crociferi, the church of **Santo Carcere** contains the prison of St. Agatha, who was martyred in AD 253.

## Influences on Traditional Sicilian Cuisine

Sicily has one of Italy's most varied cuisines. The island's unique location – marooned between North Africa, Europe, and the eastern Mediterranean – and the invaders it attracted are responsible for this culinary diversity. The earliest Western cookbook, the now lost *Art of Cooking* (5th century BC), was written by Mithaecus, a Siracusan Greek. Sicily's fertility attracted Greek colonists, who exported oil, wheat, honey, cheese, fruit, and vegetables to their homeland. The Arabs introduced oranges, lemons, eggplant, and sugar cane. Their love of sweet confections inspired *granita*, a form of flavored ice, and *cassata*, an elaborate sponge cake with ricotta and candied

A colorful selection of vegetables at a Sicilian market stand

Marzipan fruits made from almond paste

fruit. The Sicilians love to claim an Arabic origin for their ice cream, but the Greeks and Romans had created an earlier version by chilling their wine with snow from Mount Etna. Traditionally, the peasants existed on a subsistence diet, while the aristocracy enjoyed extravagant fare, and one

of the peculiarities of Sicilian food today is that it can be both frugal and handsomely ornate. All of the usual Italian dishes are available, but the more interesting meals are those that use local ingredients like swordfish, sardines, ricotta cheese, red chili peppers, eggplant, capers, olives, and almond paste to create unusual taste combinations.

Shorefront in Siracusa, one of the most beautiful cities of the ancient Greek world

## ⑱ Pantalica

Siracusa. 🚃 from Siracusa to Sortino, then 3 mile (5 km) walk to entrance (partial access), or bus from Siracusa to Ferla then 6-mile (10-km) walk to entrance. Necropolis: 🛈 Pro Loco, Ferla. **Tel** 331 152 44 24.

Remote in the desolate Monti Iblei and overlooking the Anapo River is the prehistoric **necropolis** of Pantalica – a pleasant place to walk and picnic. The dead of a large, unexcavated village (occupied from the 13th to 8th centuries BC) were buried here in cavelike tombs cut into the rock. More than 5,000 of these tombs were arranged in tiers, with a single flat stone sealing each opening.

The inhabitants of Pantalica are thought to have come from coastal **Thapsos**, which was abandoned after raids by warlike tribes from mainland Italy. The site was reinhabited in the Byzantine period, when some tombs were made into cave dwellings and chapels.

Rock-cut tombs in the prehistoric necropolis of Pantalica

Artifacts from the necropolis are displayed in Siracusa's Museo Archeologico Regionale.

Interior of Duomo in Siracusa

## ⑲ Siracusa

🏙 125,000. 🚇 🚌 🚢 🛈 Via Maestranza (0931 46 42 55). 🗓 Wed.

Siracusa (Syracuse) was the most important and powerful Greek city from the 5th to the 3rd centuries BC, and, according to the Roman consul Cicero, the most beautiful. The peninsula **Ortigia** is the hub of the old city. On the mainland, **Achradina, Tyche** and **Neapolis** have been occupied almost without a break since the expansion of the city in 480 BC. These were the years of Gelon, tyrant of Gela, when Siracusa was enriched with new temples, theaters, and dockyards. The city was a powerful force until 211 BC, when it fell to the Romans in a battle that also killed the

mathematician Archimedes, its most famous inhabitant.

The highlight of Ortigia is the extraordinary **Duomo**, begun in 1728 by architect Andrea Palma. Its Baroque facade masks the **Temple of Athena** (5th century BC), which has been absorbed into the Duomo. Facing the Ponte Nuovo are the ruins of Sicily's earliest Doric temple, the **Temple of Apollo**, which had monolithic columns.

Across from the Duomo is the **Palazzo Beneventano del Bosco** (1778–88), a bold example of Siracusan Baroque, as is **Santa Lucia alla Badia** (1695–1703). In the Municipio, a small museum records the history of Ionic temples, and the coin collection of the Galleria Numismatica records Siracusa's past wealth. The delightful **Fonte Aretusa** is frequently referred to by Classical writers as the point where Aretusa emerged from the ground, having been changed into a spring by Artemis to help her escape her lover, Alpheus.

At Ortigia's farthest point is the **Castello Maniace**, built by Frederick II around 1239. Here, too, is the **Galleria Regionale di Palazzo Bellomo**, with sculpture and paintings including the *Burial of St. Lucy* (1608) by Caravaggio.

The painting comes from the church of **Santa Lucia** in the Achradina quarter. This area was flattened during World War II, but the church survived. It is mostly 17th century with a

Norman campanile, and occupies the site where St. Lucy, patron saint of Siracusa, was martyred in AD 304. Achradina is now the center of modern Siracusa.

To the north, in Tyche, is the **Museo Archeologico Regionale Paolo Orsi**, with its important collection of artifacts from the Paleolithic to the Byzantine era, taken from southeastern sites in Sicily. Included are vases, coins, bronzes, sculpture, and fragments from Siracusan temples.

The Neapolis quarter and its **Parco Archeologico** feature the Teatro Romano, the Altar of Hieron II, and the spectacular Teatro Greco, carved from the hillside. Beyond the Nymphaeum is the 2nd-century-AD Roman amphitheater and the stone quarries – the Latomia del Paradiso, featuring the **Ear of Dionysius**. It is thought that 7,000 Athenians were incarcerated here and left to die after their calamitous defeat in 413 BC, in a battle described by Thucydides as "the greatest action in Hellenic history."

### Environs
At **Epipolae**, 5 miles (8 km) north of Neapolis, is the **Castle of Euryalus** – the most important ancient Greek fortification to have survived.

**🏛 Galleria Regionale di Palazzo Bellomo**
Palazzo Bellomo, Via Capodieci 14. **Tel** 0931 695 11. **Open** 9am–6:30pm Tue–Sun (to 1pm public hols). 🚫 ♿

**🏛 Museo Archeologico Regionale Paolo Orsi**
Viale Teocrito 66. **Tel** 0931 48 95 11. **Open** 9am–6pm Tue–Sat; 9am–1pm Sun (last adm: 1 hr before closing). 🚫 ♿

## ⓴ Noto
Siracusa. 🚩 24,000. 🚆 📷 ℹ Piazza XVI Maggio (0931 83 67 44). 🚌 Mon & 1st & 3rd Tue of the month. 🌐 comune.noto.sr.it

Noto was built from scratch in the early 18th century to replace Noto Antica, which was devastated by an earthquake in 1693. The town was comprehensively designed in Baroque style, using

The facade of the Duomo in Noto rises above a huge staircase

the local white tufa, a limestone that has turned a honey-brown color from the sun. Noto is a UNESCO World Heritage Site, but unfortunately much of its beauty is behind scaffolding due to ongoing restoration.

The twin-towered **Duomo** (completed 1770s) that dominates Noto is by architect Rosario Gagliardi, who also designed the eccentric tower facade of the seminary of **San Salvatore** (18th century) in Piazza Municipio, the convex facade of **San Domenico** (1730s) in Piazza XVI Maggio, and the oval interior of **Santa Chiara** (1730) on Corso Vittorio

Emanuele. The magnificent **Palazzo Trigona** (1781) stands on Via Cavour behind the Duomo. On Via Nicolaci, the **Palazzo Villadorata** (1730s) features a splendid facade adorned with elaborate stone carvings. At the north end of Via Nicolaci, the **Monastery of Montevergine** has a striking curved facade. In mid-May, Via Nicolaci is the site of the Infiorata flower festival. Gagliardi's church of the **Crocifisso** (1728) stands on the town's summit. It contains a sculpture of the Madonna by Francesco Laurana (1471). The **Municipio** (1740s), facing the Duomo, has a fine "billowing" first-floor design.

### Environs
The earthquake of 1693 also devastated the towns of **Modica**, around 19 miles (30 km) to the west, and **Ragusa**, a short distance farther. Like Noto, they were rebuilt in the region's rich Baroque style. Gagliardi worked on Modica's **San Giorgio** (early 18th century), Ragusa's **San Giorgio** (begun around 1746, and one of his masterpieces), and **San Giuseppe** (mid-18th century).

Boisterous carving on the facade of the Palazzo Villadorata in Noto

# SARDINIA

In his travelogue *Sea and Sardinia*, D. H. Lawrence wrote that Sardinia was "left outside of time and history." Indeed, the march of time has been slow here, and traditions from ancient Europe have survived – the legacy of invasion by Phoenicians, Carthaginians, Romans, Arabs, Byzantines, Spaniards, and Savoyards.

These traditions are displayed in Sardinia's many festivals – some soberly Christian, others with pagan roots. Several different dialects and languages are spoken in Sardinia. Catalan can be heard in Alghero, and on the island of San Pietro there is a Ligurian dialect. In the south, the traditional influences are Spanish, while conservative native strains of people and language survive in the Gennargentu mountains. Peopled by shepherds in isolated communities, this region is so impenetrable that invaders have never bothered it.

Of particular interest are the prehistoric *nuraghi* castles, villages, temples, and tombs dotted around the countryside – most notably around Barumini, north of Cagliari, and in the Valle dei Nuraghi, south of Sassari. The *nuraghi* were built by a people whose origins constitute one of the Mediterranean's great mysteries. In Cagliari, the capital of Sardinia, there is a museum with an excellent archaeological collection that offers insight into this enigmatic people.

Sassari, Oristano, Alghero, and Olbia are all centers of areas marked by their individuality. Some remarkable Pisan-Romanesque churches are located around Sassari, and here, too, dialects reveal close links with the languages of Tuscany. Olbia is a boom town made rich by tourism and the proximity of the jet-setting Costa Smeralda. Sober Nuoro with its province in the shadow of the Gennargentu mountains, by contrast, has little in common with the Sardinia of tourist brochures.

Relaxing during the day in the tiny resort of Carloforte on the Isola di San Pietro, next to Sant'Antioco

◀ The gorgeous turquoise waters of Costa Paradiso, Sardinia

# Exploring Sardinia

This island, called Sardegna in Italian, is characterized by an interior of dramatic, rolling uplands covered in *macchia* – grassland mingled with myrtle, wild thyme, prickly pears, and dwarf oaks – and a coastline of beguiling, translucent sea, isolated coves, long sandy beaches, and caves. The Gennargentu mountains, with the highest peak at 6,017 ft (1,834 m), shield a nearly impenetrable area of rural villages. In the northeast, mountains fall away dramatically to the Costa Smeralda, Sardinia's most exclusive coastal area. Farther south, the shoreline around the Golfo di Orosei is fairly unspoiled. Around Oristano in the west the land is flat, leading to the plain of Campidano, where the island's corn, fruit, and vegetables grow.

A typical scene of clothes hanging out to dry in Alghero

## Sights at a Glance

1. Costa Smeralda
2. Sassari
3. Alghero
4. Bosa
5. Nuoro
6. Cala Gonone
7. Oristano
8. Sant'Antioco
9. Cagliari

## Getting Around

Ferries from a wide range of ports on the Italian mainland dock at Cagliari, Olbia, and Porto Torres. International and domestic flights use the airports at Cagliari, Olbia, and Alghero. The island is neatly cut by the S131. It skirts the Gennargentu mountains, which are accessible only by tortuously winding passes. Branches of the S131 reach Olbia and Nuoro. Express bus services connect the major cities, while the smaller towns are linked by slow and infrequent public bus services.

**For additional map symbols** *see back flap*

Isola Asinara
la Reale
Fornelli
*Golfo*
Stintino
*dell' Asinara*
S200
Porto Torres
Sorso
Palmadula
S131
Osilo
SASSARI 2
Capo dell'
Ploac
Argentiera
S291
Olmedo
Ittiri
Ard
Grotta di
Nettuno
ALGHERO 3
Torral
S292
Va
Monteleone Rocca Doria
Ni
Montresta
Bonorv
Capo Marargiu
4 BOSA
Bosa Marina
Macome
MAR DI SARDEGNA
Cuglieri
Monte Ferru
1050m
Gl
Capo Mannu
Riola Sardo
Fordongia
Stagno di Cabras
Sola
ORISTANO 7
Sir
Santa Giusta
Arborea
S131
Capo della
Frasca
Terralba
Ur
S126
Pardu Atzei
Sar
Guspini
Capo Pecora
Villacidro
Monte Linas
1236m
Buggerru
Vallermo
Masua
S126
Iglesias
S130
Gonnesa
Sili
Portoscuso
Narcac
Carbonia
Isola di
Monte Caravit
San Pietro
Calasetta
1116
S195
SANT'ANTIOCO 8
Porto Botte
Isola di
Golfo
Sant'Antioco
di
Palmas
Teulada
Capo Teulada

resa Gallura
Capo Testa
*Isola Maddalena*
Palau
La Maddalena
*Isola Caprera*
ientu
Cannigione
Porto Cervo
**COSTA SMERALDA**
Luogosanto
San Pantaleo ①
*Galura*
Luras
Sant'Antonio
empio usania
Olbia
*Golfo Aranci*
*Golfo di Olbia*
Berchidda
Monte Limbara
1362m
Monti
Loiri
Porto S. Paolo
*Punta Timone*
*Capo Coda Cavallo*
Oschiri
Padru
San Teodoro
Monte di Alà
Budoni
*Punta la Batteria*
Pattada
Monte Lerno
1094m
Piras
Posada
Mamone
Siniscola
Osidda
Bitti
*Capo Comino*
te Rasu
259m
Bono
Orune
Irgoli
Cala Liberotto
*Monti Remule*
Orotelli
Dorgali
⑤ **NUORO**
Oliena
⑥ **CALA GONONE**
*Golfo di Orosei*
Orosei
Punta Corrasi
1463m
Orgosolo
*Grotto del Bue Marino*
Gavoi
Fonni
Urzulei
**T I R R E N O**
D E G N A
*Monti dei Gennargentu*
gono
Talana
Baunei
Santa Maria Navarrese
eo
Punta La Marmora
1834m
Seulo
Lanusei
Arbatax
Laconi
Seui
Ussassai
Bari Sardo
ao
△ Monte S. Vittoria
1212m
Nurri
Perdasdefogu
Melisenda
**M A R**
Mandas
amar
San Basilio
San Nicolò Gerrei
renti
Sant'Andrea Frius
Villaputzu
Muravera
San Sperate
Burcei
San Priamo
*Sarrabus*
Sinnai
*Capo Ferrato*
Quartu Sant'Elena
⑨ **CAGLIARI**
Geremeas
Maddalena
Spiaggia
Villasimius
*Golfo di Cagliari*
arroch
ula
*Capo di Pula*

Waves lapping at the rocks on Isola di San Pietro, northwest of Sant'Antioco

**Key**

⊟ Major highway
── Secondary road
── Minor road
── Scenic route
┈ Main railroad line
── Minor railroad line
△ Summit

0 kilometers                    50
0 miles                25

Southernmost reach of the Gennargentu Mountains

The extravagantly beautiful, macchia-scented Costa Smeralda

# ❶ Costa Smeralda

Sassari. FS 🚢 Olbia. 🚌 Porto Cervo.
🛈 AAST La Maddalena, Cava Civetta
(0789 73 63 21); AAST Palau, Via
Nazionale 94 (0789 70 95 70).
W destinationcostasmeralda.com

Stretching from the Golfo di
Cugnana to the Golfo di
Arzachena, the Costa Smeralda
was developed by a consortium of magnates in the 1950s.
One of the world's most opulent
vacation resorts, it is kept
immaculate by strict controls.

In **Porto Cervo**, the main
town, boutiques jostle with
nightclubs, fine restaurants, and
luxury hotels. It caters to the
seriously rich – billionaires,
crowned heads, and pop stars.

**Environs**
Head north to rural **Baia
Sardinia** and **Cannigione**.
From Palau ferries leave for **La
Maddalena** and **Isola Caprera**,
the home of Garibaldi and the
**Museo Nazionale Garibaldino**.

🏛 **Museo Nazionale Garibaldino**
Frazione Caprera, La Maddalena.
**Tel** 0789 72 71 62. **Open** 9am–8pm
Tue–Sun. **Closed** Jan 1, May 1, Dec 25.
🐾 🛇 W compendiogaribaldino.it

# ❷ Sassari

🜨 130,000. 🛪 FS 🚌 🛈 Viale
Caprera 36 (079 27 99 54). 🗓 Mon.
W www.provincia.sassari.it

Founded by Genoese and Pisan
merchants early in the 13th
century, Sassari is known for its
spectacular *Cavalcata Sarda*
festival on Ascension Day, and

for being the site of Sardinia's
first university. There is a
raucous, tight, church-filled
medieval quarter around
the **Duomo** (11th
century, with later,
mostly Baroque,
additions). To the
north is the huge
**Fonte Rosello**,
a late Renaissance
fountain. The **Museo
Archeologico
Nazionale "GA
Sanna"** is a good
starting point for
investigating
the region's
nuraghic history.

**Environs**
To the southeast
along the S131 is
the Pisan-Romanesque church
of **Santissima Trinità di
Saccargia** (1116), with the only
extant 13th-century fresco cycle
in Sardinia. Farther on is the
12th-century church of **San
Michele di
Salvenero**,
and at **Ardara**
the basalt-built
Romanesque
**Santa Maria
del Regno**, or
"Black Cathedral".

Façade of Santissima
Trinità di Saccargia

🏛 **Museo
Archeologico
Nazionale "GA
Sanna"**
Via Roma 64.
**Tel** 079 27 22 03.
**Open** 9am–8pm
Tue–Sun (to 2pm
Sun). 🐾 🛇

# ❸ Alghero

Sassari. 🜨 41,000. 🛪 FS 🚌
🚢 🛈 Lungomare Dante 1
(079 97 90 54). 🗓 Wed.
W comune.alghero.ss.it

Founded on a peninsula facing
the Bay of Alghero early in the
12th century, and taken from
the Genoese Dorias by the
Aragonese in 1353, Alghero
was peopled by settlers from
Barcelona and Valencia. Its
original occupants – Ligurians
and Sardinians – were expelled
with such thoroughness that
today the Catalan language and
culture is enjoying a revival and
the look of old Alghero is
consistently Spanish.

Filled with labyrinthine alleys
and cobblestone streets, the
lively port of old Alghero is
flanked by battlemented walls
and defensive towers on all but
the landward section. Facing
the Giardino Pubblico is the
massive 16th-century **Torre
di Porta Terra**, or
Jewish Tower, after
its builders. Around
the periphery of the
old town are more
towers, including
**Torre dell'Espero
Reial** and **Torre
San Giacomo** on
Lungomare
Colombo, and **Torre
della Maddalena** on
Piazza Porta Terra.

The 16th-century **Duomo** at
the bottom of Via Umberto is
predominantly Catalan-Gothic
with an Aragonese portal.
Off Via Carlo Alberto, **San

Typical houses in Alghero

The waterfront at Bosa

**Francesco** (14th century) has a pretty cloister and octagonal campanile towering over Alghero, and Baroque **San Michele** has a bright tiled dome. In Via Principe Umberto is the **Casa Doria**, the house where the pre-Hispanic rulers of Alghero lived. It has a beautiful Renaissance portal and Gothic-arched window.

### Environs

Take a boat trip or drive (the latter involves much climbing down) to the spectacular **Grotta di Nettuno**, a deep natural cave round the point of Capo Caccia, or the nearby **Grotta Verde**

## ❹ Bosa

Nuoro. 🗺 8,500. 🚊 🚌 ℹ️ Pro Loco, Via Azuni 5 (0785 37 70 43). 📅 Tue.

Bosa is a small, picturesque seaside town at the mouth of Sardinia's only navigable river, the Temo. The historic **Sa Costa** district struggles up the side of a low hill capped by the **Castello di Serravalle**, built in 1122 by the Malaspina family. The narrow passages and alleys here have changed little since the Middle Ages. By the Temo are **Sas Conzas** – the former dyers' houses and workshops.

Languishing on the riverside, the cosmopolitan **Sa Piatta** district houses the Aragonese-Gothic **Duomo** (15th century) and Romanesque **San Pietro Extramuros** (11th century), with a Gothic facade added by Cistercian monks in the 13th century.

## Nuraghi in Sardinia

The dominant feature of Sardinia is the 7,000 or so *nuraghi* dotted around the island. Dating from 1800 to 300 BC, these strange, truncated cone structures were built without any bonding from huge basalt blocks taken from extinct volcanoes. To this day, little is known about the identity of the Nuragic people. They must have been well organized and possessed remarkable engineering skills, judging by their buildings, but appear to have left no written word. The mystery of these enigmatic people has intrigued Sardinians for years.

**The individual *nuraghi*** are fairly small. A few of these structures were fortresses, equipped with wells and other defensive features.

**Su Nuraxi at Barumini** *(above)*, Serra Orrios, near Dorgali, and Santu Antine at Torralba are among the most important *nuraghe* complexes. Houses, temples, tombs, and even a theater, have been identified.

**This bronze figure** of a hero with four eyes and four arms is among the many objects and statues discovered on nuragic sites and associated with the Nuragic people.

**Key**

● Nuraghic sites

0 kilometres 100
0 miles 50

● Sassari

**Nuoro**

SARDINIA

● Oristano

**Cagliari**

Nobel Prize–winning novelist Grazia Deledda from Nuoro

# ❺ Nuoro

🚠 38,000. 🚉 🚌 ⓘ Piazza d'Italia 19 (0784 300 83). 🍴 Fri & Sat. 🎪 Aug 29: Sagra del Redentore. ⓦ comune.nuoro.it

This town, in a spectacular setting beneath Monte Ortobene and the dramatic Supramonte, was the home of Grazia Deledda, who won the Nobel Prize for Literature in 1926 for her portrayal of the power and passions in the primitive communities around her. A comprehensive collection of ethnic items, such as traditional Sardinian costumes and jewelry, can be seen in the excellent **Museo Etnografico Sardo**. Attending the *Sagra del Redentore* festival is the best way to witness the region's dancing and dialects.

**Environs**
Nuoro is on the edge of the Barbagia region, where isolated villages of shepherds have never experienced the hand of any overlord, so impenetrable are the **Gennargentu** mountains. Known to the Romans as Barbaria, it was an area they were never able to subdue. Traces of the traditional lawlessness of the Barbagia can be seen in **Orgosolo**, with its wall murals calling for Sardinia's independence. Rival clans were locked in bloody vendetta for almost 50 years, and the deeds of native bandits form part of local folklore.

In **Mamoiada**'s Feast of the Mamuthones, men in sinister masks and traditional costume perform a ritual dance ending with a symbolic "killing" of a scapegoat. The fervor of the event is indicative of the fierce folkloric tradition and deep resistance to change.

🏛 **Museo Etnografico Sardo**
Via Mereu 56. **Tel** 0784 25 70 35.
**Open** 10am–1pm & 3–8pm Tue–Sun (Oct–Mar to 7pm). 🎫 ♿
ⓦ isresardegna.it

# ❻ Cala Gonone

Nuoro. 🚠 800. 🚌 ⓘ Pro Loco, via Lamormara 108, Dorgali (0784 962 43). 🍴 daily. 🚢 from Dorgali to grottoes (Apr–mid-Oct). **Tel** 0784 933 05.

East of Nuoro, between the sea and the mountains, is the hamlet of Cala Gonone – a bustling seaside resort and fishing port, with magnificent beaches. Along the unspoiled coast are the isolated coves of **Cala Luna**, linked with Cala Gonone by a well-marked 2-hour trail, and **Cala Sisine**. The famous **Grotta del Bue Marino**, adorned with weird rock formations, can only be reached by boat.

**Environs**
To the south, the villages of **Urzulei, Baunei**, and **Santa Maria Navarrese**, along the spectacular SS125 road to Tortolì, feature breathtaking landscapes.

Ruins of Tharros near Oristano

# ❼ Oristano

Cagliari. 🚠 32,000. 🚉 🚌 ⓘ EPT, Piazza Eleonora 1 (0783 79 13 06); Pro Loco, Via Vittorio Emanuele 8 (0783 706 21). 🍴 Tue & Fri.

The province of Oristano corresponds roughly with historical Arborea, over which Eleonora ruled *(see opposite)*. She is commemorated by an 18th-century statue in **Piazza Eleonora**. On Corso Vittorio Emanuele is the 16th-century **Casa di Eleonora**, and nearby the **Antiquarium Arborense**, which has Neolithic, nuraghic, Punic, and Roman artifacts. The **Torre di San Cristoforo** (1291) in Piazza Roma was once part of Oristano's fortifications. The **Duomo** (13th century) was later rebuilt in the Baroque style. More interesting are the 14th-century churches of **Santa Chiara** on Via Garibaldi and **San Martino** on Via Cagliari.

**Environs**
The 12th-century Pisan-Romanesque **Cathedral** at Santa Giusta has columns probably taken from Tharros, an 8th-century-BC Punic settlement, 12 miles (20 km)

Entrance to the Grotta del Bue Marino, south of Cala Gonone

The tiny resort of Carloforte, the capital of Isola di San Pietro

west of Oristano on the Sinis peninsula.

### 🏛 Antiquarium Arborense
Palazzo Parpaglia. **Tel** 0783 79 12 62. **Open** Jul & Aug: 9am–2:30pm & 3:30–9pm Mon–Fri, 9am–2pm & 4–9pm Sat & Sun; Sep–Jun: 9am–8pm daily (Sat & Sun: closed 2–3pm). 🚫 🎫 ♿

## ❽ Sant'Antioco

Cagliari. 🚆 🚌 **𝒊** Pro Loco, Piazza Repubblica 31a 0781 84 05 92).

The main town on this unspoiled island is **Sant'Antioco**, once a Phoenician port and an important Roman base. Proof of almost continuous occupation is clear from the **catacombs**, a Phoenician burial place later used by Christians, under the 12th-century basilica of **Sant'Antioco Martire**. The **Museo Archeologico** has Phoenician artifacts. The Punic **Tophet** (sanctuary of the goddess Tanit) and the **necropolis** are nearby. The small **Isola di San Pietro** can be reached by ferry from Calasetta.

### 🏛 Catacombs
Piazza Parrocchia. **Tel** 0781 830 44. **Open** 9am–noon & 3:30–5:30pm Mon–Fri (to 6pm Sat); 3:30–6pm Sun & hols; summer: also 7–8pm Mon–Fri. 🎫 only. 🚫 ♿

### 🏛 Museo Archeologico
Via Regina Margherita 113. **Tel** 0783 744 33. **Open** 9am–7pm daily. **Closed** Jan 1, Easter, Dec 8, 25 & 26. 🎫 🚫 (& Tophet & necropolis). ♿

## ❾ Cagliari

🏘 165,000. ✈ 🚆 🚌 🚢 **𝒊** Piazza Matteotti ☎ (070 66 92 55). 🛍 daily; also Sun (flea) and 2nd Sun of month (antiques). 🌐 **cagliariturismo.it**

The capital of Sardinia, this site was occupied by the Phoenicians, Carthaginians, and Romans, and extensive ruins of the Phoenician city of Nora lie to the southwest of Cagliari. A 2nd-century **amphitheater** survives from the Roman era, cut from rock. Discover the town's earlier history in the **Cittadella dei Musei**, the former royal arsenal. It houses several museums, including the **Museo Archeologico Nazionale**. The nuraghic items are the most interesting in the collection, especially the bronze votive statuettes. Also in the Cittadella dei Musei is the **Pinacoteca**, an art gallery.

The old core of Cagliari has an appealing North African character. In the high **Castello** district, the Romans and, later, Pisans built defenses. The gracious **Bastione San Remy** on Piazza Costituzione offers magnificent views over the city and surrounding countryside. The **Duomo** is a 20th-century neo-Romanesque building. Flanking the entrance are two 12th-century pulpits originally destined for the cathedral in Pisa.

Nearby is the Pisan tower **Torre San Pancrazio** (14th century). Down in Stampace quarter, Piazza Yenne is the center of old Cagliari, with bars full of young crowds. Nearby, there is an elevator to the Castello quarter. From the part-ruined **Torre dell'Elefante** on Via dell'Università to the port lies the **Marina** quarter, which expanded from the old town in the 16th to 17th centuries. In Piazza San Cosimo, the 6th-century church of **San Saturnino** is a rare monument to Byzantine occupation.

### 🏛 Cittadella dei Musei
Piazza Arsenale. **Tel** 070 675 76 27. Museo Archeologico Nazionale: **Open** 9am–8pm Tue–Sun. 🚫 ♿ Pinacoteca: **Tel** 070 66 24 96. **Open** 9am–8pm Tue–Sun. **Closed** Jan 1, May 1, Dec 25. 🚫 ♿

### Eleonora of Arborea

A champion against rule from abroad, Eleonora was governing *giudicessa* (judge) of Arborea, one of four administrative divisions of Sardinia, from 1383–1404. Her marriage to Brancaleone Doria consolidated Genoese interests in Sardinia. She rallied the island to keep out Spanish invaders who tried to claim land that had been given to the Aragonese King James II. Her greatest legacy was the completion of the codifying of laws begun by her father. Written in Sardinian, they called for community of property in marriage and the right of women to seek redress for rape.

The 6th-century church of San Saturnino in Cagliari, built on a Greek-cross plan

# TRAVELERS' NEEDS

# WHERE TO STAY

People come from all over the world to visit Italy, and most Italians spend their vacations here as well, particularly in the mountains or by the sea. This means that there is a dazzling range of accommodations, from splendid hotels in old palazzi and historic residences to simple family-run *pensioni* and hostels. Most major cities also offer upscale guesthouses. Those who want vacation rentals are well served too, with everything from stately villas in Tuscany to purpose-built apartments in, or near, seaside resorts. Italian hotels can have a reputation for being expensive and short on services, but this is not always the case, and you can find excellent value in all price ranges. The hotels listed on pages 562–77 have been selected from every price category as among the best value in each area for style, comfort, or location.

The Gritti Palace, one of Venice's historic palazzi *(see p563)*

## Ratings

Hotels in Italy are classified with a rating system of one to five stars. The grading depends on the amenities offered, and each region awards stars according to slightly different criteria.

Sometimes a hotel has a lower rating than it deserves. This may be because the local tourist office has not upgraded the rating or because the hotel itself has opted to stay in a lower category to avoid higher taxes.

## Alberghi

*Albergo* is Italian for "hotel," but the term tends to refer to establishments classified as three-star or above. Room sizes vary considerably: in city centers even expensive hotels can have small rooms, especially if the hotel is located in a historic building, whereas you get far more space for your money in rural areas. *Alberghi* will have private bathrooms, with tub or shower, in all rooms. Many high-end and boutique hotels also offer spa and fitness amenities.

## Pensioni

Although the term *pensione* is no longer in official use, one- and two-star hotels still use the term to describe their status. On the whole you will find immaculate standards of cleanliness and friendly, helpful service with basic, although perfectly functional, rooms. Be aware that while your *pensioni* may be in an old building full of historic charm, this can also mean noisy, erratic plumbing and dark rooms. Many *pensioni* do not have public rooms other than a sparsely furnished breakfast room. Most will offer at least some bedrooms with a private shower although rarely a tub. If you intend to be out late, check that you'll be able to get back into the *pensione*. Not all of them are staffed after midnight or 1am, but most will at least be able to provide a key to the main door.

A *locanda* was traditionally an inn, offering cheap food and a place to sleep for the traveler. The word is still in use, particularly in central and northern Italy, but is now synonymous with *pensione* and may be more of an affectation for the benefit of the tourist.

## Chain Hotels

There are various Italian chain hotels, including **Atahotels** and **Una Hotels and Resorts**, as well as the usual big internationals. **NH Hoteles** rooms usually appeal to business travelers, and there are one or two of these hotels in most large cities. **Marriott**, **Hyatt**, and **Best Western** are international luxury chains. **Italia Lodging** caters to the more modest budget. **Relais & Châteaux** run charming hotels in historic castles, villas, and monasteries, with amenities to match.

## Meals and Amenities

There has been a general improvement in the amenities offered by Italian hotels, especially in the more modern four- and five-star hotels. However, in some older establishments there may not

Street sign showing the direction and location of hotels

◀ The popular San Carlo café on Piazza San Carlo, Turin

Romantic Hotel Villa Pagoda in Nervi, Genoa *(see p568)*

always be air-conditioning or 24-hour room service, so it's best to check before you book.

In peak season, some hotels may insist on terms including all meals *(pensione completa)* or some meals *(mezza pensione)*. Most rates include breakfast, which in many hotels will be a large buffet, although smaller hotels and *pensioni* may offer a simple continental breakfast.

For a double room, state if you want two single beds *(letti singoli)* or a double bed *(matrimoniale)*. Bathrooms in most hotels will have showers rather than bathtubs.

Most hotels offer Internet access, but it is not always free, and charges will vary. If a city center hotel does not have its own parking spaces, it may have an arrangement with a nearby garage. Check the availability and cost of parking with the hotel before making a reservation.

## Children

Italians love children, and although most hotels won't offer special amenties, kids are always welcome.

Some of the cheaper hotels may not be able to provide cribs. However, virtually all hotels will be happy to put a small bed into a double room for families traveling together. The price of this is usually an extra 30–40 percent of the double room rate per bed. Many large hotels also offer babysitting services.

## Prices

As a rule, hotels in Italy are not cheap, although prices vary considerably between regions. Hotels in major cities and resorts are likely to be more expensive. Reserving online is one way to secure a better rate, as hotel websites may offer special deals. Or you can save money by booking your hotel and flight together on most travel websites.

Prices, which include tax and service and are quoted per room, start from around €60 for a double room without a bathroom, and can rise to at least €80 with a bathroom, even for a very basic hotel. A single room will cost about two thirds of a double. Outside the big cities, €100 should get you something comfortable and often picturesque, although not particularly luxurious. For €210 and upward you can expect a good range of amenities, a pleasant or central location, and often a hotel with local or historic charm. In Rome, all campgrounds, guesthouses, and hotels must charge a city tax *(contributo di soggiorno)*. Currently, these rates are fixed at €1 per day per person for campgrounds, €2 for establishments up to and including three-star hotels, and €3 for four- and five-star hotels.

In larger hotels there is often a considerable difference in quality and price between standard and more luxurious, deluxe rooms. If you would like a view or a terrace, this is also likely to be more expensive, though for those who prefer peaceful nights, it is generally best to avoid rooms facing the street in busy cities.

Also, beware of extra charges: the minibar can be very expensive, as can the cost of parking, laundry, or making telephone calls directly from your hotel bedroom.

## Reservations

Make reservations as soon as possible, particularly if you have special requests such as a room with a view, off the street, or with a bathtub. August tends to be very busy at beach resorts, and February is peak season at mountain resorts. Peak times for cities and towns depend on their particular cultural calendars *(see pp70–73)*.

You will be asked for a deposit when you book; this can usually be paid by credit card (even in hotels that do not accept credit cards for final payment); otherwise you can use PayPal for online transactions, or transfer the money via EFT from your bank account.

Under Italian law the hotel must issue you with a receipt *(ricevuta fiscale)* for final payment, which you must keep until you leave Italy.

The Italian State Tourist Office (**ENIT**) has accommodations lists for all regions, although this might not be the most up-to-date resource. Rooms can also be booked via the **APT** (Azienda Provinciale per il Turismo).

A traditional Florentine hotel interior

The multilevel terrace of the Raphael in Rome *(see p573)*

## Checking In and Out

Italian hotels are legally obliged to register you with the police, which is why you'll always be asked for your passport when checking in. This is a mere formality, and your passport should be returned to you within an hour or two.

Checking-out time is usually before noon, although some larger hotels may extend your checking-out time upon request, but only if your room is not already reserved for another guest. All rooms must be vacated on time, but most hotels will allow you to leave your luggage in a safe place to be collected later in the day.

Al Sole, Venice *(see p563)*

## Vacation Rentals and Agriturismo

Across rural Italy, there are more than 2,000 farms, villas, and mountain chalets offering reasonably priced apartment- or hotel-style accommodations as part of the **Agriturismo** scheme. Options range from beautifully kept villas or ancient castles with first-class amenities, to simple rooms in the family home on a working farm. Some places have excellent restaurants that serve farm and local produce, while others can arrange horseback riding, fishing, or other activities

*(see p610)*. Some of these places may have a minimum stay, especially during peak season. The annual *Agriturist* publication can be found in the central tourist office in Rome, in regional offices, and in bookstores. Other options for accommodations with cooking amenities can be arranged through specialized agencies such as **Villas4you** and **Simply Travel** before you leave for Italy, but again, make sure you do this well in advance, as accommodations can fill up months ahead.

There are also so-called *residenze*, found in the ENIT accommodations lists. These are halfway between hotels and apartments, and usually offer cooking amenities and some sort of restaurant.

For stays of several months or more, accommodations agencies for apartments in the city center, as well as the nearby countryside, can be found under *Immobiliari* in the *Pagine Gialle* (Yellow Pages).

## Budget Accommodations

As well as the International Youth Hostels Association (**AIG** in Italy), tourist offices in the major cities have lists of hostels. Prices start at around €12 per person per night (€15 during peak season), and are much lower than even the cheapest *pensione*. Accom-

modations may be in single- or mixed-sex dormitories, though many hostels also have small private rooms. A room in a private house is another budget option, often offering small but clean rooms. Guesthouse accommodations are available but are of variable quality.

The **Centro Turistico Studentesco** can help students find rooms in university accommodations across Italy. This is not limited to students, particularly in the summer, when resident students are on vacation.

A peaceful alternative is to stay in a convent or monastery with guest accommodations. The rooms are clean, if a little spartan, and they are usually in a secluded area. Note that strict rules may be the price for a cheap room: most have early curfews and many will not admit members of the opposite sex even when with their spouses. There is no central agency dealing with these, but they are included in the ENIT accommodations lists for each region.

## Mountain Refuges and Campgrounds

Basic accommodations in huts and refuges are available in mountainous areas where there are hiking trails. Most of these huts are owned and run by the **Club Alpino Italiano**, headquartered in Milan.

Campgrounds abound in the mountains and around the

A boat carrying visitors' luggage to a hotel in Venice

coastal regions. Many of them offer basic accommodations in family-sized cabins *(bungalow)* as well as spaces for tents, RVs, and trailers, along with amenities such as water, electricity, and laundry. There is usually a restaurant, and, especially in campgrounds by the sea, there may also be sports amenities such as swimming pools, boat and water-sports equipment rental, and tennis courts. The **Touring Club Italiano** publishes a good list of

A high-altitude refuge in the Valsesia Alps

A Park Spa Suite bedroom in the Park Hyatt Milano *(see p566)*

campgrounds with details of amenities for each one, as does **Federcampeggio**.

## Disabled Travelers

In general, only newer hotels in Italy have amenities for disabled travelers, although older hotels will often do all they can to host people in wheelchairs by giving them downstairs rooms (when available) and helping with elevators or stairs. It is best to contact the hotel of your choice directly before making a reservation, to check whether they are accessible to wheelchairs and what amenities they have *(for more information see pp616–17).*

## Recommended Hotels

The hotels listed in this guide-book have been chosen because they represent the best Italy has to offer in hospitality, service, value, or location. A huge variety of accommodations options are covered, from simple farmhouses and alpine chalets to family-run guesthouses and luxury palaces.

Listings labeled DK Choice are outstanding in some way. They may be set in beautiful surroundings or in a historically important building, offer excellent service, have a romantic atmosphere, be particularly charming or environmentally friendly, or have a great spa. Whatever the reason, DK Choice is a guarantee of a memorable stay.

# DIRECTORY

## Chain Hotels

**Atahotels**
**Tel** 02 69 82 69 82.
**W** atahotels.it

**Best Western Hotels**
**Tel** 02 83 10 86 30.
**W** bestwestern.it

**Hyatt**
**Tel** 02 88 21 12 34.
**W** hyatt.com

**Marriott**
**Tel** 800 22 89 29 00.
**W** marriott.com

**NH Hoteles**
**Tel** 848 390 006.
**W** nh-hotels.com

**Relais & Châteaux**
**Tel** 02 62 69 00 64.
**W** relaischateaux.com

**Una Hotels and Resorts**
**Tel** 800 60 61 62.
**W** unahotels.it

## Reservations

**ENIT**
Via Marghera 2–6, 00185 Rome. **Tel** 06 497 11.
**W** enit.it

**Italian State Tourist Board**
1 Princes Street, London W1B 2AY.
**Tel** 020 7408 1254.
**W** italia.it

## Vacation Rentals and Agriturismo

**Agriturismo**
Corso Vittorio Emanuele II 101, 00186 Rome.

**Tel** 06 685 23 37.
**W** agriturist.it

**Simply Travel**
**Tel** 0871 231 40 50.
**W** thomson.co.uk

**Villas4you**
PO Box 1310, Maidstone ME14 9QH.
**Tel** 0800 096 3439.
**W** villas4you.co.uk

## Budget Accommodations

**AIG (Associazione Italiana Alberghi per la Gioventù)**
Via Nicotera 1, 00195 Rome. **Tel** 06 487 11 52.
**W** aighostels.it

**Guesthouses**
**W** bed-and-breakfast.it

**Centro Turistico Studentesco**
**Tel** 06 64 96 03 00.
**W** cts.it

**Italia Lodging**
**Tel** 06 77 25 05 43.
**W** italialodging.com

## Mountain Refuges & Campgrounds

**Club Alpino Italiano**
Via E. Petrella 19, Milan.
**Tel** 02 205 72 31. **W** cai.it

**Federcampeggio**
Via Vittorio Emanuele 11, 50041 Calenzano, Florence.
**Tel** 055 88 23 91.
**W** federcampeggio.it

**Touring Club Italiano**
Corso Italia 10, 20122 Milan. **Tel** 840 88 88 02.
**W** touringclub.it

# Where to Stay

## Venice

### CANNAREGIO: Al Saor €
B&B **Map** 3 A4
*Calle Zotti 3904/a, 30121*
**Tel** *041 296 06 54 (closed 15 days Dec)*
W alsaor.com
Many rooms at this simple and elegant guesthouse have original wood beams. Guests can have breakfast on the rooftop terrace.

### CANNAREGIO: Hotel Giorgione €€
Luxury **Map** 3 B4
*Calle dei Proverbi 4587, 30121*
**Tel** *041 522 58 10*
W hotelgiorgione.com
Stay in charming rooms in a lovely old building. There is a courtyard for alfresco dining, and a hot tub with sea water. Great breakfasts.

### CANNAREGIO: Palazzo Abadessa €€
Historic **Map** 3 A4
*Calle Priuli 4011, 30131*
**Tel** *041 241 37 84 (closed Jan 6–26)*
W abadessa.com
Charming 16th-century palace furnished with antiques and plush fabrics. Spacious rooms.

### CANNAREGIO: Ca' Sagredo €€€
Historic **Map** 3 A5
*Campo Santa Sofia 4198, 30121*
**Tel** *041 241 31 11*
W casagredohotel.com
Just across from Rialto market, this modernized 13th-century palazzo offers superb views. Frescoes decorate many rooms.

### CASTELLO: Locanda la Corte €€
Historic **Map** 3 C5
*Calle Bressana 6317, 30122*
**Tel** *041 241 13 00*
W locandalacorte.it
This is a converted 16th-century palace with a courtyard. Many rooms have charming canal or courtyard views.

### CASTELLO: Londra Palace €€
Boutique **Map** 8 D1
*Riva degli Schiavoni 4171, 30122*
**Tel** *041 520 05 33*
W londrapalace.com
Excellent service and spacious, luxurious rooms. The hotel bar is famous for its cocktails and coffee, while the restaurant offers views of San Giorgio Maggiore.

### CASTELLO: Metropole €€€
Luxury **Map** 8 D1
*Riva degli Schiavoni 4149, 30122*
**Tel** *041 520 50 44*
W hotelmetropole.com

A somewhat nondescript exterior belies the splendor within. The Citrus Garden is a verdant oasis, and the restaurant boasts a Michelin star.

### DORSODURO: Agli Alboretti €€
Pensione **Map** 6 E4
*Rio Terrà Foscarini 884, 30123*
**Tel** *041 523 00 58 (closed 20 days Jan)*
W aglialboretti.com
The simple, comfortable rooms at this hotel are equipped with a free minibar. Very helpful staff.

### DORSODURO: Instituto Artigianelli €€
Historic **Map** 6 E4
*Rio Terrà Foscarini 909/a, 30123*
**Tel** *041 522 40 77*
W donorione-venezia.it
Religious institution offering simple, modern rooms with ensuite bathrooms. Its 15th-century cloister is overlooked by the Gesuati Church cupolas.

### DORSODURO: Locanda Ca' Zose €€
B&B **Map** 6 F4
*Calle del Bastion 193/b, 30123*
**Tel** *041 522 66 35*
W hotelcazose.com
Spacious rooms in a charming guesthouse run by two sisters; in a great location for art lovers.

### DORSODURO: Locanda San Barnaba €€
Rooms with a view **Map** 6 D3
*Calle del Traghetto 2785–2786, 30123*
**Tel** *041 241 12 33*
W locanda-sanbarnaba.com
This is the perfect place to return to after a hard day's sightseeing. Spotless rooms, most overlooking the canal.

Elegant interiors and great views at the Cipriani hotel, Giudecca

### GIUDECCA: Cipriani €€€
Luxury **Map** 7 C5
*Giudecca 10, 30133*
**Tel** *041 520 77 44 (closed mid-Nov–mid-Mar)*
W hotelcipriani.com
This Venice institution is exquisite. Amenities include a free private shuttle boat to Piazza San Marco.

### LIDO: Villa Mabapa €€€
Rooms with a view
*Riviera San Nicolò 16, 30126*
**Tel** *041 526 05 90 (closed Nov–mid-Mar)*
W villamabapa.com
This attractive period villa overlooks the Venice lagoon. Meals are served in the lush, extensive garden.

### DK Choice

**MAZZORBO: Venissa** €€
Pensione **Map** 3 B4
*Fondamenta Santa Caterina 3, 30170*
**Tel** *041 527 22 81 (closed end Nov–end Feb)*
W venissa.it
A stylish option on a little-known island for those who want exclusivity. Rooms are modern and spacious. Delicious meals are served in the restaurant.

### SAN MARCO: Saturnia and International €€
Luxury **Map** 7 A3
*Via XXII Marzo 2398, 30124*
**Tel** *041 520 83 77*
W hotelsaturnia.it
Run by the same family since 1908, this hotel offers opulence wrapped in a homey setting. Antique furnishings and a pretty courtyard.

### SAN MARCO: Europa & Regina €€€
Luxury **Map** 7 A3
*Calle Larga XXII Marzo 2159, 30124*
**Tel** *041 240 00 01*
W westineuroparaginavenice.com
Stay in elegant rooms and enjoy impeccable service. Rubelli textiles, mahogany floors, and Italian marble create a touch of class in every room. There are also panoramic terraces with magnificent views.

**SAN MARCO: Gritti Palace** €€€
Luxury **Map** 6 F3
*Santa Maria del Giglio 2467, 30124*
**Tel** *041 79 46 11*
**w** thegrittipalace.com
Set in an iconic palazzo dating
back to 1475. Opulent rooms
feature period details.

**SAN MARCO: Luna Hotel
Baglioni** €€€
Luxury **Map** 7 B3
*Calle Larga dell'Ascensione 1243, 30124*
**Tel** *041 528 98 40*
**w** baglionihotels.com
Spacious, retro-chic rooms in a
historic palazzo. Arrive by water
taxi at the private jetty.

**SAN MARCO: Splendid
Venice** €€€
Luxury **Map** 7 B7
*Mercerie 760, 30124*
**Tel** *041 520 07 55*
**w** splendidvenice.starhotels.com
This hotel is comfortable and
quiet, with a well-stocked library
and peaceful reading areas.

**SAN POLO: Al Campaniel** €
B&B **Map** 6 E2
*Calle del Campaniel 2889, 30125*
**Tel** *041 275 07 49*
**w** alcampaniel.com
Rooms are spacious and bright at
this clean, cosy guesthouse on a
quiet street. The small apartment
is great for families.

**SANTA CROCE: Hotel Falier** €€
Charming **Map** 5 C1
*Salizzada San Pantalon 130, 30135*
**Tel** *041 71 08 82*
**w** hotelfalier.com
This hotel is full of light, airy
rooms and has a pretty wisteria-
filled garden. Helpful staff.

---

**DK Choice**

**SANTA CROCE: Al Sole** €€
Historic **Map** 5 C1
*Fondamenta Tolentini 134–6,
30135*
**Tel** *041 244 03 28*
**w** alsolehotels.com
Housed in Palazzo Marcello,
a 15th-century palace with a
beautiful facade and marble-
floored reception area, this
hotel offers well-appointed
rooms. Enjoy the rich breakfast
spread served in a patio garden.

---

**TORCELLO: Locanda Cipriani** €€
Rooms with a view
*Piazza Santa Fosca 29, 30012*
**Tel** *041 73 01 50 (closed Jan–mid-Feb)*
**w** locandacipriani.com
Comfortable old-world inn located
far from the madding crowd.
Famed for its quiet elegance.

Romantic natural setting of Hotel Cappella in Colfosco

# The Veneto and Friuli

**ASOLO: Albergo al Sole** €€
Rooms with a view
*Via Collegio 33, 31011*
**Tel** *0423 95 13 32 (closed Jan)*
**w** albergoalsoleasolo.com
Pleasant, spacious rooms
overlook the town square. The
restaurant terrace offers views of
the town and countryside.

**ASOLO: Villa Cipriani** €€
Historic
*Via Canova 298, 31011*
**Tel** *0423 52 34 11*
**w** villacipriani.it
Comfortable hotel in a
16th-century villa once home
to poet Robert Browning.

**CASTELROTTO:
Cavallino d'Oro** €€
Spa hotel
*Piazza Kraus 2, 39040*
**Tel** *0471 70 63 37*
**w** cavallino.it
The decor at this cosy hotel in a
pretty setting is Tyrolean-chic.
The spa is housed in the 700-
year-old wine cellar.

**CIVIDALE DEL FRIULI:
Locanda al Pomo d'Oro** €
Historic
*Piazzetta San Giovanni 20, 33043*
**Tel** *0432 73 14 89 (closed end Feb–
Mar)*
**w** alpomodoro.com
This traditional inn set on a quiet
square in the historic center
offers a number of family rooms.

**COLFOSCO: Hotel Cappella** €€
Rooms with a view
*Strada Pecei 17, 39033*
**Tel** *0471 83 61 83 (closed Sep 19–
Nov, after Easter–mid-Jun)*
**w** hotelcappella.com
At this chalet in the Dolomites,
you can choose from a variety of
different suites.

**CONEGLIANO: Il Faè** €
Rooms with a view
*Via Faè 1, San Pietro di Feletto, 31020*
**Tel** *0438 78 71 17 (closed Oct–Mar
exc Christmas)*
**w** ilfae.com
Pleasant property surrounded by
vineyards. Good views over the
foothills of the Alps.

**CORNO DI ROSAZZO:
Villa Butussi** €
Rooms with a view
*Via San Martino 29, Visinale dello
Judrio, 33040*
**Tel** *0432 75 99 22*
**w** butussi.it
A 17th-century villa converted
into a guesthouse that offers
both rooms and apartments.
Renovated suites feature Jacuzzis.

**CORTINA D'AMPEZZO:
Montana** €€
Pensione
*Corso Italia 94, 32043*
**Tel** *0436 86 21 26 (closed May & Nov)*
**w** cortina-hotel.com
In the heart of town, this hotel
has a games room, a ski depot,
and easy access to the pistes.

**CORTINA D'AMPEZZO:
Cristallo Hotel** €€€
Luxury
*Via R. Menardi 42, 32043*
**Tel** *0436 88 11 11 (closed early Oct–
mid-Dec, after Easter–mid-Jun)*
**w** cristallo.it
Some of the beautiful rooms
here have balcony views of the
Alps. Excellent amenities include
a spa and a nine-hole golf course.

**FOLLINA: Villa Abbazia** €€
Historic
*Piazza IV Novembre 3, 31051*
**Tel** *0438 97 12 77 (closed Jan–mid-
Mar)*
**w** hotelabbazia.it
This delightful 17th-century villa
has spacious rooms decorated in
English country-house style.

For more information on types of hotels *see pp558–61*

**GARDA: Locanda
San Vigilio** €€€
Rooms with a view
*Località San Vigilio 17, 37016*
**Tel** *045 725 66 88 (closed Nov–Mar)*
**W** locanda-sanvigilio.it
Exuding old-world charm, this
is one of the most exclusive
hotels on Lake Garda, with its
own port and helipad.

**MALCESINE: Sailing Center
Hotel** €€
Rooms with a view
*Via Gardesana 187, 37018*
**Tel** *045 740 00 55 (closed mid-Oct–
3rd wk Apr)*
**W** hotelsailing.com
Located on the shores of Lake
Garda, the Sailing Center Hotel
has comfortable rooms and its
own private beach.

**PADUA: Augustus Terme** €€
Spa Hotel
*Viale Stazione 150, 35036*
**Tel** *049 79 32 00 (closed Jan 10–
Feb 10)*
**W** hotelaugustus.com
The Augustus Terme is a
comfortable hotel with opulent
rooms, thermal swimming pools,
and a reputable restaurant.

**PESCHIERA DEL GARDA:
Active Hotel Paradiso & Golf** €€
Boutique
*Via Coppo 2/b, 37014*
**Tel** *045 640 58 11*
**W** activehotelparadisopeschiera.it
Amenities at this stylish hotel
with pleasant, airy rooms include
an 18-hole golf course, plus
indoor and outdoor pools.

**POVOLETTO: La Faula** €
Agriturismo
*Via Faula 5, 33040*
**Tel** *334 399 67 34 (closed Nov–early
Mar)*
**W** faula.com
Surrounded by vineyards and
farmland, this restored farmhouse
offers pleasant, rustic rooms.
Wine-tasting courses are available.

Comfortable furnishings at Hotel Laurin
in Bolzano

**TORRI DEL BENACO:
Hotel Gardesana** €
Historic
*Piazza Calderini 5, 37010*
**Tel** *045 722 54 11 (closed Nov–Mar)*
**W** gardesana.eu
A 15th-century former harbor-
master's house converted into
a friendly, comfortable hotel.

**TREVISO: Locanda da Renzo** €
B&B
*Via Terraglio 108, 31100*
**Tel** *0422 40 20 68*
**W** locandadarenzo.it
A small family-run guesthouse
with a home-cooked evening
meal available on request.

**TRIESTE: Le Corderie** €€
Boutique
*Via di Calvola 43, 34143*
**Tel** *040 322 92 77*
**W** lecorderiehotel.it
You're assured a warm welcome
at this comfortable, modern
hotel. Great breakfast.

**UDINE: Hotel Clocchiatti &
Next** €
Boutique
*Via Cividale 29, 33100*
**Tel** *0432 50 50 47 (closed last wk
Dec–1st wk Jan)*
**W** hotelclocchiatti.it
Choose between rooms with
period decor or modern fittings.
The pool is set in lush surrounds.

**VALDOBBIADENE:
Villa Barberina** €€
Historic
*Via Roma 2, 31049*
**Tel** *0423 97 24 79 (closed Dec–Mar)*
**W** villabarberina.it
In the past wealthy Venetians
would live part of the year in
their country estates. With its
elegant rooms, magnificent
grounds, and wonderful library,
this 18th-century villa gives
guests an idea of the opulence
of such residences.

**VERONA: Giulietta e
Romeo** €€
Charming
*Vicolo Tre Marchetti 3, 37121*
**Tel** *045 800 35 54*
**W** giuliettaeromeo.com
Bright, comfortable rooms and
a hearty breakfast served in a
modern space, plus a gym.

**VERONA: Il Torcolo** €€
Charming
*Vicolo Listone 3, 37121*
**Tel** *045 800 75 12 (closed mid- to
end Jan)*
**W** hoteltorcolo.it
Small, family-run hotel with
simple rooms and a pleasant
terrace where breakfast is served.

**VICENZA: Glam Boutique
Hotel** €€
Boutique
*A. Giuriolo 10, 36100*
**Tel** *0444 32 64 58*
**W** gboutiquehotel.com
This stylish hotel offers a perfect
blend of traditional and modern
decor. Bicycle rental available.

# Trentino-Alto Adige

**BOLZANO: Hotel Laurin** €€
Historic
*Via Laurin 4, 39100*
**Tel** *0471 31 10 00*
**W** laurin.it
Guests marvel at the original
Art Nouveau features of this
charming hotel. Inside, it is
all about modern comforts.

**BOLZANO: Luna-Mondschein** €€
Spa hotel
*Via Piave 15, 39100*
**Tel** *0471 97 56 42*
**W** hotel-luna.it
This stylish city-center hotel has
fabulous grounds. Guests enjoy
traditional Tyrolean cuisine and
can relax in the elegant spa.

**BRESSANONE: Hotel Dominik** €€
Rooms with a view
*Via Terzo di Sotto 13, 39042*
**Tel** *0472 83 01 44*
**W** hoteldominik.com
Furnished with antiques, most
rooms here boast views of the
river. The Wellness Zone has
an indoor pool, and there is a
sunbathing deck on the roof.

**FIE ALLO SCILIAR: Hotel
Schmung** €€
Rooms with a view
*Compatsch 12, Alpe de Siusi, 39040*
**Tel** *0471 72 79 43 (closed May & Nov)*
**W** schmung.com
Set in a protected area with
car access kept to a minimum,
this panoramic haven offers a
tranquil stay. Excellent restaurant.
Some meals included in price.

## DK Choice

**MERANO: Ottmanngut** €€
Boutique
*Via Verdi 18, 39012*
**Tel** *0473 44 96 56 (closed early
Jan–mid-Mar)*
**W** ottmanngut.it
Surrounded by lush greenery,
this family-run guesthouse is
within walking distance of the
spa town. The suites are elegant
with period furnishings and
modern conveniences. There is
also a lovely garden to relax in.

**MERANO: Hotel Castel Fragsburg** €€€
Rooms with a view
*Via Fragsburg 3, 39012*
**Tel** *0473 24 40 71 (closed Nov–Mar)*
**w** fragsburg.com
This hotel boasts some fine views. The restaurant is run by a Michelin-starred chef.

### DK Choice

**ORTISEI: Adler Dolomiti Spa & Sport Resort** €€
Spa hotel
*Via Rezia 7, 39046*
**Tel** *0471 77 50 01 (closed Apr–mid-May)*
**w** adler-dolomiti.com
Owned by the same family for generations, this is one of the finest hotels in the Dolomites. Excellent service; vast gardens.

**REDAGNO: Berghotel Zirmerhof** €€
Agriturismo
*Oberradein 59, 39040*
**Tel** *0471 88 72 15 (closed Nov–May)*
**w** zirmerhof.com
In a beautiful mountain setting, this building is 600 years old but has modern and airy interiors.

**TRENTO: Accademia** €€
Historic
*Vicolo Colico 4–6, 38122*
**Tel** *0461 23 36 00 (closed 22 Dec–6 Jan)*
**w** accademiahotel.it
Enjoy accommodations in a restored medieval building with a pleasant courtyard.

## Lombardy

**APRICA: Relais Villa Brioschi** €
Boutique
*Via Valeriana 187, 25040*
**Tel** *0342 74 56 81*
**w** relaisvillabrioschi.com
Charming rooms and apartments in a luxury Art Nouveau-style villa close to the ski slopes.

**BELLAGIO: Hotel Florence** €€
Spa hotel
*Piazza Mazzini 46, 22021*
**Tel** *031 95 03 42*
**w** hotelflorencebellagio.it
This lakeside hotel offers stylish decor, canopy beds, roll-top baths, and a gourmet restaurant.

**BELLAGIO: Grand Hotel Villa Serbelloni** €€€
Luxury
*Via Roma 1, 22021*
**Tel** *031 95 02 16*
**w** villaserbelloni.com

The outdoor pool with a view at Adler Dolomiti Spa & Sport Resort

On the promontory separating the two branches of Lake Como, this historic hotel boasts frescoed ceilings, a spa, and a lakeside pool.

**BERGAMO: Hotel Gombit** €€
Design
*Via Mario Lupo 6, 24129*
**Tel** *035 24 70 09*
**w** gombithotel.it
Located in the historic Città Alta, the Gombit gives a taste of modern Italian minimalism.

**BORMIO: Hotel Cristallo** €€
Spa hotel
*Via Milano 44, 23032*
**Tel** *0342 90 27 00*
**w** cristallohotelresidence.it
A short stroll from ski-lifts and thermal baths, this hotel offers a large garden, a ski room, and a games room.

**BRESCIA: AC Hotel Brescia** €
Design
*Via Giulio Quinto Stefana 3, 25126*
**Tel** *030 24 05 511*
**w** hotelacbrescia.com
Conveniently located for both downtown and the train station, this minimalist hotel has a fitness center and a gourmet restaurant.

**BRESCIA: Park Hotel Cà Nöa** €
Rooms with a view
*Via Triumplina 66, 25123*
**Tel** *030 39 87 62*
**w** hotelcanoa.it
Modern, bright, and comfortably furnished hotel, with a restaurant and an outdoor pool. Close to downtown and easily reached by freeway or public transportation.

**CERNOBBIO: Villa d'Este** €€€
Luxury
*Via Regina 40, 22012*
**Tel** *031 34 81*
**w** villadeste.it
This 16th-century villa set amid sumptuous Renaissance gardens has a marina, a floating pool, a

wellness and beauty center, and several restaurants.

**COLOGNE: Cappuccini Resort** €€
Historic
*Via Cappuccini 54, 25033*
**Tel** *030 715 72 54*
**w** cappuccini.it
This former monastery offers modern rooms, a wellness center, a pool and an great restaurant.

**COMO: In Riva al Lago** €
B&B
*Via Crespi 4, 22100*
**Tel** *031 30 23 33*
**w** inrivaallago.com
Centrally located, spotless rooms just steps from the lakeside and a short walk from the ferry quay and Brunate funicular.

**COMO: Hotel Firenze** €€
Rooms with a view
*Piazza Volta 16, 22100*
**Tel** *031 30 03 33*
**w** albergofirenze.it
A renovated Neo-Classical hotel located on a traffic-free downtown square.

**CREMONA: Dellearti Design Hotel** €€
Boutique
*Via Bonomelli 8, 26100*
**Tel** *0372 23 131*
**w** dellearti.com
Enjoy the sleek, modern rooms in this charming hotel close to the cathedral and medieval bell tower.

**DESENZANO DEL GARDA: Park Hotel** €€
Luxury
*Lungolago Cesare Battisti 17, 25015*
**Tel** *030 914 34 95*
**w** parkhotelonline.it
This elegant, family-run hotel has a spectacular rooftop pool and Jacuzzi with breathtaking views over Lake Garda, plus well-appointed rooms.

For more information on types of hotels *see pp558–61*

Stylish, minimalist decor at Nhow Milano in Milan

### GARDONE RIVIERA: Villa del Sogno €€€
Historic
*Via Zanardelli 107, 25083*
Tel *0365 29 01 81*
🅦 villadelsogno.it
A lakeside Neo-Classical villa with tennis courts, an outdoor pool, a spa offering massage treatments, two restaurants, and two bars.

### GARGNANO: Villa Sostaga €€€
Boutique
*Via Sostaga 19, 25084*
Tel *0365 79 12 18*
🅦 villasostaga.it
This family-run hotel offers large rooms with modern amenities and an Art Nouveau dining room.

### ISEO: Iseolago Hotel €€
Spa hotel
*Via Colombera 2, 25049*
Tel *030 98 891*
🅦 iseolagohotel.it
Extensive gardens with swimming pools, a tennis court, and a children's playground.

### DK Choice

### LIMONE SUL GARDA: Hotel Capo Reamol €
Budget
*Via IV Novembre 92, 25010*
Tel *0365 95 40 40*
🅦 hotelcaporeamol.it
This hotel's idyllic location offers breathtaking views of Lake Garda. Rooms are compact but clean. Guests enjoy a fitness room and spa services, along with a private beach and a swimming pool. Excellent value for money.

### LIVIGNO: Hotel Capriolo €
Pensione
*Via Borch 96, 23030*
Tel *0342 99 67 23*
🅦 capriololivigno.com
Family-run hotel located close to ski lifts and hiking paths. Offers traditional Valtellina cuisine.

### MANTUA: Hotel la Favorita €€
Business
*Via S. Cognetti De Martiis 1, 46100*
Tel *0376 25 47 11*
🅦 hotellafavorita.it
A modern and elegant hotel with impeccable service and an excellent restaurant.

### MANTUA: Hotel Villa dei Tigli €€
Spa hotel
*Via Cantarana 20/I, Rodigo 46040*
Tel *0376 68 49 98*
🅦 hotelvilladeitigli.it
Just 9 miles (15 km) outside Mantua, this former aristocratic villa surrounded by gardens offers comfortable rooms, a wellness spa center, and a restaurant.

### DK Choice

### MILAN: Antica Locanda Leonardo €€
Boutique
*Corso Magenta 78, 20123*
Tel *02 48 01 41 97*
🅦 anticalocandaleonardo.com
Peacefully located in an elegant 19th-century palazzo, this family-run hotel has well-decorated rooms overlooking a charming and picturesque inner garden. The staffers are helpful and friendly.

### MILAN: Antica Locanda Solferino €€
Boutique
*Via Castelfidardo 2, 20121*
Tel *02 65 70 12 9*
🅦 anticalocandasolferino.it
A welcoming guesthouse with eclectic old-world charm. Breakfast is served in your room.

### MILAN: Nhow Milano €€
Design
*Via Tortona 35, 20144*
Tel *02 48 98 861*
🅦 nh-hotels.it
Artistically decorated rooms in a renovated industrial building.

Conveniently located for the Naviglio area and its nightlife.

### MILAN: UNA Hotel Tocq €€
Business
*Via A de Tocqueville 7/D, 20154*
Tel *02 62 071*
🅦 unahotels.it
Near Garibaldi train station and right in the center of the trendy Corso Como area, this hotel offers spacious rooms and apartments.

### MILAN: Park Hyatt Milan €€€
Luxury
*Via Tommaso Grossi 1, 20121*
Tel *02 88 21 12 34*
🅦 milan.park.hyatt.com
Housed in a former bank, this elegant hotel has a spa and a gym. It is just steps away from Milan's main attractions and stores.

### PAVIA: Il Castello di San Gaudenzio €€
Historic
*Via Mulino 1, 27050*
Tel *0383 33 31*
🅦 castellosangaudenzio.com
Located between Pavia and the Oltrepò wine region, this 15th-century castle has an indoor pool, gym, and excellent restaurant.

### RANCO: Il Sole di Ranco €€
Rooms with a view
*Piazza Venezia 5, 21020*
Tel *0331 97 65 07*
🅦 ilsolediranco.it
This pleasant hotel with a pool and gardens overlooks Lake Maggiore. There is also a sauna and Turkish baths.

### RIVA DI SOLTO: Albergo Ristorante Miranda €
Pensione
*Via Cornello 7, 24060*
Tel *035 98 60 21*
🅦 albergomiranda.it
Set atop a hill overlooking Lake Iseo, the Miranda offers simple, comfortable rooms, a restaurant, a pool, and panoramic views.

### SALÒ: Hotel Laurin €€
Boutique
*Viale Landi 9, 25087*
Tel *0365 22 022*
🅦 laurinhotelsalo.com
Decorated with Art Nouveau frescoes, this romantic early 20th-century lakeside villa has a restaurant and an outdoor pool.

### SIRMIONE: Hotel Catullo €€
Historic
*Piazza Flaminia 7, 25019*
Tel *030 990 58 11*
🅦 hotelcatullo.it
This hotel offers simple rooms with balconies overlooking Lake Garda, and a lovely rooftop terrace.

**TREMEZZO: Hotel la Darsena** €€
Rooms with a view
*Via Regina 3, 22019*
**Tel** *0344 431 66*
🅦 ladarsena.it
One of the advantages of staying at this lakeside hotel-cum-restaurant is its superb location.

**TREMEZZO: Grand Hotel Tremezzo** €€€
Resort
*Via Regina 8, 22019*
**Tel** *0344 424 91*
🅦 grandhoteltremezzo.com
This prestigious lakeside hotel offers a range of well-appointed rooms, plus indoor and outdoor pools, including a floating pool in the lake, five restaurants, and a spa.

**VARENNA: Hotel du Lac** €€
Rooms with a view
*Via del Prestino 11, 23829*
**Tel** *0341 83 02 38*
🅦 albergodulac.com
Located in the medieval village of Varenna, this peaceful hotel at the edge of Lake Como boasts enchanting views. Close to good ferry connections.

# Valle d'Aosta and Piedmont

**ACQUI TERME: Hotel Rondò** €
Spa hotel
*Viale Acquedotto Romano 44, 15011*
**Tel** *0144 32 28 89*
🅦 albergorondo.it
Rooms are basic but bright, and staffers are friendly and helpful.

## DK Choice

**ALBA: Villa la Meridiana Cascina Reinè** €
Agriturismo
*Località Altavilla 9, 12051*
**Tel** *0173 44 01 12*
🅦 villalameridianaalba.it
This 18th-century villa benefits from views over the surrounding vineyards. Rooms boast antiques and there are three cosy apartments. Guests can help harvest the crop from the estate's vineyards and hunt for truffles.

**ALESSANDRIA: Hotel Alli Due Buoi Rossi** €€
Historic
*Via Cavour 32, 15121*
**Tel** *0131 51 71 71*
🅦 hotelalliduebuoirossi.com
Founded in 1741, this central hotel offers comfortable rooms, a fine dining restaurant, a bistro, and a bar.

**AOSTA: Hotel Village Aosta** €€
Resort
*Località Torrent de Maillod 1, 11020*
**Tel** *0165 77 49 11*
🅦 hotelvillageaosta.it
Offering both hotel rooms and individual chalets, this resort hotel is ideally located for both winter and summer activities. There is a Scandinavian restaurant onsite.

**ARONA: Hotel Giardino** €
Pensione
*Corso Repubblica 1, 28041*
**Tel** *0322 459 94*
🅦 giardinoarona.com
This comfortable hotel boasts splendid views across Lake Maggiore from the large terrace and grounds.

## DK Choice

**BAVENO: Hotel Splendid** €€
Resort
*Via Sempione 12, 28831*
**Tel** *0323 92 45 83*
🅦 zaccherahotels.com
This luxurious and elegant hotel has its own private beach (which has sunbeds and a private jetty) and an outdoor pool. The rooms are comfortable and well appointed – most have balconies with lakeside views. Helpful and attentive staffers provide excellent service.

**CANNOBIO: Residenza Patrizia** €€
Pensione
*Viale Vittorio Veneto 9, 28822*
**Tel** *0323 70 22 00*
🅦 residenzapatrizia.com
Inviting rooms and self-contained apartments are available at Residenza Patrizia, plus a range of amenities such as a sauna and a pool.

Stone steps leading to the charming Villa La Meridiana Cascina Reinè in Alba

**ORTO SAN GIULIO: Hotel San Rocco** €€
Historic
*Via Gippini 11, 28016*
**Tel** *0322 91 19 77*
🅦 hotelsanrocco.it
Unwind at the lakeside pool or enjoy the excellent restaurant, and views of San Giulio Island. Downtown, a pleasant walk away, offers additional eateries.

**STRESA: Hotel la Palma** €€
Resort
*Lungolago Umberto I 33, 28838*
**Tel** *0323 324 01*
🅦 hlapalma.it
This hotel offers a private beach, an outdoor pool, spa amenities and a terrace bar. There is also a well-regarded restaurant.

**TORTONA: Villa Giulia** €
Boutique
*Strada Statale per Alessandria 7/A, 15057*
**Tel** *0131 86 23 96*
🅦 villagiulia-hotel.com
Former private villa with elegant decor. Enjoy a cheerful atmosphere and an ample breakfast.

**TURIN: Albergo Serenella** €
Pensione
*Via Tarino 4, 10124*
**Tel** *011 83 70 31*
🅦 albergoserenella.com
This family-run establishment has clean and basic rooms at unbeatable prices for the city center. Prices do not change during the high season and include all charges.

**TURIN: Hotel Conte Biancamano** €
Pensione
*Corso Vittorio Emanuele II 73, 10128*
**Tel** *011 562 32 81*
🅦 hotelcontebiancamano.it
An intimate hotel with elegant decor located on the third floor of a 19th-century palazzo.

**TURIN: Grand Hotel Sitea** €€
Luxury
*Via Carlo Alberto 35, 10123*
**Tel** *011 517 01 71*
🅦 grandhotelsitea.it
Set in a Neo-Classical palazzo, this place offers elegant suites and a top-class restaurant.

**TURIN: NH Lingotto Tech** €€
Design
*Via Nizza 230, 10126*
**Tel** *011 664 20 00*
🅦 nh-hotels.com
In the refurbished FIAT factory's Lingotto building, this stunning hotel is close to transportation links to the city. Chic rooms with an industrial feel.

**TURIN: Allegro Italian**
**Golden Palace** €€€
Luxury
*Via dell'Arcivescovado 18, 10121*
**Tel** *011 551 21 11*
W goldenpalace.it
Convenient for visiting Turin's
major attractions, this centrally
located hotel offers a luxury spa,
pool, and gym, plus a restaurant.

**VARALLO SESIA: Vecchio**
**Albergo Sacro Monte** €
Pensione
*Località Sacro Monte 14, 13019*
**Tel** *0163 542 54*
W sacromontealbergo.it
Founded in 1594 for pilgrims,
this peaceful hotel located at
the entrance to the Sacro
Monte di Varallo preserve offers
comfortable, simple rooms,
a small private garden, and a
restaurant.

# Liguria

## DK Choice

**CAMOGLI: Locanda I Tre**
**Merli** €€
Rooms with a view
*Via Scalo 5, 16032*
**Tel** *0185 77 67 52*
W locandaitremerli.com
Located right on the enchanting
fishing port of Camogli, this
cosy hotel offers wonderful
views and personalized service.
Room amenities include basic
cooking amenities. A small spa
area has a Jacuzzi and a steam
bath. Ferries to Portofino and the
Cinque Terre are nearby. Parking
is available on request.

**CAMOGLI: Cenobio dei Dogi** €€€
Luxury
*Via Nicolò Cuneo 34, 16032*
**Tel** *0185 72 41*
W cenobio.it
Built for the Doges of Genoa, this
17th-century villa houses a vast
hotel with a private beach.

**FINALE LIGURE: Punta Est** €€€
Luxury
*Via Aurelia 1, 17024*
**Tel** *019 60 06 11*
W puntaest.com
Along with spectacular sea views,
this 18th-century villa offers a
heated saltwater pool, wellness
center, gardens, and Tai Chi classes.

**GENOA: Hotel Villa Pagoda** €€
Rooms with a view
*Via Capolungo 15, 16167*
**Tel** *010 372 61 61*
W villapagoda.it

With an Oriental feel, this 19th-
century villa has spectacular
views, comfortable rooms, and
a restaurant. Genoa's historic
center is easily reached by train.

**GENOA: NH Marina** €€
Rooms with a view
*Molo Ponte Calvi 5, 16124*
**Tel** *010 253 91*
W nh-hotels.com
This international hotel overlooks
the harbour and is located close
to the Aquarium, the old town,
and the markets.

**ISOLA PALMARIA: Locanda**
**Lorena** €€
Rooms with a view
*Via Cavour 4, 19025*
**Tel** *0187 79 23 70*
W locandalorena.com
Enjoy simple, comfortable rooms
and an excellent restaurant in
this beach hotel accessible only
by boat (provided by the hotel).
Rooms in a nearby residence and
a small villa are also available.

**LEVANTO: Hotel Stella Maris** €€
Boutique
*Via Marconi 4, 19015*
**Tel** *0187 80 82 58*
W hotelstellamaris.it
Close to the beach and the
Cinque Terre park, this hotel
boasts stunning Art Nouveau
interiors and a garden terrace.

**MANAROLA: Ca' d'Andrean** €
Pensione
*Via Discovolo 101, 19017*
**Tel** *0187 92 00 40*
W cadandrean.it
At this simple, good-value,
family-run guesthouse, some
rooms have a terrace and
stunning views. Breakfast is
served alfresco in summer.

Charming views from the vibrant Locanda I
Tre Merli, Camogli

**MONTEROSSO: Hotel Marina** €
Pensione
*Via Buranco 40, 19016*
**Tel** *0187 81 76 13*
W hotelmarina5terre.com
Located near the sea and the
hiking path to Vernazza, the
Marina offers elegant rooms
and an excellent restaurant.
Breakfast is served in a lemon
garden in summer.

**OSPEDALETTI: Hotel Firenze** €
Rooms with a view
*Corso Regina Margherita 97,*
*18014*
**Tel** *0184 68 92 21*
W firenze.azurline.com
This small hillside hotel offers
basic but cheerful rooms, most
of which have balconies.

**PORTO VENERE:**
**Hotel della Baia** €
Rooms with a view
*Via Lungomare 111, 19025*
**Tel** *0187 79 07 97*
W baiahotel.com
All rooms have balconies and
views over the bay. There's an
outdoor pool and a restaurant.

**PORTOFINO: Splendido** €€€
Luxury
*Salita Baratta 16, 16034*
**Tel** *0185 26 78 01*
W hotelsplendido.com
Housed in a former monastery,
the Splendido has elegantly
furnished rooms, many with
private terraces.

**RAPALLO: Hotel Italia**
**e Lido** €€
Rooms with a view
*Lungomare Castello 1, 16035*
**Tel** *0185 504 92*
W italiaelido.com
Overlooking the Gulf of Tigullio,
this hotel has bright, airy rooms
and an excellent restaurant.

**SAN REMO: Hotel Nazionale** €€
Rooms with a view
*Corso Matteotti 3, 18038*
**Tel** *0184 57 75 77*
W hotelnazionalesanremo.com
Guests at the Nazionale enjoy
a high level of service and
classically furnished rooms,
many with sea views.

**SAN REMO: Royal Hotel** €€€
Luxury
*Corso Imperatrice 80, 18038*
**Tel** *0184 53 91*
W royalhotelsanremo.com
Located right on the seafront,
the Royal Hotel is renowned
for its restaurants. Guests stay
in truly palatial rooms and
enjoy such amenities as a
great pool and spa.

**Key to prices** *see p562*

**SESTRI LEVANTE: Hotel Helvetia** €€
Boutique
*Via Cappuccini 43, 16039*
**Tel** *0185 411 75*
**w** hotelhelvetia.it
Located on the beach, this hotel boasts two pools, a sun terrace and stunning views of the bay. Excellent service.

**VENTIMIGLIA: La Riserva di Castel d'Appio** €€
Rooms with a view
*Via Peidaigo 71, 18039*
**Tel** *0184 22 95 33*
**w** lariserva.it
Enjoy panoramic views over the Italian Riviera and the Côte d'Azur at this hotel. Excellent service.

# Emilia-Romagna

**BOLOGNA: Delle Drapperie** €
Pensione
*Via Drapperie 5, 40124*
**Tel** *051 223 955*
**w** albergodrapperie.com
Painted ceilings and luxurious bathrooms characterize this well-priced option.

**BOLOGNA: Il Guercino** €
Boutique
*Via Luigi Serra 7, 40129*
**Tel** *051 369 893*
**w** guercino.it
An Indian flavor prevails at this charming hotel, which offers guests the choice of two solariums and a relaxation area.

**BOLOGNA: Indipendenza Suite** €
Pensione
*Via dell'Indipendenza 30, 40121*
**Tel** *331 4575 920*
Stay in one of four independent apartments decorated in simple, classic style.

**BOLOGNA: Commerclanti** €€
Historic
*Via de' Pignattari 11, 40124*
**Tel** *051 745 75 11*
**w** commercianti.hotelsbologna.it
Located next to Bologna's Cathedral, this hotel housed in a 13-century building is bursting with romantic details.

**BOLOGNA: Corona d'Oro** €€
Romantic
*Via Guglielmo Oberdan 12, 40126*
**Tel** *051 7457 611*
**w** hco.it
This historic hotel is decorated in an eclectic style that ranges from medieval to Art Deco. Before dinner, stop for an *aperitivo* in the glass-ceilinged atrium.

Outdoor swimming pool at La Riserva di Castel d'Appio in Ventimiglia

**BOLOGNA: Hotel Cavour** €€
Historic
*Via Goito 4, 40126*
**Tel** *051 228 111*
**w** cavour-hotel.com
This central hotel is housed in a historic building. It has elegant rooms and a small furnished terrace with great views of the towers and roofs of Bologna.

**BOLOGNA: Roma** €€
Pensione
*Via Massimo d'Azeglio 9, 40123*
**Tel** *051 226 322*
**w** hotelroma.biz
This classic pensione offers a fabulous location and delightfully quaint rooms – ask for one with a balcony.

## DK Choice

**BOLOGNA: Grand Hotel Majestic** €€€
Luxury
*Via Indipendenza, 8 40121*
**Tel** *051 225 445*
**w** grandhotelmajestic.
hotelsbologna.it
This legendary hotel expertly combines opulent old-world elegance with modern comfort and hospitality. Each room is individually decorated with lush fabrics and antique furniture. Breakfast is served on the romantic rooftop terrace with sweeping views of the city. The dining room boasts beautiful frescoes.

**FERRARA: Principessa Leonora** €€
Boutique
*Via Mascheraio 39, 44100*
**Tel** *0532 20 60 20*
**w** principessaleonoraferrara.it
A 16th-century residence exquisitely decorated with antique French tapestries and traditional furniture.

**FERRARA: Duchessa Isabella** €€€
Historic
*Via Palestro 70, 44121*
**Tel** *0532 20 21 21*
**w** duchessaisabellaferrara.it
Minute attention to detail in both decor and service. Rooms are sumptuously furnished.

**MODENA: Daunia** €
Pensione
*Via del Pozzo 158, 41125*
**Tel** *059 37 11 82*
**w** hoteldaunia.it
A simple, modern building with a restaurant. Breakfast is served in the garden, weather permitting.

**PARMA: Stendhal** €€
Romantic
*Via Giambattista Bodoni 3, 43121*
**Tel** *0521 20 80 57*
**w** hotelstendhal.it
Housed in a centrally located old palazzo, the Stendhal has eclectically decorated rooms.

**PIACENZA: San Francesco** €
Pensione
*Galleria San Francesco 2, 29121*
**Tel** *0523 32 66 88*
Excellent prices for spotlessly clean accommodations right in front of the Palazzo della Pilotta, and close to the Duomo.

**PIACENZA GENEPRETO: La Pobiella** €€
Agriturismo
*Località Pobiella 16, 29010*
**Tel** *0523 99 75 14*
This rustic stone villa is the ideal accommodations choice for a relaxed hillside holiday.

**RAVENNA: Sant'Andrea** €
Boutique
*Via Carlo Cattaneo 33, 48121*
**Tel** *0544 21 55 64*
**w** santandreahotel.com
Solid service and great value for money in this converted convent with a tranquil cloister-garden.

**RAVENNA: Cappello** €€
Romantic
*Via IV Novembre 41, 48121*
**Tel** *0544 21 98 13*
**W** albergocappello.it
The rooms in this exquisite hotel in a Renaissance building have coffered ceilings and chandeliers.

**RIMINI: Acasamia** €
Budget
*Viale Renato Parisano 34, 47921*
**Tel** *0541 39 13 70*
**W** hotelacasamia.com
Featuring bright, colorful rooms, Acasamia is located just a short stroll from the beach.

**RIMINI: Grand Hotel Rimini** €€€
Luxury
*Parco Federico Fellini 1, 47900*
**Tel** *0541 560 00*
**W** grandhotelrimini.com
Historic deluxe seaside establishment made famous by Federico Fellini. Amazing decor and ambience and a high standard of service.

# Florence

**Palazzo Guadagni** €
Historic **Map** 5 B5
*Piazza di Santo Spirito 9, 50125*
**Tel** *055 265 83 76*
**W** palazzoguadagni.com
Fantastic service, a great location, and reasonable prices, but the hotel really stands out for its terrace and loggia – a great place to relax with a glass of wine.

**Relais Il Campanile** €
B&B **Map** 6 E1
*Via Ricasoli 10, 50125*
**Tel** *055 21 16 88*
**W** relaiscampanile.it

Pleasantly bright, large rooms at the Relais Uffizi in Florence

Relais Il Campanile, housed in a 17th-century palazzo, is literally in the shadow of the Duomo, so you will get a view of it as soon as you step out of the door. Quaint rooms have wrought-iron accents.

**Residenza Johanna** €
Pensione **Map** 2 D3
*Via Bonifacio Lupi 14, 50129*
**Tel** *055 48 18 96*
**W** antichedimorefiorentine.it
Not to be confused with another *pensione* with the same name, but farther from the center, this tiny and charming hotel is fantastic value. Free parking.

**Brunelleschi** €€
Historic **Map** 6 D2
*Piazza Sant'Elisabetta 3, 50122*
**Tel** *055 273 70*
**W** hotelbrunelleschi.it
Located in a Byzantine tower, this place offers classy, opulent rooms. The two-level suite, in the tower itself, is definitely worth its steep price.

**David** €€
Pensione **Map** 4 E3
*Viale Michelangelo 1, 50125*
**Tel** *055 681 16 95*
**W** davidhotel.com
Some rooms have balconies that look out over leafy Oltrarno in this family-owned guesthouse.

**Grifone** €€
Business
*Via Gaetano Pilati 20, 50136*
**Tel** *055 62 33 00*
**W** hotelgrifonefirenze.com
The Grifone provides comfortable and spacious rooms, some with a kitchenette.

**Hotel Home** €€
Boutique **Map** 4 F2
*Piazza Piave 3, 50122*
**Tel** *055 24 36 68*
**W** hhflorence.it
This stylish hotel stands out for its white and extremely elegant decor with a minimalist touch. The suite has a private balcony with views over Florence.

## DK Choice

**Relais Uffizi** €€
Romantic **Map** 6 D4
*Chiasso del Buco 16, 50122*
**Tel** *055 267 62 39*
**W** relaisuffizi.it
Located behind the Piazza della Signoria, this hotel is fantastic value for money. All rooms are charmingly decorated, and the breakfast room looks out onto the Piazza.

**Four Seasons Hotel Firenze** €€€
Luxury **Map** 2 E4
*Borgo Pinti 99, 50121*
**Tel** *055 262 61*
**W** fourseasons.com/florence
The Four Seasons is the epitome of elegance, with silk wall hangings, frescoes, and bas-reliefs. Service is impeccable, and the restaurant is worth visiting even if you are not a guest. The hotel runs a frequent shuttle bus downtown.

**Grand Hotel Minerva** €€€
Historic **Map** 5 B2
*Piazza di Santa Maria Novella 16, 50123*
**Tel** *055 272 30*
**W** grandhotelminerva.com
A panoramic terrace with a pool gives a modern touch to one of the city's oldest hotels. The Gran Hotel Minerva's convenient location near the train station means that many sights are in walking distance.

**The Westin Excelsior** €€€
Luxury **Map** 5 A2
*Piazza d'Ognissanti 3, 50123*
**Tel** *055 271 51*
**W** westinflorence.com
Guests at the Westin Excelsior stay in sinfully opulent rooms, some with balconies that have views of the River Arno. The roof terrace is exquisitely presented.

# Tuscany

## DK Choice

**AREZZO: Badia di Pomaio** €€
Boutique
*Loc. Pomaio 4, 52100*
**Tel** *0575 35 32 10*
**W** hotelbadiadipomaio.it
This superbly converted 17th-century abbey is located in a picturesque spot amid lush gardens with a swimming pool and panoramic views of the medieval town below. Comfortable and quiet rooms with elegant furnishings. Warm and hospitable staff.

**AREZZO: Graziella**
Patio Hotel €€
Boutique
*Via Cavour 23, 52100*
**Tel** *0575 40 19 62*
**W** hotelpatio.it
This charming hotel offers a range of rooms decorated in imaginative African and Far Eastern styles. The location – next door to Piero della Francesca's frescoes – is unbeatable.

**CORTONA: Italia** €
Budget
*Via Ghibellina 5/7, 52044*
**Tel** *0575 63 02 54*
🅦 hotelitaliacortona.com
Excellent value at this lovely spot
full of character in the heart of
Cortona. There are great views
to be had from some rooms
and the restaurant.

## DK Choice

**ELBA MARCIANA: Cernia
Isola Botanica** €€
Rooms with a view
*Via San Gaetano 23, 57030*
**Tel** *0565 90 82 10*
🅦 hotelcernia.it
A lush flower-filled park and
botanical garden surround this
charming hotel. Rooms are
spacious and minimalist, with
interesting design elements.
There is a freshwater swimming
pool and wellness center.
Just a short walk from Capo
Sant'Andrea, the location is
hard to beat.

**ELBA SPARTAIA: Desiree** €€
Rooms with a view
*Spartaia, Procchio, 57030*
**Tel** *0565 90 73 11*
🅦 htdesiree.it
Guests enjoy clean rooms and
private beach access at this
comfortable hotel.

**LUCCA: Piccolo Hotel Puccini** €
Pensione
*Via di Poggio 9, 55100*
**Tel** *0583 554 21*
🅦 hotelpuccini.com
Facing Piazza Cittadella and the
statue of Puccini, this hotel is
perfectly located to get a taste
of Italian street life. The prices
may be low, but you get warm
service and charming rooms.

**MONTEPULCIANO:
San Biagio** €
Budget
*Via San Bartolomeo 2, 53045*
**Tel** *0578 71 72 33*
🅦 albergosanbiagio.it
Located just outside of the town
with glorious views, this hotel has
comfortable and neat rooms and
a heated swimming pool.

**MONTERIGGIONI:
Borgo Gallinaio** €€
Agriturismo
*Strada del Gallinaio 5, 53035*
**Tel** *0577 30 47 51*
🅦 gallinaio.it
This converted 15th-century
stone-built farmhouse is
surrounded by cypress and olive
trees. There is an outdoor pool.

Dining area with medieval details in the
Antica Residenza Cicogna, Siena

**PISA: Guerrazzi** €
B&B
*Via Francesco da Buti 4, 56125*
**Tel** *3389 32 81 69*
🅦 bbguerrazzi.hostel.com
Simple but quaint, with
comfortable, clean rooms and
a nice terrace. Lots to choose
from at breakfast, including
homemade cakes.

**PISA: Royal Victoria Hotel** €€
Historic
*Lungarno Antonio Pacinotti
12, 56126*
**Tel** *050 94 01 11*
🅦 royalvictoria.it
Housed in a 10th-century tower,
Pisa's very first hotel has stately
decor and spacious rooms.

**PISA: Relais dell'Orologio** €€€
Historic
*Via della Faggiola 12, 56126*
**Tel** *050 83 03 61*
🅦 hotelrelaisorologio.com
Built into a 14th-century tower,
this hotel has elegant rooms
and a delightful reading room.
Enjoy breakfast on the veranda.

**SAN GIMIGNANO:
Bel Soggiorno** €
Budget
*Via San Giovanni 91, 53037*
**Tel** *0577 94 03 75*
🅦 hotelbelsoggiorno.it
Run by the same family since
1886, this is a comfortable and
well-priced hotel with an
excellent restaurant.

**SAN GIMIGNANO:
Leon Bianco** €€
Rooms with a view
*Piazza Cisterna 13, 53037*
**Tel** *0577 94 12 94*
🅦 leonbianco.com
Elegant rooms with spectacular
views of the hillside piazza or
the countryside. Excellent
breakfast served on the terrace.

**SIENA: Antica Residenza
Cicogna** €
Pensione
*Via Termini 76, 53100*
**Tel** *0577 28 56 13*
🅦 anticaresidenzacicogna.it
Romantic location set in a
medieval building full of
charming details.

**SIENA: Palazzo Ravizza** €€
Romantic
*Piano dei Mantellini 34, 53100*
**Tel** *0577 28 04 62*
🅦 palazzoravizza.it
Lovely rooms with original period
furniture. Some rooms overlook
a picturesque garden.

**SIENA: Grand Hotel
Continental** €€€
Luxury
*Via Banchi di Sopra 85, 53100*
**Tel** *0577 560 11*
🅦 grandhotelcontinentalsiena.com
The most prestigious address in
Siena. This 17th-century building
has impressive frescoes and
luxurious rooms.

**VIAREGGIO: London** €€
Rooms with a view
*Viale Daniele Manin 16, 55049*
**Tel** *0584 498 41*
🅦 www.hotellondon.it
Simple, comfortable rooms and
an elegant lobby. Located a short
walk from the sea.

**VOLTERRA: Villa Rioddi** €
Historic
*Strada Provinciale del Monte
Volterrano 71, 56048*
**Tel** *0588 880 53*
🅦 hotelvillarioddi.it
This medieval 15th-century villa
offers excellent amenities, views
and a sumptuous breakfast.

**VOLTERRA: Marcampo** €€
Agriturismo
*Località San Cipriano, Podere
Marcampo 30, 56048*
**Tel** *0588 853 93*
🅦 agriturismo-marcampo.com
The pool boasts vineyards views
in this tranquil slice of Tuscan
paradise with just six rooms.

## Umbria

**ASSISI: Sole** €
Budget
*Corso Giuseppe Mazzini 35, 06081*
**Tel** *075 81 23 73*
🅦 assisihotelsole.com
The Sole offers basic but spacious
rooms in a centrally located 15th-
century building. There are great
views over the countryside and
excellent service.

**ASSISI: Le Dimore di San Crispino** €€
Romantic
*Via Sant'Agnese, 06081*
**Tel** *075 804 32 57*
W assisibenessere.it
In addition to classically decorated rooms, this hotel offers a spa, gardens, and a restaurant.

**GUBBIO: La Cinciallegre** €
Agriturismo
*Fraz. Pisciano, 06024*
**Tel** *345 062 52 29*
W lecinciallegre.it
This is a jewel hidden in the countryside. Small but cosy rooms, plus great food made on the farm. Try the quince jam.

**NORCIA: Casale nel Parco dei Monti Sibillini** €
Agriturismo
*Vocabolo Fontevena 8, 06046*
**Tel** *0743 81 64 81*
W casalenelparco.com
Countryside retreat amid amazing scenery, with canopy beds and wood-beamed ceilings. Don't miss the local delights from the kitchen.

**ORVIETO: Filippeschi** €
Budget
*Via Filippeschi 19, 05018*
**Tel** *0763 34 32 75*
W albergofilippeschi.it
Stay in basic but comfortable rooms in the historic center. Spacious lobby.

**ORVIETO: La Badia** €€
Historic
*Località La Badia 8, 05018*
**Tel** *0763 30 19 59*
W labadiahotel.it
This breathtaking hotel is built into the ruins of an 8th-century monastery, exquisitely restored and decorated with antiques.

**ORVIETO: Locanda Pallazone** €€
Agriturismo
*Località Rocca Ripesena 66, 05018*
**Tel** *0763 39 36 14*
W locandapalazzone.it
Elegant accommodations in a former cardinal's residence located on top of a hill, in the middle of vineyards. Spacious rooms and terrific views.

**PERUGIA: Castello di Monterone** €€
Historic
*Strada Montevile 3, 06126*
**Tel** *075 572 42 14*
W castellomonterone.com
This historic building is located on stunning grounds. Luxurious rooms and two first-class restaurants are among the many things to enjoy here.

**Key to prices** *see p562*

**PERUGIA: Brufani Palace** €€€
Luxury
*Piazza Italia 12, 06121*
**Tel** *075 573 25 41*
W brufanipalace.com
Sumptuous accommodations, plus a roof garden with views of the town and countryside.

**SPOLETO: Hotel Aurora** €
Budget
*Via dell'Apollinare 3, 06049*
**Tel** *0743 22 03 15*
W hotelauraspoleto.it
Comfortable rooms and great service at this central but quiet family-run hotel.

**SPOLETO: San Luca** €€
Boutique
*Via Interna delle Mura 21, 06049*
**Tel** *0743 22 33 99*
W hotelsanluca.com
Sophisticated elegance in one of the loveliest palaces in Spoleto. Excellent breakfast buffet.

**TODI CANONICA: Tenuta di Canonica** €€
Agriturismo
*Vocabolo Casalzetta 75, 06059*
**Tel** *075 894 75 45*
W tenutadicanonica.com
Sublime country residence on the site of a 9th-century farm. Superb location.

# Le Marche

**ANCONA: Grand Hotel Palace** €€
Historic
*Lungomare Luigi Vanvitelli 24, 60121*
**Tel** *071 207 35 90*
W hotelancona.it
Old-world elegance at this grand 17th-century portside palazzo. Helpful and efficient staff.

Luxuriously decorated room in the Locanda Pallazone in Orvieto

**ASCOLI PICENO: Pennile** €
Budget
*Via Gaetano Spalvieri 1, 63100*
**Tel** *0736 416 45*
W www.hotelpennile.it
This hotel charges reasonable prices for simple but well-kept rooms. All rooms feature air conditioning and Wi-Fi, plus a balcony.

### DK Choice
**ASCOLI PICENO: Villa Cicchi** €€
Agriturismo
*Via Salaria Superiore 137, 63100*
**Tel** *0736 25 22 72*
W villacicchi.it
A meticulously presented villa is at the heart of this agriturismo that combines luxury accommodations with rustic hospitality. There are magnificent grounds, a large pool, period furniture, and frescoed ceilings. Activities include trekking, wine tasting, cooking and photography courses, and yoga.

**PESARO: Bellevue** €
Resort
*Viale Trieste 88, 61121*
**Tel** *0721 690 18*
W bellevuehotel.net
Great value at this simple but accommodating beach resort with a pool. A range of child-friendly activities makes it very suitable for families.

### DK Choice
**PESARO: Alexander Museum Palace Hotel** €€
Historic
*Viale Trieste 20, 61121*
**Tel** *0721 344 41*
W alexandermuseum.it
As the name implies, these unique accommodations are part museum, part hotel. Both established and emerging Italian artists have collaborated to transform this elegant hotel into a literal work of art. Each room is different and every single design element, from the colors to the chairs and floors, is one of a kind. The sea views are a bonus.

**SAN MARINO: Hotel Joli** €
Pensione
*Viale Federico d'Urbino 36 B, 47890*
**Tel** *0549 99 10 09*
W hoteljoli.sm
This pet-friendly, family hotel offers nice rooms and a warm atmosphere. Parking is provided.

**SAN MARINO: Cesare** €€
Boutique
*Salita alla Rocca 7, 47890*
**Tel** *0549 99 23 55*
🔲 hotelcesare.com
This hotel blends convenience
with refined elegance. Rooms
are clean and bright. The staffers
are very attentive.

**URBINO: Cà Andreana** €
Agriturismo
*Via Cà Andreana 2, 61029*
**Tel** *0722 32 78 45*
🔲 caandreana.it
This farmstay is located in a
magnificent country setting
with stunning views. Rooms
are quaint and well presented.

**URBINO: Raffaello** €
Rooms with a view
*Via Santa Margherita 38, 61029*
**Tel** *0722 47 84*
🔲 albergoraffaello.com
Located near the famous artist's
childhood home. Rooms are
simple but inviting.

# Rome

## The Ancient Center

**Fortyseven** €€
Rooms with a view **Map** 6 E1
*Via Luigi Petroselli 47, 00186*
**Tel** *06 678 78 16*
🔲 fortysevenhotel.com
Stellar views of the ancient city
from this retro-styled hotel.
Elegant rooms; there are two
suites, both with private terraces.

**Hotel Forum** €€
Rooms with a view **Map** 3 B5
*Via Tor de' Conti 25, 00184*
**Tel** *06 679 24 46*
🔲 hotelforum.com
Enjoy magnificent views of
ancient Rome from a charming
terrace. Graceful interiors and
plenty of old-world charm.

**Nicolas Inn** €€
B&B **Map** 3 B5
*Via Cavour 295, 00184*
**Tel** *328 555 3004*
🔲 nicolasinn.com
Basic service, but the rooms are
pleasant and cosy, and all have
ensuite bathrooms. The hosts are
warm and friendly.

**Palazzo Manfredi** €€€
Rooms with a view **Map** 7 A1
*Via Labicana 125, 00184*
**Tel** *06 77 59 13 80*
🔲 palazzomanfredi.com
The Colosseum seems close
enough to touch at this hotel.
Elegantly decorated rooms and
excellent service.

Glass walls of the Alexander Museum Palace Hotel in Pesaro

## Around Piazza Navona

**Albergo Santa Chiara** €€
Boutique **Map** 10 D3
*Via di Santa Chiara 21, 00186*
**Tel** *06 687 29 79*
🔲 albergosantachiara.com
The lobby is the most impressive
section of this hotel; the rooms
are pleasant, with all mod cons,
but don't compare. Enjoy a drink
in the alfresco bar.

**Campo de' Fiori Hotel** €€
Rooms with a view **Map** 9 C4
*Via del Biscione 6, 00186*
**Tel** *06 68 80 68 65*
🔲 hotelcampodefiori.com
Romantically decorated rooms
with refined furnishings, and
views of rooftops and domes.

**Casa di Santa Brigida** €€
Religious institution **Map** 9 B4
*Piazza Farnese 96, 00186*
**Tel** *06 68 89 25 96*
🔲 brigidine.org
Although this is not the cheapest
convent in town, the central
location is well worth the price.
Rooms are clean and spacious,
and there is a sunny terrace.

**Hotel Sole al
Pantheon** €€
Rooms with a view **Map** 10 D3
*Piazza della Rotonda 63, 00186*
**Tel** *06 678 04 41*
🔲 solealpantheonrome.com
Gorgeous terra-cotta floors,
frescoes on the ceilings and
unparalleled views of the
bustling Piazza Navona, if you
don't mind the noise.

**Locanda Cairoli** €€
Boutique **Map** 10 D4
*Piazza Benedetto Cairoli 2, 00186*
**Tel** *06 68 80 92 78*
🔲 hotelcairoliroma.com
Locanda Cairoli is a centrally
located hotel with comfortable,
modern rooms tastefully
decorated with warm colors.

**St. George Hotel** €€
Luxury **Map** 9 A3
*Via Giulia 62, 00186*
**Tel** *06 68 66 11*
🔲 hotelindigorome.com
The decor at this elegant hotel
combines Old Masters' paintings
with art from the 1960s and '70s.

**Teatro di Pompeo** €€
Historic **Map** 9 C4
*Largo del Pallaro 8, 00186*
**Tel** *06 68 30 01 70*
🔲 hotelteatrodipompeo.it
Built on the ruins of Pompey's
ancient theater, this hotel has
simple rooms and friendly staff.

**Teatropace33** €€
Rooms with a view **Map** 9 C3
*Via del Teatro Pace 33, 00186*
**Tel** *06 687 90 75*
🔲 hotelteatropace.com
Excellent price-quality ratio
at this charming Baroque-style
hotel with elegant decor.

**Grand Hotel de la Minerve** €€€
Luxury **Map** 10 D3
*Piazza della Minerva 69, 00186*
**Tel** *06 69 52 01*
🔲 grandhoteldelaminerve.com
Excellent views from nearly every
room. The decor is luxurious and
the service is excellent.

**Raphael** €€€
Romantic **Map** 9 C2
*Largo Febo 2, 00186*
**Tel** *06 68 28 31*
🔲 raphaelhotel.com
The ivy-covered facade is the
trademark of this hotel with
gorgeous decor and a terrace.

**Sole al Biscione** €€€
Historic **Map** 9 C4
*Via del Biscione 76, 00186*
**Tel** *06 68 80 68 73*
🔲 hotelsoleroma.it
This basic but charming hotel
claims to be the oldest in Rome.
The rooms are spotless.

**For more information on types of hotels** *see pp558–61*

## Northeast Rome

### DK Choice

**Beehive**                          €
Budget                    **Map** 4 E3
*Via Marghera 8, 00185*
**Tel** *06 44 70 45 53*
W the-beehive.com
A gem of a hotel with both
private rooms and small
dormitories available. Some
rooms have ensuite bathrooms.
Extras include yoga lessons,
massage, and a café serving
organic food and drinks.

Charming outdoor garden area at Beehive, Northeast Rome

**Hostel des Artistes**              €
Budget                    **Map** 4 E2
*Via Villafranca 20, 00185*
**Tel** *06 445 43 65*
W hostelrome.com
This is a friendly hostel offering
accommodations to suit all
budgets – anything from
dorms to private rooms. Three-
star service.

**Aleph**                           €€
Luxury                    **Map** 3 B2
*Via di San Basilio 15, 00185*
**Tel** *06 42 29 01*
W hotelalephrome.com
Experience modern opulence
at this relaxing, luxurious hotel
with a spa.

**Blue Hostel**                     €€
Budget                    **Map** 4 D4
*Via Carlo Alberto 13, 00185*
**Tel** *34 09 25 85 03*
W bluehostel.it
A charming hotel housed in a
former convent in the heart of
multicultural Esquilino. Rooms
are clean and spacious.

### DK Choice

**Casa Howard**                     €€
B&B                       **Map** 3 A3
*Via di Capo le Case 18, 00187 &*
*Via Sistina 149, 00187*
**Tel** *06 69 92 45 55*
W casahoward.com
This funky B&B, inspired by
E. M. Forster's novel *Howard's
End* comprises ten uniquely
decorated rooms in two
adjacent locations, both
near the Spanish Steps.
Impeccable elegance.

**Daphne Trevi**                    €€
Boutique                  **Map** 3 B2
*Via degli Avignonesi 20, 00187*
**Tel** *06 89 34 57 81*
W daphne-rome.com
Top-notch boutique hotel with
personal service and a modern

look. They'll even give you a cell
phone for your stay.

**es hotel**                        €€
Rooms with a view        **Map** 4 E4
*Via Filippo Turati 171, 00185*
**Tel** *06 44 48 41*
W radissonblu.com/eshotel-rome
Splendid five-star hotel with
sleek modern design and all
white rooms.

**Hotel Suisse**                    €€
Pensione                  **Map** 3 A2
*Via Gregoriana 54, 00187*
**Tel** *06 678 36 49*
W hotelsuisserome.com
Great value at this elegantly
appointed hotel with 12 rooms,
babysitting services, and a
convenient location.

**Locarno**                         €€
Historic                  **Map** 2 F1
*Via della Penna 22, 00186*
**Tel** *06 361 08 41*
W hotellocarno.com
A masterpiece of Art Deco and
the location for many classic
movies, this charming hotel is
on a quiet street not far from
Via Condotti.

**Piranesi**                        €€
Boutique                  **Map** 2 F1
*Via del Babuino 196, 00187*
**Tel** *06 32 80 41*
W hotelpiranesi.com
Quiet elegance in an ideal
location. There's a roof garden,
sauna, and a solarium. It also has
a small gym.

**Residenza Cellini**               €€
Pensione                  **Map** 3 C3
*Via Modena 5, 00184*
**Tel** *06 47 82 52 04*
W residenzacellini.it
Guests at this hotel within
walking distance of the
Colosseum enjoy large, simply
furnished rooms combining
historic interiors and modern
comforts; some bathrooms
have Jacuzzi tubs.

**Aldrovandi Palace**              €€€
Luxury
*Via Ulisse Aldrovandi 15, 00197*
**Tel** *06 322 39 93*
W aldrovandi.com
A spectacular five-star hotel with
airy rooms, a swimming pool,
and views of the park.

**Babuino181**                     €€€
Boutique                  **Map** 2 F1
*Via del Babuino 181, 00187*
**Tel** *06 32 29 52 95*
W romeluxurysuites.com
Splendid modern hotel with
luxurious details, in a Renaissance
palace with a leafy roof terrace.

**Eden**                           €€€
Luxury                    **Map** 3 B2
*Via Ludovisi 49, 00187*
**Tel** *06 47 81 21*
W edenroma.com
The Eden is a grand hotel that
offers elegantly furnished rooms
and a romantic rooftop dining
area. Service is exceptional.

**Exedra**                         €€€
Luxury                    **Map** 3 C3
*Piazza della Repubblica 47, 00185*
**Tel** *06 48 93 81*
W exedra-roma.boscolohotels.
com
Lavish five-star hotel with plush
rooms, a rooftop pool, and an
award-winning spa.

### DK Choice

**Hassler**                        €€€
Luxury                    **Map** 3 A2
*Piazza Trinità dei Monti 6,
00187*
**Tel** *06 69 93 40*
W hotelhasslerroma.com
The discreet service, plush
furnishings, and stunning
bedrooms make this a firm
favorite with celebrities. Guests
can also take advantage of the
Michelin-starred Imàgora
restaurant or enjoy a cocktail in
the Hassler Bar.

**Key to prices** *see p562*

**Hotel d'Inghilterra** €€€
Romantic     **Map** 3 A2
*Via Bocca di Leone 14, 00187*
**Tel** *06 69 98 11*
W *hoteldinghilterra.com*
Spacious accommodations in
an enviable location near the
Spanish Steps. All the rooms and
suites are individually styled.

**Portrait Roma** €€€
Boutique     **Map** 3 A2
*Via Bocca di Leone 23, 00187*
**Tel** *06 69 38 07 42*
W *lungarnocollection.com*
Accommodations with style; this
hotel is owned by famed shoe
designer Salvatore Ferragamo's
family, and it shows.

**Westin Excelsior** €€€
Romantic     **Map** 3 B2
*Via Veneto 125, 00187*
**Tel** *06 470 81*
W *westinrome.com*
This favorite with honeymooners
is the perfect place to enact *la
dolce vita*.

## The Vatican and Trastevere

**Casa Internazionale delle
Donne** €
Budget     **Map** 2 D5
*Via San Francesco di Sales 1A, 00165*
**Tel** *06 689 37 53*
W *casainternazionale
delledonne.org*
This women-only hotel offers
basic rooms in quiet and central
Trastevere and also has a good
restaurant.

**Centro Diffusione
Spiritualità** €
Religious institution     **Map** 2 D5
*Via dei Riari 44, 00153*
**Tel** *06 68 80 61 22*
W *villaiari.it*
Budget accommodations
including breakfast and dinner.
There is an 11pm curfew.

**Hotel Trastevere** €
Budget     **Map** 5 C1
*Via Luciano Manara 24, 00153*
**Tel** *06 581 47 13*
W *hoteltrastevere.net*
Rooms are simple, clean, and
spacious at this hotel that offers
good value for money. Good
breakfast buffet.

**Arco del Lauro** €€
B&B     **Map** 6 D1
*Via dell'Arco de' Tolomei 27, 00153*
**Tel** *06 97 84 03 50*
W *arcodellauro.it*
Tiny hotel in a picturesque
medieval location, with simple
but lovely rooms.

**Bramante** €€
Historic     **Map** 1 C3
*Vicolo delle Palline 24, 00193*
**Tel** *06 68 80 64 26*
W *hotelbramante.com*
In the shadow of St. Peter's, this
family-run hotel has quiet and
tasteful rooms.

### DK Choice

**Donna Camilla Savelli** €€
Romantic     **Map** 5 B1
*Via Garibaldi 27, 00153*
**Tel** *06 58 88 61*
W *hoteldonnacamillasavelli.com*
Designed by Baroque genius
Borromini, this meticulously
restored monastery still belongs
to the nuns of the original
order, but is now a four-star hotel.
The cloister is a calm oasis in the
heart of the bustling city.

**Relais Casa della Fornarina** €€
Historic     **Map** 2 D5
*Via di Porta Settimiana 7, 00153*
**Tel** *06 64 56 22 68*
W *casadellafornarina.com*
This is the guesthouse where
Raphael's muse once lived.
Spacious rooms and good service.

**Residenza Arco dei Tolomei** €€
Boutique     **Map** 6 D1
*Via dell'Arco de' Tolomei 26C, 00153*
**Tel** *06 58 32 08 19*
W *inrome.info*
With classic furnishings, this tiny
hotel offers a peaceful stay and
cosy atmosphere. Regal breakfast.

**Sant'Anna** €€
Boutique     **Map** 1 C3
*Borgo Pio 134, 00193*
**Tel** *06 68 80 16 02*
W *santannahotel.net*
Modern convenience with an
old-world feel. Rooms are large,
and there is a pleasant courtyard.

Chic and comfortable sitting area at Portrait
Roma, northeast Rome

## Aventine and Lateran

**Domus Aventina** €
Budget     **Map** 5 E2
*Via di Santa Prisca 11b, 00153*
**Tel** *06 574 61 35*
W *hoteldomusaventina.com*
Simple but elegant rooms open
onto a lush courtyard. Rooms
are quiet, and a number of
attractions are in easy walking
distance. Welcoming and
helpful staff.

**Hotel San Anselmo** €€
Romantic     **Map** 6 E3
*Piazza San Anselmo 2, 00153*
**Tel** *06 57 00 57*
W *aventinohotels.com*
Four-poster beds and claw-foot
baths are available at this simple
and graceful hotel, on a
residential street and close to
many restaurants and sights.
There is also a lovely courtyard.
Parking is free.

**Villa San Pio** €€
Romantic     **Map** 6 E3
*Via Santa Melania 19, 00153*
**Tel** *06 57 00 57*
W *aventinohotels.com*
Quiet and secluded, but located
conveniently in the city center.
Good breakfasts and drinks in
the lovely garden.

## Lazio

**BRACCIANO: Villa Clementina
Spa & Resort** €€
Spa hotel
*Traversa Quarto del Lago 12, 00062*
**Tel** *06 998 62 68*
W *hotelvillaclementina.it*
Sleep in beautifully frescoed
rooms and relax on the lush
grounds, featuring a large
pool, a tennis court, and a
wellness center.

**CERVETERI L'Isola di Rosa** €
Spa hotel
*Via del Grano 20, 00052*
**Tel** *334 218 39 98 or 335 535 54 48*
W *isoladirosa.com*
An old manor house with
well-appointed rooms, L'Isola
di Rosa is located amid the
Mediterranean shrub forest
and very close to the sea.

**FRASCATI: Poggio Regillo** €
Agriturismo
*Via Pietra Porzia 30, 00044*
**Tel** *06 941 78 00*
W *poggioregillo.it*
This environmentally friendly
hotel offers excellent value for
money. There is also a self-
catering apartment for longer
stays. Pets are welcome.

For more information on types of hotels *pp558–61*

**SPERLONGA: La Nave** €€
Rooms with a view
*Via Salette 24, 04029*
**Tel** *0771 55 71 98*
W hotellanave.it
This charming beachside hotel offers simple but comfortable bungalows and has a marvellous garden in which to relax.

**TARQUINIA: Casale Poggio Nebbia** €
Agriturismo
*S.S. Aurelia km 84, 100, Loc. Farnesiana, 01016*
**Tel** *0766 84 12 68*
W poggionebbia.it
Relaxing farmstay nestled in a valley and popular with Italians. Ideal for families, it offers great views from the Tolfa Mountains up to Tyrrhenian Sea.

**TIVOLI: Palazzo Maggiore** €
B&B
*Via Domenico Giuliani 89, 00019*
**Tel** *393 10 44 937*
W palazzomaggiore.com
This attractive hotel furnished with antiques is located in the heart of town and provides the perfect base from which to explore Tivoli. Breakfast can be enjoyed on the pleasant terrace.

**TIVOLI: Grand Hotel Duca d'Este** €€
Business
*Via Tiburtina Valeria 330, 00019*
**Tel** *0774 38 83*
W ducadeste.com
Large, comfortable hotel with a fully equipped wellness center that uses the area's renowned geothermal waters.

**VITERBO: Niccolò V** €€
Spa hotel
*Strada Bagni 12, 01100*
**Tel** *0761 35 01*
W termedeipapi.it
Historic thermal baths and wellness center in an elegant four-star hotel.

# Naples and Campania

**AMALFI COAST: Hotel Desirée** €
Rooms with a view
*Via Capo 31, Sorrento, 80067*
**Tel** *081 878 15 63*
W desireehotelsorrento.com
This simple, cliff-side hotel a short walk from the center of Sorrento offers excellent value. There's an elevator to a small private beach.

**AMALFI COAST: Miramare** €€
Rooms with a view
*Via Trara Genoino, Positano, 84017*
**Tel** *089 87 50 02*
W miramarepositano.it
Rooms are brightly decorated and have picture-perfect views looking out over Positano and the ocean beyond.

**AMALFI COAST: Bellevue Syrene** €€€
Luxury
*Piazza della Vittoria 5, Sorrento, 80067*
**Tel** *081 878 10 24*
W bellevue.it
A dreamy 18th-century villa on the cliffs of Sorrento, facing Mount Vesuvius and the sea. Private beach access.

**AMALFI COAST: La Sirenuse** €€€
Luxury
*Via Cristoforo Colombo 30, Positano, 84017*
**Tel** *089 87 50 66*
W sirenuse.it
This intimate, world-class hotel offers spectacular views of Sorrento and the coast.

**CAPRI: Bellavista** €€
Boutique
*Via Giuseppe Orlandi 10, 80071*
**Tel** *081 837 14 63 or 081 837 18 21*
W bellavistacapri.com
Enjoy the spectacular views from this pleasant 1960s-style hotel in Anacapri, on a cliff that, in ancient times, was a watchtower.

**CAPRI: Grand Hotel Quisisana** €€€
Luxury
*Via Camerelle 2, 80073*
**Tel** *081 837 07 88*
W quisisana.com
Deluxe accommodations in an extraordinary setting, at the top of a picturesque street full of artisanal workshops.

**CASERTA: Amadeus** €
Boutique
*Via Giuseppe Verdi 72/76, 81100*
**Tel** *0823 35 26 63*
W hotelamadeuscaserta.it
The Amadeus is a centrally located, comfortable hotel with spacious rooms.

## DK Choice

**ISCHIA AND PROCIDA: Miramare Sea Resort & Spa** €€
Spa hotel
*Via Maddalena Comandante 29, Sant'Angelo, 80070*
**Tel** *081 99 92 19*
W miramaresearesort.it
This gorgeous old-world hotel is perched on the rocks right over the Tyrrhenian Sea. The lovely rooms, most with canopy beds and balconies, all face the sea. A short walk leads to the spa complex with thermal pools and a private beach. The ample breakfast is served on a flowering terrace with spectacular views.

**NAPLES: Decumani** €€
Historic
*Via del Grande Archivio 8, 80100*
**Tel** *081 420 13 79 or 081 410 91 44*
W palazzodecumani.com
Tasteful furnishings and elegant bathrooms in a Baroque palace amid the colorful streets of the city center.

**NAPLES: Grand Hotel Vesuvio** €€€
Rooms with a view
*Via Partenope 45, 80121*
**Tel** *081 764 00 44*
W vesuvio.it
Sumptuous lodgings with views of the gulf and Castel dell'Ovo. A pool, sauna, and Turkish baths are available.

**SALERNO: Hotel dei Templi** €€
B&B
*Via Tavernelle 64, 84063*
**Tel** *082 881 17 47*
W www.hoteldeitempli.it
Stylish hotel located just minutes from the ruined temples at Paestum. The modern furnishings are perfectly integrated with the old architecture.

Luxury suite at the Grand Hotel Vesuvio in Naples

# Abruzzo, Molise and Puglia

## DK Choice

### ALBEROBELLO: B&B Fascino Antico €
Historic
*Strada Statale 172, 74015*
**Tel** *080 432 50 89*
[W] fascinoanticotrulli.com
At this charming B&B, you can lodge in a 19th-century hut without losing the comforts of a modern holiday. Surrounded by centuries-old olive trees, the stone-built apartments face a large courtyard, and there is an outdoor pool.

### BARI: Boston €
Business
*Via Niccolò Piccinni 155, 70122*
**Tel** *080 521 66 33*
[W] bostonbari.it
Guests at the Boston enjoy functional and comfortable rooms in a convenient location.

### ISOLE TREMITI: Baely Resort €€
Resort
*Via Matteotti, 71040*
**Tel** *0882 46 37 67*
[W] baely.it
Intimate hotel with comfortable, distinctively decorated rooms. Free transportation is provided from and to the port, and there is a special buffet breakfast.

### L'AQUILA: Magione Papale €€
Boutique
*Via Porta Napoli 67, 67100*
**Tel** *0862 41 49 83 or 0862 42 21 94*
[W] magionepapale.it
Housed in a restored mill, this quaint country inn has plenty of character.

# Basilicata and Calabria

### MARATEA: La Locanda delle Donne Monache €€
Romantic
*Via Carlo Mazzei 4, 85046*
**Tel** *0973 87 61 39*
[W] locandamonache.com
There are spacious, bright rooms with four-poster beds at this 18th-century former convent. One room has a distinctive bathroom that is literally carved out of the rock. There is also a panoramic swimming pool with Jacuzzi. Cooking lessons can be arranged on request.

The stunning Art Deco style Villa las Tronas in Alghero, Sardinia

## DK Choice

### MATERA: Sassi Hotel €
Historic
*Via San Giovanni Vecchio 89, 75100*
**Tel** *0835 33 10 09*
[W] hotelsassi.it
Matera's famous rock dwellings make an evocative setting for this one-of-a-kind hotel. Each room is carved into the mountain, with distinctive vaulted stone ceilings and panoramic views of the medieval town below. Simple and classic furnishings enhance the natural elements of the 18th-century building.

### TROPEA: Cala di Volpe €€
Resort
*Località Torre Marino, 89865*
**Tel** *0963 66 92 22 or 0963 66 96 99*
[W] caladivolpe.it
A beautiful seaside resort surrounded by a lush tropical garden. Perfect for families thanks to the proximity to the beach and an amusement park.

# Sicily

### AGRIGENTO: Camere del Sud €
B&B
*Via Ficani, 92100*
**Tel** *349 638 44 24*
[W] camereasud.it
Warm, simple rooms decorated with local art in this sunny B&B with friendly, helpful owners. On the top floor there is a terrace that offers views over the city.

### ERICE: Elimo €€
Rooms with a view
*Via Vittorio Emanuele 75, 91016*
**Tel** *0923 86 93 77*
[W] hotelelimo.it
Small but lovely rooms with panoramic views of the countryside. Every room has a balcony.

### PALERMO: Principe di Villafranca €€€
Luxury
*Via Giuseppina Turrisi Colonna 4, 90141*
**Tel** *091 611 85 23*
[W] principedivillafranca.it
Elegant hotel full of intricate details and antique art and furnishings. A perfect mix of the old and the new.

# Sardinia

### ALGHERO: Villa las Tronas €€€
Spa hotel
*Lungomare Valencia 1, 07041*
**Tel** *079 98 18 18*
[W] hotelvillalastronas.it
There are scenic views at this elegant hotel, with indoor and outdoor pools, a Turkish bath, and sauna. Open year-round.

### CAGLIARI: T Hotel €€
Design
*Via dei Giudicati 66, 09131*
**Tel** *070 474 00*
[W] thotel.it
Modern design hotel with large rooms and a fitness center. Ideal for business travelers.

### COSTA SMERALDA: Nibaru €€
Resort
*Località Cala di Volpe*
**Tel** *0789 960 38*
[W] hotelnibaru.it
A tranquil oasis a short walk from the sea. Rooms are comfortable and clean, and there is a lovely pool. A wide range of water sports is on offer.

### COSTA SMERALDA: Pitrizza €€€
Luxury
*Via Nazionale 35, 07020*
**Tel** *0789 93 01 11*
[W] pitrizzahotel.com
The Pitrizza is a grand hotel with fabulous amenities and breathtaking views.

**For more information on types of hotels** *pp558–61*

# WHERE TO EAT AND DRINK

Food is a serious subject in Italy. The Italians are justly proud of their fine cuisine and wines, and many sociable hours are spent around the table. One of the great pleasures of traveling in Italy is sampling regional variations in pasta, breads, and cheeses. You don't have to head to the most expensive places for good food; a simple trattoria, which serves the local clientele, will often produce a better meal than the nearby international restaurant. However, whether it is a crowded *osteria*, a local pizzeria, or a terrace with sea views, this introduction gives plenty of practical tips on types of restaurants, ordering, and service to help you enjoy eating out in Italy.

## Places to Eat

Traditionally a trattoria and an *osteria* are cheaper and more casual alternatives to the more upscale *ristorante*.

A pizzeria is usually a cheap place to eat (as little as €18 with beer) and many serve pasta, meat, and fish dishes as well as pizzas. Pizzerias are often open in the evening only, especially those with wood-fired ovens *(forno a legna)*.

A *birreria* is another budget option, serving pasta and snacks such as sausages and burgers. An *enoteca*, or *vineria*, will offer a selection of wines to try, along with a range of light dishes. Prices vary and tend to be relatively expensive for the quantities served.

At lunchtime and in the early evening, *rosticcerie* sell roast chicken, slices of pizza *(pizza al taglio)*, and other snacks to take out. *Pizza al taglio* can also be bought straight from the baker. Many bars offer sandwiches *(panini* or *tramezzini)*, and some also serve simple hot

A restaurant in Chioggia offering a cozy environment in a vaulted room

dishes from the *tavola calda* counter for around €8.

Stop at a *gelateria* for ice cream, with a sometimes bewildering choice of different flavors, or a *pasticceria* for one of a dazzling variety of sweet and savory pastries, cakes, and cookies.

## Opening Times

Lunch is generally served between 12:30pm and 2:30pm and, particularly in the south, all other activity stops between these hours. Dinner starts at about 7:30pm and goes on until 11pm or later (in the south, eating hours tend to be later). It is not unusual to see tables still full from lunch at 4pm or diners sipping *digestivi* well after midnight.

## Reservations

Good restaurants in Italy are likely to be popular, so reserve a table in advance if you can *(prenotazione)*. Otherwise, get there early to avoid having to wait. Many restaurants close one day a week and for a few weeks in either winter or the

Villa Crespi in Piedmont, inspired by *The Arabian Nights (see p588)*

summer vacation season; this information will be included in the list of restaurants on the pages that follow, but call first if in doubt.

## The Menu

Italian meals consist of three or four courses, and restaurants generally expect patrons to order at least two, though you should not feel obligated to do so. The *antipasto* (appetizer) is followed by the *primo*, of pasta, rice, or soup. The *secondo* is the main meat or fish course, for which you will need to order vegetables *(contorni)* separately. Fruit *(frutta)*, cheese *(formaggi)*, or dessert *(dolce)* follow, with coffee and the preferred *digestivo* of the region to finish the meal.

Menus usually change with the season to make use of the freshest local produce, and the day's specials may be recited to you by the waiter rather than written down. Persevere, if you don't immediately understand, using the menu information at the beginning of each section. Try to avoid restaurants that do not state prices on their menus.

## Vegetarians

Italian restaurants offer plenty of choices for vegetarians, as the menu will always feature a selection of seasonal vegetables and beans. Many pasta and *antipasto* dishes use no meat at all and for a main course you can ask for an omelet *(frittata)* with a side of vegetables from the *contorni*. Most menus are adaptable because dishes are prepared to order – tell your waiter that you are *vegetariano* (female *vegetariana*) and they will advise you accordingly.

## Wine and Drinks

Many regions have their own *aperitivo* served before the meal and a *digestivo* for afterward. Universal alternatives are *prosecco* (dry, fizzy white wine) or an *analcolico* (nonalcoholic) aperitif, and *grappa* as a digestif. House wine (red or white) will be a simple local wine served by the liter or by the glass and will generally be perfectly palatable. In addition, all but the cheapest eateries have a range of other local and regional wines specially selected to accompany the food on the menu, with more upscale establishments also offering foreign vintages.

Tap water *(acqua del rubinetto)* is always drinkable and often very good, but Italy has a large range of mineral waters. Fizzy ones *(frizzante)* may contain carbon dioxide, while *naturale* can mean still or naturally sparkling. If you particularly want a still water, ask for *non gassata*. Espresso bars usually charge more for table service.

## Paying

Tax and service are usually included in the menu prices, but it is normal to leave a tip of around 10 percent. Note that many restaurants include a cover charge *(coperto)*, on the bill *(il conto)*, which covers bread (whether you eat it or not) and is charged per person.

Credit cards are not always accepted in Italy, particularly in smaller towns, so it is wise to check before you order.

Diners enjoying a meal alfresco in Chianti, Tuscany

## Dress

Italians generally tend to look chic but don't necessarily expect visitors to do the same. However, very scruffy or dirty clothes are unlikely to get you good, efficient, or particularly friendly service.

## Children

Children are welcome in all but high-end establishments, and restaurants are likely to be filled with extensive Italian families for Sunday lunch. Amenities such as high chairs or special menus are rare, but most places will provide a small or half portion *(mezza porzione)*.

## Smoking

Smoking is still popular in Italy. However, smoking laws now mean that all restaurants in the country are nonsmoking establishments. Unless a smokers' room is provided, you should step outside if you want to light up.

Outdoor tables at the seafood restaurant Il Riccio on Capri *(see p600)*

## Wheelchair Access

Few restaurants have special amenities for people in wheelchairs, but if you make reservations in advance, the establishment can prepare a suitable table and be ready to help when you arrive.

The charming interior of U'Giancu in Rapallo, Liguria *(see p590)*

## Recommended Restaurants

The restaurants listed in this guidebook cover a wide range of eateries, from the simple pizzeria and *tavola calda* (cafeteria) to family-run trattoria and elegant *ristorante*. Each restaurant has a cuisine type listed beneath the name of the establishment. Most of these descriptions are self-explanatory, but the *Places to Eat* section *(opposite)* will provide more information on what you can expect from the menu.

The DK Choice label indicates a restaurant that has outstanding qualities and is highly recommended. It may serve delicious local dishes, offer excellent value for money, be in a beautiful location, have a romantic atmosphere, or be particularly charming. Whatever the reason, it is a guarantee of a great meal.

# Where to Eat and Drink

## Venice

**BURANO: Da Romano** €€
Seafood
*Via Piazza Galuppi 221, 30012*
**Tel** *041 73 00 30* **Closed** *Tue; Oct–
Apr: dinner; May–Sep: Sun dinner*
A wide range of fish dishes is
served in the traditional Venetian
fashion at this historic restaurant.
Advance reservations advised.

### DK Choice

**BURANO-MAZZORBO:
Venissa** €€€
Modern Italian
*Fondamenta Santa Caterina 3,
30170*
**Tel** *041 527 22 81* **Closed** *Tue;
Nov–Mar*
Dine at the elegant Venissa
restaurant for an extra special
gastronomic experience. The
menu features a wide selection
of seafood, meat, and vegetarian
options using fresh, seasonal
ingredients grown in the
restaurant's own garden.
The menu changes daily.

**CANNAREGIO:
Trattoria da Gigio** €
Regional Italian **Map** 2 D3
*Rio Terrà San Leonardo 1594, 30121*
**Tel** *041 71 75 74* **Closed** *Sun,
Mon dinner*
Seafood is a popular option at
this simple but elegant place, as
are the generous hors d'oeuvres.

**CANNAREGIO:
Fiaschetteria Toscana** €€
Seafood **Map** 3 B5
*Salizzada San Giovanni Grisostomo
5719, 30121*
**Tel** *041 528 52 81* **Closed** *Tue, Wed
lunch; 1 wk Dec*
Try the delectable warm octopus
salad and the turbot in caper
sauce here. Reserve.

### DK Choice

**CANNAREGIO: Osteria
da Rioba** €€
Seafood
*Fondamenta della Misericordia
2553, 30121*
**Tel** *041 524 43 79* **Closed** *Mon*
This charming canalside
restaurant with friendly and
knowledgeable staff specializes
in fish, sourced daily from the
local market. Try the seafood
mosaic. Reservations are
recommended.

**CANNAREGIO:
Osteria l'Orto dei Mori** €€
Regional Italian **Map** 2 F3
*Campo dei Mori 3386, 30121*
**Tel** *041 524 36 77* **Closed** *Tue; 3 wks
Jul, 3 wks Nov*
This off-the-beaten-track *osteria*
has a refined take on local cuisine.
Elegant Modernist interiors.

**CANNAREGIO: Osteria
al Timon** €€
Regional Italian **Map** 2 E3
*Fondamenta Ormesini 2754, 30121*
**Tel** *041 524 60 66* **Closed** *lunch;
Wed; 2 wks Oct*
Fantastic range of *cicchetti* (small
plates) to accompany a glass of
wine, but also good meat dishes.

**CANNAREGIO: Vini da Gigio** €€
Regional Italian **Map** 3 A4
*Fondamenta San Felice 3628a,
30121*
**Tel** *041 528 51 40* **Closed** *Mon, Tue;
2 wks Aug*
The menu largely depends on
what Rialto market has to offer
that day. Reservations advised.

**CASTELLO:
Ristorante Giorgione** €
Regional Italian **Map** 8 F3
*Via Garibaldi 1533, 30122*
**Tel** *041 522 87 27* **Closed** *Wed*
Great neighborhood *trattoria*
serving flavorsome fish dishes,
including lasagne and risotto.

**CASTELLO: Al Covo** €€
Seafood **Map** 8 E2
*Campiello della Pescaria 3968, 30122*
**Tel** *041 522 38 12* **Closed** *Wed, Thu;
2 wks Dec–Jan, 1 wk Aug*
Tucked away behind the
Arsenale boat strip, Al Covo has
interesting tasting menus.

**CASTELLO:
Osteria di Santa Marina** €€
Regional Italian **Map** 3 B5
*Campo Santa Marina 5911, 30122*
**Tel** *041 528 52 39* **Closed** *Sun, Mon
lunch; 2 wks Jan*
A restaurant with a reputation for
its creative take on local cuisine.

**CASTELLO: Da Remigio** €€
Seafood **Map** 8 D2
*Salizzada dei Greci 3416, 30122*
**Tel** *041 523 00 89* **Closed** *Mon
dinner, Tue; 4 wks Dec–Jan*
Specials at this tiny spot include
the fish and shellfish risotto.

**CASTELLO: Ristorante Wildner** €€
Regional Italian **Map** 8 D2
*Riva degli Schiavoni 4161, 30122*
**Tel** *041 522 74 63* **Closed** *Tue;
Jan 7–carnival*

### Price Guide

Prices are based on a three-course meal
per person, with a half-bottle of house
wine, including tax and service.

| | |
|---|---|
| € | up to €40 |
| €€ | €40 to €75 |
| €€€ | over €75 |

Diners enjoy a menu of fresh
fish and locally grown organic
vegetables at this restaurant
with an interesting wine list.

**DORSODURO: Ai Gondolieri** €€
Regional Italian **Map** 6 F4
*San Vio 366, 30123*
**Tel** *041 528 63 96* **Closed** *Tue;
lunch Jul–Aug; 25 Dec.*
Regional meat and vegetable
dishes are served with flair at
this canalside restaurant.

**DORSODURO: La Rivista** €€
Modern Italian **Map** 6 E4
*Rio Terrà Foscarini 979/a, 30123*
**Tel** *041 240 14 25* **Closed** *Mon*
A welcoming restaurant offering
salads and cold platters for lunch.
In fine weather, it is possible to
eat alfresco.

**GIUDECCA:
Trattoria Altanella** €€
Regional Italian
*Rio del Ponte Lungo 268, 33035*
**Tel** *041 522 7780* **Closed** *Mon, Tue;
4 wks Dec–Jan*
A charming canalside restaurant
run by the same family for four
generations.

**GIUDECCA: Cipriani** €€€
Fine dining
*Giudecca 10, 30133*
**Tel** *041 520 77 44* **Closed** *Nov–Mar*
Guests are ferried from the San
Marco waterfront to these
exclusive island hotel restaurants.

Spectacular setting of one of the waterfront
restaurants at Cipriani, Giudecca

**SAN MARCO: Acqua Pazza** €€
Seafood　　　　　Map 7 A2
*Campo Sant'Angelo 3808, 30124*
**Tel** *041 277 06 88*　　**Closed** *Mon;*
*Jan 7–31*
This is where the Amalfi Coast
meets Venice. A different take
on fish, with wines to match.

**SAN MARCO: Gran Caffè
e Ristorante Quadri** €€€
Fine dining　　　　　Map 7 B2
*Piazza San Marco 121, 30124*
**Tel** *041 522 21 05*　　**Closed** *Mon*
Fantastic historic site now in the
capable, creative hands of star
chef Massimiliano Alajmo.

**SAN MARCO:
Trattoria Do Forni** €€€
Fine dining　　　　　Map 7 B2
*Calle dei Specchieri 468, 30124*
**Tel** *041 523 21 48*
Two dining areas with different
decors serve careful interpreta-
tions of classic Venetian cuisine.

**SAN POLO: Muro** €
Pizzeria　　　　　Map 6 E1
*Rio Terà dei Frari 2604, 30125*
**Tel** *041 524 53 10*
One of two Muro pizzerias,
popular with young locals. Huge
salads also available, along with
a wide selection of beer on tap.

**SAN POLO: Osteria da
Fiore** €€€
Fine dining　　　　　Map 6 D1
*Calle del Scaleter 2202, 30125*
**Tel** *041 72 13 08*　　**Closed** *Sun, Mon;*
*Jan 8–22; 2 wks Aug*
Many consider this the city's best
restaurant. Serves beautifully
cooked seasonal produce.

**SANTA CROCE:
Enoteca al Prosecco** €
Enoteca　　　　　Map 2 E5
*Campo San Giacomo dell'Orio
1503, 30135*
**Tel** *041 524 02 22*　　**Closed** *Sun;*
*3 wks Jan, Aug*
Enjoy light meals indoors or
outside on the square, with a
glass of excellent wine.

**SANTA CROCE: Il Rèfolo** €
Pizzeria　　　　　Map 8 E2
*Campo del Plovan 1459, 30135*
**Tel** *041 524 00 16*　　**Closed** *Mon*
Set on a picturesque square, this
modern establishment serves
innovative gourmet pizzas.

**SANTA CROCE:
Antiche Carampane** €€
Seafood　　　　　Map 2 F5
*Rio Terà Carampane 1911, 30125*
**Tel** *041 524 01 65*　　**Closed** *Sun, Mon;*
*2 wks Jan, 3 wks Aug*
Seek out this local favorite for
great fish and pasta dishes.

Tasteful interiors and charming garden at Villa Cipriani, Asolo

**SANTA CROCE:
Osteria La Zucca** €€
Regional Italian　　　Map 2 E5
*Ponte del Megio 1762, 30135*
**Tel** *041 524 15 70*　　**Closed** *Sun*
A pretty canalside restaurant
that is popular with Venetians
as well as visitors.

**TORCELLO: Locanda Cipriani** €€
Fine dining
*Piazza Santa Fosca 29, 30012*
**Tel** *041 73 01 50*　　**Closed** *Tue; Jan–Feb*
Charming and exclusive island
restaurant with a shady courtyard.

# The Veneto and
Friuli

**ARCO: Alla Lega** €
Regional Italian
*Via Vergolano 8, 38062*
**Tel** *046 451 62 05*　　**Closed** *Nov–Apr:*
*Wed; mid-Jan–mid-Mar*
Lively restaurant serving traditional
fare. Housed in an 18th-century
building with a lovely courtyard.

**ASOLO: Locanda Baggio** €
Regional Italian
*Via Bassane 1, Località Casonetto,
31011*
**Tel** *0423 52 96 48*　　**Closed** *Mon;*
*Tue lunch*
Changing seasonal menu with
innovative interpretations of
local dishes. Cooking classes
are also available.

**ASOLO: Villa Cipriani** €€
Fine dining
*Via Canova 298, 31011*
**Tel** *0423 52 34 11*
A hotel restaurant offering
creative cuisine, and overlooking
a glorious garden with breath-
taking views of the hills below.

**BASSANO DEL GRAPPA:
Antico Ristorante Cardellino** €
Regional Italian
*Via Bella Vitis 17, 36061*
**Tel** *042 422 01 44*　　**Closed** *Thu*

In spring, local white asparagus
is served here with tagliatelle,
in flans or in the traditional way,
with hard-boiled eggs.

**BASSANO DEL GRAPPA:
Osteria Trinità** €
Regional Italian
*Contrà San Giorgio 17, 36061*
**Tel** *0424 50 37 00* **Closed** *Tue dinner,*
*Wed; 3 wks Sep–Oct*
This traditional eatery serves
Venetian classics such as *pasta
e fagioli* (bean and pasta soup)
and *baccalà* (salt cod).

**BELLUNO:
Ristorante Terracotta** €
Regional Italian
*Borgo Garibaldi 61, 32100*
**Tel** *043 729 16 92*　　**Closed** *Tue, Wed*
*lunch*
Family-run restaurant specializing
in regional seasonal dishes.
Delicious selection of desserts
and an extensive wine list.

**CASTELFRANCO: Barbesin** €
Regional Italian
*Via Montebelluna di Salva Rosa 41,
31033*
**Tel** *042 349 04 46* **Closed** *Sun dinner;*
*10 days Jan, 3 wks mid-Aug*
Dishes based on local radicchio
predominate, but there are also
mixed grills and salted cod in the
Vicenza tradition.

**CHIOGGIA: Osteria Penzo** €€
Seafood
*Calle Larga Bersaglio 525, 30015*
**Tel** *041 40 09 92*　　**Closed** *Mon, Tue*
The place for traditional fare
such as squid with peas or
gnocchi with onions, mussels,
and red chicory.

**CHIOGGIA: La Taverna** €€
Seafood
*Via Felice Cavallotti 348, 30015*
**Tel** *041 40 18 06*　　**Closed** *Wed; mid-*
*Jan–mid-Feb (open daily in Aug)*
Classic seafood dishes in an
elegant setting. The outdoor
tables look over the main square.

**For more information on types of restaurants** *see pp578–9*

**CIVIDALE DEL FRIULI:**
**Al Castello**                    €€
Regional Italian
*Via del Castello 12, 33043*
**Tel** *043 273 32 42*        **Closed** *Wed;*
*2 weeks Aug*
Set in a magnificent castle, the
menu here boasts traditional
dishes and fine local wines.

**CONEGLIANO: Al Salisa**    €€
Regional Italian
*Via XX Settembre 2–4, 31015*
**Tel** *0438 242 88*          **Closed** *Wed*
An elegant restaurant housed in
a medieval building. Serving
fresh fish, game, and even sushi.

**CORMONS: Ristorante al**
**Cacciatore – La Subida**    €€
Regional Italian
*Via Subida 52, 34071*
**Tel** *048 16 05 31*   **Closed** *Tue & Wed;*
*2 wks Feb*
Inventive Friulian and Slovenian
menu that changes with the
seasons. Beautiful country setting.

**CORTINA D'AMPEZZO:**
**Ristorante El Zoco**            €
Regional Italian
*Località Cademai 18, 32043*
**Tel** *043 686 00 41* **Closed** *lunch; low*
*season: Mon*
Small but cosy restaurant on
the outskirts of trendy Cortina.
On the menu are good grilled
meats and fresh vegetables.

**CORTINA D'AMPEZZO:**
**Baita Fraina**                  €€
Regional Italian
*Località Fraina 1, 32043*
**Tel** *0436 36 34*   **Closed** *low season:*
*Mon; after Easter–May, Sep–Dec*
Attractive wood-paneled B&B
with an on-site restaurant,
panoramic terrace, and a
spacious play area for kids.

**FUMANE: Ristorante Scamperle**
**alla Rosa**                     €
Regional Italian
*Via Incisa 8, 37022*
**Tel** *045 770 10 06*        **Closed** *Mon;*
*2nd wk Jan, 2 wks mid-Aug*

One of the oldest restaurants in
the Valpolicella. All pasta, bread,
and pastries are made onsite.

**GARDA:**
**Locanda San Vigilio**          €€
Traditional Italian
*Punta San Vigilio, 37016*
**Tel** *045 725 66 88*  **Closed** *mid-Nov–*
*end Mar*
Five centuries of experience in
delighting guests with excellent
food, wine, and gorgeous views.

**GRADO: Trattoria de Toni**    €€
Seafood
*Piazza Duca d'Aosta 37, 34073*
**Tel** *043 18 01 04*         **Closed** *Wed,*
*Dec–Feb*
The house specialty here is
*boreto alla gradese*, a delicious
fish stew cooked in vinegar.

**GRANCONA: Isetta**             €
Regional Italian
*Via Pederiva 96, 36040*
**Tel** *044 488 95 21*  **Closed** *Tue & Wed*
Pretty restaurant in a hilly area
outside Vicenza. Regional food,
with emphasis on grilled meats.

**LONIGO: La Peca**            €€€
Fine dining
*Via Giovanelli 2, 36045*
**Tel** *044 483 02 14*     **Closed** *Sun (exc*
*lunch Sep–Jun), Mon; 2 wks Jun, 1 wk*
*mid-Aug*
Traditional ingredients revisited
with inventive flair. Similar mixture
of classic and creative in the decor.

**MESTRE: Osteria Vecia Posta** €€
Regional Italian
*Via Felice Cavallotti 19, 30171*
**Tel** *041 96 29 61*   **Closed** *Mon; 2 wks*
*Aug*
This eatery on a quiet square is all
about fish. Regional dishes are
served with flair, and there are
good-value set menu options.

**MIANE: Da Gigetto**            €
Regional Italian
*Via Alcide de Gasperi 5, 31050*
**Tel** *043 896 00 20*        **Closed** *Mon*
*dinner, Tue; 2 wks Jan, 1 wk Aug*

Elegant takes on local dishes with
seasonal ingredients. Try the
mushroom polenta in autumn.

**MONTECCHIA DI CROSARA:**
**Ristorante Cassandra**         €€
Regional Italian
*Via Cabalao 11, 37030*
**Tel** *045 745 02 22*  **Closed** *Mon, Tue;*
*2 wks mid-Aug*
A refined country restaurant
with a modern, interesting menu
and an outstanding wine list.

**NOVENTA PADOVANA:**
**Boccadoro**                    €€
Regional Italian
*Via della Resistenza 49, 35027*
**Tel** *049 62 50 29*   **Closed** *Wed; 1 wk*
*Jan, 3 wks Aug*
Quietly elegant family-run
restaurant offering well-balanced
fish and meat dishes.

**PADUA: Trattoria San Pietro** €
Regional Italian
*Via San Pietro 95, 35139*
**Tel** *049 876 03 30*        **Closed** *Sun,*
*3 wks Jul–Aug*
The perfect place for regional
dishes cooked with fresh local
ingredients. Informal atmosphere.

**PADUA: Da Giovanni**          €€
Regional Italian
*Via Pietro Maroncelli 22, 35129*
**Tel** *049 77 26 20*    **Closed** *Sat lunch,*
*Sun; Aug, 1 week Christmas*
Time-honored trattoria offering
classics such as homemade
pasta, risotto, and meat stews.

**RUBANO: Le Calandre**       €€€
Fine dining
*Via Liguria 1, 35030*
**Tel** *049 63 03 03*     **Closed** *Sun, Mon,*
*Tue lunch; 1st wk Jan, 3 wks Aug*
The cuisine at this three-Michelin-
starred restaurant will enchant
the senses.

### DK Choice

**SAN GIORGIO DI**
**VALPOLICELLA: Trattoria**
**Dalla Rosa Alda**             €€
Regional Italian
*Strada Garibaldi 4, 37015*
**Tel** *045 770 10 18*        **Closed** *Sun*
*dinner, Mon; Jan & Feb*
Nestled in a charming village
surrounded by vineyards, this
family-run trattoria has been
serving excellent traditional fare
for several generations.
Ingredients are carefully sourced
from local producers and the
cellars are full of carefully chosen
wines from the Valpolicella
region. There is also a beautiful
terrace where guests can eat
alfresco, weather permitting.

Guests relaxing under the shade of umbrellas at Locanda San Vigilio in Garda

**SANTA MARIA DI SALA:**
**Trattoria Barison** €
Regional Italian
*Via Ronchi 14, Borgoricco, 35010*
**Tel** *049 579 80 63* **Closed** *Mon dinner, Tue; 2 wks Jan, 3 wks Aug*
This eatery serves not only the traditional *baccalà*, but also grilled meats, cooked vegetables, and wild salads.

**SOLIGHETTO:**
**Locanda da Lino** €
Regional Italian
*Via Roma 19, 31053*
**Tel** *043 88 21 50* **Closed** *Mon; end Jan–early Feb, last 10 days Jul*
This restaurant is part of an inn overlooking the Prosecco hillsides. Homemade pasta and good grilled meats on offer.

**TREVISO:**
**Antico Ristorante Beccherie** €
Regional Italian
*Piazza Ancilotto 11, 31100*
**Tel** *0422 54 08 71* **Closed** *Tue*
The name is derived from a word in the local dialect that means "butcher's" so, not surprisingly, meat is the specialty here.

**TRIESTE: Antica Ghiacceretta** €€
Regional Italian
*Via dei Fornelli 2, 34121*
**Tel** *040 322 03 07*
Enjoy fish dishes prepared with an inventive, light touch in a modern setting. There is an excellent wine list to match.

**UDINE: Da Raffaele** €
Pizzeria
*Via Leonardo da Vinci 56, 33100*
**Tel** *043 229 58 31* **Closed** *Wed lunch*
More than just a classic pizzeria, this place boasts a traditional wood-fired oven and beer on tap.

---

**DK Choice**

**UDINE: Agli Amici** €€€
Fine dining
*Via Liguria 250, 33100*
**Tel** *043 256 54 11*
**Closed** *Apr–Oct: Sun, Mon, Tue lunch, first 3 wks Aug; Nov–Mar: Sun dinner, Mon, Tue lunch*
Agli Amici whips up a cuisine that draws on local influences, traditions, and ingredients and is served with elegance. Opt for one of the tasting menus for chance to taste a few dishes.

---

**VALEGGIO SUL MINCIO:**
**Antica Locanda Mincio** €
Traditional Italian
*Via Michelangelo Buonarroti 12, 37067*
**Tel** *045 795 00 59* **Closed** *Wed, Thu; 2 wks Feb, 2 wks Nov*

Frescoed walls, open fireplaces and an outdoor terrace. Specials include trout from Lake Garda.

**VERONA: Arche** €€
Regional Italian
*Via Arche Scaligere 6, 37121*
**Tel** *045 800 74 15* **Closed** *Sun dinner, Mon (except in summer); 2 wks Jan*
Established in 1879, this seafood restaurant serves superlative marinated rock lobster.

**VERONA: Al Bersagliere** €€
Regional Italian
*Via Dietro Pallone 1, 37121*
**Tel** *045 800 48 24* **Closed** *Sat dinner (Aug), Sun, Mon (except summer); 2 wks Aug, Dec 25–Jan 15*
This pleasantly informal, yet chic restaurant offers great risotto with Amarone and pasta dishes.

**VERONA: Il Desco** €€€
Fine dining
*Via Dietro San Sebastiano 5–7, 37121*
**Tel** *045 59 53 58* **Closed** *Sun & Mon; Jul–Aug & Dec: Mon lunch; Dec 25–Jan 15*
This elegant Michelin-starred restaurant offers a creative take on traditional dishes.

**VICENZA:**
**Antica Casa della Malvasia** €
Regional Italian
*Contrà delle Morette 5, 36100*
**Tel** *044 454 37 04* **Closed** *Mon; Jul*
Osteria serving pumpkin pancakes, local cheeses, and cold cuts, and pork fillet with truffles.

**VICENZA: Il Ceppo** €
Regional Italian
*Corso Andrea Palladio 196, 36100*
**Tel** *044 454 44 14* **Closed** *Mon*
This store-cum-bistro has local wines to accompany the food. The tasting menu is great value.

---

# Trentino-Alto Adige

---

**DK Choice**

**BOLZANO: Cavallino Bianco** €
Regional Italian
*Via dei Bottai 6, 39100*
**Tel** *0471 97 32 67* **Closed** *Sat dinner, Sun; last 2 wks Jun, Dec 24–31*
Also known by its German name, Weisses Rössl, this busy restaurant serves traditional South Tyrol fare. A large buffet breakfast is followed by good lunch options and a waiter-service dinner. The gastronomic theme evenings are popular with the locals.

---

Wood-beamed ceilings and soft lighting at the informal Al Bersagliere, Verona

**BOLZANO: Forst** €
Birreria
*Goethestrasse 6, 39042*
**Tel** *0471 97 72 43* **Closed** *Sun*
Popular restaurant serving not only the hallmark beer, but also good wines and excellent food.

**BOLZANO: Hopfen & Co** €
Birreria
*Obstplatz 17, 39100*
**Tel** *0471 30 07 88*
A sought-after brewery serving cold cuts, sausages, and desserts.

**BRESSANONE: Fink** €
Regional Italian
*Via Portici Minori 4, 39042*
**Tel** *0472 83 48 83* **Closed** *mid-Sep–Jun: Wed; 3 wks May*
Dining areas consist of elegant seating upstairs, and more casual rooms on the first floor. Classic local cuisine cooked with flair.

**BRUNICO: Oberraut** €
Regional Italian
*Via Ameto 1, Località Amaten, 39031*
**Tel** *0474 55 99 77* **Closed** *Thu; 2 wks Jan*
Nestled in the countryside, this Tyrolean-style guesthouse specializes in game and seasonal dishes.

**CALDARO: Ristorante Ritterhof** €
Traditional Italian
*Weinstrasse 1A, 39052*
**Tel** *0471 96 33 30* **Closed** *Sun dinner, Mon*
Set in a charming chalet with views over the lake. Fine fare and a menu that changes seasonally.

**CERMES: Restaurant Miil** €€
Fine dining
*Gampenstrasse 1, 39010*
**Tel** *0473 56 37 33* **Closed** *Sun, Mon*
Head to the Kränzelhof wine estate for a modern take on classic fare.

**For more information on types of restaurants** *see pp578–9*

**GUDON: Unterwirt** €€
Regional Italian
*Chiusa (Klausen), 39043*
**Tel** *0472 84 40 00* **Closed** *Sun, Mon;*
*2 wks mid-Jun*
The homemade breads are a
tasty introduction to the seasonal
menu on offer here.

**LEVICO TERME: Boivin** €
Regional Italian
*Via Garibaldi 9, 38056*
**Tel** *0461 70 16 70* **Closed** *lunch*
*(except Sun, Jul, Aug); Mon; 2 wks Jan*
Cosy *trattoria* serving classic
dishes such as potato dumplings
stuffed with cheese and walnuts.

**ROVERETO: Novecento** €
Regional Italian
*Corso Rosmini 82d, 38068*
**Tel** *0464 43 54 54* **Closed** *Sun;*
*3 wks Jan, 3 wks Jul–Aug*
Run by the Zani family, this
restaurant is renowned for its
homemade pasta and pizzas.

**TRENTO: Happy Hour** €
Seafood
*Via Perini 57, 38122*
**Tel** *0461 39 23 94* **Closed** *Sun*
*dinner, Mon*
Informal place with a menu that
changes daily, according to the
top picks from the fish market.

**TRENTO:**
**Osteria Alle Due Spade** €
Regional Italian
*Via Don Rizzi 11, 38122*
**Tel** *0461 23 43 43* **Closed** *Sun,*
*Mon lunch; last wk Jun–first wk Jul*
Welcoming cellar restaurant
serving traditional fare including
game and freshwater fish.

**VAL SENALES:**
**Zur Goldenen Rose** €
Regional Italian
*Kartaus 29, 39020*
**Tel** *0473 67 91 30* **Closed** *Apr, Nov*
Explore the surrounding
countryside and then unwind at
this excellent hotel restaurant.

# Lombardy

**BELLAGIO:**
**Albergo Ristorante Silvio** €
Regional Italian
*Via Carcano 12, 22021*
**Tel** *031 95 03 22* **Closed** *Nov–*
*mid-Mar*
Enjoy freshwater fish on a vine-
clad terrace. Offers fishing trips.

**BELLAGIO: Terrazza Barchetta** €€
Regional Italian
*Salita Mella 13, 22021*
**Tel** *031 95 13 89* **Closed** *Tue (exc*
*Jul & Aug); Nov–Easter*

The creative Mediterranean menu
includes fish and homemade
desserts. There are also rooms.

**BERGAMO:**
**Colleoni dell'Angelo** €€
Modern Italian
*Piazza Vecchia 7, 24129*
**Tel** *035 23 25 96* **Closed** *Mon; 1st wk*
*Jan*
Excellent service and imaginative
cuisine; the views over a beautiful
square enhance the experience.

**BERGAMO: Vineria Cozzi** €€
Enoteca
*Via Colleoni 22, 24129*
**Tel** *035 23 88 36* **Closed** *1 wk*
*end Jan, 1 wk Jun*
A century-old Bergamo favorite
serving local dishes.

**BERGAMO: Roof Garden** €€€
Mediterranean
*Piazzale della Repubblica 6, 24122*
**Tel** *035 36 61 59* **Closed** *Sat lunch;*
*Sun; 1st wk Jan, 1 wk Aug*
This rooftop restaurant offers
great views, a fusion of world
flavors and classic Mediterranean
dishes.

**BORMIO: Al Filò** €
Regional Italian
*Via Dante 6, 23032*
**Tel** *0342 90 17 32* **Closed** *Mon & Tue*
*lunch; 3 wks Jun, Nov*
Dishes based on game, cured
meats and mushrooms are
served in a converted barn.

**BRESCIA: Osteria delle Streghe** €
International
*Via Sorbana 72, 25125*
**Tel** *030 32 12 15* **Closed** *Sat lunch,*
*Sun; Dec 28–Jan 6*
The Osteria delle Streghe serves
a wide range of grilled meats,
including kangaroo. Reservations
are mandatory.

The entrance to Terrazza Barchetta, in
Bellagio, which specializes in local cuisine

**BRESCIA: Trattoria Mezzeria** €
Regional Italian
*Via Trieste 66, 25121*
**Tel** *030 40 306* **Closed** *Sun (dinner*
*only Nov–May); Aug*
Try the homemade *gnocchi di*
*zucca* (pumpkin dumplings) in
this busy little trattoria.

**CANTÙ: Le Querce** €
Modern Italian
*Via Marche 27, 22063*
**Tel** *031 73 13 36* **Closed** *Mon, Tue; 3*
*wks Aug; 27 Dec–6 Jan*
Set amid oak and rhododendron,
Le Querce serves local dishes and
offers a rich selection of wines.

## DK Choice

**COMO: L'Angolo del Silenzio** €
Regional Italian
*Viale Lecco 25, 22100*
**Tel** *031 377 21 57* **Closed** *Mon;*
*2 wks Aug*
This reasonably priced *osteria*,
just a few steps from the
cathedral and lake, offers homemade pasta, meat, game, and
fish dishes in a friendly atmosphere. Try the wild boar with
redcurrant sauce and Roquefort.
An inexpensive one-dish lunch
is available on weekdays and
gluten-free dishes are available
on request. Reserve ahead.

**COMO: Ristorante Sociale** €
Regional Italian
*Via Rodari 6, 22100*
**Tel** *031 26 40 42* **Closed** *Tue; 1 wk*
*Jan, last 3 wks Aug*
Sociale offers traditional Lombard
dishes. Dine in the vaulted room
or in the outdoor courtyard.

**COMO: Sant'Anna 1907** €
Regional Italian
*Via Turati 3, 22100*
**Tel** *031 50 52 66* **Closed** *Sat lunch, Sun*
Creative local cuisine, including
seafood and vegetarian options,
can be enjoyed here. Try the
spaghetti salad with two caviars.

**CREMONA: Il Violino** €€
Traditional Italian
*Via Sicardo 3, 26100*
**Tel** *0372 46 10 10* **Closed** *Sun (Jun–*
*Sep)*
Traditional local cuisine is served
in this elegant restaurant.

**GARGNANO DEL GARDA:**
**La Tortuga** €€
Modern Italian
*Via XXIV Maggio 5, 25084*
**Tel** *0365 712 51* **Closed** *Tue;*
*Mar–Oct: lunch*
Diners enjoy the light, imaginative
cuisine on offer at this renowned
lakeside restaurant.

## ISEO: Cascina Doss €€
Modern Italian
*Via Colombera 15, 25049*
**Tel** *030 98 11 11* **Closed** *Tue*
Good-quality traditional fare is served here, with excellent local wines. Monday is risotto evening.

## LAKE COMO:
**Locanda dell'Isola Comacina** €€
Seafood
*Isola Comacina, 22010*
**Tel** *034 455 083* **Closed** *Tue (Oct); Nov–Mar*
A unique experience on a wonderful island, deserted except for this spot serving fresh fish.

## LAVENO MOMBELLO:
**Trattoria Calianna** €
Regional Italian
*Via Don C Tinelli 19, 21014*
**Tel** *0332 667 315* **Closed** *Tue*
Mediterranean cuisine and local specialties such as risotto with perch, plus a relaxed atmosphere.

## LECCO:
**Antica Osteria Casa di Lucia** €€
Fine dining
*Via Lucia 27, Località Acquate, 23900*
**Tel** *0341 49 45 94* **Closed** *Sat lunch, Sun lunch; 2 wks Aug*
A superb gourmet restaurant set in a 17th-century house.

## LECCO: Mamoia Bistrot €€
Seafood
*Via Carlo Cattaneo 80, 23900*
**Tel** *0341 32 16 88* **Closed** *Mon*
Excellent fresh fish served in an informal setting. Cheaper set lunch menus are available.

## LEGNANO: Al Vintun Osteria €
Modern Italian
*Via Bramante 95, 20025*
**Tel** *0331 45 49 59* **Closed** *Sun; 1st wk Aug*
Serves Italian fish and meat dishes. A fixed-price menu is offered every Thursday evening.

## MANERBA DEL GARDA:
**Capriccio** €€€
Regional Italian
*Piazza San Bernardo 6, Località Montinelle, 25080*
**Tel** *0365 55 11 24* **Closed** *Mon–Thu (Feb), Tue dinner (Jul & Aug); Jan*
Refined dining in an elegant setting with a breathtaking view of Lake Garda from all tables.

## MANTUA:
**Antica Osteria Ai Ranari** €
Regional Italian
*Via Trieste 11, 46100*
**Tel** *0376 32 84 31* **Closed** *Mon; Jan 8–18, Jul 1–10*
Traditional Mantuan dishes, including the famous *tortelli di zucca* (pumpkin-filled pasta).

Casual dining at Pasta Madre, near Porta Romana, Milan

## MANTUA: L'Ochina Bianca €
Regional Italian
*Via Finzi 2, 46100*
**Tel** *0376 32 37 00* **Closed** *Sun dinner; lunch; Aug 1–21*
Regional dishes with a modern touch; try the local *torta sbrisolona*, a classic Mantuan sweet cake.

## MANTUA: Il Cigno Trattoria dei Martini €€
Modern Italian
*Piazza Carlo d'Arco 1, 46100*
**Tel** *0376 32 71 01* **Closed** *Mon, Tue; Aug*
Fine fare complemented by an impeccable wine list.

## MILAN: Be Bop Ristorante €
Pizzeria
*Viale Col di Lana 4, 20136*
**Tel** *02 83 76 972* **Closed** *Aug 10–20*
This restaurant offers gluten-free and vegetarian pizzas.

## MILAN: Bianco Latte €
Mediterranean
*Via Turati 30, 20121*
**Tel** *02 62 08 61 77* **Closed** *Mon dinner; 2 wks Aug*
Stop here for a hearty brunch or light dinner. Excellent coffee.

## MILAN: Erba Brusca €
Mediterranean
*Alzaia Naviglio Pavese 286, 20144*
**Tel** *02 87 38 07 11* **Closed** *Mon, Tue*
This small restaurant has its own kitchen garden, where the creative cuisine can be enjoyed alfresco.

## MILAN: Osteria Brunello €
Regional Italian
*Corso Garibaldi 117, 20121*
**Tel** *02 659 29 73*
Dishes based on Tuscan traditions; try the *pappardelle* with wild boar.

## MILAN: Pasta Madre €
Modern Italian
*Via Bernardino Corio 8, 20135*
**Tel** *02 55 19 00 20* **Closed** *Sun; 2 wks mid-Aug*

Contemporary decor with a relaxed atmosphere and creative Italian cuisine. Gluten-free desserts available.

## MILAN: Premiata Pizzeria €
Pizzeria
*Via Alzaia Naviglio Grande 2, 20144*
**Tel** *02 89 40 06 48*
A great and popular pizzeria with delicious toppings like salami, gorgonzola cheese, and truffle oil. Casual dining on shared tables.

## MILAN: Trattoria Aurora €
Traditional Italian
*Via Savona 23, 20144*
**Tel** *02 832 31 44* **Closed** *Mon dinner*
This upscale brasserie near the Navigli district offers hearty Piedmontese food. Finish your meal with a slice of *tiramisu*.

## MILAN: U Barba €
Regional Italian
*Via Decembrio 33, 20137*
**Tel** *02 45 48 70 32* **Closed** *Mon, Tue–Fri lunch; Aug 14–30*
Friendly traditional Genoese *osteria* with a bocce ball court. Great fish and game dishes. Try the freshly made gnocchi.

## MILAN:
**Alla Cucina delle Langhe** €€
Traditional Italian
*Corso Como 6, 20144*
**Tel** *02 65 54 279*
Delectable interpretations of classic Piedmontese fare, just a few steps from the outlet store 10 Corso Como.

## MILAN: Da Giacomo €€
Regional Italian
*Via Sottocorno 6, corner of Via B. Cellini, 20129*
**Tel** *02 76 02 33 13*
Close to the Duomo, this place offers simply cooked seafood in a friendly atmosphere.

**For more information on types of restaurants** *see pp578–9*

Exquisite grounds of the lovely Locanda del Pilone di Alba, Alba

**MILAN: Giglio Rosso**  €€
Fine dining
*Piazza Luigi di Savoia 2, 20124*
**Tel** *02 669 41 74*    **Closed** *Sat & Sun
lunch; Aug, Dec 23–Jan 6*
This elegant restaurant offers
innovative Tuscan dishes, staples
such as variations of risotto,
gnocchi, and ravioli.

### DK Choice

**MILAN:**
**Nobile Bistrò de Milan**  €€
Regional Italian
*Corso Venezia 45, 20121*
**Tel** *02 49 52 65 92*  **Closed** *2 wks
Aug*
This reasonably priced restaurant
is a short walk from the Montenapoleone shopping area. Well-
known Milanese chef Claudio
Sadler offers traditional regional
meat and fish dishes with
a modern twist. Continental
breakfast, lunch, afternoon tea,
*aperitivo,* and dinner are all
served in an informal atmosphere, with tables both indoors
and in a private courtyard.

**MILAN:**
**Il Ristorante Bulgari Hotel**  €€€
Fine dining
*Via Privata Fratelli Gabba 7/b, 20122*
**Tel** *02 805 80 51*
A luxury dining experience a few
steps from Via Montenapoleone.

**MILAN: Victoria**  €€€
Traditional Italian
*Via Clerici 1, 20121*
**Tel** *02 869 07 92* **Closed** *Sat lunch; Sun*
A few steps behind La Scala,
Victoria offers traditional fare
in an Art Nouveau setting.

**MONTE ISOLA: La Foresta**  €€
Regional Italian
*Via Peschiera 174, Maraglio, 25050*
**Tel** *030 988 62 10*    **Closed** *Wed;
Jan–Feb*

Family-run lakeside restaurant
serving fresh Lake Iseo fish; sun-
dried salted fish is a specialty.

**PAVIA: Le Tre Torri**  €
Pizzeria
*Via Lazzaro Spallanzani 6, 27100*
**Tel** *0382 30 28 20*    **Closed** *lunch
(Sat–Mon)*
This restaurant offers a varied
selection of pizza and pasta dishes.

**PAVIA: La Locanda
Vecchia Pavia al Mulino**  €€
Regional Italian
*Via al Monumento 5, Località
Certosa, 27012*
**Tel** *0382 92 58 94*    **Closed** *Sun
dinner, Mon; Jan 1–18, Aug 5–25*
Located on the grounds of the
Certosa di Pavia, this restaurant
serves tasty local specialties.

**SALÒ: Osteria dell'Orologio**  €
Traditional Italian
*Via Butturini 26, 25087*
**Tel** *0365 29 01 58*    **Closed** *mid-Jan–
mid-Feb, last wk Jun, Nov*
This bistro offers great-value,
traditional local cuisine and a
reasonably priced wine list.

**SALÒ:**
**Antica Trattoria alle Rose**  €€
Regional Italian
*Via Gasparo da Salò 33, 25087*
**Tel** *0365 432 20*  **Closed** *Wed; 7 Jan–
11 Feb, 2nd & 3rd wks Nov*
A traditional *trattoria* offering lake
fish, local dishes, homemade
pasta and delicious desserts.

**SALÒ: La Campagnola**  €€
Modern Italian
*Via Brunati 11, 25087*
**Tel** *0365 22 153*    **Closed** *Mon,
Tue lunch*
One of the oldest establishments
around Lake Garda, La
Campagnola has an extensive
selection of dishes, with a
separate steak menu and a good
wine list. Reserve.

## Valle d'Aosta and Piedmont

**ACQUI TERME: I Caffi**  €€
Regional Italian
*Via Scatilazzi 15, 15011*
**Tel** *0144 325 206*  **Closed** *Sun dinner
(Oct–Nov), Mon*
Piedmontese dishes revisited
with only local products, plus 600
wine labels. Impeccable service.

**ALBA:**
**Ristorante Madonna di Como**  €
Regional Italian
*Frazione Madonna di Como 31, 12051*
**Tel** *333 534 91 53*  **Closed** *Mon; 1 wk
mid-Aug*
Set in the hills above Alba and
boasting spectacular panoramic
views, this restaurant offers
regional dishes.

### DK Choice

**ALBA:**
**Locanda del Pilone
di Alba**  €€€
Regional Italian
*Strada della Cicchetta Frazione
Madonna di Como 34, 12051*
**Tel** *0173 36 66 16*    **Closed** *Tue,
Wed (Oct–Nov: Tue, Wed lunch);
Jan–Feb*
Set in a stunning location, this
converted *cascina* (barn) has
views over the Alps. The
Michelin-starred menu features
classic Piedmontese cuisine with
touches of Neapolitan cooking.
Each dish is served with a care-
fully selected wine. The desserts
are superb. Cookery classes and
wine tasting available.

**ALBA: Piazza Duomo**  €€€
Regional Italian
*Piazza Risorgimento 4, 12050*
**Tel** *0173 36 61 67*  **Closed** *Sun, Mon;
2 wks Aug, 3 wks Dec–Jan*
Gourmet fare and impeccable
service on offer near the main
square of Alba.

**ALESSANDRIA: Il Grappolo**  €€
Regional Italian
*Via Casale 28, 15121*
**Tel** *0131 25 32 17*    **Closed** *Mon
dinner, Tue*
Located in a 17th-century palace.
Offers Piedmontese food with a
modern twist; there's also a very
good wine list.

**AOSTA: Grotta Azzurra**  €
Pizzeria
*Via Croce di Città 97, 11100*
**Tel** *0165 26 24 74*    **Closed** *Wed; Jul*
Reasonably priced pizzeria in
the town center. Varied menu
features a delicious fish soup.

**AOSTA: Trattoria degli Artisti** €€
Regional Italian
*Via Maillet 5–7, 11100*
**Tel** *0165 409 60*    **Closed** *Sun lunch (except Aug); Mon; 15 days Jan, 15 days Jun*
On a cobblestone street downtown, this *trattoria* offers great homemade cakes and desserts.

**AOSTA: Il Vecchio Ristoro** €€€
Regional Italian
*Via Tourneuve 4, 11100*
**Tel** *0165 332 38*    **Closed** *Sun & Mon lunch*
This restaurant in an old watermill uses local ingredients to make creative dishes.

**ARONA: La Ruga del Corso** €€
Regional Italian
*Via Cesare Battisti 12, 28021*
**Tel** *0322 44 196* **Closed** *Tue (Oct–Mar)*
Housed in a former monastery, this place offers classic fish and meat dishes with a creative twist.

### DK Choice

**ARONA:**
**La Taverna del Pittore** €€
Fine dining
*Piazza del Popolo 39, 28041*
**Tel** *0322 24 33 66*    **Closed** *Thu*
With a veranda offering stunning views of the Rocca di Angera, this restaurant whips up creative Italian cuisine. Dishes include ravioli with truffles, *tagliolini* with lobster sauce, and grilled beef fillet with porcini mushrooms. The menu is presented on an artist's palette, recalling the restaurant's past as a meeting place for painters.

**ASTI: L'Angolo del Beato** €
Regional Italian
*Vicolo Cavalleri 2, 14100*
**Tel** *0141 53 16 68*    **Closed** *Sun; 1–6 Jan, mid-Aug*
Family-run spot in a medieval setting offering Piedmontese dishes; try the varied *antipasti*.

**ASTI: One More** €€
Traditional Italian
*Via Lungotanaro dei Pescatori, 14100*
**Tel** *0141 178 00 51*    **Closed** *Mon (Oct–May)*
A young crowd comes for beer, pizza and local fare, plus live music on the weekends.

**ASTI: Osteria da Marisa al Castello** €€
Regional Italian
*Piazza Castello 1, 14100*
**Tel** *0141 20 41 15*    **Closed** *Mon, Tue*
Set in an 18th-century castle overlooking the Monferrato hills. Excellent Piedmontese cuisine.

**BRA: Battaglino** €
Regional Italian
*Piazza Roma 18, 12042*
**Tel** *0172 41 25 09*    **Closed** *Sun dinner, Mon; 2 wks Jan, 2 wks Aug*
Traditional Piedmontese meat dishes offered in this convivial restaurant in the heart of Bra.

**BRA: Guido Ristorante** €€
Regional Italian
*Via Fossano 19, 12042*
**Tel** *0172 45 84 22*    **Closed** *lunch; Sun dinner, Mon*
Located inside the castle of Pollenzo. Refined regional meat and fish dishes a la carte, or a high-price tasting menu.

**BREUIL-CERVINIA: Al Solito Posto** €
Regional Italian
*Via Meynet 10 11021*
**Tel** *0166 94 91 26*
Charming, rustic restaurant with a good fixed-price menu.

**BREUIL-CERVINIA: Les Neiges d'Antan** €€
French
*Cretes Perreres*
**Tel** *0166 94 87 75*    **Closed** *May–mid-Jun, mid-Sep–end Oct*
This restaurant-cum-hotel serves refined rustic and rich mountain fare accompanied by great wines.

**CANNOBIO: Del Lago** €
Traditional Italian
*Via Nazionale 2, Località Carmine Inferiore, 28822*
**Tel** *0323 705 95*    **Closed** *Tue, Wed lunch; Nov–mid-Mar*
Simple yet imaginative dishes and views of Lake Maggiore.

**CANNOBIO: Osteria Vino Divino** €
Modern Italian
*Strada Valle Cannobina 1, 28822*
**Tel** *0323 719 19*    **Closed** *lunch (exc Sun); Tue (exc Jul & Aug); Nov–Mar*

Stunning views of the Rocca di Angera from La Taverna del Pittore, Arona

Traditional dishes reinvented with a twist in a converted 19th-century stable block. Good wine.

**CANNOBIO: Lo Scalo** €€
Seafood
*Piazza Vittorio Emanuele 32, 28822*
**Tel** *0323 714 80*    **Closed** *Mon & Tue lunch (mid-Sep–mid-Jul); 1 wk Feb–Mar, Nov*
Daily catch of lake fish baked in foil, plus an array of shellfish and local produce.

**CASALE MONFERRATO: La Torre** €€
Modern Italian
*Via Candiani d'Olivola 36,15033*
**Tel** *0142 702 95*    **Closed** *Tue, Wed lunch; 3 wks Aug, Dec 28–Jan 7*
La Torre offers creative regional cuisine and has a good wine list.

**CHIUSA SAN MICHELE: Ristorante Della Sacra** €
Mediterranean
*Piazzale della Sacra di San Michele, 10057*
**Tel** *011 93 98 43*    **Closed** *Mon; Tue & Wed dinner (Jul–Sep)*
Good-quality café, hotel, and restaurant next to the famous Sacra San Michele monastery.

**COGNE: Lou Rossignon** €
Traditional Italian
*Rue Mines de Cogne 22, 11012*
**Tel** *0165 740 34*    **Closed** *Tue dinner, Wed (except Aug, Sep); Jun 1–20, Nov*
Traditional Alpine and local fare in a cosy mountain taverna.

**COSSANO BELBO: Trattoria Della Posta da Camulin** €
Regional Italian
*Via Fratelli Negro 3, 12054*
**Tel** *0141 881 26*    **Closed** *Sun dinner, Mon; mid-Jul–mid-Aug*
Friendly century-old *trattoria* serving regional dishes and homemade pasta.

**COSTIGLIOLE D'ASTI: Caffè Roma** €
Traditional Italian
*Piazza Umberto I 14, 14037*
**Tel** *0141 96 65 44*    **Closed** *Mon; 1 wk end Feb, 1 wk Jun*
A wine bar at the foot of the castle with light dishes in a cosy atmosphere.

**COSTIGLIOLE D'ASTI: Cascina Collavini** €
Traditional Italian
*Strada Traniera 24, 14037*
**Tel** *0141 96 64 40* **Closed** *Tue dinner, Wed; 2 wks Jan, 2 wks Aug*
Simple, elegant restaurant in an old farmhouse. The menu features traditional regional fare. Wines come from the local vineyard.

**For more information on types of restaurants** *see pp578–9*

**COURMAYEUR: Du Tunnel** €
Pizzeria
*Via Circonvallazione 80, 11013*
**Tel** *0165 84 17 05* **Closed** *winter: Wed lunch*
A simple snack bar/pizzeria offering delicious wood-oven pizzas. Friendly and efficient staff.

**COURMAYEUR:**
**Cadran Solaire** €€
Traditional Italian
*Via Roma 122,11013*
**Tel** *0165 84 46 09* **Closed** *Tue; May, 2 wks Nov*
Local dishes including *risotto alla Valdostana* (made with Fontina cheese) served in a cosy setting.

**CUNEO:**
**Osteria Della Chiocciola** €
Regional Italian
*Via Fossano 1, 12100*
**Tel** *0171 662 77* **Closed** *Sun; 15 days Jan*
Top-quality homemade classics such as gnocchi, ravioli, and risotto are served with excellent wine.

**CUNEO: La Ciau del Tornavento** €€
Regional Italian
*Piazza Baracco 7, 12050*
**Tel** *0173 63 83 33* **Closed** *Wed, Thu lunch; Feb*
Piedmontese dishes are served in a dining room with wonderful views of rolling vineyards.

**DOMODOSSOLA: Antica**
**Ristorante Piemonte Da Sciolla** €
Regional Italian
*Piazza della Convenzione 4, 28845*
**Tel** *0324 24 26 33* **Closed** *Sun dinner, Wed; Oct–Dec 8*
Known for its local mountain fare of hearty meat and game dishes.

**IVREA: Trattoria Boccon Divino** €
Regional Italian
*Via Aosta 47,10015*
**Tel** *0125 489 98* **Closed** *Tue dinner, Sun dinner; last wk Jul, 1st wk Aug*
A small trattoria in the historic center serving regional cuisine.

**NOVARA: I Due Ladroni** €
Traditional Italian
*Corso Cavallotti 15, 28100*
**Tel** *0321 62 45 81* **Closed** *Sun; 1 wk mid-Aug*
Classic cuisine in a 16th-century palazzo in the heart of town. Excellent food with great flavors.

**NOVARA:**
**Osteria del Laghetto** €€
Regional Italian
*Via Case Sparse 11, 28100*
**Tel** *0321 47 29 62* **Closed** *Sun; 10 days Aug; Dec 24–Jan 7*
Truffles, mushrooms, and fish are on offer at this restaurant set in pretty gardens. Reserve.

Rustic and charming entrance of the popular Al Sorriso, Soriso

**ORTA SAN GIULIO:**
**Ristoro Olina** €
Traditional Italian
*Via Olina 40, 28016*
**Tel** *0322 90 56 56* **Closed** *mid-Nov–mid-Dec*
Serves homemade pasta. Local mushrooms and truffles feature on the menu, as do fish dishes.

**ORTA SAN GIULIO:**
**Villa Crespi** €€€
Modern Italian
*Via Fava 18, 28016*
**Tel** *0322 91 19 02* **Closed** *Apr–Oct: Mon, Tue lunch*
Set in a 19th-century folly, this restaurant offers high-level gastronomy and a vast wine list.

**RIVOLI: Combal.Zero** €€€
Modern Italian
*Il Castello, Piazza Mafalda di Savoia 62, 10098*
**Tel** *011 956 52 25* **Closed** *Sun, Mon; Aug*
Located on the grounds of the Castello di Rivoli, this restaurant offers a creative Italian menu.

### DK Choice

**SAINT VINCENT: Le Grenier** €€
Modern Italian
*Piazza Monte Zerbion 1, 11010*
**Tel** *0166 51 01 38* **Closed** *Mon–Thu lunch, Wed*
Soft lighting and a copper fireplace create a warm ambience in this restaurant set in a converted barn. Try the *carpaccio di filetto* (thin slices of raw beef) with curry sauce, the venison, or the *ravioli di carciofi e robiola con gamberi rossi* (pasta filled with artichokes, robiola cheese, and shrimp). There is an ample choice of Italian and French wines and a good cheese selection.

**SESTRIERE:**
**La Vineria del Colle** €€
Enoteca
*Via Assietta 1, 10058*
**Tel** *0122 764 76* **Closed** *Mon; May, Oct*
Housed in an old wine cellar next to the ski slopes, this *enoteca* combines traditional flavors with contemporary tastes.

**SORISO: Al Sorriso** €€€
Regional Italian
*Via Roma 18, 28016*
**Tel** *0322 98 32 28* **Closed** *Mon, Tue; 1 wk Jan*
Renowned for its good, creative cuisine incorporating seasonal specialties. Reserve.

**STRESA: Piemontese** €€
Regional Italian
*Via Mazzini 25, 28838*
**Tel** *0323 30 235* **Closed** *Mon; Nov–Feb*
Intimate family-run restaurant with interesting versions of local fare. There is also a pretty alfresco terrace for summer dining.

**STRESA: Il Vicoletto** €€
Modern Italian
*Vicolo del Poncivo 3, 28838*
**Tel** *0323 93 21 02* **Closed** *Nov–Mar: Thu; Jan–Feb*
Piedmontese cuisine including classic dishes with a touch of creativity. Good wine cellar.

**TORTONA: Aurora Girarrosto** €
Regional Italian
*Strada Statale per Genova 13, 15057*
**Tel** *0131 86 30 33*
The specialty here is barbecued meats, with all produce coming from local organic farmers.

**TURIN: Birilli** €€
Modern Italian
*Strada Val San Martino 6, 10131*
**Tel** *011 819 05 67* **Closed** *1st wk Jan; Oct–May: Sun dinner*
Hearty home cooking offering a good variety of pasta, grilled fish, and meat dishes.

**TURIN: La Porta Rossa** €€
Seafood
*Via Passalacqua 3/B, 10122*
**Tel** *011 53 08 16* **Closed** *Sat lunch, Sun; Aug 10–30; Dec 25–Jan 6*
Serving fresh fish accompanied by fine wines.

**TURIN: Dai Saletta** €€
Regional Italian
*Via Belfiore 37, 10126*
**Tel** *011 668 78 67* **Closed** *Sun; 2 wks Aug*
Typical *trattoria* ambience. Has a classic Piedmontese menu and a good wine list. Good selection of homemade desserts.

**TURIN: Neuv Caval 'd Bròns** €€€
Fine dining
*Piazza San Carlo 155, 10123*
**Tel** *011 53 90 30*
Set in a beautiful square, this
restaurant offers Piedmontese
dishes with an international twist.

**VENARIA REALE:**
**Il Convito della Venaria** €
Regional Italian
*Via Andrea Mensa 37g, 10078*
**Tel** *011 459 83 92*      **Closed** *Sun*
*dinner, Mon; 3 wks Feb, 1st wk Aug*
Come for meat and fish dishes or
pizza from a wood-fired oven.

**VERBANIA PALLANZA:**
**Osteria dell'Angolo** €
Regional Italian
*Piazza Garibaldi 35, 28922*
**Tel** *0323 55 63 62*   **Closed** *Mon (exc*
*dinner mid-Jul–Sep); Nov–Feb*
Typical regional taverna offering
fish dishes, and Piedmontese and
Lombard cuisine. Reserve.

**VERBANIA PALLANZA:**
**Osteria del Castello** €
Enoteca
*Piazza Castello 9, 28921*
**Tel** *0323 51 65 79*      **Closed** *Sun;*
*1 wk Dec*
A local favorite serving pasta and
Piedmontese beef. Good wine list.

**VERBANIA PALLANZA:**
**Milano** €€
Regional Italian
*Corso Zanitello 2, 28922*
**Tel** *0323 55 68 16*      **Closed** *Tue;*
*Jan, Nov*
Choose from a selection of fish
served with organic vegetables.

**VERCELLI: Acqua Pazza** €
Pizzeria
*Corso Gastaldi 25, 13100*
**Tel** *0161 21 74 20* **Closed** *Wed; 2 wks*
*Aug*
This place offers a range of pizzas
as well as Vercellese dishes.

**VERCELLI: Il Giardinetto** €
Regional Italian
*Via Sereno 3, 13100*
**Tel** *0161 25 72 30*      **Closed** *Mon;*
*1 wk Jan, 3 wks Aug*
Housed in a 19th-century villa,
this restaurant serves delicious
fare using Piedmontese delicacies.

**VERCELLI: Il Paiolo** €
Regional Italian
*Viale Garibaldi 72, 13100*
**Tel** *0161 25 05 77*      **Closed** *Thu;*
*2nd wk Jul–1st wk Aug*
A trattoria set in the rice-growing
country. Serves excellent risotto.

# Liguria

**CAMOGLI: O Magazin di**
**Camogli** €
Seafood
*Piazza Colombo 14, 16032*
**Tel** *393 923 9099*   **Closed** *Jul–Sep:*
*Mon*
This hidden-away fish bar offers
good-quality dishes in varied and
original menus.

## DK Choice

**CAMOGLI:**
**La Cucina di Nonna Nina** €€
Regional Italian
*Via Molfino 126, 16032*
**Tel** *0185 77 38 35*   **Closed** *Wed;*
*10 days Jan; 3 wks Nov*
This restaurant is on a pretty hill
and encircled by citrus and olive
trees. It produces excellent
dishes, using top-quality local
products including olive oil from
the Ligurian coast, fish bought
from local fishermen, and
organic vegetables grown in
its own garden. The focaccia,
amongst other breads, cakes
and Ligurian pasta, are all homemade on the day of serving.

**CERVO: San Giorgio** €€
Seafood
*Via Volta 19, 18010*
**Tel** *0183 40 01 75*   **Closed** *Jul & Aug;*
*Tue lunch; Oct–Easter: Mon dinner, Tue*
Popular, charming restaurant
offering simple dishes. Reserve.

**GENOA: Da Genio** €
Regional Italian
*Salita San Leonardo 61r, 16128*
**Tel** *010 58 84 63*   **Closed** *Sun; 2 wks Aug*
Sample the classic *trenette al*
*pesto* (local pasta with pesto
sauce) and fish dishes.

**GENOA: Da O' Colla** €
Regional Italian
*Via alla Chiesa di Murta 10, 16162*
**Tel** *010 740 85 79*      **Closed** *lunch;*
*Sun dinner*
Excellent home-cooked Ligurian
cuisine. Located away from the
city center, but worth the taxi fare.

**GENOA: Cantine Squarciafico** €€
Regional Italian
*Piazza Ivrea 3r, 16123*
**Tel** *010 24 70 82 3*   **Closed** *1–10 Jan*
Ligurian wine bar offering local
specialties including *stracci*
(a type of lasagne).

**LEVANTO: Cavour** €€
Regional Italian
*Piazza Cavour 1, 19015*
**Tel** *0187 80 84 97*      **Closed** *Mon;*
*Dec 15–Feb 15*
Traditional *trattoria* specializing
in local seafood dishes.

**MANAROLA: La Scogliera** €€
Regional Italian
*Via Birolli 103, 19017*
**Tel** *0187 92 07 47*      **Closed** *Nov–*
*Mar: Fri*
A pretty, family-run restaurant
renowned for seafood specialties.

**NERVI: Astor** €
Regional Italian
*Viale delle Palme 16, 16167*
**Tel** *010 32 90 11*
With magnificent views of the
sea, Astor offers local cuisine in a
simple and elegant setting.

**PORTOFINO: Da U Batti** €€
Seafood
*Vico Nuovo 17, 16034*
**Tel** *0185 26 93 79*      **Closed** *Mon;*
*Nov–mid-Jan*
A chic, intimate restaurant in one
of Liguria's most elegant towns.
Offers exceptional fish cuisine.

**PORTOVENERE: Le Bocche** €€
Regional Italian
*Calata Doria 102, 19025*
**Tel** *0187 79 06 22* **Closed** *Tue (exc Jul*
*& Aug); Jan–mid-Feb*
Delicate Ligurian fish dishes served
alfresco overlooking Portovenere.

A terrace overlooking the water, perfect for the fish dishes at Milano, in Verbania Pallanza

**PORTOVENERE: Da Iseo**  €€
Regional Italian
*Calata Doria 9, 19025*
**Tel** *0187 79 06 10* **Closed** *Wed (Sep–Jun); 20 days Nov*
This *trattoria* on the waterfront serves typical fish dishes.

**RAPALLO: U'Giancu**  €
Regional Italian
*Via San Massimo 78, 16035*
**Tel** *0185 26 05 05* **Closed** *lunch; Wed; weekends (winter).*
Ligurian specialties are served here, and the walls are full of drawings by comic masters.

**RAPALLO:**
**Hostaria Vecchia Rapallo**  €€
Seafood
*Via Cairoli 20, 16035*
**Tel** *0185 500 53* **Closed** *Oct–Mar; Mon; Jan 7–24*
This elegant restaurant offers creative seafood dishes and a good selection of wine.

**RAPALLO: La Nave**  €€
Seafood
*Via Pomaro 15, 16035*
**Tel** *0185 66 95 02* **Closed** *mid-Sep–May: Wed*
Excellent location on the beach. Sample the *frittura di pesce* (fried fish) and homemade pesto.

## DK Choice

**SANREMO:**
**Da Paolo e Barbara**  €€
Seafood
*Via Roma 47, 18038*
**Tel** *0184 53 16 53* **Closed** *lunch (open Sat & Sun lunch Nov–May); Wed, Thu*
This small family-run restaurant serves local fish, meat sourced from the nearby Langhe region, vegetables from its own farm, and homemade focaccia. Try the pasta with *gambero rosso di Sanremo* (local red prawn) or *trofie al Marò* (pasta with bean and mint sauce).

**SANREMO: Da Vittorio**  €€
Seafood
*Piazza Bresca 16, 18038*
**Tel** *0184 50 19 24* **Closed** *2 wks Nov*
A traditional favorite close to the shore. Seafood, fresh from the harbor, is the main draw.

**SANTA MARGHERITA LIGURE:**
**L'Insolita Zuppa**  €
Traditional Italian
*Via Romana 7, 16038*
**Tel** *0185 28 95 94* **Closed** *Wed (exc Jul & Aug); 2 wks Feb, last 2 wks Nov*
A cosy place offering traditional meat and fish dishes.

**SANTA MARGHERITA LIGURE:**
**Il Nostromo**  €
Seafood
*Via dell'Arco 6, 16038*
**Tel** *0185 28 16 63* **Closed** *Mon (exc Jun–Sep); Feb 15, Nov 15*
This family-run restaurant serves good portions of quality traditional Ligurian fish dishes.

**SESTRI LEVANTE:**
**Ristorante Olimpo**  €€
Mediterranean
*Via della Chiusa 28, 16039*
**Tel** *0185 426 61* **Closed** *2 Nov–Feb*
Overlooking the Baia del Silenzio, this restaurant serves fine cuisine with an emphasis on fish.

**VERNAZZA: Gambero Rosso** €€
Seafood
*Piazza Marconi 7, 19018*
**Tel** *0187 81 22 65* **Closed** *Thu; mid-Jan–Feb*
Inventive modern interpretations of Ligurian seafood dishes.

## Emilia-Romagna

**BOLOGNA:**
**Antica Trattoria della Gigina** €
Regional Italian
*Via Stendhal 1, 40128*
**Tel** *051 32 23 00*
A modern take on regional cuisine without compromising flavor.

**BOLOGNA: Battibecco**  €
Regional Italian
*Via Battibecco 4, 40123*
**Tel** *051 22 32 98* **Closed** *lunch Sat; Sun*
Classic Bolognese cuisine and seafood dishes in this centrally located, elegant restaurant.

**BOLOGNA: Pepperoni**  €
Pizzeria
*Via di Barbiano 7, 40136*
**Tel** *051 33 36 58* **Closed** *mid-Oct–mid-May: Mon*
Minimalist decor in this trendy spot serving high-quality pizzas.

**BOLOGNA: Pino**  €
Pizzeria
*Via Goito 2, 40126*
**Tel** *051 22 72 91*
This boisterous spot located in the heart of town offers first-rate pizzas topped with quality ingredients.

**BOLOGNA: Posta**  €
Regional Italian
*Via della Grada 21, 41022*
**Tel** *051 649 21 06* **Closed** *Mon, Sat lunch; last 2 wks Aug*
Enjoy Tuscan cuisine at this rustic spot with wood-beamed ceilings and terra-cotta tiled floors.

**BOLOGNA: Il Cantuccio**  €€
Seafood
*Via Volturno 4, 40121*
**Tel** *051 23 34 24* **Closed** *lunch; Mon; Aug*
Fresh Mediterranean cuisine in an intimate setting. Family-run, with courteous service.

**BOLOGNA: Cesarina**  €€
Regional Italian
*Via Santo Stefano 19, 40125*
**Tel** *051 23 20 37* **Closed** *Mon, Tue lunch*
More than 100 years old, this restaurant beside an exquisite church, offers regional dishes.

**BOLOGNA: Pappagallo**  €€
Fine dining
*Piazza della Mercanzia 3, 40125*
**Tel** *051 23 28 07*
Excellent traditional cuisine is served here, under dramatically high ceilings. The desserts on offer are delicious and the cellar is well stocked.

**BOLOGNA: Ristorante Sikelia** €€
Seafood
*Via Riva di Reno 45/B, 40124*
**Tel** *051 23 15 51* **Closed** *Mon, Sun dinner*
Excellent fish served in a city where meat reigns. Simple decor, courteous service, good prices.

Elegant seating at Sanremo's noted Da Paolo e Barbara restaurant

**BOLOGNA: Bitone** €€€
Fine dining
*Via Emilia Levante 111, 40134*
**Tel** *051 54 61 10* **Closed** *Mon, Tue; Aug*
Just outside the city center, this restaurant offers great Bolognese dishes and attentive service.

**BOLOGNA: I Portici** €€€
Fine dining
*Via dell'Indipendenza 69, 40121*
**Tel** *051 421 85* **Closed** *lunch; Mon, Sun*
The Michelin-starred chef here creates traditional Bolognese and modern Italian cuisine. Romantic setting in a former theater.

**CASTELL'ARQUATO:
Da Faccini** €€
Regional Italian
*Località S. Antonio, 29014*
**Tel** *0523 89 63 40* **Closed** *Wed; Jun, Jul*
In-season local ingredients decide the daily changing menu at this warm, family-run eatery.

**FAENZA: La Pavona** €
Regional Italian
*Via Santa Lucia 45, 48018*
**Tel** *0546 310 75* **Closed** *Tue, Sat lunch; 3 wks Jul*
Just outside the historic center, this rustic and cosy spot serves the favorites of Emilian cooking.

**FERRARA: Ca d'Frara** €
Regional Italian
*Via del Gambero 4, 44121*
**Tel** *0532 20 50 57* **Closed** *Tue, Wed lunch*
A slightly sterile atmosphere does not detract from the quality of the Emilian cuisine.

**FERRARA: Big Night, Ristorante da Giovanni** €€
Regional Italian
*Largo Castello 38, 44121*
**Tel** *0532 24 23 67* **Closed** *winter*
Large windows afford castle views at this restaurant serving traditional dishes from land and sea.

**FIDENZA FORNIO:
Osteria di Fornio** €
Regional Italian
*Via Fornio 78, 43036*
**Tel** *0524 601 18* **Closed** *Mon dinner, Tue*
Tucked away in the countryside, this restaurant has a changing menu of regional delicacies.

**MODENA: Al Boschetto da Loris** €
Regional Italian
*Via Due Canali Nord 218, 41122*
**Tel** *059 25 17 59*
This place in a 16th-century hunting lodge serves home-style cooking.

**DK Choice**

**MODENA: Osteria Francescana** €€€
Fine dining
*Via Stella 22, 41121*
**Tel** *059 22 39 12* **Closed** *Jan & Aug: Sun, Mon*
This two-Michelin-starred restaurant is experimental. The regional specialty – Parmigiano Reggiano – is available in five different stages of ageing and the most notable dishes include ravioli with veal offal, vegetables, and black truffles. Sample the marinated suckling pig with cream of fennel, and the famous Modena balsamic vinegar.

**PARMA: I Tri Siochètt** €
Regional Italian
*Strada Farnese-Vigheffio 74/a, 43125*
**Tel** *0521 96 88 70* **Closed** *2 wks Dec*
Named after the three "mad" siblings who opened this *trattoria* years ago. Hearty local cuisine.

**PARMA: Le Viole** €
Modern Italian
*Strada Nuova di Castelnuovo 60, 43126*
**Tel** *0521 60 10 00* **Closed** *Jan 15; Jul & Aug: Sun, Mon; Sep–Jun: Mon, Tue*
Seasonal produce inspires gastronomic inventions by the two sisters who run this friendly spot.

**PARMA: Parizzi** €€
Fine dining
*Strada della Repubblica 71, 43100*
**Tel** *0521 28 59 52* **Closed** *Mon; last 3 wks Aug*
Modern decor with spotlights and gold floors. A great menu of contemporary and classic dishes.

**PIACENZA: Vecchia Piacenza** €€
Modern Italian
*Via Taverna/C.ne S. Bernardo 1, 29100*
**Tel** *0523 30 54 62* **Closed** *Mon*
A husband-and-wife team combine innovative cuisine with original interior design.

**RAVENNA:
Antica Trattoria al Gallo 1909** €
Regional Italian
*Via Maggiore 87, 48123*
**Tel** *0544 21 37 75* **Closed** *Sun dinner, Mon, Tue*
The rustic exterior of this historic *trattoria* hides an Art Deco interior. Ample Emilian specialties.

**RAVENNA: Ca de Ven** €
Regional Italian
*Via Corrado Ricci 24, 48121*
**Tel** *0544 301 63* **Closed** *Mon*
Authentic eatery popular with locals. Shared tables available for a more casual dining experience.

Sophisticated ambience at the Osteria Francescana, Modena

**RAVENNA: Bella Venezia** €€
Regional Italian
*Via 4 Novembre 16, 48121*
**Tel** *0544 21 27 46* **Closed** *Sun; 3 wks Jan, 1 wk Jun*
Excellent pasta and fresh fish in a romantic, intimate setting. Great service and a central location.

**RAVENNA: Taberna Boaria** €€
Regional Italian
*Via Mentana 33, 48121*
**Tel** *0544 21 52 58* **Closed** *Tue*
This place has a classy interior and great ambience. The food includes fish and is made from the best local ingredients.

**RIMINI: Osteria de Borg** €
Regional Italian
*Via Forzieri 12, 47921*
**Tel** *0541 560 74*
A rustic setting in which to sample meat specialties, local cheeses, and cured meats.

**RIMINI: Dallo Zio** €€
Seafood
*Via Santa Chiara 16, 47921*
**Tel** *0541 78 67 47*
The cuisine at this fresh, modern spot is inspired by the classic flavors of the Adriatic.

**RIMINI: Guido** €€
Seafood
*Lungomare Guido Spadazzi 12, 47924*
**Tel** *0541 37 46 12* **Closed** *lunch (Tue–Fri), Mon; 1 wk Dec*
Cuttlefish, oysters, and calamari are just a few of the specialties served at this spot on the beach.

**RIMINI: Ristorante Molo 22** €€
Seafood
*Via Ortigara 78/80, 47921*
**Tel** *345 089 3907* **Closed** *summer: Sat dinner, Sun dinner; winter: Sat dinner, Sun dinner–Wed*
This excellent seafood restaurant on a dock (*molo*) offers a warm atmosphere and super-fresh fish.

**For more information on types of restaurants** *see pp578–9*

# Florence

**La Bussola**  €
Pizzeria  **Map** 5 C3
*Via Porta Rossa, 58 50123*
**Tel** *055 293376*
Charming, low-key pizzeria
with a wood-burning oven.
The service is excellent, and the
wine list surprisingly ample.

**Casa del Vino**  €
Enoteca  **Map** 1 C4
*Via dell'Ariento 16r, 50123*
**Tel** *055 21 56 09*  **Closed** *Thu dinner,
Sun, Mon*
Lively traditional enoteca, with
a very local clientele. Excellent
place for sandwiches and snacks.

**Il Pizzaiuolo**  €
Pizzeria  **Map** 4 E1
*Via de' Macci 113, 50122*
**Tel** *055 24 11 71*  **Closed** *3 wks Aug;
1 wk Dec*
Treat yourself to a thick-crusted
Neapolitan-style pizza.

**Ruth's**  €
Kosher/Vegetarian  **Map** 2 E5
*Via Luigi Carlo Farini 2, 50121*
**Tel** *055 248 08 88*  **Closed** *Fri dinner,
Sat lunch; Jewish festivities*
Located beside the synagogue,
this kosher restaurant serves
Jewish-inspired recipes. A good
range of vegetarian options.

**Tarocchi**  €
Pizzeria  **Map** 6 E5
*Via dei Renai 12, 50125*
**Tel** *055 234 39 12*  **Closed** *Mon*
Great prices at this off-the-beaten-
track pizzeria. Pasta dishes are
available, too.

**Trattoria Zàzà**  €
Regional Italian  **Map** 1 C4
*Piazza del Mercato Centrale 26, 50123*
**Tel** *055 21 54 11*
Traditional Florentine favorites
from land and sea, as well as
vegetarian and gluten-free dishes.

**Il Vegetariano**  €
Vegetarian  **Map** 2 D3
*Via delle Ruote 30, 50129*
**Tel** *055 47 50 30*  **Closed** *Mon, Sat &
Sun lunch; 3 wks Aug, Christmas*
There's excellent value to be
had at this long-established
restaurant. Service is meagre,
but portions are not.

**Dei Frescobaldi**  €€
Enoteca  **Map** 6 E3
*Via dei Magazzini 2, 50122*
**Tel** *055 28 47 24*  **Closed** *1 wk Jan, 3
wks Aug*
Top fine wines and meticulously
matched dishes in a historic
setting with frescoed walls.

**Da Kou**  €€
Japanese  **Map** 5 C1
*Via del Melarancio 19/r, 50123*
**Tel** *055 28 29 22*  **Closed** *Mon*
Fresh and authentic sushi
prepared with skill; portions
are generous. The decor is
modern and informal.

## DK Choice

**Alle Murate**  €€
Regional Italian  **Map** 6 E2
*Via del Proconsolo 16/r, 50122*
**Tel** *055 24 06 18*  **Closed** *Sun
lunch, Mon*
This unique restaurant offers a
one-of-a-kind opportunity to
combine Florentine art and
food. Housed in a 14th-century
palace, it boasts original frescoes
on the walls and vaulted ceilings,
hidden for centuries and
uncovered in a painstaking
restoration process. The excellent,
understated local cuisine is a
perfect companion to the
stunning early Renaissance art.

**Ora d'Aria**  €€
Modern Italian  **Map** 6 D4
*Via dei Georgofili 11/r, 50100*
**Tel** *055 200 16 99*  **Closed** *Sun, Mon
lunch; 2 wks Jan, 2 wks Aug*
Tucked away in an alley, this
place is worth a visit for its
authentic specialty dishes.

**Osteria Santo Spirito**  €€
Regional Italian  **Map** 5 A5
*Piazza Santo Spirito 16, 50125*
**Tel** *055 238 23 83*  **Closed** *lunch;
public holidays*
Tuscan specialties with a twist
at this cosy eatery.

**Pane e Vino**  €€
Modern Italian  **Map** 3 A1
*Piazza di Cestello 3/r, 50124*
**Tel** *055 247 69 56*
Family-friendly restaurant
offering traditional Florentine
dishes and more modern ones.

**Bistrò Del Mare**  €€€
Fine dining  **Map** 5 C3
*Lungarno Corsini 4/r, 50123*
**Tel** *055 239 92 24*  **Closed** *lunch
(Tue–Thu); Mon; 1 wk Aug*
Steps away from Ponte Vecchio,
this refined restaurant serves
dishes inspired by old Tuscan
recipes but brought up to date.

**Cibrèo**  €€€
Modern Italian  **Map** 4 F1
*Via Andrea del Verrocchio 8/r, 50122*
**Tel** *055 234 11 00*  **Closed** *Mon;
3 wks Aug*
This trendy place delights diners
with its contemporary take on
local cuisine.

Interiors of Pane e Vino, popular for
traditional Florentine dishes, Florence

## DK Choice

**Enoteca Pinchiorri**  €€€
Fine dining  **Map** 4 E1
*Via Ghibellina 87, 50122*
**Tel** *055 24 27 57*  **Closed** *Sun,
Mon; Aug; public holidays*
This triple Michelin-starred
restaurant is considered by
some to be the finest in Italy.
Its modern, understated interior
and soft lighting provide the
ideal setting to indulge in the
exquisite gastronomic creations
offered here. Specials include
the ravioli with *taggiasche* olives
and *burrata* cheese and the
roast pigeon with honey, spices,
and breaded aubergine. The
wine cellar is legendary. A
private dining room is available.

# Tuscany

**AREZZO:**
**Le Chiavi d'Oro**  €€
Modern Italian
*Piazza San Francesco 7, 52100*
**Tel** *0575 403 313*  **Closed** *Mon;
1 wk Feb, 1 wk Aug*
This stylish Danish-designed
restaurant is elegantly decorated
with 1960s swivel stools and
blond wood floors. The kitchen
specializes in contemporary,
regionally inspired cuisine.

**AREZZO:**
**La Lancia d'Oro**  €€
Regional Italian
*Piazza Grande 18, 52100*
**Tel** *0575 210 33*  **Closed** *Sun dinner;
Mon; 2 wks Feb, 2 wks Nov*
Hearty Tuscan meals on offer in
a stunning setting with outdoor
seating under *Vasari's Loggias*
(Vasari's Corridor).

**ARTIMINO: Da Delfina** €€
Regional Italian
*Via della Chiesa 1, 59015*
**Tel** *055 871 80 74*　　**Closed** *Mon;*
*1 wk Jan, 1 wk Feb*
The chef's creations are inspired
by his mother's cooking. Hidden
away in a delightful walled town.

**CORTONA:**
**Hostaria la Bucaccia** €
Regional Italian
*Via Ghibellina 17, 52044*
**Tel** *0575 606 039* **Closed** *Jan 15–30;*
*Dec–Feb: Mon*
This restaurant has original
features, built over a Roman road.
Home cooking is served.

**CORTONA: Il Falconiere** €€€
Fine dining
*Località San Martino 370, 52044*
**Tel** *0575 612 679*　　**Closed** *Jan 7–30*
Nestled among olive and cypress
trees, this restaurant is in a truly
idyllic setting. A great place to
sample exalted Tuscan cuisine.

**ELBA: Publius** €
Regional Italian
*Piazza del Castagneto 11, Poggio,*
*57030*
**Tel** *0565 992 08*　　**Closed** *Mon;*
*Nov–Mar*
A wide variety of dishes and an
impressive wine cellar at this
lovely restaurant with sea views.

**ELBA: La Lucciola** €€
Seafood
*Lungomare Pino Nomellini 64,*
*Marina di Campo, 57034*
**Tel** *0565 976 395*　**Closed** *Nov–Apr*
Opt for the catch of the day at
this romantic spot on the beach.

**ELBA: Stella Marina** €€
Seafood
*Via Vittorio Emanuele II 1,*
*Portoferraio, 57037*
**Tel** *0565 880 566*　　**Closed** *Mon*
Fish doesn't get much fresher
than at this tiny portside
restaurant; excellent wine list, too.

**LUCCA: Da Giulio in Pelleria** €
Regional Italian
*Via delle Conce 47, 55100*
**Tel** *0583 559 48*　　**Closed** *3 wks Jan*
Popular *trattoria* serving Tuscan
fare such as polenta and *zuppa*
*di farro* (bean and spelt soup).

**LUCCA: La Tana dell'Orco** €
Pizzeria
*Viale Regina Margherita 225, 55100*
**Tel** *389 023 32 34*　　**Closed** *Tue*
The concept is simple at this
pizzeria just outside the city walls –
minimal service and low prices.

**LUCCA: Buca di Sant'Antonio** €€
Regional Italian
*Via della Cervia 3, 55100*
**Tel** *0583 558 81*　**Closed** *Sun dinner,*
*Mon; 1 wk Jan; 1 wk Jun*
Ancient local recipes are lovingly
prepared at this historic eatery
in a medieval stable.

**MONTALCINO:**
**Il Boccon Divino** €€
Regional Italian
*Strada Provinciale Traversa dei*
*Monti 201, 53024*
**Tel** *0577 848 233*　　**Closed** *Tue*
Enjoy classic Tuscan dishes and
admire sweeping views of the
countryside. The winelist
is excellent.

**MONTE ARGENTARIO:**
**Osteria dei Nobili Santi** €€
Seafood
*Le Piane, 58019*
**Tel** *0564 833 015*　　**Closed** *Mon*
Good prices at this intimate
restaurant inside a polo club
serving plenty of delectable
fish dishes.

**MONTEPULCIANO:**
**Osteria Acquacheta** €
Regional Italian
*Via del Teatro 22, 53045*
**Tel** *0578 717 086*　　**Closed** *Tue*
This tiny, popular restaurant is
always packed. The Tuscan meat
dishes are a specialty.

**MONTEPULCIANO: La Grotta** €€
Regional Italian
*Via di San Biagio 15, 53045*
**Tel** *0578 757 479*　　**Closed** *Wed;*
*Jan; Feb*
A restaurant set in a 16th-century
building. The menu features
expertly revisited Tuscan classics.

**MONTERIGGIONI: Il Pozzo** €€
Regional Italian
*Piazza Roma 2, 53035*
**Tel** *0577 304 127*　　**Closed** *Sun*
*dinner, Mon; 2 wks Jan; 2 wks Feb*
Well located in the center of the
walled town, this rustic *osteria*
serves traditional fare.

**PIENZA: Latte di Luna** €
Regional Italian
*Via San Carlo 2, 53026*
**Tel** *0578 748 606*　　**Closed** *Tue*
Classic Tuscan dishes at this
quaint, family-friendly eatery.
Dont forget to try the locally
produced pecorino cheese.

**PISA: A Casa Mia** €
Regional Italian
*Via Provinciale Calcesana 10, 56010*
**Tel** *050 879 265*　　**Closed** *Sat lunch;*
*Sun; 1 wk Jan; Aug*
Traditional recipes are served by
warm and helpful staff in the
one-time home of the owners.

**PISA: Osteria del Porton Rosso** €
Regional Italian
*Via Porton Rosso 11, 56126*
**Tel** *050 580 566*　　**Closed** *Mon*
The menu is scrawled on a
blackboard at this eatery hidden
in the backstreets. Serves classic
Tuscan meat and seafood.

**PISA: La Taverna di Emma** €
Modern Italian
*Carlo Salomone Cammeo 50, 56122*
**Tel** *050 555 003*　　**Closed** *Sun;*
*1 wk Feb; last wk Aug*
Simple local eatery with a
talented chef who whips up
imaginative yet tradition-inspired
recipes. Gorgeous desserts.

**PISA: V. Beni** €€
Seafood
*Piazza Chiara Gambacorti 22, 56125*
**Tel** *050 250 67*　　**Closed** *Sun;*
*2 wks Aug*
Slightly off the tourist track, this
favorite with the locals is housed
in a rustic 600-year-old building.

**PISTOIA: La Bottegaia** €
Enoteca
*Via del Lastrone 17, 51100*
**Tel** *0573 365 602*　　**Closed** *Mon;*
*2 wks Aug*
Cheeses, cured meats, tempting
desserts, and, of course, a great
selection of wine at this friendly,
unpretentious wine bar.

The well-stocked wine cellar at Da Delfina in Artimino

**For more information on types of restaurants** *see pp578–9*

The traditionally decorated dining area of Osteria le Logge in Siena

**PRATO: Osteria Cibbè** €
Regional Italian
*Piazza Mercatale 49, 59100*
**Tel** *0574 607 509* **Closed** *Sun; 3 wks Aug*
Try the traditional Tuscan recipes and comforting homemade desserts at this charming eatery.

**SAN GIMIGNANO: Antica Macelleria** €
Regional Italian
*Via dei Marsili 1/3, 53037*
**Tel** *0577 942 228*
Pick your meat from the old-style butcher's counter and the chef will prepare it to your liking.

**SAN GIMIGNANO: Dorandò** €€
Regional Italian
*Vicolo dell'Oro 2, 53037*
**Tel** *0577 941 862* **Closed** *Dec–Feb*
Enjoy beautifully cooked locally sourced produce at Dorandò.

**SAN SEPOLCRO: Ristorante da Ventura** €
Regional Italian
*Via Aggiunti Niccolò 30, 52037*
**Tel** *0575 742 560* **Closed** *Sun dinner, Mon; 2 wks Aug*
Enjoy homemade delights at this family-run eatery. Try the slow-cooked veal or the truffle-filled ravioli.

**SIENA: Enoteca i Terzi** €
Enoteca
*Via dei Termini 7, 53100*
**Tel** *0577 443 29* **Closed** *Sun*
Airy, spacious wine bar with copious varieties of cheeses and smoked and cured meats.

**SIENA: Grotta Santa Caterina da Bagoga** €
Regional Italian
*Via della Galluzza 26, 53100*
**Tel** *0577 282 208* **Closed** *Sun dinner, Mon; 2 wks Jan; 1 wk Jul*
Tucked in a narrow backstreet this authentic restaurant offers good food and great service.

## DK Choice

**SIENA: Oro di Siena** €
Regional Italian
*Via Garibaldi 61–65, 53100*
**Tel** *0577 28 27 29*
A gem: a cosy restaurant, aimed at locals, serving traditional Tuscan food at reasonable prices. Don't let the unattractive exterior stop you from enjoying the homemade pastas, the *tagliata* steak and other Sienese dishes. Great service and excellent value for money.

**SIENA: La Taverna di San Giuseppe** €
Regional Italian
*Via Giovanni Duprè 132, 53100*
**Tel** *0577 422 86* **Closed** *Sun; 2 wks Jul; 2 wks Dec*
Rustic eatery with local flavors. Check out the wine cellar, carved from an ancient Etruscan dwelling.

**SIENA: Trattoria Papei** €
Regional Italian
*Piazza del Mercato 6, 53100*
**Tel** *0577 280 894*
This informal spot is run by an entire family, with mamma preparing Tuscan specialties.

**SIENA: Osteria le Logge** €€
Modern Italian
*Via del Porrione 33, 53100*
**Tel** *0577 480 13* **Closed** *Sun; 1 wk Jan*
This lovely restaurant with traditional furnishings serves novel interpretations of classic cuisine and has a fine wine list.

**SIENA: Tre Cristi** €€
Enoteca
*Vicolo di Provenzano 1–7, 53100*
**Tel** *0577 280 608* **Closed** *Sun*
Excellent seafood restaurant, away from the tourist area, with plenty of atmosphere and attentive service.

**VIAREGGIO: Cabreo** €€
Seafood
*Via Firenze 14, 55049*
**Tel** *0584 546 43* **Closed** *Sun; Nov*
The day's catch is cooked and brought straight to your plate at this authentic fish eatery. Meat dishes are available.

**VIAREGGIO: Piccolo Principe** €€€
Fine dining
*Piazza Giacomo Puccini 1, 55049*
**Tel** *0584 40 11* **Closed** *Nov–May*
Creative and sophisticated cuisine served in a rooftop garden with magnificent sea views. Its two Michelin stars are well earned.

**VOLTERRA: Enoteca del Duca** €
Enoteca
*Via di Castello 2, 56048*
**Tel** *0588 815 10* **Closed** *Tue; Jan; Feb*
Cosy wine bar serving rustic snacks. There's also an elegant restaurant for full meals in the typical Tuscan tradition.

**VOLTERRA: Il Sacco Fiorentino** €
Regional Italian
*Via Turazza 13, 56048*
**Tel** *0588 885 37* **Closed** *Tue; 1 wk Jan*
An intriguing tasting menu, as well as numerous à la carte options, offering traditional Tuscan with international touches.

# Umbria

**ASSISI: La Fortezza** €
Regional Italian
*Vicolo della Fortezza 2b, 06081*
**Tel** *075 81 29 93* **Closed** *Thu; Jul*
Mostly traditional cuisine, with some creative touches. Friendly but professional service and good price-quality ratio.

**ASSISI: I Monaci** €
Pizzeria
*Via Scalette 10, 06081*
**Tel** *075 81 25 12*
A warm and rustic pizzeria in the heart of the medieval center.

**GUBBIO: Grotta dell'Angelo** €€
Enoteca
*Via Gioia 47, 06024*
**Tel** *075 9271 747* **Closed** *Tue; Jan 7–Feb 7*
This rustic wine bar is carved into a 13th-century cave. Enjoy dining in the garden in summer.

**GUBBIO: Taverna del Lupo** €€
Regional Italian
*Via Ansidei 6, 06024*
**Tel** *075 9274 368* **Closed** *Mon*
Succulent local cuisine at this centrally located spot run by a husband-and-wife team.

**MONTEFALCO: Coccorone** €
Regional Italian
*Largo Tempestivi 11, 06036*
**Tel** *074 2379 535* **Closed** *Wed*
Traditional seasonal ingredients, including truffles and porcini mushrooms, are used to create an authentic dining experience.

**NORCIA: Il Casale degli Amici** €
Regional Italian
*Piazza San Benedetto 12, 06046*
**Tel** *0743 81 78 76* **Closed** *Wed*
Excellent Umbrian cuisine served in a simple setting in the heart of Norcia. Courteous service.

**NORCIA:**
**Taverna de' Massari** €€
Regional Italian
*Via Roma 13, 06046*
**Tel** *0743 81 62 18* **Closed** *Tue; 2 wk Jan, 1 wk Jul*
Intimate spot offering the time-honored pork dishes that make this tiny town famous.

**ORVIETO: Del Moro-Aronne** €
Regional Italian
*Via San Leonardo 7, 05018*
**Tel** *0763 34 27 63* **Closed** *Tue*
Simple, home-style cooking is served up by friendly and enthusiastic staff.

**ORVIETO: Osteria da Mamma Angela** €
Regional Italian
*Piazza del Popolo 2, 05018*
**Tel** *0763 34 27 90*
This simple trattoria in the center of town serves hearty Tuscan food at reasonable prices.

**ORVIETO: Duca di Orvieto** €€
Regional Italian
*Via della Pace 5, 05018*
**Tel** *0763 34 46 63* **Closed** *Wed*
A family-run restaurant using centuries-old local recipes. The patient staffers are happy to explain the day's specials in detail.

Traditional rustic charm at the cosy Duca di Orvieto, Orvieto

**ORVIETO: I Sette Consoli** €€
Modern Italian
*Piazza Sant'Angelo 1a, 05018*
**Tel** *0763 343 911* **Closed** *Sun dinner, Wed*
Original and imaginative cuisine in a rustic yet dignified setting. Dine in the garden in summer, weather permitting.

**PASSIGNANO SUL TRASIMENO:**
**Cacciatori da Luciano** €€€
Seafood
*Lungolago Aganor Pompilj 3, 06061*
**Tel** *075 827 210* **Closed** *Wed; Jan 6–30*
Fresh fish from the adjacent lake and delicacies from the sea are cooked using authentic recipes. Extensive wine list.

**PERUGIA: La Botte** €
Pizzeria
*Via Volte della Pace 31, 06122*
**Tel** *075 5722 679* **Closed** *Sun*
Simple, no-frills pizzeria serving delicious family recipes.

**PERUGIA: Il Falchetto** €
Modern Italian
*Via Bartolo 20, 06123*
**Tel** *075 5731 775*
Gorgeous little restaurant inside a medieval building, with seating on the piazza in summer. The menu is full of classic Umbrian dishes.

**PERUGIA:**
**Antica Trattoria San Lorenzo** €€
Modern Italian
*Piazza Danti 19/a, 06122*
**Tel** *075 5721 956*
Creative Umbrian-inspired cuisine is on offer at this cosy spot just behind the Duomo.

**PERUGIA: Borgomela** €€
Regional Italian
*Strada Tiberina Nord 224/c5, Località Tavernacce, 06134*
**Tel** *075 60 42 45* **Closed** *Sun dinner; Mon, Tue*
This family-run restaurant offers a range of traditional dishes with elegance but without pretension.

**PERUGIA: Il Gradale** €€
Modern Italian
*Strada Monteville 3, 06126*
**Tel** *075 5717 402*
This restaurant in the grand Castello di Monterone hotel delights diners with a choice of light and sophisticated dishes.

**SPOLETO: Il Tempio del Gusto** €
Modern Italian
*Via Arco di Druso 11, 06049*
**Tel** *0743 471 21* **Closed** *Thu*
Stone floors and small tables create an intimate atmosphere in this restaurant serving creative and top-notch cuisine.

**DK Choice**

**SPOLETO: Il Tartufo** €
Regional Italian
*Piazza Giuseppe Garibaldi 24, 06049*
**Tel** *0743 40 236* **Closed** *Sun dinner, Mon*
The decor may be simple, but the local truffles that this restaurant is named after make it worth a special trip. The owners, members of the family who opened the restaurant in 1927, are dedicated to creating dishes based on traditional local recipes. In good weather, it's possible to eat outside on the bustling piazza.

**TODI:**
**Antica Hostaria della Valle** €
Modern Italian
*Via Augusto Ciuffelli 19, 06059*
**Tel** *340 818 4775* **Closed** *Mon*
Imaginative gastronomic delights at this cosy and welcoming *osteria*. The homemade pasta is the star of the show.

**TODI: Umbria** €€
Regional Italian
*Via San Bonaventura 13, 06059*
**Tel** *075 894 27 37* **Closed** *Tue*
Traditional cuisine is carefully prepared at this legendary restaurant. There is a dining terrace with picturesque views.

# Le Marche

**ANCONA: La Moretta** €
Regional Italian
*Piazza Plebiscito 52, 60121*
**Tel** *071 20 23 17* **Closed** *Sun; Jan 1–6*
This traditional restaurant has been in the same family for over 100 years. Sample the excellent *stoccafisso* (dried cod) in broth.

**ANCONA: Opera Nova della Marca** €€
Modern Italian
*Via Varano 127, Località Varano, 60131*
**Tel** *071 286 10 93* **Closed** *Mon*
Super location and creative food based on traditional cuisine. Simple decor but great service.

**ANCONA: Osteria del Baffo** €€
Regional Italian
*Via Monte Venanzio 2, 60129*
**Tel** *071 349 43* **Closed** *Sun dinner; Mon*
At the end of the shoreline walk, up on a cliff, you find the best location in Ancona: a terrace with gorgeous views of the sea. Excellent fish and great service.

**ASCOLI PICENO: Nonna Nina** €
Regional Italian
*Piazza della Viola 11, 63100*
**Tel** *0736 25 15 23* **Closed** *Mon*
Popular with locals, this great
family-run restaurant serves
traditional food at reasonable
prices. Try the homemade pasta.

**ASCOLI PICENO: Del Corso** €€
Seafood
*Corso Giuseppe Mazzini 277, 63100*
**Tel** *0736 25 67 60* **Closed** *3 wks Jan,
Dec 2*
Tiny stone-walled restaurant
located in a historic palazzo. Most
dishes on the changing menu
are fish-based.

**LORETO: Andreina** €
Regional Italian
*Via Buffolareccia 14, 60025*
**Tel** *071 97 01 24* **Closed** *Tue,
Wed*
Rustic place with a few modern
touches. Serves Tuscan specialties
and tempting grilled meats.

**LORETO: Vecchia Fattoria** €
Regional Italian
*Via Manzoni 19, 60025*
**Tel** *071 97 89 76*
This converted farmhouse offers
classic regional dishes in a
welcoming family atmosphere.

**PESARO: Da Gennaro** €
Seafood
*Via Santa Marina Alta 30/1, 61100*
**Tel** *0721 273 21* **Closed** *Sun dinner,
Mon; Sep 1–20*
Perched in the mountains 4 miles
(7 km) west of the sea, this is one
of the most authentic eateries in
town.

**PESARO: Il Commodoro** €€
Enoteca
*Viale Trieste 269, 61121*
**Tel** *0721 326 80* **Closed** *Mon*
This inviting modern spot serves
up fresh fish and much more.
Cosy wine bar attached.

**PESARO: Da Alceo** €€€
Seafood
*Strada Panoramica Ardizio 101,
61100*
**Tel** *0721 513 60*
A panoramic seaside terrace
provides an exquisite setting in
which to sample some of the
best seafood in the area.

**SAN MARINO:**
**Righi la Taverna** €€€
Fine dining
*Piazzale della Libertà 10, 47825*
**Tel** *0549 99 11 96* **Closed** *Sun dinner,
Mon; Jan, Feb*
The most famous restaurant in
this republic serves a mix of age-
old and modern Italian cuisine.

**URBANIA: Big Ben** €
Regional Italian
*Corso V. Emanuele 61, 61049*
**Tel** *0722 31 97 95*
Marchegiana specialties such as
truffles, snails, and wild fennel are
offered at this restaurant.

**URBINO: Guanábana** €
Modern Italian
*Via Giuseppe Mazzini 65, 61029*
**Tel** *366 726 55 51*
This quirky little restaurant offers
an interesting fusion of local and
Venezuelan cuisines.

**URBINO: Taverna degli Artisti** €
Regional Italian
*Via Donato Bramante 52, 61029*
**Tel** *0722 26 76*
Opulent frescoed ceilings make a
dramatic contrast to the simple
home-style cooking.

**URBINO:**
**Antica Osteria da la Stella** €€
Regional Italian
*Via Santa Margherita 1, 61029*
**Tel** *0722 320228*
This historic restaurant counts
famous painters Raphael and
Piero della Francesca among its
one-time clientele. Elegant
interior with a cosy fireplace.

# Rome

## The Ancient Center

**Enoteca Provincia Romana** €
Enoteca **Map** 3 A4
*Largo di Foro Traiano 82–4, 00187*
**Tel** *06 69 94 02 73* **Closed** *Sun &
Mon dinner*
Both the wine list and the menu
are local here, and the view of
the Imperial fora is spectacular.

**Aroma** €€€
Fine dining **Map** 7 1A
*Via Labicana 125, 00184*
**Tel** *06 77 59 13 80*
Views of the Colosseum and a
seasonal menu of local favorites
prepared to the highest standards.

## Around Piazza Navona

**Acchiappafantasmi** €
Pizzeria **Map** 9 B3
*Via dei Cappellari 66, 00186*
**Tel** *06 687 34 62* **Closed** *Mon*
Its name means "ghostbusters"
and the ghost-shaped pizzas are
tasty and amusing. The rest of the
menu is full of Calabrian dishes.

**Angolo Divino** €
Enoteca **Map** 9 C4
*Via dei Balestrari 12, 00186*
**Tel** *06 686 44 13* **Closed** *Sun & Mon
lunch; Aug 10–20*

Intimate and romantic spot for
classic fare made with organic
ingredients. The warm chocolate
cake is divine, as is the wine list.

**Baffetto** €
Pizzeria **Map** 9 B3
*Via del Governo Vecchio 114, 00186*
**Tel** *06 686 16 17*
The crunchy Roman-style pizza is
said to be the best in Rome, but
be prepared to wait and to share
a table when you do get served.

**Cul de Sac** €
Enoteca **Map** 9 C3
*Piazza di Pasquino 73, 00186*
**Tel** *06 68 80 10 94* **Closed** *Dec 24,
25 & 31*
This narrow wine bar with a patio
boasts hundreds of labels, as well
as a wide variety of tasty eats,
both traditional and creative.

**Da Giggetto** €
Regional Italian **Map** 10 E5
*Via del Portico d'Ottavia 21/22, 00186*
**Tel** *06 686 11 05* **Closed** *Mon; last
2 wks Aug, Dec 24 & 31*
Dine near ancient ruins at this
Jewish-Roman eatery. Don't miss
the deep-fried artichokes.

**Nonna Betta** €
Regional Italian **Map** 10 E5
*Via del Portico d'Ottavia 16, 00186*
**Tel** *06 68 80 62 63* **Closed** *Tue*
An authentic Jewish eatery (but
without kosher certification). Don't
expect an English translation on
the menu, but the food is great.

**Old Bear** €
Regional Italian **Map** 9 C2
*Via dei Gigli d'Oro 2–4, 00186*
**Tel** *06 68 21 00 09* **Closed** *Apr;
Nov: Mon*
Dark wood beams and low ceilings
create a warm ambience. Don't
miss the Tuscan soup with truffle
oil or the truffle-flavored eggs.

Diners at the well-known Jewish-Roman
eatery Nonna Betta

### Open Baladin €
Birreria **Map** 10 D5
*Via degli Specchi 6, 00186*
**Tel** *06 683 89 89* **Closed** *Sun; 2 wks Aug, 24, 25 & 31 Dec*
More than 20 craft beers on offer, plus all-natural sodas. Staple snack food, such as sandwiches with cured meats, is served.

### Osteria del Gallo €
Regional Italian **Map** 2 E3
*Vicolo di Montevecchio 27, 00186*
**Tel** *06 687 37 81*
An informal trattoria that serves classic Roman specialties alongside fish dishes. Lots of outdoor space on the piazza.

### Il Bacaro €€
Modern Italian **Map** 10 D2
*Via degli Spagnoli 27, 00186*
**Tel** *06 687 25 54*
Romantic restaurant with dishes such as trofie with asparagus and beef *carpaccio* with truffles, plus a plethora of Roman specialties.

### Hostaria dell'Orso €€
Fine dining **Map** 9 C2
*Via dei Soldati 25c, 00186*
**Tel** *06 68 30 11 92* **Closed** *Aug*
This restaurant and nightclub in a beautiful old house, has been welcoming guests since the 1500s.

### Il Pagliaccio €€
Fine dining **Map** 9 B2
*Via dei Banchi Vecchi 129, 00186*
**Tel** *06 68 80 95 95* **Closed** *Mon & Tue lunch; Aug*
Michelin-starred restaurant serving a blend of Mediterranean and pan-Asian fare. Some tasting menus have up to 12 courses.

### Roscioli €€
Enoteca **Map** 9 C4
*Via dei Giubbonari 21, 00186*
**Tel** *06 687 52 87* **Closed** *Sun*
Part wine bar, part salumeria with drool-worthy meats and cheese and a dizzying selection of labels.

### Terra di Siena €€
Regional Italian **Map** 9 C3
*Piazza di Pasquino 77, 00186*
**Tel** *06 68 30 77 04* **Closed** *Sun in summer*
Hearty Tuscan dishes – Florentine steak and ribollita soup – in a cheerful dining room or on the lively square, near Piazza Navona.

### Camponeschi €€€
Fine dining **Map** 9 C4
*Piazza Farnese, 50/50a, 00186*
**Tel** *06 687 49 27* **Closed** *Sun*
World-class dining with a view of one of Rome's most beautiful piazzas. Try *tagliolini* with lobster and black truffles; wild game is the house specialty.

The classic exterior of La Carbonara in Northeast Rome

### La Rosetta €€€
Fine dining **Map** 9 C4
*Via della Rosetta 8/9, 00186*
**Tel** *06 686 10 02*
The daily catch is cooked in a variety of ways – or served raw as *carpaccio*. Great oysters, too.

## Northeast Rome

### Antica Birreria Peroni €
Birreria **Map** 10 F3
*Via di San Marcello 19, 00187*
**Tel** *06 679 53 10* **Closed** *Sun; Aug 2 & 5; Dec 24, 25 & 31*
Casual spot that's been serving beer for over 100 years (wine is also available). All-Italian grilled beef and pork is on the menu.

### La Campana €
Regional Italian **Map** 10 D1
*Vicolo della Campana 18, 00186*
**Tel** *06 687 52 73* **Closed** *Mon; Aug*
Packed any night of the week, this restaurant dating from 1518 is the oldest in Rome. Traditional favorites are served, plus pizza.

### La Carbonara €
Regional Italian **Map** 3 C4
*Via Panisperna 214, 00184*
**Tel** *06 482 51 76* **Closed** *Sun; Aug*
This busy *osteria* serves hearty local fare. Try the fried vegetables or the delicious carbonara.

### Cavour 313 €
Enoteca **Map** 3 C5
*Via Cavour 313, 00184*
**Tel** *06 678 54 96* **Closed** *Sun in summer*
The staff will help you select a vintage to match your food in this wood-lined wine bar.

### 'Gusto €
Pizzeria **Map** 2 F2
*Piazza Augusto Imperatore 9, 00186*
**Tel** *06 322 62 73* **Closed** *Jan 1, Dec 24*
Factory-like setting with exposed brick and iron for Neapolitan-style pizzas. Good Sunday brunch, too.

### Hang Zhou €
Chinese **Map** 4 E5
*Via Principe Eugenio 82, 00184*
**Tel** *06 487 27 32* **Closed** *Aug*
Said to offer the best Chinese food in town. The all-you-can-eat buffet is a steal; other meals are higher than average. Reserve.

### San Marco €
Pizzeria **Map** 3 C1
*Via Sardegna 38, 00187*
**Tel** *06 42 01 26 20* **Closed** *1 wk Aug; Dec 24*
A large wine bar and grill noted for its pizzas and warm service. Blackboard specials include fish and meat dishes.

### Ai Tre Scalini €
Enoteca **Map** 3 C4
*Via Panisperna 251, 00184*
**Tel** *06 48 90 74 95*
One of the hippest wine bars in town, with excellent wines, beers and savory delicacies.,

### Trimani il Wine Bar €
Enoteca **Map** 4 D2
*Via Cernaia 37b, 00185*
**Tel** *06 446 96 30* **Closed** *Sun; Jan 1; 2 wks Aug; Dec 25 & 26*
Modern wine bar with labels that pair perfectly with cold and hot dishes, as well as Italian cheeses.

### Ambasciata d'Abruzzo €€
Regional Italian
*Via Pietro Tacchini 26, 00197*
**Tel** *06 807 82 56* **Closed** *3 wks Aug*
Traditional Abruzzese dishes, such as *maccheroni* with lamb ragù, mingle with Roman favorites in a convivial setting.

### Cuoco e Camicia €€
Modern Italian **Map** 3 C5
*Via di Monte Polacco 2/4, 00184*
**Tel** *06 88 92 29 87* **Closed** *Sun, Sat lunch; 2 wks Aug*
Cheerful restaurant that prides itself on using only fresh, local ingredients. Try the octopus salad or opt for the tasting menu.

**For more information on types of restaurants** *see pp578–9*

**Doozo** €€
Japanese **Map** 3 C4
*Via Palermo 51, 00184*
**Tel** *06 481 56 55* **Closed** *Sun lunch,*
*Mon; 1 wk Aug; Dec 22–Jan 15*
Excellent sushi at this restaurant
and cultural center with a garden.
It also offers origami courses.

**Hamasei** €€
Japanese **Map** 10 F1
*Via della Mercede 35/36, 00187*
**Tel** *06 679 21 34* **Closed** *Mon; Aug*
Inventive sushi and sashimi
dishes, plus a selection of hot
meals, in a minimalist setting,
with low tables for authentic
Japanese dining.

**Imàgo** €€
Fine dining **Map** 3 A2
*Piazza Trinità dei Monti 6, 00187*
**Tel** *06 69 93 47 26* **Closed** *lunch*
Creative Italian cuisine and
exceptional views from the top
of the Spanish Steps. The desserts
are divine and the wine list is
expertly chosen.

**Osteria Margutta** €€
Modern Italian **Map** 3 A2
*Via Margutta 82b, 00187*
**Tel** *06 323 10 25* **Closed** *Sun dinner,*
*Mon lunch; 1 wk Aug*
Historic restaurant on a vine-
covered street serving classic
Roman fare with a modern twist.
The restaurant's motto is "art in
the kitchen."

**Trattoria Monti** €€
Regional Italian **Map** 4 D4
*Via di San Vito 13, 00185*
**Tel** *06 446 65 73* **Closed** *Sun dinner,*
*Mon; Aug, Dec 24–Jan 3*
The cuisine hails from Le Marche
region, and the ingredients are
all local, seasonal, and carefully
selected. A heavenly spot.

**Urbana 47** €€
Modern Italian **Map** 3 C4
*Via Urbana 47, 00184*
**Tel** *06 47 88 40 06* **Closed** *2 wks Aug*
An eclectic place with vintage
decor, serving creative and
delicious dishes that are the
result of extensive research.
Great range of desserts and
exceptional value.

**Oliver Glowig** €€€
Fine dining
*Via Ulisse Aldrovandi 15, 00197*
**Tel** *06 321 61 26* **Closed** *Sun & Mon*
*in winter, Sun only in summer*
The chef is German, but the
menu is 100% Mediterranean
at this luxury hotel restaurant.
Try delicacies such as scampi
with artichoke heart and *burrata*
cheese, or fish dishes combining
Roman and Sicilian traditions.

Sleek interiors at the Japanese restaurant Doozo, northeast Rome

# The Vatican and Trastevere

**Antica Osteria Rugantino** €
Roman **Map** 6 D1
*Via della Lungaretta 54, 00153*
**Tel** *06 581 85 17*
Specializing in pasta dishes, this
rustic place serves traditional
Roman fare in a typical Trastevere
setting. Pleasant outdoor patio.

**Bir and Fud** €
Birreria **Map** 2 E5
*Via Benedetta 23, 00153*
**Tel** *06 589 40 16* **Closed** *Dec 25 & 31*
Boutique beers and microbrews
accompany crusty pizzas and
gourmet fries at this popular and
hip joint in Trastevere.

**Brasserie 4.20** €
Birreria **Map** 5 C3
*Via Portuense 82, 00153*
**Tel** *06 58 31 07 37*
Craft beers from around the
world are paired with snacks
such as burgers, fries, and
hotdogs at this welcoming spot.

**Da Gildo** €
Regional Italian **Map** 2 D5
*Via della Scala 31/a, 00153*
**Tel** *06 580 07 33* **Closed** *Thu*
Quirky decoration and a cosy
outdoor seating area. Try the
divine *gnocchi alla romana* (baked
*gnocchi* with cheese on top).

**Ivo a Trastevere** €
Pizzeria **Map** 5 C1
*Via di San Francesco a Ripa 158, 00153*
**Tel** *06 581 70 82* **Closed** *Tue*
A wide range of snacks and
thin-crusted pizza have this
eatery bustling with locals.

**Meridionale** €
Southern Italian **Map** 5 C1
*Via dei Fienaroli 30/a, 00153*
**Tel** *06 589 71 96*
All pasta is homemade at this
modern restaurant attracting

a youthful crowd. Creative
specialties include a shellfish
pasta dish and pasta with
octopus. For dessert, try the
superb *tiramisù*.

**Panattoni L'Obitorio** €
Pizzeria **Map** 5 C1
*Viale di Trastevere 53, 00153*
**Tel** *06 580 09 19* **Closed** *Wed;*
*Aug 10 & 28*
Nicknamed "the morgue" for
its long marble-top tables.
Try the *supplì al telefono* (fried
rice balls).

**Dar Poeta** €
Pizzeria **Map** 2 E5
*Vicolo del Bologna 45, 00153*
**Tel** *06 588 05 16* **Closed** *Dec, 24 & 31*
Perfect balance between thick-
and thin-crusted pizza at this
joyfully hectic spot. The buffalo
mozzarella topping is unmatched.

**Il Sorpasso** €
Roman **Map** 1 C2
*Via Properzio 31–33, 00193*
**Tel** *06 89 02 45 54* **Closed** *Sun*
Il Sorpasso delivers simple
dishes that are big on flavor.
Everything is made using fresh,
organic ingredients sourced from
the surrounding countryside.

**Trattoria da Lucia** €
Regional Italian **Map** 5 B1
*Vicolo del Mattonato 2b, 00153*
**Tel** *06 580 36 01* **Closed** *Mon; 2 wks*
*Aug; Dec 24, 25 & 31*
Simple pasta dishes, as well as
more hearty meals and delicious
homemade desserts, are served
in a traditional setting.

**Antico Arco** €€
Fine dining **Map** 5 A1
*Piazzale Aurelio 7, 00152*
**Tel** *06 581 52 74* **Closed** *1 Jan*
Truffles and tuna tartare are
made to perfection at this
romantic restaurant with a
superb wine list.

### Arlù €€
Regional Italian **Map** 1 C3
*Borgo Pio 135, 00193*
**Tel** *06 686 89 36* **Closed** *Sun lunch; Jan 1; 2 wks Aug; Dec 25 & 26*
The most authentic restaurant in the area. A husband-and-wife team serves up delectable cuisine. Great choice of drinks and desserts.

### Isole di Sicilia €€
Regional Italian **Map** 5 B1
*Via Garibaldi 68, 00153*
**Tel** *06 58 33 42 12* **Closed** *Mon–Fri lunch*
The elaborate dishes here are inspired by the cuisine of the tiny islands around Sicily. The antipasto, in particular, is exceptional.

### DK Choice

**Osteria La Gensola** €€
**Roman and Sicilian** **Map** 6 D1
*Piazza della Gensola 15, 00153*
**Tel** *06 581 63 12*
An intimate, family-run space specializing in raw fish dishes and wonderful pastas, such as the *tagliolini* with calamari.

### Spirito Divino €€
Modern Italian **Map** 6 D1
*Via dei Genovesi 31, 00153*
**Tel** *06 589 66 89* **Closed** *Sun*
Fine dishes served in a converted medieval synagogue; take a peek in the 2,000-year-old wine cellar.

### Taverna Trilussa €€
Regional Italian **Map** 2 E5
*Via del Politeama 23, 00153*
**Tel** *06 581 89 18* **Closed** *lunch; Sun; 3 days mid-Aug; Dec 24, 25 & 31*
Locals flock here for sublime pasta dishes and decadent desserts.

### Antica Pesa €€€
Fine dining **Map** 5 B1
*Via Garibaldi 18, 00153*
**Tel** *06 580 92 36* **Closed** *Sun; Jan 1*
Enjoy exquisite cuisine – including a delicious *millefoglie* cake – in a beautifully decorated restaurant covered with murals.

### Settembrini €€€
Modern Italian
*Via Luigi Settembrini 21, 00195*
**Tel** *06 323 26 17* **Closed** *Sun, Sat lunch; 2 wks Aug*
Creative Italian cuisine that is as beautiful as it is tasty. Try the raw fish platter or the lobster.

## Aventine and Lateran

### Angelina a Testaccio €
Regional Italian **Map** 6 D3
*Via Galvani 24, 00153*
**Tel** *06 57 28 38 40* **Closed** *Sat & Sun lunch*

The gem of Testaccio, this shabby-chic bistro in a former industrial butchery offers great meat dishes and a tempting Sunday brunch.

### Oasi della Birra €
Birreria **Map** 6 D3
*Piazza Testaccio 39, 00153*
**Tel** *06 574 61 22* **Closed** *1 wk Aug; Dec 24 & 25*
This trendy bar offering Belgian craft beers and platters starts serving in the early afternoon.

### Checchino dal 1887 €€
Regional Italian **Map** 6 D4
*Via di Monte Testaccio 30, 00153*
**Tel** *06 574 38 16* **Closed** *Sun, Mon; Aug*
Lovingly prepared hearty Roman dishes, including artichoke specialties, make this restaurant a local favorite.

## Farther Afield

### La Gatta Mangiona €
Pizzeria
*Via Federico Ozanam 30, Monteverde Nuovo, 00152*
**Tel** *06 534 67 02* **Closed** *Jan 1; Aug 10–25; Dec 24–26 & 31*
This popular place dishes up pizzas with creative toppings, plus appetizers like fried cod fish and fried zucchini flowers.

### DK Choice

**Mó Mó Republic** €
Pizzeria
*Piazza Forlanini 10, Monteverde Nuovo, 00151*
**Tel** *06 537 30 87*
A 19th-century mansion is the setting for this trendy pizzeria. Huge chandeliers add to the ambience. In summer, start with an *aperitivo* on the lawn. Pasta, meat and fish are also available.

### Osteria Flaminio €
Modern Italian
*Via Flaminia 297, 00196*
**Tel** *06 323 69 00*
Trek north of the center to try the innovative Italian cuisine on offer here. The ambience is modern and pleasant, and the wine list spans the entire peninsula, from the Alps to Sicily.

### Osteria Scaloni €€
Traditional Roman
*Via Carlo Mirabello 8, 00195*
**Tel** *06 372 1593*
Simple, local dishes are given a new lease on life with unexpected ingredients and creative touches. The specialty is fish, and the wine list is excellent.

### DK Choice

**La Pergola** €€€
Fine dining
*Via Alberto Cadlolo 101, 00136*
**Tel** *06 350 91* **Closed** *Sun, Mon*
Rome's finest restaurant, La Pergola is also the only one to earn the coveted three Michelin stars. Chef Heinz Beck dazzles with exquisite Mediterranean creations. Perched atop Monte Mario hill, it offers great views of St. Peter's Basilica. There is also an award-winning wine cellar.

## Lazio

### BRACCIANO: Quattro Castagni €
Regional Italian
*Via Olmata Tre Cancelli 7, 00062*
**Tel** *06 99 84 91 55* **Closed** *Tue*
This eatery specializes in wild game and meat dishes, plus fried vegetables, all served in a rustic setting with exposed stonework.

### CASTELLI ROMANI FRASCATI: Pezzafina €
Modern Italian
*Vicolo Manara 2, 00044*
**Tel** *335 657 23 30* **Closed** *lunch daily, Sun*
This chic restaurant in a former wine cellar offers daring ingredient combinations, whilst retaining the traditional flavors.

### CERVETERI: Trattoria Zi Maria €
Regional Italian
*Via Sasso Manziana 2, 00050*
**Tel** *06 99 07 90 29* **Closed** *Tue*
Specialties here include venison with wild berries and risotto with strawberries and stinging nettles.

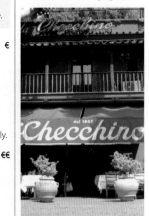

Exterior of the friendly Checchino dal 1887, known for its filling Roman dishes

For more information on types of restaurants *see pp578–9*

**GAETA: Narì** €
Seafood
*Via Duomo 15, 04024*
**Tel** *0771 46 30 94* **Closed** *Mon*
Excellent fish and pasta dishes
in the medieval center of Gaeta.
Favorites include anchovy
balls, fish soup, and roasted king
shrimp. Excellent value, too.

**OSTIA: La Bussola** €€
Seafood
*Lungomare A. Vespucci 72, 00122*
**Tel** *06 56 47 08 67* **Closed** *Mon*
Inspired by the recipes of the
owners' great aunt. Try the
gnocchi with octopus and the
fish stew, or stop by for an aperitif
of oysters and white wine.

**SERMONETA: Il Giardino del
Simposio** €€
Modern Italian
*Via della Conduttura 1, 04010*
**Tel** *339 284 69 05* **Closed** *Mon & Tue;
Jan & Feb: Sat & Sun*
Innovative dishes such as pasta
with fresh ricotta and wild fennel
served amid the trees of a
picturesque garden.

**SPERLONGA: Gli Archi** €€
Traditional Italian
*Via Ottaviano 17, 04029*
**Tel** *0771 54 83 00* **Closed** *Wed; Jan*
Simple traditional cuisine in the
heart of this seaside village. For
dessert, try the delicious mousse
made with buffalo ricotta cheese.
Outdoor seating in warm weather.

**TARQUINIA: Lupo di Mare** €
Italian
*Strada Porto Clementino 21, 01016*
**Tel** *347 545 81 84*
This poolside restaurant specializes
in traditional fish cuisine. Try the
antipasto Lupo di Mare, consisting
of mussels, couscous, squid,
oysters, calamari, and shrimp.

**TIVOLI: Avec 55** €€
Modern Italian
*Via Domenico Giuliani 55, 00019*
**Tel** *0774 31 72 43* **Closed** *Mon*

The gastronomic creations at this
"cooking workshop" (as the owners
call it) are paired with great wine.

**TIVOLI: La Sibilla** €€
Regional Italian
*Via della Sibilla 42, 00019*
**Tel** *0774 33 52 81* **Closed** *Mon*
Fine views of the Roman ruins
provide a great setting to indulge
in high-quality regional cuisine.

### DK Choice

**VITERBO: Il Labirinto** €
Pizzeria
*Via di San Lorenzo 46, 00100*
**Tel** *0761 30 70 26* **Closed** *Mon*
Enjoy a variety of traditional
*bruschette*, pizza, pasta, and
main courses. The outdoor
seating area is next to a quaint
fountain and a medieval church.

**VITERBO: Ristorantino
La Torre** €
Fine dining
*Via della Torre 5, 01100*
**Tel** *0761 22 64 67* **Closed** *Mon
lunch; Sun; 3 wks Aug*
The chef and sommelier create
an unforgettable dining
experience at this vibrant spot.

**VITERBO: Villa San Michele** €€
Fine dining
*Via de la Quercia, Vitorchiano, 01030*
**Tel** *0761 37 34 41* **Closed** *Mon, Tue*
The menu at this elegant country
villa includes smoked baby
calamari au gratin, and risotto
with squash and anchovies.

# Naples and Campania

**AMALFI:
Da Ciccio Cielo Mare Terra** €€
Regional Italian
*Via Nazionale per Sorrento, 84011*
**Tel** *089 83 12 65* **Closed** *Tue; Jan, Nov*

Great views of the coastline are
matched by the delicious food.

**AMALFI: La Caravella** €€€
Fine dining
*Via Matteo Camera 12, 84011*
**Tel** *089 87 10 29* **Closed** *Tue; Jan, Nov*
The Michelin-starred chef here
uses local flavors to exalt the
regional cuisine.

**BENEVENTO: Pascalucci** €€
Regional Italian
*Via Appia 1, 82010*
**Tel** *0824 77 84 00* **Closed** *winter*
Simple recipes prepared with
fresh local ingredients.

**CAPRI: Da Gelsomina** €€
Regional Italian
*Via Migliara 72, 80071*
**Tel** *081 837 14 99* **Closed** *Tue;
Jan–Feb*
Much of the produce is grown
onsite at this delightful restaurant.

**CAPRI: Da Paolino** €€
Regional Italian
*Via Palazzo a Mare 11, 80073*
**Tel** *081 837 61 02* **Closed** *Oct–Apr*
Rustic country restaurant with
rich regional cuisine.

**CAPRI: L'Olivo** €€€
Fine dining
*Via Capodimonte 14, 80071*
**Tel** *081 978 01 11* **Closed** *mid-Oct–
mid-Apr*
Uses saffron, bergamot, fava
beans, and asparagus to make
gorgeous flavor combinations.

**CAPRI: Il Riccio** €€€
Seafood
*Via Grotta Azzurra 11, 80071*
**Tel** *081 837 13 80* **Closed** *Nov–Mar*
Pleasant atmosphere in which to
enjoy exceptional seafood dishes.

**CASERTA: Antica Locanda** €
Regional Italian
*Piazza della Seta 7, 81100*
**Tel** *0823 30 54 44* **Closed** *Sun dinner;
Mon; Aug; Dec 24 & 31*
Simple, characterful *osteria* with
rustic details. Southern Italian
cooking and excellent risotto.

**CASERTA: Leucio** €
Seafood
*Via Giardini Reali 86, 81100*
**Tel** *0823 30 12 41* **Closed** *Sun dinner;
Mon; 1 wk Aug*
Exceptional prices at this simple
fish restaurant run by a father
and son. Also serves great pasta.

**CASERTA: Le Colonne** €€
Fine dining
*Viale Giulio Douhet 7, 81100*
**Tel** *0823 46 74 94* **Closed** *Tue*
Indulge in superbly reinterpreted
local cuisine in a luxurious setting.

Romantic dining amid lemon trees at Da Paolino, Capri

Sunny patio of the Neapolitan gem, Il Comandante

### ISCHIA AND PROCIDA:
**Lo Scoglio** €
Seafood
*Via Cava Ruffano 58, Sant'Angelo, 80077*
**Tel** *081 999529*
Stunningly located on a rock jutting over the sea, this simple restaurant serves quality fish. There is also a good selection of wine.

### ISCHIA AND PROCIDA:
**La Stadera** €
Enoteca
*Via C. Maddalena 15, Sant'Angelo, 80070*
**Tel** *081 99 98 93*
Narrow alleys lead to this *enoteca*, where the owners delight in pairing delicious food with unusual wines and liqueurs.

### ISCHIA AND PROCIDA:
**La Tinaia** €
Pizzeria
*Via Matteo Verde 39, Forio, 80075*
**Tel** *081 99 84 48* **Closed** *Dec 24*
Fantastic thick-crusted pizza, as well as pasta and seafood. Basic but friendly service.

### ISCHIA AND PROCIDA:
**Alberto** €€
Modern Italian
*Via Cristoforo Colombo 8, Ischia, 80077*
**Tel** *081 98 12 59* **Closed** *Nov–Mar*
Sample creatively reinterpreted traditional Italian seafood specialties at this lovely beach-front restaurant.

### ISCHIA AND PROCIDA:
**Gorgonia** €€
Seafood
*Via Marina di Corricella 50, Procida, 80079*
**Tel** *081 810 10 60*
Opt for the catch of the day at this delightful restaurant set high above a picturesque bay.

### ISCHIA AND PROCIDA:
**Il Mosaico** €€€
Fine dining
*Piazza Bagni, Casamicciola Terme, 80074*
**Tel** *081 99 47 22* **Closed** *lunch; Wed; mid-Oct–Mar*
Rich Neapolitan cuisine inspires this multitalented chef's innovative and exquisite menu. The wine list is excellent and the desserts are divine.

### DK Choice

### ISCHIA AND PROCIDA:
**Umberto a Mare** €€€
Fine dining
*Via del Soccorso 2, Forio, 80075*
**Tel** *081 99 71 71* **Closed** *Nov–Mar*
Time seems to stand still as you take a seat on the tiny terrace that juts out over the sea in the shadow of the evocative Santa Maria del Sorrorso church. The tasting menus feature gastronomic delights from all over the Mediterranean. The wine selection is outstanding, and staffers attend to every need.

### NAPLES: Di Matteo €
Pizzeria
*Via dei Tribunali 94, 80138*
**Tel** *081 455 262* **Closed** *Sun*
A Naples institution serving classic chewy pizza and tasty *fritti* (fried food). Popular with locals and celebrities.

### DK Choice

### NAPLES: Da Michele €
Pizzeria
*Via Cesare Sersale 1, 80139*
**Tel** *081 553 92 04* **Closed** *Sun*
A trip to Naples wouldn't be complete without a Margherita here, probably the most famous pizzeria in the world. Come early, or be prepared to wait outside. Only Margherita and Marinara pizzas are served.

### NAPLES: La Notizia €
Pizzeria
*Via Michelangelo da Caravaggio 53, 80126*
**Tel** *081 714 21 55* **Closed** *Mon; Aug; Dec 24*
Tiny pizzas with intense flavors at this popular spot, considered one of the world's best pizzerias.

### NAPLES: La Piazzetta €
Regional Italian
*Via Nazario Sauro 21, 80132*
**Tel** *081 764 61 95*
Traditional local fare and pizzas at this quaint restaurant designed to look like a small-town piazza.

### NAPLES: Sorbillo €
Pizzeria
*Via dei Tribunali 32, 80138*
**Tel** *081 033 10 09* **Closed** *Sun; 1 wk Feb*
A comfortable setting, good pizza and attentive service for a great price.

### NAPLES: La Cantinella €€
Fine dining
*Via Cuma 42, 80132*
**Tel** *081 764 86 84* **Closed** *Sun dinner*
A bamboo forest is re-created in this award-winning restaurant with an imaginative chef.

### NAPLES: Kukai Nibu €€
Japanese
*Via Carlo de Cesare 52, 80132*
**Tel** *081 41 19 05*
Generous portions of sushi and sashimi; a glass kitchen allows diners a great view of the action.

### NAPLES: La Scialuppa €€
Seafood
*Piazzetta Marinari 5, 80132*
**Tel** *081 764 53 33* **Closed** *Mon; Jan*
Right on the gulf, this traditional restaurant serves fresh fish, as well as pasta and pizza.

### NAPLES: Il Comandante €€€
Fine dining
*Via Cristoforo Colombo, 80133*
**Tel** *081 017 50 01* **Closed** *Tue*
The chef at this Michelin-starred restaurant creates exquisite dishes from a few basic ingredients.

### NAPLES: Palazzo Petrucci €€€
Modern Italian
*Via Posillipo 16, 80123*
**Tel** *081 575 75 38* **Closed** *Sun dinner, Mon lunch; Aug 2–4; Dec 25*
This Michelin-starred restaurant in a splendid villa on the sea serves modern fare from local produce.

### POSITANO: Rada Restaurant €
Regional
*Via Grotte dell'Incanto 51, 84017*
**Tel** *089 87 58 74* **Closed** *Oct–Apr*
Wine bar with panoramic sea views. The wine cellar is carved right into the hillside rock.

### POSITANO: Chez Black €€
Seafood
*Via del Brigantino, 84017*
**Tel** *089 87 50 36* **Closed** *mid-Jan–mid-Feb*
Idyllic beachfront location. Serves traditional fish recipes.

### POSITANO: Zass €€
Fine dining
*Via Laurito 2, 84017*
**Tel** *089 87 54 55*
Mouthwateringly delicious examples of regional cuisine. Desserts to die for.

### SALERNO: Addor I Pizza €
Pizzeria
*Piazza San Francesco d'Assisi, 84122*
**Tel** *089 24 18 76* **Closed** *Sun lunch*
Courteous service in this tiny
pizzeria that also serves pasta.

### SALERNO: Osteria Dedicato
a mio Padre €€
Seafood
*Vicolo Giudaica 8, 84100*
**Tel** *089 23 15 55* **Closed** *Sun*
Numerous varieties of fresh fish,
served up in a cosy setting in the
heart of the historic center.

### SALERNO: Il Timone €€
Seafood
*Via Generale Clarke 29/35, 84131*
**Tel** *089 33 51 11* **Closed** *Mon;*
*Aug 15–31*
Friendly, bright seafood restaurant
with fast, courteous service.

### SORRENTO: Zi'ntonio €
Regional Italian
*Via Luigi De Maio 11, 80067*
**Tel** *081 878 16 23*
Local dishes served in a room
with exposed tufa blocks and
wood-beamed ceilings.

### SORRENTO: La Basilica €€
Regional Italian
*Via Sant'Antonino 28, 80067*
**Tel** *081 877 47 90*
It's possible to dine until 1am at
this restaurant. Fish, meat, and
vegetarian options in classic
regional style.

### SORRENTO: Il Buco €€
Modern Italian
*Il Rampa Marina Piccola 5, 80067*
**Tel** *081 878 23 54* **Closed** *Wed; Jan*
Elegant yet informal restaurant
housed in the cellar of an ancient
monastery. A perfect blend of
tradition and more daring cuisine.

---

# Abruzzo, Molise, and Puglia

### ALBEROBELLO: Trullo d'Oro €
Regional Italian
*Via Felice Cavallotti 27, 70011*
**Tel** *080 432 18 20* **Closed** *Mon*
Local cuisine in the characterful
setting of an authentic *trullo*.
Great *antipasto* spread.

### ALBEROBELLO: Il Poeta
Contadino €€
Fine dining
*Via Indipendenza 21, 70011*
**Tel** *080 432 19 17* **Closed** *Mon (exc*
*Aug); Jan (exc group reservations)*
Awarded a Michelin star for its
delectable regional cuisine and
heavenly desserts. The location
is stunning.

Homey setting for regional cuisine at Il Cortiletto, Lucera

### BARI:
Osteria delle Travi "Il Buco" €
Regional Italian
*Largo Ignazio Chiurlia 12, 70122*
**Tel** *339 157 88 48* **Closed** *Sun*
*dinner, Mon*
Authentic home-style cooking in
the old Pugliese-style *osteria*.

### BARI: Biancofore €€
Modern Italian
*Corso Vittorio Emanuele II 13, 70122*
**Tel** *080 523 54 46* **Closed** *Mon*
People come to one of the best
eateries in Bari for modern takes
on traditional dishes, coupled
with an extensive wine list.

### GARGANO PENINSULA:
Medioevo €
Regional Italian
*Via Castello 21, 71037*
**Tel** *0884 56 53 56* **Closed** *Nov:*
*dinner; Dec–Feb: Mon*
This simple *osteria* uses the best
seasonal produce available. Meat
and soup are specialties.

### GARGANO PENINSULA:
Al Dragone €€
Regional Italian
*Via Duomo 8, 71019*
**Tel** *0884 70 12 12* **Closed** *Apr–Nov:*
*Tue; Dec–Mar*
Dining in this restaurant built into
a natural cave is an experience in
itself. Delicious regional dishes
and a good wine list.

### GARGANO PENINSULA:
Porta di Basso €€
Seafood
*Via Cristoforo Colombo 38, 71010*
**Tel** *0884 35 51 67*
Creative reinterpretations of
Pugliese fish recipes. Located
on a cliff above the sea.

### ISOLE TREMITI: La Nassa €
Seafood
*Via Aldo Moro 24, 71040*
**Tel** *0882 46 33 45* **Closed** *Easter;*
*Apr–Oct*
Nestled in a lush garden, this
restaurant offers fresh fish served
in the simple but rich tradition.

### L'AQUILA: L'Unico Posto €
Mediterranean
*Viale Croce Rossa 30/a, 67100*
**Tel** *347 483 13 20*
Kebabs, spit-roasted meat and
ribs – a meat lover's heaven.

### L'AQUILA: Elodia €€
Fine dining
*Via Valle Perchiana 22, 67100*
**Tel** *0862 60 68 30* **Closed** *Mon, Tue*
Gourmet interpretations of great
local recipes; delicious desserts.
Reservations essential.

### LECCE: Osteria degli Spiriti €
Regional Italian
*Via Cesare Battisti 4, 73100*
**Tel** *0832 24 62 74*
Local cuisine served in a high-
ceilinged trattoria that was once
a warehouse.

### LUCERA: Il Cortiletto €
Regional Italian
*Via Famiglia de Nicastri 26, 71036*
**Tel** *0881 54 25 54* **Closed** *Sun dinner*
Regional favorites with original
touches. The short weekly menu
is described by the staff.

---

### DK Choice

**LUCERA: Le Delizie di Bacco** €
Gourmet pizzeria
*Via Luigi Zuppetta 27, 71036*
**Tel** *329 029 43 55* **Closed** *Tue*
A pizzeria like no other, this tiny
place only serves pizza *al taglio*
(by the slice). But they are made
with the best ingredients in the
most traditional way, even if
owner Luigi experiments with
taste combinations. The inside is
decorated like an artist's studio,
and service is kind and helpful.

---

### OSTUNI: Osteria Piazzetta
Cattedrale €
Modern Italian
*Largo Arcidiacono T. Trinchera 7,*
*72017*
**Tel** *0831 33 50 26* **Closed** *Tue*
This elegant restaurant serves local
cuisine with a modern touch.

**OSTUNI:**
**Osteria del Tempo Perso**    €€
Modern Italian
*Via Gaetano Tanzarella Vitale 47,
72017*
**Tel** *0831 30 48 19*    **Closed** *Mon;
Jan 15–20*
Set in an antique mill, the dishes
are reinventions of classic recipes.

**OSTUNI: Porta Nova**    €€
Seafood
*Via Gaspare Petrarolo 38, 72017*
**Tel** *0831 33 89 83*
A fine fish restaurant with lovely
views from its large terrace.

**OTRANTO: Peccato di Vino**    €€€
Modern Italian
*Via Rondachi 7, 73028*
**Tel** *0836 80 14 88*    **Closed** *Tue*
One of the finest restaurants in
town, serving creative Pugliese
cuisine in a jovial atmosphere.

**SULMONA: Pensavo Peggio**    €
Regional Italian
*Via Barbato 1, 67039*
**Tel** *347 995 43 89*
Simple but wholesome food in
a rustic setting. Don't miss the
*maltagliati alla crema di pistacchi*
(pasta with pistachio cream).

**TARANTO: Al Canale**    €€
Seafood
*Scesa Vasto, 74100*
**Tel** *099 476 42 01*    **Closed** *Sun
dinner; Nov 1–15*
Delicious fish dishes are served at
this cheeful restaurant by the sea.

**TARANTO:**
**Trattoria al Gatto Rosso**    €€
Regional Italian
*Via Cavour 2, 74123*
**Tel** *099 452 98 75*    **Closed** *Sun
lunch, Mon*
Innovative contemporary cuisine
based on local recipes.

**TRANI: Torrente Antico**    €€€
Fine dining
*Via Edoardo Fusco 3, 70059*
**Tel** *0883 48 79 11*    **Closed** *Mon*
Light and modern versions of
Puglia's traditional recipes at the
finest restaurant in the area.

# Basilicata and Calabria

**MARATEA:**
**Il Giardino di Epicuro**    €
Regional Italian
*Contrada Massa Piano, 85046*
**Tel** *0973 87 01 30*    **Closed** *Jan,
Feb, Nov*
The owner's mother creates
heavenly traditional meals.

**MARATEA: Zà Mariuccia**    €€
Seafood
*Via Grotte 2, 85040*
**Tel** *0973 87 61 63*    **Closed** *Mon;
mid-Oct–Mar*
Make a reservation to secure one
of the few terrace tables with fine
sea views. Top-notch local seafood
with an excellent wine list.

**MARATEA: Taverna Rovita**    €€€
Regional Italian
*Via Rovita 12, 85046*
**Tel** *0973 87 65 88*
Serves tempting meat and fish
dishes and homemade pasta
with seasonal ingredients.

**MATERA: Alle Fornaci**    €
Seafood
*Piazza Cesare Firrao 5/7, 75100*
**Tel** *0835 33 50 37*    **Closed** *Mon*
Fresh fish from the Ionian and
Tyrrhenian seas is brought in
daily for the no-fuss dishes.

**MATERA: Don Matteo**    €€
Modern Italian
*Via San Potito 12, 75100*
**Tel** *0835 34 41 45*    **Closed** *lunch*
Dine inside a *sassi* (characteristic
stone dwelling). A modern take
on traditional local recipes.

## DK Choice

**MELFI: La Villa**    €
Regional Italian
*Contrada Cavallerizza, 85025*
**Tel** *0972 23 60 08*    **Closed** *Sun
dinner, Fri; 2 wks mid-Jul*
Set in the heart of the countryside, this rustic restaurant mills its
own flour and grows its own
grapes. Every ingredient used
is local, and the traditional
recipes are executed with
attention to detail. The family
who run the estate treat guests
like family members.

The warmly lit entrance to seafood
restaurant Porta Nova in Ostuni

**MELFI: Novecento**    €
Regional Italian
*Contrada Incoronata, 85025*
**Tel** *0972 23 74 70*
Authentic local cuisine served in
a welcoming restaurant. Worth
the trek outside town.

**MELFI: La Grotta Azzurra**    €€
Regional Italian
*Via Carmine 13, 85025*
**Tel** *0972 23 81 34*
Bring a big appetite to this
excellent restaurant with hearty
Lucano specialties. Heavenly
desserts and a good wine list.

**REGGIO DI CALABRIA:**
**L'Angolo dell'Antica Villa**    €
Seafood
*Via Zaleuco 7, 89125*
**Tel** *0965 209 55*    **Closed** *Sun;
first wk Jan*
Sicilian cuisine, based mostly on
fish, is on offer in this welcoming
restaurant with a good Calabrian
wine list.

**REGGIO DI CALABRIA:**
**Bistrot 15**    €€
Bistro
*Via Nazionale Pellaro 15, 89134*
**Tel** *0965 35 03 41*    **Closed** *May–Sep;
Dec–Feb: Mon*
Innovative and artistic seafood
served in a modern setting.
Worth the short journey out
of the center.

**ROSSANO: Bella Napoli**    €
Pizzeria
*Via Capri 5, 87067*
**Tel** *0983 51 01 53*
Authentic Neapolitan-style pizzas
are served in generous portions.
Pasta and meat dishes are also on
the menu.

**ROSSANO: Trattoria Amici di
Bacco**    €
Regional Italian
*Via Carducci 2, 87067*
**Tel** *0983 50 01 14*
Simple and reliable trattoria that
serves typical Rossanese dishes.
Ask for any fresh fish on offer.

**TROPEA: La Lamia**    €
Modern Italian
*Largo Vulcano, 89861*
**Tel** *0963 612 74*
Both meat and fish dishes
feature heavily on the menu at
this characteristic and popular
neighborhood *osteria*.

**TROPEA: Al Pinturicchio**    €
Pizzeria
*Via Dardano, 89861*
**Tel** *0963 60 34 52*
Come early to this popular
pizzeria, where tables spill out
onto the narrow street.

**TROPEA: Pimm's** €€
Seafood
*Largo Migliarese 10, 89861*
**Tel** *0963 66 61 05*     **Closed** *Mon*
Elegant and quiet restaurant in the heart of town.

**VENOSA: Locanda Accademia dei Piacevoli** €€
Modern Italian
*Via Discesa Capovalle 1, 85029*
**Tel** *0972 360 82*     **Closed** *Mon; first 2 wks Nov*
Small gourmet restaurant set in a tiny stone house.

# Sicily

**AGRIGENTO: Kokalos** €€
Regional Italian
*Via Alfredo Capitano 3*
**Tel** *0922 60 64 27*
Traditional Sicilian cuisine using local ingredients such as oranges, almonds, and sun-dried tomatoes.

**AGRIGENTO: Trattoria dei Templi** €€
Seafood
*Via Panoramica Valle dei Templi 15, 92100*
**Tel** *0922 40 31 10*
This inviting restaurant overlooking the temples offers expertly prepared seafood specialties.

**CATANIA: La Siciliana** €
Regional Italian
*Viale Marco Polo 52, 95126*
**Tel** *095 37 64 00*     **Closed** *Sun dinner, Mon*
Classic Sicilian recipes, including dishes specific to the town. One of Catania's best restaurants.

**CATANIA: Il Cuciniere** €€
Modern Italian
*Via Finocchiaro Aprile 110, 95129*
**Tel** *095 747 07 02*     **Closed** *Sun*

Erice's Monte San Giuliano restaurant, serving local dishes

The chef here uses traditional Sicilian ingredients in unique ways, such as fish with Modica chocolate.

**CEFALÙ: La Brace** €
Bistro
*Via 25 Novembre 10, 90015*
**Tel** *0921 42 35 70*     **Closed** *Mon, Tue; Dec 15–Jan 15*
Hints of the Orient mingle with local flavors at this bistro hidden away in the historic center.

**ENNA: Ariston** €
Regional Italian
*Piazza Napoleone Colajanni 6, 94100*
**Tel** *0935 260 38*
Fresh local ingredients from land and sea are served by enthusiastic staff at this friendly spot.

**ERICE: Monte San Giuliano** €
Regional Italian
*Vicolo San Rocco 7, 91016*
**Tel** *0923 86 95 95*     **Closed** *Mon; Nov 15*
The remarkable terrace-garden here is an ideal setting to enjoy some authentic local cuisine.

**ERICE: Osteria di Venere** €€
Regional Italian
*Via Roma 6, 91016*
**Tel** *0923 86 93 62*
Sample diverse Mediterranean cuisine including homemade pasta and grilled seafood.

**MARSALA: Garibaldi** €
Regional Italian
*Piazza dell'Addolorata 1, 91025*
**Tel** *0923 95 30 06*     **Closed** *Sat lunch, Sun dinner*
A dizzying selection of regional favorites, and fish cooked any way you please.

**MESSINA: La Durlindana** €
Regional Italian
*Via Nicola Fabrizi 143, 98123*
**Tel** *090 641 31 56*
This modern restaurant with an open kitchen offers regional dishes and wines.

**MESSINA: Piero** €€
Regional Italian
*Via Ghibellina 119, 98123*
**Tel** *090 640 93 54*     **Closed** *Aug*
This restaurant has been serving large plates of fish, big salads, and hearty meat dishes since its opening in 1962.

**MONREALE: Taverna del Pavone** €
Regional Italian
*Vicolo Pensato 18, 90046*
**Tel** *091 640 62 09*     **Closed** *2 wks Jan, 2 wks Jul*
Sample authentic, no-frills Sicilian specialties served in a cosy and friendly setting.

**PALERMO: Antico Caffè Spinnato** €
Enoteca
*Via Principe di Belmonte 111, 90139*
**Tel** *091 749 51 04*     **Closed** *Christmas*
Come for the wines, liqueurs, and espresso, but stay for the *cassata* (traditional Sicilian dessert), *cannoli* (fried pastry with a creamy filling), and gelato.

**PALERMO: Bye Bye Blues** €€
Fine dining
*Via del Garofalo 23, 90149*
**Tel** *091 684 14 15*     **Closed** *Mon; 2 wks Jan*
Fantastic prices for a Michelin-starred restaurant. Diners can watch their dishes being prepared in the kitchen.

**PALERMO: Carizzi d'Amuri** €€
Modern Italian
*Via Lungarni 21, 90133*
**Tel** *091 61 61 388*   **Closed** *lunch; Tue*
The relaxed, modern setting is perfect for a romantic meal. The food is traditional Sicilian with a contemporary twist.

**PALERMO: Sapori Perduti** €€
Modern Italian
*Via Principe di Belmonte 32, 90139*
**Tel** *091 32 73 87*     **Closed** *Mon; Aug*
Modern design goes hand-in-hand with expertly prepared modern Italian cuisine.

**PALERMO: Lo Scudiero** €€
Seafood
*Via Filippo Turati 7, 90139*
**Tel** *091 58 16 28*     **Closed** *Sun; 2 wks Aug*
The impeccable and attentive service is almost as refreshing as the delectable fish.

**SIRACUSA: Enoteca Solaria** €
Enoteca
*Via Roma 86, 96100*
**Tel** *0931 46 30 07*
The oldest wine bar in the city, with labels from Italy and France.

**SIRACUSA: Oinos** €€
Modern Italian
*Via della Giudecca 69/75, 96100*
**Tel** *0931 46 49 00*
Intimate and informal setting for a variety of modern dishes based on recipes from across Italy. There is also a good range of beverages to accompany meals.

**SIRACUSA: Porta Marina** €€
Regional Italian
*Via dei Candelai 35, 96100*
**Tel** *0931 225 53*     **Closed** *Mon; 2 wks Feb*
A lovely restaurant set in a crumbling early Renaissance palazzo. It offers good value for the quality of food it serves.

## DK Choice

**TAORMINA: Al Duomo**  €€
Seafood
*Vico Ebrei (Piazza Duomo), 98039*
**Tel** *0942 62 56 56*
The picturesque location for
this restaurant is a terrace in
Taormina's most beautiful
piazza, with the backdrop of
a 12th-century cathedral.
Classic and modern fish dishes
are whipped up by the chefs
with enthusiasm. The kitchen is
open well past midnight.

**TAORMINA: Principe Cerami**  €€€
Fine dining
*Piazza San Domenico 5, 98039*
**Tel** *0942 61 31 11* **Closed** *lunch, Mon*
Uber-refined Sicilian fare is served
on a heavenly terrace overlooking
crystal waters. Reserve early.

**TRAPANI: Taverna Paradiso**  €€
Seafood
*Lungomare Dante Alighieri 22, 91100*
**Tel** *0923 223 03*
Ask one of the friendly staff for
recommendations at this lovely
eatery with super-fresh fish.

# Sardinia

**ALGHERO: Quintilio**  €€
Modern Italian
*Via El Trò 44, Grotte di Costa, 07041*
**Tel** *330 258 608*
Enjoy a meal or a cocktail while
watching the sun set over the sea.

**ALGHERO: Al Tuguri**  €€
Seafood
*Via Maiorca 113, 07041*
**Tel** *079 97 67 72* **Closed** *Sun;
mid–Dec–Mar*
Just a few tables are available in
this cosy seafood restaurant.

**BOSA:
Mannu da Giancarlo e Rita**  €€
Seafood
*Viale Alghero 14, 08013*
**Tel** *0785 37 53 06* **Closed** *winter*
A modern restaurant where
Lobster dominates the menu.

**CAGLIARI:
La Stella Marina di Montecristo** €
Seafood
*Via Sardegna 140, 09124*
**Tel** *347 578 89 64* **Closed** *Sun*
A simple *osteria* offering cordial
service. Wild game on Thursdays.

**CAGLIARI: Dal Corsaro**  €€
Modern Italian
*Viale Regina Margherita 28, 09124*
**Tel** *070 66 43 18* **Closed** *Sun;
3 wks Jan*

Buzzing atmosphere at Hivaoa, Costa Smeralda

Sardinian classics are re-created
with a contemporary twist.

**CALA GONONE: Il Pescatore**  €€
Seafood
*Lungomare Acqua Dolce 1, 08022*
**Tel** *0784 931 74*
A seaside spot serving classic
Sardinian fish dishes.

**COSTA SMERALDA:
Corbezzolo**  €€
Seafood
*Piazzetta della Fontana, Baia
Sardinia, 07021*
**Tel** *0789 998 93* **Closed** *Dec–May*
Classic fish dishes served on a
terrace with stunning sea views.

**COSTA SMERALDA: Hivaoa**  €€
Pizzeria
*Via della Marina, Porto Cervo, 07021*
**Tel** *0789 914 51*
Dine on a breezy terrace. Pizza,
pasta, and excellent seafood.

## DK Choice

**COSTA SMERALDA:
Pedristellas**  €€
Regional Italian
*Via Monte Ladu, Porto Rotondo,
07026*
**Tel** *377 236 92 01* **Closed** *winter*
Literally "rocks and stars" in the
Sardinian dialect, this restaurant
is set in a rock garden dotted
with centuries-old pine trees.
The tables, lighting, and mean-
dering paths complement the
natural setting. It offers traditional
Sardinian dishes, perfectly cooked.

**COSTA SMERALDA:
Stella di Gallura**  €€
Regional Italian
*Loc. Monte Ladu, Porto Rotondo,
07026*
**Tel** *0789 344 02* **Closed** *winter*
Dine by the poolside and sample
delicious regional dishes.

**COSTA SMERALDA:
Da Giovannino**  €€€
Fine dining
*Piazza Quadra 10, Porto Rotondo,
07026*
**Tel** *0789 352 80* **Closed** *winter*
High-profile restaurant with a
pretty garden. Excellent
Mediterranean cuisine.

**COSTA SMERALDA:
Spinnaker**  €€€
Seafood
*Res. Alba Ruja, Porto Cervo, 07020*
**Tel** *0789 912 26* **Closed** *winter*
One of the Emerald Coast's best-
known restaurants. Excellent
seafood and impeccable staff.

**NUORO: Il Rifugio**  €€
Regional Italian
*Via Antonio Mereu 28, 08100*
**Tel** *0784 23 23 55* **Closed** *winter*
An ample variety of classic
Sardinian dishes served in a pretty,
romantic setting. Excellent pizza.

**ORISTANO: Craf da Banana**  €€
Regional Italian
*Via de Castro S. A. 34, 09170*
**Tel** *0783 42 01 82* **Closed** *winter*
Wild game is the house specialty
at this friendly basement eatery.

**SANT'ANTIOCO:
Moderno da Achille**  €€
Regional Italian
*Via Nazionale 82, 09017*
**Tel** *0781 831 05* **Closed** *winter*
Tasty Sardinian cuisine expertly
prepared by a talented chef who
makes each dish his own. A very
elegant setting.

**SASSARI: Il Vecchio Mulino**  €€
Regioanl Italian
*Via Frigaglia 5, 07100*
**Tel** *079 492 03 24* **Closed** *Sun,
Mon lunch, Fri dinner*
The setting in an old mill is perfect
for the excellent regional dishes.
Great value and huge portions.

**For more information on types of restaurants** *see pp578–9*

# SHOPPING IN ITALY

Italy is known for its quality designer goods, ranging from chic clothing and sleek cars to stylish household items. There is a strong tradition of craftsmanship, often from family-run businesses, and there are numerous markets selling regional specialties. Aside from the town markets, it is not a country for bargains, but there's plenty to look at even for those not planning to buy. If you come from outside the European Union, you may be able to claim back the 21 percent IVA tax (sales tax). Make sure you leave time at your departure airport to fulfill all administrative requirements.

Fresh vegetables on display at a Venetian market stall

## Opening Hours

Opening hours for stores are usually 9:30am–1pm and around 3:30–8pm, Tuesday to Saturday and Monday afternoons. However, storekeepers are increasingly using more flexible hours. There are few department stores, but most large towns will have a Standa, Upim, Coin, or Rinascente. These stores are often open nonstop (*orario continuato*) from 9am to 8pm, Monday through Saturday. Music- and bookstores sometimes stay open after 8pm and on Sundays.

## Food Stores

Even though there are supermarkets throughout Italy, the specialty stores, although more expensive, are still the most interesting way to shop. A *forno* has the best bread and a *macellaio* has the finest meat (go to a *norcineria* for pork products). Vegetables are freshest from market stands or the *fruttivendolo*. You can buy cakes at the *pasticceria*, milk at the *latteria*, and pasta, ham, cheese, and general foods at the often impressively stocked *alimentari*. Here you can also buy wine, but for a wider choice, head for the *enoteca*, *vineria*, or *vinaio*, where you can sometimes taste the wine before purchasing.

## Markets

All towns have regional weekly markets. Large towns will have several small daily markets followed by a weekly flea market, usually on Sunday. In this guide the main market days are listed under each town. Traders set up at 5am and start to clear away at about 1:30pm. Food is sold by the *etto* (100 grams, or 3.5 oz) and the *chilo* (kilo, or 2.2 pounds) (*see p617*), or in numbers (two onions, etc.). Food stands selling seasonal products generally have fresher and cheaper produce than the stores. Bargaining is not customary when buying food, but it is worth asking for a discount (*sconto*) for clothes.

## Seasonal Produce

To make the most of Italian food, try to buy and eat what is in season. Grapes and mushrooms are best in fall, while spring is the season for asparagus and strawberries. In winter, vegetables such as Roman artichokes, cauliflower, and broccoli are at their best, as are lemons from Amalfi and Sicilian blood oranges. Summer is the time for plums, pears, and cherries, as well as zucchini, eggplant, tomatoes, and melons.

## Clothes and Designer Stores

Italy is renowned worldwide for its fashion industry. Milan is the fashion capital and Via Monte Napoleone, in the city center, is lined with designer boutiques. All large towns will have a selection of designer stores, usually located near each other. Less expensive clothes

Souvenir store in Ostuni, near Brindisi, Puglia

are available in markets and many department stores, where the styles tend to be more conventional. Italy is also famous for leather shoes and purses, the prices of which tend to be reasonable.

Sales *(saldi)* are held in summer and winter. Second-hand stores can be expensive, but the quality and condition of the clothes are usually very good. Larger markets have stands piled high with used clothes. Rummage through and you will often find bargains.

Colorful store display of leather purses in Florence

### Jewelry Stores and Antiques Shops

Glitzy gold jewelry is very popular in Italy and every *gioielleria* (jewelry store) will have a wide selection. For more unusual items, try the *bigiotteria* or artisan stores *(oreficeria)*. Antiques shops like *Antichità* and *Antiquariato* sell furniture and ornaments of varying quality and prices. You will rarely find bargains in Italy, except perhaps at the *fiere dell'antiquariato* (antiques fairs), held throughout the year all over the country.

### Interior Design and Homewares

Interior design is another Italian sector where top names demand extravagant prices, with many stores concentrating on modern, high-tech styles. There are household stores in cities and towns throughout the

An elegant designer clothing boutique in Treviso

country. Italian kitchenware is particularly striking, with its stainless steel and copper pots, pans, and utensils. For the lowest prices, avoid the tourist stores and, if possible, buy directly from the manufacturer. Less expensive items include the characteristic brown espresso and cappuccino cups sold in all markets.

### Regional Specialties

Many of Italy's regional specialties are world famous: Parma ham, Chianti wine, olive oil, and *grappa*. Regional desserts and candies, including the Sienese *panforte* and Sicilian marzipan, are also well-known, as are cheeses such as Gorgonzola from Lombardy and Parmesan from Emilia-Romagna.

Traditional crafts endure, and range from delicate lacework and glassware in the Veneto to leatherwork, jewelry, and marbled paper in Florence. Italian ceramics include elaborate Tuscan pottery, hand-painted dishes around Amalfi, and De Simone's stylized designer plates from Sicily.

Display of decorative glazed pottery from Tuscany

### Size Chart

For Australian sizes follow the British and American conversions.

**Women's dresses, coats, and skirts**

| Italian | 36 | 38 | 40 | 42 | 44 | 46 | 48 |
|---|---|---|---|---|---|---|---|
| British | 8 | 10 | 12 | 14 | 16 | 18 | 20 |
| American | 4 | 6 | 8 | 10 | 12 | 14 | 16 |

**Women's shoes**

| Italian | 36 | 37 | 38 | 39 | 40 | 41 |
|---|---|---|---|---|---|---|
| British | 3 | 4 | 5 | 6 | 7 | 8 |
| American | 5 | 6 | 7 | 8 | 9 | 10 |

**Men's suits**

| Italian | 44 | 46 | 48 | 50 | 52 | 54 | 56 | 58 (size) |
|---|---|---|---|---|---|---|---|---|
| British | 34 | 36 | 38 | 40 | 42 | 44 | 46 | 48 (inches) |
| American | 34 | 36 | 38 | 40 | 42 | 44 | 46 | 48 (inches) |

**Men's shirts** (collar size)

| Italian | 37 | 38 | 39 | 41 | 42 | 43 | 44 | 45 (cm) |
|---|---|---|---|---|---|---|---|---|
| British | 14 | 15 | 15¹/₂ | 16 | 16¹/₂ | 17 | 17¹/₂ | 18 (inches) |
| American | 14 | 15 | 15¹/₂ | 16 | 16¹/₂ | 17 | 17¹/₂ | 18 (inches) |

**Men's shoes**

| Italian | 39 | 40 | 41 | 42 | 43 | 44 | 45 | 46 |
|---|---|---|---|---|---|---|---|---|
| British | 6 | 7 | 7¹/₂ | 8 | 9 | 10 | 11 | 12 |
| American | 7 | 7¹/₂ | 8 | 8¹/₂ | 9¹/₂ | 10¹/₂ | 11 | 11¹/₂ |

# ENTERTAINMENT IN ITALY

Italians exude strong national pride and passion about all aspects of their cultural heritage. One of Europe's key centers of culture since Roman times, Italy was the cradle of the Renaissance, and it is known today as the home of opera and a mixed bag of regional styles of folk music. The country holds one of the most acclaimed international film festivals and every town boasts a *teatro*, an elaborate classical venue with mixed programs incorporating every aspect of classic and traditional culture. Add to this the many street festivals and fairs, often in celebration of food, wine, and *la dolce vita*, and you will never have a dull moment.

## Practical Information

Most venues have online reservations or a dedicated phone line to call. However, major events and most opera performances tend to sell out well in advance, so it is wise to reserve through ticket agencies such as **Ticket One**, which may still have availability when the venue itself has sold out.

To find out what's happening in Italy during your stay, check the Italian tourism website (www.italia.it) or pick up a copy of *Dove*, a monthly publication about culture, travel, and gastronomy that also highlights the month's events in Rome and Milan.

*Il Corriere della Sera*, Italy's oldest daily newspaper, has sections on events and culture; its ViviMilano website (www.corriere.it/vivimilano) is a mine of information on events taking place in the fashion capital. Another website (www.romaturismo.it) offers excellent service for Rome.

Tourist information offices (*see p617*) will also provide information on programs, events, and venues, as will the **Italian State Tourist Board**. Few Italian venues provide easy access for people with restricted mobility. The situation improves a little in the summer, when many events are held outside.

## Opera and Classical Music

Italy has some of the world's most beautiful and historic opera houses. Venice's **La Fenice**, destroyed by fire in 1996, has been restored to its former splendor, and **Teatro alla Scala** (*see p197*) in Milan also underwent a major renovation. In addition to the original building, there is also an extra theater, **Teatro degli Arcimboldi**, allowing the Scala to host more performances.

Verona hosts a summer season of opera and classical music in the outdoor **Arena di Verona** (*see p147*), while Rome's venues include the open-air **Baths of Caracalla** (*see p441*), the breathtaking Renzo Piano-designed auditorium **Parco della Musica**, and the **Teatro dell'Opera**.

In May and June, Florence's **Maggio Musicale** (*see p70*) is packed with opera, ballet, and classical performances.

Poster advertising the Venice Film Festival

## Rock, Jazz, and Contemporary Music

Large concerts tend to be held in classic theaters or in sports stadiums. The **Arena di Verona** hosts big names in summer, as does the **Stadio Olimpico** in Rome. In Milan, the **Forum di Assago** sports stadium is a popular venue. Tickets for concerts are sometimes sold in record stores.

World-class jazz performers gather annually in Perugia for the **Umbria Jazz** festival in July. The website provides booking details and information.

## Theater and Ballet

Italy has the highest concentration of traditional theaters in Europe, offering a mix of theater, dance, and classical music all under one roof. All theaters also host ballet performances, mainly by international touring troupes. The **Scala**'s ballet company has gained international renown. Both tradition and innovation can be seen at the international festival of ballet that takes place at Genoa's **Teatro Carlo Felice** in July.

The opera festival in Verona attracts huge crowds to the Roman arena

## Cinema

One of the highlights of the cinema year is the **Venice Film Festival** *(see p71)*, which takes place from August to September. The Rome International Festival of Cinema *(see p72)* also draws major movie stars. A smaller International Film Festival *(see p71)* is held in Taormina, Sicily, while Florence has the Festa dei Popoli *(see p72)* in winter.

A thrilling moment in the Sienese Palio race held in Piazza del Campo

## Regional Dance, Music, and Festivals

Seasonal festivals are either religious, relating to patron saints, or food-oriented. The best known is Carnevale (literally "farewell to meat") *(see p73)*, which celebrates the end of winter and introduces Lent. Venice holds the most opulent and the oldest masquerade party, while Viareggio, in Tuscany, is famous for its lively themed floats.

Another festival highlight is the Palio of Siena *(see pp71 and 345)*, a bareback horse race that takes place twice a year in one of Italy's most beautiful squares. For further details on festivals throughout Italy, see pp70–73.

*An elaborate Carnival mask*

Every region in Italy has its own ancient music and dance, but the best known is the *tarantella*, a lively dance and rhythmic song from Puglia *(see p515)*. Legends trace the origins of the name to the tarantula spider, since victims of a tarantula bite would perform a frenzied dance in order to sweat out the poison.

## Culture

Spectating, whether at sporting events, rural festivals, or even grand events, is what entertainment is all about. And part of this, of course, involves that very Italian pastime – seeing and being seen. You can witness this in daily life in the café culture – visit any of the large cities' popular squares, such as Piazza di Spagna or Piazza Navona in Rome, Piazza del Duomo in Milan, or Piazza San Marco in Venice, and you will see people of all ages parading around in their best clothes. This is referred to as *la passeggiata*, a walk around that becomes a ritual on weekends, along the seafront and lakeside promenades in summer and in city and town centers.

Another aspect of daily life is the *aperitivo*. This ritual of joining friends for an early evening drink after work or before going on to dinner or to a nightclub is back in fashion. Bars provide abundant finger-food buffets to accompany the drinks, which are generally priced higher than at other times of day. This trend has spawned lounge clubs in the major cities.

# DIRECTORY

# Theme Vacations and Outdoor Activities

Italy offers an amazing variety of cultural, sporting, and leisure activities. However, many schools and groups require annual membership and short-term activities are often expensive and difficult to find. Information on current leisure and sporting events in a specific region is available from the tourist office listed for each town in this guide. For details on annual festivals, see *Italy Through the Year* on pages 70–73. The following suggestions include some of the most popular as well as some more unusual pursuits.

Bicycling on the tree-lined flatlands of the Po Delta

## Walking, Bicycling, and Horseback Riding

Some Italian branches of the **World Wide Fund for Nature (WWF)** organize walks and treks. **Club Alpino Italiano (CAI)** runs trekking and climbing excursions and the **Italian Birds Protection League (LIPU)** arranges nature walks and bird-watching trips. The military *IGM* maps are the most

detailed, but unfortunately are only available from specialty map stores.

Bicycling is popular despite Italy's mountainous landscape. Travel bookstores stock publications with suggested routes, such as the Po Delta, which has miles of scenic flatlands.

Many horseback riding schools organize trips, which are also advertised in the local press. For general information, contact the **Federazione Italiana Sport Equestri**.

## Mountain Sports

The most well-equipped and famous ski resorts are in the Dolomites, in the Italian Alps, and around Turin, the city chosen to host the 2006 Winter Olympics. There are also smaller and less expensive resorts in the Apennines and in Sicily. Package ski vacations, arranged from outside Italy, offer the best deals.

Group hiking tour in the Dolomites of Trentino-Alto Adige *(see p86)*

The **Federazione Arrampicata Sportiva Italiana** has a list of mountain-climbing schools that arrange climbs for all abilities.

Ski lift near the Falzarego Pass, in the heart of the Dolomites

## Archaeological Digs

The British monthly magazine *Archaeology Abroad*, available in the UK, gives a comprehensive list of archaeology groups and digs worldwide. In Italy, the **Gruppo Archeologico Romano** runs two-week digs in various regions. There are summer and winter digs, for both adults and children. The group has contacts with local archaeological organizations as well.

## Italian Language and Culture

For a wide selection of material on courses and schools in Italy, contact the Italian consulate in your home country. The **Società Dante Alighieri** provides courses in the Italian language, history of art, literature, and culture. There are both full- and part-time courses available, for every level. Language schools abound in Italy's main cities and are advertised in the Yellow Pages *(Pagine Gialle)* or foreign-language bookstores and newspapers. For young students, **Intercultura** will organize weekly, monthly, and year-long exchanges, including language courses, accommodations with Italian families, and enrollment in Italian schools. Cooking vacations

A lesson in Italian cookery in Sicily

run by English-speaking experts in Italian cooking have become very popular. **Tasting Places**, for example, has wine tours and week-long courses in Italian cuisine, and provides beautiful accommodations. The course locations include the Veneto, Sicily, Tuscany, and Umbria. Wine-tasting tours are organized by local tourist boards. The Università per Stranieri in Perugia runs courses in Italian, art history, and literature (www.unistrapg.it).

## Water Sports

Most lakes and many seaside resorts rent out sailboats, canoes, and windsurfing equipment. Lessons and courses are organized by clubs, which usually require membership. For a list of authorized associations, contact the **Federazione Italiana Canoa Kayak** and the **Federazione Italiana Vela**. Weekend and weekly sailing vacations and courses are featured in the magazine *Avventure nel Mondo*, and most travel agents have a selection of sailing vacations.

Swimming pools are expensive in Italy and many do not accept people on a daily basis. You often have to pay a membership fee and a monthly tariff. Some of the luxurious hotels open their pools to the public in summer, but at pricey rates. Water parks are popular and provide pools, slides, wave machines, and games. Before diving into any lakes or rivers (and even the sea near main towns), it is best to check that the water is not polluted. The **Federazione Italiana di Attività**

Subacquee runs diving courses, and can give information on all local centers.

## Air Sports

There are schools nationwide that offer hang-gliding and flying courses, but the minimum duration of each course is one month. For information and a list of schools, contact the **AeroClub Italia**. You must be licensed before you can fly, and all crafts must be registered with AeroClub.

## Other Sports

Playing golf

Golf is a popular sport in Italy, and there are plenty of courses to choose from. Home membership and handicap are often required for daily access to a club. Italian tennis clubs usually operate on a membership basis, unless you are invited as a member's guest. The national **Federazione Italiana di Tennis** has a list of all the tennis clubs in Italy. The opportunity to watch a professional soccer game should not be missed. Seats can be scarce, so buy tickets in advance from the stadium. Most Serie A games are played on Sundays, with international games taking place on Tuesdays and Wednesdays.

Sailing in Italy is a popular leisure activity and competitive sport

## DIRECTORY

**AeroClub Italia**
Via Cesare Beccaria 35a, 00196 Rome. **Tel** 06 36 08 46 01.
w aeci.it

**Club Alpino Italiano**
Via E. Petrella 19, Milan.
**Tel** 02 205 72 31. w cai.it

**Federazione Arrampicata Sportiva Italiana**
Via del Terrapieno 27, 40127 Bologna. **Tel** 051 601 48 90.
w federclimb.it

**Federazione Italiana Attività Subacquee**
Via A. Doria 8, Milan.
**Tel** 02 670 50 05. w fias.it

**Federazione Italiana Canoa Kayak**
Viale Tiziano 70, 00196 Rome.
**Tel** 06 36 85 81 88; 06 36 85 41 75.
w federcanoa.it

**Federazione Italiana Sport Equestri**
Viale Tiziano 74, 00196 Rome.
**Tel** 06 83 66 84 41. w fise.it

**Federazione Italiana di Tennis**
Stadio Olimpico, Rome.
**Tel** 06 98 37 21 44.
w federtennis.it

**Federazione Italiana Vela**
Piazza Borgo Pila 40, Genoa.
**Tel** 010 54 45 41. w federvela.it

**Gruppo Archeologico Romano**
Via Contessa di Bertinoro 6, 00162 Rome. **Tel** 06 638 52 56.
w gruppoarcheologico.it

**Intercultura**
Via Venezia 25, 00184 Rome.
**Tel** 06 48 88 24 01; 339 565 0573.
w intercultura.it

**Italian Birds Protection League (LIPU)**
Via Udine 3a, 43122 Parma.
**Tel** 0521 27 30 43. w lipu.it

**Società Dante Alighieri**
Piazza Firenze 27, 00186 Rome.
**Tel** 06 687 36 94. w ladante.it

**Tasting Places Cookery and Wine Tours**
w tastingplaces.com

**World Wide Fund for Nature**
Via Po 25c, 00198 Rome.
**Tel** 06 84 49 71. w wwf.it

# SURVIVAL GUIDE

# PRACTICAL INFORMATION

Ask any Italian and they will almost certainly tell you that Italy is the most beautiful country in the world. They may not be far wrong. However, the charm and allure of Italy may help to veil some of her numerous practical problems. Getting any kind of information is rarely straightforward;

public offices and banks are nearly always crippled by long lines and bureaucracy; and the postal service is renowned for its inefficiency. This section, together with some forward planning and a little patience, should help you cope with some of Italy's idiosyncrasies.

Tourists crossing the Ponte della Paglia in Venice *(see p113)*

## When to Visit

The northern part of Italy is generally more temperate than the south, which has a Mediterranean climate. From June through September the weather is hot everywhere and, in peak summer, also humid. Seaside resorts tend to get very busy. Spring and fall are ideal for visiting cities as temperatures are milder, making sightseeing much more comfortable.

Italy's towns and historic sites are popular attractions and it is worth considering this when planning your trip. Most sights are open year-round, except on some public holidays *(see p73)*, and most close one day a week. Rome, Florence, and Venice are all crowded from spring through October and it is advisable to reserve a hotel well in advance. In August the cities are generally slightly less busy, abandoned by their inhabitants for the summer vacation.

In February, Venice triples its population during Carnevale *(see p73)* and at Easter, Rome is overrun by pilgrims and tourists. Winter can be bitterly cold, especially in the north, and

December through March is the time of year for skiing in the high-altitude resorts of the Italian Alps. *The Climate of Italy* on pages 76–7 takes a detailed look at the country's regional weather.

## Visas and Permesso di Soggiorno

European Union nationals and citizens of the US, Canada, Australia, and New Zealand do not need visas for stays of up to three months. Most European Union (EU) visitors need only a valid passport.

All visitors should check requirements with the Italian embassy before traveling and, officially, declare themselves to the Italian police within eight days of arrival. If you are staying in a hotel or campground, this will be done for you by the staff; otherwise you will need to contact the local *Questura* (police station) yourself. Anyone wishing to stay in Italy for more than three months will have to obtain a *permesso di soggiorno*. Non-EU citizens must apply for one within eight days

of arrival. You can apply for a residence permit at any main police station. In some cases you can obtain a kit containing the necessary application form from main post offices. You must apply for the correct permit, either a permit to work *(lavoro)* or a permit to study *(studio)*. The necessary documentation is listed on the *Questura* website *(see p617)*.

To apply for a study permit, it is necessary to get a letter from the relevant school or university at which you intend to study. This then has to be sent to the Italian consulate in your own country of origin to obtain an official covering letter, or declaration.

You will also need some form of guarantee that your medical bills will be paid if you become ill or have an accident. A comprehensive insurance policy for the length of your stay will usually be sufficient.

## Travel Safety

Visitors can get up-to-date travel safety information from the State Department in the US , the Foreign and Commonwealth Office in the UK, and the Department of Foreign Affairs and Trade in Australia.

Rome's renowned Tazza d'Oro café, an ideal rest stop after sightseeing

◀ The wonderful view from the A22 highway that carves through the mountains and vineyards that surround Bolzano

## Customs

On 30 June 1999, the intra-EU Duty and Tax Free Allowances, better known as duty-free and mainly affecting such high-tax items as alcohol, perfumes, and tobacco, were abolished. However, for EU residents the amount of these goods that can be imported for personal use has increased.

Consulates can generally provide up-to-date information on particular customs regulations. To find out what you can take back from Italy to non-EU countries, contact that particular country's customs department, which will be able to advise you.

**Sign for tourist information**

## Tax Exemption

Sales tax (IVA in Italy) ranges from about 22 per cent, with a reduced rate of 4–10 per cent on some items. Non-European Union citizens making purchases in Italy can claim an IVA rebate, provided the total expenditure in the one store is over €155. It is a long process, and it is easier to get a refund if you shop where you see the "Euro Free Tax" sign, rather than from a market stall. In this instance, show your passport to the store clerk, complete a form, and the IVA will be deducted from your bill. Alternately, present a customs officer with your purchases and their receipts on your departure from Italy. He or she will stamp the receipts, which you then send to the vendor. A refund should eventually be sent to you.

## Tourist Information

The national tourist board, **ENIT**, has a good website as well as branches in capital cities worldwide, and offers general information on Italy. For specific requests, contact the local tourist offices. The addresses and telephone numbers are listed under each town or city, directly under the title, and they are plotted on the town and city maps. An **EPT** (Ente Provinciale di Turismo) has information on its town and surrounding province, whereas an **APT** (Azienda di Promozione Turistica) deals exclusively with individual towns. Both offices help with practical information such as hotel bookings and tours. They also provide free maps and guidebooks in various languages. The EPT and APT can refer you to local tour guides and advise on trips and excursions.

Small towns will have a Pro Loco, a tourist office run by the local administration, which is sometimes open only during the tourist season. It is usually located in the town hall.

## Tours

Many tour companies organize bus tours, with English-speaking guides, that include all the main tourist attractions in Italy. Companies such as UK-based **Leger Holidays** offer bus tours that span the country. If you want something a little more personal and off the beaten track, check the local pages of national newspapers for tour groups or organizations. Local tourist boards will also be able to advise you. Always employ official guides and be sure to establish the fee in advance. For information on special interest vacations, such as sporting or cultural activities, turn to pages 610–11.

**A guided group tour on the streets of Rome, near Vatican City**

**Daytime sightseeing on a tranquil canal in Venice**

## Sightseeing Opening Hours

Italian museums, particularly in the northern and central regions of the country, mostly conform to regulations, opening from 9am to 7pm daily, except Mondays. In winter, museums may revert to slightly earlier closing times, particularly on Sunday, so it is best to check. In Rome many are open daily.

Privately run and smaller museums set their own opening times, so it is best to phone in advance to avoid disappoint-ment. Archaeological sites are generally open from 9am to one hour before sunset, daily, except Mondays. Churches tend to open from about 7am to 12:30pm and 4 to 7pm. However, they often prefer not to let tourists in during services, so Sunday is not the best day to visit.

## Admission Charges

Sightseeing fees range from €2 to €14. Churches are usually free, but some expect a donation, and you will need coins to illuminate some works of art. Reductions for students are not always offered, but many state-run museums and archaeological sites allow free entry for visitors under 18 and over 60 or 65 years of age. Large groups are often entitled to a discount as well. If reductions are available, you will need to show a valid form of identification.

## Etiquette and Tipping

People in Italy are friendly toward foreign visitors. On entering a store or bar it is customary to greet people with a general *buon giorno* (good morning) or *buona sera* (good evening), and the same applies when leaving. They will also try to be helpful when asked directions in the street. If your Italian is slight, simply saying *scusi*, followed by the name of the place you wish to go to, will often suffice. *Grazie* (thank you) is replied to with *prego* (you're welcome).

Tipping in restaurants is expected when the 10–15 percent service is not included. However, as much as 10 percent would be considered generous, and a tip is often not expected at all in more basic restaurants. Taxi drivers and hotel porters expect a few euros if they have been helpful. You could simply round the check up to the nearest €2.

Italians are very dress-conscious and unusual clothes do get noticed. Be aware that in places of worship you should cover your torso and upper arms; shorts and skirts must reach below the knee.

Smoking is forbidden in all buildings open to the public (including offices, stores, bars, and restaurants). However, it is tolerated in outdoor public places, whereas drunkenness is definitely frowned upon.

Unacceptable dress in church: both sexes are required to cover torsos and upper arms

A student relaxing in the sun in Gaiole in Chianti

## Religious Services

Around 35 percent of the population is practicing Catholic. Sunday Mass is celebrated throughout the country, while in the principal churches, services are also held during the week. In major cities some churches, such as the church of Santa Susanna (Via XX Settembre 14) in Rome, offer services and confession in English. For some visitors, a trip to Rome will include an audience with the pope (see p423).

With increasing numbers of foreigners making their home in Italy, all the main religious beliefs are also represented. For details contact the main centers in Rome.

## Student Information

The national student travel organization, **CTS** (Centro Turistico Studentesco), has branches throughout Italy and Europe. They issue the International Student Identity Card (ISIC) and the Youth International Educational Exchange Card (YIEE). Both can be used, along with a passport, for discounts at museums and other tourist attractions. The ISIC card also gives holders access to a free 24-hour telephone helpline in cases of emergency. As well as issuing youth cards, CTS offers cut-rate car rental and will organize vacations and courses. For details

ISIC card

about youth hostels, contact the **Associazione Italiana Alberghi per la Gioventù** (the Italian YHA), providing that you are a current member.

## Traveling with Children

On the whole, Italians love children, to an extent that sometimes seems over-indulgent. Most trattorias and pizzerias welcome them and there are no rules excluding children from bars; however, high chairs are rare. Hotels also welcome children, but smaller establishments may have limited amenities. Some of the more upscale hotels will arrange a babysitting service. Very few museums, on the other hand, provide special child-oriented activities. It is common to see children playing outside fairly late at night, especially in summer. Most towns have city parks with playgrounds, and many have summer amusement parks. Regular stops for *gelato* are guaranteed to go down well with youngsters. For young swimmers, the calm Mediterranean is ideal, though care should always be taken.

## Disabled Travelers

Awareness of the needs of mobility-impaired travelers is improving in Italy, especially in major cities, with ramps being added to museums and some churches. Trains and buses are also becoming more wheelchair-friendly. In Milan **AIAS**

(Associazione Italiana Assistenza Spastici) and in Rome **CO.IN. Sociale** and **Roma per Tutti** provide information and general assistance. **Trenitalia** offers help on international and domestic routes with reservations and assistance at stations.

## Public Restrooms

*Gabinetto* or *bagno pubblico* means "public restroom", though signs often say "WC." Tourist cities have well-marked public restrooms that charge around €1. Some have cleaning staff on hand and a tip may be left. Italian cafés usually have a restroom for their customers, but it is worth checking first. Old-style "crouch" toilets are still common.

## Electrical Adapters

The voltage in Italy is 220 volts, with two-pin round-pronged plugs, so it is a good idea to bring a universal adapter with you or buy one in the country. Most hotels with three or more stars have hair-dryers and electrical outlets in all bedrooms, but check the voltage first, to be safe.

## Italian Time

Italy is 1 hour ahead of Greenwich Mean Time (GMT). The clocks are put forward 1 hour in March and back in October. For example: New York is 6 hours behind Italy; London is 1 hour behind; while Sydney is 9 hours ahead.

## Responsible Travel

Local attitudes toward environmental issues are developing rather slowly in Italy, despite the efforts of many concerned groups. However, there are opportunities for low-impact travel and alternative green options available.

Staying at family-run guest-houses instead of international hotel chains helps support local economies. National and regional parks award eco labels to hotels and guesthouses that adhere to EU rules governing sustainable tourism, which cover issues such as energy- and water-saving, waste disposal, and use of local products. The **Agriturismo** *(see p560)* offers countrywide farmstays. These are a great way of enjoying the countryside

and experiencing local traditions, as well as helping supplement the income of small farm owners. Amenities vary and some farms offer visitors the opportunity to help out or enjoy pursuits such as horseback riding.

Farmers' markets and growers who sell their produce direct to the public are now more common, guaranteeing fresh, seasonal produce. Look for the label *biologico* when searching for organic produce.

## Conversion Chart

**Imperial to Metric**
1 inch = 2.54 centimeters
1 foot = 30 centimeters
1 mile = 1.6 kilometers
1 ounce = 28 grams
1 pound = 454 grams
1 pint = 0.57 liter
1 gallon = 4.6 liters

**Metric to Imperial**
1 centimeter = 0.4 inch
1 meter = 3 feet 3 inches
1 kilometer = 0.6 mile
1 gram = 0.04 ounce
1 kilogram = 2.2 pounds
1 liter = 1.8 pints

# DIRECTORY

## Questura and Permits

ⓦ poliziadistato.it

ⓦ portale immigrazione.it

ⓦ esteri.it/visti

## Customs and Tax

ⓦ agenziadogane. gov.it

## Travel Safety

**US Dept. of State**
ⓦ travel.state.gov

**UK Foreign and Commonwealth Office**
ⓦ gov.uk/foreign-travel-advice

**Australia Dept. of Foreign Affairs & Trade**
ⓦ dfat.gov.au
ⓦ smartraveller.gov.au

## Tourist Information and Tours

**APT Florence**
Via Cavour 1r. **Map** 2 D4.
**Tel** 055 29 08 32.
ⓦ firenzeturismo.it

**APT Siena**
Piazza Duomo 1. **Tel** 0577 28 05 51. ⓦ terresiena.it

**APT Venice**
Piazza San Marco 71f.
**Map** 7 B2. **Tel** 041 529 87 11. ⓦ turismovenezia.it

**ENIT**
ⓦ italia.it

**IAT Milan**
Galleria Vittorio Emanuele (corner Piazza Scala).
**Tel** 02 88 45 55 55.
ⓦ visitamilano.it

**Leger Holidays**
**Tel** 01709 385 733.
ⓦ leger.co.uk

## Rome Tourist Office

Termini Station, Platform 24. **Map** 4 D3. **Tel** 06 06 08.
ⓦ turismoroma.it

## Religious Organizations

**Catholic**
Ufficio Informazioni Vaticano, Piazza San Pietro, Vaticano, Rome. **Map** 1 B3. **Tel** 06 69 88 16 62.

**Jewish**
Unione delle Comunità Ebraiche Italiane, Lungotevere Sanzio 9 **Map** 5 C1. **Tel** 06 45 54 22 00.

**Muslim**
Centro Islamico Culturale d'Italia, Viale della Moschea 85. **Tel** 06 80 82 258.

## Students

**Associazione Italiana**

## Alberghi per la Gioventù

Via Nicotera 1, Rome.
**Map** off 2 D1. **Tel** 06 487 11 52. ⓦ aighostels.com

**CTS**
Via Solferino 6a, Rome.
**Map** 4 D3. ⓦ cts.it

## Disabled Travelers

**AIAS**
Via P. Mantegazza 10, Milan. ⓦ aiasmilano.it

**CO.IN.Sociale**
Via E. Giglioli 54a, Rome.
ⓦ coinsociale.it

**Roma per Tutti**
ⓦ romapertutti.it

## Responsible Travel

**National Association for Agritourism**
ⓦ agriturist.it

# Personal Security and Health

Although Italy is generally a safe place for visitors, it is wise to keep a watchful eye on your personal belongings, especially in the larger towns and cities. There is a conspicuous police presence throughout the country and, in the event of an emergency or crime, any of the police officers described in this section will be able to assist you and tell you where to go to report an incident. If you fall ill, pharmacies are a good first stop where medically trained staff can give advice or tell you where to find further help. In an emergency, the Emergency Room (*Pronto Soccorso*) of any hospital will treat you, and it is likely that you will encounter English-speaking staff, especially in large towns.

*Commissariato di Polizia* – a police station

Police car

Green Cross ambulance in Venice

Roman fire truck

## Personal Property

Petty theft such as pickpocketing, bag snatching, and car theft is common in Italian cities. In the event of a theft you must report it within 24 hours to the nearest *questura* or *commissariato di polizia* (police station). If possible, show them some ID.

Avoid leaving anything visible in an unattended car, including a car radio. If you have to leave luggage in a car, find a hotel that has private parking. When making a purchase, always check your change and do not keep wallets in back pockets, especially on buses or in other crowded places. "Fanny packs" and money belts are a favorite target for pickpockets, so try to keep them hidden. When

walking, hold bags and cameras in front of you and on the inside of the pavement so as not to tempt motorized snatchers, and do not show expensive cameras and video equipment in areas off tourist routes.

If attacked, never attempt to hang on to your things, as you could be seriously injured and dragged along the street.

Avoid carrying large sums of money – take out only what you need for the day. It is advisable to get comprehensive travel insurance that covers theft of personal possessions in addition to covering cancellation/delay of flights, loss/damage of luggage, money and other valuables, as well as personal liability and accidents. It should include cover for legal assistance and advice.

If you do need to make an insurance claim for stolen or lost property, you must get a copy of the report *(denuncia)* from the police station when you report the incident. In case of lost passports, go to your embassy or consulate; for lost credit cards or travelers' checks, contact the issuing company's nearest office.

If you do not have insurance cover, contact your embassy as soon as possible after an incident, such as an accident,

occurs. The embassy can offer advice and should provide you with a list of English- and Italian-speaking lawyers who are knowledgeable about both the Italian and English legal systems.

## Personal Security

Although petty crime in cities is frequent, violent crime in Italy is rare. However, it is common for people to raise their voices aggressively during an argument. Usually, remaining calm and being polite will help to defuse the situation.

Always be wary of unofficial tour guides, taxi drivers, or strangers who wish to assist you or advise you on accommodations, restaurants, or stores, as they may expect something in return. Decline their offers politely but firmly.

The brass band of the *carabinieri* performing in high uniform

## Women Travelers

Women traveling on their own in Italy are likely to meet with a lot of attention. This is often more of an irritation than a danger, but it is best to keep away from lonely, unlit streets and areas near train stations at night, and to carry an alarm or whistle and be equipped with the telephone numbers of your hotel and a local taxi service. Walking quickly and purposefully is a good way to avoid any unwanted attention. The staff at hotels and restaurants generally treat single female guests and customers with extra care and attention.

## The Police

There are several different police forces in Italy and each one fulfils a particular role. The State police, *la polizia*, wear blue uniforms and drive blue cars. They deal with most crimes.

The *carabinieri* are militarily trained, with dark blue and black uniforms with red striped pants. These officers deal with a variety of offenses, from organized crime to speeding, and can also conduct random security checks.

The *guardia di finanza* are the financial police (dealing with fraud), and wear grey uniforms with yellow striped pants. The *vigili urbani*, or the municipal traffic police, wear blue and white uniforms in winter and white during the summer.

Even though they are not official police officers, the *vigili urbani* can issue heavy fines for traffic and parking offenses. They can usually be spotted patrolling the streets, enforcing laws or directing traffic. Officers from any of the forces will be able to help in an emergency.

Outside a Florentine pharmacy with a green cross sign

## Medical Treatment

Emergency medical care in Italy is free for all EU and Australian citizens, thanks to reciprocal agreements. The EHIC European Health Insurance Card, which is available from the **UK Department of Health** offices, website or from a main post office, covers emergencies only; private medical insurance is needed for all other types of treatment. The card comes with a booklet that contains general health advice and information about how to claim free medical treatment when traveling abroad. You may find you have to pay and reclaim the money later. Australians need to apply to **Medicare**.

Municipal police officer

Non-EU citizens should try to arrive in Italy with comprehensive private medical insurance to cover all eventualities. If you do need emergency treatment, go to the *Pronto Soccorso* (Emergency Room) of the nearest hospital.

If necessary, you will be referred to the appropriate specialist or department within the same structure.

As an alternative, ask your hotel to call the night doctor – *guardia medica* – who can be consulted on the phone.

No inoculations are needed for Italy, but mosquito repellent is advisable in summer. Repellent creams and sprays are found in pharmacies, as are electrical repellers that burn pellets to deter the bugs.

## Pharmacies

Various medical products, including homeopathic medications, are available in any pharmacy *(farmacia)*, but a prescription is often required. Qualified staff will offer advice for minor ailments and common illnesses and provide appropriate medicines. Thanks to a night rota *(servizio notturno)*, there is always a pharmacy open in all cities and most towns. Those that are open at night are listed in the local pages of daily newspapers and on all pharmacy doors.

Pharmacies also sell toiletries and beauty items. Common non-prescription pharmaceutical products such as aspirin are also sold at lower prices in many large supermarkets.

# Banking and Local Currency

Virtually all Italian hotels, many stores, large restaurants, and gas stations accept major credit cards. Only in the more off-the-beaten-track locations will you have difficulties without cash in euros, though some establishments will offer a discount for payments made in cash, especially in low season. When you pay with a credit card, you might be asked to show identification, such as your passport. Foreign currency can be changed in banks, although these are often crowded and service tends to be slow. All banks have ATMs (*bancomat*) that will accept cards with a PIN.

Most machines also accept MasterCard, VISA, and American Express cards. Although banks often have the best exchange rates, bureaux de change and foreign exchange machines can be more convenient.

ATM, which also accepts VISA and MasterCard

## Changing Money

Banking hours are somewhat restrictive and can also be slightly erratic so it is safest to acquire a small amount of local currency before you arrive in Italy. Exchange rates will vary from place to place.

Traveler's checks are no longer in common use in Italy. Few stores will accept them (or even know what they are). A more modern alternative to the traveler's check is a prepaid currency card. You can apply online for a card, preload money from your checking account and convert it into euros. You can then use the card much like a debit card in stores, restaurants, bars, and ATMs. They can be topped up at any time and cancelled if stolen. As they are not connected to a bank account, they minimize the risks of fraud.

Bureaux de change can be found in all main towns. Although they are easier to use,

they usually have worse exchange rates and charge more commission than banks.

## Regional Differences in Cost of Living

The north is generally more expensive than the south, but there are many exceptions. Restaurants and hotels off the beaten track are usually better value, and buying locally made produce is cost effective if you avoid obvious tourist traps.

## Banking Hours

Banks are usually open between 8:30am and 1:30pm, Monday through Friday. Most also open for an hour in the afternoon, from about 2:15pm to 3pm or 2:30pm until 3:30pm, depending on the bank. All banks close on weekends and for public holidays, and they also close early the day before a major

Metal-detecting security doors found at most banks

holiday. Bureaux de change, however, are often open all day, and in some places they also stay open until late at night.

## Using Banks

For security purposes, most banks have electronic double doors with metal detectors, that allow one person in at a time. Metal objects and bags should first be deposited in the lockers located in the lobby. Press the button to open the outer door, then wait for it to close behind you. The inner door then opens automatically. Do not be alarmed by the heavily armed guards you will see patrolling most banks in Italy.

Changing money at a bank can be a frustrating process involving endless form-filling and standing in line. First you have to go to the window that displays the *cambio* sign and then to the *cassa* to obtain your money. If in doubt, ask someone in order to avoid waiting in the wrong line.

If you need to have money sent to you in Italy, banks at home can transfer money to an Italian bank, but it can take up to a week. American Express, Thomas Cook, and Western Union all provide swifter money transfer services, with a charge to the sender.

## ATMs

Withdrawing cash from an ATM (automatic teller machine) with a credit card is a straightforward process. Choose your language on the screen and follow the instructions. You will need to enter your PIN, so make sure you know it. Should your card be swallowed up by an ATM for some reason (for example if you used an incorrect PIN), it may be sent back to the issuing bank. However, if the bank is open do ask inside. Costs for cash withdrawals are set by your bank, so check before you travel. It may be advisable to take out a largish amount of money in one go, but bear in mind that ATMs may run out of bills on weekends.

## The Euro

The euro (€) is the common currency of most of the European Union. It came into general circulation on January 1, 2002, initially for 12 participating countries. Italy was one of those 12 countries taking the euro.

EU members using the Euro as sole official currency are known as the Eurozone. Several EU members have opted out of joining this common currency. Euro bills are identical throughout the Eurozone countries, each one including designs of fictional architectural structures. The coins, however, have one side identical (the value side) and one side with an image unique to each country. Bills and coins are exchangeable in each participating country.

### Bank Notes

Euro bills have seven denominations. The €5 bill (gray in color) is the smallest, followed by the €10 bill (pink), €20 bill (blue), €50 bill (orange), €100 bill (green), €200 bill (yellow) and €500 bill (purple). All bills show the 12 stars of the European Union.

€5 bill

€10 bill

€20 bill

€50 bill

€100 bill

€200 bill

€500 bill

€2 coin

€1 coin

50 cents

20 cents

10 cents

5 cents

2 cents

1 cent

### Coins

The euro has eight coin denominations: €1 and €2; 50 cents, 20 cents, 10 cents, 5 cents, 2 cents, and 1 cent. The €2 and €1 coins are both silver and gold in color. The 50-, 20- and 10-cent coins are gold. The 5-, 2- and 1-cent coins are bronze.

# Communications and Media

Although the Italian postal service is known for being very slow, Italy's other forms of communication, at least in the cities, are more efficient. Fax machines, courier services, and telephones are all widespread, and Internet points are available throughout Italy. Foreign-language newspapers and magazines are on sale in all cities and most large towns. Both state-run and privately owned television stations exist, but only satellite television and radio stations broadcast foreign-language programs.

Telephone company logo

### Telephones

The Italian national telephone company, Telecom Italia, dismantled the last remaining telephone booths in 2014, so it's best to rely on your cell phone, either by setting up a roaming agreement with your provider at home or by purchasing a local SIM card. TIM and Vodafone are the country's main providers..

country code when you are calling from abroad.

Cell phone numbers always start with a 3 and are not preceded by a 0.

### Cell Phones

There are four main GSM frequencies (Global System for Mobile Communications) in use around the world, so, to guarantee that your phone will work, make sure you have a quad-band phone. Tri-band phones from outside the US are also usually compatible but, because the US uses two frequency bands itself, a US tri-band phone may only have limited global coverage. Contact your service provider for clarification.

To use your cell phone abroad you may need to get "permission" from your network operator, as often they need to enable "roaming" for your phone.

Currently, you are charged for the calls you receive in addition to the calls you make, and you

Telephone sign

### International and Local Telephone Calls

A cheap and efficient way to make an international call is to buy an international calling card, which can be purchased at tobacconists or news-stands.

Rates are slightly higher when using it to call a cell phone. Be sure to check with your hotel before using a card from your room, because additional charges may be applied.

To make a local call, always dial the area code preceded by 0, even if you are calling a number within the same town. The 0 before the local area code also needs to be dialed after the

have to pay a substantial premium for the international leg of the call.

Another option is to purchase a local SIM card – the electronic chip that links your phone to a particular network – that can be topped up with credit and uses the local cell phone networks. You can only do this if your handset is "unlocked" – some operators lock their phones to specific networks.

It is worth checking your insurance policy for coverage in case your cell phone is stolen. You should also keep your network operator's helpline number handy in case of emergencies.

### Email and Internet

Internet and email services are widely available throughout Italy, particularly in urban areas, so it should not be difficult to access email accounts or connect to the web. Telecom Italia, the iltalian national phone company, has set up Internet services in the country's major train stations and public phone centers. Internet time can be purchased using a regular phone card.

Some major chains of Internet points sell magnetic cards with credit that can be used in any of their stores throughout Italy. **Internet Train**, with branches in over 40 towns, is the most visible. Visit its website for a full list of stores. In addition, small Internet points are very common. These are usually clustered around train stations, cheap hotels, and university areas and can range from the back room of a café or bar to the corner of a laundromat. Users can buy computer time in blocks as short as 15 minutes. Student discounts are usually available, and the cost per

Using an Internet café in Rome

minute decreases as the amount of time purchased increases.

Many hotels have Wi-Fi, so travelers who bring their own laptop can have easy access. You'll probably need a plug adaptor, too. Remember that with **Skype** or **Voip Stunt** installed it's possible to make phone calls over the Internet with the help of a small microphone. Calls are free between Skype users.

## TV and Radio

Television channels in Italy include the state-owned RAI (Uno, Due, and Tre) and Mediaset (Retequattro, Canale Cinque, and Italia Uno). There are also many local channels. Most foreign programs are dubbed into Italian, although satellite channels, such as BBC World News, Sky, and CNN, show news and sports programs in English. There are three national radio stations and hundreds of local stations.

A selection of newspapers available at a newsstand

## Newspapers

There are several national daily newspapers, including *La Stampa, Il Corriere della Sera,* and *La Repubblica.* Papers with the most detailed news of Italy's major cities include *Il Mattino* for Naples, *Il Messaggero* for Rome, *La Nazione* for Florence, and *Il Giornale* for Milan.

All newspapers will have local pages and listings for movies, theaters, main concerts, and other cultural events. In Rome and Milan, *La Repubblica* also publishes regular "what's on and where to go" supplements called *TrovaRoma* and *ViviMilano* respectively. Florence's *Firenze*

*Spettacolo* has weekly entertainment listings magazines. The latter also has a useful restaurant section and a summary of listings in English at the back.

British and American papers, such as the *International Herald Tribune, The Guardian,* and *USA Today,* are readily available and tend to arrive in the main cities at around midday on the day of publication.

## Post Offices

Local post offices open from 8:25am to 1:50pm weekdays, and from 8:25am to noon on Saturday. Main city post offices are open from 8:25am to 7pm nonstop. Many tobacconists also sell stamps.

The Vatican City and the state of San Marino have their own mail systems and stamps. Bear in mind that letters bearing San Marino or Vatican stamps can only be posted in San Marino and Vatican mailboxes.

The red mailboxes (blue in the Vatican) usually have two slots, labeled *per la città* (for the city only) and *tutte le altre destinazioni* (for all other destinations).

Italian mail is notorious for its unreliability, and letters can take between four days and two weeks to arrive.

For a faster service it is better to send letters by express mail services such as *Postacelere* (for letters) and *Paccocelere* (for larger packages). Both services are based at all main post offices and guarantee delivery within 24 to 72 hours. They are far less expensive than private couriers. Another reliable option is recorded delivery *(raccomandata).* Anything of value should be sent by insured post *(assicurata).*

City letters · Other destinations

Italian mailbox

## DIRECTORY

Always remember to use the full area code (including the first zero), even when phoning within a city.

### Useful Numbers

**Information**
**Tel** 1254 (Option 1).

**Multilingual Information**
**Tel** 1254 (Option 2).

**Operator Services**
**Tel** 170 (also for collect and calling card calls).

**American Operators**
**Tel** 800 17 24 44 (AT&T).
**Tel** 800 17 24 01 (Verizon).
**Tel** 800 17 24 05 (Sprint).

**Australian Operators**
**Tel** 800 17 26 10 (Telstra).
**Tel** 800 17 26 11 (Optus).

### Country Codes

To call Italy from these countries, dial the code and then the full area code (including the 0) and the number.
**Tel** 0 1139 – US & Canada
**Tel** 00 39 – UK
**Tel** 00 39 – Ireland
**Tel** 00 1139 – Australia

### Email and Internet

**Internet Train**
w internettrain.it/dovesiamo.html

**Skype**
w skype.com

**Voip Stunt**
w voipstunt.com

### Mail and Couriers

**Italian Post Office**
w poste.it

### Private Couriers

**DHL**
**Tel** 199 19 93 45.
w dhl.it

**Fedex**
**Tel** 199 15 11 19.
w fedex.com

**UPS**
**Tel** 02 30 30 30 39.
w ups.com

# TRAVEL INFORMATION

Italy has transportation systems of varying efficiency, from the modern road, bus, and rail networks of the north to the slower systems of the south. Numerous airlines operate flights to several of the country's major airports. Within Italy itself, the national carrier Alitalia and several smaller companies provide an extensive network of domestic flights. Connections by road to the rest of Europe are good, though Alpine roads can be adversely affected by the weather in winter. Freeways and other roads within the country are generally good, but can be busy on weekends and at peak periods. Italy also has an efficient system of ferries connecting Sicily, Sardinia, and many of the smaller off-shore islands. Many of these are car ferries, and are busy in summer.

## Green Travel

An excellent public transportation network makes traveling in Italy – without using high-impact flights or long car drives – quite straightforward. Train and bus systems both offer regular and reliable services and are reasonably priced. Connections with major European cities are good and travelers can often choose between day services on the Eurocity trains and overnight services on the EuroNight trains. There are also high speed trains, known as the *Alta Velocità* (*see pp628–9*).

In places where only a few people use a service (such as to outlying settlements in the Alps and Apennines), some authorities have set up a *servizio a chiamata* (demand-responsive service), whereby passengers call a toll-free number to reserve a vehicle. This results in cost savings for the administration and a reduction in carbon emissions, plus passengers get a personalized taxi for the price of a one-way bus ticket. Within cities, less polluting vehicles such as battery- or methane-powered buses and *vaporetti* have been introduced.

Bicycle tracks and bicycle rental points are increasing in number, and many cities such as Milan and Rome have plenty of rental points and marked safe tracks. The Trentino-Alto Adige regions are especially well organized, with long-distance bicycle routes. For a small charge bicycles can be transported on many regional and international trains.

## Arriving by Air

*Rome's Leonardo da Vinci (Fiumicino) and Milan's Malpensa are the key airports for long-haul flights into Italy. Milan's Linate airport handles some European flights, and most European airlines also fly to Venice, Turin, Naples, and Pisa (for Florence). Many airlines are now flying regularly to smaller cities such as Florence, Genoa, Bologna, Verona, and Bergamo, while charter flights serve summer destinations in peak season such as Catania, Olbia, and Rimini.*

The bright hall at Fiumicino airport, Rome

## Long-Haul Flights

If you are flying from the United States, **Delta** and **United Airlines** operate regular direct scheduled flights to Rome and Milan, with services from New York, Philadelphia, Los Angeles, Boston, and Chicago. **Air Canada** flies from Montreal and Toronto, while **Qantas** flies from Sydney and Melbourne.

Regular service between Rome and Milan and New York, Boston, Chicago, Miami, and Toronto is also offered by the Italian state airline, **Alitalia**.

It may, however, be more convenient and cheaper for long-haul passengers to take a budget flight to London, Frankfurt, Paris, Athens, or Amsterdam and then continue to Italy from there.

## European Low-Cost Flights

It has never been so easy to get to Italy by air. **British Airways** and **Alitalia** and its partners fly to major destinations in Italy from large European cities. However, low-cost, "no-frills" airlines offer many more destinations.

From the UK, **Ryanair** flies to more than 20 airports (including Genoa, Rome-Ciampino, Turin, and Venice-Treviso) out of Stansted; while **easyJet**, from Gatwick, Luton, or Stansted, serves Rome-Ciampino, Milan, Venice, Pisa, Palermo, and Naples, and also Rome, Olbia, and Pisa from Bristol. **Meridiana** flies to Florence and Olbia from Gatwick and, like **Blu-Express**, also offers a number of domestic flights.

An airplane at Rome's Fiumicino airport

## Tickets and Fares

Fares vary enormously according to season and supply and demand. You can usually get the best deals by reserving online well in advance.

Consult a good travel agent or check availability on the Internet. If you are based in the UK, it may be worthwhile to scour the small ads of newspapers for charter and discounted scheduled flights on major routes. Most charters leave from Gatwick or Luton, and may land at a city's second (and often less convenient) airport. Fares tend to vary greatly during the year, but the most expensive periods are during the summer months and over the Christmas and Easter holidays. Where applicable, ask for available student discounts.

## Package Vacations

Package vacations to Italy are usually cheaper than traveling independently, unless you are traveling on a tight budget and are prepared to make use of youth hostels and campgrounds. Rome, Florence, and Venice are often offered as separate or linked package deals, and many operators have packages to the Tuscan and Umbrian countryside, Sicily, the Italian Lakes, the Italian Riviera, Naples, and the Amalfi Coast. In winter, ski packages are available to many Alpine resorts. Special interest packages, such as cooking, walking, and art tours, are common.

In cities, different tour operators may use different hotels, so it is worth researching the most pleasant (and centrally located) accommodations options. Many operators include transfers from the airport to your hotel. Some include tour guides.

## DIRECTORY

### Green Travel

**Bicycling in Trentino**
W visittrentino.it

### Airlines

**Air Canada**
W aircanada.com

**Alitalia**
Tel 89 20 10. W alitalia.com

**Blu-Express**
W blu-express.com

**British Airways**
Tel 02 69 63 36 02.
W britishairways.com

**Delta**
W delta.com

**easyJet**
W easyjet.com

**Meridiana**
W meridiana.it

**Qantas**
W qantas.com

**Ryanair**
W ryanair.com

**United Airlines**
W united.com

| Airport | Information | Distance to city center | Taxi fare to city center | Public transportation to city center |
|---|---|---|---|---|
| Rome (Fiumicino) | 06 659 51 W adr.it | 22 miles (35 km) | €48 | FS 30 mins |
| Rome (Ciampino) | 06 659 51 W adr.it | 9 miles (15 km) | €35 | M 45 mins |
| Milan (Linate) | 02 23 23 23 W milano linate-airport.com | 5 miles (8 km) | €20 | 15 mins |
| Milan (Malpensa) | 02 23 23 23 W milano malpensa-airport.com | 31 miles (50 km) | €90 | FS M 60 mins |
| Pisa (Galileo Galilei) | 050 84 91 11 W pisa-airport.com | 1 mile (2 km) | €10 | FS to Pisa: 10 mins FS to Florence: 80 mins |
| Venice (Marco Polo) | 041 260 92 60 W veniceairport.it | 8 miles (13 km) | €35 (€100 water taxi) | 60 mins 20 mins |
| Venice (Treviso) | 0422 31 51 11 W trevisoairport.it | 15 miles (25 km) | €70 to Venice | to Treviso: 20 mins to Venice: 70 mins |
| Verona | 045 809 36 666 W aeroportoverona.it | 7 miles (12 km) | €25 | 15 mins |
| Bergamo | 035 32 63 23 W orioaeroporto.it | 3 miles (5 km) | €18 | 25 mins |
| Turin | 011 567 63 61 W aeroportoditorino.it | 9 miles (15 km) | €30 | 20 mins |
| Naples | 081 789 61 11 W aeroportodinapoli.it | 4 miles (7 km) | €20 | 30 mins |
| Palermo | 091 702 02 73 W gesap.it | 21 miles (35 km) | €40–€45 | 50 mins 1 hr |

# Arriving by Sea, Rail, and Road

Italy is served by an extensive network of roads, railroads, and international ferry lines. Road and rail links cross into the country from France, Switzerland, Austria, and Slovenia, and there are train services from as far afield as Budapest, London, and Barcelona. Road connections into the country are generally of freeway standard, though delays can occur at some of the many Alpine passes and tunnels during bad weather or peak summer vacation periods.

Self-service help points with train information on screens

Ticket windows at Florence's Santa Maria Novella train station

## Arriving by Car

Most roads into Italy from the rest of Europe involve Alpine crossings by tunnel or mountain pass. The notable exceptions are from Slovenia in the northeast (on the A4 freeway) and the French Riviera route that enters Italy as the A10 freeway at Ventimiglia.

The most popular route from Geneva and southeast France, via the Mont Blanc tunnel and A5 freeway, enters Italy close to Aosta and Turin. The Gotthard Base tunnel also runs between Switzerland and Italy and is 35 miles (57 km) long. Another approach from Switzerland uses the St. Bernard Pass and tunnel.

Farther east, the main route from Austria and southern Germany crosses the Brenner Pass and heads down to Verona on the A22 freeway via Trento and the Adige valley. The passes are rarely closed for bad weather, but snow and fog can make progress slow on the winding roads through the mountains. Most freeways are toll-roads that you pay as you exit.

## Arriving by Train

After air travel, arriving by train is the least painful way to reach Italy. Countless services (including many sleepers) link Italian towns and cities with places as far afield as Brussels, Budapest, and Barcelona. Connections from Paris (and London, via Eurostar) run to Turin, Milan, Venice, Bologna, Florence, or along Italy's west coast, via Genoa and Pisa, to Rome and Naples. Trains also run from German, Swiss and other northern European cities

Platform sign

Exit sign

A Frecciargento train on the track at Venice train station

to Milan, Turin, Venice, and Verona. There are also direct services from Vienna, Spain, and the south of France. Motorail connections exist from several centers in northern Europe and the Channel ports.

The popularity of low-cost airlines has forced international train travel to be a little more competitive – if reserved online. Special discount fares, however, are often available for senior travelers and for people under 26.

Trains can be extremely busy during peak periods, particularly on Friday and Sunday evenings, and during the Christmas and Easter holiday periods. July and August can also be frantically busy, especially on routes from Germany and ports connecting with Greek ferries in the south. Reservations on most services are advisable.

## Arriving by Boat

Most people arriving in Italy by boat do so from Greece, using services from Corfu and Patras to Brindisi and other southeastern ports. Boats are crowded in summer, as are connecting train services from Brindisi to the rest of Italy.

Other international connections include ferries from Malta and North African ports to Palermo, Naples, and various southern Italian ports. Boats also run from towns in the south of France to Genoa, Livorno, and ports on the Italian Riviera, and from the Croatian coast across the Adriatic to Venice.

## Arriving by Bus

Bus travel to Italy is relatively cheap, but long journey times make it one of the least comfortable ways to travel. The travel time from London to Milan is about 24 hours, and it is about 33 hours from London to Rome. A night on the road is thus unavoidable. **Eurolines** runs buses from London's Victoria Coach Station to most of Italy's major cities as far as Rome and Naples (a change at Milan or Paris is often necessary). Buses travel via Dover, Calais, Paris, and Dijon and it is useful to have some euros with you for stops en route. Travel around Italy by long-distance bus is feasible with **SITA**.

Tourist buses parked in Venice's bus station

# Traveling by Ferry

Italy's large number of offshore islands have led to a large and well-developed network of ferries, as well as ferry services to the rest of Europe and North Africa.

One of the Moby Lines car ferries that sail the Mediterranean

### Ferries

Car ferries are a convenient link with the beautiful islands scattered off the Italian mainland. Boats for Sardinia leave from Civitavecchia (north of Rome), Livorno, and Genoa, and depart for Sicily from Naples and Reggio di Calabria. Ferries run from the major Sicilian ports to the Egadi and the Aeolian archipelagoes, as well as to countless other small islands around Sicily (although be aware that ferries to the smaller islands do not always carry cars).

Boats also ply between Elba and Piombino, as well as to the smaller islands of the Tuscan archipelago such as Capraia. Ferries run from ports close to Rome to Ponza and its surrounding islands, and from Naples to Capri and Ischia. On the east coast the Tremiti islands are linked to ports on the Gargano peninsula.

Hydrofoils are increasingly complementing conventional ferries, particularly on the busy routes to Capri and Ischia. Hydrofoils, and ferries, also run on some of Italy's lakes, such as Como and Garda.

Lines for ferries are common in summer, so make reservations well in advance if you plan to travel in July or August, especially if taking a vehicle. Ferry services are more frequent and reliable in summer than in winter.

Reservations can be made online, through travel agents, or with a ferry line's agent in your own country. Ticket prices can vary according to the time of year but are generally reasonable. To check schedules and fares, visit the relevant website.

## DIRECTORY

### Arriving by Train

**Ferrovie dello Stato**
Tel 89 20 21 (in Italy).
W trenitalia.com

### Arriving by Bus

**Eurolines**
W eurolines.co.uk

**SITA**
W sitabus.it

### Ferries

**Corsica Sardinia Ferries**
Tel 199 400 500.
W corsicaferries.it
Civitavecchia/Livorno – Golfo Aranci

**Grandi Navi Veloci**
Tel 010 209 45 91.
W gnv.it Genoa/Civitavecchia – Palermo Genoa – Porto Torres/Olbia

**Moby Lines**
Tel 199 303 040.
W mobylines.it
Piombino – Elba
Genoa/Livorno – Olbia

**SNAV**
Tel 081 428 55 55.
W snav.it
Ancona – Split
Naples/Sorrento – Capri/Ischia
Naples – Aeolian Islands

**Tirrenia**
Tel 892 123; 02 26 30 28 03. W tirrenia.it
Bari – Durazzo
Genoa – Porto Torres
Civitavecchia – Olbia
Naples – Palermo/Cagliari
Cagliari – Palermo

**Venezia Lines**
Tel 041 882 11 01.
W venezialines.com
Venice – Rabac
Venice – Porec/Rovinj/Pula
Bari – Durazzo

# Traveling by Train

Train travel is one of the best ways to explore Italy. Tickets are inexpensive, services frequent, and the trains are some of the most modern in Europe. Services can be busy, but the days of rampant overcrowding are mostly over. Tracks often run through lovely countryside, from mountain lakes to rolling plateaus, and they provide more convenient links between cities than roads or air travel. Only in the south, or deeply rural areas, are services slow and infrequent.

A Eurostar – one of Italy's fastest trains

## The Network

Italy's railroad network is largely an integrated state-run system operated by **Trenitalia** of the Ferrovie dello Stato (FS), which has introduced superfast services reducing travel times between major cities. In this, it competes with the **NTV** consortium, whose trains are known as **Italo** by most people. Smaller privately run lines also fill crucial gaps left by the FS, but through tickets are generally available where travel involves both networks. State and private lines often share the same main station (*stazione*), and also charge similar fares.

## Trains

Trenitalia and NTV (Italo) take advantage of the *Alta Velocità* (AV) network between major cities in the north and also south as far as Naples. These, the fast Eurostar (ES), and a handful of other special high-speed trains always require advance seat reservations. Intercity (IC) trains and Eurocity (EC) trains stop only at major stations and require a supplement (*un supplemento*) to be paid on top of the standard ticket price (supplements can be bought on the train, but are considerably more expensive).

*Regionali* and *Interregionali* trains make more stops and require no supplement.

All AV, ES, EC, and Intercity trains are usually air-conditioned. Branch line cars can still be ancient.

Amenities for mobility-impaired passengers include assistance at stations, exits on all fast trains, and international services. For assistance, ask at the special *Sale Blu* (Blue Halls) in main train stations.

## Tickets, Fares and Timetables

Tickets (*biglietti*) are available as one-way (*andata*) or round-trip (*andata e ritorno*) in first class (*prima classe*) or second class (*seconda classe*). They can be bought at some travel agents or at any station ticket office (*biglietteria*).

At major stations there are automated ticket machines, and you can also buy tickets through the Trenitalia app for iPhone and the ProntoTreno app for Android and other devices. Please note that you must be registered on the Trenitalia website in order to use the app, so it is wise to register before departure. Be sure to validate all non-digital tickets on both outbound and return journeys, or you will be fined. A ticket's validity usually starts on the day of purchase, so be sure to specify the day of travel when buying tickets. Fares are calculated on a kilometric basis and are among the cheapest in western Europe. Many discounted fares are offered, including special family tickets. Some online ticket purchases also carry discounts.

Getting refunds involves a complicated process – ask at the *Assistenza* counter at major stations. It is very important, therefore, to buy the correct ticket before traveling.

If you plan to use trains often, visit www.trenitalia.com for the online timetable.

## Passes

The most useful pass for visitors is the **Interrail Pass**, which gives unlimited travel for consecutive or nonconsecutive days over varying periods, with special rates for those under 26. It can be purchased online or at most main stations and various agencies outside Italy. An Interrail One Country Pass allows travel on any five or ten days within a specific period within one country.

## Validity and Reservations

One-way or round-trip tickets are valid for up to two months from the date of purchase. If a seat reservation is made with the ticket, however, the date you wish to travel will be stamped automatically on the ticket. Reservations are automatic on AV and Eurostar services, and they are a good idea on all trains on and around public holidays. Reservations can be made at most main stations or online.

The concourse at Stazione Termini, Rome

## Discounts

The Smart Price deal offers discounts on international trains between Italy and various European countries. One-way prices range from €19 to €70, though there are additions for couchettes and sleeper cars. Tickets can be bought at major stations or on the Trenitalia website, though a fixed number are available, so reserve ahead.

## Luggage Storage

Main city stations usually have luggage storage. Most are staffed (but the smaller stations have self-service lockers), and you may need to present identification when depositing or picking up bags. Fees are calculated per bag and by the number of hours they are left.

## Scenic Railroad Routes

Italy's varied geography makes for some memorable train trips across the length and breadth of the country. The glacially shaped Adige Valley between Bolzano and Verona in the north is thick with apple orchards and surrounded by soaring alpine peaks, with the pretty Trento-Male line branching off it. The Tuscan countryside south of Florence boasts views of hill-towns and rolling wheatfields, while close by in Lazio the Roma Nord-Viterbo line winds its way through beautiful rural scenery.

Farther south, trains cross the Straits of Messina to Sicily on a special ferry, while a narrow-gauge line circles Mount Etna. For steam train enthusiasts, there are trips run by the **FTI (Ferrovie Turistiche Italiane)** groups in the north through alpine foothills and past picturesque lakes, as well as in the countryside outside Siena.

## Machines for Trenitalia Train Tickets

These machines are easy to use, and most have instructions on screen in a choice of six languages. They accept coins, bills, and credit cards.

**1** Touch screen: choose destination, train, and ticket type, make seat reservations, and choose payment method.

**2** Insert coins here.

**3** Insert bills here.

**4** Make payment with credit card: use touch pad with slot for card below.

**5** Receive train tickets, seat reservations, and change here.

## DIRECTORY

### Trains

**Erail Travel Ltd**
**Tel** 020 7619 1083 (UK).
**w** erail.co.uk

**FTI (Ferrovie Turistiche Italiane)**
**w** ferrovieturistiche.it

**Interrail Pass**
**w** interrail.eu

**NTV (Italo)**
**w** italotreno.it

**Trenitalia**
Information for travel all over Italy. **Tel** 89 20 21.
**w** trenitalia.com

## Italy's Principal FS Network

The Italian state railroad network operates various types of services. Check what is available before buying your ticket.

**Key**

● Main stations

○ Other stations

— Principal railroad route

- - Route over water

# Traveling by Car

A motoring tour is a practical way of exploring the country, though you should take into account high gas prices, parking difficulties, driving restrictions in cities, and the Italians' occasionally erratic approach to driving. A car is invaluable in the countryside and for extensive touring, but less useful in major towns and cities, due to congestion and the fact that most city centers are off-limits to non-residents' cars.

One-way street

Blue signs showing main highways and green signs showing freeways

Automatic tollbooths on the freeway outside Florence

## What to Take

Drivers from outside Italy who bring their own foreign-registered cars into the country must carry a Green Card (for insurance purposes), all the vehicle's registration documents, and a full, valid driver's license (*patente* in Italian). Any EU nationals who do not have the standard EU "pink" license and are planning to stay for more than six months will need an Italian translation of their license, obtainable from most automobile organizations or from the Italian state tourist office in your home country. A red warning triangle and fluorescent vests must also be carried at all times, for use in the event of a breakdown or emergency.

## Gas

Gas *(benzina)* in Italy is some of the most expensive in Europe (diesel, or *gasolio*, is a little cheaper). Although many gas stations are now self-service, it is still common to be served by an attendant. Most gas stations follow normal business hours, so make sure you have a full tank before lunchtime or on public holidays. On highways gas stations tend to be open 24 hours a day. Credit and debit cards are usually accepted.

## Roads

Italy has a good network of freeways, though many have a total of only four lanes, often leading to congestion. Busy routes include the A1 from Bologna to Florence and between Bologna, Parma, and Milan. Tolls are payable on most freeways *(autostrade)*, again leading to congestion at tollbooths *(Alt Stazione)* at busy periods. Payment is made at the end of the journey with cash, credit card, or pre-paid magnetic VIA cards, available

### Rules and Regulations

Drive on the right, use the left lane only for passing, and yield to traffic from the right. Seat belts are required for all passengers in the front and back. Heavy fines are levied for using a cell phone while driving. Headlights must be turned on even during the day on highways and outside built-up areas. The speed limit in urban areas is 30 mph (50 km/h); outside urban areas it is 70 mph (110 km/h) on divided highways and 55 mph (90 km/h) on other secondary roads. On freeways the limit is 80 mph (130 km/h) for vehicles over 1100cc and 70 mph (110 km/h) for those under 1100cc.

from tobacconists and the **ACI**. There is a congestion charge in Milan (7:30am–7:30pm Mon–Fri); phone 800 437 437 or visit www.comunemilano.it/ecopass before entering the city.

Secondary highways are known as *Nazionali* (N) or as *Strade Statali* (SS), and vary enormously in quality. Mountain roads are usually good, but distances can be deceptive. In winter, snow chains are mandatory on many higher routes.

Back roads can offer incredible views, but there are often hairpin bends. Sound your horn when approaching a blind bend and flash your lights at night. Roads known as *strade bianche*, or "white roads" have only a gravel surface. These are often narrow and steep, but usually passable to cars. Avoid driving in unfamiliar areas of the countryside at night.

No stopping

End of speed restriction

Pedestrian-only street – no traffic

Give way to oncoming traffic

No parking

Danger (often with description)

Logo for international car rental company Europcar

## Car Rental

Car rentals (autonoleggio) in Italy are expensive, and should be organized beforehand through package airfare-plus-rental deals or advance reservations with rental agencies that have branches in Italy. For on-the-ground rentals, Italian firms may be cheaper than big international names. Agencies are listed in the Yellow Pages (Pagine Gialle) under Autonoleggio. Most airports have car rental offices on site.

To rent a car in Italy you must usually be over 21 (sometimes older) and have held a valid driver's license for at least a year. Visitors from outside the EU must have an international license, though in practice not all rental agencies insist on this. Check the fine print of the agreement for insurance coverage.

## Accidents and Breakdowns

If you have an accident or a breakdown, switch on your hazard warning lights and place a warning triangle 164 ft (50 m) behind your car. Then (for break-downs) call the **ACI** emergency number (803 116) or emergency services (112 or 113). The ACI will tow any foreign-registered car free to the nearest ACI-affiliated garage. They also do free repairs for members of affiliated auto-mobile associations, such as the AAA in the US.

If you have an accident, stay calm, and do not admit liability or make any statements that might incriminate you later. Simply exchange car and insurance details, names, and addresses.

## Parking

Parking in most Italian cities and large towns is a problem. Many historic centers have restricted daytime access and baffling one-way systems. Other areas may be reserved for residents' parking (marked riservato ai residenti). Most towns have metered park-ing areas that charge an hourly fee, paid with coins, cards, or coupons bought from tabacchi. Cars can be towed away or have their wheels clamped, especially in areas marked zona rimozione, particularly on street-cleaning days. Call the municipal police (vigili) to retrieve your car.

Official parking area patrolled by attendant

## Safety

Car theft is rife in Italy. Never leave anything in your car, and (if possible) always remove radio-CD players and GPS devices. Leave your car in a guarded parking lot whenever you can. Be especially careful driving at night, when Italian driving is more cavalier than usual, and when many traffic lights switch to flashing amber. Hitchhiking (autostop) is not a good idea (and is not common), certainly never for women on their own.

## DIRECTORY

### Car Rental

**Avis**
Tel 06 45 21 08 391.
W avisautonoleggio.it

**Europcar**
Tel 199 307 030.
W europcar.it

**Hertz**
Tel 199 11 22 11.
W hertz.it

**Maggiore**
Tel 199 151 120.
W maggiore.it

**Sixt**
Tel 06 65 21 11 (Rome).
W sixt.it

### Emergencies

**ACI emergency**
Tel 80 3116. W aci.it

**Police**
Tel 112 or 113.

**Ambulance**
Tel 118.

## Distance Chart

| Rome | | | | | | | | | | | |
|---|---|---|---|---|---|---|---|---|---|---|---|
| **286** 178 Ancona | | | | | | | | | | | |
| **748** 465 | **617** 383 Aosta | | | | | | | | | | |
| **383** 238 | **219** 136 | **401** 249 Bologna | | | | | | | | | |
| **645** 401 | **494** 307 | **449** 279 | **280** 174 Bolzano | | | | | | | | |
| **278** 173 | **262** 163 | **470** 292 | **106** 66 | **367** 228 Florence | | | | | | | |
| **510** 317 | **506** 315 | **245** 152 | **291** 181 | **422** 262 | **225** 140 Genoa | | | | | | |
| **601** 373 | **614** 382 | **1220** 758 | **822** 511 | **1097** 682 | **871** 541 | **1103** 685 Lecce | | | | | |
| **575** 357 | **426** 265 | **181** 113 | **210** 130 | **295** 183 | **299** 186 | **145** 90 | **1029** 639 Milan | | | | |
| **219** 136 | **409** 254 | **959** 596 | **594** 369 | **856** 532 | **489** 304 | **714** 444 | **393** 244 | **786** 488 Naples | | | |
| **673** 418 | **547** 340 | **110** 68 | **332** 206 | **410** 255 | **395** 245 | **170** 106 | **1150** 715 | **138** 86 | **884** 549 Turin | | |
| **530** 329 | **364** 226 | **442** 275 | **154** 96 | **214** 133 | **255** 158 | **397** 247 | **967** 601 | **273** 170 | **741** 460 | **402** 250 Venice | |

**10 Distance in kilometres**
10 Distance in miles

# Traveling within Cities

The best ways of getting around Italian cities differ from place to place. In Rome buses are most useful, in Milan the metro is more efficient, and in Venice you will need to take a boat to get around. Streetcars still run in some cities, such as Milan and Rome. Cars are a liability almost everywhere, unlike walking, which in many cases is the easiest way to negotiate the tight historic cores of Italian towns and cities. Florence and Rome have a large limited-traffic zone, and most towns now have a pedestrian-only area in the center.

A Roman bus in the red and gray livery of ATAC

One of the distinctive orange city buses, central Verona

## Buses and Streetcars

Virtually every Italian city and large town has a bus system. Most are cheap, comprehensive, and as efficient as traffic and narrow streets will allow, and systems vary only slightly from city to city. Bus stops are known as *fermate*, and increasingly (notably in Rome) list full details of the routes they serve. Buses *(autobus)* usually run from about 6am to midnight, and there are night buses *(servizio notturno)* in larger cities. If you arrive in a town by train, stations are invariably linked to the center by shuttle buses from the front of the station (tickets are usually available from the station bar or tobacconist).

## Tickets

Tickets *(biglietti)* must be bought before boarding the bus, and can be found at kiosks belonging to the bus company (ATAF in Florence, ATAC in Rome), bars, newsstands, or tobacconists

displaying the bus company's sticker. A few cities also have on-street vending machines around main transportation hubs. It is often worth buying more than one ticket at a time, as outlets often close in the afternoon or early evening. Discounted tickets *(un blocchetto* or *un carnet)* and day- or weeklong visitors' tickets and passes *(una tessera* or *tesserino)* are also available. In some cities tickets are valid for any number of trips within a given time. The ATAC website (www.atac.roma. it) has more details on bus services in Rome.

## Using Buses and Streetcars

Board buses via the front and rear doors, and exit via the central doors. Buses usually have a driver and no conductor (night buses may have a conductor from whom tickets can be bought). Tickets must be validated by

Bus stop displaying the route

punching them in machines at the front or rear of the bus. There are large on-the-spot fines if you are caught without a properly validated ticket. The front, low seats on buses are for people with children, the elderly, and the disabled.

Most larger cities have transportation information offices at the main train station or piazza that provide free maps, timetables, and tickets.

The majority of city buses are painted bright orange and display the final destination *(capolinea)* on the front.

## Metropolitana

Subway systems, known as *metropolitana (la metro* for short), are found in Rome and Milan. Rome's network consists of two lines, A and B, which converge at Stazione Termini, the city's central train station. A third "C" line is under construction, with some stations already operational. Several stations are useful for key sights, and at peak times the lines provide the best way of crossing the city quickly. Stations are fairly dingy – though rarely dangerous – and the train cars can be stiflingly hot in summer. In Milan there are three principal lines – MM1 (the red line), MM2 (green), and MM3 (yellow) – that meet at the hub stations of Stazione Centrale, Duomo, Cadorna, and Loreto.

Metro sign

Termini metro station, Rome

An official taxi waiting at a pedestrian crossing

These three lines give easy access to the majority of the city's main sights.

Metro tickets in both cities are available from the same sources as bus and streetcar tickets, and from machines and ticket offices in subway stations. Tickets in Rome are valid for 100 minutes for one metro journey only, but can be used on any number of bus and streetcar trips. One-, three-, and seven-day tickets are also available and offer unlimited metro, bus, and streetcar travel. In Milan, by contrast, ordinary metro tickets are valid for 90 minutes for one metro journey and can also be used on the buses and streetcars.

Stay on the sidewalk at all costs

Marginally less dangerous to cross

(churches, museums, and other places of interest are often indicated by yellow signs). Always carry your valuables well out of sight. The best times to walk are in the cool of the morning, or in the early evening, when you can join in the pre-dinner stroll known as the *passeggiata*.

## Taxis

Only accept rides in official taxis. Most drivers are honest, but there are many supplements that can be legitimately levied. Generally an extra charge is made for each piece of luggage placed in the

trunk, for rides between 10pm and 7am, on Sundays and public holidays, and for travel to and from airports.

In theory, taxis cannot be hailed. Take one at an official taxi stand (usually found at the train station or main piazza, or close to key tourist sights), or reserve one by phone. When you order a taxi by phone, take the driver's code name, e.g., Napoli 18. If you call a cab, the meter will start at the time of your call.

## Bicycle Rental

Many towns and cities, especially those popular with visitors, have stands and stores offering bicycles and scooters for rent. You can usually rent hourly or by the day, and you may have to leave your passport with the store as a deposit. Be very careful, however, if riding a bicycle in the busy traffic of the larger towns and cities.

**BikeMi** in Milan provides access to bicycles at various places in the city. The initial fee is €4.50 a day (€9 a week), which covers the first 30 minutes. Rates are then 50 cents for 30 minutes, rising to €2 per hour after the first 2 hours. You can register by phone (02 48 60 76 07) or via the website (www.bikemi.it).

## Walking

Walking can be a wonderful way to explore Italy's historic towns and cities, most of whose historic centers are smaller than you might expect. Traffic can be a curse, however, especially in narrow streets (Rome is worst in this respect), but many cities are introducing pedestrian-only areas or cutting down on car access around key tourist sights. On certain Sundays (*domenica a piedi*), entire town centers may be designated traffic-free zones.

Italian towns have plenty of shady squares and cafés to escape the heat of the summer sun, and churches and cathedrals also provide cool retreats from the rigors of sightseeing. Most sights are well marked

## Long Distance Transportation: Buses

Long-haul buses (*pullman* or *corriere*) between towns and cities operate in a similar way to local buses, though you can usually buy tickets on board, and services are often run by different companies who use different-colored buses (blue is the most common color for *pullman*, orange for city buses). Buses in some areas may be run by

Rome–Gubbio bus

several companies (notably around Florence and in Tuscany), and not all of them operate from the same terminals. Long distance routes often depart from outside train stations, or from a town's main piazza. If in doubt, ask at a local tourist office. Reduced schedules may be operating on weekends, when bus company offices are closed.

**Rome**

**COTRAL**
Tel 800 174 471
or 06 72 05 72 05.
 cotralspa.it

**Tuscany**
**Sita**
Tel 800 37 37 60.
w sitabus.it

**Tra-In**
Tel 0577 20 41 11.
w trainspa.it

**National & International**

**Eurolines**
Tel 0861 199 19 00.
w eurolines.it

# Traveling Around Venice

For visitors to Venice, the *vaporetti* or waterbuses *(see pp140–41)* provide an entertaining form of public transportation, although most journeys within the city can usually be covered more quickly on foot. The main route through the city for the *vaporetti* is the Grand Canal. Waterbuses also supply a useful service connecting outlying points on the periphery of Venice, and linking the city to the islands in the lagoon. The most important service from a visitor's point of view is the No. 1. This operates from one end of the Grand Canal to the other and travels slowly enough for you to admire the parade of palaces at the waterside *(see pp92–5)*.

Vaporetto stop at the Giardini Pubblici, Venice

A *vaporetto* or waterbus

The smaller, sleeker *motoscafo*

## Hours of Service

The main routes run every 10 to 20 minutes until the early evening. Services are reduced after midnight, but they run all night. From June through September the services are more frequent and certain routes are extended. Time-tables are available at main landing stages. Be warned: May through September the main routes and island boats are very crowded.

## The Boats

The original *vaporetti* were steam-powered (*vaporetto* means "little steamer"); today they are mostly diesel-run motorboats, with a handful of electric, battery-powered prototypes. Although all the boats tend to be called *vaporetti*, the word only really applies to the large, wide boats that are used on slow routes, such as No. 1. These boats provide the best views. *Motoscafi* are the slimmer, smaller boats that look old but actually go at a fair pace, while *motonavi* are the two-tier boats that run to the islands. To visit the islands of Murano, Burano, or Torcello, take the LN Line, which departs from San Zaccaria and Fondamenta Nuove.

## Types of Tickets

If booths at landing stages are closed, one-way tickets can be purchased on board at no extra charge – the tickets are valid for 75 minutes from the time of purchase. A good way to save

money, however, is by buying a travel card, which is available in one-, two, and three-day variants. Such a card entitles the holder to unlimited travel on most lines. A one-way or round-trip journey supplement to/from Marco Polo airport can also be added to the price of the card (see www.veneziaunica.it).

If you are staying more than a few days, it is worth buying a weekly season ticket (*abbonamento*), available from ticket offices, though non-residents are charged €60 for the privilege. Holders of Rolling Venice cards (which come with information packs and discounts for 6- to 29-year-olds) can buy a three-day youth pass. Tickets include carriage of one piece of luggage, so be prepared to buy another ticket for extra items.

## Vaporetto Information

**ACTV (Venezia Unica office)** Piazzale Roma, Venice. **Map** 5 B1. **Tel** 041 24 24. 🔳 **actv.it**

## Traghetti

*Traghetti* are gondola ferries that cross the Grand Canal at seven different points, providing a useful service for pedestrians. Few tourists make use of this cheap (about €2 per trip), constant service. Points where *traghetti* cross the Grand Canal are marked on the Street Finder maps *(see pp130–39)*. A gondola on yellow street signs points to *traghetti* stops.

A two-tier *motonave* boat

## Gondolas

Gondolas are a luxury form of transportation used only by visitors and Venetians at weddings. Before boarding, check the official tariffs and agree a price with the gondolier. Official costs are around €80 for 40 minutes, rising to €100 after 7pm. During low season, you may be able to negotiate a lower fee, and a journey shorter than the usual 40 minutes.

## Water Taxis

For those with little time and sufficient funds, the fastest and most practical means of getting from A to B in Venice is by water taxi. The craft are sleek, white or polished wood motorboats, and all are equipped with a cabin.

They zip efficiently to and from the airport in only 20 minutes. There are 16 water-taxi ranks, including one at the airport and one at the Lido.

A waterbus gliding past the Palazzo Ducale, on Venice's Grand Canal

Beware of extra charges for transporting luggage, waiting, night service, and for calling out a taxi. When the *vaporetti* go on strike, taxis are scarce.

### Water-Taxi Stands

**Radio Taxi (all of Venice)**
**Tel** 041 522 23 03.

**Piazzale Roma**
**Map** 5 B1. **Tel** 041 71 69 22.

A motor boat on a canal in Venice

## The Main Routes

**Route 1** This is the slow boat down the Grand Canal, stopping at every landing stage. The route starts at Piazzale Roma, travels the length of the Grand Canal, then from San Marco it heads east to the Lido.

**Route 2** The 2 is the faster route down the Grand Canal. With an extension to the Lido during the summer months, the route serves San Zaccaria, continuing westward along the Giudecca Canal to Tronchetto and Piazzale Roma, then down the Grand Canal back to San Zaccaria.

**Routes 4.1, 4.2, 5.1, 5.2, and 6** These lines all sail around the central islands. The circular *Giracittà* routes 4.1-4.2 provide a scenic tour of Venice and Murano, while lines 5.1-5.2 and 6 also extend to the Lido.

**Routes 12, 14** The 12 departs from the Fondamenta Nuove and runs to the main islands in the northern lagoon – Murano, Mazzorbo, and Burano (with a connection to Torcello) – then calls at Punta Sabbioni. The 14 takes you to the Lido, before concluding at San Zaccaria.

## Using the Vaporetti

**1** Tickets are available at most landing stages, some bars, stores, and tobacconists displaying the ACTV sign. It is also possible to buy them on board. The price of a ticket remains the same whether you are going one stop or traveling the whole line.

P.le Roma Parisi

**2** Signs on the landing stage tell you the direction of the boats stopping there.

**3** Imob electronic chip tickets are in use and should be validated before each journey at the electronic machines on the landing stages. Inspectors rarely board the boats and this makes it surprisingly easy to hop on and off the boats without a validated ticket. However, there are steep fines for any passengers caught without tickets.

**4** An indicator board at the front of each boat gives the line number and main stops (ignore the black numbers on the boat's side).

**5** Each landing stage has its name clearly marked on a board. Most stops have two landing stages and it is quite easy, particularly if it is crowded and you can't see which way the boat is facing, to board a boat traveling in the wrong direction. It is helpful to watch which direction the boat is approaching from; if in doubt, check with the boatman.

# General Index

# Acknowledgments

Dorling Kindersley would like to thank the following people whose contributions and assistance have made the preparation of this book possible.

## Contributors
**Paul Duncan** is an expert on art and architectural history and has published guides to Sicily and Italy's hill-towns.
**Tim Jepson**, formerly Rome correspondent for the *Sunday Telegraph*, has written guides to Tuscany, Umbria, Rome and Venice, a complete guide to Italy, *Italy by Train* and *Wild Italy*, a guide to Italy's nature reserves.
**Andrew Gumbel**, former Reuters correspondent in Rome, has written a number of guide books and is the correspondent for the *Independent* in Rome.
**Christopher Catling** has written guides to Florence and Tuscany, the Veneto and the Italian Lakes and is particularly interested in archaeology.
**Sam Cole** works for Reuters in Rome, where he has lived for some years, and contributes regularly to guidebooks on Rome and the Lazio region.

## Additional Contributors
Dominic Robertson, Mick Hamer, Richard Langham Smith, Gillian Price.

## Additional Photography
Francesco Allegretto, Giuseppe Carfagna & Associati, Peter Chadwick, Andy Crawford, Philip Dowell, Mike Dunning, Philip Enticknap, Steve Gorton, John Heseltine, Dave King, Neil Mersh, Anna Mockford, Roger Moss, Poppy, Rough Guides/ James McConnachie, Roger d'Olivere Mapp, Martin Richardson; Kim Sayer, Helena Smith, James Stevenson, Clive Streeter, Jo-Ann Titmarsh, David Ward, Matthew Ward, Christine Webb.

## Additional Illustrations
Andrea Corbella, Richard Draper, Kevin Jones Associates, Chris Orr and Associates, Robbie Polley, Simon Roulstone, Martin Woodward.

## Cartographic Research
Jane Hugill, Samantha James, Jennifer Skelley.

## Revisions Team
Ashwin Raju Adimari, Tora Agarwala, Beverley Ager, Gillian Allan, Gaye Allen, Douglas Amrine, Emma Anacootee, Emily Anderson, Hansa Babra, Claire Baranowski, Peter Bently, Marta Bescos Sanchez, Sonal Bhatt, Uma Bhattacharya, Tessa Bindloss, Hilary Bird, Sally-Ann Bloomfield, Samantha Borland, Isabel Boucher, Hugo Bowles, Reid Bramblett, Caroline Brooke, Nick Bruno, Paola Cacucciola, Stefano Cavedoni, Margaret Chang, Susi Cheshire, Elspeth Collier, Sherry Collins, Lucinda Cooke, Cooling Brown, Imogen Corke, Michelle Crane, Gary Cross, Felicity Crowe, Cristina Dainotto, Federico Damonte, Peter Douglas, Mandy Dredge, Stephanie Driver, Julia Dunn, Michael Ellis, Adele Evans, Mariana Evmolpidou, Danny Farnham, Alice Fewery, Emer FitzGerald, Karen Fitzpatrick, Sarah Fraser, Kyra Freestar, Anna Freiberger, Camilla Gersh, Jackie Gordon, Angela-Marie Graham, Caroline Greene, Vanessa Hamilton, Amy Harrison, Sally-Ann Hibbard, Elinor Hodgson, Tim Hollis, Paul Jackson, Gail Jones, Bharti Karakoti, Roberta Kedzierski, Sumita Khatwani, Amy Knauff, Steve Knowlden, Shikha Kulkarni, Rahul Kumar, Suresh Kumar, Jude Ledger, Leonie Loudon, Siri Lowe, Carly Madden, Hayley Maher, Nicola Malone, Sarah Martin, Georgina Matthews, Alison McGill, Ferdie McDonald, Sam Merrell, Ian Midson, Rebecca Milner, Adam Moore, Cherrye Moore, Daniel Mosseri, John Murphy, Cristina Murroni, Jennifer Mussett, Claire Naylor, George Nimmo, Catherine Palmi, Tiffany Parks, Helen Partington, Alok Pathak, Julia Paynton, Susie Peachey, Alice Peebles, Tamsin Pender, Helen Peters, Marianne Petrou, Gillian Price, David Pugh, Alessandra Pugliese, Rada Radojicic, Jake Reimann, Catherine Richards, David Roberts, Evelyn Robertson, Ellen Root, Carolyn Ryden, Simon Ryder, Giuseppina Russo, Collette Sadler, Sands Publishing Solutions, Baishakhee Sengupta, Ankita Sharma, Marcella Simoni, Kunal Singh, Rituraj Singh, Kate Singleton, Ellie Smith, Susana Smith, Alison Stace, Solveig Steinhardt, Donald Strachan, Hugh Thompson, Rachel Thompson, Jo-Ann Titmarsh, Nikky Twyman, Conrad Van Dyk, Elaine Verweymeren, Ingrid Vienings, Karen Villabona, Stewart J Wild, Rebecca Winke, Debra Wolter, Veronica Wood, Sophie Wright.

Dorling Kindersley would also like to thank the following for their assistance: Azienda Autonoma di Soggiorno Cura e Turismo, Napoli; Azienda Promozione Turistica del Trentino, Trento; Osservatorio Geofisico dell'Università di Modena; Bell'Italia; Enotria Winecellars.

## Photography Permission
Dorling Kindersley would like to thank the following for their assistance and kind permission to photograph at their establishments: Assessorato Beni Culturali Comune di Padova. Le Soprinten-denze Archeologiche di Agrigento, di Enna, di Etruria Meridionale, per il Lazio, di Napoli, di Pompei, di Reggio Calabria e di Roma. Le Soprintendenze per i Beni Ambientali e Architettonici di Bolzano, di Napoli, di Potenza, della Provincia di Firenze e Pistoia, di Ravenna, di Roma, di Siena e di Urbino. Le Soprintendenze per i Beni Ambientali, Architettonici, Artistici e Storici di Caserta, di Cosenza, di Palermo, di Pisa, di Salerno e di Venezia. Le Soprintendenze per i Beni Artistici e Storici della Provincia di Firenze e Pistoia, di Milano e di Roma. Also all the other churches, museums, hotels, shops, restaurants, galleries and sights too numerous to thank individually.

## Picture Credits
a-above; b-below; c-centre; f-far; l-left; r-right; t-top.

Works of art have been reproduced with the permission of the following copyright holders: © ADAGP, Paris and DACS, London 2006 *Bird in Space* by Constantin Brancusi 109cl; © DACS, 2006 *Mother and Son* by Carlo Carrà 203tl.

Dorling Kindersley would like to thank the following for their assistance: **Eric Crighton:** 87cra, **FIAT:** 224c, **Gucci**

Ltd: 43cr, **Prada, Milan:** 43c, **National Archaeological Museum, Naples:** 499br, **National Maritime Museum:** 44cla, **Royal Botanic Gardens, Kew:** 87ca, **Science Museum, Telecom Italia:** 622tr.

The publisher would like to thank the following individuals, companies and picture libraries for permission to reproduce their photographs: **123RF.com:** Lianem 337br; **Accademia Italiana:** Sue Bond 499c; **Actv S.p.A:** 634br, 635crb; **AFE, Rome:** 42cb, 43tl; Giuseppe Carfagna 198br, 206br, 222tl, 222br, 225bl, 226cla, 229tl, 239tr, Claudio Cerquetti 72tc, 73bl, 73tr; Enrico Martino 62clb, 70tr; Roberto Merlo 240bl, 243tl, 243br; Piero Servo 271t, 273bl, Gustavo Tomsich 231tl; **APT Turin:** 228bl, 228tr; **Archivio APT Monregalese:** 233tr; **Action Plus:** Mike Hewitt 74cla; Glyn Kirk 75tr; **Alamy Images:** Peter Adams Photography 16bl; Archivart 443cl; Arco Images GmbH 17cr; Krys Bailey 618cl, Adriano Bacchella 185tl, Bluered 329tl; Tibor Bognar 114br; Enrico Caracciolo 253c; Caro 582bl; Cristina Fumi 28br; CuboImages srl 261tr; FALKENSTEINFOTO 51c; funkyfood London – Paul Williams 96–7; gkphotography 83cl; Jack Hobhouse 626 cla; INTERFOTO 225cr; Jon Arnold Images Ltd. 8–9; Brian Johnson 629c, Norma Joseph 368; Jtb Media Creation, inc. 13br; Justin Kase ztwoz 627cl; Lanmas 425cb; Theodore Liasi 618cla, LOOK Die Bildangentur der Fotografen GmbH 142; David Lyons 13tl, 24, 212–13; Marka 17tr; Steven May 634cla; David Noton Photography 258, 318; Chuck Pefley 26tr; Prisma Bildagentur AG 410; Robert Harding Picture Library Ltd. 173cr; Robert Harding World Imagery 170; tbkmedia.de 603bc; Travel Pictures 15tr; travelstock44 577tr; vario images GmbH & Co.KG/Ulrich Baumgarten 620cl; Steve Vidler 398cla; Ross Warner 95bl; Woodstock 548; **Alamy Stock Photo:** CFimages 622bl, epa european pressphoto agency b.v. 367bl, North Wind Picture Archives 161br, J. Schwanke 351cr. **Alexander Museum Palace Hotel:** 573tr; **Allsport:** Mark Thompson: 75ca; **Ancient Art and Architecture:** 485br; **Antica Residenza Cicogna:** 571tc; **Archiv für Kunst und Geschichte, London:** 32bl, 38b, *Rossini* (1820), Camuccini, Museo Teatrale alla Scala, Milan 40br, 41bl, 45br, *Pope Sixtus IV Naming Platina Prefect of the Library*, Melozzo da Forlì (1477), Pinacoteca Vaticana, Rome 48cla, *Statue of Augustus from Prima Porta* (1st century AD) 53tl, *The Gift of Constantine* (1246), Oratorio di San Silvestro, Rome 54cl, *Frederick I Barbarossa as a Crusader* (1188), Biblioteca Apostolica Vaticana, Rome 57bl, *Giving the Keys to St Peter*, Perugino (1482), Sistine Chapel, Vatican, Rome 60cla, 60bl, *Machiavelli*, Santi di Tito, Palazzo Vecchio, Florence 61br, Andrea Palladio, Meyer 62cb, *Goethe in the Campagna*, Tischbein (1787), Stadelsches Kunstinstitut, Frankfurt 64cl, *Venetian Carnival in the Eighteenth Century*, Anon (19th century) 64clb, *Bonaparte Crossing the Alps*, David, Schloss Charlottenburg, Berlin 65cr, 65bl, 110tr, 110bl, 203bc, 470bl, *Archimedes*, Museo Capitolino, Rome 485bl, 509tc, 513cl; Stefan Diller *St Francis Appearing to the Brothers at Arles* (1295–1300), San Francesco, Assisi 57tl; Erich Lessing Margrave *Gualtieri of Saluzzo Chooses the Poor Farmer's Daughter, Griseldis, for his Wife, di Stefano*, Galleria dell'Accademia Carrara, Bergamo 38crb, *The Vision of St Augustine* (1502), Carpaccio, Chiesa di San Giorgio degli Schiavoni, Venice 61cr, 226bl, 272b, 495cr; **Archivio IGDA, Milan:** 208cl, 208br, 209bc, 525br; **Emporio Armani:** 43tc; **Artemide, GB Ltd:** 43clb.

**Badio & Coltibuono:** 579; **Beehive, Rome:** 574; **Al Bersagliere:** 583tr; **Mario Bettella:** 539clb, 546c; **La Biennale di Venezia:** 608cra; **Frank Blackburn:** 271c; **Osvaldo Böhm, Venice:** 93tc, 98c, 115tc; **Bridgeman Art Library, London/ New York:** 50c, Ambrosiana, Milan 199tl; Bargello, Florence 283bc, 287c; **Bibliothèque Nationale, Paris:** *Marco Polo with Elephants and Camels Arriving at Hormuz, Gulf of Persia, from India, Livre des Merveilles Fr 2810 f.18v* 45tr; British Museum, London *Etruscan Vase Showing Boxers Fighting* 49tl, *Flask Decorated with Christian Symbols* 54tl, *Greek Attic Red-Figure Vase depicting Odysseus with the Sirens, Stamnos* 485cb; Galleria dell'Accademia Carrara, Bergamo 205tc; Galleria degli Uffizi, Florence 30tc, 30tr, 33tl, 33cb, *Self-Portrait*, Raphael Sanzio of Urbino 61bl, 291br, 293bc; K & B News Photo, Florence 280tl; Santa Maria Novella, Florence 301bl; Museo Civico, Prato 332bl; Ravenna 272tr; Louvre, Paris *Statuette of Herakles Brandishing his Club*, Classical Greek, Argive period 484tc; Mausoleo di Galla Placidia, Ravenna 272tr; Museo di San Marco, Florence 301bl; Musée d'Orsay, Paris – Giraudon *Les Romains de la Decadence*, Thomas Couture 399tr; Museo delle Sinopie, Camposanto, Pisa 31clb; Palazzo dei Normanni, Palermo *Scene with Centaurs from the Room of King Ruggero* 527b; Pinacoteca di Brera, Milan 202cla, 202bl, 203ca, Private Collection *Theodoric I* (AD 455–526) *Ostrogothic Kinfg of Italy* 54br; San Francesco, Arezzo 31tr; San Francesco, Assisi 359cb; San Sebastiano, Venice 33crb; San Zaccaria, Venice 37c, 37tr, 103cr; Santa Croce, Florence 288bl, 289cl; Santa Maria Gloriosa dei Frari, Venice 32tr; Santa Maria Novella, Florence 31cla; Scrovegni (Arena) Chapel, Padua 31tr; Scuola di San Giorgio degli Schiavoni, Venice 124b; Staatliche Museen, Berlin *Septimius Severus and Family* 53b; Vatican Museums and Galleries, Rome 425bl; Walker Art Gallery, Liverpool *Aeschylus and Hygieia* 484bc; **British Museum, London:** 50cl; **Brufani Palace:** 572bc.

**Capitoline Museum, Rome:** 391cr; **Hotel Cappella Romantik:** 563tr; **Demetrio Carrasco:** 106br, 634tr; **Cephas Picture Library** Mick Rock: 28tl, 186tr, 187bl, 187tr, 255tl, 255tr; **Foto Elio e Stefano Ciol:** 81cra, 168bc, 168br, 169bl, 169bc, 169br; **Hotel Cipriani, Guidecca:** 562bc; Fortuny Restaurant 580br; **Villa Cipriani:** 581tr; **Il Comandante:** 601tr; **Comune di Asti:** 72cl; **Consorzio Motoscafi Venezia:** 634clb; **Corbis:** Assignments Photographers/Bryn Colton 184cla; Dave Bartruff 480cla; Owen Franken 252cla, 253tl, 481c; Michelle Garrett 481tl; In Pictures/Michael Aitchison 16tr; John Heseltine 382cla; Robert Harding World Imagery/Jeremy Bright 112cla; Robert Holmes 83tl; Hemis/ Stefano Torrione 556–7; Frank Krahmer 2–3; Jose Fuste Raga 180–81; Reuters/ Tony Gentile 383tl; Sylvain Sonnet 378–9, 400; Hubert Stadler 543crb; **Il Cortiletto:** 602tr; **Giancarlo Costa:** 39cr, 39cra, 39tl, 79c.

**Il Dagherrotipo:** 549b, 628bl; Archivio Arte 211tl; Archivio Storico 39br, 210br, 265bc; Alberto Berni 229cl; Riccardo Catani 505b; Marco Cerruti 182cla, 217crb, 219br, 220cl; Antonio Cittadini 193tr, 196bl, 206tl; Gianni Dolfini 554bl; Riccardo d'Errico 74tr, 251tl, 272cl; Maurizio Fraschetti 500br; Diane Haines 177br, 611bc; Maurizio Leoni 71c; Marco Melodia 510clb, 510br, 511cb, 551tr, 610cl; Stefano Occhibelli 73c, 405bl; 256t, 517tr; Donato Fierro Perez 537cb; Marco

Ravasini 174tl, 553cr; Giovanni Rinaldi 29t, 70bl, 71tl, 183bl, 235b, 402c, 371tr, 377tl, 470cr, 503tc, 511c, 537cr, 555tl, 555crb; Lorenzo Scaramella 472cr; Stefania Servili 176tl; **Da Delfina:** 593bl; **Chris Donaghue The Oxford Photo Library:** 121cla; **Doozo, Rome:** 598tr; **Dreamstime:** 88and84 143b; Abey79 12br; Giuseppe Anello 541bl; Ange84 476–7; Antonella865 635tr; Artzzz 627tr; Arzan 51cb; Elisa Bistocchi 506tr; Bokstaz 625tl; Bopra77 506bl; Cipriansalceanu 12tl; Eddygaleotti 490tr; Christa Eder 86tr; Fotoclipge 75cra; Rostislav Glinsky 5cr, 626bc; Gmv 214; Yulia Grigoryeva 487b; Marco Guidi 71tr; Jayk67 328cl; Jborzicchi 74c; Kcho 467tl; Libux77 80bl; Elisa Locci 552br; Lornet 391crb; Luis2007 624cr; Stefano Marinari 338br; Mcristale 157tr; Krisztian Miklosy 340–341; minnystock 319b; Mirohasch 11br; Guido Nardacci 467cr; Pavlinec 544–5; Picturemakersllc 615bc; Romitas 635cla; Rostislav Glinsky 626bc; Rundywong 234; Sergey02 434; Sborisov 386; Spongecake 191b; Stefano Tinti 618br; **Duca di Orvieto:** 596bc.

**Electa:** 160c, 161c, 161tc; **ET Archive:** 40bc, 49c, 53cr, 56–7c, 61tl, 63tl, 67bc, 416tr, 485cra, 535br; **Mary Evans Picture Library**: 38bl, 45ca, 66b, 66crb, 67cr, 68cb, 84tr, 324cla, 330tc, 395cra, 397bl, 413br, 446clb, 515cr, 515br, 554tl.
**Ferrari**: 42b; **Archivio Storico Fiat, Turin**: 68tr; **Fiat Press Office:** 224ca; **APT Folignate e Nocera Umbra:** 365tr; by kind permission of **Fondazione Arena di Verona:** Gianfranco Fainello 608bl; **Werner Forman Archive:** 49br, 55tr, 439br; **Fotolia:** LianeM 14tr; **Consorzio Frasassi:** 376br.

**Studio Gavirati, Gubbio:** 356c; **APT Genova:** Roberto Merlo 242bl; **Getty Images:** Peter Adams 504; Barclay / Stringer 94cla; Daryl Benson 91tr; Mel Curtis 464; De Agostini / A. Dagli Orti 41c; DEA / A. DAGLI ORTI 93cla; Rick Dole 75c; Robert Everts 190; Julian Finney 74bc; Godong 46; Robert Harding 10cla; Hulton Archive / Stringer 68br, 94br, 357br; Francesco Iacobelli 352; The Image Bank/Andrea Pistolesi 82cla; Adam Jones 248–9; Michal Krakowiak 486; Leemage 68cla; Bryn Lennon 74clb; Jean-Pierre Lescourret 14bl; David Lyons 526; Maremagnum 623cl; Clive Mason 75cb; Sergio Pitamitz 78–9; Olaf Protze 259b; Roy Rainford 15cb; Stefano Scata 518; SOPA RF/SOPA/Franco Cogoli 88; Stone/Simone Huber 609tr; Stringer 69tl; Steve Sucsy 246–7; Bob Thomas 69clb; Guy Vanderelst 418; Roger Viollet 68c; **Giraudon, Paris:** *Aphrodite Persuading Helen to Follow Paris to Troy*, Museo Nazionale di Villa Giulia, Rome 49clb, *Pharmacy*, Museo della Civiltà Romana 52cb, *Grandes Chroniques de France*; *Coronation of Charlemagne in St Peter's by Leon III*, Musée Goya, Castres 55tl, *Taking of Constantinople*, Basilica of St John the Evangelist, Ravenna 57cr, *Dante's Hell with Commentary of Guiniforte delli Bargigi* (Ms2017 fol 245), Bibliothèque Nationale, Paris 58crb, *Portrait of St Ignatius of Loyola*, Rubens, Musée Brukenthal, Sibiu 63ca, *Charles III's Fleet at Naples 6th October 1759*, Joli de Dipi, Museo del Prado, Madrid 64tr, *Inauguration of the Naples-Portici Railway*, Fergola (1839), Museo Nazionale di San Martino, Naples 66clb, *Piedmontese and French at the Battle of San Martino in 1859* Anon, Museo Centrale del Risorgimento, Rome 67tl, 110crb, 111tl, 203cr; **Alinari-Giraudon:** *St Mark Appearing to the Venetians Looking for His Body*, Tintoretto (1568), Brera Art Gallery, Milan 33tr, *Shrine*, House of the Vettii, Pompeii 53cb, *St Gregory in his Study* (Inv 285), Pinacoteca

Nazionale, Bologna 55bl, *Portrait of Victor Emmanuel II*, Dugoni (1866), Galleria d'Arte Moderna, Palazzo Pitti, Florence 111br, 203tl, *Louis II of Gonzaga and his Court*, Andrea Mantegna (1466–74), Museo di Palazzo Ducale, Mantova 8–9, 291tl–tc; *History of Pope Alexander III: Building of the City of Alexandria*, Aretino Spinello (1407), Palazzo Pubblico, Siena 59cr; **Alinari-Seat-Giraudon:** 231c; **Flammarion-Giraudon:** *Poem by Donizo in Honour of Queen Matilda*, Biblioteca Apostolica, Vatican 56ca; **Lauros-Giraudon:** *Portrait of Francis Petrarch* 58bc, *Liber notabilium Philippi Septimi, francorum regis a libris Galieni extractus* (Ms 334 569 fig17), Guy of Pavia (1345), Musée Condé, Chantilly 59bl, *Gallery of Views of Ancient Rome*, Pannini (1758), Musée du Louvre, Paris 64–5c, *Four Angels and Symbols of the Evangelists*, 36tr, 37t; **Orsi-Battaglini-Giraudon:** *Madonna of the Shadow*, Museum of San Marco, Florence 36c, *Supplice de Savonarola* Anon 60clb; **Grand Hotel Vesuvio:** 576bl; **The Ronald Grant Archive:** 69bc; Paramount *The Godfather Part III* (1990) 539br; Riama *La Dolce Vita* (1960) 68cra; TCF *Boccaccio '70 The Name of the Rose* (1986) 38cla; **Gritti Palace:** 95 cl; **Palazzo Venier dei Leoni, Peggy Guggenheim Collection, Venice:** 95cla.

**Photo Halupka:** 124tr; **Robert Harding Picture Library:** 41br, 195br, 394cl, 423br, 610bl; Dumrath 273crb; Gavin Hellier 12crb; 610tr; Roy Rainford 503cr; **John Heseltine:** 471tr; **Hivaoa:** 605tr; **Hotel Castel Fragsburg:** 565tr. **Hotel Raphaël – Relais & Châteaux:** 560tl; **Hotel Villa Pagoda:** 559tl; **HSL:** 631tl.

**Icona Roma:** 4cla; **The Image Bank, Milan:** 199br; **Index, Florence:** 286c, 331tr, 331cr; **Istituto e Museo di Storia della Scienza di Firenze:** Franca Principe 44br, 289c; **iStockphoto. com:** ROMAOSLO 465b.

**Tim Jepson:** 355tr.

**Frank Lane Picture Agency:** 220tr, 221tl, 221ca, 221cr; M Melodia/Panda 510cla; **La Riserva di Castel D'appio:** 569tr; **Hotel Laurin, Bolzano:** 564bl; **Locanda del Pilone di Alba:** 586tl; **Locanda I Tre Merli:** 568bc.

**Magnum, London:** Abbas 68crb; **The Mansell Collection:** 56clb; **Marconi Ltd:** 44cl; **Marka:** L Barbazza 101tr; E Cerretelli 125br; M Motta 619tc; **Masterstudio, Pescara:** 508cr; su concessione del **MAXXI:** Roberto Galasso 445tl; **Milano:** 589bl; **Ministero per i Beni Culturali e Ambientali:** *The Last Supper*; da Vinci, Leonardo 204b; **Mirror Syndication International:** 44c; **Foto Modena:** 270tl, 375c; **Monte san Giuliano:** 604bl; **Tony Mott:** 474t; **Museo Diocesano di Rossano:** 524tl.

**NHPA:** Laurie Campbell 87crb; Gerard Lacz 87br; Silvestris Fotoservice 87cr; **Grazia Neri:** Marco Bruzzo 72br; Cameraphoto 112bl; Marcello Mencarini 92br; **Newimage s.r.l:** Rolando Fabriani 606cla; **Nhow Milano:** 566tl; **Nippon Television Network:** 428–9 all pics, 430bl; **Peter Noble:** 322tr, 345br; **Nonna Betta:** 596br.

**L'Occhio di Cristallo/Studio Fotografico di Giorgio Olivero:** 233bl; **APT Orvieto:** Massimo Roncella 362tr; **Osteria**

Francescana: 591tr; Osteria Le Logge: 594tl.
Padova – Musei Civici – Cappella Scrovegni: 81cr, 160 all pics, 161cra, 161crb, 161bl; Padova – Musei Civici Agli Eremitani: 162tr, 162c; Palazzo Grassi S.p.A: Thomas Mayer 109br; Pane e Vino: 592tc; Pasta Madre: 585tr; Da Paolo e Barbara: Toni Meneguzzo 590br; Da Paolino: 600bl; Luciano Pedicini – Archivio dell'Arte: 366bl, 408tr, 479tc, 494tr, 494cl, 494clb, 495tl, 495ca, 495br, 497tr, 534b; APT Pesaro – Le Marche: 372br; Pictures Colour Library: 50clb, 552tl; Andrea Pistolesi: 25; PNALM Archive: in association with www. abruzzonatura.com 510bc; Polis Photo Library; Portrait Suites, Rome: 575bc.

Sarah Quill, Venice: 94t, 98bc, 104tl. Relais Uffizi, Florence: 570bl; Rex Features: 41tl; Steve Wood 43tr; Reuters: Toru Hanai 74crb; Ferran Paredes 75tl; Il Riccio Restaurant: 579bc.

Sauraya & Moroni Milton: 42cr; Scala Group S.p.A: 30bl, 31br, 32br, 33ca, 33bl, 92cla, 56bl, 402cla, *Portrait of Claudio Monteverdi*, Domenico Feti, Accademia, Venice 40bl, *Portolan of Italy* (16th century), Loggia dei Lanzi, Firenze 295bl, Museo Correr, Venice 47b, *Etruscan Bronze Liver*, Museo Civico, Piacenza 48clb, *Earrings*, Museo Etrusco Guarnacci, Volterra 48br, 48r–9c, *Crater from Pescia Romana*, Museo Archeologico, Grosseto 49bc, *Terracotta Vase in the Shape of an Elephant*, Museo Nazionale, Naples 50cr, *Cicero denounces Catiline*, Palazzo Madama, Rome 51tl, 51bl, *Circus Scene Mosaic – Gladiator Fight*, Galleria Borghese, Rome 52ca, 52br, *Theodolinda Melts the Gold for the New Church* (15th century), Famiglia Zavattari, Duomo, Monza 54clb, 54–5, 55br, *Tomb Relief depicting a School*, Matteo Gandoni, Museo Civico, Bologna 56bc, *Detail from an Ambo of Frederick II* (13th century), Cattedrale, Bitonto 57cb, *Guidoriccio da Fogliano at the Siege of Note Massi*, Simone Martini, Palazzo Pubblico, Siena 58clb, 59tl, *Return of Gregory XI from Avignon* Giorgio Vasari, Sala Regia, Vatican 59crb, 60br, 60r–61ci, 61crb, *Clement VII in Conversation with Charles V*, Giorgio Vasari, Palazzo Vecchio, Florence 62cla, *Portrait of Pierluigi da Palestrina*, Istituto dei Padri dell'Oratorio, Rome 62br, *Revolt at Masaniello*, Domenico Gargiulo, Museo di San Martino, Naples 63crb, 64br, 65tl, 65crb, 66cla, 66–7c, 67crb, 99cla, 104c, 122br, 150cla, 226tr, 230br, 264tl, 267tl, 269tr, 273tl, 278cla, 278bl, 279tr, 280c, 280bl, 281tl, 281b, 284cl, 286tc, 287tr, 287br, 290cl, 290cb, 290br, 291ca, 291cb, 292tr, 292b, 293tr, 293cl, 295bl, 296cl, 296bc, 297tr, 297clb, 298tr, 298cl, 299tc, 300cl, 302–3 all, 305clb, 306tr, 306cla, 306c, 307tl, 307cl, 307bl, 329c, 329br, 334–5 all, 336tl, 336br, 342bl, 344tl, 345cl, 348cla, 349br, 358clb, 358br, 359bl, 362bl, 363cl, 374tr,
375tl, 375bc, 381br, 388cl, 404bl, 406tr, 408cl, 415c, 420cla, 421bl, 421tl, 423tl, 424tr, 424c, 425cr, 427tr, 427clb, 427br, 431cla, 431br, 494bc, 515clb, 517tl, 533b, 534tr, 540tc, 541tr, 542bc, 553bc; Science Photo Library: Argonne National Laboratory 45cr; John Ferro Sims: 369b, 546bl; Agenzia Sintesi, Rome: Antonella Girolamo 618clb; Al Sorriso: 588tc; Mario Soster di Alagna: 561cl; Frank Spooner Pictures: Gamma 69tr; STA Travel Group: 616crb; Tony Stone Images: 87cla; Stephen Studd 35tr, 189cr; Agenzia Fotografica Stradella, Milan: Bersanetti 195tl; Francesco Gavazzini 221br; F Giaccone 530cla; Mozzati 263bc, 374bc; Massimo Pacifico 511tl; Ettore Re 503crb; Ghigo Roli 503bl; Giulio Vegi 537ca; Amedeo Vergani 218br, 238tl; SuperStock: age fotostock 383c.

Tasting Italy: Martin Brigdale 611tl; Tate Gallery Publications: 68bl; Taverna del Pittore: 587bc; Tipsimages: Mario Verin 612–13; Touring Club of Italy: 208cb, Cresci 538ca; Archivio Città di Torino Settore Turismo: 225tl; Davide Bogliacino 217tr; Travel Library: 279cb; Fototeca APT del Trentino: Foto di Banal 178tl; Foto di Faganello 177tr, 179cr.

U'Giancu Restaurant: 579cr. Vela SpA: 635cr, 635br; Villa Crespi: 578bl; Villa Foscari: © Villa Foscari La Malcontenta, photo by Noboru Inoue, A+U 164TL; Villa Meridiana Cascina Reine: 567. Edizione White Star: Giulio Veggi 79; Peter Wilson: 5t.

**Front Endpaper:** Alamy Images: David Noton Photography Rftl, Lcra, Norma Joseph Rcla, Rcra, LOOK Die Bildagentur der Fotografen GmbH Rtr, Robert Harding World Imagery Rtl, Woodstock Lfclb; Corbis: SOPA RF/SOPA/Franco Cogoli Rftr, Sylvain Sonnet Lfbr; Dreamstime: Gmv Ltc, Rudywong Lca; Getty Images: Peter Adams Rfcra, Mel Curtis Lbr, Robert Everts Lcla, Michal Krakowiak Lfcrb, David Lyons Rfbr, Stefano Scata Rfcrb.

**Back Endpaper:** Alamy Images: Jon Arnold Images Ltd Rcrb, Prisma Bildagentur AG Rtr; Corbis: Sylvain Sonnet Lca; Dreamstime.com: Rbl; Getty Images: Guy Vanderelst Ltl.

**Cover images:** Front & spine: Alamy Stock Photo: Jan Wlodarczyk; Back: Dreamstime: 68573553.

**Map cover:** Alamy Stock Photo: Jan Wlodarczyk

All other images © **Dorling Kindersley**. For further information: www.dkimages.com

## Special Editions of DK Travel Guides

DK Travel Guides can be purchased in bulk quantities at discounted prices for use in promotions or as premiums. We are also able to offer special editions and personalized jackets, corporate imprints, and excerpts from all of our books, tailored specifically to meet your own needs.

To find out more, please contact:
*in the United States* **specialsales@dk.com**
*in the UK* **travelguides@uk.dk.com**
*in Canada* DK Special Sales at **specialmarkets@dk.com**
*in Australia* **penguincorporatesales@penguinrandomhouse.com.au**

# Phrase Book

## In an Emergency

| | | |
|---|---|---|
| Help! | **Aiuto!** | eye-yoo-toh |
| Stop! | **Ferma!** | fair-mah |
| Call a doctor. | **Chiama un medico.** | kee-ah-mah oon meh-dee-koh |
| Call an ambulance. | **Chiama un' ambulanza.** | kee-ah-mah oon am-boo-lan-tsa |
| Call the police. | **Chiama la polizia.** | kee-ah-mah lah pol-ee-tsee-ah |
| Call the fire department. | **Chiama i pompieri.** | kee-ah-mah ee pom-pee-air-ee |
| Where is the telephone? | **Dov'è il telefono?** | dov-eh eel teh-leh-foh-noh? |
| The nearest hospital? | **L'ospedale più vicino?** | loss-peh-dah-leh-pee oo vee-chee-noh? |

## Communication Essentials

| | | |
|---|---|---|
| Yes/No | **Sì/No** | see/noh |
| Please | **Per favore** | pair fah-vor-eh |
| Thank you | **Grazie** | grah-tsee-eh |
| Excuse me | **Mi scusi** | mee skoo-zee |
| Hello | **Buon giorno** | bwon jor-noh |
| Goodbye | **Arrivederci** | ah-ree-veh-dair-chee |
| Good evening | **Buona sera** | bwon-ah sair-ah |
| morning | **la mattina** | lah mah-tee-nah |
| afternoon | **il pomeriggio** | eel poh-meh-ree-joh |
| evening | **la sera** | lah sair-ah |
| yesterday | **ieri** | ee-air-ee |
| today | **oggi** | oh-jee |
| tomorrow | **domani** | doh-mah-nee |
| here | **qui** | kwee |
| there | **la** | lah |
| What? | **Quale?** | kwah-leh? |
| When? | **Quando?** | kwan-doh? |
| Why? | **Perchè?** | pair-keh? |
| Where? | **Dove?** | doh-veh? |

## Useful Phrases

| | | |
|---|---|---|
| How are you? | **Come sta?** | koh-meh stah? |
| Very well, thank you. | **Molto bene, grazie.** | moll-toh beh-neh, grah-tsee-eh |
| Pleased to meet you. | **Piacere di conoscerla.** | pee-ah-chair-eh dee coh-noh-shair-lah |
| See you later. | **A più tardi.** | ah pee-oo tar-dee |
| That's fine. | **Va bene.** | va beh-neh |
| Where is/are ...? | **Dov'è/Dove sono ...?** | dov-eh/doveh soh-noh? |
| How long does it take to get to ...? | **Quanto tempo ci vuole per andare a ...?** | kwan-toh tem-poh chee voo-oh-leh pair an-dar-eh ah ...? |
| How do I get to ...? | **Come faccio per arrivare a ...?** | koh-meh fah-choh pair arri-var-eh ah ...? |
| Do you speak English? | **Parla inglese?** | par-lah een-gleh -zeh? |
| I don't understand. | **Non capisco.** | non ka-pee-skoh |
| Could you speak more slowly, please? | **Può parlare più lentamente, per favore?** | pwoh par-lah-reh pee-oo len-ta-men-teh pair fah-vor-eh? |
| I'm sorry. | **Mi dispiace.** | mee dee-spee-ah-cheh |

## Useful Words

| | | |
|---|---|---|
| big | **grande** | gran-deh |
| small | **piccolo** | pee-koh-loh |
| hot | **caldo** | kal-doh |
| cold | **freddo** | fred-doh |
| good | **buono** | bwoh-noh |
| bad | **cattivo** | kat-tee-voh |
| enough | **basta** | bas-tah |
| well | **bene** | beh-neh |
| open | **aperto** | ah-pair-toh |
| closed | **chiuso** | kee-oo-zoh |
| left | **a sinistra** | ah see-nee-strah |
| right | **a destra** | ah dess-trah |
| straight ahead | **sempre dritto** | sem-preh dree-toh |
| near | **vicino** | vee-chee-noh |
| far | **lontano** | lon-tah-noh |
| up | **su** | soo |
| down | **giù** | joo |
| early | **presto** | press-toh |
| late | **tardi** | tar-dee |
| entrance | **entrata** | en-trah-tah |
| exit | **uscita** | oo-shee-ta |
| restroom (toilet) | **il gabinetto** | eel gah-bee-net-toh |
| free, unoccupied | **libero** | lee-ber-oh |
| free, no charge | **gratuito** | grah-too-ee-toh |

## Making a Telephone Call

| | | |
|---|---|---|
| I'd like to place a long-distance call. | **Vorrei fare una interurbana.** | vor-ray far-eh oona in-tair-oor-bah-nah |
| I'd like to make a collect call. | **Vorrei fare una telefonata a carico del destinatario.** | vor-ray far-eh oona teh-leh-fon-ah-tah ah kar-ee-koh dell dess-tee-nah-tar-ree-oh |
| I'll try again later. | **Ritelefono più tardi.** | ree-teh-leh-foh-noh pee-oo tar-dee |
| Can I leave a message? | **Posso lasciare un messaggio?** | poss-oh lash-ah-reh oon mess-sah-joh? |
| Hold on. | **Un attimo, per favore.** | oon ah-tee-moh, pair fah-vor-eh |
| Could you speak up a little please? | **Può parlare più forte, per favore?** | pwoh par-lah-reh pee-oo for-teh, pair fah-vor-eh? |
| local call | **telefonata locale** | te-leh-fon-ah-tah loh-cah-leh |

## Shopping

| | | |
|---|---|---|
| How much does this cost? | **Quant'è, per favore?** | kwan-teh pair fah-vor-eh? |
| I would like ... | **Vorrei ...** | vor-ray |
| Do you have ...? | **Avete ...?** | ah-veh-teh ...? |
| I'm just looking. | **Sto soltanto guardando.** | stoh sol-tan-toh gwar-dan-doh |
| Do you take credit cards? | **Accettate carte di credito?** | ah-chet-tah -teh kar-teh dee creh-dee-toh? |
| What time do you open/close? | **A che ora apre/chiude?** | ah keh or-ah ah-preh/kee-oo-deh? |
| this one | **questo** | kweh-stoh |
| that one | **quello** | kwell-oh |
| expensive | **caro** | kar-oh |
| cheap | **a buon prezzo** | ah bwon pret-soh |
| size (clothes) | **la taglia** | lah tah-lee-ah |
| size (shoes) | **il numero** | eel noo-mair-oh |
| white | **bianco** | bee-ang-koh |
| black | **nero** | neh-roh |
| red | **rosso** | ross-oh |
| yellow | **giallo** | jal-loh |
| green | **verde** | vair-deh |
| blue | **blu** | bloo |

## Types of Stores

| | | |
|---|---|---|
| antiques dealer | **l'antiquario** | lan-tee-kwah-ree-oh |
| bakery | **il forno /il panificio** | eel forn-oh /eel pan-ee-fee-choh |
| bank | **la banca** | lah bang-kah |
| bookstore | **la libreria** | lah lee-breh-ree-ah |
| butcher | **la macelleria** | lah mah-chell-eh-ree-ah |
| cake shop | **la pasticceria** | lah pas-tee-chair-ee-ah |
| delicatessen | **la salumeria** | lah sah-loo-meh-ree-ah |
| department store | **il grande magazzino** | eel gran-deh mag-gad-zee-noh |
| fishmonger | **il pescivendolo** | eel pesh-ee-ven-doh-loh |
| florist | **il fioraio** | eel fee-or-eye-oh |
| greengrocer | **il fruttivendolo** | eel froo-tee-ven-doh-loh |
| grocery store | **alimentari** | ah-lee-men-tah-ree |
| hairdresser | **il parrucchiere** | eel par-oo-kee-air-eh |
| ice-cream parlor | **la gelateria** | lah jel-lah-tair-ee-ah |
| market | **il mercato** | eel mair-kah-toh |
| newsstand | **l'edicola** | leh-dee-koh-lah |
| pharmacy | **la farmacia** | lah far-mah-chee-ah |
| post office | **l'ufficio postale** | loo-fee-choh pos-tah-leh |
| shoe store | **il negozio di scarpe** | eel neh-goh-tsioh dee skar-peh |
| supermarket | **il supermercato** | eel su-pair-mair-kah-toh |
| tobacconist | **il tabaccaio** | eel tah-bak-eye-oh |
| travel agency | **l'agenzia di viaggi** | lah-jen-tsee-ah dee vee-ad-jee |

## Sightseeing

| | | |
|---|---|---|
| art gallery | **la pinacoteca** | lah peena-koh-teh-kah |
| bus stop | **la fermata dell'autobus** | lah fair-mah-tah dell ow-toh-booss |
| church | **la chiesa** | lah kee-eh-zah |
| | **la basilica** | lah bah-seel-i-kah |
| closed for holidays | **chiuso per le ferie** | kee-oo-zoh pair leh fair-ee-eh |
| garden | **il giardino** | eel jar-dee-no |
| library | **la biblioteca** | lah beeb-lee-oh-teh-kah |
| museum | **il museo** | eel moo-zeh-oh |
| train station | **la stazione** | lah stah-tsee-oh-neh |
| tourist information | **l'ufficio di turismo** | loo-fee-choh dee too-ree-smoh |

## Staying in a Hotel

| | | |
|---|---|---|
| Do you have any vacant rooms? | **Avete camere libere?** | ah-veh-teh kah-mair-eh lee-bair-eh? |
| double room | **una camera doppia** | oona kah-mair-ah doh-pee-ah |
| with double bed | **con letto matrimoniale** | kon let-toh mah-tree-moh-nee-ah-leh |
| room with two beds | **una camera con due letti** | oona kah-mair-ah kon doo-eh let-tee |
| single room | **una camera singola** | oona kah-mair-ah sing-goh-lah |
| room with a bath, shower | **una camera con bagno, con doccia** | oona kah-mair-ah kon ban-yoh, kon dot-chah |
| porter | **il facchino** | eel fah-kee-noh |
| key | **la chiave** | lah kee-ah-veh |
| I have a reservation. | **Ho fatto una prenotazione.** | oh fat-toh oona preh-noh-tah-tsee-oh-neh |

## Eating Out

| | | |
|---|---|---|
| Have you got a table for…? | **Avete un tavolo per …?** | ah-veh-teh oon tah-voh-loh pair …? |
| I'd like to reserve a table. | **Vorrei riservare un tavolo.** | vor-ray ree-sair-vah-reh oon tah-voh-loh |
| breakfast | **colazione** | koh-lah-tsee-oh-neh |
| lunch | **pranzo** | pran-tsoh |
| dinner | **cena** | cheh-nah |
| The check, please. | **Il conto, per favore.** | eel kon-toh pair fah-vor-eh |
| I am a vegetarian. | **Sono vegetariano/a.** | soh-noh veh-jeh-tar-ee-ah-noh/nah |
| waitress | **cameriera** | kah-mair-ee-air-ah |
| waiter | **cameriere** | kah-mair-ee-air-eh |
| fixed-price menu | **il menù a prezzo fisso** | eel meh-noo ah pret-soh fee-soh |
| dish of the day | **piatto del giorno** | pee-ah-toh dell jor-no |
| appetizer | **antipasto** | an-tee-pass-toh |
| first course | **il primo** | eel pree-moh |
| main course | **il secondo** | eel seh-kon-doh |
| vegetables | **il contorno** | eel kon-tor-noh |
| dessert | **il dolce** | eel doll-cheh |
| cover charge | **il coperto** | eel koh-pair-toh |
| wine list | **la lista dei vini** | lah lee-stah day vee-nee |
| rare | **al sangue** | al sang-gweh |
| medium | **al puntino** | al poon-tee-noh |
| well-done | **ben cotto** | ben kot-toh |
| glass | **il bicchiere** | eel bee-kee-air-eh |
| bottle | **la bottiglia** | lah bot-teel-yah |
| knife | **il coltello** | eel kol-tell-oh |
| fork | **la forchetta** | lah for-ket-tah |
| spoon | **il cucchiaio** | eel koo-kee-eye-oh |

## Menu Decoder

| | | |
|---|---|---|
| l'acqua minerale gassata/naturale | **lah-kwah mee-nair-ah-leh gah-zah-tah/nah-too-rah-leh** | mineral water fizzy/still |
| agnello | **ah-niell-oh** | lamb |
| aceto | **ah-cheh-toh** | vinegar |
| aglio | **al-ee-oh** | garlic |
| al forno | **al for-noh** | baked |
| alla griglia | **ah-lah greel-yah** | grilled |
| l'aragosta | **lah-rah-goss-tah** | lobster |
| arrosto | **ar-ross-toh** | roast |
| la birra | **lah beer-rah** | beer |
| la bistecca | **lah bee-stek-kah** | steak |
| il brodo | **eel broh-doh** | broth |
| il burro | **eel boor-oh** | butter |
| il caffè | **eel kah-feh** | coffee |
| i calamari | **ee kah-lah-mah-ree** | squid |
| i carciofi | **ee kar-choff-ee** | artichokes |
| la carne | **la kar-neh** | meat |
| carne di maiale | **kar-neh dee mah-yah-leh** | pork |
| la cipolla | **la chip-oh-lah** | onion |
| i contorni | **ee kon-tor-nee** | vegetables |
| i fagioli | **ee fah-joh-lee** | beans |
| il fegato | **eel fay-gah-toh** | liver |
| il finocchio | **eel fee-nok-ee-oh** | fennel |
| il formaggio | **eel for-mad-joh** | cheese |
| le fragole | **leh frah-goh-leh** | strawberries |
| il fritto misto | **eel free-toh mees-toh** | mixed fried dish |
| la frutta | **la froot-tah** | fruit |
| frutti di mare | **froo-tee dee mah-reh** | seafood |
| i funghi | **ee foon-ghee** | mushrooms |
| i gamberi | **ee gam-bair-ee** | shrimp |
| il gelato | **eel jel-lah-toh** | ice cream |
| l'insalata | **leen-sah-lah-tah** | salad |

| | | |
|---|---|---|
| il latte | **eel laht-teh** | milk |
| lesso | **less-oh** | boiled |
| il manzo | **eel man-tsoh** | beef |
| la melanzana | **lah meh-lan-tsah-nah** | eggplant |
| la minestra | **lah mee-ness-trah** | soup |
| l'olio | **loh-lee-oh** | oil |
| il pane | **eel pah-neh** | bread |
| le patate | **leh pah-tah-teh** | potatoes |
| le patatine fritte | **leh pah-tah-teen-eh free-teh** | French fries |
| il pepe | **eel peh-peh** | bell pepper |
| la pesca | **lah pess-kah** | peach |
| il pesce | **eel pesh-eh** | fish |
| il pollo | **eel poll-oh** | chicken |
| il pomodoro | **eel poh-moh-dor-oh** | tomato |
| il prosciutto cotto/crudo | **eel pro-shoo-toh kot-toh/kroo-doh** | ham cooked/cured |
| il riso | **eel ree-zoh** | rice |
| il sale | **eel sah-leh** | salt |
| la salsiccia | **lah sal-see-chah** | sausage |
| le seppie | **leh sep-pee-eh** | cuttlefish |
| secco | **sek-koh** | dry |
| la sogliola | **lah soll-yoh-lah** | sole |
| i spinaci | **ee spee-nah-chee** | spinach |
| succo d'arancia/di limone | **soo-koh dah-ran-chah/dee lee-moh-neh** | orange/lemon juice |
| il tè | **eel teh** | tea |
| la tisana | **lah tee-zah-nah** | herbal tea |
| il tonno | **eel ton-noh** | tuna |
| la torta | **lah tor-tah** | cake/tart |
| l'uovo | **loo-oh-voh** | egg |
| vino bianco | **vee-noh bee-ang-koh** | white wine |
| vino rosso | **vee-noh ross-oh** | red wine |
| il vitello | **eel vee-tell-oh** | veal |
| le vongole | **leh von-goh-leh** | clams |
| lo zucchero | **loh zoo-kair-oh** | sugar |
| gli zucchini | **lyee dzu-kee-nee** | zucchini |
| la zuppa | **lah tsoo-pah** | soup |

## Numbers

| | | |
|---|---|---|
| 1 | **uno** | oo-noh |
| 2 | **due** | doo-eh |
| 3 | **tre** | treh |
| 4 | **quattro** | kwat-roh |
| 5 | **cinque** | ching-kweh |
| 6 | **sei** | say-ee |
| 7 | **sette** | set-teh |
| 8 | **otto** | ot-toh |
| 9 | **nove** | noh-veh |
| 10 | **dieci** | dee-eh-chee |
| 11 | **undici** | oon-dee-chee |
| 12 | **dodici** | doh-dee-chee |
| 13 | **tredici** | tray-dee-chee |
| 14 | **quattordici** | kwat-tor-dee-chee |
| 15 | **quindici** | kwin-dee-chee |
| 16 | **sedici** | say-dee-chee |
| 17 | **diciassette** | dee-chah-set-teh |
| 18 | **diciotto** | dee-chot-toh |
| 19 | **diciannove** | dee-chah-noh-veh |
| 20 | **venti** | ven-tee |
| 30 | **trenta** | tren-tah |
| 40 | **quaranta** | kwah-ran-tah |
| 50 | **cinquanta** | ching-kwan-tah |
| 60 | **sessanta** | sess-an-tah |
| 70 | **settanta** | set-tan-tah |
| 80 | **ottanta** | ot-tan-tah |
| 90 | **novanta** | noh-van-tah |
| 100 | **cento** | chen-toh |
| 1,000 | **mille** | mee-leh |
| 2,000 | **duemila** | doo-eh mee-lah |
| 5,000 | **cinquemila** | ching-kweh mee-lah |
| 1,000,000 | **un milione** | oon meel-yoh-neh |

## Time

| | | |
|---|---|---|
| one minute | **un minuto** | oon mee-noo-toh |
| one hour | **un'ora** | oon or-ah |
| half an hour | **mezz'ora** | medz-or-ah |
| a day | **un giorno** | oon jor-noh |
| a week | **una settimana** | oona set-tee-mah-nah |
| Monday | **lunedì** | loo-neh-dee |
| Tuesday | **martedì** | mar-teh-dee |
| Wednesday | **mercoledì** | mair-koh-leh-dee |
| Thursday | **giovedì** | joh-veh-dee |
| Friday | **venerdì** | ven-air-dee |
| Saturday | **sabato** | sah-bah-toh |
| Sunday | **domenica** | doh-meh-nee-kah |

# Central Rome

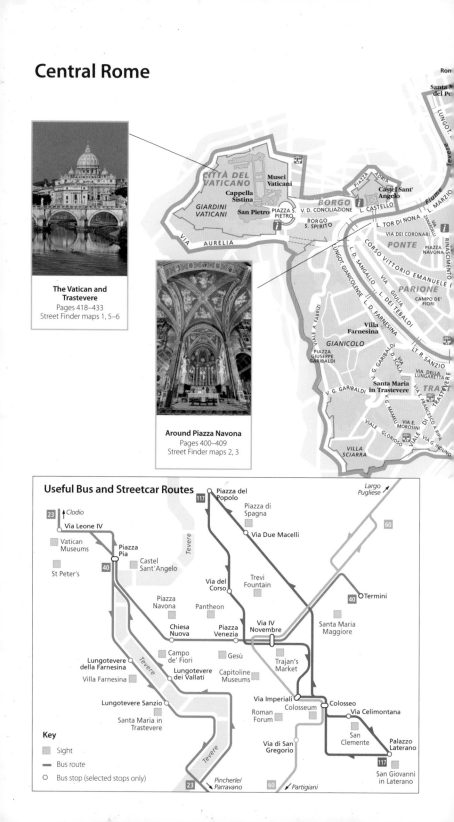

**The Vatican and Trastevere**
Pages 418–433
Street Finder maps 1, 5–6

**Around Piazza Navona**
Pages 400–409
Street Finder maps 2, 3

## Useful Bus and Streetcar Routes

**Key**

- Sight
- Bus route
- Bus stop (selected stops only)